# Aristotle

# *Nicomachean Ethics*

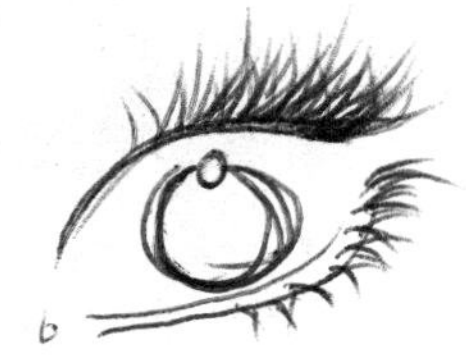

# Aristotle

# *Nicomachean Ethics*

Translated
With Introduction and Notes
By

C. D. C. Reeve

Hackett Publishing Company, Inc.
Indianapolis/Cambridge

Printed in the United States of America

17 16 15 14 1 2 3 4 5 6 7

For further information, please address
Hackett Publishing Company, Inc.
P.O. Box 44937
Indianapolis, Indiana 46244-0937

www.hackettpublishing.com

Composition by Aptara, Inc.

**Library of Congress Cataloging-in-Publication Data**

Aristotle.
[Nicomachean ethics. English]
Nicomachean ethics / Aristotle; translated with introduction and notes by C.D.C. Reeve.
pages cm
Includes bibliographical references and index.
ISBN 978-1-62466-117-4 (pbk.)—ISBN 978-1-62466-118-1 (cloth)
1. Ethics. I. Reeve, C. D. C., 1948 translator. II. Title.
B430.A5R438 2014
171'.3—dc23 2013037301

The paper used in this publication meets the minimum requirements of American National Standard for Information Sciences—Permanence of Paper for Printed Library Materials, ANSI Z39.48–1984.

♾

*For*

Ela
&
Pavlos

τοῦ καλοῦ ἕνεκα

# Contents



## Nicomachean Ethics

### Book I: Happiness and the Soul

## Book II: Virtue of Character



## Book III: Action and the Virtues of Character



## Book IV: Virtues of Character

## Book V: Justice



## Book VI: Virtues of Thought

# Preface

Readers of the *Nicomachean Ethics* in translation find themselves in territory whose apparent familiarity is often deceptive and inimical to proper understanding: *politikê* isn't quite politics, *epistêmê* isn't quite science, *praxis* isn't quite action, *theôria* isn't quite theory, *eudaimonia* isn't quite happiness, *ergon* isn't quite function, *aretê* isn't quite virtue. Even what the *Ethics* is about isn't quite ethics. A worthwhile translation must try to compensate for this deceptive familiarity without producing too much potentially alienating distance and strangeness in its place.

Accuracy and consistency in translation is essential to achieving this goal, obviously, but so too are extensive annotation and commentary. Much of this, however, can consist, as it does here, of texts selected from other works of Aristotle. While traveling through the region of the Aristotelian world the *Ethics* describes, the reader can thus travel through other regions of it, thereby acquiring an ever widening and deepening grasp of the whole picture—something that is crucial, in my view, to understanding any part of it adequately or, perhaps, at all.

To make the journey a convenient one, footnotes and glossary entries are replaced by sequentially numbered endnotes, so that the information most needed at each juncture is available in a single place. The non-sequential reader interested in a particular passage will find in the detailed Index a guide to places where focused discussion of a term or notion occurs. In the case of key terms, indeed, these passages are quoted so that the entry becomes a sort of glossary by Aristotle himself. The Introduction describes the book that lies ahead, explaining what it is about, what it is trying to do, what sort of evidence is relevant to its evaluation, and what sort of person has access to such evidence. It isn't a comprehensive discussion of all the important topics the *Ethics* contains, nor an attempt to situate Aristotle's thought in the history of ethical thought more generally. Many books are readily available that attempt these tasks, including some by me. Nor is it, I should add, an expression of scholarly consensus on the topics it does discuss—insofar as such a thing exists—but rather my own particular take on them.

Some readers will, I have assumed, be new to the *Ethics,* without much background in ancient Greek philosophy, so I have tried to keep their needs in mind. I have also had in mind, though, the needs of more advanced students, who require an English version that is sufficiently reliable and informed for their purposes.

I have benefited from the work of previous translators, including David Ross, H. Rackham, Martin Ostwald, Terence Irwin, Roger Crisp, and Christopher Rowe. The commentaries by J. A. Stewart in English and by R. A. Gauthier and J. Y. Jolif in French, as well as the notes in John Burnet's edition, were an invaluable resource, as was, in the case of Books II–IV, the edition of C. C. W. Taylor; in the case of Book VI, that of L. H. G. Greenwood; and in the case of Books VIII–IX, that of Michael Pakaluk. The collection of essays on Book VII edited by Carlos Natali was also of great assistance. Information on these and other relevant works can be found in Further Reading.

Having often served as reader of other people's translations, I can attest to the hard work it involves when done carefully. I am especially indebted, therefore, to Pavlos Kontos, who has read every line of this translation at least twice and often many more times, suggesting improvements and correcting errors. I am lucky to have had the benefit of his deep knowledge of Greek and of his devotion to a text we both love. I am even luckier that in the process of working together we have become close friends. I include him in the dedication, in inadequate recognition of what his aid and friendship, always unstintingly given, have meant to this book and to me.

Equal devotion to Greek philosophical texts, albeit of a different sort, has been demonstrated by Jay Hullett and Deborah Wilkes and their colleagues at Hackett Publishing Company, who have been my publishers, supporters, and friends for over twenty-five years.

While I was at work on the *Ethics* I had the good fortune to teach joint seminars on it with Mariska Leunissen and Michael Ferejohn and to profit from discussions with them and with some of the students, auditors, and visiting speakers involved—including John Cooper, Pierre Destrée, Daniel Devereux, Gary Gala, Devin Henry, Richard Kraut, Daniel Moseley, Christiana Olfert, and Katja Vogt. Pierre, in particular, sent me many helpful comments on small points and large (that "incontinence" is missing from the translation is due to him) as subsequently on Book I did Mariska and James Lesher. I am grateful to Alex Rosenberg, chair of the Philosophy Department of Duke University, for providing funds for one of the seminars and to Marc Lange, chair of the Philosophy Department of the University of North Carolina at Chapel Hill, for matching those funds, for the grant of a semester's research leave, and for many other kindnesses.

I renew my thanks to ΔKE, the first fraternity in the United States to endow a professorial chair, and to the University of North Carolina for awarding it to me. The generous research funds, among other things, that the endowment makes available each year have allowed me to travel to conferences and to acquire books, computers, and other research materials and assistance, without which my work would have been much more difficult.

All these debts are dwarfed, however, by the debt I owe to Aristotle himself and to his teacher Plato. I have spent much of the past forty years in the company of these great philosophers and in thinking along with them have participated to some extent in the life they—quite reasonably in my experience—thought happiest.

# Abbreviations

*Aristotle*

| | |
|---|---|
| *APo.* | *Posterior Analytics* |
| *APr.* | *Prior Analytics* |
| *Cael.* | *De Caelo (On the Heavens)* |
| *Cat.* | *Categories* |
| *DA* | *De Anima (On the Soul)* |
| *Div. Somn.* | *On Divination in Sleep* (Ross) |
| *EE* | *Eudemian Ethics* |
| *Fr.* | *Fragments* (Rose) |
| *GA* | *Generation of Animals* |
| *GC* | *On Generation and Corruption* (Joachim) |
| *HA* | *History of Animals* (Balme) |
| *IA* | *Progression of Animals (De Incessu Animalium)* |
| *Insomn.* | *On Dreams* (Ross) |
| *MA* | *Movement of Animals* (Nussbaum) |
| *MM* | *Magna Moralia** (Susemihl) |
| *Mem.* | *On Memory* (Ross) |
| *Met.* | *Metaphysics* |
| *Mete.* | *Meteorology* |
| *Mu.* | *De Mundo** |
| *NE* | *Nicomachean Ethics* |
| *PA* | *Parts of Animals* |
| *Ph.* | *Physics* |
| | *Peri Ideôn* (Fine) |
| *Po.* | *Poetics* |
| *Po. II* | *Poetics II* (Janko) |
| *Pol.* | *Politics* |
| *Pr.* | *Problems** |
| *Protr.* | *Protrepticus* (Düring) |

| | |
|---|---|
| *Resp.* | *On Respiration* |
| *Rh.* | *Rhetoric* |
| *SE* | *Sophistical Refutations* |
| *Sens.* | *Sense and Sensibilia* |
| *Somn.* | *On Sleep* |
| *Top.* | *Topics* |

(An asterisk indicates a work whose authenticity has been seriously questioned.)

I cite and translate the *Oxford Classical Texts* (OCT) editions of these works, where available, otherwise the editions noted:

Balme, D. M. *Aristotle: Historia Animalium* (Cambridge, 2002).

Düring, Ingemar, *Aristotle's Protrepticus: An Attempt at Reconstruction* (Göteborg, 1961).

Fine, Gail, *On Ideas: Aristotle's Criticism of Plato's Theory of Forms* (Oxford, 1993).

Janko, Richard, *Aristotle on Comedy: Towards a Reconstruction of "Poetics II"* (Berkeley, 1984).

Joachim, H. H., *Aristotle on Coming-to-be and Passing-away* (Oxford, 1926).

Mayhew, Robert, *Aristotle: Problems* (Cambridge, Mass., 2011).

Nussbaum, Martha C., *Aristotle's De Motu Animalium: Text with Translation, Commentary, and Interpretative Essays* (Princeton, 1978).

Rose, V., *Aristotelis Fragmenta,* 3rd ed. (Leipzig, 1886).

Ross, W. D., *Aristotle Parva Naturalia* (Oxford, 1955).

Susemihl, F., *Aristotelis Magna Moralia* (Leipzig, 1883).

*Plato*

| | |
|---|---|
| *Ap.* | *Apology* |
| *Chrm.* | *Charmides* |
| *Cra.* | *Cratylus* |
| *Cri.* | *Crito* |
| *Euthd.* | *Euthydemus* |
| *Euthpr.* | *Euthyphro* |
| *Grg.* | *Gorgias* |
| *Hp. Ma.* | *Hippias Major* |

| | |
|---|---|
| *La.* | *Laches* |
| *Lg.* | *Laws* |
| *Ly.* | *Lysis* |
| *Men.* | *Meno* |
| *Phd.* | *Phaedo* |
| *Phlb.* | *Philebus* |
| *Prt.* | *Protagoras* |
| *Rep.* | *Republic* |
| *Smp.* | *Symposium* |
| *Ti.* | *Timaeus* |

## Other Abbreviations

Aspasius = Aspasius, *On Aristotle's "Nicomachean Ethics" 1–4, 7–8*. Translated by David Konstan (Ithaca, 2006).

DK = H. Diels and W. Kranz, eds. *Die Fragmente der Vorsokratiker,* 6th ed (Berlin: 1951).

# Introduction

## *Life and Works*

Aristotle was born in 384 BC to a well-off family living in the small town of Stagira in northern Greece. His father, Nicomachus, who died while Aristotle was still quite young, was allegedly doctor to King Amyntas of Macedon. His mother, Phaestis, was wealthy in her own right. When Aristotle was seventeen his guardian, Proxenus, sent him to study at Plato's Academy in Athens. He remained there for twenty years, initially as a student, eventually as a researcher and teacher.

When Plato died in 347, leaving the Academy in the hands of his nephew, Speusippus, Aristotle left Athens for Assos in Asia Minor, where the ruler, Hermias was a patron of philosophy. He married Hermias' niece, Pythias, and had a daughter by her, also named Pythias. Three years later, in 345, after Hermias had been killed by the Persians, Aristotle moved to Mytilene on the island of Lesbos, where he met Theophrastus, who was to become his best student and closest colleague.

In 343 Aristotle seems to have been invited by Philip of Macedon to be tutor to the latter's thirteen-year-old son, Alexander, later called "the Great." In 335, Aristotle returned to Athens and founded his own institute, the Lyceum. While he was there his wife died and he established a relationship with Herpyllis, also a native of Stagira. Their son Nicomachus was named for Aristotle's father, and the *Nicomachean Ethics* may, in turn, have been named for him or transcribed by him. In 323 Alexander the Great died, with the result that anti-Macedonian feeling in Athens grew stronger. Perhaps threatened with a formal charge of impiety (X 7 1177$^{b}$33n), Aristotle left for Chalcis in Euboea, where he died twelve months later, in 322, at the age of sixty-two.

Legend has it that Aristotle had slender calves, small eyes, spoke with a lisp, and was "conspicuous by his attire, his rings, and the cut of his hair." His will reveals that he had a sizable estate, a domestic partner, two children, a considerable library, and a large circle of friends. In it Aristotle asks his executors to take particular care of Herpyllis. He directs that his slaves be freed "when they come of age" and that the bones of his wife, Pythias, be mixed with his "as she instructed."

Although the surviving writings of Aristotle occupy almost 2,500 tightly printed pages in English, most of them are not works polished for publication but sometimes incomplete lecture notes and working papers: the *Ethics* itself shows signs of hasty editing (the two treatments of "pleasure" are often cited in this regard). This accounts for some, though not all, of their legendary difficulty. It is unfair to complain, as a Platonist opponent did, that Aristotle "escapes refutation by clothing a perplexing subject in obscure language, using darkness like a squid to make himself hard to catch," but there is darkness and obscurity enough for anyone, even if none of it is intentional. There is also a staggering breadth and depth of intellect. Aristotle made fundamental contributions to a vast range of disciplines, including logic, metaphysics, epistemology, psychology, ethics, politics, rhetoric, aesthetics, zoology, biology, physics, and philosophical and political history. When Dante called him "the master of those who know," he was scarcely exaggerating.

## What the Nichomachean Ethics Is

One thing we might mean by the *Nicomachean Ethics* is what we now find inscribed on the pages that make up Ingram Bywater's Oxford Classical Text (OCT) edition of the Greek text, first published in 1894, which is the basis of the present translation. This is the descendant of texts derived—via manuscripts copied in the Byzantine period (from the tenth to the fifteenth centuries AD)—from manuscripts that derive from the edition of Aristotle's works produced by Andronicus of Rhodes in the first century BC. Bywater's edition, like most other modern editions, records in the textual apparatus at the bottom of the page various manuscript readings alternative to the one he prints in the body of his text. In some cases, I have preferred one of these readings and have indicated this in the notes.

Divisions of the text into books and chapters are the work of editors, not the work of Aristotle himself. In the case of the *Nicomachean Ethics,* indeed, two different divisions into chapters exist, both mediaeval in origin. The one preferred by Bywater and most Anglophone scholars is recorded in the chapter headings together with the book number (for example, VII 2 = Book VII Chapter 2). Also present in Bywater's text, as in all worthwhile modern editions, are the page numbers of Immanuel Bekker, *Aristotelis Opera* (Berlin: 1831 [1970]). Citations of Aristotle's works are standardly made to this edition in the form of abbreviated title, book number (when the work is divided into books), chapter number, page number, column letter, and line number. The page number, column letter, and line number appear between upright lines in the present translation (for example, |1094$^{a}$1|) at the end of the first line in a column to which they apply, and as line numbers alone thereafter. These numbers refer to the Greek text, however, and so are approximate—though usually closely so—in the translation. Occasional material in square brackets in the translated text is my addition.

The *Nicomachean Ethics* shares three of its central books (V–VII) with another treatise thought to be authentic, the *Eudemian Ethics* (perhaps so called because it was transcribed or edited by Eudemus, a Lyceum member), which is widely, though not universally, believed to predate the *Nicomachean*. A third work, the so-called *Magna Moralia,* or *Great Ethics,* is largely authentic in content but is generally thought not to be by Aristotle himself. There are important differences between these works, to be sure, some of them significant, but there is also a massive and impressive overlap in overall perspective. The spuriousness of a fourth short work, *On Virtues and Vices,* has never been seriously contested.

The second thing we might mean, and are perhaps more likely to mean, by the *Nicomachean Ethics* is the work itself, so to speak, namely, the more abstract thing that is embodied in a good Greek text and (ideally) in any translation of it. Aristotle identifies this as a contribution to "our philosophy of human affairs" (X 9 1181$^{b}$15) and subsequently refers to it as included among "those philosophical works of ours in which we draw distinctions concerning ethical matters" (*Pol.* III 12 1282$^{b}$19–20). In the discussion that begins in the opening chapter of the *Ethics* and ends in its successor, he says that the method of inquiry—the *methodos*—pursued in it is "a sort of politics (*politikê*)" (*NE* I 2 1094$^{b}$11). Since politics is the same state of the soul as practical wisdom (*phronêsis*), politics is presumably a sort of practical wisdom as well or some sort of contribution to it (VI 8 1141$^{b}$23–24).

What is politics, though? What does it consist in? To what evidence is it answerable? How should its success or failure be determined?

## *Aristotelian Sciences*

Aristotle usually divides the bodies of knowledge he refers to as "sciences" (*epistêmai*) into three types: theoretical, practical, and productive (crafts). But when he is being especially careful, he also distinguishes within the theoretical sciences between the *strictly theoretical* ones (astronomy, theology), as we may call them, and the *natural* ones, which are like the strictly theoretical ones in being neither practical nor productive but are unlike them in consisting of propositions that—though necessary and universal in some sense—hold for the most part rather than without exception:

> If all thought is either practical or productive or theoretical, natural science must be a theoretical science. But it theorizes only about being that is capable of being moved and only about substance that, in accord with its account, holds for the most part, since it is not separate [from matter]. We must not fail to notice, though, the way the what it is to be [that is, the essence] and its account hold, since without this,

> inquiry achieves nothing. But of things defined, that is, what something is, some are like snub, some like concave. These differ because snub is bound up with matter (for snubness is concavity *in a nose*), while concavity is without perceptible matter. If then all natural things are like snub (for example, nose, eye, face, flesh, bone and, in general, animal, or leaf, root, bark, and, in general, plant; since none of these can be defined without reference to movement but always have matter), it is clear how we must inquire about and define what a natural thing is. It is also clear that it belongs to the natural scientist in a way to provide theoretical knowledge even of the soul, that is, of so much of it as is not without matter. That natural science is a theoretical science, then, is evident from these considerations. But mathematics is also theoretical—although whether its objects are unmoving and separate from matter is not clear at present. But what *is* clear is that some parts of mathematics theorize about them *insofar as* they are unmoving and *insofar as* they are separate. But if there is some being that is eternal and unmoving and separate, the knowledge of it belongs to a theoretical science—not, however, to *natural* science nor to mathematics but to a science prior to both. . . . If, then, there is no substance other than those beyond those constituted by nature, natural science will be the primary science. But if there is an unmoving substance, the science of this will be prior and will be primary philosophy. (*Met.* VI 1 1025$^{b}$25–1026$^{a}$30)

When we hear, as we quickly do (*NE* I 3 1094$^{b}$14–22), that because the subject matter of politics, which consists of noble, just, and good things and the like, admits of so much difference and variability, its claims hold for the most part, we should bear in mind that all the natural sciences—which for us are the paradigm cases of science—are in a similar boat. Psychology, however, has an interestingly mixed status, part strictly theoretical, part natural (*DA* I 1 403$^{a}$3–$^{b}$16).

When science receives its focused discussion in the *Ethics*, however, Aristotle is explicit that if we are "to speak in an exact way and not be guided by mere similarities" (VI 3 1139$^{b}$19), we should not call anything a science unless it deals with eternal, entirely exceptionless facts about universals that are wholly necessary and do not at all admit of being otherwise (1139$^{b}$20–21). Since he is here explicitly epitomizing his more detailed discussion of science in the *Posterior Analytics* (1139$^{b}$27), we should take the latter too as primarily a discussion of science in the exact sense, which it calls *epistêmê haplôs*—unconditional scientific knowledge. It follows—and we should acknowledge this—that only the strictly theoretical sciences are sciences in the exact sense. Hence politics is not such a science and neither are physics or biology or any other natural science.

Having made the acknowledgement, though, we must also register the fact—since it is a fact—that Aristotle himself mostly does not speak in the exact way but instead persistently refers to bodies of knowledge other than the strictly theoretical sciences as *epistêmai*. His division of the *epistêmai* into theoretical, practical, and productive is a dramatic case in point. But so too is his use of the term *epistêmê* within the *Ethics*, which we first encounter (*NE* I 1 1094$^a$7) being applied to medicine, shipbuilding, generalship, and household management, which are a mix of bodies of practical knowledge (household management) and bodies of productive knowledge (shipbuilding). For that matter, politics itself is introduced in answer to a question about "which of the *epistêmai* or capacities" (1094$^a$26) has the human good as its proper end or target, and is implicitly identified as a practical science a few lines later (1094$^b$4–5). Even boxing and wrestling are classed as *epistêmai* (*Cat.* 10b3–4).

So the interesting question isn't whether politics is a science, since the answer to that is obvious: it is not a science if we are being absolutely exact about the matter, but it is a science if we allow ourselves to be guided by the similarities between it and the strictly theoretical sciences—or by Aristotle's own general use of the term *epistêmê*, on the assumption that he himself was guided by these. The interesting question—and it *is* interesting—is, what are these similarities? Just how like a canonical or theoretical science is politics?

An Aristotelian science of any sort, including a theoretical one, is a state of the soul, not a body of propositions in a textbook—although the state does involve having an assertoric grasp of a set of true propositions (VI 3 1139$^b$14–16). Some of these propositions are indemonstrable starting-points, which are or are expressed in definitions, and others are theorems demonstrable from these starting-points. We can have scientific knowledge only of the theorems, since—exactly speaking—only what is demonstrable can be scientifically known (VI 6). Thus when we read in the *Physics* that we "should not try to resolve everything but only what is falsely drawn from the relevant starting-points" (I 1 185$^a$14–15), it seems to be this notion of a science and of a scientist's task that is being presupposed. Yet—in what is clearly another lapse from exact speaking—Aristotle characterizes "the most exact of the sciences," which is theoretical wisdom (*sophia*), as also involving a grasp by understanding (*nous*) of the truth where the starting-points themselves are concerned (VI 7 1141$^a$16–18). He does the same thing in the *Metaphysics,* where theoretical wisdom is the *epistêmê* that provides "a theoretical grasp of the primary starting-points and causes"—among which are included "the good or the for sake of which" (I 2 982$^b$7–10). Indeed, the grasp we have of such starting-points must result in their being "better known" than the theorems we demonstrate from them if we are to have any scientific knowledge of the exact sort at all (*NE* VI 3 1139$^b$34).

How like that is politics? Are there starting-points here too and theorems demonstrable from them? We might think this is an easy question to answer. After all, the method of inquiry the *Ethics* employs is a sort of politics, yet it doesn't seem to include any demonstrations whatsoever. For a demonstration is, among other things, a deductively valid argument that is syllogistic in form, and deductions of any sort are scarcely to be found in the *Ethics*. This is also a problem with the vast majority of Aristotle's works, even those that are usually classed as "scientific treatises"—for example, *Meteorology* and *Parts of Animals*. For none of them seems to fit the description of a science as developed in the *Posterior Analytics*. People have certainly tried to find elements of demonstration and axiomatic structure in these treatises, as they have in the *Ethics*, but the results are somewhat underwhelming. In large part, this is because the search is somewhat misconceived from the outset.

If we think of a science in the exact sense as consisting exclusively of what is demonstrable, as we have seen that Aristotle himself sometimes does, we will be right to conclude that a treatise without demonstrations in it cannot be scientific. But if, as he also does, we include knowledge of starting-points as parts of science, we will not be right, since a treatise could contribute to a science not by demonstrating anything but by arguing to the starting-points themselves—an enterprise which couldn't possibly consist of demonstrations from those starting-points, since these would be circular. Arguments leading *from* starting-points and arguments leading *to* starting-points are different (I 4 1095$^a$30–32), we are invited not to forget, just as we are told that happiness (*eudaimonia*) is a starting-point (I 12 1102$^a$2–4), that a major goal of the *Ethics* is to give a clear account of what happiness really is, so as to increase our chances of achieving it (I 2 1094$^a$22–26), and that because establishing starting-points is "more than half the whole" (I 7 1098$^b$7), we should "make very serious efforts to define them correctly" (1098$^b$5–6). We might reasonably infer, therefore, that the *Ethics* is a sort of science precisely because it contributes to the correct definition and secure grasp of starting-points without which no science can exist. The same idea might be employed in the case of many of Aristotle's other treatises. They too, we might suppose, are scientific in just this sense.

But even if politics has starting-points, it still would not be a science unless it were possible to demonstrate theorems from these. Yet here too we seem to face an obstacle. For Aristotle tells us that we cannot demonstrate things whose starting-points admit of being otherwise (VI 5 1140$^a$33–35), that politics is the same state of the soul as practical wisdom (VI 8 1141$^b$23–24), and that the starting-points of practical wisdom do admit of being otherwise (VI 5 1140$^a$30–$^b$4). Elsewhere, though, he allows that there *can* be demonstrations of what admits of being otherwise provided it holds for the most part—as the starting-points and theorems of politics are said to do (I 3 1094$^b$19–22):

> What admits of being otherwise is spoken of in two ways: in one, it means what holds for the most part, that is, when the necessity has gaps (*dialeipein*)—for example, a man's turning grey or growing or decaying, or, in general, what belongs to something by nature (for this does

> not belong by continuous necessity, since a human being does not exist forever, although if a human being does exist, it belongs either necessarily or for the most part); in the other, it means what is indeterminate, which is what is capable of being thus or not thus—for example, an animal's walking or an earthquake's taking place while it is walking, or, in general, what is the result of luck (for it is not more natural for it to be that way rather than the opposite). . . . Science and demonstrative deductions are not concerned with things that are indeterminate, because the middle term is irregular, but there is scientific knowledge of what happens by nature, and argument and investigations are pretty much concerned with things that are possible in this way. (*APr.* I 13 32$^{b}$4–21)

Apparently, then, the notion of a demonstration is a bit like that of a science. Speaking exactly, there are demonstrations only in the theoretical sciences, since—speaking exactly again—these alone are sciences. Speaking less exactly, though, there are also demonstrations in other bodies of knowledge. Thus we find Aristotle referring to practical demonstrations (*NE* VI 11 1143$^{b}$2), contrasting the undemonstrated sayings and beliefs of practically-wise people with things they can demonstrate (1143$^{b}$11–13), telling us about practical deductions (VI 12 1144$^{a}$31–32), and contrasting what are clearly theoretical deductions with productive ones (VII 3 1147$^{a}$25–$^{b}$1). We hear too about starting-points in politics and about reaching conclusions from them (I 3 1094$^{b}$21–22), and about supposedly having reached some (see I 8 1098$^{b}$9–10). Finally—and this is as much a reminder as anything else—if we do not allow there to be demonstrations of what admits of being otherwise in the sense of holding for the most part, it isn't just politics that will lose its putative scientific status; natural science will too.

A penultimate problem. Scientific knowledge seems to be exclusively about universals—about what is common to many particulars (VI 6 1140$^{b}$31, X 9 1180$^{b}$15–16). Yet politics, to the extent that it is the same state as—or is a part of—practical wisdom, must also deal with particulars (VI 7–8). It seems an easy inference that politics cannot be a science. The first point to make in response is that even theoretical sciences, though they deal with eternal and unchangeable necessary truths about universals and have no grasp "on any of the things from which a human being will come to be happy" (VI 12 1143$^{b}$19–20), can be "coincidentally useful to us where many of the necessities of life are concerned" (*EE* I 6 1216$^{b}$15–16). Knowledge of astronomy, for instance, helped Thales to make a killing in the olive business (*NE* VI 7 1141$^{b}$4n). The second point to make is that Aristotle allows that sciences dealing with universals can also deal—albeit coincidentally—with (perishable) particulars: "There is neither demonstration nor unconditional scientific knowledge of what is subject to passing away, but only the coincidental sort, because it does not hold of this universally, but at some time (*pote*) and in some way (*pôs*)" (*APo.* I 8 75$^b$24–26). The scientific theorem that all light meats are healthy may enable me to infer that this meat is healthy now, but it doesn't tell me whether it will still be healthy tomorrow (it may have rotted in the meantime) or whether, though it is healthy for most people, it is healthy for me (I may have a fever that makes meat of any sort a bad choice).

While each of these points does something to take the edge off our problem, even collectively they do not seem to go quite far enough. And the reason they don't is this: It is quite possible to have scientific knowledge of universals without knowing how to apply it in particular cases, but it is not possible to have practical wisdom—or, therefore, a grasp of politics—without knowing this. In fact, it is almost the other way around:

> Nor is practical wisdom knowledge of universals only. On the contrary, it must also know particulars. For it is practical, and action is concerned with particulars. That is why, in other areas too, some people who lack knowledge—most of all, those with experience—are more effective *doers* of action than are others who have knowledge. For if someone knows that light meats are digestible and healthy but is ignorant about which sorts of meat are light, he will not produce health; but someone who knows that bird meats are healthy will produce health more. But practical wisdom is practical, so one must possess both sorts of knowledge—or this one more. (*NE* VI 7 1141$^b$14–21)

At the same time, knowledge of universals is a crucial part of politics. This emerges most clearly in the final discussion in the *Ethics,* where we learn not only about the importance of experience of particulars to politics but also about the need to "take steps toward the universal" (X 9 1180$^b$21), on the grounds that "the best supervision in each particular case" will be provided by the person who has "knowledge of the universal and knows what applies in all cases or in these sorts (since the sciences are said to be—and actually are—of what is common)" (1180$^b$13–16).

Once we register the fact that politics must include both a scientific knowledge of universals and an experience of particulars that enables us to apply those universals correctly to them, we can see that it is something like an applied science as opposed to a pure one. And this seems to be what Aristotle has in mind by classifying it as *practical*—that is to say, as bearing on *praxis*, or action, and so on the particulars with which action is irremediably concerned. When we look for the similarities that may justify him in classifying it as a practical *science*, then, we must look not at its particularist component but at its universalist one, since a science, as we saw, is always of what is universal. A practical science, in other words, might to some extent be usefully thought of as a combination of something like a theoretical science (in any case, in the sense in which natural science is theoretical) and the experience-based knowledge of how to apply it.

What the universalist component of politics consists in is uncontroversial, since Aristotle tells us plainly that it is *nomothetikê,* or legislative science:

> Maybe, then, someone who wishes to make people—whether many or few—better because of his supervision should also try to acquire legislative science, if it is through laws that we can become good. For producing a noble disposition in anyone whatever—in anyone put before him—is not a matter for some random person, but if indeed anyone can do it, it is a person who knows, just as in medicine and in all other matters that involve a sort of supervision and practical wisdom. (X 9 1180$^{b}$23–28)

What legislative science does, as its name suggests, is to produce a set of universal laws—for "all law is universal" (V 10 1137$^{b}$13)—that will "make citizens good by habituating them" (II 1 1103$^{b}$3–4). Thus one very important subset of these laws bears on education, since "what produces virtue as a whole are the actions that are ordained by the laws concerned with education that looks to the common good" (V 2 1130$^{b}$25–26). Another subset, however, governs the actions of already-educated adults:

> It is not enough, presumably, that when people are young they get the correct nurture and supervision. On the contrary, even when they have grown into manhood they must continue to practice the same things and be habituated to them. And so there will need to be laws concerning these matters as well and, in general, then, concerning all of life. (X 9 1180$^{a}$1–4)

The phrase "concerning all of life" nicely captures the ideal extent of the laws: "It is above all appropriate that correctly established laws themselves define all the things they possibly can and leave the fewest possible to the judges" (*Rh.* I 1 1354$^{a}$31–33), since "human wish . . . is not a safe standard" (*Pol.* II 10 1272$^{b}$6–7).

We are now able to solve a final problem. Theorems in canonical theoretical sciences are not just universal, they are also necessary: they are about relations between universals that do not "*at all* admit of being otherwise" (*NE* VI 3 1139$^{b}$20–21). The theorems of natural science too, although not as strictly necessary as this, also describe relations between universals that are far from simply being matters of luck or contingency. Were it otherwise, there would, as we noticed, simply be no such thing as natural *science*. Obviously the theorems of politics, which are universal laws, are not like either of these, since they govern voluntary action, which, as something whose starting-point is in us, is up to us to do or not to do (III 5 1113$^{b}$7–8). This difference, however, is due to a difference in direction of fit. Theorems of a theoretical science *describe* how things must be; practical laws *prescribe* how they must be. Thus when Aristotle gives an example of an ethical proposition, it is this: "whether we *should* obey our parents or the laws, if they disagree" (*Top.* I 14 105$^b$22–23). What practical laws prescribe will be correct, if it is what the virtues require of us (*NE* V 2 1130$^b$22–24), and it will be what the virtues require of us if it is what the practical wisdom they presuppose would prescribe, and it will be what practical wisdom would prescribe if it is what best furthers happiness or the human good (VI 9 1142$^b$31–33, 10 1143$^a$8). For the law owes its compulsive force to the fact that it is "reason that derives from a sort of practical wisdom and understanding" (X 9 1180$^a$21–22).

Although it is through laws that we can "become good" (X 9 1180$^b$25), it is not just through any old laws. Rather, we need *correct* laws—laws that really do further happiness by inculcating genuine virtues. The question arises, therefore, of how such laws are to be found. A good place to start, Aristotle thinks, is by collecting the laws and constitutions that are in use in different places, as well as those ideal ones suggested by wise people, such as Plato, who have thought a lot about the topic. But this by itself will not be enough, since selecting the best ones from these requires "correct discernment" (X 9 1181$^a$17), making the collection itself all but useless to "those who lack scientific knowledge" (1181$^b$6). For what selection of the best ones clearly requires is knowledge of what virtue and vice—what goodness—really are, so that we can see which laws and constitutions really do further their acquisition by those brought up and living under them. In Aristotle's view, there is only one such constitution:

> The only constitution that is rightly called an aristocracy is the one that consists of those who are unconditionally best as regards virtue. . . . For only here is it unconditionally the case that the same person is a good man and a good citizen. (*Pol.* IV 7 1293$^b$3–6; compare *NE* V 7 1135$^a$5)

Thus when the topic of the best constitution is taken up in the *Politics*, Aristotle begins by noting that "anyone who intends to investigate the best constitution in the proper way must first determine which life is most choiceworthy" (VII 1 1323$^a$14–17), referring us for a fuller discussion to "external accounts," whose topics significantly overlap those of the *Ethics*. Other constitutions, however—and this is a point that we shall return to in a moment—can come close enough to the best one that something approximating full virtue can be acquired in them; these are the non-deviant constitutions (kingship, aristocracy, and polity) described in VIII 10 and, in greater detail, in the relevant parts of the *Politics*.

It is scarcely a step at this point to see what the *Ethics* contributes to legislative science. After all, the *Ethics* is devoted to defining the virtues of character, which are starting-points of politics (*Met.* XIII 4 1078$^b$17–30, quoted below), as well as to correctly and clearly defining the yet more fundamental starting-point, happiness, which is the end or target that politics aims at (I 2 $1094^{a}26$–$^{b}7$). The *Ethics* is a contribution to the philosophy of human affairs, as we saw, and "the political philosopher is the architectonic craftsman of the end to which we look in calling each thing unconditionally bad or good" (VII 11 $1152^{b}1$–3)—namely, happiness.

This helps us to understand something that is much more mysterious than is usually recognized, namely, how it is that Aristotle can do the following three things: First, characterize the *Ethics* as "not undertaken for the sake of theoretical knowledge . . . but in order to become good people, since otherwise there would be nothing of benefit in it" (II 2 $1103^{b}26$–29; also I 3 $1095^{a}5$–6). Second, insist that we become good in large part through habituation, not through reading books (II 2 $1103^{b}23$–25). And, third, that we must already have been "nobly brought up if, where noble things, just things, and the topics of politics as a whole are concerned, we are to be an adequate audience" (I 4 $1095^{b}4$–6). For "argument and teaching . . . do not have strength in everyone," but only in those whose souls have been "prepared beforehand through habits to enjoy and hate in a noble way, like earth that is to nourish seed" and may not even be comprehensible to anyone else (X 9 $1179^{b}23$–31). The heavy lifting of the *Ethics*' practicality is done, then, not so much by the book itself, which presupposes an already existing noble condition in a comprehending reader, but by the contribution it makes to legislative science, ensuring that the laws it selects will habituate people in genuine virtues and that it will have as its end happiness correctly conceived and clearly defined.

Because the heavy lifting is done by legislation and habituation, it matters enormously that the legislation and habituation in question is not required to be of the ideal or very best sort available only in a true aristocracy of virtue. For such a constitution does not exist, and never has existed. But even if it had, Aristotle was not brought up in it—Stagira and Athens were certainly not such true aristocracies—and his audience and fellow Lyceum members weren't either. What *is* required, though, is that we not be "disabled in relation to virtue" (I 9 $1099^{b}19$), that we have the natural resources needed to develop it—which may include possession of the so-called natural virtues (VI 13 $1144^{b}5$–6), that we have been sufficiently well brought up that we do not, like children, pursue each thing in accord with our feelings, but rather form our desires and perform our actions to some extent at least "in accord with reason" (I 3 $1095^{a}4$–11), and that we have "sufficient experience of the actions of life," since "the arguments are in accord with these and concerned with these" ($1095^{a}3$–4). Aristotle doesn't go into detail in the *Ethics* about just how much experience of just what sorts of actions we need, but there is a suggestion in the *Politics* that we may not have it until we have reached the age of around fifty. Because our nature, upbringing, and experience are unlikely to have been ideal, moreover, we must not expect too much, but rather "be content if, when we have all the things through which it seems we become decent people, we achieve some share of virtue" (X 9 1179$^{b}$18–20).

We turn now to the particularist part of politics, which is concerned with deliberation: "Of the practical wisdom concerned with the city, the architectonic part is legislative science, while the part concerned with particulars has the name common to both—'politics.' This part is practical and deliberative, since a decree is doable in action, as the last thing" (VI 1141$^{b}$24–28). Precisely because this part is particularist, it cannot itself be a science, since—to repeat—sciences are always (anyway non-coincidentally) about universals. Nonetheless it is some sort of knowledge or ability that makes its possessor a competent deliberator—someone who is reliably able to deliberate correctly by working out the best means to the best end (VI 9 1142$^{b}$28–33), this being happiness or the human good. Since only a practically-wise person is in this position and since practical wisdom is as much if not more concerned with particulars than with universals, the function of such a person is "most of all . . . to deliberate well" (VI 7 1141$^{b}$9–10).

Now the sphere of deliberation is the part of what admits of being otherwise that deliberators can change through their own actions (III 3 1112$^{a}$30–34). Hence it is also the sphere of the practical and productive sciences which help deliberators to make good choices within that sphere. But once these sciences are factored into the equation, the scope of deliberation within the sphere is affected, so that as their scope expands, that of deliberation contracts:

> There is no deliberation, however, where sciences that are both exact and self-sufficient are concerned—where writing the letters of the alphabet is concerned, for example, since we have no hesitation about what way to write them. We do deliberate, however, about those things that come about through ourselves, but not always in the same way (for example, about the things that medicine or moneymaking deals with). And we deliberate more about navigation than about athletic training, insofar as navigation is less exactly developed. Further, deliberation is involved in a similar way where the rest are concerned, but more where crafts are concerned than sciences, since we are more hesitant about them. (*NE* III 3 1112$^{a}$34–$^{b}$9)

As Aristotle succinctly puts it at one point: "Craft does not deliberate" (*Ph.* II 8 199$^{b}$28). He means, as we see, that a craft, insofar as it is exact, fully developed, and self-contained, does not do so.

Even when the productive sciences are less exact or developed, however, as is true, for example, of medicine and wealth acquisition, their universal laws should generally be followed:

> Those who think it advantageous to be ruled by a king hold that laws speak only of the universal, and do not prescribe with a view to actual circumstances. Consequently, it is foolish to rule in accord with written rules in any craft, and doctors in Egypt are rightly allowed to abandon the treatment prescribed by the manuals after the fourth day (although, if they do so earlier, it is at their own risk). It is evident for the same reason, therefore, that the best constitution is not one that follows written rules and laws. All the same, the rulers should possess the universal reason as well. And something to which feeling is entirely unattached is better than something in which it is innate. This element does not belong to the law, whereas every human soul necessarily possesses it. But perhaps, to balance this, it should be said that a human being will deliberate better about particular cases. In that case, it is clear he must be a legislator, and laws established, although they must not be in control insofar as they deviate from what is best, since they should certainly be in control everywhere else. (*Pol.* III 15 1286$^{a}$9–25; also 16 1287$^{a}$33–1287$^{b}$5)

It is when the universal laws fail us—as the Egyptian doctors imagine them doing by the fourth day of a patient's unresponsiveness to the prescribed treatment—that deliberation comes into play. It is then that the practical wisdom possessed by the better practitioners of the science becomes important. We "speak of people as practically-wise *in some area*, when they rationally calculate well about what furthers some excellent end, concerning which no craft [prescription] exists" (*NE* VI 5 1140$^{a}$28–30).

The element in practical wisdom that is particularly involved in the kinds of cases where the end is "living well as a whole" (VI 5 1140$^{a}$27–28) is decency (*epieikeia*):

> All law is universal, but about some sorts of things it is not possible to pronounce correctly in universal terms. . . . So whenever the law makes a universal pronouncement and a particular case arises that is contrary to the universal pronouncement, at that time it is correct (insofar as the legislator has omitted something, and he has made an error in pronouncing unconditionally) to rectify the deficiency—to pronounce what the legislator himself would have pronounced had he been present and would have put into his law had he known about the case. . . . And this is the very nature of what is decent—a rectification of law insofar as it is deficient because of its universality. For this is also the cause of not everything's being regulated by law—namely, that there are some cases where it is impossible to establish a law, so that decrees (*psêphismata*) are needed. For the standard of what is indeterminate is itself indeterminate, just like the lead standard used in Lesbian building. For the standard is not fixed but adapts itself to the shape of the stone and a decree adapts itself to the things themselves. (V 10 1137$^{b}$13–32)

Though this comment applies primarily to the context of political deliberation by members of a city's ruling deliberative body, it is the model for Aristotle's account of an individual agent's deliberation as well. This is particularly clear when an individual's action-controlling beliefs—the guiding premises of his deliberative reasoning—are analogized to decrees (VII 9 1151$^b$15, 10 1152$^a$20–21). But it is similarly in operation when the last thing reached in deliberation is identified as a decree (VI 8 1141$^b$26–28). Practical wisdom is a prescriptive virtue (VI 10 1143$^a$8) indeed because it issues in decrees which, like laws, have prescriptive force.

The picture that finally emerges of politics, therefore, is of a science that has three elements. The first is legislative science, which, since it issues universal laws that have the right sort of modal status (allowing for differences of direction of fit), makes politics similar enough to a canonical theoretical science to justify its classification as a science. The second is deliberative ability (*bouleutikê*), which is particularistic enough to justify its classification as practical. The third is the judicial science (*dikastikê*), which is primarily exercised in the administration of legal justice (*dikê*) (VI 8 1141$^b$33). But this is a picture of politics that has, as it were, a concealed element, which is the one providing an argument for the starting-points—happiness, the virtues—that are crucial to it. These, we learned, it was the job of the method of inquiry used in the *Ethics* to provide. We must now see what that job consists in.

## *The Foundations of Politics*

We know that scientific starting-points cannot be demonstrated. They are what we construct demonstrations from not to. Of scientific starting-points, therefore, we have understanding, not scientific knowledge (VI 6 1141$^a$7–8)—even if, when we do have understanding of them combined with demonstrations from them, what we have is a more exact form of such knowledge (VI 7 1141$^a$16–18). It is in this less exact way, remember, that we saw we should speak when considering the scientific status of politics. How, then, do we get this understanding? Where do we start the process? "We must," Aristotle says, "start from things that are knowable. But things are knowable in two ways, since some are knowable to us, some unconditionally. So presumably we should start from things knowable to us" (I 4 1095$^b$2–4). For the sake of clarity, let us call these *raw starting-points*. These are what we start from when we are arguing to *explanatory scientific starting-points*. It is crucial not to confuse the two.

In the case of the method of inquiry developed in the *Ethics*, we are told that a raw starting-point is "the fact that something is so" (I 4 1095$^b$6; also I 7 1098$^b$2–3) and that this fact concerns "noble things, just things, and the topics of politics as a whole" (1095$^b$5–6). But since no explicit examples are given of these starting-points, we need to do some detective work to get a better understanding of what exactly they are.

An important clue to their nature derives from the way that we gain access to them: "it is virtue, whether natural or habituated, that teaches correct belief about the starting-point" (VII 8 1151$^a$18–19). Hence Aristotle's insistence on the importance of being well or nobly brought up: "it makes no small difference whether people are habituated in one way or in another way straight from childhood; on the contrary, it makes a huge one—or rather, *all* the difference" (II 1 1103$^b$23–25). Equally important is the account of the way that failure to be brought up well affects or blocks our access to raw starting-points:

> Ordinary people naturally obey not shame but fear, and abstain from base things not because of their shamefulness but because of the sanctions involved. For living by feeling as they do, they pursue the pleasures that are properly their own as well as the things through which these come about, and avoid the opposing pains. Of what is noble and what is truly pleasant, however, they have no understanding at all, not having tasted it.
>
> What sort of argument, then, could reform such people? For it is not possible—or not easy—to alter by argument what has long since been locked up in traits of character. (X 9 1179$^b$11–16)

By being habituated badly where pleasures and pains are concerned, people are prevented from experiencing what is noble and truly pleasant. When such people read in the *Ethics* that we should sacrifice wealth, power, honor, the satisfaction of their appetites, and other such so-called external goods (I 8 1098$^b$12–16n) in order to gain what is noble for ourselves, they should suppose it mere words (X 8 1179$^a$22). After all, their own life experience, which is what casts "the controlling vote" (1179$^a$20) in practical matters, tells them in no uncertain terms that words is all it is. For ordinary people "judge by external goods, since these are the only ones they can perceive" (1179$^a$16), and so when they see someone who lacks these, they cannot see how he could be happy, and when they see him sacrifice these for the sake of what is noble they cannot do otherwise than take him to be sacrificing his self-interest for an empty dream (IX 8).

One kind of raw political starting-point, then, is a belief about the sort of value that noble things (as well as just things) have. People who have been correctly habituated to enjoy and hate in a noble way see correctly that these things are intrinsically valuable or choiceworthy for their own sake and that they are more valuable than external goods. People who have been inadequately habituated cannot see this and so reject one of the raw starting-points of politics right off the bat. When they read the *Ethics*, therefore, they simply cannot see the truth in it, and so it is of no practical value to them. They do what virtue requires of them to the extent that they do from fear of penalties rather than for the sake of what is noble (X 9 1180ª4–5).

Happiness is also a raw starting-point of politics (I 12 1102ª2–4), about which people quite reasonably get "their suppositions . . . from their lives" (I 5 1095ᵇ15–16). Hence happiness too can seem as variable as good things generally (I 3 1094ª16–17). As a result, ordinary people—anyway "the most vulgar ones"—suppose that happiness is pleasure, since their bad habituation, especially where bodily pleasures and pains are concerned, leads them exclusively to pursue "money, honors, and bodily pleasures . . . on the supposition that they are the best goods" (IX 8 1168ᵇ16–18). Yet, as Aristotle points out, they "have an argument for their choice," since people in positions of power, like Sardanapalus, who are able to do what they want, pursue these goods too. It is this argument that makes their views worth examining (I 4 1095ª28–30). The same goes for people whose upbringings have lead them to pursue honor as if it were the best good.

Raw political starting-points, we now see, are socially mediated and language mediated facts (or putative facts) that are accessible only to properly socialized subjects and so only to subjects who are members of societies—that is, of groups that socialize or habituate their members into some common form of life. Here is Aristotle himself on the topic:

> A voice (*phônê*) is an indicator of what is pleasant or painful, which is why it is also possessed by the other animals (for their nature goes this far: they not only perceive what is pleasant or painful but also indicate them to each other). But rational speech (*logos*) is for making clear what is beneficial or harmful, and hence also what is just or unjust. For it is special to human beings, in comparison to other animals, that they alone have perception of what is good or bad, just or unjust, and the rest. And it is community in these that makes a household and a city. (*Pol.* I 2 1253ª10–18)

It follows, then, that the beliefs of properly socialized subjects—or the way things noble, just, and so on appear to them as a result of such socialization—are the rawest data available. It is to these that politics is ultimately answerable. That is why the *Ethics* invariably appeals to what socialized subjects say or think or to how things seem or appear to them (for example, I 8 1098ᵇ9–12).

It is useful to juxtapose this picture of the *Ethics* to a picture Aristotle gives of the canonical sciences and of the importance in them of experience and ultimately of perception:

> What causes our inability to take a comprehensive view of the agreed-upon facts is lack of experience. That is why those who dwell in more intimate association with the facts of nature are better able to lay down [explanatory] starting-points which can bring together a good many of these, whereas those whom many arguments have made unobservant

> of the facts come too readily to their conclusions after looking at only a few facts. (*GC* I 2 316ᵃ5–10)

We might advisedly see "those who dwell in more intimate association with the facts of nature," in other words, as the equivalent in a canonical science of the well brought up or properly socialized and habituated subjects of the *Ethics*, who, "because they have an eye formed from experience, . . . see correctly" (VI 11 1143ᵇ13–14). And one reason we might do so is that canonical scientists too are socialized subjects, albeit of a somewhat specialized sort. For it is only within scientific communities or communities of knowledge that, through complex processes of habituation and teaching, canonical scientists are produced: we learn science from other scientists (X 9 1180ᵇ28–34). But communities of knowledge, both in Aristotle's view and in reality, are parts of the political community and are regulated and sustained by it. When we first meet politics, in fact, it is as an architectonic science that oversees the others, ensuring that all sciences work together to further human happiness (I 2 1094ᵃ26–ᵇ7).

Because the things that appear to be so to appropriately socialized subjects are the raw starting-points in canonical sciences just as much as in politics, the only difference between them lying in the sort of socialization involved, we must be careful not to think of an appeal to "the things we say (*ta legomena*)" (I 8 1098ᵇ10, VII 1 1145ᵇ20) as an appeal to evidence of a sort quite different from the sort appealed to in a canonical science. We are not in the one case appealing to conceptual considerations or "intuitions," and in the other case to empirical facts or findings. We are not looking at analytic matters as opposed to synthetic ones. Instead, what we have in both cases are socially mediated facts, some closer to the conceptual or the analytic, some closer to the empirical or synthetic. Political subjects who disagree about the intrinsic choiceworthiness of what is noble, for example, are not disagreeing about a concept or about the meaning of a word but are disagreeing about a substantive issue concerning how to live. Aristotle's account of happiness and his definition of virtue of character as a sort of medial state are to be evaluated not by appeal to our intuitions but by appeal to the facts of our lives (X 8 1179ᵃ17–22).

The significance of these conclusions about raw political starting-points and the kinds of subjects who can detect them is most easily seen when we run across—as readers of the secondary literature on the *Ethics* inevitably will—topics related to the "foundations" of Aristotle's ethics. Often a central exhibit in these discussions is the famous function (*ergon*) argument (I 7 1097ᵇ22–1098ᵃ20), where it is thought that the notion of a function is introduced into politics as something already so grounded in the facts (or putative facts) of Aristotle's biological or metaphysical investigations that politics then inherits these grounds and becomes hostage to these facts—facts that are not themselves political facts or putative facts. Another frequent exhibit is the use Aristotle makes, at various junctures, of his own account of the soul—an account supported not by political facts or putative facts, apparently, but by biological or psychological ones (I 13 1102$^{a}$14–26).

What these discussions fail to give proper weight to is the difference between *empirical* foundations, or the facts to which politics or any other body of knowledge is ultimately answerable, and *explanatory* foundations, or the explanatory notions that politics makes use of in explaining those facts. To be sure, these notions may also often play explanatory roles in various other Aristotelian bodies of knowledge, including various theoretical sciences, and may for that reason recommend themselves to Aristotle for use elsewhere. It would be strange if it were otherwise. These notions may well, then, be epistemically sanctioned within these other bodies of knowledge too, providing correct explanations of the relevant sorts of facts. But this does not mean that politics must be committed to them as fixed points of its own explanatory enterprise. Rather it takes them on board wholly and entirely as answerable to raw political starting-points and must reject them if they prove inadequate for those purposes. In the only really important sense, then, politics has political facts as its sole foundations. Biology, metaphysics, and other bodies of knowledge have no foundational role in politics whatsoever.

## *Explanatory Starting-points and Dialectic*

In the case of canonical sciences, the most important explanatory starting-points consist of definitions that specify the genus and differentiae of the real (as opposed to nominal) universal essences of the beings with which the science deals (*APo.* II 10 93$^{b}$29–94$^{a}$19). Since scientific definitions must be apt starting-points of demonstrations, this implies, Aristotle thinks, that the "extremes and the middle terms must come from the same genus" (I 7 75$^{b}$10–11). As a result, a single canonical science must deal with a single genus (I 28 87$^{a}$38–39). The conclusion we reached earlier—that politics deals with and is empirically based only on political facts—thus marks another potential similarity between politics and a canonical science, since it suggests that politics does deal with a single genus and so meets a crucial condition definitive of a canonical science.

It should come as no surprise, then, that in defining the virtues of character, which are the explanatory starting-points of politics and are those states of the soul with which noble and just actions must be in accord, Aristotle first specifies their genus (*NE* II 5 1106$^{a}$12–13). They are, he says, states (*hexeis*)—where a state is a condition "by dint of which we are well or badly off in relation to feelings" (1105$^{b}$25–26). Then, making use of the so-called doctrine of the mean, he goes on to tell us what the differentiae are of the states that are virtues: "Virtue . . . is a deliberately choosing state, which is in a medial condition in relation to us, one defined by a reason and the one by which a practically-wise person would define it" (II 6 1106$^{b}$36–1107$^{a}$1). At that point he implies he has discovered virtue's "essence (*ousia*) and the account (*logos*) that states its what it is to be (*to ti ên einai*)" (1107$^{a}$6–7). It is just what a definition or account in a canonical science is supposed to do (*APo.* II 3 90$^{b}$16, 10 93$^{b}$29).

There is an important difference, though, which Aristotle takes pains to register but whose significance is nonetheless easy to miss. If politics is a science at all, it is a practical one, which aims to make us good. This means that the definitions it produces must be of a sort that can guide the actions of politicians, legislators, and individual agents. They must, in a word, be definitions that can be put into practice. Thus Aristotle's major criticism of Plato's views on the form of the good is that it is impractical: "even if there is some single good predicated in common of all intrinsic goods, a separable one that is itself an intrinsic good, it is clear that it will not be something doable in action or acquirable by a human being. But that is the sort we are now looking for" (*NE* I 6 1096$^{b}$32–35). Moreover, it is even impractical in a more attenuated sense, namely, as a sort of regulative ideal, unachievable in action yet guiding it from beyond. For to treat it as such results in a clash with the productive sciences as these are actually practiced, since the practitioners of the productive sciences, though seeking some good, ignore the form of the good altogether, "yet for all craftsmen not to know—and not even to look for—so important an aid would hardly be reasonable" (1097$^{a}$6–8).

It is true that Aristotle's own definition of happiness as activity of the soul in accord with the best and most complete virtue seems to end up entailing that a certain theoretical activity—the contemplation of the god—is the best kind of happiness (X 7–8). But it is not a theoretical definition for all that, if by "theoretical" we mean, as we should, that truth alone is the measure of its correctness. What matters most is that what it defines, unlike Plato's good itself, is something we can put into practice—something we can *do*. That is why the measure of its success is an entirely practical one: "When we examine what has been previously said, . . . it must be by bringing it to bear on the facts of our life, and if it is in harmony with the facts, we should accept it, but if it clashes, we should suppose it mere words" (X 8 1179$^{a}$20–22). With similar concerns in mind, Aristotle prefaces his definition of virtue of character with an account of how we think such virtue is acquired (II 1) and with a reminder that the goal of the *Ethics* is practical, not theoretical (II 2). When the definition is finally developed (II 5–6), we see that it is in keeping with these prefatory comments, since it is one that can guide us in both inculcating and maintaining the virtues of character in others and in ourselves (II 9).

Nowadays philosophy is for the most part a theoretical subject with few pretensions to having much bearing on practical affairs. So it is easy to forget that Aristotle thinks of some branches of philosophy, anyway, in quite a different way. His discussion of voluntariness and involuntariness, for example, is intended to be "also useful to legislators regarding honors and punishments" (III 1 1109$^{b}$34–35). When we evaluate that discussion, therefore, we shouldn't just do so in standard philosophical fashion—by looking for clever counter-examples, however far fetched they might be. We should think rather of how well it would work in practical life, where the far fetched seldom occurs and requires special provision when it does. Here the discussion of decency (V 10) should serve as our guide.

Understanding, then, that definitions of starting-points in politics must be practical, let us return to the question of how we arrive at these definitions by beginning from raw starting-points. Well, first we have to have the raw starting-points ready to hand. Aristotle is clear about this, as he is indeed about what is supposed to happen next:

> The method (*hodos*) is the same in all cases, in philosophy as well as in the crafts or any sort of learning whatsoever. For one must observe for both terms what belongs to them and what they belong to, and be supplied with as many of these terms as possible. . . .When it is in accord with truth, it must be from the terms that are catalogued (*diagegrammenôn*) as truly belonging, but in dialectical deductions it must be from premises that are in accord with [reputable] belief. . . . Most of the starting-points, however, are special to each science. That is why experience must provide us with the starting-points where each is concerned—I mean, for example, that experience in astronomy must do so in the case of astronomical science. For when the appearances had been adequately grasped, the demonstrations in astronomy were found in the way we described. And it is the same way where any other craft or science whatsoever is concerned. Hence if what belongs to each thing has been grasped, at that point we can readily exhibit the demonstrations. For if nothing that truly belongs to the relevant things has been omitted from the collection, then concerning everything, if a demonstration of it exists, we will be able to find it and give the demonstration, and if it is by nature indemonstrable, we will be able to make that evident. (*APr.* I 30 46$^{a}$3–27)

So once we have a catalogue of the raw starting-points, the demonstrative explanation of them from explanatory scientific starting-points is supposedly fairly routine. We should not, however, demand "the cause [or explanation] in all cases alike. Rather, in some it will be adequate if the fact that they are so has been correctly shown (*deiknunai*)—as it is indeed where starting-points are concerned" (I 8 1098$^{a}$33–$^{b}$2). But what exactly is it to show a starting-point correctly or adequately? It can't be to demonstrate it, we know that.

Aristotle describes what he is undertaking in the *Ethics* specifically as a "method of inquiry (*methodos*)," as we saw, and as a contribution to the "philosophy of human affairs." And to the explanatory scientific starting-points of these, he claims, there is a unique route:

> Dialectic is useful as regards the philosophical sciences because the capacity to go through the puzzles on both sides of a question will make it easier to discern what is true and what is false in each. Furthermore, dialectic is useful as regards the first starting-points (*ta prôta*) where each science is concerned. For it is impossible to say anything about these based on the starting-points properly belonging to the science in question, since these starting-points are the first ones of all, and it is through reputable beliefs (*endoxa*) about each that it is necessary to discuss them. This, though, is a task special to, or most characteristic of, dialectic. For because of its ability to examine (*exetastikê*), it has a route toward the starting-points of all methods of inquiry. (*Top.* I 2 101$^{a}$34–$^{b}$4)

Prima facie, then, the *Ethics* should correctly show the explanatory starting-points of politics by going through puzzles and solving them by appeal to reputable beliefs. But before we rush to the *Ethics* to see whether that is what we do find, we need to be clearer about what exactly we should be looking for. Writers on Aristotle's method of ethics often go astray by failing to do this.

Dialectic is recognizably a descendant of the Socratic elenchus, which famously begins with a question like this: *Ti esti to kalon?* What is the noble? The respondent, sometimes after a bit of nudging, comes up with a universal definition, what is noble is what all the gods love, or whatever it might be (I adapt a well-known answer from Plato's *Euthyphro*). Socrates then puts this definition to the test by drawing attention to some things that seem true to the respondent himself but which conflict with his definition. The puzzle, or *aporia,* that results from this conflict then remains for the respondent to try to solve, usually by reformulating or rejecting his definition. Aristotle understood this process in terms that reveal its relationship to his own:

> Socrates occupied himself with the virtues of character, and in connection with them became the first to look for universal definitions. . . . It was reasonable that Socrates should inquire about the what it is. For he was inquiring in order to deduce, and the starting-point of deductions is the what it is. For there are two things that may be justly ascribed to Socrates—inductive arguments and universal definition, since both are concerned with starting-points of science. (*Met.* XIII 4 1078$^{b}$17–30; also I 6 987$^{b}$1–4)

In Plato too dialectic is primarily concerned with scientific starting-points, such as those of mathematics, and seems to consist in some sort of elenchus-like process of reformulating definitions in the face of conflicting evidence so as to render them puzzle free (*Rep.* VII 532a1–533d1). Aristotle can reasonably be seen, then, as continuing a line of thought about dialectic, even if in works such as the *Topics* and the *Sophistical Refutations* he contributes greatly to its exploration, systemization, and elaboration.

Think now about the respondent's first answer, his first definition: what is noble is what the gods love. Although it is soon shown to be incorrect, there is something quite remarkable about its very existence. Through experience shaped by acculturation and habituation involving the learning of a natural language the respondent is confident that he can say what nobility is. He has learned to apply the word "noble" to particular people, actions, and so on correctly enough to pass muster as knowing its meaning, knowing how to use it. From these particular cases he has reached a putative universal, something the particular cases have in common, but when he tries to define that universal in words, he gets it wrong, as Socrates shows. Here is Aristotle registering the significance of this: "What is knowable to each person at first is often knowable to a very small extent and possesses little or nothing of what is real [or true]. All the same, we must start from what is but badly knowable to us and try . . . to proceed through this to a knowledge of what is entirely knowable" (*Met.* VII 3 1029$^b$8–12).

The route by which the respondent reaches the universal that he is unable to define correctly is what Aristotle calls "induction" (*epagôgê*), or that variant of induction, which also involves the shaping of feelings and the development of character, namely, habituation (*ethismos*). This begins with (1) perception of particulars, which leads to (2) retention of perceptual contents in memory, and, when many such contents have been retained, to (3) an experience, so that for the first time "there is a universal in the soul" (*APo.* II 19 100$^a$3–16). The universal reached at stage (3), which is the one the respondent reaches, is described as "indeterminate" and "better known by perception" (*Ph.* I 1 184$^a$22–25). It is the sort of universal, often quite complex, that constitutes a nominal essence corresponding to the nominal definition or meaning of a general term. Finally, (4) from experience come craft knowledge and scientific knowledge, when "from many intelligible objects arising from experience one universal supposition about similar objects is produced" (*Met.* I 1 981$^a$5–7).

The *nominal* (or analytic, meaning-based) definition of the general term "thunder," for example, might pick out the universal *loud noise in the clouds*. When science investigates the things that have this nominal essence, it may find that they also have a real essence or nature in terms of which their other features can be scientifically explained:

> Since a definition is said to be an account of what something is, it is evident that one sort will be an account of what its name, or of what some other name-like account, signifies—for example, what "triangle" signifies. . . . Another sort of definition is an account that

> makes clear the explanation of why it exists. So the former sort signifies something but does not show it, whereas the latter will evidently be like a demonstration of what it is, differing in arrangement from a demonstration. For there is a difference between giving the explanation of why it thunders and saying what thunder is. In the first case you will say: because fire is being extinguished in the clouds. And what is thunder? The loud noise of fire being extinguished in the clouds. Hence the same account is given in different ways. In one way it is a continuous demonstration, in the other a definition. Further, a definition of thunder is "a noise in the clouds," and this is a conclusion of the demonstration of what it is. The definition of an immediate item, though, is an indemonstrable positing (*thesis*) of what it is. (*APo.* II 10 93$^{b}$29–94$^{a}$10)

A real (or synthetic, fact-based) definition, which analyzes this real essence into its "constituents (*stoicheia*) and starting-points" (*Ph.* I 1 184$^{a}$23), which will be definable but indemonstrable, makes intrinsically clear what the nominal definition made clear to us only by enabling us to recognize instances of thunder in a fairly—but imperfectly—reliably way. As a result, thunder itself, now clearly a natural and not just a conventional kind, becomes better known not just to us but entirely or unconditionally (*NE* I 4 1095$^{b}$2–8). These analyzed universals, which are the sort reached at stage (4), are the ones suited to serve as starting-points of the sciences and crafts: "People with experience know the fact that but not the explanation why, whereas those with craft knowledge know the explanation why, that is, the cause" (*Met.* I 1 981$^{a}$28–30).

Socrates too, we see, wanted definitions that were not just empirically adequate but also explanatory. Thus in telling Euthyphro what he wants in the case of piety, he says that he is seeking "the form itself *by dint of* which all the pieties are pieties" (*Euthphr.* 6d10–11). That is why he rejects the definition of piety as being what all the gods love. This definition is in one way correct, presumably, in that if something is pious, it is necessarily loved by all the gods, and vice versa, but it isn't explanatory, since it doesn't tell us what it is about pious things that makes all the gods love them, and so it does not identify the form by dint of which they are pious (9e–11b).

Let's go back. We wanted to know what was involved in showing a scientific starting-point. We were told how we could *not* do this, namely, by demonstrating it from scientific starting-points. Next we learned that dialectic had a route to it from reputable beliefs. At the same time, we were told that induction had a route to it as well—something the *Ethics* also tells us: "we get a theoretical grasp of some starting-points through induction, some through perception, some through some sort of habituation, and others through other means" (I 7 1098$^{b}$3–4). This suggests that induction and dialectic are in some way or other the same process. It is a suggestion to keep in mind.

What shows a Socratic respondent to be wrong is an example that the respondent's definition does not fit. The presentation of the example might be quite indirect, however. It might take quite a bit of stage setting, elicited by the asking of many questions, to bring out a puzzle. But if the example is one the definition does not fit, it shows that the universal grasped by the respondent and the definition he produces are not entirely or unconditionally knowable and that his state is not one of clear-eyed understanding:

> A puzzle in thought reveals a knot in its subject matter. For thought caught in a puzzle is like people who are tied up, since in either case it is impossible to make progress. That is why one must get a theoretical grasp on all the difficulties ahead of time, both for these reasons and because those who inquire without first going through the puzzles are like people who don't know where they have to go, and, in addition, don't even know whether they have found what they were inquiring about, since the end is not clear to them. But to someone who has first gone through the puzzles it is clear. (*Met.* III 1 995$^a$30–$^b$2)

But lack of such clear-eyed understanding of a scientific starting-point has serious downstream consequences:

> If we are to have scientific knowledge through demonstration, . . . we must know the starting-points better and be better convinced of them than of what is being shown, but we must also not find anything more convincing or better known among things opposed to the starting-points from which a contrary mistaken conclusion may be deduced, since someone who has unconditional scientific knowledge must be incapable of being convinced out of it. (*APo.* I 2 72$^a$37–$^b$4; also see *NE* VI 3 1139$^b$33–35)

If dialectical examination reveals a puzzle in a respondent's thought about a scientific starting-point, then he cannot have any unconditional scientific knowledge even of what he may well be able to demonstrate correctly from it. Contrariwise, if dialectical examination reveals no such puzzle, then he apparently does have clear-eyed understanding, and his route to what he can demonstrate is free of obstacles.

At the heart of dialectic, as Aristotle understands it, is the dialectical deduction (*dialektikos sullogismos*). This is the argument lying behind the questioner's questions, partly dictating their order and content and partly determining the strategy of his examination. In the following passage it is defined and contrasted with two relevant others:

> Dialectical arguments are those that deduce from reputable beliefs in a way that reaches a contradiction; peirastic arguments are those that deduce from those beliefs of the respondent that anyone must know (*eidenai*) who pretends to possess scientific knowledge . . . ;

> contentious (*eristikos*) arguments are those that deduce or appear to deduce from what appear to be reputable beliefs but are not really such. (*SE* 2 165ᵇ3–8)

If we think of dialectical deductions in this way, a dialectician, in contrast to a contender, is an honest questioner, appealing to genuinely reputable beliefs and employing valid deductions. "Contenders and sophists use the same arguments," Aristotle says, "but not to achieve the same goal. . . . If the goal is apparent victory, the argument is contentious; if it is apparent wisdom, sophistic" (11 171ᵇ27–29). Nonetheless, Aristotle does also use the term *dialektikê* as the name for the craft that honest dialecticians and sophists both use: "In dialectic a sophist is so called on the basis of his deliberate choice, and a dialectician is so called not on the basis of his deliberate choice but on the basis of the capacity he has" (*Rh.* I 1 1355ᵇ20–21). If dialectic is understood in this way, a dialectician who deliberately chooses to employ contentious arguments is a sophist (I 1 1355ᵃ24–ᵇ7). We need to be careful, therefore, to distinguish *honest dialectic* from what we may call *plain dialectic*, which—like all crafts—can be used for good and ill (*NE* V 1 1129ᵃ13–17).

The canonical occasion for the practice of the Socratic elenchus, obviously, is the examination of someone else. But there is nothing to prevent a person from practicing it on himself: "How could you think," Socrates ask Critias, "that I would refute you for any reason other than the one for which I would refute myself, fearing lest I might inadvertently think I know something when I don't know it?" (*Chrm.* 166c7–d2). Dialectic is no different in this regard:

> The premises of the philosopher's deductions, or those of a person who is investigating by himself, though true and knowable, may be refused by the respondent because they lie too near to the original proposition, and so he sees what will happen if he grants them. But the philosopher is unconcerned about this. Indeed, he will presumably be eager that his axioms should be as familiar and as near to the question at hand as possible, since it is from premises of this sort that scientific deductions proceed. (*Top.* VIII 1 155ᵇ10–16)

What we are to imagine, then, is that the political philosopher, to focus on him, surveys the raw political starting-points (the empirical foundations of politics), constructing detailed catalogues of these. He then tries to formulate definitions of the various universals involved in them that seem to be candidate scientific starting-points (virtue, happiness, and so on), testing these against the raw political starting-points by trying to construct demonstrations from them. But these definitions will often be no more than partial; our political philosopher is on his way to complete definitional starting-points, just as the demonstrations will often be no more than proto or nascent demonstrations. The often rudimentary demonstrations that we find in Aristotle's scientific treatises are parts of this process of arguing to not from starting-points. We argue to them in part by seeing whether or to what extent we could demonstrate from them.

So, first, we have the important distinction between dialectic proper, which includes the use of what appear to be deductions from what appear to be reputable beliefs, and honest dialectic, which uses only genuine deductions from genuine reputable beliefs. Second, we have the equally important distinction between the use of dialectic in examining a potentially hostile respondent and its use by the philosopher in a perhaps private pursuit of the truth. Third, we have an important contrast between honest dialectical premises and philosophical ones or scientific ones. Honest dialectical premises are reputable beliefs, philosophical and scientific premises must be true and knowable. Fourth, we have two apparently equivalent routes to scientific starting-points, one inductive, which starts from raw political starting-points, and the other dialectic, which starts from reputable beliefs.

According to the official definition, genuine reputable beliefs are "things that are believed by everyone, by the majority, or by the wise—either by all of them, or by most, or by the most well known and most reputable" (*Top.* I 1 $100^b$21–23). Just as the scientist should have a catalogue of scientific truths ready to hand from which to select the premises of his demonstrations, so a dialectician ought also to select premises "from arguments that have been written down and produce catalogues (*diagraphas*) of them concerning each kind of subject, putting them under separate headings—for example, 'Concerned with good,' 'Concerned with life'" (*Top.* I 14 $105^b$12–15). We should be reminded of the collections of laws and constitutions that enjoy "a good reputation (*eudokimountas*)," from which the legislative scientist selects the best ones (*NE* X 9 $1181^a$12–$^b$12).

Clearly, then, there will be considerable overlap between the scientist's catalogue of raw starting-points and the honest dialectician's catalogue of genuine reputable beliefs. For, first, things that are believed by reputably wise people are themselves reputable beliefs, and, second, any respondent would accept "the beliefs of those who have investigated the subjects in question—for example, on a question of medicine he will agree with a doctor, and on a question of geometry with a geometer" (*Top.* I 10 $104^a$8–37). The catalogues also differ, however, in that not all reputable beliefs need be true. If a proposition is a reputable belief, if it would be accepted by all or most people, it is everything an honest dialectician could ask for in a premise, since his goal is simply this: to reveal by honest deductions that a definition offered by any respondent whatsoever conflicts—if it does—with other beliefs that the respondent has. That is why having a complete or fairly complete catalogue of reputable beliefs is such an important resource for a dialectician. It is because dialectic deals with things only "in relation to belief," then, and not as philosophy and science do, "in relation to truth" (*Top.* I 14 105ᵇ30–31) that it needs nothing more than reputable *beliefs*.

Nonetheless, the fact that all or most people believe something leads us "to trust it as something in accord with experience" (*Div. Somn.* 1 426ᵇ14–16), and—since human beings "are naturally adequate as regards the truth and for the most part happen upon it" (*Rh.* I 1 1355ᵃ15–17)—as containing some truth. That is why having catalogued some of the things that people believe happiness to be, Aristotle writes: "Some of these views are held by many and are of long standing, while others are held by a few reputable men. And it is not reasonable to suppose that either group is entirely wrong, but rather that they are right on one point at least or even on most of them" (*NE* I 8 1098ᵇ27–29). Later he generalizes the claim: "things that seem to be so to everyone, these, we say, are" (X 2 1172ᵇ36–1173ᵃ1). Raw starting-points are just that—raw. But when refined, some shred of truth is likely to be found in them. So likely, indeed, that if none is found, this will itself be a surprising fact needing to be explained: "when a reasonable explanation is given of why an untrue view appears true, this makes us more convinced of the true view" (VII 14 1154ᵃ24–25). It is in the perhaps mere grain of truth enclosed in a reputable belief that a philosopher or scientist is interested, then, not in the general acceptability of the surrounding husk, much of which he may discard.

The process of refinement in the case of a candidate explanatory starting-point is that of testing a definition of it against reputable beliefs. This may result in the definition being accepted as it stands or in its being altered or modified. The same process applies to the reputable beliefs themselves, since they may conflict not only with the definition but also with each other. Again, this may also result in their being modified, often by uncovering ambiguities within them or in the argument supporting them or by drawing distinctions that uncover complexities in these. Thus Aristotle's view that it is "from oneself that all the features fitted to friendship also extend to others" is in accord with the reputable beliefs embodied in "all the proverbs" (IX 8 1168ᵇ5–10). But both conflict with the view that there is something shameful about being a self-lover, since a base person "does all his actions for the sake of himself," whereas a decent one "seems to act because of what is noble . . . and for the sake of a friend, disregarding his own interests" (1168ᵃ31–35). As a result, "it is reasonable to be puzzled . . . as to which side we should follow, since both carry conviction." Hence to ease our puzzlement not just in this case but in all others like it, "we need to draw distinctions in connection with the arguments and determine to what extent and in what ways they grasp the truth. If, then, we were to find out what those on each side mean by 'self-love,' perhaps this would be clear" (1168ᵇ10–15). By the end of the chapter, this is precisely what has been accomplished. If, as ordinary people do, we think of self-lovers as those who gratify the nonrational part of their soul (as if it were their true self) with money, honors, and bodily pleasures (as if these were the greatest goods), we can see why they are right to think that "self-love" is a term of reproach. But if we recognize that noble things are better than these other goods, and that the true self is the understanding, we will also see what is wrong in their view and what is right in the opposing one, and agree that we should be "self-lovers" in that sense of the term.

A more extreme possibility, as we saw, is that a reputable belief isn't modified at all but is rejected entirely and has its appearance of truth explained away. This is what happens in the case of bodily pleasures. These are not more choiceworthy, Aristotle argues, yet they appear to be. So we must explain away their false appearance of choiceworthiness, one source of which is that they "knock out pain," and "get their intensity (which is why they are pursued) from the fact that they appear alongside their contrary" (VII 14 1154$^a$26–31). Sometimes all the reputable beliefs on a certain topic stemming from a certain group can be excluded *en masse*:

> To investigate all the beliefs about happiness held by different people is superfluous, since little children, sick people, and lunatics apparently have many views, but no one with any understanding would go through these. For these people need not arguments but, in some cases, time in which to mature, in others, medical or political correction [or punishment]—for a drug is no less correctional than a flogging. Similarly there is no need to investigate the beliefs of the majority, since they speak baselessly on pretty much every topic but most of all this one. On it, only the beliefs of wise people need be investigated. (*EE* I 3 1214$^b$28–1215$^a$2)

We might see Aristotle's account of the distorting effects on beliefs about happiness of inadequate habituation where pleasures and pains are concerned as the justification of this bold claim. Readers who think that Aristotle gives the life of indulgence shrift that is much too short (see *NE* I 5 1095$^b$19–22, X 6 1176$^b$9–1177$^a$1) should not overlook its bearing on their concern. False consciousness, at least in one of its forms, was as familiar to Aristotle as it subsequently became to Hegel and Marx.

The canonical occasion for the use of honest dialectic, as of the Socratic elenchus and plain dialectic, is the examination of a respondent. The relevant premises for the questioner to use, therefore, are the reputable beliefs in his catalogue that his respondent will accept. Just how wide this set of beliefs is in a given case depends naturally on how accessible to the untrained subject the subject matter is on which he is being examined. In this regard our target candidate science, politics, is in a somewhat special position, since all adequately socialized subjects have access to the relevant subject matter and are even likely to have received some—however vestigial—training in politics itself. That is no doubt why Socrates' respondents are so confident, prior to examination, that they do know how to define the virtues. We might usefully compare the case of religious beliefs about the nature of human beings and the origins of life and cosmos in a society where all the citizens practice the same religion and all the schools teach it. In other more esoteric areas the class of reputable beliefs may be substantially narrower. We may all have some beliefs about thunder and other phenomena readily perceptible to everyone, that are—for that very reason—reputable. But about Mandelbrot sets, Bell's theorem, and messenger RNA we may have none at all.

When a scientist is investigating by himself, the class of premises he will select from is the catalogue of *all* the raw starting-points of his science, despite a natural human inclination to do otherwise:

> Yet . . . people seem to inquire up to a certain point but not as far as it is possible to take the puzzle. It is what we are all inclined to do, to make our inquiry not with an eye to the thing itself but with an eye to the person who says things that contradict him. For even a person inquiring on his own continues up to the point at which he is no longer able to contradict himself. That is why a person who is going to inquire correctly should be able to raise objections to a position by using objections that are proper to the relevant genus, and this will be when he has acquired a theoretical grasp of all the differentiae. (*Cael.* II 13 $294^{b}6$–13)

Hence our scientist will want to err on the side of excess, adding any reputable belief that appears to have any relevance whatsoever, to his catalogue. When he formulates definitions of candidate scientific starting-points from which he thinks he can demonstrate the raw ones, he must then examine himself to see whether he really does in this case have the scientific knowledge he thinks he has. If he is investigating together with fellow scientists, others may examine him: we all do better with the aid of co-workers (*NE* X 7 $1177^{a}34$), among whom time figures as one (I 7 $1095^{a}23$–24). What he is doing is using honest dialectic on himself or having it used on him. But this, we see, is little different from the final stage—stage (4)—of the induction we looked at earlier. Induction, as we might put it, is, in its final stage, (possibly self-directed) honest dialectic.

In a famous and much debated passage of the *Ethics*, Aristotle writes:

> We must, as in the other cases, set out the things that appear to be so and first go through the puzzles, and, in that way show preferably all the reputable beliefs about these ways of being affected, or, if not all of them then most of them, and the ones with the most control. For if the objections are resolved and the reputable beliefs are left standing, that would be an adequate showing. (VII 1 $1145^{b}1$–7)

The specific topic of the comment is "these ways of being affected," which are self-control and its lack as well as resilience and softness. Some people think that the comment applies only to this topic and should not be generalized, even though "as in the other cases" surely suggests a wider scope. And as we can now see, that scope *is* in fact entirely general, since it describes the honest dialectical or inductive route to the starting-points of *all* the sciences and methods of inquiry, with *tithenai ta phainomena* ("set[ting] out the things that appear to be so") describing the initial phase in which the raw starting-points are collected and catalogued.

Earlier we asked whether the *Ethics* took a route like this to the starting-points of politics. Now that we know what exactly it is we are asking, we must follow in Aristotle's footsteps to see what the answer is. If it turns out to be yes, as we have already seen reason to think it will be, that will mark another important point of similarity between politics and a canonical science, increasing our rising confidence that it is in fact a science, albeit a practical one.

## The Route the Ethics Takes

On the basis of the function argument (I 7 1097$^b$22–1098$^a$20), Aristotle defines happiness as (roughly speaking) rational activity in accord with virtue. Although he doesn't explicitly identify this definition in terms of genus and differentiae, as he does in the case of the definition he gives of virtue of character, it seems clear that rational activity is the genus and virtue the differentia. In I 8 he shows that this definition is in accord with reputable beliefs about happiness, which are the relevant raw starting-points, and to that extent explains them. Happiness as so defined, however, "needs external goods to be added" (1099$^a$31–32). This is what leads some people actually to identify happiness with good luck (1099$^b$7–8). It is also—as the beginning of I 9 notes—what leads people to puzzle about whether happiness is acquirable by learning, habituation, or training on the one hand, or by luck or divine dispensation on the other.

Aristotle's response to this puzzle reveals what truth there is in each of the options and how that core of truth (the refined data) is consistent with his definition. In the process, as we are about to see, the definition gets refined too. The dialectical nature of the process is not quite as obvious here as in the discussion of self-love (IX 8), but it reveals the same need "to draw distinctions" (IX 8 1168$^b$12–13).

At the beginning of I 10 a new puzzle, explicitly identified as such (1100$^a$31), arises about the bearing of luck on happiness—this one generated by the reputable opinion of Solon that we should wait to see the end of a person's life before calling him happy. In the course of discussing it a third puzzle, again identified as such (1100$^a$21), arises about the effects of the welfare of descendants on the happiness of someone who has died. By the time he has gone through these puzzles and shown what truth there is in the raw reputable opinions, Aristotle is able to produce a subtle and nuanced account of the effects of luck on human life and then, in light of it, to somewhat modify his definition of happiness:

> What, then, prevents us from calling happy the person who is active in accord with complete virtue and is adequately supplied with external goods, not for some random period of time but in a complete life? Or must we add that he will continue living like that and die accordingly, since the future is obscure to us and we suppose happiness to be an end and complete in every way? If so, we shall call blessed those living people who have and will continue to have the things we mentioned—blessed, though, in the way human beings are. (I 10 1101ᵃ14–21)

The original definition, remember, made no mention of external goods or of the distinctive way, somewhat vulnerable to luck, that human beings are happy.

In I 13, Aristotle introduces some clearly empirical facts about the soul that he will need throughout the rest of the *Ethics,* especially the distinction between the part of the soul that has reason—which will later be divided into the scientific part and the deliberative part (VI 1 1139ᵃ3–14)—and the desiring part which, though it doesn't have reason itself, can listen to it. The major difference between the self-controlled person and the virtuous one will turn out to be that the desiring part of the former listens less well to the rational part than does the desiring part of the latter (I 13 1102ᵇ13–28).

Aristotle says that while someone who is to have knowledge of politics must "get a theoretical grasp on what concerns the soul," that is, psychology, his grasp should be for the sake of producing human virtue and happiness in citizens and "of an extent that is adequate to the things being looked for" (1102ᵃ23–25). The discussion of lack of self-control involves some quite sophisticated material (VII 2–3), as does the discussion of pleasure (X 1–5)—itself a topic on which politics must get a theoretical grasp (VII 11 1152ᵇ1–2) and with which the entire *Ethics* "both as a contribution to virtue and as a contribution to politics" is concerned (II 3 1105ᵃ5–6, 10–13). This political psychology, whatever exactly its precise extent and level of exactness, is part of what we earlier called the explanatory foundations of politics, answerable only to raw political starting-points (even if there is also considerable overlap between these and raw psychological ones). In fact, political psychology can even make contributions of its own to psychology—the discussion of lack of self-control may be a case in point (see, for example, VII 3 1146ᵇ31–1147ᵇ19).

Many other elements in the *Ethics* seem to have a status similar to that of psychology, although it is sometimes less easy to see what body of knowledge they belong to or whether they are really part of the explanatory foundations or of the empirical ones. A few examples will show how diverse and hard to categorize these are: some ends are activities while others are works beyond the activities (I 1 1094a4–5); some things are knowable to us, others unconditionally (I 4 1095b2–3); a human being is by nature political (I 7 1097b11); the most estimable sciences are more steadfast, because the blessed live most of all and most continuously in accord with them (I 10 1100b15–16); there are three proper objects of choice: what is noble, what is advantageous, and what is pleasant (II 3 1104b30–31); the things that come about in the soul are of three types: feelings, capacities, and states (II 5 1105b20); in everything continuous and divisible, it is possible to take more, less, and equal (II 6 1106a26–27); nature is more exact and better than any craft (1106b14–15); the causes of things seem to be: nature, necessity, luck, understanding, and everything that comes about through ourselves (III 3 1112a31–33); parts of the soul have knowledge of something on the basis of a certain similarity and kinship with it (VI 1 1139a8–11); there are things that are far more divine in nature than human beings—the most evident ones being those from which the universe is composed (VI 7 1141a34–b2); the objects in mathematics are given through abstraction (VI 8 1142a18); it is from particulars that universals come and the perception of them is understanding (VI 11 1143b4–5); there are two ways of presenting premises (VII 3 1146b35–1147a1); hypotheses are starting-points in mathematics (VII 8 1151a16–17); all things by nature have something divine in them (VII 13 1153b32); the god always enjoys a single simple pleasure (VII 14 1154b26); what is lovable is either good, pleasant, or useful (VIII 2 1155b18–19); a man and a woman have a different virtue and a different function (VIII 7 1158b17–18); the better person should be more loved than loving (1158b25); each person would seem to be his understanding part, or it most of all (IX 4 1166a22–23); what the producer is in capacity, his work is in activity (IX 7 1168a7); a capacity is brought back to its activity (IX 9 1170a17–18); being determinate is characteristic of the nature of the good (20–21); every process is in time and is of an end, and is complete when it has produced what it seeks to produce (X 4 1174a19–21); the virtue of understanding is separated (X 8 1178a22); the gods exercise a sort of supervision over human affairs (X 8 1179a24–25). About some of these, Aristotle is clear that we should look elsewhere in his works for an exact account of them (X 4 1174b2–3, 8 1178a23), but the fact remains that each is a potential target of honest dialectical scrutiny and that each must earn its political keep. It may not be by appeal to raw political starting-points, however broadly conceived, that these explanatory starting-points are best criticized or defended, but in the end it is the political ones they must, as parts of politics, help explain.

In II 1–4, Aristotle argues that we acquire justice and temperance by doing just and temperate actions, and similarly for all the other virtues of character.

Then in II 4 he confronts a puzzle (1105ª17) about this that someone might raise on the basis of the apparently sensible claim that to do just or temperate actions we must be already just or temperate. To solve the puzzle Aristotle introduces a distinction between doing just or temperate actions, which is possible without being just or temperate, and doing them as a just or temperate person would do them, which isn't (1105ᵇ5–12). This distinction is crucial for understanding how virtue differs from self-control.

The definition of virtue of character formulated in II 5–6 is tested by appeal to reputable beliefs about the individual virtues in III 1–V 8 without explicit mention of puzzles. But when we reach V 9–11, we are again in puzzle land—first, concerning the adequacy of the definition of suffering an unjust action (V 9 1136ª10, 23, ᵇ1, 15, and V 10 1138ª26–28), then concerning various apparently conflicting truths about justice and decency (V 10 1137ᵇ6, 11). Similarly, once the definitions of the virtues of thought have been developed and discussed in VI 1–11, VI 12–13 raises a series of puzzles about what use they are (VI 12 1143ᵇ18, 36).

The discussion of self-control and the lack of it in VII 1–10, referred to in the previous section, is a recognized showcase of the importance of puzzles and dialectic in the *Ethics*. Later we have a puzzle about whether friends really do wish the greatest good to their friends (VIII 7 1159ª5–7), puzzles about the allocation of goods among friends (IX 2 1164ᵇ2) and the dissolution of friendships (IX 3 1165ª36), the marvelous puzzle about whether a person should love himself most of all (IX 8 1168ª28), and finally the puzzle about whether friends share our burden when we are suffering (IX 11 1171ª30). The mark of all these puzzles—indeed the defining marks of a puzzle as opposed to some other sort of problem—is that there is a conflict between views, all of which carry conviction (IX 8 1168ᵇ10–12), which cannot be resolved simply by appeal to explanatory starting-points because it is these they challenge.

The fact that the *Ethics* explicitly refers to puzzles over thirty times is one measure of the importance of honest dialectic in it. But if we take this as the only measure, we are likely not to recognize the honest dialectic present in the many discussions in which no puzzles arise because none are encountered. This would be a mistake, as we saw, that our understanding of the *Ethics* would inherit from a mistake we had already made about the nature of honest dialectic and its role in all canonical sciences. When appearances, or what appears so, or what is evident to properly socialized subjects is appealed to—as happens hundreds of times in the *Ethics*—honest dialect is silently there, even if no puzzles are present.

With that caveat in mind, let us return to the question we started with. Does the *Ethics* take an honest dialectical route to the theoretical starting-points of politics? Now that we have traveled that route armed with a proper understanding of honest dialect, we can see that it does. Hence politics is, in this respect too, similar to a canonical Aristotelian science.

Is politics, then, sufficiently similar to count as a science—provided that we *are* guided by similarities and are not speaking in an exact way? If we look, as we should, to politics' universalist component, the answer is that politics is as much like a canonical theoretical science as a natural science is. If we look to politics' particularist component, the answer is that it is not a science. All of which is to say that politics is a *practical* science, one with both a universalist and a particularist component. The contribution the *Ethics* makes to this science, so conceived, is to give it its capstone or "head"—a clear-eyed understanding of its primary starting-points (VI 7 1141ᵃ19) that is at once true and (unlike Plato's form of the good) practical. But a contribution to politics is also perforce a contribution to practical wisdom, since politics and practical wisdom are the same state of the soul (VI 8 1141ᵇ23–24). It isn't just to the politician that the *Ethics* speaks, therefore, but to every properly socialized ethical agent.

## *Where the Route Leads*

The *Ethics* begins with the raw political starting-points available to properly socialized subjects, and follows a route to properly scientific explanatory starting-points, a route that is in essence inductive and dialectical. But to where does that route finally lead?

What scientific investigation of ourselves and the world tells us, Aristotle thinks, is that our understanding (*nous*) is a divine element in us, and the one with which we are most identified:

> It would seem too that each person actually *is* this, if indeed it is the controlling and better element. So it would be strange if he were to choose not his own life but that of something else. Moreover, what we said before will fit now as well. For what properly belongs to each thing by nature is best and most pleasant for each of them. For each human being, then, the life in accord with understanding is so too, if indeed this most of all is a human being. Hence, this life will also be happiest. (X 7 1178ᵃ2–8; also *Protr.* B58–70)

Active understanding in accord with theoretical wisdom, moreover, as our function brought to completion in accord with the best and most complete virtue, is the best kind of happiness, provided it extends through a complete life (X 7 1177ᵇ24–26). Since practical wisdom has happiness as its defining target and teleological starting-point, it must aim to further contemplation, the leisure time required for it, and the relevant sort of completeness of life—at any rate, when circumstances permit.

When practical wisdom finds itself in such circumstances, the universal laws it must enact in its guise as politics include those pertaining to the education of (future) citizens in the virtues of character and thought and to the various so-called external goods, such as wealth and so on, needed for virtuous activities, long life, and, indeed, for life itself (VI 13 1145$^a$6–11). Practical wisdom should maximize the cultivation of the character and its virtues, since "a happy life for human beings is possessed more often by those who have cultivated their character and thought to an extreme degree" (*Pol.* VII 1 1323$^b$1–3). As to activities, practical wisdom should aim to have us spend the greatest possible amount of time on the leisured ones, and of these, contemplation in accord with theoretical wisdom, since "those to whom it more belongs to contemplate, it also more belongs to be happy, not coincidentally but rather in accord with contemplation, since this is intrinsically estimable" (*NE* X 8 1178$^b$29–31).

But a human being is a political animal. He needs family, friends, fellow citizens, and other external goods if he is to be able to contemplate, and cannot survive on a diet of contemplation alone, since his nature, unlike a god's, is not self-sufficient for it (X 8 1178$^b$33–1179$^a$9). Insofar as he is human, therefore, he will deliberately choose to do actions that are in accord with virtue of character. If, as may happen because of uncontrollable circumstances, such actions fail to achieve the leisure needed for contemplation, they nonetheless, as intrinsically valuable themselves, constitute a kind of happiness second in quality only to the best kind of happiness constituted by contemplation itself. The life in which it is achieved, even if no better kind of happiness is thereby furthered, is, Aristotle says, "happiest, but in a secondary way . . . since the activities in accord with it are [merely] human" (X 8 1178$^a$9–10).

The life consisting of unleisured practical political activity in accord with practical wisdom and the virtues of character is thus the altogether happiest one, when—because it is led in a city with the best constitution, ideally situated and provisioned with external goods—it succeeds in achieving the best kind of happiness for its possessor. This complex life—part practical, part contemplative—is the best human life that practical wisdom, which is the best kind of practical knowledge, can arrange.

How well does this conclusion fit with our own conception of happiness and happy lives? The first point to make is that our conception is unsettled and disputed. Nonetheless being happy seems to be a favorable emotional state or state of feeling of some sort. If someone emotionally endorses his life so that he is cheerful or joyful rather than sad, is engaged in it so that he is absorbed by it rather than bored or alienated, and is attuned to it so that he is relaxed rather than anxious or stressed—or is these things more than their contraries—he is happy. Perhaps those who think that *eudaimonia* is pleasure (I 4 1095$^a$22–23) come close to thinking of it as we think of happiness. Yet pleasure doesn't seem to be happiness, even if it is somehow involved in it. One can be unhappy even though one is regularly experiencing pleasures. An intense pleasure, such as orgasm, need not make one very happy. Being in constant pain is not the same as being unhappy, although it can, of course, be a source of unhappiness. Those who think the *eudaimôn* life is the political life or the contemplative one seem yet further away from thinking of them as happy lives. For nothing about these lives seems to ensure that those who live them will necessarily be in a favorable emotional state—an excellent politician or philosopher can be sad, alienated, or anxious. Worthwhile lives they may be, but a life can be worthwhile without being happy.

Aristotle's own account of *eudaimonia* avoids some of these problems of its fit with happiness, in part because it intentionally incorporates elements of the other conceptions, since these—simply because of their appeal to the many or the wise—amount to *endoxa,* or reputable opinions about *eudaimonia*, which sound dialectical methodology must respect:

> Again, all the things that are looked for where *eudaimonia* is concerned apparently hold of what we have said it is. For to some it seems to be virtue, to others practical wisdom, to others some sort of theoretical wisdom, while to others it seems to be these, or one of these, involving pleasure or not without pleasure. Other people include external prosperity as well. Some of these views are held by many and are of long standing, while others are held by a few reputable men. And it is not reasonable to suppose that either group is entirely wrong, but rather that they are right on one point at least or even on most of them. (I 8 1098$^{b}$22–29)

As a result Aristotle sees as an important point in favor of his account of *eudaimonia* as activity in accord with the best and most complete virtue, that it makes pleasure intrinsic to the *eudaimôn* life:

> The things that are pleasant to ordinary people, however, are in conflict because they are not naturally pleasant, whereas the things pleasant to lovers of what is noble *are* naturally pleasant. And actions in accord with virtue are like this, so that they are pleasant both to such people and intrinsically.
>
> Their life, then, has no need of a pleasure that is superadded to it, like some sort of appendage, but has its pleasure within itself. (I 8 1099$^{a}$11–16)

Although he is not equally explicit that his account also incorporates such truth as there is in the view of those who make *eudaimonia* reside in honor—the virtue of character that attracts it, and the practical wisdom that goes along with it—or in theoretical wisdom, he is explicit that any adequate account would have to do so. In any case, his own two-tiered conception—consisting of the second-best sort of *eudaimonia* (activity in accord with full virtue of character) that is for the sake of the very best sort (activity in accord with theoretical wisdom)—does seem designed to meet this adequacy condition.

Because the Aristotelian *eudaimôn* life is intrinsically pleasant or enjoyable, it is plausibly seen as cheerful or joyful, especially since—as in accord with correct reason, whether deliberative or architectonic—it would seem to be reflectively endorsed by the agent in a way that these emotions evidence. For the same reason, the *eudaimôn* person seems unlikely to be bored, alienated, or anxious about living the life he has been trained and habituated to live and has chosen as best. Although *eudaimonia* is an activity, not a favorable emotional state, it wouldn't be *eudaimonia* if it did not involve such a state by being the actualization of it. In this regard, *eudaimonia* is like the simple pleasures it may at times involve—pleasant and valuable in part because evoking desire. Nonetheless, the activity itself in which *eudaimonia* consists is relatively more important than the enjoyment of it, since it is better to do the noble things that the virtuous person would do, even if it makes one sad, bored, and anxious (as might be true of the self-controlled person), than to do something else that inspires the contrary feelings (as might be true of the one who lacks self-control). For Aristotelian *eudaimonia,* the noble activity counts for more than the emotional state it evokes in the agent. That is why Aristotle cites with approval the words of Hesiod:

> Best of all is the one who understands everything himself,
> Good too is that person who is persuaded by one that has spoken
> well.
> But he who neither understands it himself nor listening to another
> Takes it to heart, that one is a useless man. (*NE* I 4 1095$^b$10–11)

Because happiness does consist in a favorable emotional state, moreover, what evokes it can vary from person to person, and—arguably—the person himself or herself is the final authority on its existence: if someone feels happy, he is happy. These, too, are important points of difference with Aristotelian *eudaimonia.* A further difference seems more important still. When we say that someone is happy, we describe his life in psychological terms. We do not in the relevant sense evaluate it. A happy life needn't be successful or accomplished or admirable. It need not amount to much. The very modest can be very happy, while the driven, the brilliant, the heroic, the creative, and even the saintly may have a much harder time of it. Children can be happy, dogs, too, it seems, but neither can be *eudaimôn.* Aristotelian *eudaimonia* has a large perfectionist element, in other words, that happiness seems to lack.

We might want to acknowledge this element by translating Aristotelian *eudaimonia* as "flourishing." But one advantage of "happiness" over these alternatives is that it highlights the importance of a favorable emotional state—of endorsement and engagement—to the *eudaimôn* life. In addition, what evokes that emotional state should be the best good for a human being—a kind of active living in accord with virtue, in which the state is realized and expressed. So conceived, *eudaimonia* surely has a lot to recommend it as the goal of life.

When we see what Aristotle thinks *eudaimonia* consists in, however, a question arises: how seriously can we take that recommendation? Could contemplation really be happiness of the best kind? At the end of the *Ethics,* Aristotle tells us, as we saw, that we should evaluate his account by "bringing it to bear on the facts of our life, and if it is in harmony with the facts, we should accept it, but if it clashes, we should suppose it mere words" (X 8 1179ᵃ20–22). But that just seems to make matters worse. For who among us lives the contemplative life or can claim on the basis of experience that it is the happiest of all? At the same time, few will want to consider the *Ethics* mere words on these grounds. They will be more inclined to turn toward the second best kind of *eudaimonia,* which consists in activity in accord with practical wisdom and the virtues of character. For them, Book VI and not Book X might reasonably be treated as the argumentative culmination of the work—the place where the account of the virtues of character is completed by the account of the correct reason with which they must be in accord. There is an important sense, then, in which practical wisdom—politics—is not simply a central topic of the *Ethics* but its most valuable legacy.

# *Nicomachean Ethics*

# Book I

## I 1

Every craft and every method of inquiry and likewise |1094a1| every action and deliberate choice seems to seek some good.[1] That is why they correctly declare that the good is "that which all seek."[2]

A certain difference, however, appears to exist among ends.[3] For some are activities while others are works of some sort beyond the activities themselves.[4] But wherever there are ends beyond the actions, in those cases, the works are naturally better than the activities. But since there are many sorts of actions and of crafts and sciences, their ends are many as well. For health is the end of medicine, a ship of shipbuilding, victory of generalship, and wealth of household management.[5]

Some of these fall under some one capacity, however, as bridle making falls under horsemanship, along with all the others that produce equipment for horsemanship, and as it and every action in warfare fall under generalship, and, in the same way, others fall under different ones.[6] But in all such cases, the ends of the architectonic ones are more choiceworthy than the ends under them, since these are pursued for the sake also of the former.[7] It makes no difference, though, whether the ends of the actions are the activities themselves or some other thing beyond them, just as in the sciences we have mentioned.[8]

## I 2

If, then, there is some end of things doable in action that we wish for because of itself, and the others because of it, and we do not choose everything because of something else (since if *that* is the case, it will go on without limit so that the desire will be empty and pointless), it is clear that this will be the good—that is, the best good.[9] Hence regarding our life as well, won't knowing the good have great influence and—like archers with a target—won't we be better able to hit what we should?[10] If so, we should try to grasp in outline, at least, what the good is and to which of the sciences or capacities it properly belongs.[11]

It would seem to be the one with the most control, and the most architectonic one.[12] And politics seems to be like this, since it is the one that prescribes which of the sciences need to exist in cities and which ones each group in cities should learn and up to what point.[13] |1094b1| Indeed, we see that even the capacities that are generally most honored are under it—for example, generalship, household management, and rhetoric.[14] And since it uses the other practical sciences and, furthermore, legislates about what must be done and what avoided, its end will circumscribe those of the others, so that it will be the human good.[15]

For even if the good is the same for an individual and for a city, that of a city is evidently a greater and, at any rate, a more complete good to acquire and preserve.[16] For while it should content us to acquire and preserve this for an individual alone, it is nobler and more divine to do so for a nation and city. And so our method of inquiry seeks the good of these things, since it is a sort of politics.[17]

## I 3

Our account will be adequate if its degree of perspicuity is in accord with its subject matter.[18] For we must not look for the same degree of exactness in all accounts, any more than in all products of the crafts.[19]

Noble things and just things, which are what politics investigates, admit of so much difference and variability that they seem to exist by conventional law alone and not by nature.[20] Good things seem to admit of variability in the same way too, because they result in harm in many cases, since some have in fact been destroyed because of wealth, others because of courage. So it should content us, in an account that concerns and is in accord with such things, to show the truth roughly and in outline, and—in an account that concerns things that hold for the most part and is in accord with them—to reach conclusions of the same sort too.[21] It is in the same way, then, that we also need to take each of the things we say. For it is characteristic of a well-educated person to look for the degree of exactness in each kind of investigation that the nature of the subject itself allows.[22] For it is evident that accepting persuasive arguments from a mathematician is like demanding demonstrations from a rhetorician.[23]

But each person correctly discerns the things he knows and is a good discerner of these. Hence a person well educated in a given area is a good discerner *in that area,* while a person well educated in all areas is an unconditionally good discerner.[24] |1095a1| That is why a young person is not a suitable audience for politics.[25] For he has no experience of the actions of life, and the accounts are in accord with these and concerned with these.[26]

Further, since he tends to follow his feelings, it will be pointless and not beneficial for him to be in the audience, since the end is not knowledge but action.[27] And it makes no difference whether he is young in years or immature in character, since the deficiency is not a matter of time but is due to living and pursuing each thing in accord with his feelings. For to people like that, knowledge turns out to be profitless in just the way it does to those who lack self-control.[28] For those who form their desires and do their actions in accord with reason, however, it will be of great benefit to know about these things.

So much for the prefatory remarks concerning the audience, how our discussion is to be received, and what we are proposing to do.

## I 4

Let us, then, resume our account. Since every sort of knowledge and every deliberate choice reaches after some good, let us say what it is politics seeks—that is, what the topmost of all the good things doable in action is.

About its name, most people are pretty much agreed, since both ordinary people and sophisticated ones say it is "happiness" and suppose that living well and doing well are the same as being happy.[29] Concerning happiness, however, and what it is, they are in dispute, and ordinary people do not give the same answer as wise ones. For ordinary people think it is one of the plainly evident things, such as pleasure or wealth or honor—some taking it to be one thing, others another. And often the same person thinks it is different things, since when he gets a disease, it is health, whereas when he is poor, it is wealth. But when these people are conscious of their own ignorance they are wonder-struck by those who proclaim some great thing that is over their heads. And some people did used to think that, beyond these many good things, there is another intrinsically good one that causes all of them to be good.[30]

Now it is presumably quite pointless to inquire into all these beliefs, and enough to inquire into those that are most prevalent or that seem to have some argument for them.[31]

We must not let it escape our notice, however, that arguments leading from starting-points and arguments leading to starting-points are different.[32] For Plato too was rightly puzzled about this and would inquire whether the route was leading from starting-points or to starting-points—as, in a stadium racecourse, that of the athletes may lead away from the starting-point toward the boundary or in the reverse direction. We must indeed start from things that are knowable. But things are knowable in two ways, since some are knowable to us, some unconditionally.[33] So presumably we should start from things knowable to us.

That is why we must be nobly brought up if, where noble things, just things, and the topics of politics as a whole are concerned, we are to be an adequate audience.[34] For the starting-point is the fact that something is so, and, if this is sufficiently evident, we do not also need the explanation of why it is so.[35] A nobly brought up person, then, either has the starting-points or can easily get hold of them. And as for someone who neither has nor can get hold of them, he should listen to Hesiod:

> Best of all is the one who understands everything himself,
> Good too is that person who is persuaded by one that has spoken well.
> But he who neither understands it himself nor listening to another
> Takes it to heart, that one is a useless man.[36]

## I 5

But let us take up our account at the point where we digressed.[37] People seem (which is not unreasonable) to get their suppositions about the good—that is, happiness—from their lives.[38] For ordinary people, the most vulgar ones, suppose it to be pleasure. And that is why the life they like is the life of indulgence. For there are three lives that stand out: the one we just mentioned, the political, and, third, the contemplative.[39]

Now ordinary people do seem wholly slavish, because the life they deliberately choose is one that is characteristic of grazing cattle. They have an argument for their choice, though, because many of those in positions of authority feel the same as Sardanapalus.[40]

Sophisticated people, on the other hand, and doers of action, deliberately choose honor, since it is pretty much the end of the political life. It, however, is apparently more superficial than what we are looking for, since it seems to be in the hands of the honorers more than of the honorees, whereas we have a hunch that the good is something that properly belongs to us and is difficult to take away.[41] Further, people seem to pursue honor in order to be convinced that they are good—at any rate, they seek to be honored by practically-wise people, among people who know them, and for virtue.[42] It is clear, then, that according to them, at least, virtue is better.

Maybe one might even suppose that *it* is more the end of the political life than honor is. But even virtue is apparently too incomplete, since it seems possible to have virtue even while sleeping or being inactive throughout life or while suffering evils and bad luck of the worst sort. Someone who was living like *that*, however, |**1096a1**| no one would call happy unless he was defending a thesis at all costs.[43] That is enough about these issues, since they have also been adequately discussed in the works that are in circulation.[44]

The third life is the contemplative one, which we shall undertake to investigate in what follows.

The life of a moneymaker is in a way forced, and wealth is clearly not the good we are looking for, since it is useful and for the sake of something else.[45] Hence we might be more inclined to suppose that the things already mentioned are the end, since they are liked because of themselves. But they are apparently not the end either—indeed, many arguments have been presented against them. So we may set them aside.[46]

## I 6

But perhaps we had better investigate the universal good and go through the puzzles concerning the way in which it is said of things, even if this sort of inquiry is an uphill one because the men who introduced the forms were friends of ours.[47] Yet it would seem better, perhaps, and something we should do, at any rate when the preservation of the truth is at stake, to confute even what is properly our own, most of all because we are philosophers. For while we love both our friends and the truth, it is a pious thing to accord greater honor to the truth.

Those, then, who introduced this view did not posit forms for things among which they spoke of prior and posterior, which is why they did not furnish a form of the numbers.[48] But the good is said of things in the categories of what it is, quality, and relation, and what is intrinsically—that is, substance—is naturally prior to relation (for a relation would seem to be an offshoot or coincidental attribute of what is), so that there will not be some common form set over these.[49]

Further, good is said of things in as many ways as being. For it is said of things in the category of what it is (for example, the god and the understanding), in that of quality (the virtues), in that of quantity (the moderate amount), in that of relation (the useful), in that of time (the opportune moment), in that of place (a livable dwelling), and so on.[50] Thus it is clear that it will not be some common universal—that is, a "one."[51] For then it would not be said of things in all the categories but only in one.

Further, if of things that are in accord with one form there is also one science, then of all goods there would also be some one science.[52] But as things stand there are many, even of goods in one category—for example, of the opportune moment (for in war it is generalship but in disease medicine) and of the moderate amount (in food it is medicine but in physical exertion athletic training).

We might also raise puzzles about what they even mean by *each-thing-itself* if indeed of both human-itself and human there is a single account—namely, that of human.[53] For insofar as each is human, they will not differ at all, and neither will the corresponding "ones," insofar as each is good.

Neither will the good-itself be more of a good by being eternal, if indeed a long-lasting white thing is no whiter than an ephemeral one.

The Pythagoreans seem to have something more convincing to say about this, since they place the One in the column of goods—indeed, Speusippus seems to have followed their lead.[54]

But let us leave these topics for another discussion.

A controversial point, however, does lie concealed in what we have said, because their arguments are not concerned with *every* good. Those said of things in accord with one form are those pursued and liked as intrinsic goods, whereas those that tend to produce or safeguard these, or to prevent their contraries, are said to be good because of these and in a different way.[55] It is clear, then, that "good" would be said of things in two ways, that is, of some as intrinsic goods, of others as goods because of these. So let us separate off the intrinsic goods from the ones that produce a benefit, and investigate whether intrinsic goods are said to be good in accord with a single form.

The intrinsic ones, though, what sorts of things should we suppose them to be? Or aren't they the ones that are pursued on their own as well, such as thinking, seeing, and certain pleasures and honors? For even if we do pursue these because of other things, we might nonetheless suppose them to belong among the intrinsic goods. Or does nothing else belong there except the form? In that case, the form will be pointless.[56] But if these other things belong among the intrinsic ones, the same account of the goodwill have to show up in all of them, just as that of whiteness does in snow and white lead. In fact, though, the accounts of honor, practical wisdom, and pleasure differ and are at variance regarding the very way in which they are goods.

Hence the good is not something common and in accord with a single form.

But how, then, is it said of things? For at least it does not seem to be a case of homonymy resulting from luck.[57] Is it, then, that all goods at least derive from or are related to a single thing? Or is it more a matter of analogy? For as sight is in the case of body, so understanding is in the case of soul, and so on for other things in other cases.[58]

But perhaps we should leave these questions aside for now, since an exact treatment of them more properly belongs to a different branch of philosophy.[59] Similarly in the case of the form. For even if there is some single good predicated in common of all intrinsic goods, a separable one that is itself an intrinsic good, it is clear that it would not be doable in action or acquirable by a human being.[60] But that is the sort that is being looked for.

Maybe someone might think it better to get to know the form in connection with the goods that *are* acquirable and doable in action. For they might think that by having it as a paradigm, we shall also better know those things that are good for us and—knowing them—aim at and hit them. This argument certainly has some plausibility but it seems to clash with the sciences. For each of these, though it seeks some good and looks for how to supply whatever is lacking, leaves aside knowledge of the form. And yet for all craftsmen not to know—and not even to look for—so important an aid would hardly be reasonable.

There is a puzzle too about how a weaver or a carpenter will benefit, as regards his own craft, from knowing the good-itself or how anyone will be a better doctor or a better general from having seen the form-itself. For the doctor does not even seem to investigate health in that way but, rather, human health, or perhaps, rather, the health of this human being, since it is the particular human being that he treats.

So much, then, for these topics.

## I 7

Let us return to the good we are looking for and what it could possibly be. For it is apparently different in different actions and different crafts, since it is one thing in medicine, a different one in generalship, and likewise for the rest. What, then, is the good characteristic of each? Or isn't it the thing for whose sake the rest of the actions are done? In medicine this is health, in generalship victory, in building a house, and in other crafts something else, and in every action and deliberate choice it is the end, since it is for the sake of the end that everyone does the rest of the actions. So if there is some end of all the things doable in action, this will be the good doable in action, and if there are more than one, it will be these.

Taking a different course, then, our account has reached the same conclusion.[61] But we should try to make this yet more perspicuous.

Since there are evidently many ends, and we choose some of them because of something else, as we do wealth, flutes, and instruments generally, it is clear that not all ends are complete. But the best one is apparently something complete.[62] So if one thing alone is complete, this will be what we are looking for, but if there are more, it will be the most complete of them.

We say that what is intrinsically worth pursuing is more complete than what is worth pursuing because of something else, that what is never choiceworthy because of something else is more complete than things that are both intrinsically choiceworthy and choiceworthy because of it, and that what is unconditionally complete, then, is what is always intrinsically choiceworthy and never choiceworthy because of something else.

Happiness seems to be most like this, since *it* we always choose because of itself and never because of something else. But honor, pleasure, understanding, and every virtue, though we do choose them because of themselves as well (since if they had no further consequences, we would still take each of them), we also choose for the sake of happiness, supposing that because of them we shall be happy. Happiness, on the other hand, no one chooses for the sake of these things or because of anything else in general.

The same conclusion also apparently follows from self-sufficiency, since the complete good seems to be self-sufficient. By "self-sufficient," however, we mean not self-sufficient for someone who is alone, living a solitary life, but also for parents, children, wife, and friends and fellow citizens generally, since a human being is by nature political.[63] Of these, some defining mark must be found, since, if we extend the list to ancestors and descendants and to friends' friends, it will go on without limit.[64] But we must investigate this on another occasion. In any case, we posit that what is self-sufficient is what, on its own, makes a life choiceworthy and lacking in nothing, and this, we think, is what happiness is like.

Further, we think it is the most choiceworthy of all things, when not counted among them—for if it is counted among them, it clearly would be more choiceworthy with the addition of the least of goods. For what is added would bring about a superabundance of goods, and of goods, the greater one is always more choiceworthy.[65]

Happiness, then, is apparently something complete and self-sufficient, since it is the end of what is doable in action.

But to say that happiness is the best good is perhaps to say something that is apparently commonplace, and we still need a clearer statement of what it is. Maybe, then, this would come about if the function of a human being were grasped.[66] For just as for a flute player, a sculptor, every craftsman, and in general for whatever has some function and action, the good—the doing well—seems to lie in the function, the same also seems to hold of a human being, if indeed there is some function that is his.

So are there some functions and actions of a carpenter and of a shoemaker but none at all of a human being? And is he by nature inactive? Or, rather, just as of eye, hand, foot, and of each part generally there seems to be some function, may we likewise also posit some function of a human being that is beyond all these?[67]

What, then, could this be? For living is evidently shared with plants as well, but we are looking for what is special.[68] Hence we must set aside the living that consists in nutrition and growth. Next in order is some sort of perceptual living.[69] But this too is evidently shared with horse and ox and every animal.

There remains, then, some sort of practical living of the part that has reason. And of what has reason, one part has it by dint of obeying reason, the other by dint of actually having it and exercising thought.[70] But "living" is said of things in two ways, and we must take the one in accord with activity, since it seems to be called "living" in a fuller sense.[71]

If, then, the function of a human being is activity of the soul in accord with reason or not without reason, and the function of a sort of thing, we say, is the same in kind as the function of an excellent thing of that sort (as in the case of a lyre player and an excellent lyre player), and this is unconditionally so in all cases when we add to the function the superiority that is in accord with the virtue (for it is characteristic of a lyre player to play the lyre and of an excellent one to do it well)—if all this is so, and a human being's function is supposed to be a sort of living, and this living is supposed to be activity of the soul and actions that involve reason, and it is characteristic of an excellent man to do these well and nobly, and each is completed well when it is in accord with the virtue that properly belongs to it—if all this is so, the human good turns out to be activity of the soul in accord with virtue and, if there are more virtues than one, then in accord with the best and most complete.[72] Furthermore, in a complete life, for one swallow does not make a spring, nor does one day.[73] Nor, similarly, does one day or a short time make someone blessed and happy.[74]

Let the good, then, be sketched in this way, since perhaps we should outline first and fill in the details later. It would seem, though, that anyone can develop and articulate the things in the outline that have been correctly done, and that time is a good discoverer and co-worker in such matters. This is even the source of advances in the crafts, since anyone can produce what is lacking.[75]

We must also remember what was said before and not look for the same exactness in everything but, in each case, the one that is in accord with the subject matter and the degree sought by the method of inquiry that properly belongs to it.[76] For a carpenter and a geometer inquire differently about the right angle. A carpenter does so to the degree that is useful for his work, whereas a geometer inquires about what it is or what sort of thing, since he is a contemplator of the truth.[77] We must do things in just the same way, then, in other cases, so that side issues do not overwhelm the works themselves.[78]

Nor should we demand the cause in all cases alike.[79] Rather, in some cases it will be adequate if the fact that they are so has been correctly shown—as it is indeed where starting-points are concerned.[80] And the fact that something is so is a first thing and a starting-point.[81]

We get a theoretical grasp of some starting-points through induction, some through perception, some through some sort of habituation, and others through other means.[82] In each case we should follow the method of inquiry suited to their nature and make very serious efforts to define them correctly. For they are of great and decisive importance regarding what follows. It seems indeed that the starting-point is more than half the whole and that many of the things we were inquiring about will at the same time become evident through it.

## I 8

We must investigate it, however, not only in accord with the conclusions and premises of our argument but also in accord with the things we say about it.[83] For all the data are in tune with a true view, whereas they soon clash with a false one.[84]

Goods, then, have been divided into three sorts, with some said to be external, some relating to the soul, and some to the body.[85] The goods relating to soul are most fully such, and, we say, are goods to the highest degree, and we take the actions and activities of the soul to be goods relating to soul.[86] So what we have said is correct, according to this view at least, which is long standing and agreed to by philosophers.[87]

It is correct even in saying that actions and activities of some sort are the end, since that way the end turns out to be one of the goods relating to soul, and not one of the external ones.

The saying that someone who is happy both lives well and does well is in tune with our argument too, since happiness has been pretty much defined as a sort of living well and doing well.

Again, all the things that are looked for where happiness is concerned apparently hold of what we have said it is. For to some it seems to be virtue, to others practical wisdom, to others some sort of theoretical wisdom, while to others it seems to be these or one of these involving pleasure or not without pleasure. Other people include external prosperity as well. Some of these views are held by many and are long standing, while others are held by a few reputable men. And it is not reasonable to suppose that either group is entirely wrong but, rather, that they are right on one point at least or even on most of them.[88]

Now with those who say that happiness is virtue or some sort of virtue, our argument is in tune, since activity in accord with virtue is characteristic of that virtue.[89] But it makes no small difference, presumably, whether we suppose the best good to consist in virtue's possession or in its use—that is, in the state or in the activity.[90] For it is possible for someone to possess the state while accomplishing nothing good—for example, if he is sleeping or out of action in some other way. But the same will not hold of the activity, since he will necessarily be doing an action and doing it well. And just as in the Olympic Games it is not the noblest and strongest who get the victory crown but the competitors (since it is among these that the ones who win are found), so also among the noble and good aspects of life it is those who act correctly who win the prizes.

Further, their life is intrinsically pleasant. For being pleased is among the things that belong to soul, and to each person what is pleasant is that thing by reference to which he is said to be a lover of such things—as, for example, a horse in the case of a lover of horses, and a play in that of a lover of plays. In the same way, just things are pleasant to a lover of justice and the things in accord with virtue as a whole are pleasant to a lover of virtue.

The things that are pleasant to ordinary people, however, are in conflict because they are not naturally pleasant, whereas the things pleasant to lovers of what is noble are naturally pleasant. And actions in accord with virtue are like this, so that they are pleasant both to such people and intrinsically.

Their life, then, has no need of a pleasure that is superadded to it, like some sort of appendage, but has its pleasure within itself. For besides what we have already said, the person who does not enjoy doing noble actions is not good. For no one would call a person just who did not enjoy doing just actions, or generous if he did not enjoy doing generous ones, and similarly as regards the others.

If that is so, however, actions in accord with virtue will be intrinsically pleasant. But they are also good, of course, and noble as well. Further, they are each of these things to the highest degree, if indeed an excellent person discerns them correctly—and he does discern them that way.[91]

Hence happiness is what is best, noblest, and most pleasant. And these qualities are not distinguished in the way the Delian inscription says:

> The noblest thing is the most just; the best, to be healthy.
> The most pleasant, however, is to get the thing we desire.

For the best activities possess them all.[92] And it is these—or the one among them that is best—that we say is happiness.

All the same, it apparently needs external goods to be added, as we said, since it is impossible or not easy to do noble actions without supplies.[93] For just as we perform many actions by means of instruments, we perform many by means of friends, wealth, and political power. Then again there are some whose deprivation disfigures blessedness, such as good breeding, good children, and noble looks.[94] For we scarcely have the stamp of happiness if we are extremely ugly in appearance, ill-bred, living a solitary life, or childless, and have it even less, presumably, if our children or friends are totally bad or were good but have died.

Just as we said, then, happiness does seem to need this sort of prosperity to be added.[95] That is what leads some to identify good luck with happiness and others to identify virtue with happiness.[96]

## I 9

It is also what leads people to puzzle about whether happiness is something acquirable by learning or by habituation or by some other sort of training, or whether it comes about in accord with some divine dispensation or even by luck.[97]

Well, if anything is a gift from the gods to human beings, it is reasonable to suppose that happiness is also god given—especially since it is the best of human goods. Perhaps this topic properly belongs more to a different investigation, yet even if happiness is not a godsend but comes about through virtue and some sort of learning or training, it is evidently one of the most divine things, since virtue's prize and end is evidently something divine and blessed.[98] At the same time, it would also be something widely shared, since it is possible for it to be acquired through some sort of learning or supervision by all those not disabled in relation to virtue.[99]

If it is better to acquire it in that way than to be happy by luck, |20| however, it is reasonable to suppose that this is how we do acquire it, if indeed what is in accord with nature is by nature in the noblest possible condition. Similarly with what is in accord with craft or with any cause whatsoever—above all, what is in accord with the best one. To entrust what is greatest and noblest to luck would strike a very false note.

The answer we are looking for is also entirely evident from our argument. |25| For we have said that happiness is a certain sort of activity of the soul in accord with virtue, while of the remaining goods, some are necessary conditions of it, others are by nature co-workers and useful as instruments. This also would agree with what we said at the start.[100] For we took the end of politics to be the best end. And its supervision aims above all at producing |30| citizens of a certain sort—that is, good people and doers of noble actions.[101]

It makes perfect sense, then, that we do not say that an ox, a horse, or any other animal whatsoever is happy, since none of them can share in this sort of activity. This is the |1100b1| explanation of why a child is not happy either, since he is not yet a doer of such actions because of his age. Children who are said to be blessed are being called blessed because of their prospects, since for happiness there must be, as we said, both complete virtue and a complete life.[102] For many reversals of fortune |5| and all sorts of lucky accidents occur in life, and the most prosperous may meet with great disasters in old age—just as is said of Priam in the story of the events at Troy.[103] And no one counts someone happy who has suffered strokes of luck like that and dies in a wretched way.[104]

## I 10

Are we then to count no other human being happy either, |10| as long as he is still living but—in accord with Solon's advice—must we see the end?[105] And if we are indeed to accept his view, is it really that someone is happy only when he *is* dead? Or is that, at any rate, a completely strange notion—most of all for those who say, as we do, that happiness is a sort of activity?

Even if we do not say that the dead are happy, however—and this is not what Solon means either, |15| but only that when a human being has died it will at that point be safe to call him blessed (since he is then outside the reach of bad things and misfortunes)—that is also something we might dispute to some extent. For to some extent it does seem that something may prove good or bad for someone who is dead, if indeed there are also good or bad things for someone who is living but not actively perceiving them—for example, honor and dishonor, and children or descendants generally who do well or who suffer misfortunes.

But this also raises a puzzle. For it is possible for many reversals of fortune involving his descendants to befall someone who has lived a blessed life until old age and died accordingly. Some of his descendants may be good people and get the life they deserve while to others the contrary may happen. And it is clear that the degree of separation between them and their ancestors admits of all sorts of variation. But it would be strange, surely, if the dead person changed along with them and was happy at one time and wretched at another. Yet it would also be strange if what happens to descendants did not affect their ancestors to any extent or for any period of time.

But we should go back to the first puzzle. For maybe from it we will also be able to get a theoretical grasp on what we are now inquiring about. Suppose that we must wait to see the end in each case and at that point call someone blessed—not as then being blessed but because he was so before. Would it not be strange, then, if when he is happy, we cannot truly attribute to him what he actually possesses, because of our not wishing to call the living happy because of reversals of fortune, |**1100b1**| and because we suppose that happiness is something steadfast and in no way easy to reverse, whereas the same person's luck often turns completely around? For it is clear that if we were to be guided by luck, we would often have to say that the same person is happy and then wretched turn and turn about, thereby representing the happy person as a sort of chameleon and as someone with unsound foundations.[106]

Or is it that to be guided by luck is not at all correct? For it is not in *it* that living well and living badly are to be found but, rather, a human life needs this to be added, as we said, whereas it is activities in accord with virtue that control happiness and the contrary ones its contrary.[107] The puzzle we are now going through further testifies to our argument for this. For none of the functions of human beings are as stable as those concerned with activities in accord with virtue, since they seem to be more steadfast even than our knowledge of the sciences. And of these sciences themselves, the most estimable are more steadfast, because the blessed live most of all and most continuously in accord with them.[108] This would seem to be the cause, indeed, of why forgetfulness does not occur where they are concerned.[109]

What we are inquiring about, then, will be characteristic of the happy person, and throughout life he will be as we say. For he will always or more than anyone else do actions and get a theoretical grasp on things in accord with virtue, and will bear what luck brings in the noblest way and, in every case, in the most suitable one, since he is "good, four-square, beyond blame."[110]

Many things happen in accord with luck, however, that differ in greatness and smallness. But small strokes of good luck or similarly of the opposite clearly will not have a strong influence on his way of living, whereas great and repeated ones, when good, will make his life more blessed, since by nature they help to adorn it, and his use of them is noble and excellent. If they turn out the reverse, though, they reduce or spoil his blessedness, since they involve pain and impede many activities. All the same, even in these cases nobility shines through when someone calmly bears repeated strokes of great bad luck—not because he is insensitive to suffering but because of being well bred and great-souled.

If, however, it is activities that control living, as we said, no blessed person will ever become wretched, since he will never do hateful or base actions.[111] For a truly good and practically-wise person, we think, will bear what luck brings graciously and, making use of the resources at hand, will always do the noblest actions, just as a good general makes the best uses in warfare of the army he has and a good shoemaker makes the best shoes out of the hides he has been given, and the same way with all other craftsmen.

If this is so, however, a happy person will never become wretched—nor *blessed* certainly—if he runs up against luck like Priam's. He will not, then, be variable or easily subject to reversals of fortune, since he will not be easily shaken from his happiness by just any misfortunes[112] that chance to come along but only by great and repeated ones. And from these he will not return to being happy again in a short time but—if indeed he does do so—in a long and complete one in which he achieves great and noble things.

What, then, prevents us from calling happy the person who is active in accord with complete virtue and is adequately supplied with external goods not for some random period of time but in a complete life? Or must we add that he will continue living like that and will die accordingly, since the future is obscure to us and we suppose happiness to be an end and complete in every way? If so, we shall call "blessed" those living people who have and will continue to have the things we mentioned—blessed, though, in the way human beings are.[113]

So much for our determinations on these topics.

## I 11

The view that the luck of someone's descendants and all his friends have not the slightest effect on him is evidently a view too inimical to friendship and one that is contrary to the beliefs held on the subject.[114] But since the things that happen are many and admit of all sorts of differences, and some of them get through to us more and others less, it is evidently a long—even endless—task to distinguish all the particular cases, and it will perhaps be enough to speak about the matter in universal terms and in outline.

If, then, of even the misfortunes that affect the person himself, some have a certain weight and a strong influence as regards his life, whereas others seem to have a lighter one, the same also holds for what affects all his friends. And for each incident, it makes a difference whether it involves the living or the dead—much more than whether the unlawful and terrible deeds in tragedies have happened beforehand or are enacted on the stage.

Our deductive argument, then, must also take account of this difference, but even more account, perhaps, of the results of going through the puzzles about whether the dead share in any good thing or in any of the opposite ones.[115] For it seems likely from these considerations that even if anything at all does get through to them, whether good or the opposite, it is something feeble and small, either unconditionally so or so for them. Or if it is not like that, it is of a size and sort, at any rate, that does not make happy those who are not happy or take away the blessedness of those who are. It does, then, contribute something to the dead, apparently, when their friends do well and similarly when they do badly, but something of such a sort and size that it neither makes the happy ones unhappy nor does anything else of this sort.

## I 12

Having made these determinations, let us investigate whether happiness is included among praiseworthy things or, rather, among estimable ones, since it is clear at least that it is not included among capacities.[116]

Well, apparently all the things that are praiseworthy are praised for being of a certain quality and for standing in a certain relation to something. For we praise the just person and the courageous one—in fact, the good person and his virtue generally—because of his actions and his works, also the strong person and the good runner, and so on in each of the other cases, because he is naturally of a certain quality and stands in a certain relation to something good or excellent.[117] This is also clear from awards of praise involving the gods. For these are evidently ridiculous if it is by reference to us that they are awarded. But this happens because awards of praise involve such a reference, as we just said.[118]

If praise is of things like this, it is clear that of the best things there is no praise but something greater and better—as is in fact evident. For we call the gods both blessed and happy and call the most divine of men this as well. Similarly in the case of goods too. For we never praise happiness as we praise justice, but call it blessed since it is a more divine and better thing.[119]

It seems, in fact, that Eudoxus advocated in the correct way the cause of pleasure in the competition for supreme excellence.[120] For not to praise pleasure, while including it among the goods, is to reveal, he thought, that it is better than things that are praised, in the way that the god and the good are, since it is to these that the others are referred.[121]

For praise is properly given to virtue, since we are doers of noble actions as a result of it, whereas encomia are properly given to its works, in like manner both to those of the body and those of the soul.[122] But perhaps an exact treatment of these topics more properly belongs to those who work on encomia. It is clear to us from what we have said, however, that happiness is included among things both estimable and complete. |**1102a1**|

This also seems to hold because happiness is a starting-point, since it is for the sake of it that we all do all the other actions that we do, and we suppose that the starting-point and cause of what is good is something estimable and divine.[123]

## I 13

Since happiness is some activity of the soul in accord with complete virtue, we must investigate virtue, since maybe that way we will also get a better theoretical grasp on happiness. It seems too that someone who is truly a politician will have worked most on virtue, since he wishes to make the citizens good and obedient to the laws.[124] A paradigm case is provided by the Cretan and Spartan legislators and by any others there may have been that are like them.[125] If this investigation belongs to politics, however, it is clear that our present inquiry will be in accord with the deliberate choice we made at the start.[126]

It is also clear that the virtue we must investigate is human virtue. For it is in fact the human good we are looking for, and human happiness. By "human virtue," though, we mean not that of the body but that of the soul; and happiness, we say, is an activity of the soul. But if all this is so, it is clear that a politician must in a way know about what pertains to the soul, just as someone who is going to take care of people's eyes must know about the body generally—more so, indeed, to the extent that politics is more estimable and better than medicine—and that doctors (the ones who are more sophisticated) occupy themselves greatly with knowing about the body.[127] It is also for a politician, then, to get a theoretical grasp on what concerns the soul. But his theoretical grasp should be for the sake of the things in question and of an extent that is adequate to the things being looked for, since a more exact treatment is perhaps harder work than the topics before us require.

Enough has been said about some aspects of the soul in the external accounts too, and we should make use of these—for example, that one part of the soul is nonrational whereas another part has reason.[128] Whether these are distinguished like the parts of the body or like anything else that is divisible or whether they are two in definition but inseparable by nature (like convex and concave in a curved surface) makes no difference for present purposes.[129]

Of the nonrational part, one part seems to be shared and vegetative—I mean, the cause of nutrition and growth. For this sort of capacity of soul is one that we suppose is present in all things that take in nourishment, even embryos, and that this same one is also present in completely grown animals, since that is more reasonable than to suppose a different one to be present in them.

Hence the virtue of this capacity is apparently something shared and not distinctively human. For this part and this capacity seem to be most active in sleep, and a good person and a bad one are least clearly distinguished during sleep (leading people to say that the happy are no different from the wretched for half their lives, which makes perfect sense, since sleep is idleness of the soul in that respect with reference to which it is said to be excellent or base), unless—to some small extent—some movements do get through to us and, in this way, the things that appear in the dreams of decent people are better than those of any random person.[130] But that is enough about these things, and we should leave the nutritive part aside, since by nature it has no share in human virtue.[131]

Another natural constituent of the soul, however, also seems to be nonrational, although it shares in reason in a way. For we praise the reason—that is, the part of the soul that has reason—of a person with self-control and of a person without it, since it exhorts them correctly toward what is best. But they also have by nature something else within them besides reason, apparently, which fights against reason and resists it. For exactly as with paralyzed limbs (when their owners deliberately choose to move them to the right, they do the contrary and move off to the left), so it is in the case of the soul as well, since the impulses of people who lack self-control are in contrary directions. In the case of the body, to be sure, we see the part that is moving in the wrong direction, whereas in the case of the soul we do not see it. But presumably we should nonetheless acknowledge that in the soul as well there is something besides reason, countering it and going against it. How it is different, though, is not important.

But this part apparently also has a share of reason, as we said, at any rate, it is obedient to the reason of a self-controlled person.[132] Furthermore, that of a temperate and courageous person, presumably, listens still better, since there it chimes with reason in everything.

Apparently, then, the nonrational part is also twofold, since the vegetative part does not share in reason in any way but the appetitive part (indeed, the desiring part as a whole) does so in some way, because it is able to listen to reason and obey it.[133] It has reason, then, in the way we are said to have the reason of our fathers and friends and not in the way we are said to have that of mathematics.[134] The fact, though, that the nonrational part is persuaded in some way by reason is revealed by the practice of warning people and of all the different practices of admonishing and exhorting them.

If we should say that it too has reason, however, then the part that has reason will be double as well—one part having it fully and within itself, the other as something able to listen to it as to a father.

Virtues are also defined in accord with this difference, since we say that some are of thought, others of character. Theoretical wisdom, comprehension, and practical wisdom are virtues of thought; generosity and temperance virtues of character.[135] For when we talk about someone's character we do not say that he is theoretically-wise or has comprehension but that he is mild-mannered or temperate. But we do also praise a theoretically-wise person with reference to his state, and—among the states—it is the praiseworthy ones that we call virtues.

# Book II

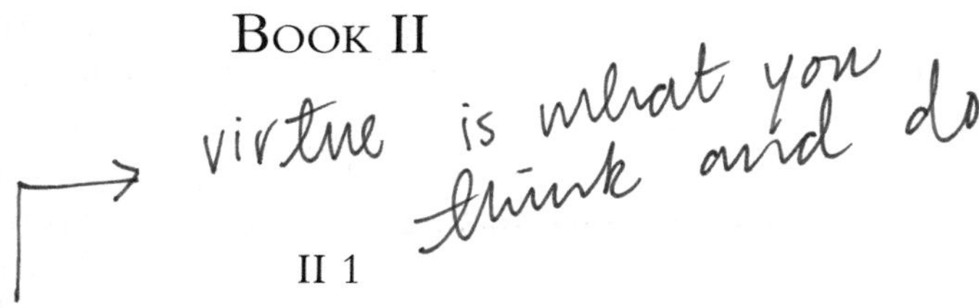
virtue is what you think and do

## II 1

Virtue, then, is twofold, of thought and of character.[136] That of thought both comes about and grows mostly as a result of teaching, which is why it requires experience and time.[137] That of character (*êthikê*), on the other hand, results from habit (*ethos*)—indeed, this is the source of the name *êthikê*, which derives with a minor variation from *ethos*.

From this it is also clear that none of the virtues of character comes about in us naturally, since nothing natural can be habituated to be otherwise—for example, a stone that naturally moves downward cannot be habituated to move upward, not even if to habituate it you threw it upward ten thousand times, nor will fire move downward, nor can anything else that is naturally one way be habituated into being another way.[138] Hence the virtues come about in us neither by nature nor against nature, rather we are naturally receptive of them and are brought to completion through habit.[139]

Further, in the case of things that are provided to us by nature, we first receive the capacities for them and later exhibit the activities. (This is clear in the case of the perceptual capacities. For it was not from frequent acts of seeing or of hearing that we acquired the perceptual capacities, rather it was the reverse—we used them because we had them, we did not have them because we used them.) The virtues, by contrast, we acquire by first engaging in the activities, as is also true in the case of the various crafts.[140] For the things we cannot produce without learning to do so are the very ones we learn to produce by producing them—for example, we become builders by building houses and lyre players by playing the lyre. Similarly, then, we become just people by doing just actions, temperate people by doing temperate actions, and courageous people by doing courageous ones.[141]

What happens in cities also testifies to this, since legislators make citizens good by habituating them; that is to say, this is the *wish* of every legislator, and those legislators who do not do it well fail in their purpose, and it is in this respect that one constitution differs from another, a good one from a base one.[142]

Further, it is from the same things and through the same things that each virtue both comes about and is ruined. The case of a craft is similar as well, since it is from playing the lyre that both good and bad lyre players come about. And something analogous holds in the case of builders and all the rest, since it is from building houses well that good builders arise and from doing so badly, bad ones.

If it were otherwise, there would have been no need whatsoever of a teacher, but they would all have been born either good or bad at their craft. This, then, is also how it is with the virtues, since it is from acting as we do in our transactions with other human beings that some of us become just and others unjust, and from acting as we do in terrible circumstances and from becoming habituated to feel fear or confidence that some of us become courageous and others cowards.[143] Something similar also holds of circumstances involving appetites and those involving feelings of anger, since some people become temperate and mild-mannered, whereas others become intemperate and irascible—the one group from conducting themselves in one way in such circumstances, the other from doing so in another way. In a word, then, states come about from activities that are similar to them.

That is why the activities must exhibit a certain quality, since the states follow along in accord with the differences between these. So it makes no small difference whether people are habituated in one way or in another way straight from childhood; on the contrary, it makes a huge one—or rather, *all* the difference.[144]

## II 2

Since, then, the present work is not undertaken for the sake of theoretical knowledge, as our others are (for we are engaging in the investigation not in order to know what virtue is but in order to become good people, since otherwise there would be nothing of benefit in it), we must investigate what relates to actions, that is, in what way they are to be done.[145] For actions also control what sorts of states will come about, as we said.[146]

That we should act in accord with the correct reason, though, is a common view and is to be taken as basic—we shall talk about it later, both about what the correct reason is and about how it is related to the various virtues.[147]

Let us take it as agreed in advance, however, that the entire account of issues relating to the actions we must do has to be stated in outline and not in an exact way, and—as we said at the start—the sorts of accounts we demand should be in accord with the subject matter.[148] For things in the sphere of action and advantageous things have no fixed identity, just as healthy ones have none.

While that is what the universal account is like, |5| the account dealing with particular cases is still less exact. For these do not fall under any craft or any set of rules whatsoever, and the agents themselves always have to inquire to find out what it is opportune to do, just as in the case of medicine and navigation. But even though this *is* what the present |10| account is like, it must still try to provide help.

First, then, we must get a theoretical grasp on the fact that states like these are naturally ruined by deficiency and excess (for we must use evident cases to testify on behalf of obscure ones), just as we see happen in the cases of strength and health.[149] For both athletic training regimens that are excessive and those that are deficient |15| will ruin our strength, and routines of drinking and eating too much will ruin our health, whereas those involving proportionate amounts produce, increase, and preserve it.

It is also that way, then, with temperance, courage, and the other virtues. For someone who avoids and fears everything and endures nothing |20| becomes cowardly, whereas someone who fears nothing at all and goes to face everything becomes rash. Similarly, someone who indulges in every pleasure and abstains from none becomes intemperate, whereas someone who avoids all of them, as boorish people do, becomes insensible in a way.[150] Temperance, then, and courage are ruined by |25| excess and deficiency and are preserved by the medial condition.

It is not only that the coming about, growth, and ruin of the virtues result from the same things and are caused by the same things, however, but also that their activities are found in the same ones, since this holds in the other more evident cases as well—for example, in that of strength. |30| For strength comes about from taking much food and enduring much exertion, and it is a strong person who is most capable of doing these very things.

It is also that way in the case of the virtues, since from abstaining from pleasures we become temperate and, having become so, are most capable of abstaining from them. Similarly, |35| in the case of courage, since if we are habituated to despise frightening things |1104b1| and to endure them, we become courageous and, having become so, are most capable of enduring frightening things.

## II 3

We must take the pleasures and pains that supervene on a person's works as an indication of his states.[151] For someone who abstains from bodily |5|

pleasures and enjoys doing just this is temperate, whereas someone who is annoyed is intemperate, and someone who endures terrible things and enjoys doing so—or at least is not pained by it—is courageous, whereas someone who is pained is cowardly.[152] For virtue of character is concerned with pleasures and pains.[153] Indeed, it is because of pleasure that we do base actions and because of pain that we abstain from doing noble ones. That is why we must be brought up in a certain way straight from childhood, as Plato says, so as to enjoy and be pained by the things we should, since this is what the correct education is.[154]

Further, the virtues are concerned with actions and feelings, and every feeling and every action entails pleasure and pain.[155] That is also why virtue is concerned with pleasures and pains. Punishments also reveal this, since they take place by means of pleasure and pain. For punishments are medical treatments of a sort, and medical treatments are naturally effected by means of contraries.[156]

Further, as we said just now, the sorts of things that by nature cause every state of soul to become worse or better are the ones the state is by nature related to and the ones it is concerned with.[157] Again, it is because of pleasures and pains that people become base—by pursuing and avoiding these, either the ones they shouldn't or when they shouldn't or in the way they shouldn't or in whatever other ways are distinguished in the account. That is also why people define the virtues as a sort of absence of feeling or a sort of being at rest. But they do not define them well if they say this unconditionally and do not add "as we should" or "as we shouldn't" and all the other distinctions.

Hence we may take it that virtue is the sort of state concerned with pleasures and pains that is a doer of the best actions, and that vice is the contrary state.[158]

It will become evident to us from the following considerations, in fact, that virtue and vice are concerned with the same things. For there are three proper objects of choice and three of avoidance: what is noble, what is advantageous, and what is pleasant, and their contraries, what is shameful, what is harmful, and what is painful.[159] Where all these are concerned, a good person is able to be correct and a bad one unable not to err—most of all, though, where pleasure is concerned, since it is both shared with animals and entailed by every object of choice. For what is noble or what is advantageous appears pleasant too.

Further, |1105a1| pleasure has grown up with all of us from infancy. That is why it is difficult to rub out this feeling that is dyed into our lives.[160] Also, we measure our actions, some more and others less, by the standard of pleasure and pain. That is why, then, our entire work must be concerned with these, since whether someone enjoys or is pained well or badly makes no small difference in his actions.

Further, it is more difficult to fight against pleasure than to fight against spirit, just as Heraclitus says, and both craft and virtue are always concerned with what is more difficult, since to do well what is more difficult is in fact a better thing.[161] So that is also why our entire work, both as a contribution to virtue and as a contribution to politics, must be concerned with pleasures and pains, since someone who uses these well will be good and someone who uses them badly will be bad.

Let us say, then, that virtue is concerned with pleasures and pains, that the things from which it comes about are also the ones by which it is increased and (if they come about differently) ruined, and that the things from which it has come about are also the ones concerning which it is active.

## II 4

Someone might raise a puzzle, however, about how we can claim that people must do just actions to become just, and temperate ones to become temperate. For if people are doing what is just or temperate, they are already just and temperate, in the same way that if they are doing what is grammatical or musical, they already know grammar or music.

Or doesn't that hold in the case of the crafts either? For it is possible to produce something grammatical either by luck or on someone else's instruction. Someone would be a grammarian, then, if he produced something grammatical and produced it in the way a grammarian would. And this is to do it in accord with the craft knowledge of grammar that is internal to himself.

Further, the case of crafts is *not* similar to that of virtues. For the things that come about by means of the crafts have their goodness internal to them, and thus it is enough if they come about in such a way as to be in a certain state. The things that come about in accord with the virtues, by contrast, are done justly or temperately not simply if they are in a certain state but if the one who does them is also in a certain state. First, if he does them knowingly; second, if he deliberately chooses them and deliberately chooses them because of themselves; and third, if he does them from a stable and unchangeable state.[162]

Where the various crafts are concerned, these factors do not count, except |**1105b1**| for the knowing itself. Where the virtues are concerned, however, knowing has little or no strength, whereas the other factors have not just a little but, rather, *all* the significance, and these are the very ones that come about from frequently doing just and temperate actions.[163]

Actions are said to be just and temperate, then, when they are the sort that a just or a temperate person would do, whereas a just or temperate person is not the one who does these actions but the one who, in addition, does them in the way a just or temperate person does them.[164] So it is correct to say that a person comes to be just from doing just actions, and temperate from doing temperate ones, and that from not doing them no one could have even the prospect of becoming good.

Ordinary people, however, do not do these actions but, taking refuge in argument, think that they are doing philosophy and that this is the way to become excellent—thus behaving a bit like sick people who listen carefully to their doctors but do none of the things that are prescribed.[165] So just as people who take care of themselves in that way will not have a body that is in a good state, people who do philosophy in a similar way will not have souls that are in a good one either.

## II 5

Next we must investigate what virtue is. Since the things that come about in the soul are of three sorts—feelings, capacities, and states—virtue will be one of these.[166]

By feelings I mean appetite, anger, fear, confidence, envy, enjoyment, love, hatred, longing, jealousy, pity, and generally whatever entails pleasure and pain. By capacities I mean that by dint of which we are said to be susceptible to these feelings—for example, by dint of which we are capable of feeling anger, or pain, or pity.[167] By states I mean the things by dint of which we are well or badly off in relation to feelings—for example, in relation to anger, if we feel it too intensely or too weakly, we are in a bad state; if we feel it to a medial degree, we are in a good one; and similarly in relation to the others.

Virtues and vices are not feelings, then, because we are not called "excellent" or "base" on account of our feelings, whereas we are so called on account of our virtues. Nor are we praised or blamed on account of our feelings (for it is not the person who fears or gets angry who is praised nor the person who simply gets angry who is blamed but, rather, the one who gets angry in a certain way). We *are* praised or blamed, though, on account of our virtues and vices. |**1106a1**|

Further, we become angry or feel fear without deliberate choice, whereas the virtues are deliberate choices of a sort—or, rather, not without deliberate choice. Besides, we are said to be moved on account of our feelings, but on account of our virtues and vices we are said not to be moved but, rather, to be disposed in a certain way.[168]

For these reasons virtues are not capacities either. For we are not called "good" for having the capacity simply to feel things, nor are we called "bad," nor are we praised or blamed. Further, we have the capacities by nature, whereas we do not become good or bad by nature—we talked about this earlier.[169]

If, then, the virtues are neither feelings nor capacities, it remains for them to be states. We have now said what the genus of virtue is.[170]

## II 6

We should not say only that virtue is a state, however, but also what sort of state it is.

We should say, then, that every virtue, regardless of what thing it is the virtue of, both completes the good state of that thing and makes it perform its function well—as, for example, the virtue of an eye makes both the eye and its function excellent, since it is by dint of the eye's virtue that we see well. Similarly the virtue of a horse makes the horse excellent—that is, good at running, carrying its rider, and standing firm against enemies. If, then, this holds in every case, the virtue of a human being will also be the state by dint of which he becomes a good human being and will perform his own function well. How that will come about, we have already said.[171] But it will also become evident if we get a theoretical grasp on the sort of nature that virtue has.

In everything continuous and divisible, then, it is possible to take more, less, and equal, and these either *in relation to the thing itself* or *in relation to us*—where equal is some sort of mean between excess and deficiency.[172] By "the mean in relation to the thing," I mean what is equidistant from each of its two extremes, which is precisely one in number and the same for all. The mean in relation to us, by contrast, is what takes neither too much nor too little.[173] It is not one thing and is not the same for all. For example, if ten are many and two are few, we take six as the mean in relation to the thing, since it exceeds and is exceeded by an equal amount. That is the mean in accord with arithmetical proportion. But the mean in relation to us must not be ascertained in that way. For if ten minae is lot to eat and two minae a little, the trainer |**1106b1**| will not prescribe six minae.[174] For that is presumably also a lot or a little for the person who is to eat it—a little for Milo but a lot for someone starting his athletic training regimen.[175] Similarly in the cases of running and wrestling. In this way, then, everyone with scientific knowledge avoids excess and deficiency and looks for the mean and chooses it—the mean not in the thing but in relation to us.

If, then, every science does complete its function well in this way, looking to the mean and bringing its works into conformity with it—which is why people regularly say of works that are well made that nothing could be taken away or added, since excess and deficiency ruin what is well done whereas the medial condition preserves what is well done, and good craftsmen, as we say, accomplish their works by looking to the mean—and if virtue is more exact and better than any craft, just as nature also is, virtue will be able to aim at and hit the mean.[176]

I am speaking of virtue of character, since it is concerned with feelings and actions and it is in these that there is excess, deficiency, and the mean. For example, it is possible to feel fear and confidence, appetite, anger, pity, and pleasure and pain generally, both too much and too little and in both ways not well.

To feel such things when we should, though, about the things we should, in relation to the people we should, for the sake of what we should, and as we should is a mean and best and precisely what is characteristic of virtue.

Similarly where actions are concerned, there is excess, deficiency, and the mean.[177] But virtue is concerned with feelings and actions in which excess is in error and subject to blame, as is deficiency, whereas the mean is subject to praise and is on the correct path (and both these features are characteristic of virtue).[178] Hence virtue is a sort of medial condition because it is able to aim at and hit the mean.

Further, it is possible to err in many ways (for the bad belongs to what is without a limit, as the Pythagoreans portrayed it, and the good to what is determinate), whereas there is only one way to be correct.[179] That is why erring is easy and being correct difficult, since it is easy to miss the target but difficult to hit it. So because of these facts too, excess and deficiency are characteristic of vice, whereas the medial condition is characteristic of virtue: "for people are good in one simple way, but bad in all sorts of ways."[180]

Virtue, then, is a deliberately choosing state, which is in a medial condition in relation to us, one defined by a reason and the one by which a practically-wise person |**1107b1**| would define it.[181] Also, it is a medial condition between two vices, one of excess and the other of deficiency. Further, it is also such a condition because some vices are deficient in relation to what the relevant feelings and actions should be and others are excessive, but virtue both finds the mean and chooses it.

That is why—as regards its essence and the account that states its what it is to be[182]—virtue is medial, but, in relation to the best and doing well, it is extreme.

But not every action or every feeling admits of the medial condition, since in some cases they are named in such a way that they are united with baseness from the start—for example, spite, shamelessness, and envy, and (in the case of actions) adultery, theft, and murder. For all these and things like them—and not the excessive varieties of them or the deficient ones—are said to be what they are because they are base. It is never possible, then, to be correct where they are concerned but it is necessary always to be in error. Nor is there a doing well or not well where such things are concerned (committing adultery with whom we should, when we should, in the way we should), but, rather, simply to do any of these things is to err.[183]

So it is like thinking that there are also medial conditions and an excess and a deficiency where unjust and cowardly and intemperate actions are concerned—since that way, at any rate, there will be a medial condition of excess and of deficiency and an excess of excess and a deficiency of deficiency. But just as in temperance and courage there is no excess and deficiency, because the mean is in a way an extreme, so in these other cases too there is no mean and no excess or deficiency either, but, however they are done, they are errors. For, putting it generally, there is neither a medial condition of excess and deficiency nor excess and deficiency of a medial condition.

## II 7

We should state this not only in universal terms, however, but we should also state how it fits the particular virtues and vices. (For in accounts concerned with actions, whereas the universal ones are common to more cases, the ones that apply to a part are truer, since actions are concerned with particulars and our account should be in harmony with them.)[184] We should ascertain these, then, from the chart.[185]

Where feelings of fear and confidence are concerned, then, courage is the medial condition, whereas of those people who are excessive, the one who is excessive in his fearlessness is nameless |**1107b1**| (many indeed are nameless), the one who is excessive in his confidence is rash, and the one who is excessively fearful and deficient in confidence is cowardly.

Where pleasures and pains are concerned (not all of them and even less so where pains are concerned), the medial condition is temperance and the excess is intemperance. But people deficient in pleasure are scarcely found, which is why people of that sort have not even acquired a name. Let us call them "insensible."[186]

Where giving and getting wealth are concerned, the medial condition is generosity, whereas the excess and deficiency are wastefulness and acquisitiveness.[187] In the case of these states, people are excessive and deficient in contrary ways, since the wasteful person is excessive in giving wealth and deficient in getting it, whereas the acquisitive person is excessive in getting it but deficient in giving.[188] (For the moment we are speaking in outline and in headline form, satisfying ourselves with just this much. A more exact definition of these virtues will come later.)

Where wealth is concerned there are also other dispositions: the medial condition is magnificence (for the magnificent person differs from a generous one, since the former is concerned with great sums, the latter with small), the excess is tastelessness and vulgarity, and the deficiency is niggardliness. These vices differ from the ones where generosity is concerned. How they differ will be discussed later.

Where honor and dishonor are concerned, the medial condition is greatness of soul, whereas the excess is called a sort of conceitedness, and the deficiency smallness of soul. And just as we said generosity was related to magnificence, differing from it in being concerned with small sums, so there is also something related in this way to greatness of soul (which is concerned with great honor) that is concerned with small honor. For we can desire honor as we should or more or less than we should. A person who is excessive in these desires is said to be an honor lover, whereas someone who is deficient in them is indifferent to honor, and the medial person nameless. Also nameless are the corresponding dispositions, with the exception of that of an honor lover, which is called "love of honor." This is why the extremes lay claim to the middle ground—that is, we sometimes say that a medial person is an honor lover and sometimes that he is indifferent to honor, and sometimes we praise an honor lover and sometimes one who is indifferent to honor. Why we do this will be discussed in what follows. For now, let us speak about the rest in the way we have laid down.[189]

There is also excess and deficiency and a mean where anger is concerned, but, since these are pretty much nameless, and since a medial person is said to be mild-mannered, let us call the medial condition "mild-mannerdness." Of those at the extremes, let an excessive one be irascible and his vice irascibility, and a deficient one inerascible and his vice inerascibility.

There are also three other medial conditions that have a certain similarity to each other but differ from each other. For all of them are concerned with communal relations in words and actions, but they differ because one is concerned with the truth in them while the others are concerned with what is pleasant—in amusements, in the case of one, and in what bears on life generally, in the case of the other. So let us talk about these too in order to see more clearly that in all cases the medial condition is praiseworthy, whereas the extremes are neither praiseworthy nor correct but blameworthy. Now of these, most are also nameless. But we should try, just as in the other cases, to make up names for them ourselves for the sake of perspicuity and ease in following.

Where truth is concerned, then, let us call a medial person "a truthful sort," and let us call the mean "truthfulness."[190] Pretense that exaggerates will be boastfulness and a person who has it will be boastful. Pretense that minimizes will be self-deprecation and a person who has it will be a self-deprecator.

Where what is pleasant in amusements is concerned, a medial person is witty and the disposition is wit. The excess is buffoonery and one who has it is a buffoon, whereas a deficient person is a sort of boor and the state is boorishness. Where the remainder of what is pleasant is concerned (that in life generally), let us call "friendly" a person who is pleasant in the way we should be and the medial condition friendliness. An excessive person (if he is not so for the sake of something specific) will be ingratiating or (if he is so for his own benefit) a flatterer. And a deficient person (who is unpleasant in everything) will be a quarrelsome sort of person and disagreeable.

There are also medial conditions in feelings and concerned with feelings.[191] For shame is not a virtue, yet a person with a sense of shame is praised as well. And in these cases, in fact, one person is said to be medial, whereas another is said to be excessive (as in the case of a bashful person, who is ashamed of everything). Someone who is deficient in shame or who does not feel it at all is shameless. And a medial person is said to have a sense of shame.

Indignation is a medial condition between envy and spite, all of which are concerned with pleasure and pain at what happens to neighbors. The indignant person is pained by those who do well undeservedly. The envious person exceeds him in being pained by everyone's doing well, whereas the spiteful person is so deficient in being pained that he even enjoys this.

There will be an opportunity to discuss these issues later. But, where justice is concerned, since the term is not said of things only unconditionally, we shall (after that) distinguish its two varieties and say in what way each is a medial condition—and, similarly, where the virtues of reason are concerned.[192]

## II 8

There are three dispositions, then, two of which are vices (one of excess and the other of deficiency) and one a virtue (the medial one), and all of them are opposed to each other in a way, since the extremes are contrary both to the mean and to each other, and the mean to the extremes.

For just as what is equal is greater when compared to what is smaller and smaller when compared to what is greater, so the mean states are excessive both in feelings and in actions when compared to the deficiencies and deficient when compared to the excesses. For a courageous person appears rash when compared to a coward and cowardly when compared to a rash one. Similarly, a temperate person appears intemperate when compared to an insensible person and insensible when compared to an intemperate one, and a generous person appears wasteful when compared to an acquisitive person and acquisitive when compared to a wasteful one. That is why each of the extreme people pushes a medial one toward the other extreme—that is to say, a coward calls a courageous person "rash" and a rash person calls him "a coward" and analogously in the other cases.

While they are opposed to each other in this way, however, the greatest contrariety is that of the extremes when compared to each other rather than when compared to the mean, since they are further from each other than from the mean (as what is great is further from what is small and what is small further from what is great than either is from what is equal).

Further, when compared to the mean, some extremes appear to have a certain similarity to it, as rashness does when compared to courage or wastefulness when compared to generosity. The greatest dissimilarity, however, appears to be that of the extremes when compared to each other. But things that are furthest from each other are defined as contraries, so that things that are further apart are also more contrary.

When compared to the mean, the deficiency is more opposed, in some cases, and the excess, in others. For example, in the case of courage, it is not rashness (the excess) that is more opposed but cowardice (the deficiency), whereas, in the case of temperance, it is not insensibility (the deficiency) but intemperance (the excess).

Two things explain why this comes about. One derives from the thing itself. For because it is closer to the mean and more similar to it, we regard not it but its contrary as more opposed to the mean. For example, since rashness seems to be more like courage and closer to it, and cowardice less similar, we regard cowardice as more opposed, since things further from the mean seem to be more contrary to it. This, then, is one explanation, deriving from the thing itself.

The other derives from ourselves, since the things that we ourselves are naturally more inclined toward are the ones that appear more contrary to the mean. For example, we are naturally more inclined toward pleasures, which is why we are more easily drawn toward intemperance than toward moderation. So it is these things that we say are more contrary—the ones to which we are more addicted. That is why it is intemperance (the excess) that is more contrary to temperance.

## II 9

We have spoken adequately about these topics, then, saying that virtue of character is a medial condition and in what way, that it is a medial condition between two vices (one of excess and the other of deficiency), and that it is such because it is able to aim at and hit the mean both in feelings and in actions.

That is why it takes work to be excellent, since in each case it takes work to find the mean [*meson*]—for example, not everyone can find the midpoint [*meson*] of a circle, but, rather, someone with knowledge.[193] In the same way, getting angry is also something everyone can do and something easy, as is giving or spending money. Determining whom to give it to, though, and how much, when, for the sake of what, and in what way—that is no longer something everyone can do or something easy. That is why doing it well is a rare thing and a praiseworthy and noble one.

Hence a person who is aiming to hit the mean must first steer clear of what is more contrary to it, as Calypso too advises: "from that surge and spray keep your ship well clear."[194] For one of the extremes is more in error, the other less. So since it is extremely difficult to hit the mean, the second best course, as they say, is to ascertain the lesser of the evils, and that will best be done in the way we say.

We should also investigate what we ourselves are easily drawn toward, since different people are naturally inclined toward different things. This will become known to us from the pleasure and pain that the things bring about in us. And it is in the contrary direction that we should drag ourselves off, since it is by pulling well away from error that we shall attain the mean—as people do in rectifying distortions in pieces of wood.[195]

In everything, though, we must most of all guard against what is pleasant (that is, against pleasure), since we are not unbiased judges of it. So precisely the way the elders of the people felt about Helen,[196] that is the way we ourselves should feel about pleasure, and on each occasion we should repeat what they uttered, since that way we shall send it off and be less in error.

To speak in headline form: if we do these things, we shall be most able to hit the mean. But presumably it is difficult to hit it, most of all in particular cases, since it is not easy to define how, with whom, about what, or for how long a time we should be angry. We ourselves indeed sometimes praise people who are deficient in anger, saying that they are mild-mannered, and sometimes those who are harsh, calling them "manly."

It is not a person who deviates a little—whether toward excess or toward deficiency—who is blamed, however, but one who does so a lot, since someone like that does not escape notice. But up to what point and to what extent a person's deviation is blameworthy is not easy to define in an account—nor indeed is anything else among perceptibles, for such things lie in the particulars, and their discernment lies in perception.[197]

This much, then, makes clear that the mean state is praiseworthy in all cases but that we should sometimes incline toward excess and sometimes toward deficiency, since that way we shall most easily hit the mean and what constitutes doing well.

# Book III

## III 1

Since virtue is concerned with feelings and actions, then, and it is the voluntary ones that are praised and blamed, while the involuntary ones elicit sympathetic consideration and are sometimes even pitied, it is perhaps necessary for those who are investigating issues relating to virtue to make some determinations about what is voluntary and what involuntary.[198] This is also useful to legislators regarding honors and punishments.

Now what is involuntary seems to be what comes about by force or because of ignorance. Also, what is forced is what has an external starting-point, that is, the sort of starting-point where the agent, or the one being affected, contributes nothing—as, for example, if the wind or human beings with control over him took him off somewhere.[199]

Actions done because of fear of greater evils or because of something noble—for example, if a tyrant with control over your parents and children orders you to do something shameful and, if you do it, they will be saved, whereas, if you do not do it, they will be put to death—give rise to disputes about whether the actions are involuntary or voluntary.[200]

The same sort of dispute also arises where cases of throwing cargo overboard in a storm are concerned, since, unconditionally speaking, no one throws it overboard voluntarily, but to preserve himself and all the rest, anyone with understanding does do it.

These sorts of actions are mixed, then, although they more closely resemble voluntary ones, since they are choiceworthy at the time when they are done and the end of the actions is in accord with the opportune moment. Both "voluntary" and "involuntary," then, should be ascribed with reference to the time at which the agent does these actions. And the agent does do them voluntarily, since the starting-point of his moving his instrumental parts in actions of this sort is in fact internal to himself, and—since the starting-point is internal to himself—it is also up to him whether to do them or not. Such actions, then, are voluntary.[201] Unconditionally, though, they are presumably involuntary, since no one would choose anything of this sort for what it intrinsically is.[202]

People are sometimes even praised for actions of this sort, when they endure something shameful or painful for great and noble things, whereas if it is the reverse, they are blamed, since to endure the most shameful things for something not at all noble or only moderately so is characteristic of a base person. And to some people it is not praise we give but, rather, sympathetic consideration, when someone does some action he shouldn't do because of things that overstrain human nature and that no one could endure.

In some cases, however, there is presumably no being compelled. On the contrary, rather than do them we should die having suffered the most terrible things. For the things that compelled Euripides' Alcmaeon to kill his mother are evidently ridiculous.[203]

But it is sometimes difficult to distinguish what should be chosen for what or what should be endured for what, and more difficult still to stand by what we have determined, since the expected consequences are for the most part painful and what we are compelled to do shameful. That is what leads people to give praise or blame to those who are compelled or not.

What sorts of things, then, should we say are forced? Or is it that things are unconditionally forced, when their cause lies in external factors and the agent contributes nothing? But the ones that are intrinsically involuntary, though choiceworthy on this occasion for these things, and where the starting-point is internal to the agent—these, though intrinsically involuntary, are, on this occasion and done for these things, voluntary. But they more closely resemble voluntary ones, since the actions lie in the particulars and these particular actions are voluntary.[204] What sorts of things should be chosen for what, though, is not easy to give an account of, since there are many differences that lie in the particulars.

If someone were to say that pleasant things and noble things force us (since they are external and compel us), then for him everything would be forced, since everyone does every action for the sake of these.[205] Moreover, people who are forced to act and act involuntarily find it painful, whereas those who act because of what is pleasant or what is noble do it with pleasure. It is ridiculous, then, for the agent to hold external things responsible but not himself for being easily ensnared by such things, and to hold himself responsible for his noble actions but pleasant things responsible for his shameful ones.[206]

That which comes about by force, then, seems to be that whose starting-point is external, nothing being contributed by the one who is forced.

All of what is done because of ignorance, however, is *not voluntary,* although it is *contra-voluntary* when involving pain and regret.[207] For a person who has done whatever it is because of ignorance, but sees nothing repulsive in his action, has not acted voluntarily, because he did not know what he was doing. But neither has he acted contra-voluntarily, because he is not pained by it. Of those people, then, who act because of ignorance, the one who regrets what he did seems a contra-voluntary agent. The one who does not regret, since he is a different case, let him be a non-voluntary agent. For since he is different, it is better for him to have a special name.

Acting because of ignorance, however, seems to be different from acting in ignorance. For the person who is drunk or angry does not seem to act because of ignorance but because of one of the aforementioned conditions, although he does not act knowingly but in ignorance.[208] Now every depraved person is ignorant of the things he should do and the things he should abstain from, and it is because of this sort of error that unjust people—and bad people generally—come about.[209]

But a case is not meant to be called "involuntary" if someone is ignorant of what things are advantageous. For ignorance in our deliberate choice is not a cause of something's being involuntary but of depravity, and neither is ignorance of the universal (since people are blamed for ignorance of this sort) but, rather, ignorance of the particulars in which the action lies and with which it is concerned. For in these lie the basis for both pity and |1111a1| sympathetic consideration, since it is a person who is ignorant of one of these who acts involuntarily.

So perhaps it is not a bad thing to make some determinations about these, what they are and how many they are. When someone acts, then, we can ask [1] who? [2] what? and [3] concerning what? or [4] in what? and sometimes [5] with what? (for example, with what instrument?), [6] for the sake of what? (for example, preservation), and [7] in what way? (for example, weakly or intensely).[210]

Now no one who is not a madman could be ignorant about all of these nor, clearly, about [1] who is doing it. For how could he be ignorant about *himself*? But about [2] what he is doing, he might be ignorant, as when people say that things "just slipped out" while they were talking or that they "didn't know they were a secret," as Aeschylus said about the Mysteries or that they "wished to do a demonstration and it went off," as the man said about the catapult.[211] Or someone might think that [3–4] his son was the enemy, as Merope did, or [5] that a spear had a guard on the point or that the stone was pumice stone or he might give someone a drink [6] with a view to preserving his life but end up killing him or [7] mean to give someone a light tap (as sparring partners do) and knock him out.[212]

Now since about all these things ignorance is possible and these are the ones in which the action lies, a person who is ignorant of one of them seems to have acted involuntarily—most of all so if he is ignorant of the ones with most control. And the ones with most control seem to be the ones in which the action occurs and what it is for the sake of.[213] What is called "involuntary" on the basis of this sort of ignorance, then, must also cause pain and regret.

Because what is involuntary consists, then, of what comes about by force or because of ignorance, what is voluntary would seem to be what has its starting-point in the agent himself, when he knows the particulars in which the action lies.

For actions done because of spirit or appetite are presumably not correctly said to be involuntary. For, first of all, none of the other animals will then act voluntarily and neither will children. Second, are none of the actions we do because of appetite or spirit done voluntarily, or are the noble ones voluntary and the shameful ones involuntary? Or is that certainly ridiculous, since they have a single cause? But presumably it is strange to call the things we should desire "involuntary." And we should be angry at certain things and have an appetite for certain ones, such as health and learning. It also seems that involuntary things are painful, whereas those in accord with appetite are pleasant.

Further, what difference in involuntariness is there between errors made on the basis of rational calculation and those made on the basis of spirit? Both indeed are to be avoided. But the nonrational feelings seem to be no less human, with result that |1111b1| actions resulting from spirit and appetite are no less the actions of human beings. So it would be strange to count them as involuntary.

## III 2

Now that we have made these determinations about what is voluntary and what involuntary, the next task is to discuss deliberate choice, since it seems to belong most properly to virtue and to be a better discerner of people's characters than their actions are.[214]

Deliberate choice, then, is apparently something voluntary, although not the same as what is voluntary, which extends more broadly. For children and other animals share in what is voluntary but not in deliberate choice, and sudden actions are voluntary, we say, but are not in accord with deliberate choice.[215]

Those who say that deliberate choice is appetite, spirit, wish, or some sort of belief do not seem to be correct.[216] For deliberate choice

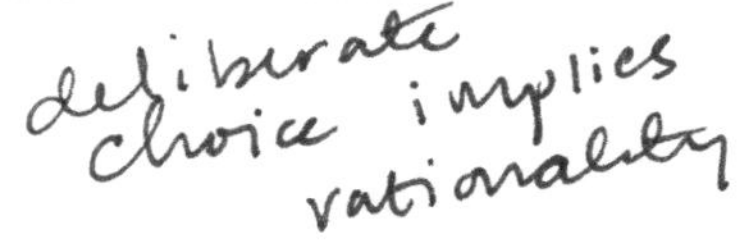


is not something shared by nonrational creatures, whereas appetite and spirit are. Also, a person who lacks self-control acts from appetite but not from deliberate choice, whereas a person who has self-control does the reverse, acting from deliberate choice but not from appetite. Also, appetite is contrary to deliberate choice but not to appetite.[217] Also, appetite is concerned with what is pleasant and what is painful, whereas deliberate choice is concerned neither with what is painful nor with what is pleasant. Still less is deliberate choice spirit, since actions done because of spirit seem least of all to be in accord with deliberate choice.

Then, again, it is not *wish* either, although it appears to be a close relative of it. For there is no deliberate choice of impossible things, and if someone were to say he was deliberately choosing them, he would seem silly. But there is wish for impossible things—for example, immortality.[218] There is also wish concerning the sorts of things that could never come about through ourselves—for example, that a certain actor or athlete should win a victory prize. No one deliberately chooses things like that, but things he thinks can come about through him. Further, wish is more for the end, whereas deliberate choice is of the things that further the end. We wish to be healthy, for example, but we deliberately choose the things through which we shall be healthy. We wish to be happy too, and say so, whereas it is not fitting to say that we deliberately choose to be happy, since deliberate choice generally seems to be concerned with what is up to us.

Neither, then, would it seem be belief. For belief seems to be concerned with all things and no less concerned with eternal ones and impossible ones than with ones that are up to us. And beliefs are divided into false and true, not into bad and good, whereas deliberate choices are more divided into bad and good.

Presumably no one does claim that deliberate choice is the same as belief in general, but neither is it the same as a specific sort of belief. For it is by deliberately choosing good things or bad things that we are people of a certain sort, not by believing them. Also, we deliberately choose to take or avoid some such thing, whereas we have beliefs about what it is or to whose advantage it is or in what way. But whether to take it or avoid it is scarcely something we hold a belief about. Also, deliberate choice is praised more for being of what it should be of, or for correctness in this sense, whereas belief is praised for being true. Also, we deliberately choose things that we most know to be good, whereas we have beliefs about things we scarcely know to be good. Also, the people who make the best deliberate choices do not seem to be the same as the ones who form the best beliefs, on the contrary, some people form better beliefs but because of vice choose what they shouldn't.

Whether there is belief preceding deliberate choice, though, or following it, makes no difference, since it is not this we are investigating but whether deliberate choice is the same as a specific sort of belief.

What, then, or what sort of thing, is deliberate choice, since it is none of the ones we mentioned? To be sure, it is something voluntary, apparently, although not everything voluntary is deliberately chosen. Well, is it something reached by prior deliberation at least? For deliberate choice involves reason and thought and even its name [*prohairesis*] seems to indicate something's being chosen [*haireton*] before [*pro*] other things.

## III 3

Do people deliberate about everything, and is everything a proper object of deliberation or are there some things about which there is no deliberation?[219] And presumably we should call "a proper object of deliberation" not what a silly sort of person or a madman would deliberate about but what a person with understanding would.

No one deliberates about [1] eternal things, then, about the universe, for example, or about the fact that the diameter and sides of a square are not proportionate; or about [2a] things that include change but that always come about in the same way, whether from necessity (or indeed [2b] by nature) or due to some other cause, such as the solstices or the risings of the heavenly bodies; or about [3] things that happen sometimes in one way, sometimes in another, such as droughts and rains; or about [4] things that come about by luck, such as discovering a treasure; or about all human affairs either—for example, no Spartan deliberates about the best form of government for the Scythians, since none of these things comes about through ourselves.[220]

We do deliberate, though, about things that are up to us and doable in action, and these in fact are the remaining ones. For the causes of things seem to be nature, necessity, luck, and, furthermore, understanding and everything that comes about through a human being.[221] Among human beings, however, each group deliberates about what is doable in action through itself.

There is no deliberation, however, where sciences that are both exact and self-sufficient are concerned— where writing the letters of the alphabet is concerned, for example, since we have no hesitation about what way to write them.[222] We do deliberate, however, about those things that come about through ourselves but not always in the same way (for example, about the things that medicine or moneymaking deals with). And we deliberate more about navigation than about athletic training, insofar as navigation has been less exactly worked out. Further, deliberation is involved in a similar way where the rest are concerned but more where crafts are concerned than sciences, since we are more hesitant about them.[223]

Deliberation is found, then, in the sphere of what holds for the most part but where it is unclear what way things will turn out and where there is an element of indefinability.[224] And we call on partners in deliberation on important questions, when we mistrust ourselves as not being adequate to determine the answer.

We deliberate not about ends, though, but about the things that further ends. For a doctor does not deliberate about whether to cure or an orator about whether to persuade or a politician about whether to produce good government, nor do any of the rest deliberate about their end.[225] Rather, they take the end for granted and investigate in what way and through which things it will come about. And if it appears that it can come about through several, they investigate through which ones it will most easily and best come about. But if it is brought to completion through only one, they investigate in what way it will come about through this and through which things it, in turn, will come about, until they arrive at the first cause, which is the last thing in the process of discovery. For a deliberator seems to inquire and analyze in the way we said just as though he were dealing with a diagram—but whereas it is evident that not all inquiry is deliberation (for example, mathematical inquiry), all deliberation is inquiry. And the last thing found in the analysis seems to come first in bringing about the result.[226]

Also, if people encounter something impossible, they give up (for example, if wealth is needed but there is no way to provide it), whereas if it appears possible, they set about doing the action. But possible things are ones that could come about through ourselves. For what comes about through our friends comes about through ourselves in a way, since the starting-point is in us.[227]

We inquire sometimes about instruments, sometimes about what way they are to be used, and similarly for the rest—sometimes through whom, sometimes in what way, and sometimes through which things.[228]

It seems, then, as we said, that a human being is a starting-point of actions and that deliberation is about what is doable in action by him, while the actions are for the sake of other things.[229] For what is deliberated about is not the end but the things that further ends, and neither, of course, is it particulars (for example, whether this thing is a loaf or whether it is cooked in the way it should be), since these are matters for perception. |1113a1| And if we deliberate at every point, we shall go on without limit.

Proper objects of deliberation and proper objects of deliberate choice are the same, except that proper objects of deliberate choice are already something determinate, since it is what has been discerned as a result of deliberation that is a proper object of deliberate choice. For each of us stops inquiring about what way to act when he brings back the starting-point to himself and, within himself, to the leading element, since this is what deliberately chooses.[230] This is also clear from the ancient constitutions that Homer described, since the kings announced to the common people what kings had deliberately chosen.[231]

Since a proper object of deliberate choice is a proper object of deliberation and of desire that is among the things that are up to us, deliberate choice too will be a deliberative desire of things that are up to us. For having discerned as a result of deliberation, we desire in accord with our deliberation.[232]

So much, then, by way of an outline of deliberate choice, of the things it is concerned with and that it is about the things that further ends.

## III 4

Wish is for the end, as we said, but some people think it is for the good, others that it is for the apparent good.[233]

For those who say that the proper object of wish is the good, it follows that when someone who has not deliberated correctly wishes for something, what he wishes for is not a proper object of wish at all (for if it is a proper object of wish, it will also be a good thing, but, as it happens, it was a bad one).[234]

For those, on the other hand, who say that the proper object of wish is the apparent good, it follows that nothing is by nature a proper object of wish, but what seems good to each person is so, with different things—even contrary ones, as it happens—appearing so to different ones.[235]

Supposing, then, that these results do not satisfy us; should we say that unconditionally and in truth the proper object of wish is the good, but to each person it is the apparent good? To an excellent person, it is what is truly the proper object; to a base one, it is whatever random thing it happens to be. It is just the same in the case of bodies. The things that are healthy for those in good condition are the things that are truly healthy, whereas for those that are diseased, it is different ones, and similarly with bitter, sweet, hot, heavy, and each of the others. For an excellent person discerns each of them correctly and, in each case, what is true is apparent to him.

For each state has its own special set of things that are pleasant or noble, and an excellent person is perhaps distinguished most by his seeing what is true in each case, since he is like a standard and measure of them.[236] In the case of ordinary people, however, deception seems to come about because of pleasure, which appears to be a good thing when it is not. So they choose what is pleasant as good |1113b1| and avoid what is painful as bad.

## III 5

Since, then, wish is for the end, and the proper objects of deliberation and of deliberate choice are things that further the end, actions concerned with these will be in accord with deliberate choice and voluntary. Also, the activities of the virtues are concerned with these things.

Virtue too is up to us, then, and, similarly, vice. For where acting is up to us, so is not acting, and where saying "No" is up to us, so is saying "Yes." Hence if acting, when it is noble, is up to us, not acting, when it is shameful, will also be up to us. And if not acting, when it is noble, is up to us, acting, when it is shameful, will also be up to us. But if doing noble actions or doing shameful ones is up to us and, similarly, also not doing them (which was what being good people and being bad people consisted in), then being decent or base will be up to us.[237]

Saying that no one "is voluntarily wicked or involuntarily blessed" seems to be partly false and partly true, since, while no one is involuntarily blessed, depravity is a voluntary thing.[238]

Or should we dispute what has been said just now and say that a human being is *not* a starting-point or begetter of his actions as of his children?[239] But if what we have said does appear to be the case and we cannot bring back our actions to any starting-points beyond the ones in us, then, since they are indeed things that have their starting-points in us, they themselves are also up to us and voluntary.[240]

The behavior of private individuals and of legislators themselves seems to testify to this. For they punish and take revenge on anyone who does a depraved action, provided it was not forced or done because of ignorance for which he himself was not responsible, whereas they honor anyone who does noble actions, on the supposition that this will encourage the one and prevent the other. Furthermore, no one encourages us to do actions that are neither up to us nor voluntary, on the supposition that for us to be persuaded not to feel hot, suffer, feel hungry, or anything of this sort is pointless, since being persuaded will not make us feel these things any less.

In fact, they also punish someone for ignorance itself, if he seems to be responsible for the ignorance—as, for example, when penalties are doubled in cases of drunkenness.[241] For the starting-point is in the agent, since not to get drunk was in his control and that was what was responsible for his ignorance. Also, they punish someone for ignorance of something in the laws that should be known and that is not difficult, and similarly in other cases where someone seems to be ignorant because of neglectfulness, on the supposition that it is up to him not to be ignorant, since to take care was in his control.

Presumably, though, he is the sort of person not to take care. But people are themselves responsible for becoming like that because of living in a loose way, and for being unjust or intemperate because of evildoing or because of spending their time drinking and the like, since it is the activities in each case that produce people of the corresponding character. This is clear from those who practice for any sort of competition or action, since they practice the relevant activity continually. So to be ignorant that, in each case, it is from engaging in the activity that the corresponding state comes about, is the mark of an altogether insensible person.

Further, it is unreasonable to suppose that a person who is acting unjustly does not wish to be unjust or that someone doing intemperate actions does not wish to be intemperate. But if someone non-ignorantly does the actions that will result in his being unjust, he will be voluntarily unjust. This does not mean that if he merely wishes, he will stop being unjust and will be just instead. For a diseased person will not be healthy that way either, even if, as it happens, he is diseased voluntarily because of living a life that lacks self-control and disobeying his doctors. At one time, certainly, it was possible for him not to be sick. Once he has let himself go, however, it is no longer possible, just as when someone has let a stone go it is no longer possible for him to call it back. All the same, throwing it was up to him, since the starting-point was in him.[242] In the same way it was possible at the start for an unjust and an intemperate person not to become like that, which is why such people are voluntarily unjust and intemperate. But once they have become like that, it is no longer possible not to be.

It is not only vices of the soul that are voluntary, though, but in some cases vices of the body are as well—these being the ones we also admonish. For no one admonishes people who are naturally ugly but, rather, those who are so because of lack of athletic training or neglectfulness. Similarly in the case of those who are weak or disabled, since no one would admonish someone who was naturally blind or blind as the result of a disease or as the result of a blow but would rather pity them, whereas those who are so as a result of drunkenness or of other sorts of intemperance that everyone would admonish.[243] Of the vices of the body, then, it is the ones that are up to us that are admonished, while those that are not up to us are not. And if that is so, then in other cases too the vices that are admonished will be the ones that are up to us.

Suppose that someone were to say that everyone seeks the apparent good but that we do not control its appearance. Instead, whatever sort of person each of us happens to be also determines the sort of end that appears to him. Well, if each individual is somehow responsible for his own state of character, he is also somehow responsible for the appearance in question. If not, no one is responsible for his own evildoing but does evil things because of ignorance of the end, thinking that because of doing them he will achieve what is best for him. His seeking of the end in question is not self-chosen, rather, we must be born possessed of a sort of sight by which to discern correctly and choose what is truly good, and a person in whom this by nature operates correctly is naturally well disposed. For this is what is greatest and noblest and is not the sort of thing we can get from someone else or learn but the sort of thing whose condition at birth is the one in which it will later be possessed and, when it is naturally such as to be in a good and noble condition, will be the naturally good disposition in its complete and true form.[244]

If all this is true, then, how will virtue be any more voluntary than vice? For to both the good and the bad alike the end appears—or is determined by nature or by whatever it is—and whatever other actions they do, they do with reference to that end. If it is not by nature, then, that the end appears to each person in whatever way it does, but there is also something contributed by the person himself or, if the end is something natural, but an excellent person's virtue is voluntary because he does the rest of the actions voluntarily, vice will be no less voluntary than virtue. Similarly, in the case of the bad person there is something that comes about in his actions through himself, even if not in his end. So if, as is said, the virtues are voluntary (since we are in a way ourselves contributing causes of our states and it is by being people of a certain sort that we suppose the end to be of a certain sort), the vices will also be voluntary, since the two are alike.

We have now discussed in outline the virtues collectively and their genus, saying that they are medial conditions and states, that the sorts of things they arise from are the very sorts virtues lead us to do in accord with themselves, and that they are up to us and voluntary and such as the correct reason prescribes.

Actions and states are not voluntary in the same way, since we control our actions from their starting-point up to their end because we know the particulars. With states, however, we control their starting-point but the particulars of their development are not known to us any more |**1115a1**| than with diseases. But because it was up to us to use the states in a given way or not in that way, they are voluntary.

Let us resume and, where each particular virtue is concerned, say what it is, what it is concerned with, and in what way. It will be clear at the same time how many there are.

## III 6

And let us first do this where courage is concerned. Well, that there is a medial condition concerned with feelings of fear and confidence is something that has already become evident. It is clear too that what we fear are frightening things and that these—unconditionally speaking—are bad things. That is why people define fear as expectation of what is bad.

Now we certainly do fear all bad things (for example, disrepute, poverty, disease, friendlessness, and death) but they do not all seem to be the concern of a courageous person. For there are some we should in fact fear, where fearing is noble and not fearing shameful—for example, disrepute. For a person who fears this is decent and has a sense of shame, whereas one who does not fear it is shameless. But some do say that such a person is courageous, by extension of the term, since he has some similarity to a courageous person. For a courageous person is also in a way fearless.

Poverty, however, is presumably something we should not fear, as is disease or things generally that are not the results of vice or of ourselves. But a person who is fearless where they are concerned is not courageous either, although he too is called so by similarity. For some people who are cowards when facing the dangers of warfare are generous and face the loss of wealth with good confidence.[245]

Neither, then, is a person cowardly if he fears wanton aggression against his children or wife or if he fears envy or anything like that. Nor is he courageous if he is confident when he is about to be flogged.[246]

What sorts of frightening things, then, is a courageous person concerned with? Or isn't it with the greatest ones? For no one is better at enduring frightening things. And the most frightening one is death, since it is a boundary point and for the dead person it seems that nothing is any longer either good or bad.

But a courageous person would not seem to be concerned with death in all circumstances either—for example, on the sea or in sickness. In what sorts, then? Or isn't it in the noblest ones? And deaths that occur in war are of that sort, since they occur in the face of the greatest and noblest danger, and this fits with the honors awarded in cities and by monarchs.[247]

The person who is called "courageous" in the full sense, then, is the one who is unanxious where noble death is concerned and the things that are an imminent threat of death. And the things that occur in war are most of all of this sort.[248]

On the sea too, of course, and in facing diseases, a courageous person is unanxious but not in the way that seamen are. For whereas courageous people have despaired of preserving their life and are repelled by a death of this sort, seamen remain optimistic in keeping with their experience.[249] At the same time, people also show courage in circumstances in which a display of prowess is possible or in which it is noble to die, and neither holds when we come to ruin in these two ways.[250]

## III 7

What is frightening is not the same for everyone, though some sorts of things, we say, are actually beyond the human level. These, then, *are* frightening to everyone—at any rate, to everyone with understanding. And those that are on the human level differ in magnitude, that is, some are more frightening, some less, and similarly with things that inspire confidence.

A courageous person, however, is as undaunted as a human being can be. So though he will also fear such things, he will endure them in the way he should, in the way reason prescribes, and for the sake of what is noble, since this is the end characteristic of virtue.

We can fear frightening things more, however, and we can fear them less. Furthermore, we can also fear things that are not frightening as if they were. And the way error comes about is that we fear what we shouldn't, in the way we shouldn't, when we shouldn't, or something else of that sort. Similarly with the things that inspire confidence.

So a person is courageous who endures and fears the things he should, in the way he should, when he should, and is similarly confident, since a courageous person feels and acts as things merit and in the way reason prescribes.

But the end of every activity is what is in accord with the corresponding state. This also holds, then, for a courageous person. But courage is something noble.[251] The corresponding end, then, is also such, since each thing is defined by its end. It is for the sake of what is noble, then, that a courageous person endures things and does the actions that are in accord with courage.

Among those who go to excess, the one who is excessive in his fearlessness is nameless (we said earlier that many are nameless) but would be some sort of madman or insensitive to suffering if he feared nothing—"neither earthquake nor waves," as they say of the Celts.[252] But one who is excessively confident concerning frightening things is rash.

A rash person also seems to be a boaster and a pretender to courage. At any rate, the way that a courageous person is concerned with frightening things is the way a rash person wishes to appear to be concerned with them, and thus he imitates a courageous person in those situations where he is able. That is why most rash people are actually rash cowards, since, while they are rash in such situations, they do not endure frightening things.

An excessively fearful person, on the other hand, is a coward, since he fears the things he shouldn't, in the way he shouldn't, and all the other things of that sort follow in his case. He is also deficient in confidence, but his being excessive in the pains he feels is more evident.

A coward, then, is in a way despondent, since he fears everything. And a courageous person is the contrary way, since to be confident is the mark of an optimistic person.

So a coward, a rash person, and a courageous person are all concerned with the same things but have states that are differently related to them, since the others are excessive and deficient but a courageous person has the mean state that is related in the way it should be. Rash people are also impetuous and wish for dangers ahead of time but shrink from them when in their midst, whereas courageous people are quick spirited when there are things to be accomplished but at peace beforehand.

As we said, then, courage is a medial condition concerned with things that inspire confidence and fear in the circumstances we have described, and courage makes choices and endures things because it is noble to do so or shameful not to. Also, dying to avoid poverty, erotic desire, or something painful is the mark not of a courageous person but, rather, of a coward. For to flee from painful labors is a mark of softness, and someone like that faces up to death not because it is noble but because he is fleeing something bad.

## III 8

Courage, then, is something of this sort. But there are other things so called, which are of five sorts. First comes political courage, since it is most like courage.[253] For citizens seem to endure dangers because of the penalties prescribed by the laws, because of people's reproaches, and because of the honors involved. And that is why the most courageous seem to be those among whom cowards are dishonored and courageous people honored.

Homer too depicts people of this sort—for example, Diomedes and Hector: "Polydamas will be the first to heap disgrace on me," and "One day Hector will say among the Trojans 'The son of Tydeus fleeing me.'"[254] This is most similar to the sort we previously discussed, because it seems to come about because of virtue, since it comes about because of a sense of shame, because of a desire for something noble (since honor is that), and to avoid reproach (since reproach is shameful).[255]

Someone might also put in the same class those who are compelled by their rulers. But these are not as good, because they do what they do not because of a sense of shame but because of fear and in order to avoid not the shameful but the painful. For the people in control compel them to do it in the way that Hector does: "If I see anyone cringing in fear far away from the battle, he will not, you can be sure, avoid being thrown to the dogs."[256] And commanders who beat people if they retreat are doing the same thing, as are those who draw up their men in front of trenches or things of that sort, since they are all exerting compulsion. We should be courageous not because of compulsion, however, but because it is noble.

Experience in particular areas also seems to be courage, which is why Socrates too thought that courage is scientific knowledge.[257] Different sorts of people have experience in different areas but in matters of warfare, it is the professional soldiers. For there seem to be many occasions that are empty of danger in war and the professional soldiers are most capable of seeing these at a glance.[258] They appear courageous, then, because the others do not know what sorts of situations these are. Moreover, as a result of their experience, they are most capable of attacking and of defending—capable of using their weapons and having the sorts that are strongest both for attacking and for defending. They are like armed men, then, contending with unarmed ones, or trained athletes against private individuals, since in contests of this sort as well it is not the most courageous who are the best fighters but those whose strength is greatest and whose bodies are in the best condition.

Professional soldiers turn out to be cowards, however, when the danger overstrains them and they are inferior in numbers and equipment, since they are the first to flee, whereas the citizens stand their ground and are killed—as happened at the temple of Hermes.[259] For to the citizens, fleeing is shameful and death is more choiceworthy than preserving their life at this cost, whereas the others were from the very start facing up to danger on the supposition of being stronger, and when they come to know the truth, they flee, fearing death more than shame. But a courageous person is not like that.

People also count spirit as courage, since those who act because of spirit—like wild beasts that rush at the people who have wounded them—also seem to be courageous, because courageous people are spirited as well, since spirit is most ready to meet dangers. Again, Homer attests to this: "he put strength into his spirit," "rage and spirit he aroused," "bitter rage breathed through his nostrils," and "his blood boiled."[260] For all such expressions seem to signify the arousal of spirit and its impulse.

Now courageous people act because of what is noble, and spirit is their co-worker. Wild beasts, however, act because of pain, since they act because they have been struck or because they are frightened. For if they are in a forest, at any rate, they do not attack. Now it is not courage to rush into danger because of suffering pain or because of being driven on and impelled by spirit while foreseeing none of the terrible outcomes, since that way even hungry *donkeys* would be courageous, since they do not stop grazing when they are beaten. Adulterers also do many daring things because of their appetite. The courage that is caused by spirit does seem to be the most natural sort, though, and to really be courage once deliberate choice and the end are added.[261]

Human beings also suffer pain when they are angered, of course, and take pleasure in revenge. But people who fight because of these, though they may be good fighters, are not courageous, since they do not fight because of what is noble or in the way reason prescribes but because of feeling. Still, they have something similar to courage.

Optimistic people are not courageous either, then, since it is because they have often been victorious and over many opponents that they are confident in facing dangers. But they are similar to courageous people, because both are confident. Whereas courageous people are confident because of what we just mentioned, however, optimistic ones are confident because they think they are the strongest ones and that nothing will happen to them. (Drunks also behave in this sort of way, since they become optimistic.) When things do not turn out as expected, though, they flee. But it is characteristic of a courageous person, as we saw, to endure things that are and appear frightening to a human being, because it is noble to do so or shameful not to.

That is why it seems to be characteristic of a more courageous person to be fearless and calm in the face of frightening things that are sudden than of those that are clear beforehand, since doing so was more the result of his state of character, because it was less the result of preparation. For when things are evident beforehand we can deliberately choose what to do in accord with rational calculation and reason as well, whereas when they happen suddenly we must do so in accord with our state of character.

Ignorant people also appear courageous and are not far removed from optimistic ones but are inferior to them insofar as ignorant people have no sense of self-worth, whereas the others do. That is why optimistic people stand their ground for a time, whereas once those who are deceived recognize that the situation is other than they supposed, they flee (which is precisely what happened to the Argives when they fell upon the Spartans taking them for Sicyonians).[262]

We have said, then, what sort of people courageous ones are, as well as the ones that seem to be courageous.

## III 9

Although courage is concerned with things that inspire confidence and with frightening things, it is not concerned with both equally but more with frightening ones. For a person who is calm in the face of frightening things, and is in the state he should be in where they are concerned, is courageous more than a person who is so in the face of things that inspire confidence. It is for enduring painful things, then, as we said, that people are called "courageous." That is why courage involves pain, indeed, and is justly praised, since it is more difficult to endure painful things than to abstain from pleasant ones.

Nonetheless the end that is in accord with courage would seem to be pleasant but to be obscured by the circumstances, as also happens in athletic contests, since to boxers the end is pleasant—namely, the end for which they fight, namely, the victory crown and the honors. But being struck by blows makes them suffer, if indeed they are made of flesh and blood, and is painful—as too is all their exertion. And because there is a lot of all that, the end for which they fight, because it is small in extent, appears to have nothing pleasant about it.[263]

If the same is also true where courage is concerned, then death and wounds will be painful to a courageous person and he will suffer them involuntarily. But he will endure them because it is noble to do so or shameful not to. Indeed, the more he is possessed of virtue in its entirety and the happier he is, the more he will be pained at the prospect of death, since to someone like that living is most worthwhile, and this one will be *knowingly* depriving himself of the greatest goods, which is a painful thing. He is no less courageous because of that, however, but perhaps even more so, because he chooses what is noble in war in preference to those goods. It is not true, then, in the case of all the virtues that it is pleasant to actively exercise them, except insofar as doing so attains the end.

Presumably, there is nothing to prevent the best professional soldiers from being not people like that but, rather, the sort who are less courageous but possess no other good, since these are ready to face dangers and trade their lives for small profits.

So much for courage, then, since it is not difficult to get at least an outline of what it is from what has been said.

## III 10

After courage let us discuss temperance, since courage and temperance seem to be the virtues of the nonrational parts.[264]

Now we have already said that temperance is a medial condition concerned with pleasures (for it is less concerned—and not in the same way—with pains). Intemperance also appears in this area. With what *sorts* of pleasures temperance is concerned, we must now determine.

Let us distinguish, then, between pleasures of the soul and those of the body. Consider, for example, love of honor and love of learning. For in the case of each of these two, a person disposed to the love enjoys them without his body being affected at all but, rather, his thought. But people concerned with pleasures like this are called neither temperate or intemperate. The same holds for those concerned with any of the other non-bodily pleasures, since if people are lovers of stories and inveterate gossipers, spending their days concerned with whatever random things are happening, we call them idle chatterers, not intemperate. Nor do we call people intemperate if they are pained over matters of wealth or friends. |**1118a1**|

With pleasures of the body, however, temperance *would* seem to be concerned—but not with all of these pleasures either. For people who enjoy objects of sight, such as colors, shapes, or a painting, are called neither temperate or intemperate, yet it would seem possible, even in these cases, to enjoy them in the way we should or to do so excessively or deficiently. Similarly where the objects of hearing are concerned, since no one calls intemperate those who enjoy melodies or drama excessively or temperate those who enjoy these in the way they should. Nor do we do this where smells are concerned, except coincidentally, since people who enjoy the smells of apples, roses, or incenses are not called intemperate but, rather, the ones who enjoy those of perfumes or gourmet dishes.[265] For intemperate people enjoy these, since through them they are reminded of the objects of their appetites. We also see other people enjoying the smells of food when they are hungry, but to enjoy such things is characteristic of an intemperate person, since, in his case, these are the objects of his appetite.

Nor in the case of the other animals is pleasure taken in these perceptual capacities, except coincidentally. For what the dogs enjoy is not the smell of a hare but to eat it up, although the smell is what made them perceive it. Nor is the lowing of an ox what a lion enjoys but its meat. The fact that the ox was nearby is something that the lion perceived because of the sound, and thus the lion appears to enjoy the sound itself. Similarly, what he enjoys is not seeing "a deer or a wild goat" but making a meal of it.[266]

Temperance and intemperance are concerned with the sorts of pleasures that the rest of the animals share in as well (which is why they appear slavish and beast-like), namely, touch and taste.[267] They appear, though, to make little or no use even of taste. For the use of taste is to discern flavors, as people do when testing wines, or chefs when preparing gourmet dishes. But discerning such things is scarcely what people enjoy—at any rate, intemperate ones don't. On the contrary, what they enjoy is indulging in them—which enjoyment, whether in eating and drinking or in the so-called pleasures of Aphrodite, comes about wholly through touch.[268] That is why a certain gourmand prayed for his gullet to become longer than a crane's, showing that it was the touching that gave him pleasure.[269] Intemperance, then, is related to the most widely shared of the perceptual capacities and so would justly seem to be disgraceful, because it characterizes us not insofar as we are human beings but insofar as we are animals.[270]

To enjoy such things, then, and to like them most, is beast-like. For the pleasures of touch that are most appropriate to free people must in fact be excluded, such as the ones produced in gyms by massaging and heating, since the touching that is characteristic of the intemperate person does not concern the body generally but only certain parts of it.[271]

## III 11

Some appetites seem to be shared, others to be peculiar to individuals and acquired. For example, the appetite for nourishment is natural, since everyone has an appetite for dry or liquid food, sometimes both, when he is in need of them, and for "bed," as Homer puts it, when he is young and in his prime.[272] But not everyone has an appetite for this or that sort of nourishment or for sex with the same people. That is why such an appetite seems to be peculiarly its possessor's. Nonetheless, it does at least have something natural about it as well, since, though different things are pleasant to different people, there are also some things that everyone finds more pleasant than they do random ones.

Now in the case of the natural appetites, few people make errors and only in one direction—that of excess. For to eat or drink random things until we are overfull is to exceed the quantity that is in accord with nature, since a natural appetite is for the replenishment of a need.[273] That is why people who do this are called "gluttons," because they glut their belly beyond what they should.[274] Those who turn out like this are utterly slavish people.

Where the pleasures peculiar to individuals are concerned, however, many people do make errors and in many ways. For people are called "lovers of such and such" because they enjoy the sorts of things they shouldn't or do so more than ordinary people do or do so not in the way they should. And intemperate people go to excess regarding all these, since they actually enjoy some things that they shouldn't (ones they should hate, indeed) and if there are some things of the sort in question that they should enjoy, they enjoy them more than they should and more than ordinary people do.

It is clear, then, that intemperance is excess where pleasures are concerned and is blameworthy. Where pains are concerned we are not said to be temperate—as we are said to be courageous—for enduring them, nor intemperate for not doing so. Rather, an intemperate person is so called for being more pained than he should at not getting pleasant things (indeed, the pain too is produced in him by the pleasure), and a temperate one for not being pained at the absence of pleasure or at abstaining from it.

An intemperate person, then, has an appetite for all pleasant things or for the most pleasant ones, and appetite leads him to choose these before the others.[275] That is why he is pained both when he fails to get them and when he has an appetite for them (since appetite involves pain), though it does seem strange to be pained *because of pleasure*.

People who are deficient where pleasures are concerned and who enjoy them less than they should, scarcely occur, since that sort of insensibility is not human. For even the rest of the animals distinguish among foods and enjoy some but not others. Indeed, if there is someone to whom nothing is pleasant and who does not distinguish between one thing and another, he would be far from being human. This sort of person has not acquired a name, though, because he scarcely ever occurs.

A temperate person, however, is in a medial state concerning these matters, since he does not take pleasure in the things the intemperate person most enjoys but is, rather, repelled by them. Neither does he take it in those things generally that he shouldn't nor get intense pleasure from anything of that sort nor become pained by its absence. He does not have an appetite for them, or only moderately, and not more than he should, when he shouldn't, or in any of those ways generally. But pleasant things that are conducive to health or a good state, these he will desire moderately and in the way he should, as he will the other pleasant things that do not impede these or are not contrary to what is noble or beyond his means. For a person who desires them the other way likes such pleasures more than they deserve, whereas a temperate person is not like that but instead loves them in the way the correct reason prescribes.

## III 12

Intemperance seems a more voluntary thing than cowardice does, since it comes about because of pleasure, cowardice because of pain, and of these, pleasure is something choiceworthy, pain something to be avoided. Moreover, pain causes degeneration from, or destruction of, the natural state of a person who has it, whereas pleasure does nothing of the sort. Intemperance, then, is a more voluntary thing. That is why it is a more disgraceful one. For it is actually easier to be habituated to resist pleasures, since many pleasant things occur in our lives, and the circumstances of habituation involve no dangers, whereas with frightening things it is the reverse.

It would seem, however, that cowardice and the particular actions of cowardice are not voluntary in the same way, since cowardice itself is without pain but the actions cause degeneration because of the pain involved, with the result that people even throw away their weapons and do other unseemly things. That is why the actions seem to be forced.

For an intemperate person it is the reverse. The particular actions seem voluntary (since the agent has the corresponding appetite and desire), whereas intemperance generally seems less so (since no one has an appetite to be intemperate).

We also apply the name "intemperance" to children's errors, as they have a certain similarity to it.[276] Which is called after which makes no difference for present purposes, although it is clear that what is posterior is called after what is prior. The transfer of the name, in any case, seems not to be a bad one. For something that desires shameful things and has a tendency to grow large should be disciplined, and appetite and children are most like this, since children also live in accord with appetite and it is mostly in them that the desire for pleasure is found.

So if the appetitive element is not obedient and subordinate to the ruling element, it will grow and grow. For the desire for pleasure is insatiable and, from indiscriminate sources in someone who lacks understanding and the activity of appetite, causes its congenital tendency to grow, and if the appetites are large and intense, they even knock out rational calculation. That is why they should be moderate and few and not oppose reason in any way (this is the sort of thing we call "obedient" and "disciplined") and just as a child should live in accord with the commands of his tutor so the appetitive element too should be in accord with reason.[277]

Hence a temperate person's appetitive element should be in harmony with reason. For the target of both is what is noble, and a temperate person has an appetite for the things he should and in the way and when he should, which is just what reason, for its part, prescribes.

So much, then, for temperance.

# Book IV

## IV 1

Let us next discuss generosity. Well, it seems to be the medial condition concerned with wealth, since a generous person is praised not in matters of warfare or in those in which a temperate person is praised or, again, in legal judgments but rather where giving or getting wealth are concerned—most of all, the giving of it.[278] By wealth we mean everything whose worth is measured by money.

Wastefulness and acquisitiveness are excesses and deficiencies concerning wealth. Acquisitiveness, for its part, we ascribe always to those who take wealth more seriously than they should, whereas in ascribing wastefulness to people we sometimes combine several things, since we call people who lack self-control "wasteful," as we do those who spend on intemperate extravagances.[279] That is why they seem to be the basest of people, since they have many vices at the same time.

The name, then, does not properly belong to them, since by someone's being wasteful we mean to denote someone having one vice—that of ruining his substance.[280] For a wasteful person is one who is being destroyed through himself, |**1120a1**| and the destruction of one's substance seems to be a sort of self-ruination, on the supposition that living depends on it. That, then, is what we take wastefulness to be.

Things that have a use can be used well or badly, and wealth is something that has a use. But the best user of each thing is the one who has the virtue concerned with it. Wealth, then, will also be best used by a person who has the virtue concerned with wealth. And this is a generous person.

Using wealth seems to consist in spending and giving it, whereas getting it and safeguarding it seem more a matter of possession. That is why it is more characteristic of a generous person to give to the people he should than to get from the ones he should and not get from the ones he shouldn't. For it is more characteristic of virtue to be a benefactor rather than to be a beneficiary and to do noble actions rather than not to do shameful ones. And it is clear enough that giving entails benefaction and doing noble actions, whereas getting entails being a beneficiary and not acting shamefully.

Also, gratitude goes to the person who gives, not to the one who does not get. Praise goes more to him too. Also, not getting is easier than giving, since people part with what properly belongs to them less readily than they avoid getting what belongs to others. Also, those who give are the ones called "generous," whereas those who do not get are praised—not for being generous but, if for anything, for justice. And those who do get are not praised at all. Also, of all virtuous people, generous ones are pretty much the most loved, since they are beneficial and their being so lies in their giving.

Actions in accord with virtue are noble and for the sake of what is noble. And a generous person will give for the sake of what is noble and will do so correctly. He will give to the people he should, in the amount he should, when he should, and so on for all the other things that correct giving entails. And he will do it with pleasure or without pain, since what is in accord with virtue is pleasant or without pain, and least of all is it painful.

A person who gives to the people he shouldn't, by contrast, or not for the sake of what is noble but due to some other cause, will not be called "generous" but, rather, something else, and neither will someone who finds giving painful, since he would choose wealth over noble action, and that is not characteristic of a generous person.

A generous person will not get from the sources he shouldn't either, since that sort of getting is not characteristic of someone who does not pay honor to wealth. Nor will he be fond of asking for favors, since it is not characteristic of a benefactor to readily accept being a beneficiary. But he will get from the sources he should (for example, from his own possessions), regarding this not as noble but as necessary, in order to have something to give. Nor will he neglect his own possessions, since of course he wishes to assist others by means of them. Nor will he give to random people—in order that he be able to give to the ones he should when he should and where it is noble to do so.

What is exceedingly characteristic of a generous person is even to be excessive in giving, so that he leaves less for himself, since it is characteristic of a generous person not to look out for himself. But it is on the basis of his wealth that someone is said to have generosity. For what is generous lies not in the size of what is given but in the state of the giver and is in accord with the giver's wealth. Nothing prevents a person who gives less from being more generous, then, if he has less from which to give.

Those who have not acquired their wealth themselves but inherited it seem to be more generous, since they have no experience of need. Also, everyone likes his own works more, as parents and poets do.[281] It is not easy either for a generous person to be wealthy, since he is neither a getter nor a safeguarder of wealth but is lavish with it and pays honor to it not because of itself but for the sake of giving. That is why people complain about luck, saying that those who are most deserving of wealth are the least wealthy. But it is not surprising that this should happen, since we cannot have wealth if we do not supervise things in such a way as to have it—just as with everything else.

All the same, a generous person will not give to those he shouldn't, when he shouldn't, and so on. For if he did, he would no longer be acting in accord with generosity, and, if he spent on those things, he would have nothing to spend on the ones he should. For as we said, a generous person is one who spends in accord with his wealth and on the things he should, whereas a person who spends excessively is wasteful. That is why tyrants are not called "wasteful," since it does not seem easy for their giving and spending to exceed the size of their possessions.

Since generosity is a medial condition, then, concerned with the giving and getting of wealth, a generous person will both give and spend on the things he should and as much as he should, alike in matters small and great, and with pleasure. He will also get from the sources he should and as much as he should. For since the virtue is a medial condition concerned with both giving and getting, he will do both in the way he should, since giving that is decent entails the same sort of getting, and the getting that is not of that sort is contrary to decent giving. So the giving and getting that entail each other are found at the same time in the same person, whereas those that are contrary to each other clearly aren't.

If it should happen that a generous person *does* spend in a way contrary to the way he should and to the correct way, |**1121a1**| he will be pained—but moderately so and in the way he should, since it is characteristic of virtue to be pleased and pained at the things we should and in the way we should. Also, a generous person is easy to deal with in matters of wealth. In fact, he is susceptible of being treated unjustly, since he does not pay honor to wealth and is more annoyed if he has not spent what he should than he is pained if he has spent what he shouldn't and, in that respect, is not satisfied with Simonides.[282]

A wasteful person, for his part, errs in these matters too, since he is neither pleased nor pained at the things he should or in the way he should. This will become more evident as we proceed.

We have said, then, that wastefulness and acquisitiveness are excesses and deficiencies in two things—giving and getting. (For we put spending under giving.) In fact, wastefulness is excessive in giving and not getting but deficient in getting, whereas acquisitiveness is deficient in giving and excessive in getting—but only in small matters.

Certainly the two characteristics of wastefulness are scarcely ever coupled, since it is not easy, while getting from nowhere, to give to everyone. For private individual donors (precisely the people, in fact, who seem to be wasteful) soon outstrip their wealth. And yet this sort of person would seem to be better than an acquisitive person—and not just by a little bit, since he is easily cured, both by age and by poverty and is able to reach the mean. For he has the characteristics of a generous person, since he both gives and does not get, though he does neither in the way he should or well. If, then, he were changed in this respect either through habituation or in some other way, he would be generous, since he will give to the people he should and will not get from the sources he shouldn't. That is why he does not seem to be of base character, since to be excessive in giving and in not getting is characteristic not of a depraved or ill-bred person but of a silly one. But someone wasteful in this way does seem much better than an acquisitive person both because of what we have just said and because he benefits many people, while an acquisitive person benefits no one—not even himself.

However, the majority of wasteful people, as we said, also get from the sources they shouldn't and are, in that respect, acquisitive. They become acquisitive because they wish to spend but are not readily able to do so, because they soon outstrip their resources. So they are compelled to seek provision from elsewhere. At the same time, because they actually think contemptuously of what is noble, |**1121b1**| they also get from any source regardless, since they have an appetite for giving but how and from what source they give makes no difference to them.[283]

That is why their acts of giving are not generous, either, since they are not noble, done for the sake of what is noble, or done in the way they should be. On the contrary, these people sometimes enrich those who should be poor, giving nothing to people of moderate character but a lot to flatterers or people who provide pleasure of some other sort. That is why most of them are intemperate—because they spend readily and on intemperate extravagances, they are prone to expenditures, and because they do not live with an eye to what is noble, they incline toward pleasures.

A wasteful person who is left untutored changes in this direction, then, but, with supervision, he could reach the mean and be as he should.

Acquisitiveness, however, is both incurable (since old age and any sort of incapacity seem to make people acquisitive) and a more natural part of human nature than wastefulness, since ordinary people are more disposed to love wealth than to give it away. Acquisitiveness is also widespread and multiform, since there seem to be many ways of being acquisitive. For it consists in two things—deficiency in giving and excess in getting—and so does not come about in its entirety in all cases but sometimes in separate bits, with some people tending to excessive getting, others to deficient giving.

For people who are called "misers," "tightfisted people," "skinflints," and the like are all deficient in giving but they do not seek what belongs to others or wish to get it—in some cases because of some sort of decency and being wary of what is shameful. For there are those who seem to guard their property—at least this is what they say—in order not to be compelled to do anything shameful.[284] These include the cheeseparer (so called because of his excessive reluctance to give anything away). But there are also those who because of fear keep their hands off what belongs to others, on the supposition that it is not easy for someone to take another's property without their taking his, so they are satisfied neither to get from others nor to give to them.[285]

The other sort, by contrast, are excessive in getting, because they get anything and from any source—those, for example, who work in unfree occupations, such as pimps and everyone of that sort, and loan sharks, who lend small amounts at high interest.[286] For all these people get from sources they shouldn't and in amounts they shouldn't.

What they apparently have in common is their love of shameful profit, since they all put up with reproach for the sake of profit—and a small profit at that. For those who, on a vast scale, get from sources they shouldn't and get things they shouldn't—such as tyrants who sack cities and plunder temples—are not called "acquisitive" but, rather, are called "wicked," "impious," and "unjust." However a gambler and a robber *are* included among the acquisitive, since they are lovers of shameful profit.[287] For it is for the sake of profit that both ply their trades and put up with reproach, robbers facing the greatest dangers for the sake of what they can get, gamblers profiting from their friends—the very people they should be giving to. Both gamblers and robbers, then, are lovers of shameful profit, since they wish to profit from the sources they shouldn't. All such ways of getting, then, are acquisitive. And it makes perfect sense that acquisitiveness is said to be the contrary of generosity, since it is a greater evil than wastefulness and people err more in its direction than with respect to what we have described as wastefulness.

So much, then, for generosity and the vices opposed to it.

## IV 2

The next thing to discuss would seem to be magnificence, indeed, since it too seems to be a virtue concerned with wealth. But unlike generosity magnificence does not extend to all actions involving wealth but only to those actions concerned with expenditure and, in these, it surpasses generosity in its magnitude. For, as the name itself [*megaloprepeia*] indicates, it involves expenditure that is appropriate [*-prepeia*] in its magnitude [*megalo-*]. But the magnitude is relative, since equipping a trireme does not involve the same expenditure as paying for a religious delegation.[288] What is appropriate, then, is relative to the agent himself, what the action lies in, and what it concerns.[289]

Someone who, in matters that are small or moderate, spends in accord with worth—like the one who "gave to many a vagabond"—is not called "magnificent," but someone who does so in great ones is.[290] For a magnificent person is generous, but that does not mean that a generous person is magnificent.

The deficiency corresponding to this state is niggardliness, while the excess is vulgarity, tastelessness, and other things of that sort, which involve people being excessive not in the magnitude of their spending on the things they should but in being extravagant in circumstances they shouldn't and in ways they shouldn't. We shall talk about these topics later.[291]

A magnificent person is like someone with scientific knowledge, since he is able to get a theoretical grasp on what is appropriate and spend great sums in a suitable way. For as we said at the start, the state is defined by its activities and by its objects.[292] Now a magnificent person's expenditure is great and appropriate. His works, then, are also like that, since that is the way the expenditures will be great and appropriate to the work. Thus the work should be worthy of the expenditure and the expenditure should be worthy of the work—or even exceed it. And the magnificent person will incur such expenditure for the sake of what is noble, since this is a feature common to the virtues. Further, he will do it with pleasure and lavishly, since exact accounting is niggardly. And he will investigate how what he accomplishes can be noblest and most appropriate rather than how much it costs or how to do it most cheaply.

It is necessary, then, for a magnificent person to be generous too. For a generous person will also spend as much as he should and in the way he should, and it is in these aspects of expenditure that the "greatness (*mega*)" of a "magnificent (*megaloprepês*)" person—that is, its magnitude (*megethos*)—is found (since generosity concerns the same sorts of expenditures), and from the same expenditure it produces a more magnificent work. For the virtue of a possession and of a work are not the same. A possession that is worth the most is the most estimable (for example, gold), whereas the most estimable work is the one that is great and noble (since the contemplation of it is wondrous and what is magnificent is something wondrous). Also, the virtue of a work—its magnificence—lies in its magnitude.

This is found in the sorts of expenditure that are called "estimable"—for example, those concerning the gods (votive offerings, ritual objects, and sacrifices). And, similarly, those expenditures concerning the entirety of what is worshipped and cases where there is acceptable competition for the honor of furthering the common good—for example, when people think they should fund a chorus extravagantly, equip a trireme, or provide a feast for the city.[293]

In all cases, though, as we said, expenditure is relative to the agent, both who he is and what resources he has (since the expenditure must be worthy of both) and appropriate not to the work alone but to the one producing it as well. That is why a poor person cannot be magnificent, since he does not have the resources to spend great amounts in an appropriate way. Someone who tries to do so is silly, since it is contrary to his worth and to what he should do, whereas to spend correctly is to do so in accord with virtue. But spending great amounts is appropriate to those who already have such resources through themselves or their ancestors or connections or to those who are well bred or reputable or anything else of that sort, since all these things involve magnitude and worthiness.

A magnificent person, then, is most of all someone like that, and magnificence is found most of all in these sorts of expenditures, as we said, since these are the greatest and generally most honored. But it is also found in private expenditures of the sort that come about only once, such as a wedding or something else like that, or something (if there is something) that the entire city or the most worthy people in it are eager for—concerned with receiving or sending off foreign guests, say, and giving gifts or receiving them in return. For it is not on himself that a magnificent person spends but on common goods, and so his gifts have something of the character of votive offerings.[294] It is also characteristic of a magnificent person to provide himself with a house fitted to his wealth (since it is also an adornment of a sort) and, where such things are concerned, to prefer to spend on those works that will be long lasting (since those are the noblest) and, in each case, to spend what is appropriate (since the same things are not fitting for gods and human beings or for a temple and a tomb).

Also, since each expenditure is great in relation to its kind, the unconditionally most magnificent one is great in relation to a great work. And what is most magnificent here or there is what is great in relation to these or those things, and greatness in the work is different from greatness in the expenditure.[295] For a very noble ball or oil flask has the sort of magnificence characteristic of a child's gift, but its price is not something great or generous. That is why it is characteristic of a magnificent person, in relation to whatever kind of thing he produces, to produce it magnificently (since that sort of thing is not easily surpassed) and in such a way that its worth is in accord with his expenditure.

Such, then, is a magnificent person.

A person who is excessive and vulgar exceeds by spending more than he should, as we said, since in matters of small expenditure, he spends a lot and is improperly extravagant—for example, by giving the members of his dining club a feast appropriate for a wedding, or, when he funds a chorus for a comedy, bringing them onstage dressed in purple, as they do in Megara.[296] And he will produce everything of this sort not for the sake of what is noble but to demonstrate his wealth, and thinking that he will be wondrous because of it. And where he should spend a lot his expenditure is small, and where he should spend a little it is great.

A niggardly person, on the other hand, will be deficient with regard to everything and, despite having spent the greatest sums, will destroy something noble over a small detail, both hesitating to produce the thing he should and investigating how to spend as little as possible, both complaining about that and always thinking that he is producing something greater than he should.

These states, then, are vices, but at least they do not incur reproach, because they are neither harmful to a neighbor nor too unseemly.

## IV 3

Greatness of soul [*megalopsuchia*], even from its name, seems to be concerned with great things [*megala*], and our first task is to grasp what sorts of things these are.[297] And it makes no difference whether we investigate the state or the person who is in accord with it.[298]

A great-souled person seems, then, to be someone who thinks himself worthy of great things and is worthy of them. For a person who does the same but not in accord with his worth is silly, whereas no one who is in accord with virtue is silly or lacks understanding.[299] So a great-souled person is the one we mentioned. For a person who is worthy of small things and thinks himself worthy of them, is temperate but not great-souled. For greatness of soul requires magnitude, just as nobility of appearance requires a large body, whereas small people are elegant and well proportioned but not noble in appearance.

A person who thinks himself worthy of great things when he is unworthy of them, is conceited, whereas not everyone who thinks himself worthy of greater things is conceited.[300] A person who thinks himself worthy of smaller things than he is, is small-souled, whether he is worthy of great or moderate things, but also if he is worthy of small ones and thinks himself worthy of ones that are yet smaller. Also, the person who is most small-souled of all would seem to be the one who is worthy of great things. For what would he do if he were not worthy of so much?[301] A great-souled person, then, is extreme in terms of greatness but medial in being as he should, since the things he thinks himself worthy of are in accord with his worth, whereas the others are excessive or deficient.

If, then, he thinks himself worthy of great things and is worthy of them, and most of all so if he is worthy of the greatest things, he will be most concerned with one thing. For worth is relative to external goods, and we would take the greatest of these to be the one we award to the gods, the one that the most worthy people most pursue, and the one awarded as the prize for the noblest accomplishments. But honor is like that, since it surely is the greatest of external goods.[302] It is with honor and dishonor, then, that the great-souled person is concerned in the way he should be. Argument aside, indeed, great-souled people also appear to be concerned with honor, since it is most of all of honor that they think themselves worthy—but in accord with their worth.[303] A small-souled person, on the other hand, is deficient both relative to himself and relative to a great-souled person's worth, whereas a conceited person is excessive relative to himself but at least not relative to a great-souled one.[304]

A great-souled person—if indeed he is worthy of the greatest things—will be the best person, since the better person is always worthy of what is greater and is always the best of what is greatest. Hence a truly great-souled person must be good. Indeed, it would seem characteristic of a great-souled person to be great in each virtue. And so it would never be fitting for a great-souled person to flee with his arms pumping like a runner's or to do injustice. For the sake of what things will he do shameful actions, indeed, when to him, at any rate, none of them is something great? Also, if one investigates particular cases, it appears that a great-souled person would appear completely ridiculous if he were not good. Nor would he be worthy of honor if he were base, since honor is a prize of virtue and is awarded to good people. Greatness of soul, then, seems to be like a sort of adornment of the virtues, since it makes the virtues greater and does not come about without them. That is why it is difficult to be truly great-souled, since it is not possible without noble-goodness.[305]

It is with honor and dishonor, then, that a great-souled person is most concerned. And he will be moderately pleased by great honors conferred by excellent people, thinking that he is getting what properly belongs to him—or actually less, since no honor can match the worth of virtue that is complete in every way. Nevertheless, he will accept it at least because they have nothing greater to award him. But honor that comes from random people or for small accomplishments, he will treat with total contempt, since it does not match his worth. Similarly with dishonor, since it cannot justly attach to him.

It is most of all with honor, then, as we said, that a great-souled person is concerned. Nevertheless, his state concerning wealth and positions of power will be a moderate one—as it will be where good luck or bad luck are concerned (whichever way it turns out to be).[306] So he will not be overjoyed by good luck or over pained by bad luck. For his state of mind, even where wealth is concerned, is not to think of it as the greatest thing. For positions of power and wealth are choiceworthy because of honor (at any rate, those who have them wish to be honored because of them), and so, to a person for whom even honor is a small thing, these other things will be small as well. That is why great-souled people seem to be arrogant.

It seems that good luck also contributes to greatness of soul. For the well bred are worthy of honor, as are those who hold positions of power or who are wealthy, since they are in a superior position and whatever is superior with respect to some good is generally more honored. That is why these things make people more great-souled, since they are honored by some people.[307] In truth, however, only a good person is worthy of honor, although someone who has both goodness and these other things is considered more worthy of it. But people who possess these other good things without possessing virtue are not justified in thinking themselves worthy of great things and cannot correctly be called "great-souled," since without virtue that is complete in every way, it is impossible. In fact, people who do possess these other good things are among the ones who become arrogant and wantonly aggressive, since without virtue they cannot easily handle good luck in a suitable way. And when they cannot handle it and consider themselves superior to other people, they despise them, although their own actions are no better than those of a random person. For they imitate a great-souled person without really being like him, although they do it where they can. They do not act in accord with virtue, then, although they do despise others. For a great-souled person is justified in despising others, since his beliefs are true, but ordinary people despise others in a random way.

A great-souled person does not brave danger in small matters, nor is he a lover of danger, because there are few things he honors. But he does brave great dangers, and, when he does, he is unsparing of his life, on the supposition that it is not worthwhile to live at any price. He is also the sort of person who is a benefactor but is ashamed to be a beneficiary, since the former is characteristic of a superior, the latter of an inferior. In fact, he reciprocates benefits with bigger ones, since that way the one who started the process will owe him a further debt and be the beneficiary.

Great-souled people also seem to remember the benefits they bestow but not the ones they have received (for the beneficiary is inferior to the benefactor, and a great-souled person wishes to be superior) and are pleased to hear about the former but displeased to hear about the latter. That is why Thetis does not mention to Zeus the benefactions she had provided on his behalf, nor did the Spartans mention theirs to the Athenians, but only the ones they received.[308] It is also characteristic of a great-souled person to ask for nothing or hardly anything but to offer his services eagerly, and to exhibit his greatness to those with a reputation for great worth or those who are enjoying good luck but to moderate his greatness to those in the middle. For it is a difficult and a dignified thing to show oneself superior to the former but an easy one to do so to the latter and, while adopting a dignified manner toward the former is not ill bred, to do so toward humble people is vulgar, like displaying strength against the weak. Also, it is characteristic of a great-souled person not to go in for things that are generally honored or for things where others have first place, and to be inactive or delay acting except where there is great honor or a great thing to be accomplished, and to be a doer of few actions but of great and notable ones.

It is also necessary that he be open about his hatreds and loves (for keeping them from being noticed is characteristic of a fearful person, as is neglecting the truth rather than his reputation) and that he speak and act openly (for, because he is someone who despises people, he is a free-speaker and tells the truth except when he is being self-deprecating in the presence of ordinary people).[309] Also, he is incapable of fashioning his way of living to suit another person, unless he be a friend, since to do so would be slave-like (which is why all |**1125a1**| flatterers are menial and all humble people are flatterers). Nor is he prone to wonder, since to him nothing is great. Nor is he someone who remembers past wrongs, since it is not characteristic of a great-souled person to dwell on things (least of all bad ones) but, rather, to disregard them. Nor is he someone fond of conversation about people. For he will not talk either about himself or about someone else, since he cares neither about winning praise for himself nor about how to get other people blamed.

On the other hand, he is not given to praise, which is why he also does not speak badly of people—even of his enemies, unless because of wanton aggression.[310] Where things that are necessary or small are concerned, he is least likely to complain or ask for help, since to do so is characteristic of someone who takes such things seriously. He is also the sort of person whose possessions are more noble and purposeless than purposeful and beneficial, since that is more characteristic of self-sufficient people.

The movements characteristic of a great-souled person seem to be slow, his voice deep, and his speech steady. For a person who takes few things seriously is not the sort to hurry, nor is someone who thinks that nothing is all that great inclined to be tense. But shrillness of voice and hastiness come about because of these.

So that is what a great-souled person is like. A deficient one is small-souled, an excessive one conceited. Now people of these sorts do not seem to be bad either (since they are not evildoers) but to be in error.[311] For a small-souled person who is worthy of good things will deprive himself of the things he is worthy of and thus does seem to have something bad in him, stemming from his not thinking of himself as worthy of good things and from being ignorant of himself. For otherwise he would have reached out for the things he was worthy of, since they are certainly good ones. Nevertheless, people like that do not seem to be silly, at least, but, rather, to be lacking in self-esteem. Their belief about themselves actually seems to make them worse, though. For each sort of person seeks what is in accord with his worth, but these people avoid even noble actions and pursuits because they think they are unworthy of them, and similarly external goods.

Conceited people *are* silly and ignorant of themselves, and obviously so. For they try for things that are generally honored when they are not worthy of them and then are found out. And they adorn themselves with clothes and accessories and things of that sort, and since they wish their good luck to be evident, they talk about it, thinking they will be honored because of it.

Smallness of soul is more opposed to greatness of soul than conceitedness is,for it comes about more often and is worse.[312]

Greatness of soul is concerned with great honor, then, as we said.

## IV 4

There also seems to be a sort of virtue concerned with honor, as we said in |**1125b1**| our first remarks, that would seem to be related to greatness of soul in much the way that generosity is related to magnificence.[313] For both of these virtues escape greatness but, where moderate and small matters are concerned, they dispose us to be the way we should. And just as in getting and giving wealth there is a medial condition, an excess, and a deficiency, so in the case of honor as well we can desire it more or less than we should or from the sources and in the way we should. For we blame the honor lover for seeking honor more than he should or from sources he shouldn't, and we also blame the person who is indifferent to honor for deliberately choosing not to be honored even for noble things. Sometimes, though, we praise an honor lover as manly and a lover of what is noble, and someone who is indifferent to honor as moderate and temperate—as we also said in our first remarks.[314]

Since a person can be called a "lover of such and such" in more than one way, however, it is clear that we do not always apply the term "love of honor" to the same thing. Instead, when we are praising, we apply it to loving honor more than ordinary people do; when we are blaming, to loving it more than we should. But since the medial condition is nameless, the extremes dispute with each other as if it did not exist. Where there is excess and deficiency, however, there is also a mean. And people do desire honor both more than they should and less. There is also the case, then, of those who desire it in the way they should. So it is this state that is praised, since it is a medial condition concerned with honor, although a nameless one. Compared to love of honor, it appears as indifference to honor; compared to indifference to honor, as love of honor; and compared to both, as somehow both.

The same would seem to hold of the other virtues too. But here the extreme people seem opposed to each other because the mean has not been given a name.

## IV 5

Mild-mannerdness is a medial condition concerned with anger (the mean is actually nameless, as pretty much are the extremes, so we transfer the term "mild-mannered" to the mean, although it leans toward the deficiency, which is itself actually nameless).[315] The excess might be said to be a sort of irascibility [*orgilotês*], since the feeling here is anger [*orgê*], although the things that produce it are many and various.

A person who gets angry about the things he should, with the people he should, and, furthermore, in the way he should and both when and for as long as he should is praised. He, then, would be mild-mannered if indeed mild-mannerdness is praised. For being mild-mannered means being calm and not being led by feelings but displaying anger in the way, about the things, and for the length of time that the reason prescribes. It seems to err more toward the deficiency, though, since the mild-mannered person is not revengeful but, rather, considerate to others.

The deficiency, however, whether it is a sort of inerascibility or whatever, is blamed. For people who are not angry at the things they should, seem silly, as do the ones who are not angry in the way they should, when they should, or with the people they should. Someone like that seems not to be perceptive or not to feel pain or—as he is not angry—not to be the sort to defend himself. But for someone to put up with insulting treatment and to stand by watching while this happens to those who are his kin is slavish.

The excess comes about in all these respects (that is, with the people it shouldn't, about things it shouldn't, more than it should, and more quickly and for a longer time) but at least they are not found in their entirety in the same person. For that would not be possible, since what is bad ruins even itself, and if all the parts of it are present, it becomes unbearable.

Irascible people certainly become angry quickly and with people they shouldn't, about things they shouldn't, and more than they should, but they do stop quickly—and this is their best feature. In their case, this comes about because they do not bottle up their anger but retaliate openly, because of the quickness of their spirit, and then stop.

Hypercholeric people [*akrocholoi*] are excessively quick-spirited because they are irascible toward everything and on every occasion—hence their name [*akros* ("extreme") + *cholos* ("gall")].

Bitter people are difficult to make up with and stay angry for a long time, since they bottle up their spirit.[316] It stops when they retaliate, though, since taking revenge puts a stop to their anger by producing pleasure in place of pain. But if that does not come about, they hold a grudge. For because their anger is not open, no one tries to persuade them to give it up, and to digest anger inside ourselves takes time. People like this are the most troublesome to themselves and to their closest friends.

We call "harsh" those who display anger at the things they shouldn't, both more than they should and for a longer time, and who do not become reconciled without taking revenge or exacting punishment.[317]

We regard the excess as more opposed to mild-mannerdness. For the excess actually comes about more often, since it is more human to want revenge. Also, harsh people are worse to share a life with.

What we said even in our previous remarks is also clear from the present ones.[318] For it is not easy to define in what way, with whom, about what, and for how long we should be angry and up to what point someone is doing so correctly or in error. For someone who deviates a little—whether toward the more or toward the less—is not blamed, since sometimes we praise those who are deficient in anger and call them "mild-mannered" and sometimes we call those who display anger "manly," on the supposition that they are capable of ruling. How far, then, and in what way someone must deviate to be blameworthy is not easy to define in an account, for it lies in the particulars, and it is in perception that their discernment lies.[319]

But this much is clear at least, that the mean state is praiseworthy and that it is in accord with the mean state that we are angry with the people we should, about the things we should, in the way we should, and so on, whereas the excesses and the deficiencies are blameworthy—weakly if they are small, more if they are more, and very if they are large. So it is clear that we should cling to the mean state.

So much, then, for our discussion of the states concerned with anger.

## IV 6

In social interaction (that is, living with others and sharing in words and actions) some people seem to be ingratiating. These are people who praise everything in order to give pleasure and are never a hindrance, thinking that they should cause no pain to those they meet. People of the contrary sort, who are a hindrance in everything and think nothing of causing pain, are called "disagreeable" and "quarrelsome."

That the aforementioned states are blameworthy, then, is clear enough, as is the fact that the one in a mean between them is praiseworthy—the one in accord with which we approve of the things we should, in the way we should, and are likewise repelled by them. No name has been given to this state, but it seems most of all like friendship. For this is the sort of person—the one in accord with the mean state—that we tend to call "a decent friend," once affection is added.

The mean state differs from friendship, however, because it is without feeling and affection for those it relates to. For it is not because of loving or feeling enmity that this person approves of each thing in the way he should but because of the sort of person he is. For he will do so alike where those he does not know and those he does know are concerned or where intimates and non-intimates are concerned, except that in each case he will do it in the way that is fitting. For being thoughtful to intimates is not the same as being thoughtful to strangers, nor, again, is causing pain the same in both cases.

Putting it in universal terms, then, we have said that he will relate to others in the way he should and—referring to what is noble and to what is beneficial—will aim either at not causing pain or at causing pleasure.[320] For he would seem to be concerned with pleasures and pains that come about in social interaction, and in such cases, if it is not noble (or is harmful) to cause pleasure to others, he will be repelled and will deliberately choose to cause pain. And so if someone is doing something unseemly (and not just a little unseemly at that) or something that causes harm, and opposing it will cause little pain, he will not approve but, rather, be repelled.

He will relate differently to people of worth and to random ones, and to those more and those less well known to him, and similarly as regards the other relevant differences, allocating to each group what is appropriate and choosing as an intrinsic good to cause pleasure and to be wary of causing pain—but in a way that is guided by the consequences (I mean, what is noble and what is advantageous), if these are greater.[321] And, for the sake of great pleasure in the future, he will cause small pain now.

That, then, is what the medial person is like, although he has not been given a name. Among those who cause pleasure to others, a person who aims at being pleasant, not because of something else, is ingratiating, while someone who does so to get some benefit for himself (in terms of wealth or what comes because of wealth) is a flatterer. As for a person who is repelled by everything, we have said that he is disagreeable and quarrelsome. The extremes appear to be opposed to each other, however, because the mean is nameless.[322]

## IV 7

Concerned with pretty much the same things is the medial condition between boastfulness and self-deprecation, which is also nameless.[323] But it is not a bad idea to go through states of this nameless sort as well, since we shall know more about issues relating to character if we have gone through each particular one, and we shall be more convinced that the virtues are medial states if we see that this holds in the case of all of them. In regard to living with others, then, those who engage in social interaction with a view to causing pleasure and pain have been discussed. Now let us discuss those who are true or false in words and actions alike and in their pretensions about themselves.

A boaster, then, seems to be someone who pretends to have reputable qualities that he does not have or to have greater ones than he has, whereas a self-deprecator seems to be the reverse and to disavow or belittle those qualities he has. A medial person, however, seems to be himself, so to speak—truthful in life and word, acknowledging as his the qualities he really has, and neither magnifying nor diminishing them.

It is possible, though, to do each of these things either for the sake of something further or of nothing further. But each sort of person speaks and acts in accord with the sort of person he is and lives that way too, provided he is not acting for the sake of something further. What is false, however, is intrinsically base and blameworthy, whereas what is true is intrinsically noble and praiseworthy. Thus a person who is truthful, since he is medial, is also praiseworthy, whereas the ones who are false are blameworthy—and boasters more so. But before we discuss these two, we should discuss the person who is truthful.

For we are not talking about a person who is truthful in his agreements or in matters that contribute to justice or injustice (since these would belong to a different virtue) but about someone who, in situations in which there is nothing of that sort to make a difference, is truthful both in word and life because that is what his state of character is like. And someone like that would seem to be decent. For a lover of truth, since he is truthful even in situations where it makes no difference, will be even more truthful in those where it does make a difference. For in these cases he will be wary of falsehood as a shameful thing, since he was already being wary of it intrinsically. And someone like that is praiseworthy. But he is more inclined toward telling less than the truth, since this appears more suitable, because the extremes are more offensive.

A person who not for the sake of anything pretends to more than he has is like someone base (since otherwise he would not enjoy being false) but is more vain and foolish, apparently, than bad. If it is for the sake of something, someone who does it for reputation or honor is not extremely blameworthy, whereas someone who does it for money or for things that fetch money is more unseemly.[324] (It is not by dint of his capacity that someone is a boaster, however, but by dint of his deliberate choice, since it is in accord with his state of character that he is a boaster, and by being that sort of person).[325] In the same way, someone may be false because he enjoys the falsehood itself or because he desires reputation or profit.

Now those who boast for the sake of reputation pretend to the sorts of qualities that are praiseworthy or that are thought to make us happy, whereas those who boast for profit pretend to the qualities that indulge their neighbors and that are possible to avoid being detected for not really possessing, such as those of a prophet, a wise person, or a doctor.[326] That is why most boasters pretend to qualities like this, since it is in them that the aforementioned features are found.

Because self-deprecators play down their qualities in what they say, they appear to have more sophisticated characters, since they do not seem to speak for the sake of profit but, rather, to avoid pomposity. But it is most of all the reputable qualities that they utterly deny, as indeed Socrates used to do.[327]

Those who disavow small and obvious qualities, however, are called "affected" and are more easily despised—in fact doing so sometimes appears to be boastfulness, as when people wear Spartan dress, since both the excess and the extreme deficiency are boastful.[328] But people who use self-deprecation in a moderate way, in regard to qualities that are not excessively pedestrian and obvious, appear sophisticated.

It is a boastful person, though, who appears to be opposed to a truthful one, since he is worse.

## IV 8

Since life also includes relaxation and the latter includes pastimes that involve amusement, it seems that here too there is a sort of social interaction that is suitable, and sorts of things we should say and ways we should say them, and similarly for listening. The sort of people we speak to or listen to also makes a difference. And clearly where these things are concerned there is also excess and deficiency in relation to a mean.

People who go to excess in trying to cause laughter seem to be buffoons and vulgar, doing anything to cause a laugh and aiming at producing laughter rather than at saying things that are gracious and do not cause pain to the butt of their jibing.[329] But those who never say anything to cause laughter themselves and are repelled by those who do, seem boorish and stiff. People who are amusing in a gracious way, on the other hand, are called "witty" [*eutrapeloi*], as they are quick on the return [*eutropoi*]. For things of this sort seem to be movements of people's characters, and just as their bodies are discerned from their movements, so are their characters. Since occasions for causing laughter are prevalent, however, and most people enjoy amusement and jibing more than they should, buffoons are also called "witty" because they are thought sophisticated. But that there is a difference here, and no small one, is clear from what we have said.

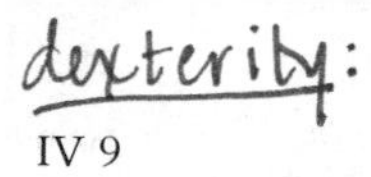



Dexterity is also something that properly belongs to the medial state, since it is characteristic of a person who is dexterous to say and to listen to the sorts of things that are fitting for those who are decent and free. For there are some things that it is appropriate for such a person to say as part of amusement, and also to listen to, and the amusement of the free person differs from that of the slavish one, and that of the well-educated person from that of the uneducated one.[330] We can also see this from old-style and new-style comedies, since in the former what caused laughter was shameful language, whereas in the latter it is more innuendo, and there is no small difference between these as regards graciousness.[331]

Should a person who jibes well be defined then as saying things that are not unsuitable for a free person or that do not cause pain to his listener or even delight him?[332] (Or is that sort of thing indeterminate, since different things are hateful and pleasant to different people?) And he will listen to the same sorts of things, since the sorts he can endure listening to seem to be the sorts that he produces himself.[333]

Now he will not produce every sort. For jibes are a type of abuse, and some types of abuse are forbidden by legislators, so presumably should some types of jibing. A sophisticated and free person, then, will be like that, since he is a sort of law for himself. That, then, is what a medial person is like, whether he is said to be dexterous or witty.

A buffoon cannot resist what causes laughter—sparing neither himself nor anyone else if he can produce a laugh and saying the sorts of things that a sophisticated person would never say and some he would not even listen to.

A |**1128b1**| boor, on the other hand, is useless in social interaction of this sort, since he contributes nothing and is repelled by everything. It seems, though, that relaxation and amusement are necessary in life.

The medial conditions in life that we have discussed, then, are three, and all of them are concerned with sharing in certain sorts of words and actions. They differ because one is concerned with truth, whereas the others are concerned with pleasure. Of those concerned with pleasure, one is found in amusements, the other in social interaction in the rest of life.

## IV 9

Shame is not properly spoken about as a sort of virtue, since it is more like a feeling than a state.[334] Shame is defined as a sort of fear of disrepute at any rate, and its effects are somewhat similar to those of the fear of frightening things. For people who are ashamed of themselves blush, and those who fear death turn pale. Both shame and fear appear, then, to be somehow bodily, which seems to be precisely what is characteristic of a feeling rather than a state.

The feeling is fitting not to every age, however, but to the young. For we think that young people should have a sense of shame because they live by their feelings and so make many errors but are restrained by shame.[335] Also, we praise those young people who have a sense of shame. No one would praise an older person for being prone to shame, however, since we think that he shouldn't do any action that gives rise to shame.

For shame is not something characteristic of a decent person either, if indeed it is a response to base actions. (For these actions should not be done. And whether they are truly shameful or reputed so makes no difference, since neither should be done, and so a decent person should not feel shame.) In fact, shame is characteristic of a base person, since he is the sort to do shameful actions. But to be the sort of person who feels ashamed once he does an action like that and then thinks himself to be decent because of it, is strange. For shame is felt toward voluntary actions, and a decent person will never voluntarily do base actions.

But shame will be hypothetically decent, in the sense that if someone were to do such actions, he would feel ashamed. But this hypothetical character is not possible where the virtues are concerned. And even if shamelessness is something base, as is not being ashamed of doing shameful actions, it still does not follow that a person who is ashamed of doing these actions is decent.

At any rate, even self-control is not a virtue but a sort of mixed virtue. It will be discussed later.[336] Now, though, let us talk about justice.

# Book V

## V 1

|1129a1| As regards justice and injustice, we must investigate what sorts of actions they are concerned with, what sort of medial state justice is, and what that which is just is a mean between. And let our investigation follow the same method of inquiry as our preceding discussions.

We see, then, that what everyone means to say about justice is that it is the sort of state from which people are doers of just things—that is, from which they do just actions and wish for what is just. It is the same way where injustice is concerned—it is the state from which people do injustice and wish for what is unjust. That is why the first thing we should do in our outline is to assume these things.

For capacities and sciences do not operate in the same way as states. For the same capacity or science seems to result in contraries, whereas a state that is contrary to another does not result in contraries—for example, from health we do not do contrary actions but, rather, healthy ones only (for we say that someone is walking in a healthy way when he walks in the way a healthy person would).

So a state that is contrary to another can often be known from its contrary, and states, often from their underlying conditions.[337] For if the good state is evident, the bad one also becomes evident, and from what conduces to the good state, the good state becomes evident, and from it, the things that conduce to it. For if the good state is firmness of flesh, the bad state must indeed be flabbiness of flesh, and what produces the good state must be what produces firmness in flesh.

It for the most part follows that if one of a pair of contraries is said of things in more than one way, the other is also said of things in more than one way—for example, if "just" is, "unjust" is as well.

It seems, though, that "justice" and "injustice" *are* said of things in more than one way but that the homonymy escapes notice because of their closeness and is less clear than when the ways are further apart (for here there is a big difference in their appearance)—as, for example, the clavicle of an animal and the thing we open a door with are said to be "keys" homonymously.[338]

Let us find out, then, the number of ways in which someone is said to be unjust. Well, an unlawful person seems to be unjust, as does a greedy or unfair one, so it is clear that a lawful person will be just and so will a fair one.[339] Hence what is just will be what is lawful and what is fair, and what is unjust will be what is unlawful and what is unfair.

Since an unjust person is greedy, however, he will be concerned with goods—not with all of them but with those that are matters of good and bad luck, which are always good, unconditionally speaking, but for this or that person, not always so. (These are the ones we human beings pray for and pursue. But we shouldn't. Instead, we should pray that unconditionally good things will also be good for us, while choosing the ones that are good for us.)

An unjust person does not always choose more. Instead, he actually chooses less in the case of the unconditionally bad things. But because the lesser evil also seems somehow good and greed is for what is good, he seems to be greedy. In fact, he is unfair, since this term circumscribes the two cases and is what they have in common.

But since, as we saw, an unlawful person is unjust and a lawful one just, it is clear that all lawful things are somehow just, since the things defined by legislative science are lawful and each of these, we say, is just. The laws, for their part, pronounce about all matters, aiming either at the common advantage of all or at that of the best people or of those who—in accord with their virtue or in accord with some other such thing—are in control.[340] So, in one way, the things we call "just" are the ones that produce and safeguard happiness and its parts for the political community.[341]

The law, however, also prescribes that the works of a courageous person be done (for example, not breaking rank or fleeing or throwing down one's weapons), as well as those of a temperate person (for example, not committing adultery or wanton aggression) and those of a mild-mannered one (for example, not striking people or verbally abusing them). Similarly, where the other virtues and types of depravity are concerned, the law orders some things and forbids others—correctly, if established correctly, less well if carelessly formulated.

This sort of justice, then, is complete virtue—not unconditionally but in relation to another person. And that is why justice often seems to be the most excellent of the virtues, with the result that "neither the evening star nor the morning star is so wondrous," and, as the proverb says, "in justice is all virtue summed."[342] And it is complete virtue in the highest degree, because it is the complete use of complete virtue.[343] It is the complete use because someone who possesses it is able to use his virtue in relation to another person and not solely with regard to himself. For many people are able to use their virtue in what properly belongs to themselves but unable to do so in issues relating to another person.

And that is why Bias' saying, "ruling office shows forth the man," seems good, since a ruler is automatically in relation to another person and in a community with him.[344] It is also because of this very same thing that justice, alone of the virtues, seems to be the good of another, because it is in relation to another person, since it does what is advantageous for someone else, whether ruler or community member.[345]

The worst sort of person, then, is the one who uses his depravity both in relation to himself and in relation to his friends, whereas the best sort is not the one who uses his virtue in relation to himself but the one who uses it in relation to another person, since *that* is difficult work.[346]

This sort of justice, then, is not a part of virtue but is virtue as a whole, nor is the injustice contrary to it a part of vice but is vice as a whole.

Besides, the difference between virtue and justice of this sort is clear from what we have said, since they are the same state but their being is not the same.[347] Instead, insofar as the state is in relation to another person it is justice, whereas insofar as it is unconditionally a state of a certain sort, it is virtue.

## V 2

What *we* are looking for, however, is the justice that is a part of virtue, since there is one, so we say, and similarly where the injustice that is a part of vice is concerned.

An indication of their existence is this: a person whose activities are in accord with the other sorts of depravity actually does an unjust action but is not at all greedy—for example, someone who throws down his shield because of cowardice, who engages in verbal abuse because of harshness, or who does not help someone with his wealth because of acquisitiveness. On the other hand, when someone is greedy, often his action is not in accord with any of these vices and certainly not with all of them. Yet it is in accord with some sort of wickedness, at least, since we blame it—namely, with injustice. Hence there is another sort of injustice that is a part of the whole, and another way for something to be unjust by being a part of what is unjust in the sense of being unlawful.

Further, if one person commits adultery for profit and makes money on it, while another does it—spending and so losing money on it—because of appetite, the latter would seem to be intemperate rather than greedy and the former to be unjust but not intemperate. Hence it is clear that this is because the former does it to make a profit.

Further, where every other sort of unjust action is concerned, its coming about is always attributed to some particular sort of depravity—for example, if someone has committed adultery, to intemperance; if he broke rank, to cowardice; |30| or if he struck someone, to anger. But if the action was one of making a profit, it is attributed to no sort of depravity besides injustice.

So it is evident that there is another sort of injustice beyond injustice as a whole, that is a part of it. It has the same name, because its definition places it in the same genus, since they both exercise their capacity in relation to another person. |**1130b1**| The former is concerned with honor, wealth, or preservation (or—if we had a name for it—whatever includes all these) and is concerned with them because of the pleasure of making a profit, while the latter is concerned with all the things that are the concern of an excellent person.[348] |5|

It is clear, then, that there are several sorts of justice and that there is a distinct sort beyond virtue as a whole. What it is and what sort of thing, we must now ascertain.

Well, in the case of what is unjust, we distinguished between what is unlawful and what is unfair, and in the case of what is just, between what is lawful and what is fair.[349] The injustice discussed above is the unlawful sort. Since |10| the unfair and the unlawful are not the same, however, but differ as part from whole (since everything unfair is unlawful but not everything unlawful is unfair), so this unfair sort of what is unjust and of injustice are not the same but different from the other sort, the former as parts, the latter as wholes. For this injustice is a part of injustice as a whole, and similarly this justice is a part |15| of justice as a whole. Hence we must also speak about the justice that is a part, about the injustice that is a part, and about what is just and what is unjust in this way.

We may set aside, then, the justice and injustice that are prescribed in accord with virtue as a whole, since the first is the use of virtue as a whole in relation to another person and the second the use of vice. |20| And it is evident how we should distinguish what is just and what is unjust in accord with these. For the majority of lawful actions are pretty much the ones prescribed by virtue as a whole, since the law prescribes living in accord with each virtue and forbids living in accord with each sort of depravity.

Moreover, what produces virtue as a whole are the actions that are ordained by the laws |25| concerned with education that looks to the common good.[350] (Whether the education concerned with a particular individual, on the basis of which he is unconditionally a good man, is a matter for politics or for another science, is something we must determine later.[351] For being a good man is presumably not in every case the same as being a good citizen.[352])

One form of the justice that is a part, and of what is just in this way, is the form found in the allocation of honor, wealth, or any of the other things that are to be divided among members of a constitution, since, in the case of these things, it is possible for one person to have a share that is equal or unequal to another's.

Another form is rectification in transactions. Of it, there are two parts, since some transactions are voluntary, others involuntary. The voluntary ones are such things as selling, buying, lending with interest, pledging, giving free use of something, depositing, and hiring out (these are called "voluntary" because the starting-point of the transactions is voluntary). Of the involuntary ones, some are clandestine (for example, theft, adultery, poisoning, pimping, enticing away slaves, murder by treachery, and betrayal), whereas others involve force (for example, assault, imprisonment, murder, abduction, disabling, verbal abuse, and insulting treatment).

## V 3

Since an unjust person is unfair and what is unjust is unfair, it is clear that there is also a mean between the unfair extremes. This is what is fair or equal.[353] For in any sort of action in which there is too much and too little, there is also what is fair or equal. So if what is unjust is unfair, what is just is fair or equal—which is precisely what everyone believes even without argument.

Since what is fair is a mean, what is just will be a mean of some sort. What is fair or equal, however, involves at least two terms. It is necessary, therefore, for what is just to be both a mean and fair or equal, and relative—that is, for certain people. And insofar as it is a mean, it will be between certain extremes (too much and too little); and insofar as it is fair or equal, it will involve two shares; and insofar as it is just, it will be so for certain people. Hence it is necessary for what is just to involve at least four terms: the people for whom it is just, which are two, and the things involved (the shares), which are two.

Also, the fairness or equality will be the same for the people and for the shares involved. For the latter (the shares involved) will stand in the same relationship to each other as the people, since if the people are not equal, they will not have equal shares. Indeed, it is from this that quarrels and complaints arise, when either equals get unequal shares (that is, get them in an allocation) or unequals get equal ones.

Further, this is clear from its being in accord with worth. For everyone agrees that what is just in allocations should be in accord with some sort of worth. But they are not all talking about worth of the same sort. Instead, to supporters of democracy, worth lies in freedom; to some supporters of oligarchy, in wealth; to others, in good breeding; and to supporters of aristocracy, in virtue.[354]

Hence what is just is a proportion of some sort. For being proportionate is special not to number consisting of units alone but to number in general, since proportion is equality of ratios and involves at least four terms.[355] (That a divided proportion involves four terms is clear. But so does a continuous proportion. For it uses one term as two, that is, it mentions it twice—for example, as line A is to line B, so line B is to line C. Line B, then, has been mentioned twice. So if line B is put in twice, the terms in the proportion will be four.)

Also, what is just will involve at least four terms, and the ratio is the same, since the people and the shares involved are similarly divided. Hence as term A is to term B, so term C is to term D; and hence, taking them alternately, as A is to C so B is to D. Hence the whole (A + C) will also be so related to the whole (B + D). This is precisely the way the allocation couples them and if it puts them together that way, couples them justly.

Hence the coupling of A with C and that of B with D is what is just in allocation. And what is just in this way is a mean, whereas the unjust is contrary to what is proportionate. For what is proportionate is a mean and what is just is proportionate. (Mathematicians call this sort of proportion "geometrical," since in the geometrical sort, the relation of whole to whole is precisely the relation of each part to each part.) But our proportion is not continuous, since there is not a single numerical term for person and share.

What is just, then, is this: what is proportionate. What is unjust, on the other hand, is what is contrary to what is proportionate. Hence one share becomes too large and the other too small, which is precisely what actually happens in the case of injustice. For the person doing the injustice gets too much of what is good, while the one treated unjustly gets too little. In the case of what is bad, it is the reverse. For the lesser evil in the ratio becomes a good in relation to the greater evil (for the lesser evil is more choiceworthy than the greater, what is choiceworthy is a good, and what is more so is a greater one).

This, then, is one form of what is just.

## V 4

The remaining form is rectificatory, which is found in transactions, both voluntary and involuntary. And this form of what is just is different from the previous one. For what is just in an allocation from common funds is always in accord with the aforementioned proportion, since if in fact the allocation is from wealth that is common, it will be in accord with precisely the same ratio as the original investments in it have to each other. And the injustice that is opposed to this form of justice is the one contrary to that proportion.

What is just in transactions, on the other hand, is a sort of equality and what is unjust a sort of inequality—although one in accord not with the previous proportion but in accord with the arithmetic one. For it makes no difference whether a decent person has defrauded a base person or a base person has defrauded a decent one; or whether a decent person committed adultery or a base one. For the law looks only to the difference created by the harm done but treats the people involved as equals, if one is doing an injustice and the other is suffering it; that is, if one is doing a harm and the other is suffering it.

What is unjust in this way, since it is a case of inequality, the judge tries to make equal. For even when one person is struck and another does the striking or one actually kills and the other is killed, the suffering and the action constitute unequal parts in a division, and the judge tries to make them equal with respect to the loss by subtracting from the agent's profit.

For when we are describing such cases in simple terms, even if the terms do not properly apply in some of them, we speak of the "profit," for example, for the one striking the blow, and the "loss" for the one suffering it. It is after what was suffered has been measured, at any rate, that the second is called "a loss" and the first "a profit."

So what is equal is a mean between too much and too little. But too much and too little constitute a profit or a loss in contrary ways—too much good or too little bad constitutes a profit and the opposite a loss. A mean here, as we saw, is what is equal, and it, we say, is just. So what is just in a rectification will be a mean between loss and profit.

That is why when people are involved in dispute they take refuge in a judge. Going to a judge, however, is going to justice, since a judge is meant to be, as it were, justice ensouled.[356] Also, they seek a judge as an intermediary—in fact, some people call judges "mediators," on the supposition that a person who can hit the mean is the one who will hit what is just.[357] Hence what is just is a mean in some way, if indeed a judge is also one.

The judge, however, equalizes things exactly as if they were a line divided into unequal segments and what he had done was subtract from the larger segment the amount by which it exceeded the half line and added it to the smaller segment. And when the whole has been divided in two, then people say that each "has his own share" when he gets what is equal—where what is equal is a mean between too much and too little that is in accord with the arithmetic proportion.

(That is why it is called *dikaion* ["just"], because it consists in dividing *dicha* ["in two"], as if we had said *dichaion* and as if a *dikastês* ["judge"] was a *dichastês*. For when a certain amount is subtracted from one of two equal things and added to the other, the second exceeds the first by two times that amount, since if the amount had been subtracted from the one but not added to the other, the second would have exceeded the first by only one times the amount. Hence the second was exceeding the mean by one times the amount and the mean |**1132b1**| was exceeding the thing from which something was subtracted by one times the same amount.[358]

Hence this is the way to come to know what to subtract from the one who has too much and what to add to the one who has too little. For to the latter there must be added the amount by which the mean exceeds it, while the amount by which the mean is itself exceeded must be subtracted from the greatest share.[359] Let the lines AA′, BB′, CC′, and DD′ be equal to each other. From AA′ let AE be subtracted and let CD be added to CC′, so that the whole line DCC′ exceeds EA′ by the segment CD and CF, then AE will exceed BB′ by CD.[360] |**1132b9**|

This also holds in the case of the various crafts, since they would have been ruined if the producer did not produce something of both a certain size and a certain quality and if the recipient did not receive this and in that size and that quality.[361]

These terms "loss" and "profit" are derived from voluntary exchange, since having more than our own share is called "making a profit," while having less than the one had at the start is called "suffering a loss"—as it is, for example, in buying and selling and other transactions in which the law grants immunity.[362] When neither too much nor too little results, however, but the same as was given, the parties say they have what is their own and are neither suffering a loss nor making a profit. So what is just is a mean between a certain sort of profit and loss in matters that are counter to what is voluntary, consisting in having an equal amount both before and after the transaction.[363]

## V 5

It seems to some people, however, that reciprocity is unconditionally just, which is precisely what the Pythagoreans asserted, since they defined what is just unconditionally as what stands in a reciprocal relation to another. But reciprocity does not fit either the case of what is just in an allocation or the case of what is just in a rectification, since in many ways it clashes with them. (And yet people interpret even Rhadamanthys' line about justice—"If a person suffered what he did, right justice would be done"—as saying that it fits what is just in a rectification at least.[364]) For example, if a ruling officer strikes someone, he should not be struck in return; and if a ruling officer was the person struck, the one who struck him should not only be struck back but punished too. Further, voluntariness and involuntariness make a great difference.

In communities based on exchange, however, what binds the parties together is what is just in this way, namely, reciprocity that is proportionate and not equal. For it is proportionate reciprocity that keeps a city together. For people either seek to return evil for evil (and if they do not, it seems like slavery) or good for good (and if they do not, no giving in exchange takes place), and it is by giving in exchange that they keep together. That is why cities erect the temple of the Graces [*Charites*] in a conspicuous place, in order that there might be a return for what is given. For this is the special characteristic of gratitude [*charis*], since we should not only do a service in return for someone who has done us a favor [*ho charisamenos*] but, on another occasion, start by doing a favor too.

What produces proportionate exchange is diagonal coupling. Let A be a builder, B a shoemaker, C a house, and D a shoe. The builder, then, must get from the shoemaker the shoemaker's work and give him his own work in return. So if there is first proportionate equality and then reciprocity is achieved, the condition we mentioned will be met. But if not, there is no equality and nothing to keep the parties together, since there is nothing to prevent the work of one of them from being more excellent than that of the other. These works, then, must be equalized.[365] For it is not from two doctors that a community comes about but from a doctor and a farmer and, in general, from people who are different and not equal. And these must be equalized. That is why everything that is exchanged must be in some way commensurable.

It is for this purpose that money has been introduced and becomes a sort of mean. For since it measures everything, it also measures excess and deficiency and how many shoes are equal to a house or food. Just as builder is to shoemaker, then, so must such and such number of shoes be to a house or food. For if this does not happen, there will be no exchange and no community. And it will not happen unless the things in question are in some way equal. Hence they must all be measured by some one thing, as we said before. In truth, this one thing is need, which binds everything together. For if people neither needed things nor needed them to a similar extent, either there would be no exchange or not the same one.[366] But as a sort of exchangeable representative of need, money came into existence on the basis of convention and is called "money" [*nomisma*] because of this, because it exists not by nature but by conventional law [*nomos*], and changing it or rendering it useless is up to us.[367]

Reciprocity will exist, then, when equalization has taken place, with the result that just as farmer is to shoemaker, so a farmer's work is to a shoemaker's. But we must not introduce them as terms in the figure of proportion when they have already made the exchange (otherwise one extreme will have both of the excess amounts) but when they both still have what is their own. That way they will be equals and community members, because this sort of equality can come about in their case: A is a farmer, C food, B a shoemaker, and D his equalized work. But if reciprocity could not be achieved in this way, there would be no community.

That it is need that binds them together, since it is, as it were, one thing, is made clear by the fact that when the parties are not in need of each other—whether mutual or one-sided—they make no exchange, just as when someone needs what one has oneself, for example, when people permit the export of corn in return for wine.[368] Hence this proposed exchange must be equalized. And in the name of future exchange, even if we need nothing now, were we to need something in the future, money acts as a sort of pledge that it will be available to us, since it must be possible for the person who brings *it* to get what he wants.

The same thing also happens to money, certainly, since it does not always have equal purchasing power. All the same, it tends to be rather steadfast. That is why everything must be assigned a price, since that way there will always be exchange, and—if it exists—community. Money, then, acts like a measure that by making things proportionate equalizes them. For there would be no community without exchange, no exchange without equality, and no equality without proportionality. In truth, to be sure, it is impossible that things so different should become proportionate, but in relation to our needs they can become adequately so.

There must, then, be some single measure, but it will be one based on a hypothesis, which is why it is called "money" [*nomisma*].[369] For money makes everything proportionate, since everything is measured in money. A is a house, B ten minae, C a bed: A is half of B, provided a house is worth five minae, or is equal to them, and the bed C is a tenth part of B. It is clear, therefore, how many beds equal a house—five. And that this is how exchange took place before there was money is clear, since it makes no difference whether it is five beds in return for a house, or the value of five beds.

We have now said what it is for something to be unjust and what it is for it to be just. And with these defined, it is clear that just action is a mean between doing injustice and suffering injustice, since the one involves having too much and the other having too little.

Justice is something medial, not in the same way as the other virtues but because it is productive of a mean, and injustice of the extremes.[370] Also, justice is the state in accord with which a just person is said to do in action what is just and to do so in accord with his deliberate choice; and to allocate things—whether to himself and another or to two other people—not in such a way that too much of what is choiceworthy goes to himself and too little to his neighbor; and the reverse with what is harmful, but rather the proportionately equal amount to both—and similarly where the allocation is to two other people.

Injustice, which is the contrary, is related in that way to what is unjust, while what is unjust is excess and deficiency of what is beneficial and what is harmful, contrary to what is proportional. So injustice is excess and deficiency because it is productive of excess and deficiency. In the agent's own case, this is an excess of what is unconditionally beneficial and a deficiency of what is harmful. In the case of other people, it is generally the same, but it can be contrary to what is proportional in either of the two directions. In the case of an unjust action, getting too little is what constitutes suffering injustice, while getting too much constitutes doing injustice.

So much for justice and injustice, then, what the nature of each is, and similarly for what, in universal terms, is just and what unjust.

## V 6

Since it is possible to do injustice without yet being unjust, what sorts of unjust actions must someone do to be already unjust in terms of each of the particular sorts of injustice—to be, for example, a thief, an adulterer, or a pirate? Or is that not at all the way in which they differ? For someone might in fact have sex with a woman knowing who she is, but not because deliberate choice was the starting-point of his action but because feeling was. He is doing injustice, certainly, but he is not unjust—as, for example, someone is not a thief although he did steal, nor an adulterer although he did commit adultery, and similarly in the other cases.

Now we have previously said how reciprocity is related to what is just. But we must not forget that we are inquiring about both what is unconditionally just and what is politically just. The latter is found where people share a communal life with a view to self-sufficiency and are free and equal, either proportionately or arithmetically.[371] So those who are not like that have nothing politically just in their relations with each other, only what is just in a way and by a certain similarity.[372] For what is just can exist only among people whose relations with each other are subject to law, and law only among those where there can be injustice, since a judicial proceeding is what discerns what is just and what is unjust. Where injustice exists among people, doing injustice also exists among them (although, where doing injustice exists among them, there is not always injustice), and doing injustice consists in allocating to oneself too many of the things that are unconditionally good and too few of those that are unconditionally bad.[373]

That is why it is not a human being we allow to rule but reason, because a human being does so for himself and thus becomes a tyrant.[374] A ruler by contrast is a guardian of what is just and, if of what is just, also of what is equal. He seems never to get a greater share for himself, if indeed he is just (since he does not allocate a larger share of what is unconditionally good to himself, unless it is proportionate to himself—which is why he seems to labor for someone else—and it is because of this that people say that justice is the good of another, as we also said earlier).[375] Hence some sort of wage must be given to him, and this is honor and privilege. And people for whom such things are not enough are the ones who become tyrants.[376]

What is just for a master of slaves or for a father is not the same as these other sorts but similar to them. For there is no unqualified injustice in relation to what is one's own, and our possession or our child, until it reaches a certain age and has been separated, is like a part of us.[377] No one, however, deliberately chooses to harm himself. That is why there is no injustice in relation to oneself and hence nothing politically unjust or politically just either. For what is politically just, we saw, is what is in accord with law and exists among those who are naturally subject to law, and these are people sharing equally in ruling and being ruled.[378] That is why what is just is found more in relation to a wife than in relation to a child or possessions, since that is what is just in a household. And it too is different from what is politically just.[379]

# V 7

Of what is politically just, one part is natural, the other legal. The natural one is the one that has the same force everywhere and not because it does or does not seem to have it, whereas the legal is the one where at the start it makes no difference whether it enjoins one thing or another, but once people establish it, it does make a difference—for example, that a mina is the amount of a ransom, or that a goat should be sacrificed and not two sheep. Further, what is legally just includes both laws passed for particular cases (for example, that sacrifices be offered to Brasidas) and enactments in the form of decrees.[380]

Some people think, though, that all cases of legal justice are like this, since what is natural is unchangeable and has the same force everywhere, just as fire burns here and in Persia; whereas what is just they see as changing. This is not the case, however, but in a way it is. Among the gods it is presumably not at all this way, but among us, while there is such a thing as what is natural, everything is nevertheless changeable. All the same, we do find what is natural and what is not natural here. But of the things that admit of being otherwise, it is clear what sort are natural and what sort are not natural but rather legal and conventional, if indeed both are similarly changeable. And the same distinction will apply in other cases. For the right hand is naturally stronger, yet it is possible for everyone to become ambidextrous.[381]

The sorts of things that are just by being in accord with convention and what is advantageous, however, are like measures, since measures for wine and for corn are not the same everywhere |**1135a1**| but are bigger in wholesale buying and selling and smaller in retail. Similarly, things that are not naturally just but are so for certain humans are also not the same everywhere, since even constitutions are not the same everywhere, although only one is everywhere naturally best.[382]

Each type of what is legally just is like a universal in relation to particulars, since the things that are done in action are many, but each type is one thing—a universal, in fact. For an unjust action (*adikêma*) and what is unjust are different as are a just action (*dikaiôma*) and what is just. For what is unjust is so by nature or by constitutional arrangement, whereas this same thing, when done, is an unjust action but, before it was done, it was not yet one but rather something unjust.[383] Similarly with a just action, although here the common type is more usually called a *dikaiopragêma*, whereas it is the rectification of an unjust action that is called a *dikaiôma*.

Later we must investigate each of these to see what sorts of forms they have, how many there are, and what they are concerned with.[384]

# V 8

Given that just and unjust actions are the way we said they are, a person does an unjust action (*adikei*) or does a just action (*dikaiopragei*) when he does these voluntarily. But when he does them involuntarily, he neither does an unjust action nor a just action, except coincidentally. For people do in fact do actions that are coincidentally just or unjust.

An unjust action, however, and a just action are defined by what is voluntary and what is involuntary, since it is when the action is voluntary that it is blamed, and it is then, at the same time, also an unjust action.[385] And so it is possible for something to be unjust without yet being an unjust action, if it is not voluntary as well. What I mean by voluntary, as was also said earlier, is what is up to the agent and done knowingly—that is, not in ignorance of the one affected, the instrument, or the end (for example, whom he is striking, with what, and for the sake of what), and where each of these is neither coincidentally so nor so by force.[386] For example, if someone were to take the hand of another person and use it to strike a third, the second would not be acting voluntarily, since it was not up to him. It is also possible that the one being struck is his father, whereas the agent, while knowing that he is striking a human being or one of the people present, does not know that it is his father. Similar distinctions must also be made in the case of the end and concerning the action as a whole.

What is done in ignorance, then, or not in ignorance but not up to the agent, or what is done by force, is involuntary. For there are in fact many natural processes that we either do or undergo knowingly, none of which are either voluntary or involuntary—for example, aging or dying.

Both unjust actions and just actions alike can also be coincidentally such. For someone might return a deposit involuntarily and because of fear, and someone like that should not be said either to be doing what is just or to be doing a just action, except coincidentally. Similarly we should also say that someone who fails to return a deposit, because he is under compulsion and acting involuntarily, is only coincidentally doing what is unjust or doing an unjust action. Of our voluntary actions, though, we do some having deliberately chosen them (namely, the ones where there is prior deliberation), whereas we do others not having deliberately chosen them (namely, the ones where there is no prior deliberation).

There are three sorts of harm, then, that are found in communities. Those involving ignorance are *errors* when the one affected, what he is doing, the instrument, or the end is not as the agent thought. For he thought, for example, that he was not hitting or not with this or not this person or not for the sake of this, but, instead, the actual result happened not to be as he thought (for example, he hit not in order to wound but in order to provoke) or not the person he thought or not with the instrument he thought.

When the harm is contrary to reasonable expectation, it is a misfortune. By contrast, when it is not contrary to reasonable expectation but involves no vice, it is an error. For someone commits an error when the starting-point of its cause is in himself, but it is a misfortune when the starting-point is outside him.

When an agent harms knowingly but without prior deliberation, it is an unjust action—for example, acts done because of spirit or other feelings that are necessary and natural to human beings. For people who do these sorts of harms and commit these sorts of errors are doing what is unjust, and their actions are unjust actions; however they are not yet unjust or wicked because of this. For the harm was not done because of depravity. But when it is done as a result of deliberate choice, the agent is unjust and depraved.

That is why acts done as a result of spirit are correctly judged not to be premeditated, since their starting-point is not the agent who acts as a result of spirit but the one who made him angry. Further, the dispute is not about whether the event took place or not but about what is just, since the anger is at the apparent injustice. For the parties are not disputing about whether the event took place or not, as in transactions, where—unless they are doing it because of forgetfulness—one of the parties must be depraved.[387] Instead, the parties agree about the things themselves but dispute about which action was just (whereas a person who deliberately harms another is not ignorant about this), so that one party thinks he has been done an injustice, whereas the other denies it.[388]

If a person harms as a result of deliberate choice, however, he acts unjustly, and |**1136a1**| it is by doing unjust actions of this sort, when they are contrary to what is proportionate or to what is equal, that the unjust person is actually unjust. Similarly a person is just when he does just actions as a result of deliberate choice, whereas he does just actions if he merely acts voluntarily.

Some involuntary actions merit our sympathetic consideration, whereas others do not merit our sympathetic consideration.[389] Errors that people make not only in ignorance but also because of ignorance merit sympathetic consideration, whereas when errors are made not because of ignorance but in ignorance caused by a feeling that is neither natural nor human, they do not merit sympathetic consideration.

## V 9

Someone might raise some puzzles, however, about whether we have adequately defined what suffering an unjust action is and what doing an unjust action is. He might ask, first of all, whether things are as Euripides suggests in the strange lines:

> "I killed my own mother: short the tale."
> "A voluntary thing on both your parts or an involuntary one?"[390]

For is it really possible to suffer an unjust action voluntarily? Or is it impossible and, instead, always involuntary, just as doing an unjust action is always voluntary? And is it always one or the other or is it sometimes voluntary and sometimes involuntary?[391]

It is similar in the case of suffering a just action. For doing a just action is always voluntary, so that it is reasonable for there to be a similar opposition in either case and for suffering an unjust action and suffering a just action to be either something voluntary or something involuntary. For it would seem strange, even in the case of suffering a *just* action, if it were always voluntary, since some people suffer a just action involuntarily.[392]

Next, we might also go through the following puzzle about whether every person who has suffered something unjust has suffered an unjust action or whether the case of suffering one is just like the case of doing one. For it is possible to share coincidentally in what is just in both directions, and similarly, it is clear, in the case of what is unjust. For doing something that is unjust is not the same as doing an unjust action, nor is suffering something unjust the same as suffering an unjust action. Similarly in the case of doing a just action and suffering a just action. For it is not possible to suffer an unjust action without someone's doing an unjust action or to suffer a just action without someone's doing a just action.

But if to do what is unconditionally an unjust action is to harm someone voluntarily; and if "voluntarily" means for someone to know the one affected, the instrument, and the way; and if a person who lacks self-control harms himself voluntarily; then he would voluntarily suffer an unjust action and it would be possible for someone to do an unjust action to himself. This is also one of the puzzles that are raised, namely, whether it is possible for someone to do an unjust action to himself. Further, someone could, because of lack of self-control, be voluntarily harmed by someone else, so that it would be possible to suffer an unjust action voluntarily.

Or is this definition incorrect, and to "harming while knowing the one affected, the instrument, and the way," should we add "against the wish of the one affected"? Then someone is harmed and suffers unjust things voluntarily, but no one suffers an unjust action voluntarily. For no one wishes to suffer such an action, not even a person who lacks self-control, who instead acts contrary to his wish, since no one wishes for what he does not think to be excellent, and a person who lacks self-control does not do what he thinks he should do.

A person who gives away what is his own, as Homer says Glaucus gave to Diomedes "gold for bronze, a hundred oxen's worth for nine," is not suffering an unjust action voluntarily, since to give is up to the agent.[393] To suffer an unjust action, however, is not up to the agent, but there must be someone there to do the action. Where suffering an unjust action is concerned, then, it is clear that it is not voluntary.

Further, of the puzzles we deliberately chose to discuss, two remain, namely, whether the person doing the unjust action is the one who allocates a larger share to someone contrary to his worth or is the one who has the larger share, and whether it is possible to do an unjust action to oneself.[394] For if the first alternative is possible and it is the allocator who does the unjust action and not the one who has the larger share, then if someone knowingly and voluntarily allocates a larger share to someone else than he does to himself, this person does an unjust action to himself, which is precisely what moderate people seem to do, since a decent person tends to take less than his share. Or is that too simple? For it may be that the decent person is getting a larger share of a different good—for example, of reputation or of what is unconditionally noble. Further, the puzzle is resolved by appeal to our definition of what it is to do an unjust action.[395] For he suffers nothing contrary to his own wish, so that he suffers no unjust action—at least, not because of what he does. Rather, if indeed he suffers anything, it is harm alone.

It is evident that the allocator of the larger share does in fact do an unjust action but that the person who has the larger share does not always do one. For it is not the person to whom the unjust share belongs who does the unjust action but the one who voluntarily does the unjust action, namely, the one from whom, as the starting-point of the action, it derives, and the starting-point is in the allocator, not in the recipient.[396]

Further, things are said to "do" things in many ways (there is even a way in which soulless things "do" the killing, or someone's hands, or a servant at his master's orders), so the recipient, though he does not "do" an unjust action, does "do" what is unjust.

Further, if the allocator gave his judgment in ignorance, he does not do an unjust action, according to what is legally just, nor is his judgment unjust. In a way, it is unjust, since legal justice is different from what is just in the primary way. However, if he knowingly gave an unjust judgment, he himself is greedy either for a favor or for revenge. The person, then, who has given an unjust judgment because of these things has also got more than his share, exactly as if he had got part of the proceeds of an unjust action. For having given the judgment about land because of these things, he got not land but money.

Human beings think that doing unjust actions is up to them. That is why they also think that what is just is easy. But it isn't. Having sex with a neighbor's wife, striking someone standing nearby, or putting money in someone's hand is easy and is up to ourselves. But doing them because of being in a certain state is not easy and not up to ourselves.

Similarly, human beings think that to know what is just and what is unjust we need not be at all wise, because the things the law pronounces about are not difficult to comprehend (although these do not constitute what is just except coincidentally). But knowing the way actions must be done and things must be allocated if they are to be just—*that* takes more work than knowing what things are healthy. For even in their case, while knowing that honey, wine, hellebore, cautery, and surgery are healthy things is easy, knowing the way these must be allocated with a view to health and to whom and when takes as much work as being a doctor.

Because of this, they also think that to do unjust actions is no less characteristic of a just person than of an unjust one, because the just person is no less—but even more—able to do each of these actions.[397] For he is able to have sex with a woman and strike blows, and a courageous person is able to throw down his shield and turn and run in this direction or that. But doing cowardly actions or unjust actions is not doing things of this sort except coincidentally; on the contrary, it involves being in a certain state when we do them.[398] In the same way, doing medical actions or curing someone does not consist in performing a surgery or not performing one; or giving drugs or not giving them; but in doing them in a certain way.

What is just is found among people who have a share in unconditionally good things, who can have an excess of these or a deficiency, since for some beings (as presumably for gods) there is no such thing as an excess of them, whereas for others (the incurably bad ones) no amount of them is beneficial but they are all harmful, and, for yet others, they are beneficial up to a point.[399] That is why what is just is something human.

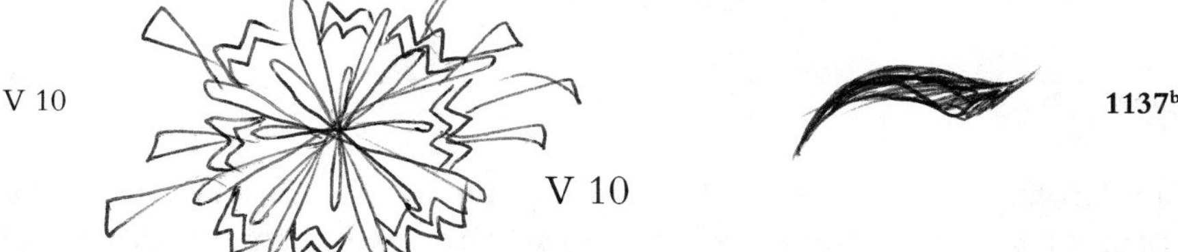

## V 10

We must next say something about decency and what is decent—about the way decency is related to justice and the way what is decent is related to what is just. For on investigation these appear to be neither unconditionally the same nor different in genus. For sometimes we praise what is decent and a decent man, so that we even transfer the term "decent" to other things we are praising, in place of "good," making it clear that what is more decent is better. But sometimes, on following out the argument, it appears strange that what is decent, if it is something apart from what is just, should be something praiseworthy. For either what is just is not something excellent or what is decent isn't, if it is different from what is just; or if both are excellent, they are the same.[400]

It is pretty much because of these considerations, then, that a puzzle arises about what is decent. Yet in a way they are all correct and none is contrary to any of the others. For what is decent, although better than what is in a certain way just, is still just and is not better than what is just by way of being a thing of a different genus. Hence what is just and what is decent are the same, and while both are excellent, what is decent is more excellent.

What produces the puzzle is that while what is decent is just, it is not what is just according to the law but, rather, a rectification of what is legally just. The cause of this is that all law is universal, but about some sorts of things it is not possible to pronounce correctly in universal terms. So in the sorts of cases where it is necessary to pronounce in universal terms but not possible to do so correctly, the law picks what holds for the most part, not unaware of the error involved. And it is no less correct for doing so, since the error is not in the law or in the legislator but in the nature of the thing itself. For what is doable in action consists of this sort of subject matter right from the outset.[401] So whenever the law makes a universal pronouncement and a particular case arises that is contrary to the universal pronouncement, at that time it is correct (insofar as the legislator has omitted something and he has made an error in pronouncing unconditionally) to rectify the deficiency—to pronounce what the legislator himself would have pronounced had he been present and would have put into his law had he known about the case.

That is why what is decent is just and better than what is in a certain way just. It is not better than what is unconditionally just, however, but only better than the sort that, because it pronounces universally, makes an error. And this is the very nature of what is decent—a rectification of law insofar as it is deficient because of its universality. For this is also the cause of not everything's being regulated by law—namely, that there are some cases where it is impossible to establish a law, so that decrees are needed. For the standard of what is indeterminate is itself indeterminate, just like the lead standard used in Lesbian building.[402] For the standard is not fixed but adapts itself to the shape of the stone, and a decree adapts itself to the things themselves.

What it is to be decent, then, and that it is both just—and better than what is in a certain way just—is clear. And it is also evident from this what a decent person is. For the person who deliberately chooses to do—and actually does—decent things and is not a stickler for justice in the bad way but takes less than his due even if he has the law on his side, is decent and his state is decency, which is a sort of justice and not some different state.

## V 11

Whether it is possible to do an unjust action to oneself or not is evident from what has been said.[403]

First, some just actions are the ones in accord with any virtue that are required by law. For example, the law does not allow the killing of oneself, and those things whose killing it does not allow, it forbids.[404] Further, whenever, contrary to the law, someone harms another person, not in return for a harm, and does so voluntarily, he does an unjust action (and the one who does it voluntarily is the one who does it knowing the person affected and the instrument used). But someone who, because of anger, cuts his own throat does this voluntarily, contrary to the correct reason, and this the law does not allow. Hence he does an unjust action. But to whom? Or is it to the city and not to himself? For he suffers it voluntarily, and no one suffers an unjust action voluntarily. That is why the city imposes a penalty and why a certain dishonor attaches to a person who has done away with himself, on the supposition that he is doing something unjust to the city.

Further, insofar as an unjust agent is only unjust and not wholly base, it is not possible for him to do an unjust action to himself. (This is different indeed from the former case, since the person who is unjust in this way is wicked in the same way as a coward, not by possessing wickedness as a whole, and so it is also not in accord with it that he does the unjust action). For that would be for the same thing to have been taken away from and added to the same person at the same time, and this is impossible. Rather, when something is just or when something is unjust, there must always be more than one person involved.[405]

Further, an unjust action is voluntary, done from deliberate choice, and initiatory.[406] For a person who acts because of something he suffered and who does the same thing back does not seem to do an unjust action. If he does it to himself, however, he is suffering and doing the same thing at the same time.

Further, it would be possible to suffer an unjust action voluntarily.

Besides, no one does an unjust action without doing one of the particular sorts of unjust action, and no one commits adultery with his own wife or breaks into his own house or steals his own property.

The puzzle about doing an unjust action to oneself is generally resolved, however, by reference to the definition concerned with suffering an unjust action voluntarily.[407]

It is also evident that both the doing of the unjust action and the suffering of the unjust action are base, since the second involves having less and the first having more than what is a mean (which is like health in the case of medicine, or good physical condition in that of athletic training). All the same, the doing of the unjust action is worse. For doing an unjust action involves vice and is blameworthy, and the vice is either complete and unconditional or close to it (since not every voluntary unjust action involves injustice), whereas suffering an unjust action involves neither vice nor injustice. So suffering an unjust action is intrinsically less base—coincidentally, though, there is nothing to prevent it from being a greater evil. But what happens coincidentally is of no concern to craft. Rather, it says that pleurisy is a worse malady than a stumble, and yet the latter might turn out to be coincidentally worse (if the stumbler, because of his fall, was captured or killed by his enemies).

By transference, though, and by similarity, what is just is found not in a person's relations to himself but among his parts—not what is just in every way but what is just in the way found in the mastery of slaves or in household management. For in these accounts the part of the soul that has reason is distinguished from the nonrational part.[408] People look at *these* and it seems to them that just actions can occur in a person's relations to himself, because it is possible for each of the parts to suffer things that are contrary to its own desires, so that there is something just in their relations with each other, like that between ruler and ruled.

Where justice and the others—the virtues of character—are concerned, then, let them be defined in the foregoing way.

# Book VI

## VI 1

Since we have previously said that we should choose the mean, not the excess and not the deficiency, and the mean is as the correct reason says, let us distinguish this.[409] For in the case of all the states we have discussed, and as regards the others as well, there is some target on which a possessor of the reason keeps his eye as he tightens or loosens, and there is some sort of defining mark of the medial states, which we say are between excess and deficiency since they are in accord with the correct reason.[410]

But though this is true to say, it is not at all perspicuous. For in the other types of supervision where there is scientific knowledge, it is also true to say that we should exert ourselves or relax neither too much nor too little but mean amounts and in the way the correct reason says.[411] If we know only this, however, we are no better off—for example, as regards what sorts of treatments to apply to the body, if we are told that we should apply those that medicine prescribes and in the way the one who possesses it would. That is why, with regard to the states of the soul as well, we should not only assert this much of the truth but also determine what the correct reason is and what its defining mark.

In distinguishing the virtues of the soul we said that some are virtues of character and some of thought.[412] **|1139a1|** The virtues of character, we have discussed. So let us now speak about the others as follows, after first saying something about the soul. Previously, then, we said that there are two parts of the soul, one that has reason and one that lacks reason.[413] Let us now divide in the same way the part that has reason. Let us take it that there are two parts that have reason—one through which we get a theoretical grasp on those beings whose starting-points do not admit of being otherwise and one through which we do so on those that do admit of being otherwise, since where beings differ in kind, parts of the soul that differ in kind are naturally suited to each of them, since it is on the basis of a certain similarity and kinship that they have knowledge.[414]

Let us call one of these "the scientific part" and the other "the rationally calculative part." For deliberating is the same as rationally calculating, and no one deliberates about what does not admit of being otherwise.[415] So the rationally calculative part is one distinct part of the part that has reason.

Hence we must ascertain what the best state of each of these parts is, since this is the virtue of each of them and the virtue relates to the proper function.

## VI 2

Three things in the soul control action and truth—perception, understanding, and desire.[416] Of these, perception is not a starting-point of any action. This is clear from the fact that wild beasts have perception but do not share in action.

What assertion and denial are in the case of thought, that, in the case of desire, is precisely what pursuit and avoidance are. So, since virtue of character is a deliberately choosing state and deliberate choice is deliberative desire, it follows that both the reason must be true and the desire must be correct, if indeed the deliberate choice is to be an excellent one, and the very things the one asserts, the other must pursue.[417] This, then, is practical thought and truth. In the case of thought that is theoretical, however, and neither practical nor productive, the good state and the bad state are truth and falsity (since that is the function of every part involving thought) but in the case of the part involving practical thought, the good state is truth in agreement with correct desire.

Of action, then, the starting-point—the source of the movement, not what it is for the sake of—is deliberate choice, and of deliberate choice, the starting-point is desire and reason that is for the sake of something. That is why, without understanding and thought on the one hand and a state of character on the other, there is no deliberate choice, since there is no doing well in action or its contrary without thought and character.[418] Thought by itself, however, moves nothing. But the one that is for the sake of something and practical does. Indeed, it even rules productive thought. For every producer produces for the sake of something, and what is unconditionally an end (as opposed to in relation to something and for something else) is not what is producible but what is doable in action. For doing well in action is the end, and the desire is for it. That is why deliberate choice is either desiderative understanding or thought-involving desire, and this sort of starting-point is a human being.[419]

Nothing that happened in the past, though, is an object of deliberate choice—for example, nobody deliberately chooses to have sacked Troy. For nobody deliberates about what happened in the past but they deliberate about what will happen in the future and what admits of being otherwise, and what is past does not admit of not having happened. That is why Agathon is correct:

> Of one thing alone is even a god deprived,
> To make undone what is done and finished.[420]

Of both of the parts that involve understanding, then, the function is truth. So the states in accord with which each most grasps the truth are, in both cases, their virtues.

## VI 3

Let us start, then, from a more general perspective and speak afresh about these. Let the states in which the soul grasps the truth by way of assertion and denial be five in number: craft knowledge, scientific knowledge, practical wisdom, theoretical wisdom, and understanding. For supposition and belief admit of falsehood.[421]

Now what scientific knowledge is, will be evident from the following, if one is to speak in an exact way and not be guided by mere similarities. For we all suppose that what we know scientifically does not at all admit of being otherwise, whereas, in the case of things that do admit of being otherwise, whenever they fall outside our theoretical grasp it escapes notice whether they hold or not.[422] Hence what admits of being known scientifically is by necessity. Hence it is eternal. For the things that are unconditionally necessary are all eternal, and eternal things cannot come to be or pass away.

Further, all scientific knowledge seems to be teachable, and what can be known scientifically to be learnable. It is from things already known, however, that all teaching proceeds, as we also say in the *Analytics*, since some is through induction and some by deduction.[423] Now induction leads to the starting-point, that is, the universal, whereas a deduction proceeds from universals. Hence there are starting-points from which a deduction proceeds that are not reached by deduction. Hence induction must provide them.

Hence scientific knowledge is a state affording demonstrations and has the other features included in the definition we give in the *Analytics*, since it is when someone is convinced in a certain way and the starting-points are known to him that he has scientific knowledge.[424] For if they are not better known than the conclusion, it is in a coincidental sense that he will have scientific knowledge.

Let scientific knowledge, then, be defined in this way.

## VI 4

What admits of being otherwise includes both what is producible and what is doable in action. But production and action are different (about them we rely also on the external accounts), so that the practical state involving reason is also different from the productive state involving reason.[425] And nor is one included in the other.[426] For action is not production and production is not action. Since, then, building, for example, is one sort of craft and is precisely a productive state involving reason, and since there is no craft that is not a productive state involving reason and no such state that is not a craft, a craft is the same as a productive state involving true reason.

Every craft is concerned with coming to be, that is, with crafting things and getting a theoretical grasp on how something may come to be that admits of being and of not being and whose starting-point is in the producer and not in the product.[427] For things that are or come to be by necessity are not the concern of craft, nor are things that are in accord with nature (since they have their starting-point within themselves).[428] Since, then, production and action are different, it is necessary that craft be concerned with production but not with action.

And in a certain way, craft and luck are concerned with the same things; as Agathon says, "Craft loves luck and luck craft."

A craft, then, as we said, is some sort of state involving true reason concerned with production, and craft incompetence is the contrary, a state involving false reason concerned with production.[429] Both are concerned with what admits of being otherwise.

## VI 5

Where practical wisdom is concerned, we may get hold of it once we get a theoretical grasp on what sort of person we say is practically-wise. It seems, then, to be characteristic of a practically-wise person to be able to deliberate correctly about what is good and advantageous for himself, not partially (for example, about what sorts of things further health or further strength) but about what sorts of things further living well as a whole. An indication of this is that we also speak of people as practically-wise in some area, when they rationally calculate well about what furthers some excellent end, concerning which no craft exists.[430] Hence in the case of the whole too it is the deliberative person who will be practically-wise.

Also, nobody deliberates about things that cannot be otherwise or about things that do not admit of being done in action by himself. So, since scientific knowledge involves demonstration, and the things whose starting-points admit of being otherwise cannot be demonstrated (for all of them also admit of being otherwise) and it is not possible to deliberate about what holds by necessity, practical wisdom cannot be either scientific knowledge or craft knowledge—not scientific knowledge because what is doable in action admits of being otherwise, not craft knowledge because action and production differ in kind. Hence the remaining possibility is for practical wisdom to be a true state involving reason, a practical one, concerned with what is good or bad for a human being.[431] For the end of production is something other than production, while that of action is not something other than action, since doing well in action is itself action's end.

That is why we think Pericles and people of that sort to be practically-wise—because they have a theoretical grasp on what is good for themselves and for human beings, and we think household managers and politicians are like that.[432]

That is also why we call temperance (*sôphrosunê*) by this name, as being what preserves practical wisdom (*sôzousan tên phronêsin*).[433] And it does preserve the sort of supposition in question. For what is pleasant or painful does not ruin or distort every sort of supposition (for example, that triangles do or do not contain two right angles) but it does do this to the one about what is doable in action. For the starting-points of things doable in action are the end for which the things doable in action are done. But once someone is ruined by pleasure or pain, to him it does not appear a starting-point or that it is for the sake of *it* and because of *it* that he should choose and do everything, since vice is ruinous of the starting-point.[434] So practical wisdom must be a true state involving reason, concerned with human goods, and practical.[435]

Well, of craft knowledge there is certainly a virtue, whereas of practical wisdom there is not one. And, in the case of a craft, someone who makes errors voluntarily is preferable but with practical wisdom he is less so, as is also the case with the virtues. It is clear, then, that it is some sort of virtue and not a craft.

Since there are two parts of the soul that have reason, however, it must be a virtue of one of them—namely, of the part that forms beliefs. For belief is concerned with what admits of being otherwise, as too is practical wisdom.

But it is not a state involving reason only. An indication of this is that there is forgetfulness of a state like that, but of practical wisdom there isn't.[436]

## VI 6

Since scientific knowledge is supposition about universals and things that are by necessity, and since there are starting-points of what can be demonstrated, and so in all sciences (since scientific knowledge involves reason), about the starting-point of what is scientifically known there can be neither scientific knowledge nor craft knowledge nor practical wisdom, since what is scientifically known is demonstrable and the other two deal with what admits of being otherwise.[437]

Neither, then, is there theoretical wisdom regarding starting-points, since it is characteristic of a theoretically-wise person to have a demonstration of certain things.

If, then, the states by which we grasp the truth and never have false views about what cannot—or indeed can—be otherwise are scientific knowledge, practical wisdom, theoretical wisdom, and understanding, and it cannot be any of the three of these (by the three I mean practical wisdom, scientific knowledge, and theoretical wisdom), the remaining alternative is for understanding to be of starting-points.

## VI 7

Wisdom in crafts we ascribe to the most exact practitioners of the relevant craft (for example, calling Phidias a wise sculptor in stone and Polyclitus a wise sculptor in bronze), here signifying nothing else by wisdom, indeed, than that it is the virtue of a craft.[438] There are, however, some people we think are wise about things as a whole, not wise in some area or wise in some other particular way, as Homer says in the *Margites*: "him the gods made neither a digger nor a ploughman nor wise in any other particular way."[439] So, it is clear that theoretical wisdom must be the most exact of the sciences.[440]

Hence a theoretically-wise person not only must know what follows from the starting-points but also must grasp the truth where the starting-points are concerned. So theoretical wisdom must be understanding plus scientific knowledge—scientific knowledge, having a head as it were, of the most estimable things.[441] For it would be strange to think—if anyone does—that politics or practical wisdom is most excellent, unless the best thing in the universe is a human being.[442]

Now if health or goodness is different for human beings than for fish, for example, but whiteness and straightness are always the same, anyone would say that theoretical wisdom is the same for all but that practical wisdom is different, since the one who has a theoretical grasp of the good of a given sort of being is the one human beings would call "practically-wise," and it is to him that they would entrust such matters.[443] That is why even some of the wild beasts are said to be practically-wise—those that appear to have a capacity for forethought about their life.[444]

It is evident too that theoretical wisdom cannot be the same as politics. For if people are to call the science that deals with what is beneficial to themselves "theoretical wisdom," there will be many theoretical wisdoms, since there will not be one dealing with the good of all animals but a different one for each sort.[445] For there is not even one science of medicine for all beings. And if human beings are the best of the other animals, it makes no difference, since there exist other things that are far more divine in nature even than human beings—the most evident ones, certainly, being those from which the universe is composed.[446]

From what has been said, then, theoretical wisdom is clearly scientific knowledge combined with understanding of the things that are naturally most estimable. That is why Anaxagoras and Thales and people of that sort are said to be wise—but not practically-wise when we see them to be ignorant of what is advantageous to themselves—and why what they know is said to be extraordinary, wondrous, difficult, and worthy of worship but useless, because it is not human goods they seek.[447]

Practical wisdom, on the other hand, is concerned with human affairs and what can be deliberated about. For of a practically-wise person we say that most of all this is the function—to deliberate well. And nobody deliberates about what cannot be otherwise or about the sorts of things that do not lead to some specific end, where this is something good, doable in action. The unconditionally good deliberator, however, is the one capable of aiming at and hitting, in accord with rational calculation, the best for a human being of things doable in action.

Nor is practical wisdom knowledge of universals only. On the contrary, it must also know particulars. For it is practical, and action is concerned with particulars. That is why, in other areas too, some people who lack knowledge—most of all, those with experience—are more effective *doers* of action than are others who have knowledge.[448] For if someone knows that light meats are digestible and healthy but is ignorant about which sorts of meat are light, he will not produce health; but someone who knows that bird meats are healthy will produce health more.[449] But practical wisdom is practical, so one must possess both sorts of knowledge—or this one more.[450]

But here too there will be a sort that is architectonic.[451]

## VI 8

Politics and practical wisdom are the same state, but their being is not the same.[452] Of the practical wisdom concerned with the city, the architectonic part is legislative science, while the part concerned with particulars has the name common to both—"politics."[453] This part is practical and deliberative, since a decree is doable in action, as the last thing.[454] That is why only these people are said to take part in politics, since it is only they who do things in just the way handicraftsmen do.

It also seems that the practical wisdom concerned with oneself as an individual is most of all practical wisdom, and it is this that has the name common to all the sorts. Of the other sorts, one is household management, another legislative science, another politics, and of the latter, one part is deliberative and the other judicial.[455]

Now knowledge of what is good for oneself will certainly be one type of knowledge, but it admits of much difference.[456]

It certainly seems that someone who knows about and spends his time on the things that concern himself is practically-wise and that politicians are busybodies. That is why Euripides says:

> How can I be practically-wise, when I could have minded my
> own business,
> and been numbered among the ranks of the army,
> sharing equally?
> For those who aim too high and occupy themselves too
> much. . . .[457]

For people seek what is good for themselves and think that this is what they should do. From this belief, then, has come the view that such people are the ones with practical wisdom. And yet a person's own welfare cannot be achieved, presumably, without household management or without a constitution. Further, how the things that pertain to his own welfare are to be managed is unclear and must be investigated.

An indication of what has been said is that while young people become geometers and mathematicians and wise in such things, they do not seem to become practically-wise. The explanation is that practical wisdom is concerned also with particulars, knowledge of which comes from experience. But there is no young person who is experienced, since it is quantity of time that produces experience.

(Indeed, we might also investigate why it is that a child can become a mathematician but not a theoretically-wise person or a natural scientist. Or isn't it that the objects in mathematics are given through abstraction, while the starting-points in theoretical wisdom or natural science come from experience, so that the young lack conviction there but only talk the talk, whereas in mathematics it is quite clear to them what each of the objects is?)[458]

Further, the error in deliberation may be either about the universal or about the particular—in supposing either that all heavy types of water are bad or that this particular water is heavy. But that practical wisdom is not scientific knowledge is evident.[459] For it is concerned with the last thing, as we said, since what is doable in action is such. It stands opposed, then, to understanding.[460] For understanding is of the terms for which there is no reason, but practical wisdom concerns the last thing, of which there is not scientific knowledge but rather perception—not the perception of special objects but like the sort by which we perceive that the last thing among mathematical objects is a triangle, since there too will come a stopping point. Practical wisdom, however, is more this perception, but it is of a different form than the other.[461]

## VI 9

Inquiry and deliberation are different, since deliberation is inquiry *of a certain sort*. But we must also grasp what good deliberation is, whether some sort of scientific knowledge or belief or good guesswork or some other kind of thing.

Well, scientific knowledge it certainly isn't. For people do not inquire about things they know. But good deliberation is a sort of deliberation and a deliberator inquires and rationally calculates. However, it is not good guesswork either. For good guesswork is without reason and is also something quick, whereas one deliberates for a long time. And it is said that we should act quickly on the results of our deliberation but deliberate slowly.

Further, readiness of wit is different from good deliberation, and being ready witted is a sort of good guesswork.[462]

Nor, again, is good deliberation any sort of belief. On the contrary, since a bad deliberator makes an error and a good one deliberates correctly, it is clear that good deliberation is some sort of correctness—correctness neither of scientific knowledge nor of belief. For of scientific knowledge there is no correctness (since there is no error either), and of belief the correctness is truth. Furthermore, everything about which there is belief is already determined. However, without reason there is no good deliberation either.[463]

Hence it remains for it to be correctness of thought, since thought is in fact not yet assertion.[464] For while belief is not inquiry but already a sort of assertion, a deliberator, whether he deliberates well or badly, is inquiring about something and rationally calculating.

But good deliberation is a certain sort of correctness of deliberation. That is why we must inquire first what this correctness is and what it concerns.[465] Since correctness is of more than one sort, however, it is clear that it will not be any and every sort. For a person who lacks self-control or a base person will reach as a result of rational calculation what he proposes should be done and so will have deliberated correctly but will have got hold of something very bad.[466] But it seems to be a good thing to have deliberated well. For it is this sort of correctness of deliberation that is good deliberation—the sort that reaches something good.

We can also reach this by a false deduction, however—that is, reach the thing that should be done but not by the means we should, the middle term being false. It follows that this is not yet good deliberation—where one reaches what should be done, yet not by the means we should.

Further, one person may deliberate a long time to reach it, while another does so quickly. So the former is not yet a case of good deliberation, which is correctness in accord with what is beneficial and about what to do, how to do it, and when to do it.

Further, it is possible to deliberate well either unconditionally or to further a specific end. Unconditionally good deliberation correctly furthers the unconditional end, the specific sort, some specific end. If it is characteristic of practically-wise people to have deliberated well, then good deliberation will be the sort of correctness that is in accord with what is advantageous in furthering the end about which practical wisdom is true supposition.

## VI 10

Comprehension too, that is, good comprehension—the state by which we say people comprehend or comprehend well—is not the same as scientific knowledge as a whole |**1143a1**| nor as belief (since if it were, everyone would have comprehension), nor is it any one of the sciences dealing with a particular area, as medicine is concerned with healthy things, geometry with magnitudes.[467] For comprehension is not concerned with what always is and is unchanging, nor is it concerned with just any of the things that come to be but with those one might puzzle and deliberate about.[468] That is why it is concerned with the same things as practical wisdom, although comprehension is not the same as practical wisdom. For practical wisdom is prescriptive, since what *should* be done or not is its end, whereas comprehension is discerning only. (For comprehension and good comprehension are the same, as are those with comprehension and those with good comprehension.)

Comprehension is neither having practical wisdom nor acquiring it. But just as learning something is called "comprehension" when one is using scientific knowledge, it is also so called when one is using belief to discern what someone else says about matters with which practical wisdom is concerned—that is, discern correctly (*kalôs*). For "well (*eu*)" is the same as "correctly (*kalôs*)" here. And this is where the name "comprehension (*sunesis*)"—in the sense of what makes people have good comprehension (*eunsunetoi*)—came from, namely, the comprehension involved in learning. For we often call learning "comprehending."

## VI 11

What is called "consideration (*gnômê*)," due to which, people are said to be sympathetically considerate (*sungnômones*) and to have consideration, is the correct discernment of what is decent. Here is an indication of this: we say that it is the decent person, above all, who is sympathetically considerate, and that to be decent in certain cases is to be sympathetically considerate. Sympathetic consideration, then, is the correct consideration that discerns matters of what is decent. And the correct sort is the one that arrives at the truth about them.

All these states are quite reasonably taken to tend in the same direction, since we attribute consideration, comprehension, practical wisdom, and understanding to the same people and say they actually have consideration and understanding when they are practically-wise and able to comprehend.[469] For all these capacities are concerned with things that come last, that is, particulars. And it is in being discerning in matters with which a practically-wise person is concerned that someone exhibits comprehension and sound consideration or sympathetic consideration, since decency is common to all good people in relation to another person. And among particulars—that is, things that come last—are all the things doable in action. For a practically-wise person must also know these, and comprehension and consideration are concerned with things doable in action; and these are things that come last.

Also, understanding is concerned with things that come last in both directions.[470] For concerning the primary terms and the things that come last, there is understanding but no reason—that is to say, on the one hand, in the case of demonstrations, understanding is of the unchanging and primary terms; on the other hand, in the case of those that are practical, it is of the last thing and the one that admits of being otherwise and the other premise, since these are starting-points of the end, as it is from particulars that universals come.[471] So of these we must have perception, and this is understanding.[472] That is why these things even seem to be natural—and why, while nobody seems wise by nature, people do seem to have consideration, comprehension, and understanding by nature.

An indication of this is that we also think these states correspond to the stages of life and that a particular stage brings understanding and consideration, as if nature were the cause. That is why understanding is both starting-point and end, since demonstrations are from these and concerned with these.[473] So we should attend to the undemonstrated sayings and beliefs of experienced and older people or practically-wise ones, no less than to the demonstrations, since, because they have an eye formed from experience, they see correctly.

We have said, then, what practical wisdom and theoretical wisdom are and what each of them is concerned with and that each is the virtue of a different part of the soul.

## VI 12

We might, however, go through some puzzles about what use they are. For surely theoretical wisdom will not have a theoretical grasp on any of the things from which a human being will come to be happy (since it is not concerned with anything's coming to be). Practical wisdom, though, certainly does have this. But what do we need it for? For if practical wisdom is indeed the virtue concerned with things just and noble and good for a human being and these are the ones it is characteristic of a good man to do, and knowledge of them in no way makes us better *doers* of them (if indeed states are what the virtues are), then it will be exactly the same as in the case of things relating to health or things relating to good physical condition (I mean those so called not for producing the state but for resulting from it), since we are in no way better doers of them because of knowing medicine or physical training.

If, on the other hand, we are to say that being practically-wise is useful not for this but for becoming good, to those who are excellent it will be of no use. Further, it will be of none to those who are not such, since it will make no difference whether they have it themselves or they put their trust in others who have it—that is, it would be enough for us to do just as we also do in the case of health. For we wish to be healthy but, all the same, we do not learn medicine.

In addition to all this, it would seem absurd if practical wisdom, though inferior to theoretical wisdom, were to have more control than it. Yet it is what produces a thing that rules and issues prescriptions concerning it. About these topics, then, we must speak, since so far we have only raised the puzzles relating to them.

Well, first, let us say that these states must be intrinsically choiceworthy (since each is the virtue of one of the two parts that have reason) even if neither of them produces anything at all.

Next, they do indeed produce something; not, however, as medicine produces health but as health does. *That* is also how theoretical wisdom produces happiness, since as a part of virtue as a whole, by being possessed and actualized, it produces happiness.[474]

Further, our function is completed in accord with practical wisdom and virtue of character. For virtue makes the target correct, and practical wisdom what furthers it.[475] Of the fourth part of the soul, the nutritive, there is no virtue of this sort, since there is no action that is up to it to do or not do.

With regard to our being in no way better doers of noble actions and just actions because of practical wisdom, let us start a little further back, taking the following as a starting-point. For we also say that some people who do just things are still not just (for example, those who do what is prescribed by the laws either involuntarily, because of ignorance, or because of something else, and not because of the actions themselves), even though they at least do the actions they should and do everything an excellent person must do. Likewise, it seems, there is the case of being so disposed, when doing all these actions, as to be a good person—I mean, for example, to do them because of deliberate choice and for the sake of what is done in the actions themselves.

Virtue, then, makes the deliberate choice correct, but as to whatever should naturally be done for the sake of carrying it out—that is not the business of virtue but of a different capacity. However, we must get scientific knowledge of these things and discuss them in a more perspicuous way.

There is, then, a capacity called cleverness, and this is the sort of thing that, when it comes to the things that further hitting a proposed target, is able to do these and to hit upon them.[476] If, then, the target is a noble one, this capacity is praiseworthy, but, if it is a base one, it is unscrupulous.[477] That is why both practically-wise people and unscrupulous ones are said to be clever.[478] Practical wisdom, however, is not the capacity of cleverness but does not exist without this capacity.[479]

But the state, the one pertaining to this eye of the soul, does not come about without virtue, as we have said and is clear.[480] For practical deductions have a starting-point, "since the end—that is, the best one—is such and such," whatever it may be (let it be any random thing for the sake of argument); this, however, is not apparent except to a good person, since depravity produces distortion and false views about practical starting-points.[481] So it is evident that it is impossible to be practically-wise without being good.

## VI 13

Virtue, then, must also be investigated again. For virtue is also in much the same situation: as practical wisdom is related to cleverness—not the same but similar—so natural virtue is related to full virtue. For everyone thinks that each character trait is possessed in some way naturally, since we are in fact just, disposed to temperance, courageous, and the rest straight from birth.[482] All the same, we look for what is fully good to be something else and for such qualities to be possessed in another way. For to both children and wild beasts these natural states also belong; but without understanding they are evidently harmful.[483] At any rate, this much we can surely see: that just as a heavy body moving around without sight suffers a heavy fall because it has no sight, so it happens in this case too.

But if someone should acquire understanding, it makes a difference in his action; and his state, though similar to the one he had, will then be full virtue. So, just as in the case of the part that forms beliefs there are two forms of condition (cleverness and practical wisdom), so also in the part responsible for character there are two (natural virtue and full virtue), and of these, full virtue does not come into being without practical wisdom.

That is why indeed some people say that all the virtues are types of practical wisdom and why, in one sense, Socrates used to inquire correctly but, in another sense, erroneously.[484] For in thinking that all the virtues were types of practical wisdom, he was in error, but in saying that they did not exist without practical wisdom, he spoke correctly.

Here is an indication of this: even now everyone, when defining virtue and having named the state and what it is concerned with, adds "the one in accord with the correct reason"—and the correct one is the one in accord with practical wisdom. It would seem, then, that all people somehow have a hunch that this sort of state is virtue—the one in accord with practical wisdom.

We, however, should go a little further. For it is not the state that is only *in accord with* the correct reason that is virtue but the one that also *involves* the correct reason. And the correct reason about such matters is practical wisdom. Socrates, then, thought that the virtues *were* cases of reason (all being cases of scientific knowledge), whereas we think that they *involve* reason.[485]

It is clear, then, from what we have said, that it is neither possible to be fully good without practical wisdom nor practically-wise without virtue of character. And in this way we can also resolve the argument by which someone might contend dialectically that the virtues are separate from each other on the grounds that the same person is not naturally well disposed in the highest degree where all of them are concerned, so that he will at some point have acquired one when he has not yet acquired another.[486] In the case of the natural virtues, indeed, this is possible, but in the case of those in accord with which someone is called "unconditionally good," it is not possible, since at the same time that practical wisdom, which is one state, is present, they will all be present.

And it is clear that even if practical wisdom were not practical, we would need it because it is the virtue of its part; clear too that deliberate choice will not be correct without practical wisdom or without virtue, since virtue makes us do the actions that the end consists in whereas deliberate choice makes us do the actions that further it.[487]

But yet it does not control either theoretical wisdom or the better part any more than medicine controls health, since it does not use it but sees to its coming into being. So it prescribes for its sake, but not to it. Besides, it would be like saying that politics rules the gods, because it prescribes with regard to everything in the city.

# Book VII

## VII 1

Next we must make a fresh start and say that the things having to do with character that are to be avoided are of three forms: vice, lack of self-control, and beastliness.[488] It is clear what the contraries of two of these are, since we call the one virtue and the other self-control. Where the contrary of beastliness is concerned, it would most fit the case to speak of a virtue that is beyond us, one of a heroic even a divine sort—as when Homer has Priam say that Hector was exceptionally good: "nor did he seem the son of a mortal man but, rather, one of a god."[489] So if, as they say, human beings become gods because of an extreme of virtue, it is clear that the state opposed to the type that is beast-like will be of this sort.[490] And just as there is in fact neither vice nor virtue of a wild beast, neither is there of a god.[491] But his state is more estimable than virtue, while that of a wild beast is of a different kind than vice.[492]

Since it is a rare thing indeed for there to be a divine man (which is what the Spartans tend to call someone they particularly admire, saying in their dialect that he is a *seios anêr*), so the beast-like type is also a rare occurrence among human beings.[493] It occurs most among non-Greeks, although some cases come about because of disease or disability. We also use "beast-like" as a term of abuse for those who exceed human beings in their vice. But about this disposition we shall have to make some mention later on, whereas about vice we spoke earlier.[494]

But about lack of self-control and softness (or effeminacy), we must now speak, as well as about self-control and resilience, since we must not suppose that either of the two is concerned with the same states as virtue and depravity or that it is of a different kind than the other.[495]

We must, as in the other cases, set out the things that appear to be so and first go through the puzzles, and in that way show preferably all the reputable beliefs about these ways of being affected, or if not all of them then most of them, and the ones with the most control.[496] For if the objections are resolved and the reputable beliefs are left standing, that would be an adequate showing.[497]

Now, both self-control and resilience seem to be excellent things and praiseworthy ones, whereas lack of self-control and softness seem to be base as well as blameworthy.[498]

Also, a self-controlled person seems to be the same as one who is also such as to stand by his rational calculation, and a person who lacks self-control seems to be the same as one who is also such as to depart from his rational calculation.[499] A person who lacks self-control, knowing that the actions he is doing are base, does them because of feeling, whereas one who has self-control, knowing that his appetites are base, does not follow them, because of his reason.

Also, some people say that a temperate person is self-controlled and resilient, some saying that all of the latter sort are temperate, others that they aren't, but all also saying that an intemperate person lacks self-control and that one who lacks self-control is intemperate, lumping both together. Others, however, say these sorts of people are different. Sometimes, they say that it is impossible for a practically-wise person to lack self-control, although sometimes they say that some people who are practically-wise and clever do lack self-control.

Further, people are said to lack self-control regarding spirit, honor, and profit.

These then are the things that are said.[500]

## VII 2

Someone might be puzzled about what sort of correct supposition a person has when he acts in a way that is not self-controlled.[501]

Some people certainly deny that he can have scientific knowledge, for it would be terrible, as Socrates used to think, for scientific knowledge to be in someone but controlled by something else and dragged around like a slave.[502] For Socrates used wholly to combat this account, on the supposition that there is no such thing as lack of self-control. For no one, while supposing that he is doing so, acts contrary to what is best but acts that way only because of ignorance.

This argument certainly contradicts what plainly appears to be the case, and so we must inquire about the way the agent is affected, if he acts because of ignorance, as to what manner of ignorance it turns out to be. For *before* he is affected, at any rate, it is evident that an agent who lacks self-control does not think that he should do the action.

There are some people who concede some parts of this but not others, since they agree that nothing is stronger than scientific knowledge but do not agree that no one acts contrary to what he believes to be better and, because of this, they say that it is not when a person who lacks self-control has scientific knowledge that he is controlled by pleasures but when he has belief.

Yet if it is belief, not scientific knowledge (if it is not a strong supposition that is resisting but a weak one, like that found in people who hesitate), there will be sympathetic consideration for failure to stand by such beliefs in the face of strong appetites. But for depravity there is no sympathetic consideration, nor for any other blameworthy thing.

What, then, if practical wisdom is what is doing the resisting? For it is something very strong. But that would be a strange thing, since the same person would be at the same time practically-wise and lacking in self-control, and no one would say that it is characteristic of a practically-wise person to do the worst actions voluntarily. Besides, it was shown earlier that a practically-wise person is a doer of action (for he is concerned with last things) and has the other virtues.[503]

Further, if someone cannot be self-controlled unless his appetites are strong and base, a temperate person will not be self-controlled or a self-controlled one temperate, since it is not characteristic of a temperate person to have appetites that are too strong or ones that are base. Yet they must be both. For if his appetites are good, the state that prevents him from following them must be base, so that not all self-control will be excellent.[504] On the other hand, if they are weak and not base, self-control will be nothing dignified, whereas if they are base and weak, it will be nothing great.

Further, if self-control makes someone such as to stand by every belief, it is base—for example, if it makes him do so even when the belief is false. Also, if lack of self-control makes a person such as to depart from every belief, there will be a sort of lack of self-control that is excellent. For example, Neoptolemus in Sophocles' *Philoctetes,* since he is praiseworthy for not standing by what Odysseus persuaded him to do, because it pains him to tell a falsehood.[505]

Further, a certain sophistical argument constitutes a puzzle.[506] For because they wish to refute in a way that is contrary to beliefs in order to be clever when they engage in ordinary discussions, the resulting deduction turns into a puzzle.[507] For thought is tied up when it does not wish to stand still, because what has been concluded is not pleasing but cannot move forward, because of its inability to resolve the argument. There is a certain argument, then, from which it follows that foolishness combined with lack of self-control is virtue. For because of lack of self-control an agent acts contrary to the ways he supposes he should, but what he supposes is that bad things are good and that he should not do them, with the result that he does the good and not the bad actions.

Further, a person who, by being persuaded and by deliberate choice, does or pursues pleasant things seems to be better than someone who does them not because of rational calculation but because of lack of self-control.[508] For the first one is more easily cured, because he might be persuaded to act otherwise. A person who lacks self-control, on the other hand, is subject to the proverb: "When water is choking you, what will wash it down?" For if he had been persuaded to do what he is doing, he would have stopped if he was persuaded to act otherwise. But he is already persuaded, yet nonetheless does something else.[509]

Further, if there is lack of self-control and self-control concerning all things, who is it that is unconditionally lacking in self-control? For no one has every sort of lack of self-control. And yet we do say that some people are unconditionally such.

These, then, are the sorts of puzzles that arise, and thus some things must be confuted, others left standing, since the resolution of a puzzle constitutes a discovery.[510]

## VII 3

We must investigate first, then, whether a person who lacks self-control acts knowingly or not and in what way knowingly and second, what sorts of things should we take a person who lacks self-control and a person who has it to be concerned with—I mean, whether they are concerned with every sort of pleasure and pain or with some determinate sorts. Also, we must investigate a self-controlled person and a resilient one to see whether they are the same or different; and similarly where other matters germane to this theoretical investigation are concerned.

The starting-point of the investigation is whether a person who has self-control and a person who lacks it differ in the things they are concerned with or in the way they are concerned with them—I mean, whether a person who lacks self-control lacks it solely by being concerned with such-and-such things or solely by the way he is concerned with them, or as a result of both. Next, whether there is lack of self-control and self-control concerning all things, or not. For a person who unconditionally lacks self-control is not concerned with all things but, rather, with the very same ones as an intemperate person, nor does he unconditionally lack self-control by having a state that is unconditionally related to these (since then it could be the same as intemperance) but, rather, by having one related to them in a certain way. For an intemperate person is deliberately choosing when he is led on, since he believes that he should always pursue what is pleasant at present. One who lacks self-control does not think this but pursues anyway.

As regards the view that it is contrary to true belief but not to scientific knowledge that people act without self-control—well, it makes no difference to the argument. For some people with belief are not hesitant but think they know in the most exact way.[511] If, then, it is because of the weakness of their convictions that those with belief are more likely than those with scientific knowledge to do actions contrary to their supposition, scientific knowledge will be no different here from belief. For some people have no less conviction about what they believe than others do about what they know scientifically—something Heraclitus makes clear enough.[512]

But since we speak of knowing scientifically in two ways (since both the person who has but is not using his scientific knowledge and the one who is using it are said to know scientifically), there will be a difference between having knowledge of and not actively contemplating and having knowledge of and actively contemplating the actions we should not do (for this is what seems bizarre, although not if we are *not* actively contemplating them).

Further, since there are two ways of presenting premises, nothing prevents |**1147a1**| someone who has both from acting against his scientific knowledge, provided he makes use of the universal one but not of the partial one, since here the particulars are what is doable in action.[513] And there is also a difference as regards the universal one. For one part is directed to the agent himself and the other to the thing itself—for example, that dry foods are advantageous for all human beings and that he himself is a human being or that this sort of food is dry. But whether this is of that sort—*that* is what the agent either does not have or is not activating.[514] Between these ways, then, there is an enormous difference, so that to know in the way described seems not at all strange but, in the other way, amazing.

Further, human beings can have scientific knowledge in a way other than the ones we have just described. For among those who have but are not using it we see a difference in the having of the state, so that someone both has it in a way and does not have it—for example, if he is sleeping, mad, or tipsy.[515] But surely this is the way people who are indeed in the grip of their feelings are disposed. For spirited feelings, sexual appetites, and some things of this sort clearly alter the condition of the body as well and in some people even produce states of madness.[516] Clearly, then, we should say that people who lack self-control have scientific knowledge in a way similar to these people.

The fact that they talk the talk that stems from scientific knowledge signifies nothing, since those in the grip of their feelings can recite demonstrations and verses of Empedocles.[517] And those who have first learned something string the words together but do not yet know what they have learned, since it must grow to be a natural part of them, and that takes time.[518] So we must suppose that those who are acting without self-control are also talking like actors on a stage.[519]

Further, we might look into the cause of acting without self-control by appealing to natural science. For one is a universal belief, whereas the other is concerned with particulars, which perception already controls.[520] But when a single belief comes about from these, the soul, in one sort of case, necessarily asserts what has been concluded, whereas in productive cases it acts straightaway.[521] For example, if everything sweet should be tasted and this (as one of the particulars) is sweet, it is necessary for someone who is able and not prevented also to do this at once.[522] So when one universal premise is in the agent preventing tasting, as well as another (that everything sweet is pleasant) and this is sweet (and this one is active) and there happens to be an appetite in him, the one premise says, "Avoid this!" but the appetite leads him on (since each of the parts can move), the result is that from reason, in a way, and from belief he acts without self-control.[523] The belief, however, is not intrinsically but coincidentally contrary (since what is contrary is the appetite, not the belief) to the correct reason.

(So it is also because of this that wild beasts do not lack self-control, namely, that they do not have a universal supposition but only imagination and memory of particulars. As for how the ignorance of an agent who lacks self-control is resolved and he recovers his scientific knowledge, the account is the same as in the case of a tipsy person and a sleeping one and is not special to this way of being affected; it is one we must hear from the natural scientists.[524])

Since the final premise both is a belief about something perceptible, however, and controls the action, either an agent who lacks self-control does not have this or he has it in such a way as not to have scientific knowledge of it but, rather, to talk the talk, like a tipsy person with the verses of Empedocles.[525] And because the last term is not universal and does not seem to be scientifically knowable in the way the universal is, even the result Socrates was looking for would seem to come about. For neither is it full scientific knowledge that seems to be actively present when this way of being affected comes about, nor is *it* what is dragged around because of feeling but, rather, the perceptual sort.[526]

So much, then, for knowing and not knowing and for how it is possible to know and yet to act without self-control.

# VII 4

We must next discuss whether there is someone who unconditionally lacks self-control (or whether all people who lack self-control do so partially), and if there is, concerning what sorts of things.

That there are people who have self-control and are resilient where pleasures and pains are concerned as well as people who lack self-control and are soft, is evident. Some of the things productive of pleasure are necessary, however, and others are intrinsically choiceworthy but can be taken to excess. The necessary ones are the bodily ones (I mean such things as the ones concerned with food and our sexual needs, that is to say, such bodily ones as we took temperance and intemperance to be concerned with).[527] Others, though, are not necessary but intrinsically choiceworthy (I mean, for example, victory, honor, wealth, and other such things as are good and pleasant).

So, then, when people, contrary to the correct reason that is in them, go to excess in relation to the intrinsically choiceworthy ones, we do not say they unconditionally lack self-control but add that they lack self-control regarding wealth, profit, honor, or spirit. We do not say that they unconditionally lack self-control, on the supposition that they are different and that they are called "lacking in self-control" by similarity to those who unconditionally lack it (like the victor at the Olympic Games called "Human," since, in his case, the common account differed only slightly from the special one, but was different all the same).[528]

An indication of this is that lack of self-control, whether unconditional or partial, is blamed not only as an error but also as a sort of vice, whereas none of these other people is blamed.[529]

In the case of the types of pleasures and pains concerned with bodily gratifications, though—the ones that we say a temperate and an intemperate person are concerned with—a person who, without having deliberately chosen, goes to excess in pursuing these pleasant things and avoiding the painful ones (hunger, thirst, heat, cold, and all those concerned with touch and taste), but contrary to his deliberate choice and thought, is called "lacking in self-control," not with regard to such-and-such additional thing that he lacks self-control about, such as anger, but unconditionally and solely so.[530]

An indication of this is that people are also called "soft" where these sorts of bodily pleasures and pains—but not any of the others—are concerned.[531]

It is because of this too that we put people who lack self-control and intemperate ones in the same class (and also self-controlled people and temperate ones), but none of the others.[532] This is because the former are concerned, in a way, with the same pleasures and pains. But though these people are concerned with the same things, they are not concerned with them in the same way, rather, one of them acts from deliberate choice, whereas the other does not act from deliberate choice.[533] That is why we should say that someone who has no appetite or only a weak one for excessive pleasures yet pursues them and avoids moderate pains is more intemperate than someone who does so because of intense appetite. For what would such a person do if he came to develop a vigorous appetite for the necessary pleasures and felt a strong pain at their lack?

Some appetites and pleasures have objects that are noble and excellent as a kind, since some pleasant things are naturally choiceworthy (whereas others are the contrary and others in between). We distinguished this group earlier—for example, wealth, profit, victory, and honor.[534] Where all things of this sort are concerned, and all the in-between ones, people are blamed not for being affected by them (that is, having an appetite for them and loving them) but for being affected in a certain way—to wit, excessively.

I mean those who are either controlled by or pursue some of these naturally noble and good things, contrary to reason—for example, those who are more serious about honor than they should be or about children and parents. For though these are indeed good things and people are praised for being serious about them, all the same there is a sort of excess even in their case—as, for example, if someone were to be like Niobe and get in a fight even with the gods, or to behave toward his father like Satyrus, the so-called father lover did—since Satyrus seemed to be utterly stupid about him.[535] So there is no depravity where these appetites and pleasures are concerned, because of what we have just said, namely, that each of them is naturally choiceworthy because of itself, but their excesses are base and to be avoided.

Similarly, there is no lack of self-control here either, since lack of self-control is not only something to be avoided but also blameworthy. Because of the similarity in the way of being affected, however, people do speak of lack of self-control with an addition where each is concerned. It is like the case of a bad doctor or a bad actor. We would not say that either was unconditionally bad, because neither of these conditions is badness, but only something similar to it by analogy. So it is likewise clear that the conditions we must alone suppose to be self-control and the lack of it are the ones concerned with the same things as temperance and intemperance. We do, however, speak of self-control or the lack of it concerning spirit, by similarity with these. That is why we add the qualification and say "lacking in self-control with regard to spirit," just as "with regard to honor" or "with regard to profit."

## VII 5

Some things are naturally pleasant, and of these, some are unconditionally pleasant, while others are so with reference to particular kinds both of animals and of human beings. Other things are not naturally pleasant but come to be so—some because of a disability, some because of habit, some because of depraved natures. That is why where each of these is concerned, we also see corresponding states. I mean the beast-like ones—for example, that of the female who people say used to rip open pregnant women and devour their children; or the pleasures said to be enjoyed by some of the savages who live around the Black Sea, some of whom eat raw meats, some human flesh, while others are said to reciprocally lend their children to each other to be eaten at festivities; or what they say about Phalaris.[536] These states are beast-like.

Some, however, come about because of diseases (even because of madness, in some cases, like the man who sacrificed and ate his mother, or the one who ate the liver of his fellow slave). Others are morbid conditions arising from habit—for example, plucking out one's hair or chewing on one's nails or even on charcoal and earth and besides these, sexual intercourse between males. In some cases, these come about naturally; in some as a result of habit—for example, those who have suffered wanton aggression from childhood on.[537] Now if nature is the cause, no one would call these people lacking in self-control any more than one would call women such because they have the passive rather than the active role in copulation. The same goes for those who are in a morbid condition because of habit.[538]

So on the one hand having any of these conditions is outside the marks definitive of vice, just as beastliness also is. On the other hand having them and either not controlling them or being controlled by them is not unconditional lack of self-control but lack of self-control by resemblance, as someone who is in this condition where spirited feelings are concerned should be called "lacking in self-control by way of his feelings" but not "unconditionally lacking in self-control."[539]

Of all the excesses of vice (in fact of foolishness, cowardice, intemperance, and harshness), some are beast-like, whereas others are morbid conditions.[540] For someone who is naturally the sort of person to fear everything—even the squeak of a mouse—is cowardly with a beast-like cowardice, whereas the individual who was afraid of his weasel was so because of a disease.[541] Of foolish people as well, those who are naturally without rational calculation and so live by perception alone—like some distant races of non-Greeks—are beast-like, while others are foolish because of diseases, such as epilepsy, or because of morbid madness.[542]

Of these conditions, however, there are some it is possible to have sometimes without being controlled by them (I mean, for example, if Phalaris had an appetite for eating a child or for some strange sexual pleasure, but controlled himself). But it is also possible to be controlled by them and not only to have them.

So just as in the case of depravity, where the sort that is on a human level is unconditionally called depravity and the other sort so called with an addition to the effect that it is beast-like or a morbid condition but not unconditionally depraved, so in the same way it is clear that lack of self-control too is in some cases beast-like and in others a morbid condition, whereas unconditional lack of self-control is that which is in accord with what is human intemperance only.[543]

So it is clear that lack of self-control and self-control are concerned only with the very same things as intemperance and temperance, and that where the other things are concerned there is another form of lack of self-control that is so called by transference and not unconditionally.

## VII 6

That spirit's lack of self-control is also less shameful than appetite's, is something that we should now get a theoretical grasp on.[544] For spirit seems to listen somehow to what reason says but to mishear it, like hasty servants who run off before they hear the whole of what is said and then make an error in carrying out the instructions or dogs that before investigating to see if it is a friend bark at a sound alone.[545] In the same way spirit, because of its hot and hasty nature, does hear, but does not hear the prescription and so impulsively rushes off to exact revenge. For reason or imagination reveals that we have been a victim of wanton aggression or contemptuous treatment, and spirit—as if deducing that this sort of thing must be fought against—becomes very harsh straightaway.[546] Appetite, on the other hand, only needs reason or perception to say that this is pleasant, and it impulsively rushes off to indulge itself. So spirit follows reason, in a way, but appetite does not.[547] So lack of self-control regarding the latter is more shameful. For someone who lacks self-control regarding spirit gives in to reason in a way, whereas the other one gives in to appetite and not to reason.

Further, there is more a feeling of sympathetic consideration for people who follow natural desires, since there is more even in the case of those appetites that are common to all, and to the extent that they are common.[548] But spirit is more natural—as is harshness—than are appetites for excess and for things that are not necessary.[549] It is like the case of the son defending himself for beating his father: "Yes indeed I did beat him," he said, "but he beat his father, and *he* beat his," and, pointing to his own young child, he said, "and he'll beat me when he becomes a man— it runs in the family." Or the man, being dragged by his son, who used to urge him to stop at the front door since that was as far as he had dragged his own father.

Further, people who are more given to plotting are more unjust. Well, the spirited person does not plot, and neither does spirit. On the contrary, it is forthright. Appetite, though, is like what they say about Aphrodite, "a weaver of guile, indeed, from Cyprus sprung," and like what Homer says of her embroidered girdle: "an allurement that steals understanding from the minds of the most practically-wise."[550] So if this sort of lack of self-control is in fact more unjust and more shameful than lack of self-control regarding spirit, it is unconditional lack of self-control and, in a way, vice.

Further, no one is pained at committing wanton aggression, but whoever does something out of anger is pained by doing it, whereas a wantonly aggressive person does what he does with pleasure. So if those acts at which it is most just to be angry are more unjust, so also is the lack of self-control that comes about because of appetite, since there is no wanton aggression in spirit.[551]

Accordingly, it is clear that lack of self-control regarding appetites is more shameful than lack of self-control regarding spirit, and that self-control and lack of self-control are concerned with appetites and pleasures that are bodily.

There are differences among these appetites and pleasures, however, that we need to grasp. For as we said at the start, some of them are human and natural both in kind and magnitude, some are beast-like, while some are present because of incapacities or diseases. Temperance and intemperance are concerned only with the first of these. That is why we do not say that wild beasts are either temperate or intemperate except by transference, that is, if one whole sort of animals differs from another in wanton aggression, as it may be, or destructiveness or omnivorousness. For they do not have deliberative choice or rational calculation, but are a degeneration from nature, like madmen among human beings.[552]

Beastliness is a lesser thing than evil (although it is more frightening), since the better thing has not been ruined, as in the human case, but is just not present.[553] So it is like comparing something soulless to something ensouled, to see which is worse. For the baseness of what does not possess the starting-point is always less destructive, and understanding is the starting-point.[554] So the comparison is similar to that between injustice and an unjust human being.[555] For there is a way in which each is worse—for an evil human being will do ten thousand times as much evil as a beast.[556]

## VII 7

Where the pleasures and pains that come about through touch and taste are concerned, as well as the appetites for them and the avoidances of them (the ones we earlier defined as the concern of intemperance and temperance), it is possible for someone to be in a state such that he gives in even to those that ordinary people are stronger than or controls even those to which ordinary people give in. Of these, a person concerned with pleasures lacks self-control in the first case and has it in the second, whereas one concerned with pains is soft or resilient, respectively. The state of most people lies in between these, even though they may incline more toward the worse ones.

Some pleasures are necessary, however, and others are not, and the former are so, up to a point, whereas neither their excesses nor their deficiencies are necessary. Similarly, where both appetites and pains are concerned. Hence a person who pursues the excesses of pleasures (or does so to excess) and does so because of deliberate choice, because of the pleasures themselves and not because of any further consequence, is intemperate.[557] For he necessarily has no regrets and so is incurable. For the sort of person who has no regrets is incurable. (A person who is deficient is his contrary, while one in a mean is temperate.) Similarly for someone who avoids bodily pains not because he gives in but because of deliberate choice.

(Of those who do not act from deliberate choice, one is led on because of the pleasure, another because he is avoiding the pain that comes from appetite, so that these differ from each other. Everyone would think someone to be worse, however, if he did a shameful action with either no or weak appetite than if he did it with intense appetite, and worse for striking someone when he was not angry than for doing it when he was angry. For what would he have done if he had felt these things? That is why an intemperate person is worse than one who lacks self-control.)

Of the cases mentioned, then, one person has more of a kind of softness, whereas the other is intemperate.[558]

A person with self-control is the opposite of a person without it, and a resilient one is the opposite of one who is soft. For being resilient consists in resisting, self-control in controlling. And resisting is different from controlling, just as not giving in is different from being victorious. That is why self-control is more choiceworthy than resilience.

Someone who is deficient concerning the things that ordinary people both |1150b1| struggle against and can do so successfully is soft and effeminate, since effeminacy is a sort of softness. Such a person trails his cloak on the ground in order not to suffer the pain of lifting it up, and, while acting like a sick person, does not think himself to be wretched, similar to a wretched one though he is.

Similar things hold where self-control and lack of self-control are concerned. For if someone gives in to strong or excessive pleasures or pains, it is not something to wonder at. Rather, it merits sympathetic consideration provided that he struggles against them—as the Philoctetes of Theodectes does when bitten by the snake or as Cercyon does in the *Alope* of Carcinus or like people trying to restrain their laughter who suddenly burst out laughing, as happened to Xenophantus.[559] But it is something to wonder at if he does this where things that ordinary people can successfully struggle against are concerned and if he gives in to and cannot struggle successfully against these—unless it is because of his congenital nature or because of disease—as there is congenital softness in Scythian kings—or as female differs in relation to male in this regard.[560]

An amusement-lover also seems to be intemperate, but is actually soft. For amusement is a loosening up, if indeed it is a relaxation, and an amusement-lover is one of those who goes to excess where relaxation is concerned.

One type of lack of self-control is impetuosity, another is weakness. For some people, though they have deliberated, do not stand by the results of their deliberations because of what they are feeling, whereas others, because they have not deliberated, are led on by what they are feeling. For just as those who tickle first cannot be tickled back, some of these people, if they are aware of it beforehand and have seen it coming and have roused themselves and their capacity for rational calculation ahead of time, do not give in to what they are feeling, whether pleasant or painful.[561]

It is most of all quick-spirited and passionate people who are lacking in the self-control that is impetuous lack of self-control.[562] For it is because of the hastiness in the one case and because of the intensity in the other that they do not wait for reason, because they are the sort of people who follow appearances.

## VII 8

An intemperate person, as we said, is not the sort to have regrets, since he stands by his deliberate choice, whereas anyone who lacks self-control is the sort of person who invariably has regrets.[563] That is why things are not the way we suggested in listing the puzzles.[564] Instead, the intemperate person is incurable, whereas the one who lacks self-control is curable. For depravity resembles diseases like dropsy or consumption, while lack of self-control is like epilepsy. For depravity is continuous wickedness; lack of self-control discontinuous wickedness. In fact, lack of self-control and vice are wholly different in kind, since vice escapes its possessor's notice, whereas lack of self-control does not escape it.

Among people who lack self-control themselves, those who depart[565] are better than those who have |**1151a1**| the reason but do not stand by it, since the latter give in to a weaker way of being affected and do not act without prior deliberation as the former sort do. For a person who lacks self-control is like those who get drunk quickly and on a little wine or on less wine than ordinary people.[566]

That lack of self-control is not a vice is evident, although perhaps it is one *in a way*. For lack of self-control is contrary to deliberate choice, whereas vice is in accord with deliberate choice. Nevertheless, lack of self-control is similar to vice, at least, as regards their actions. It is like what Demodocus said about the Milesians:

> The Milesians aren't stupid people
> But they do precisely what stupid people do.[567]

In the same way, people who lack self-control are not unjust but will do unjust actions.

A person who lacks self-control is the sort who pursues bodily pleasures that are excessive and contrary to the correct reason but not because he is persuaded that he should. An intemperate person, on the other hand, is persuaded, because he is the sort of person to pursue them. So a person who lacks self-control is easily persuaded to change; an intemperate one isn't. For virtue preserves the starting-point, whereas depravity ruins it, and in actions the end for which we do them is the starting-point, just as hypotheses are in mathematics.[568] Reason, then, does not teach the starting-points either in the case of mathematics or in the present one. Instead, it is virtue, whether natural or habituated, that teaches correct belief about the starting-point.[569] A person of that sort is temperate and his contrary intemperate.

But there is also a person who, because of feeling, departs contrary to the correct reason, who is controlled by that feeling to the extent of not acting in accord with the correct reason but not so as to be the sort of person who is persuaded that he should pursue such pleasure and not control it. This is a person who lacks self-control. He is better than an intemperate person and is not unconditionally base, since the best thing is preserved in him—the starting-point.

Another sort of person is contrary to this one. He stands firm and does not depart—at least, not because of feeling.

It is evident from these considerations, then, that the state of a person who has self-control is excellent and that the state of one who lacks self-control is base.

## VII 9

Now, is a self-controlled person one who stands by any reason whatsoever and any deliberate choice whatsoever or is it one who stands by the correct deliberate choice? And is someone lacking in self-control if he does not stand by any deliberate choice whatsoever or any reason whatsoever or must it be a reason that is not false and a correct deliberate choice? This was the puzzle we raised earlier.[570] Or is it that a person with self-control or a person without it only coincidentally stands by any reason or deliberate choice whatsoever but intrinsically stands by the true reason and the correct deliberate choice? For if someone chooses or pursues this because of that, he pursues and chooses the second intrinsically and the first coincidentally. But what is intrinsic, we say, is unconditional. So there is a way in which it is any belief whatsoever that a person with self-control stands by and one without self-control departs from, but unconditionally it is the true belief.

There are some people, though, who are the sort to stand by their belief, whom we call stubborn—the ones who are difficult to persuade into something and not easy to persuade out of it. In some respects such a person is similar to a self-controlled one (just as a wasteful person is to a generous one, and a rash person to a confident one), but in many respects he is different. For it is by feeling and appetite that a self-controlled person is not moved, since he will be easily persuaded when occasion arises, whereas it is by reason that stubborn people are not moved, since they acquire appetites, at any rate, and many of them are led on by pleasures.

It is opinionated people, unlearned ones, and boorish ones who are stubborn. Opinionated ones are such because of pleasure and pain, since they enjoy being victorious if they are not persuaded to change their views and are pained if their own beliefs lack control, insofar as these are like decrees.[571] As a result they are more like a person who lacks self-control than like one who has it.

There are some people, however, who do not stand by their beliefs, but not because of lack of self-control—for example, Neoptolemus in Sophocles' *Philoctetes*.[572] Although it was because of pleasure that he did not stand firm, it was a noble pleasure. For telling the truth was a noble thing to him, but he had been persuaded by Odysseus to lie. For not everyone who does something because of pleasure is intemperate, base, or lacking in self-control—only someone who does so because of a shameful pleasure.

Since there is also a sort of person who enjoys bodily pleasures less than he should and does not stand by his reason, a person with self-control is a mean between this one and one who lacks it. For a person who lacks self-control does not stand by his reason because of too much of something, this one because of too little. One with self-control, by contrast, stands firm and does not change because of either. Now if indeed self-control is something excellent, both of these contrary states must be base, as they in fact appear to be. But because the other state appears in only a few people and on rare occasions, the result is that just as temperance seems contrary only to intemperance, self-control seems contrary only to lack of self-control.

Since many things are called what they are by similarity, it is by similarity too that we have come to speak of the self-control of a temperate person. For both a self-controlled person and a temperate one are the sorts of people to do nothing contrary to their reason because of bodily pleasures. But a self-controlled one has base appetites, whereas a temperate one does not, and a temperate one is the sort not to feel pleasure contrary to his reason, whereas the self-controlled one is the sort to feel such pleasure but not be led by it.

A person who lacks self-control and an intemperate person are also similar, even though they are different. Both pursue bodily pleasures, but an intemperate one does it while also thinking he should; one who lacks self-control does it while not thinking so.

## VII 10

Nor is it possible for the same person to be at once practically-wise and lacking in self-control, since it has been shown that a person is at once practically-wise and excellent in character.[573] Further, a person is not practically-wise by knowing alone but also by being a doer of the relevant action, but a person who lacks self-control is not a doer of the relevant action. (Nothing prevents a *clever* person from lacking self-control, though. This is why some people are sometimes thought to be both practically-wise and lacking in self-control, because cleverness and practical wisdom differ in the way we described in our initial account, that is, they are close as regards reason, but different as regards deliberate choice.[574]) Nor, of course, is a person who lacks self-control like someone who knows and is actively contemplating what he knows, but, rather, he is like someone asleep or tipsy.

Also, he acts voluntarily (for in a way he acts knowing both what he is doing and for the sake of what), but he is not a wicked person, since his deliberate choice is decent.[575] So he is half wicked. And he is not unjust, since he is not a plotter.[576] For one sort of person who lacks self-control does not stand by the results of his deliberation, while the other, the passionate one, is not the sort to deliberate at all.

In fact a person who lacks self-control is like a city that passes all the decrees it should and has excellent laws, but puts them to no use—as in Anaxandrides' jibe, "the city willed it, that cares no whit for laws."[577] A wicked person, by contrast, is like a city that puts its laws to use but puts to use wicked ones.

Lack of self-control and self-control are concerned with what exceeds the state of ordinary people, since a self-controlled person stands firm more than most people are capable of doing; one who lacks self-control does so less.

The sort of lack of self-control that is found in passionate people is more easily cured than the sort found in those who deliberate but do not stand firm, and those who lack self-control through habituation are more easily cured than people who naturally lack self-control, since habit is easier to change than nature. In fact, the reason why habit is also difficult to change is that it resembles nature, as Evenus too says:

> It comes with longtime training, friends,
> And this for human beings as their nature ends.[578]

We have now said what self-control is, what lack of self-control, what resilience, and what softness, and how these states are related to each other.

## VII 11

Having a theoretical grasp on pleasure and pain is part of being a political philosopher, |1152b1| since he is the architectonic craftsman of the end to which we look in calling each thing unconditionally bad or good.[579]

Further, it is actually a necessary requirement that we investigate them, since we have not only taken it that virtue and vice of character are concerned with pains and pleasures, but most people say that happiness involves pleasure.[580] That is why a *makarios* ("blessed") person is so called, after ***chairein*** ("to enjoy").

Now to some people it seems that [1] no pleasure is a good, either intrinsically or coincidentally, since the good and pleasure are not the same, while to others it seems that [2] some pleasures are good but that most are base. Further, there is a third of these views, that [3] even if all pleasures were good things, all the same it is not possible for the best good to be pleasure.

[1] Pleasure is not a good at all. Why? [1a] Every pleasure is a perceived coming to be in the natural state, but no coming to be is the same kind of thing as its end—for example, no process of building is the same kind of thing as a house.[581] Further, [1b] a temperate person avoids pleasures.[582] Further, [1c] a practically-wise person pursues what is painless, not what is pleasant.[583] Further, [1d] pleasures impede thinking, and the more we enjoy them, the more they do so—for example, sexual pleasure (for no one is capable of actively understanding anything in the midst of *it*).[584] Further, [1e] there is no craft of pleasure, and yet everything good is the work of some craft.[585] Further, [1f] children and wild beasts pursue pleasures.

The reasons for [2], the view that not all pleasures are excellent, are that [2a] there are also pleasures that are actually shameful and objects of reproach, and [2b] there are pleasures that are harmful (for some pleasant things cause diseases).

The reason for [3], the view that pleasure is not the best good, is that it is not an end but a coming to be.

These, then, are pretty much the things that are said.

## VII 12

But that it does not follow from these arguments that [1] pleasure is not a good—or [3] even that it is not the best good—is clear from these next considerations.

[Against 1a] First, since what is good is so in two ways (unconditionally and to some particular person), natures and states will be correspondingly divisible and so also will processes and comings to be. So some of the ones that seem to be bad will be unconditionally bad, although for some particular person they are not bad but instead worthy of choice by him. Some, though, are not choiceworthy even to a particular person but only so at a particular time and for a short period and not always.[586] And some are not even pleasures but only appear to be—those that involve pain and are curative, for example, the ones sick people undergo.[587]

[Against 1a] Further, since one sort of good is an activity and another sort is a state, restorations to our natural state are only coincidentally pleasures. The activity in the case of the appetites belongs to the residual state and nature, although there are in fact pleasures without pain or appetite, such as the activities of contemplation, where there is no lack in the natural state.[588] An indication of this is that people do not enjoy the same thing while a lack in their natural state is being replenished as they do when it has been restored. Rather, when it has been restored, they enjoy things that are unconditionally pleasant, but when it is being replenished they enjoy their contraries too—for example, sharp and bitter things, none of which is either naturally pleasant or unconditionally pleasant. So the pleasures gotten from them are not so either, since as pleasant things differ from each other, so also do the pleasures arising from them.

[Against 1a and 3] Further, it is not necessary for something else to be better than pleasure in the way that the end, some people say, is better than its coming to be. For pleasures are not comings to be nor do they all involve comings to be, but, rather, they are activities and an end, and they do not occur when we come to be something but when we use something.[589] Also, not all pleasures have something else as end but only those that lead to the completion of our nature. That is why it is not correct to say that pleasure is a perceived coming to be, but we should better say that it is an activity of a natural state and that it is unimpeded instead of perceived.[590] But it seems to some people to be a coming to be, because it is fully good. For they think an activity is a coming to be, whereas in fact it is something different.

[Against 2b] To say that pleasures are bad because some of them cause diseases is the same as saying that healthy things are bad because some of them are bad in relation to moneymaking. Both of them are bad in the relevant respect, but they certainly are not *bad* on account of this, since even contemplation is sometimes harmful to health.[591]

[Against 1d] Neither practical wisdom nor any state whatsoever is impeded by the pleasure specific to it but only by alien ones. For the pleasure arising from contemplation and learning will make us contemplate and learn all the more.[592]

[Against 1e] The fact that no pleasure is the work of a craft, is what we would quite reasonably expect, since there is no craft of any other activity either, but only of the corresponding capacity—although the crafts of the perfumer and the gourmet chef do seem to be crafts of pleasure.[593]

[Against 1b, c, f] The arguments that a temperate person avoids pleasure, that a practically-wise person pursues a painless life, and that children and wild beasts pursue pleasure, are all resolved in the same way. For we have said in what way pleasures are good and in what way not all of them are unconditionally good, and it is the latter sort that both wild beasts and children pursue, and it is painlessness in their case that a practically-wise person pursues.[594] These are the ones involving appetite and pain, that is, the bodily ones (since they are of that sort) and their excesses, regarding which the intemperate person is intemperate. That is why a temperate person avoids *these* pleasures, since there are pleasures that are characteristic of a temperate person too.

## VII 13

Moreover, it is also agreed that pain is a bad thing, and something to be avoided. For one sort of pain is an unconditionally bad thing, while another is bad by being in some way an impediment to activity. But the contrary of what is to be avoided—insofar as it is something to be avoided and bad—is a good. So pleasure must be a sort of good. For the resolution of this argument that Speusippus used to propose does not in fact resolve it—namely, that it is just like the case of what is greater being the contrary of what is less and of what is equal.[595] For he would not say that pleasure is intrinsically bad.[596] And even if some pleasures are bad, nothing prevents a pleasure of some sort from being the best good, just as some science might be the best good even if some sciences are bad.

Presumably, though, it is even necessary that if there are indeed unimpeded activities of each state, no matter whether happiness is the activity of all of them or of one of them in particular, then this activity, insofar as it is unimpeded, is the most choiceworthy. But this *is* pleasure.[597] So the best good might be some sort of pleasure, even if most pleasures turned out to be bad—even unconditionally bad.

It is because of this in fact that everyone thinks that the happy life is a pleasant one and—quite reasonably—weaves pleasure into happiness.[598] For no activity is complete when it is impeded, and happiness is something complete.[599] This is why a happy person needs to have goods of the body and external goods—the ones luck brings—in addition, so that he will not be impeded in the corresponding ways.[600] (People who claim that a person who is being broken on the rack or succumbing to great misfortunes is happy provided that he is good are talking nonsense, whether they mean to or not.[601])

In fact because a happy person needs the goods that fortune brings in addition, some people think that good luck is the same as happiness. But it isn't. For even good luck is an impediment when it is excessive, and presumably it should no longer by rights be called *good* luck. For the defining mark of *good* luck is determined by relation to happiness.

Also, the fact that all things—both wild beasts and human beings—pursue pleasure is an indication that pleasure is in some way the best good: "No rumor comes entirely to nought that many peoples spread. . . ."[602] But since the same nature or state neither is nor seems to be the best for all, neither do they all pursue the same pleasure, although all do pursue pleasure. And perhaps they are actually pursuing not the one they think or would say that they were pursuing but the same pleasure, since all things by nature have something divine in them.[603] But the bodily pleasures have stolen the name "pleasure," because we most often direct our course toward them and because all share in them. So, because these are the only ones people know, they think that they are the only pleasures.

It is also evident that if pleasure is not a good and an activity, it will not be the case that a happy person is living pleasantly.[604] For what would he need pleasure for, if indeed it is not a good and a happy person may even be living painfully? For pain is neither a bad thing nor a good one, if indeed pleasure is neither of these. So why would he avoid it? The life of an excellent person is not more pleasant either, then, if its activities are not so too.

## VII 14

Where the bodily pleasures are concerned, then, there is a question to be investigated by those who say that some pleasures are intensely choiceworthy (for example, the noble ones), but not the bodily ones—that is, the ones with which an intemperate person is concerned: Why is it that the contrary pains are bad? For good is contrary to bad.

Or are the necessary pleasures good in this way, namely, that even what is not bad is good? Or are they good up to a point? For of some states and processes there cannot be an excess that is better, and so there cannot be an excess of their pleasure either, whereas of others there can be such an excess, and so there can be one of their pleasure too.[605] Of the goods of the body, however, there can be an excess, and it is by pursuing the excess, not the necessary pleasures, that a base person is base. For everyone enjoys gourmet dishes, wines, and sexual relations in some way or other, although not everyone does so in the way he should.

In the case of pain, the contrary is true. For it is not just the excess a base person avoids but pain generally, since pain is not contrary to excess except to someone who pursues excess.

We should not only state the true view, however, but also the explanation of the false one, since that contributes to our conviction. For when a reasonable explanation is given of why an untrue view appears true, this makes us more convinced of the true view. So we should say why it is that bodily pleasures appear more choiceworthy.

Well, the first reason, then, is that bodily pleasure knocks out pain. Because of excessive pain, in fact, people pursue excessive pleasure—and bodily pleasure generally—as if it were a cure. But these curative pleasures get their intensity (which is why they are pursued) from the fact that they appear alongside their contrary.

(Indeed pleasure seems to be no excellent thing, as we said, because of the following two considerations.[606] Some are the actions of a base nature—whether congenital, as with a wild beast, or by habituation, like the actions of base human beings. Others are curative of something lacking, and being in the good state is better than coming to be in it, but these occur in the process of coming to completion and so are coincidentally excellent.)

Further, bodily pleasures are pursued because of their intensity by people incapable of enjoying other sorts. At any rate, they contrive certain thirsts for themselves.[607] Now when these are harmless, this is unobjectionable (although when they are harmful, it is base), since not only do they have nothing else to enjoy but also what is neither pleasant nor painful is painful to many of them because of their nature.[608] For a living thing is always suffering, as the natural scientists also testify, since seeing and hearing, they claim, are painful. But we have already become habituated to them, as they say.[609] Similarly, during their youth—because they are growing—people are in a condition that is like tipsiness, and so youth is a pleasant thing.[610] People who are naturally passionate, on the other hand, are always in need of a cure, since even their body is constantly stinging them because of its mix, and so they are always in a state of intense desire.[611] But pain is driven out both by the contrary pleasure and by any random one, provided it is a strong one. It is for these reasons in fact that such people become intemperate and base.

Pleasures that do not involve pain, however, have no excess. These are among the things naturally and not coincidentally pleasant.

By coincidentally pleasant things, I mean the curative ones, since being cured happens to coincide with a certain activity of the part of us that remains healthy, and because of this it seems to be pleasant.[612] By things naturally pleasant, on the other hand, I mean those that bring about action in a nature of a corresponding sort.

In no case, though, is the same thing always pleasant, because our nature is not simple but also has another element in it, in that we are mortals.[613] As a result, if one of the two is doing something, it is contrary to the nature of our other nature, and when the two are equally balanced, what we are doing seems neither painful nor pleasant. For if the nature of some being were simple, the same action would always be most pleasant.

That is why the god always enjoys a single simple pleasure.[614] For there is not only an activity of moving but also an activity of unmoving, and pleasure is found more in rest than in movement. "Change in all things is sweet," as the poet says, because of a sort of wickedness.[615] For just as a wicked human being is an easily changeable one, a nature that needs change is also wicked, since it is neither simple nor decent.

We have now discussed self-control and lack of self-control as well as pleasure and pain, and said what each of them is and in what ways some of them are good and others bad. It remains for us to discuss friendship too.[616]

# Book VIII

## VIII 1

The next topic we should discuss is friendship, since friendship is a sort of virtue or involves virtue. Furthermore, it is most necessary as regards living.[617] For no one would choose to live without friends, even if he had all the other good things. For even wealthy people and those who are rulers or hold positions of power seem to need friends most. For what benefit is such prosperity once the opportunity to be a benefactor—which occurs most and is most praiseworthy when it is toward friends—is removed? Or in what way could their prosperity be protected and safeguarded without friends? For the greater their prosperity is, the more precarious it is.

In poverty too, as in all other misfortunes, people think friends to be their only refuge. Also, friends are necessary to young people with a view to the avoidance of error, to old ones with a view to being taken care of and being given aid with the actions they have to leave unaccomplished because of their weakness, and to those in their prime with a view to doing noble actions—for when "two go together" they are better able both to understand and to act.[618]

Also, friendship seems to be naturally present in parent for offspring and offspring for parent, not only among human beings but also among birds and most of the animals and among members of the same race toward each other—most of all among human beings (which is why we praise lovers of mankind).[619] Even on our travels, we can see how every human being is kin and friend to every other human being.

It also seems that friendship holds cities together and that legislators take it more seriously than justice.[620] For concord seems to be something like friendship, and this is what they seek most, whereas faction, because it is enmity, they most seek to drive out.[621] Also, if people are friends, there is no need for justice, whereas people who are just need friendship in addition to justice.[622] Also, of just things the most just of all seem to be fitted to friendship.[623]

Friendship is not only something necessary, however, but also something noble, since we praise those who love their friends and many-friendedness seems to be something noble. And, further, it is the same people we consider to be good men and friends.

There are, however, quite a few disputes about friendship.[624] For some suppose that it is a sort of likeness and that those who are alike are friends. Whence the sayings, "like is drawn to like," "birds of a feather flock together," and so on.[625] Others, on the contrary, say that people who are alike are proverbial potters to each other.[626]

Also, where these issues are concerned, some people conduct their inquiry at a higher level and one that is more deeply natural. Euripides says that "earth is in love with rain," when it has become parched, and that "the majestic heaven, when filled with rainwater, is in love with falling on earth."[627] Heraclitus too says that "opposition unites," that the noblest harmonies arise from discord, and that everything comes about through strife.[628] Others, on the contrary, including Empedocles, say that like seeks like.[629]

Now, the puzzles of natural science we may set aside, since they do not properly belong to the present investigation. Those that concern human affairs, though, and pertain to characters and feelings, *these* we should investigate—for example, does friendship come about among all sorts of people or are depraved people incapable of being friends? Also, is there one form of friendship or more than one? (For some people think that there is one form, because friendship admits of differences in degree.[630] But they have been convinced by an inadequate indication, since things that differ in form also admit of differences in degree. But we have spoken about these earlier.[631])

## VIII 2

Maybe these issues will become evident, however, if we first come to know the proper object of love.[632] For not everything is loved, it seems, but only what is lovable, and this is either good or pleasant or useful. But what would seem to be useful is that through which some good or some pleasure comes about, so that what are lovable as ends are what is good and what is pleasant.

Is it, then, what is good that people love? Or what is good for themselves? For sometimes these clash. Similarly, where what is pleasant is concerned. It seems indeed that what each person loves is what is good for himself and that while what *is* good is unconditionally lovable, what is good for each person is lovable to himself. (In fact, each person loves not what is really good for him but what appears good to him. But that will make no difference, since "what is lovable" will then be "what appears lovable."[633])

Though there are three things because of which people love, the way of loving that is appropriate for soulless objects is not called friendship since there is no reciprocal loving involved and no wishing for the object's good (for it would presumably be ridiculous for someone to wish good things to his wine, but if indeed it happens, it is for its preservation that he wishes, in order to have it for himself). But to a friend, it is said, we must wish good things for his own sake. Those who wish good things to someone in this way, however, if the same wish is not reciprocated, are said to have *goodwill* toward him, since friendship is said to be reciprocated goodwill.[634]

Or should we add "that does not go unawares"? For many have goodwill toward people they have never seen but take to be decent or useful, and one of the latter might feel the same way |**1156a1**| toward one of them. That these people have goodwill toward each other is evident, but how could we call them friends when they are unaware of how they are mutually disposed? Hence friends must have goodwill (that is, wish good things) for each other because of one of the things we mentioned, and not be unaware of it.[635]

## VIII 3

But these things differ in form from each other, hence so do the ways of loving and the friendships. There are, then, three forms of friendship, equal in number to the proper objects of love, since in the case of each proper object of love there is a corresponding way of reciprocal loving that does not go unawares, and those who love each other wish good things to the other in the way in which they love.[636] Now, those who love another person because of his utility do not love each other for themselves but only insofar as some good comes to them from each other. Similarly with those who love because of pleasure, since they like witty people not for having a character of a certain sort but because they find them pleasant.

Those who love because of utility, then, feel affection because of what is good for themselves, and those who love because of pleasure do so because of what is pleasant to themselves and not insofar as the beloved is who he is but insofar as he is useful or pleasant.

These friendships are in fact coincidentally friendships, then, since a person who is beloved in that way is loved not insofar as he is precisely who he is but insofar as he provides some good, in the one case, or some pleasure, in the other.

Such friendships are prone to dissolve easily, then, because of the friends not remaining the same, since when they are no longer pleasant or useful to each other they stop loving. Utility indeed does not endure, but differs from time to time. So when the things because of which they were friends have been removed, the friendship breaks off as well, inasmuch as the friendship was in accord with these things.

This sort of friendship seems to come about among older people most of all (since at that age it is not pleasure they pursue but what is beneficial), also among those in their prime or youth who pursue what is advantageous. But such people scarcely ever live together, since sometimes they are not even pleasant to each other. Nor, then, do they need this sort of social interaction unless they are advantageous to each other, since they are pleasant to each other only to the extent that they have an expectation of some good. It is also among these friendships that people put guest-friendship.[637]

Friendship between young people seems to exist because of pleasure, since they live in accord with their feelings and pursue most of all what is pleasant for themselves and present at hand. As they grow older, though, their pleasures also become different. That is why they quickly become friends and quickly stop being so. For the friendship changes along with what is pleasant, and that sort of pleasure changes quickly. Also, young people are prone to erotic desire. For erotic friendships are largely in accord with feeling and exist because of pleasure. That is why they love and quickly stop loving, often changing in a single day. But they do wish to spend their days together and to live together, since that is how they get what is in accord with their friendship.

Complete friendship, however, is the friendship of good people who are alike in virtue. For each alike wishes good things to the other insofar as he is good, and each is intrinsically good. And those who wish good things to their friends for the friends' own sake are friends most of all, since it is because of themselves and not coincidentally that they are disposed in this way. So their friendship lasts as long as they are good—and virtue is something steadfast.[638] Also, each of them is unconditionally good and is so to his friend, since good people are both unconditionally good and beneficial to each other. They are likewise pleasant as well. For good people are both unconditionally pleasant and pleasant to each other, since to each his own actions and those similar to them are pleasurable, and the actions of good people are the same or similar.

This sort of friendship is with good reason steadfast, since it joins together within it all the qualities that friends should have. For every sort of friendship exists because of some good or because of pleasure, whether unconditionally or for the person loving, and is in accord with some likeness between the parties. But to this sort of friendship all the qualities we mentioned belong, because of the friends themselves. For in this sort of friendship the other qualities also are alike in both parties, and what is unconditionally good is also unconditionally pleasant, and these are the most proper of all objects of love. Loving, then, and friendship too, exist most and at their best between people like these.

Friendships like these are likely to be rare, however, since there are few such people. Furthermore, time and intimacy are needed in addition. For as the proverb says people cannot know each other until they have "eaten the canonical amount of salt together."[639] They cannot accept each other, then, or be friends either until each appears lovable to the other and gains his trust.

Those who quickly do for each other things fitted to friendship, on the other hand, wish to be friends, but are not friends unless they are also lovable and know this. For though the wish for friendship comes about quickly, friendship does not.

## VIII 4

So this form of friendship is complete both as regards time and as regards the rest, and in all of them each party gets the same or similar things from the other, which is precisely what should happen between friends.

The friendship that exists because of pleasure bears a similarity to the complete sort of friendship, since good people are also pleasant to each other. Similarly with the sort that exists because of utility, since good people are also useful to each other. And between these sorts of friends, friendships are also most lasting when the parties get the same thing—for example, pleasure—from each other, and not only that but also get it from the same thing, as happens with witty people, for example, and not as with a lover and his boyfriend.[640] (For these do not take pleasure in the same things, but one takes pleasure in looking at the other, whereas the other takes pleasure in being taken care of by his lover. As the boy's bloom fades, however, sometimes the friendship also fades, since the lover does not take pleasure in seeing the boy, and the boy does not get taken care of by his lover. On the other hand, many do remain friends, if as a result of their intimacy they come to feel affection for each other's character, having similar characters themselves.)

Those who exchange not pleasure but utility in their erotic friendships are and remain friends to a lesser degree: people who are friends because of utility break off their friendship as soon as the advantage is at an end, since it was not to each other that they were friends but to gain.

Because of pleasure and because of utility, in fact, even base people can be friends with each other, as can decent people with base ones, and ones who are neither bad nor decent with a person of any sort whatever. It is clear, though, that only good people can be friends because of themselves, since bad ones find no enjoyment in each other unless some benefit might come of it.

Also, the friendship of good people is the only sort that is immune to slander, since it is not easy to trust anyone about a person we have ourselves put to the test over a long period of time. Also, there *is* trust between them, and the conviction that "he would never do an injustice," and all the other things required in a true friendship. But in the other sorts of friendship there is nothing to prevent things like these from happening.

For people apply the name "friends" even to those who feel affection because of utility, just as they do with cities (since alliances come about between cities for the sake of what is advantageous), and also apply it to those who feel affection for each other because of pleasure (just as in the case of children). So presumably we too should call such people "friends," while saying that there are more forms of friendship than one. Friendship in the primary and full sense is that between good people insofar as they are good, while the rest are friendships by similarity to it. For it is insofar as there is something good in their relationship, and so some similarity to the primary case, that they are friends, since what is pleasant is also good to lovers of pleasure.

The latter sorts of friendship are scarcely ever joined together, nor do the same people become friends because of utility and because of pleasure, since things that are coincidental to a subject are scarcely ever coupled.

With friendships divided into these forms, base people will be friends because of pleasure or because of utility, since that is the respect in which they are alike. But good people will be friends because of themselves, since they will be friends insofar as they are good. So they are friends unconditionally, whereas the others are friends coincidentally and by similarity to these.

## VIII 5

Just as with the virtues, where some people are called good with regard to a state, others with regard to an activity, so it is with friendship too. For the ones who live together find enjoyment in each other and provide the requisite good things.[641] The ones who are asleep or in separate places, on the other hand, though not actively doing them, have the state that would result in their doing the things fitted to friendship, since being in separate places does not break off friendship unconditionally but rather its activity. But if the absence goes on for a long time, it seems to make people forget even their friendship. Hence the saying, "many a friendship has broken off for want of conversation."[642]

Neither older people nor sour-tempered ones seem fitted for friendship. For there is little pleasure to be found in them, and no one can spend his days with what is painful or with what is not pleasant, since it is evident that nature most avoids what is painful and seeks what is pleasant.[643] (People who approve of each other yet do not live together seem to have goodwill rather than friendship. For nothing is so fitted to friendship as living together, since while people who are in need desire benefit, even the blessed desire to spend their days together, since a solitary life suits them least of all.) But passing the time with each other is not possible for people who are not pleasant and do not enjoy the same things, which is precisely what companionate friendship seems to involve.

Now the friendship of good people is most of all friendship, as we have often said. For what is lovable and what is choiceworthy seems to be what is unconditionally good or pleasant, and what is so to each person seems to be what is good or pleasant for himself—and a good person is lovable and worthy of choice to another good person on both grounds.

Loving seems to be a feeling, whereas friendship seems to be a state, since loving seems to be no less directed toward soulless things. Reciprocal loving, though, involves deliberate choice, and deliberate choice stems from a state.[644] Also, when people wish good things to their beloveds for their beloveds' own sake, that they do so is not in accord with a feeling but with a state. Also, in loving their friend they love what is good for themselves, since a good person, in becoming a friend, becomes a good for the person for whom he is a friend. So each of the two both loves what is good for himself and makes an equal return in the good he wishes and in what is pleasant (for friendship is said to be equality), and it is most of all in the friendship of good people that these qualities are found.[645]

## VIII 6

Among sour-tempered or older people, friendship less often comes about, insofar as they are disagreeable and find less enjoyment in social interaction, since these are the qualities that seem to be most fitted to friendship and productive of it. That is why young people become friends quickly, whereas older ones do not (since people do not become friends with those they find no enjoyment in), and neither for similar reasons do sour-tempered ones. Instead such people can have goodwill toward each other, since they wish each other good things and meet each other's needs, but they are scarcely friends, because they do not spend their days together and do not find enjoyment in each other—which are precisely the things that seem most fitted to friendship.

To be a friend to many people, however, in a way that accords with complete friendship, is not possible, just as it is not possible to be in love with many people at the same time. For erotic love is like an excess, and something of that sort naturally comes about in relation to a single person.[646] And it is not easy for many people to please the same person intensely at the same time, nor, presumably, for them to be good. But he must actually acquire experience of them and become intimate with them, which is very difficult. If, however, the friendship exists because of pleasure or because of utility, it is possible for many people to please someone, since there are many of the requisite sorts and the services involved take little time.

Of these, the one that exists because of pleasure is more like friendship, when they both get the same things from each other and find enjoyment in each other or in the same things. The friendships of young people are like this, since the element of generosity is found more in these. The sort that exists because of utility, by contrast, is characteristic of businesslike people. Also, blessed people, although they have no need of useful friends, do need pleasant ones, since they wish to have people to live together with, and, while they can bear what is painful for a short time, no one could withstand it continuously—not even the good itself, if it were painful to him.[647] That is why they seek friends who are pleasant. But presumably they should seek friends who are also good—and furthermore good *for them*. For that way they will have everything that friends should have.

People in positions of authority appear to make use of distinct groups of friends, since some are useful, others pleasing, but the same people are scarcely ever both. For they do not look for friends who are both pleasant and virtuous or those who are useful with a view to noble actions, but rather they look for witty people when it is pleasure they are seeking or those, on the other hand, who are clever at doing the actions prescribed, and these qualities are scarcely ever found together.

Although we did say that an excellent person is both pleasant and useful at the same time, still that sort of person does not become a friend to a superior unless the latter is superior in virtue too (otherwise he does not achieve proportionate equality as an inferior).[648] But superiors like that are scarcely ever found.

Now the sorts of friendships we have discussed are in accord with equality, since both parties get the same and wish the same to each other, or trade one thing for another—for example, pleasure for benefit. But that these are both lesser friendships and less lasting ones, we have already said.[649] Because of their similarity and dissimilarity to the same thing, indeed, they seem both to be and not to be friendships. For insofar as they are similar to friendship in accord with virtue they are apparently friendships (since one of them involves pleasure and the other utility, and friendship in accord with virtue also involves these), but insofar as friendship in accord with virtue is immune to slander and steadfast, whereas these sorts change quickly, and differ from it in many other ways, they are apparently not friendships, because of their dissimilarity to it.

## VIII 7

A different form of friendship, however, is the one in accord with superiority—for example, of a father for his son, of older for younger generally, of man for woman, and of any sort of ruler for someone he rules. These, though, also differ from each other, since the friendship of parents for children is not the same as that of ruler for ruled, but neither are those of father for son and son for father, or those of man for woman and woman for man. For of each of the parties involved there is a different virtue and a different function—different too are the things because of which they love.[650] So the ways of loving and the friendships are also different.

Each, then, does not get the same things from the other and should not look for them either. But when children render to their parents what should be rendered to begetters, and parents render to their children what should be rendered to offspring, the friendship between them will be steadfast and decent. In all friendships in accord with superiority, however, the loving should be proportionate too—for example, the better person should be more loved than loving, as should the more beneficial one, and similarly in each of the other cases. For when loving is in accord with worth, a sort of equality comes about, and that seems to be characteristic of friendship.[651]

What is equal, though, does not seem to be the same in matters of justice and in friendship, since in matters of justice equality is primarily equality in worth and secondarily equality in quantity, whereas in friendship equality is primarily equality in quantity and secondarily equality in worth. This is made clear when a great disparity in virtue, vice, resources, or something else comes about, since then the parties are no longer friends and do not even claim that they deserve to be. This is most evident in the case of the gods, since they are the most superior to us in all good things. But it is also clear in the case of kings, since people who are much inferior to them do not claim that they deserve to be their friends either, nor do worthless people claim that they deserve to be friends with the best or wisest ones. In cases like this there is no exact definition of the point up to which people can remain friends, since much can be taken away and the friendship still last, but if the separation is large—for example, between us and a god—it no longer does.[652]

Whence in fact the puzzle arises as to whether friends really wish the greatest of goods to their friends (for example, that they be gods), since then they will no longer be friends to them nor good things either, then, since friends are good things.[653] If, then, we were correct to say that one friend wishes good things to the other for the other's own sake, it should be the case that the other remains whatever sort of thing he is. It is to him insofar as he is a human being, then, that he will wish the greatest goods. But perhaps not all of them, since it is most of all for himself that each person wishes good things.[654]

## VIII 8

Ordinary people, because of their love of honor, seem to wish to be loved more than to love. That is why ordinary people love flattery. For a flatterer is a friend who is inferior, or pretends to be so and to love more than he is loved. Being loved, though, seems close to being honored, which is of course what ordinary people seek.

It does not seem to be because of itself, however, that they choose honor, but rather coincidentally. For ordinary people enjoy being honored by those in positions of authority because of what they expect, since they think that if they need something they will get it from these. It is as an indication of benefits to be received, then, that they enjoy the honor. Those who desire honor from decent and knowledgeable people, on the other hand, are seeking to confirm their own beliefs about themselves. What they enjoy, then, is that they are good, and that happens thanks to their trusting the discernment of those who say this. Being loved, though, is something people intrinsically enjoy. That is why being loved would seem to be better than being honored, and friendship to be intrinsically choiceworthy.

But friendship seems to consist more in loving than in being loved. An indication of this is that it is in loving that mothers take enjoyment. For mothers sometimes give away their own children to be reared by others, and though they love them (since they know who they are), they do not look for reciprocal love (if love in both directions is impossible). Instead it seems enough for them to see that their children are doing well, and they themselves love their children even if these render up none of the things appropriate to a mother because of their ignorance of who she is.

Since friendship consists more in loving, however, and those who love their friends are praised, loving seems to be the virtue characteristic of friends, so that it is those in whom love comes about in accord with worth who are steadfast friends and have a steadfast friendship.[655] It is in this way that even |**1159b1**| unequals will best be friends, since in this way they will be equalized.

Equality and likeness is friendship, and most of all the likeness of those who are alike in virtue. For since they are steadfast in themselves, they also remain steadfast to each other, and they neither need base services nor provide such services themselves, but even prevent them, so to speak.[656] For it is characteristic of good people neither to commit errors themselves nor to allow their friends to do so. Depraved people, by contrast, do not have anything stable about them, since they do not remain even like themselves.[657] Instead, they become friends for a short time, while they are enjoying each other's depravity.

Useful and pleasant people last longer as friends, since they do so for as long as they provide each other with pleasures or benefits. The friendship that exists because of utility, however, seems to come about most of all from contraries (for example, of poor for rich, or unlearned for knowledgeable), since whatever someone needs he seeks, giving something else in return. Here we might also include lover and boyfriend, and beautiful and ugly. That is why lovers also sometimes appear ridiculous by claiming that they deserve to be loved in the same way as they love. If they were lovable in a similar way, they should perhaps claim they deserve this, but when they are nothing of the sort, it is ridiculous to do so.

Presumably, a contrary does not intrinsically seek its contrary, however, but rather does so coincidentally, and the desire is instead for the mean, since this is something good—for example, for what is dry the good is not to become wet but rather to reach the mean, and similarly for what is hot and the rest. Well, we may set aside these issues, since they belong to another discussion entirely.[658]

## VIII 9

It does seem, though, as we said at the start, that friendship and justice are concerned with the same things and involve the same people.[659] For in every community there seems to be some sort of justice and some sort of friendship as well. At any rate, people address their fellow sailors or fellow soldiers as friends, and those in other sorts of communities do likewise. And the extent to which they share things communally is the extent of their friendship, since it is also the extent of justice.[660] The proverb "what friends have they have in common" is correct too, since it is in community that friendship lies.

But whereas brothers and companions have everything in common, others have only specified things—more in some cases, fewer in others, since some friendships are in fact greater in extent, others less. What is just differs too, since it is not the same for parents toward children as for brothers toward each other |**1160a1**| or the same for companions as for fellow citizens, and similarly in the case of the other sorts of friendships as well.

Injustice toward each of these, then, is also different, and grows when it is toward those who are more fully friends—for example, it is a more terrible thing to rob a companion of his money than to rob a fellow citizen or not to give aid to a brother than not to give it to a stranger or to strike one's father than to strike anyone whomever. Justice too naturally increases along with the friendship, since it involves the same people and has an equal extension.

All communities seem to be parts of the political community, however, since people consort together for some advantage and to provide themselves with something for their life. And the political community too seems both to have come together at the start and to remain in existence, for the sake of what is advantageous.[661] For legislators also aim to hit this, and what is for the common advantage is said to be just.[662]

Now other communities seek what is advantageous in some area—for example, sailors seek what is advantageous on a voyage related to some moneymaking occupation or something of that sort, whereas fellow soldiers seek what is advantageous in war, whether money, victory, or taking a city; and similarly with members of tribes or demes.[663] Some communities, though, seem to come about because of pleasure—namely, religious guilds and dining clubs, since these come about for the sake of sacrifices and companionship.[664] All of these, however, seem to be subordinate to the political community, since it seeks not the advantage that is present at hand but the one that is for all of life. . . [even when its members are] performing sacrifices, arranging gatherings related to these, giving honors to the gods, and providing pleasure-involving relaxations for themselves.[665] For ancient sacrifices and gatherings seemed to take place after the harvesting of the crops, as a sort of offering of first fruits, since it was at these times that people were most at leisure.

All these sorts of communities, then, are evidently parts of the political community, and the various sorts of friendship will follow upon the various sorts of community.

## VIII 10

There are three forms of constitution and an equal number of deviations—ruined versions, as it were—of these.[666] The forms of constitution are kingship, aristocracy, and, thirdly, one based on property assessments, which it seems proper to call "timocracy," though most people usually call it "polity."[667]

Of these, the best is kingship, the worst timocracy. The deviation from kingship is tyranny. For though both are monarchies, they differ greatly, since the tyrant targets his own advantage, a king that of the ones he rules. For a person is not a king unless he is self-sufficient and superior in all good things, and someone like that needs nothing in addition and so will not target what would benefit himself but what would benefit those he rules, since a king who is not like this would be some sort of titular king.[668] Tyranny is the very contrary of this, since the tyrant pursues what is good for himself. Also, it is more evident in its case that it is the worst, and the worst is the contrary of the best.[669]

From kingship a constitution changes to a tyranny, since the baseness characteristic of monarchy is tyranny and a depraved king becomes a tyrant. From aristocracy it changes to oligarchy due to the vice of the rulers, who allocate what belongs to the city contrary to worth, giving all or most of the good things to themselves and offices always to the same people, considering the acquisition of wealth to be their most important concern. The rulers are few, then, and depraved people rather than the most decent ones. From timocracy it changes to democracy, since these are neighbors. For timocracy too is meant to be rule by the majority, and all those meeting the property assessment are equal. Democracy is least depraved, since it deviates only a little from a form of polity. Constitutions change most of all in these ways, then, since these changes are smallest and easiest.

Resemblances—and, as it were, paradigms—of these constitutions can also be found in households. For the community of a father in relation to his sons takes the shape of a kingship, since it is for his children that a father cares; that is why Homer too calls Zeus "father," since kingship is meant to be paternal rule.[670] Among the Persians, however, the rule of a father is tyrannical, since they use their sons as slaves. Also tyrannical is the rule of a master in relation to slaves, since it is the advantage of the master that is served in it. But whereas this form of rule is apparently correct, the Persian form is apparently erroneous, since when the people ruled are of different types, the forms of rule are different.

The community of man and woman is apparently aristocratic, since the man rules in accord with his worth and in those matters in which a man should rule, whereas whatever is fitting for a woman he gives over to her. If on the other hand the man controls everything, he changes it into an oligarchy, since he makes it contrary to worth and not dependent on who is better.[671] Sometimes, though, women rule because they are heiresses. Their rule, then, is not in accord with virtue but exists because of wealth and power, as in oligarchies.

The community of brothers is like a timocracy, since brothers are equals except insofar as they differ in age. That is why if their ages differ greatly, their friendship is no longer a brotherly one. Democracy, however, is found most of all in masterless habitations (since there everyone is on an equal footing), and in those in which the ruler is weak and everyone has authority.[672]

## VIII 11

In each of the constitutions there is evidently friendship to the extent that there is justice. The friendship of a king toward those he rules is in accord with his superiority as a benefactor. For he treats those he rules well, if indeed he is good, and supervises them to ensure that they do well, just as a shepherd does his sheep. Whence Homer also calls Agamemnon "shepherd of the people."[673]

Paternal friendship is also like this, but differs in the magnitude of the benefactions, since a father is a cause of existence (which seems to be the greatest service) as well as of nurture and education. And these services are attributed to ancestors too. It is by nature, moreover, that a father is fit to rule his sons, ancestors to rule descendants, and a king those he rules.[674]

These friendships are in accord with superiority, which is also why parents are honored. What is just, then, in these relationships is not what is the same for the two parties but rather what is in accord with their worth, since the friendship is that way too.

Also, the friendship of a man toward a woman is the same as in an aristocracy, since it is in accord with virtue, with more good going to the better and what is fitting going to each. And what is just is that way too.

The friendship of brothers is like companionate friendship, since they are equals and of an age, and people like that are for the most part similar in feelings and character. The friendship that accords with timocracy is like this too, since the citizens are meant to be equal and decent, ruling in turn and on equal terms. Their friendship, then, is that way too.

In the deviations, however, just as justice is found only to a small extent, so too is friendship, and it is found least in the worst one, since in tyranny there is little or no friendship.[675] For in cases where there is nothing in common between ruler and ruled, there is no friendship, since there is no justice either—for example, of craftsman toward instrument, soul toward body, or master toward slave.[676] *Benefited* by their users all these things certainly are, but there is no friendship |**1161b1**| toward soulless things nor justice either. Neither is there friendship toward a horse or an ox, or toward a slave insofar as he is a slave, since there is nothing in common between the parties. For a slave is an ensouled instrument, an instrument a soulless slave. Insofar as he is a slave, then, there is no friendship toward him, but insofar as he is a human being there is.[677] For there seems to be some sort of justice on the part of any human being toward anyone capable of participating in a community of law and convention, and of friendship too, then, to the extent that he is a human being.

The various forms of friendship and justice are found to a small extent even in tyrannies, then, whereas in democracies they are found to a greater extent, since in the case of those who are equal, the things they have in common are many.

## VIII 12

It is in community, then, that every form of friendship lies, as we said.[678] But we might distinguish the cases of familial and companionate friendship. Political friendships, by contrast, as well as tribal friendships, friendships between fellow sailors, and all friendships of this sort do seem to be more like communal ones, since they seem to be in accord with some sort of agreement. Guest-friendship might also be ranked with these.

Familial friendships also seem to be multiform, although all derive from paternal friendship. For parents feel affection for their children as being something of themselves, and children feel it for their parents as those they come from. But parents know better what has come from them than their offspring know that they have come from these. Also, an offspring is more intimately attached to what it comes from than what it comes from is to what produced it. For what comes from something properly belongs to what it comes from (as a tooth or hair or whatever else does to what has it), whereas what something comes from does not properly belong to it at all, or does so to a lesser extent. Also, there is the quantity of time involved. For parents feel affection for their offspring straight from birth, whereas children feel it for parents when time has passed and they have acquired comprehension or perception. From these observations it is also clear why mothers love their children more.

Parents love their children, then, as they love themselves, since what has come from them is like another (by being separated from them) "themselves," and children love parents as being what brought them into the world.[679] Brothers love each other as having been brought into the world by the same parents. For because their relationship to their parents is one and the same, they become one and the same too. Hence we speak of "one and the same blood," "one and the same root," and so on. They are one and the same in some way, then, even though divided in two.

Joint nurture and being of an age are major factors in friendship, since "age makes for fellowship," and those who live intimately become companions. That is also why fraternal friendship and companionate friendship are similar. And cousins and other relatives derive their intimate attachment from that of brothers, since it exists because they come from the same ones. But some are closer kin and others more distant depending on their closeness to or distance from their initial common ancestor.

The friendship of children toward parents, as of human beings toward gods, is as toward something good and superior, since they are the producers of the greatest goods and the cause of their existence and nurture as well as of their education, once born. And this form of friendship also includes pleasure and utility more than does the friendship of strangers, insofar as they have more of a common life.

Fraternal friendship has the features found in companionate friendship (most of all when the parties are decent, and generally when they are similar to one another) to the extent that brothers are closer kin to each other and feel affection for each other from birth, and to the extent that those who come from the same parents and have been jointly nurtured and similarly educated are more similar in character and their test of each other over time is longest and most stable.

Among other relatives too the features fitted to friendship are also proportionate.[680]

Between a man and a woman, friendship seems to hold by nature, since a human being seems to be by nature more couple forming than political to the extent that household is prior to and more necessary than city, and reproduction is a characteristic more common to animals.[681] Now with the other animals, their community only goes as far as reproduction, whereas human beings share a household not only for the sake of reproduction but also for the sake of various things necessary for life. For straight from the beginning their functions are divided, those of a man being different from those of a woman, so they assist each other by putting their special ones into the common enterprise.[682] Because of this, both utility and pleasure seem to be found in this form of friendship. It may also exist because of virtue, however, if both parties are decent. For there is a virtue characteristic of each, and they can enjoy something like this. And children seem to be a bond of union, which is why childless unions are more quickly dissolved. For children are a good common to both, and what is common holds things together.

As for how a man should live his life in relation to a woman, and generally speaking a friend in relation to a friend, there is apparently no difference between inquiring about this and inquiring about how he will do so justly, since this is not the same, apparently, for a friend toward a friend as toward a stranger, a companion, or a classmate.

## VIII 13

There are three forms of friendship, as we said at the start, and in each, some are friends in accord with equality while others are so in accord with superiority.[683] For, similarly, good people become friends as do better ones and worse ones, and similarly with pleasant people too and those who become friends because of utility, who may be equal or different in the benefits they confer. Equal partners, then, must equalize their loving and everything else in accord with equality, while unequal ones must return what is proportionate, given the sorts of superiority involved.

Complaints and grievances arise only or mostly in friendships that are in accord with utility. And quite reasonably so. For those who are friends because of virtue are eager to provide benefits for each other, since this is characteristic of virtue and friendship, and when *that* is what people are competing about, there can be no complaints or quarrels. For no one is repelled by someone's loving him or providing benefits for him but, rather, insofar as he is a sophisticated person, he responds by providing benefits in turn. And the one who excels the other does not complain about his friend, because he gets what he is seeking, for each of them desires what is good.[684]

Complaints scarcely ever arise, either, in friendships that exist because of pleasure, since what both parties desire they get at the same time, if they enjoy passing the time together. And a person who complained about someone who did not delight him would appear ridiculous, when he is free not to spend his days with him.

Friendship that exists because of utility, however, is prone to complaints. For since they are making use of each other for their own benefit, they always need more, thinking that they have less than is proper, and raising a grievance that they are not getting as much as they need, though they claim that they deserve it. Those who are providing the benefits, on the other hand, are unable to provide as much as the recipients need.

It seems that just as justice is twofold, one sort unwritten and the other in accord with the law, so in the case of friendship in accord with utility, one sort is ethical in character and the other sort legal in character. Now complaints most arise when the partners do not begin and dissolve their association in accord with the same sort of this friendship.

The sort that is legal in character is one on specified terms; one sort consists entirely in businesslike hand-to-hand exchange, the other is freer as to time, albeit based on a quid-pro-quo contract. In the latter, the debt is clear and not disputable but the deferral of repayment is fitted to friendship. That is why in some places there cannot be judicial proceedings over these, but, rather, people think that those whose transactions were based on trust should be content with that.[685]

The sort that is ethical in character is not one on specified terms but, rather, each gives a gift or whatever as to a friend, yet he claims that he deserves to get back an equal amount or more, on the supposition that he was not giving but making a loan.

In a case where one party does not begin and dissolve the association on the same terms, there will be complaint. (This happens because all or most people, while they wish for what is noble, deliberately choose what is beneficial. And while it is noble to provide benefits not because they will be repaid, it is being the recipient of a benefaction that is beneficial.) |**1163a1**|

If the recipient can, then, he should make a return of equal worth to what he has received and do so voluntarily (since he should not make the other party an involuntary friend).[686] He must suppose, then, that he was in error at the start and received a benefit from someone he should not have received it from, since it was not from a friend or from someone doing it because of itself. And he must dissolve the association as if the benefaction had been provided on specified terms and agree that he will make repayment when he is able. But if he is unable, not even the giver could claim he deserves it. So if possible he should repay. At the start, though, he should investigate from whom he is receiving benefactions and on what terms, so that he may either accept them on those terms or not.

It is disputable whether we should measure by the benefit to the recipient and make repayment in accord with that or measure by the beneficence of the giver. For recipients say that they got from the benefactors the sorts of things that were small things for the benefactors and that they could have gotten them from someone else—minimizing the matter. The givers, conversely, say they were the biggest things for them, could not have been gotten from others, and were given in times of danger or of similar sorts of need.

Well, when the friendship exists because of utility, shouldn't the recipient's benefit be the measure of it? For he was the one in need of it and the giver assists him on the supposition that he will get an equal return. So the assistance has been precisely as great as the benefit received, and the recipient should repay, then, as much as he got out of it—or even more, since that is a nobler thing to do.

In friendships in accord with virtue, on the other hand, there are no complaints. Rather the measure would seem to be the deliberate choice of the giver, since the controlling element of virtue and character lies in deliberate choice.[687]

## VIII 14

Disputes also arise in friendships in accord with superiority, since each of the two parties claims that he deserves to have more, and when this happens the friendship is dissolved. For the better party thinks it appropriate that he have more, since more should be allocated to the one who is good, and the partner who confers greater benefits thinks similarly. For a useless person, they say, should not have an equal share, since then it becomes a charity and not a friendship, if what results from it is not in accord with the worth of the parties' functions.[688] For they think that just as in a community formed with a view to making money, where those who contribute more get more, so it should be in a friendship too.[689] But the person in need, or the worse party, takes the converse position. For the function of a good friend is to assist those who are in need, since what, they ask, is the benefit of being the friend of an excellent person or one in a position of power if you are going to get nothing out of it?[690]

Now it would seem that the thought of each party about his deserts are correct, and that more should be allocated to each of them from the friendship—not more of the same thing, however, but more honor to the superior party and more profit to the one in need. For honor is the privilege appropriate to virtue and beneficence, whereas profit is the assistance appropriate to need.[691]

It is apparently this way in constitutions as well, since someone who contributes nothing good to the common good is given no honor. For a common good is given to a person who benefits the common good, and honor is a common good.[692] For one cannot at the same time receive money from communal sources *and* receive honor, since no one endures getting the smaller share in everything. To the person who gets a smaller share where money is concerned, then, they allocate honor, and to the person willing to accept gifts, money. For what is in accord with worth equalizes and preserves the friendship, as we said.[693] This, then, is also how we should associate with unequals: the party who is benefited in regard to wealth or in regard to virtue should give honor in return, making what repayment he can.

For friendship seeks what is possible, not what is in accord with worth, since that is not even possible in all cases, such as in cases of honor to the gods or to parents. For here no one could ever make a return of equal worth, but someone who serves them as far as he can seems to be decent. That is why it would seem that son is not free to disown father, whereas father is free to disown son.[694] For a debtor must repay, and since nothing a son has done is worthy of the benefits he has already received, he is always in debt. A creditor, however, is free to remit a debt, and so, then, is a father. At the same time, presumably, it seems that no one would disclaim a son who was not one utterly excessive in his depravity. For quite apart from their natural friendship, it is human not to reject assistance. For the son, however, if he is depraved, providing goods to his father is something to avoid or not take seriously. For while ordinary people wish to receive benefits, they avoid providing them on the supposition that they involve no gain.

So much, then, for our discussion of these topics.

# Book IX

## IX 1

In all friendships between dissimilars, what is proportionate equalizes and preserves the friendship, as we said.[695] For example, in political friendship a shoemaker gets a payment for his shoes in accord with their worth, and so do a weaver and the rest.[696] Now in these cases, money is provided as a common measure, and so it is this, then, that everything is referred to and measured by.

In erotic friendships, however, the lover sometimes complains that while his own love is beyond measure he is not reciprocally loved (even when, as it happens, he has nothing lovable about him), whereas the boyfriend complains that his lover had earlier promised everything but now delivers nothing. These sorts of things happen when the lover loves the boy because of pleasure, whereas the boy loves him because of utility, and these are no longer possessed by both of them.[697] For when a friendship exists because of these, it is dissolved when the things for whose sake they loved do not occur. For it was not the parties themselves who were the objects of affection but their qualities, which were not steadfast. That is why such friendships are not steadfast either. But friendship of character, because it is intrinsic friendship, does endure, as we said.[698]

Disputes arise when the things the parties get are different and not what they desire, since it is like getting nothing at all when we do not get what we seek. Consider, for example, the man who promised a lyre player that the better he played the more he would get, but when dawn came and the lyre player asked for what the man had promised, the man said that he had given pleasure in return for pleasure.[699] Now if this was what each of them had wished, that would have been enough. But if one wished for delight, the other for profit, and the one has what he wished for while the other hasn't, matters conducing to their community will not be correctly arranged. For it is what each person happens to need that he is in fact intent on—at any rate, it is for this that he gives what he does.

Which of them, though, is to fix its worth, the one giving first or the one who has gotten first? For the one giving first would seem to turn it over to the other. This is precisely what they say Protagoras used to do.[700] For whenever he taught anything at all, he used to invite the learner to assess how much the things he got to have scientific knowledge of seemed to be worth and accepted that amount. But in cases like this, some people prefer the saying, "to a man his wage."[701] It makes perfect sense, though, that those who get the money first and then do none of the things they said they would do, because of the extreme nature of their promises, are subject to complaint, since they do not deliver what they agreed to. This, however, is what the sophists are presumably compelled to do, because no one would pay them money for what they do scientifically know.[702] So they take the wage, do not do what they said, and—as makes perfect sense—get involved in complaints. But where there is no contract of services to be rendered, those who, because of the other parties themselves, give first are not subject to complaint, as we said, since this is characteristic of friendship in accord with virtue.[703] And the payment for it should be in accord with deliberate choice, since this is characteristic of a friend and of virtue.[704] This, it seems, is also the way it should be when the parties have formed a community for the purposes of philosophy. For the worth of philosophy is not measured in money, nor will honor serve as its counterweight, but it is perhaps enough—as in the case of gods and parents—to do what we can.[705]

If the giving was not of this sort but with a view to some return, presumably the return should ideally be one that each of them thinks to be in accord with worth. But if they do not agree on this, it would seem to be not only necessary but also just that the one who got first should fix its worth. For if the other gets in return as much benefit as he did, or as much as he would have given for the pleasure, he will have gotten a worthy return.

Indeed, this is apparently what happens with buying and selling things. And in some places there are laws prohibiting judicial proceedings in voluntary transactions, on the supposition that we should dissolve a community with someone we trusted in the same way as we formed it.[706] For the law considers it more just for the person to whom something is turned over to fix its worth than for the person who turns it over to do so. For most things are not priced equally by those who have them and those who wish to get them, since to each party their own belongings and the things they give appear to be worth a lot. All the same, payment is made in whatever amount is fixed by the ones who get them. But presumably the price should not be what a thing appears to be worth once the getter has it but the price he put on it before he had it.

## IX 2

Puzzles also arise in cases of the following sort. Whether, for example, a person should allocate everything to his father and obey him in everything or put his trust in a doctor when he is sick and elect as a general someone capable in warfare.[707] Similarly, whether he should do a service for a friend rather than for an excellent person and return a favor to a benefactor rather than do one for a companion, if he cannot do both.

All such matters are difficult to determine with any exactness, aren't they? For they involve all sorts of differences both in greatness and smallness and in nobility and necessity.[708] But that we should not return everything to the same person is clear enough, and we should for the most part return benefactions rather than do a favor for a companion, just as we should repay a loan to the one to whom we owe it rather than give it to a companion.[709] But presumably not even this is always so—for example, should someone who has been ransomed from pirates ransom his ransomer in return, whoever he is (or if the latter has not been captured but is asking to be paid, repay him), or should he, rather, ransom his father? For it would seem that you should ransom your father rather than even yourself.

Well, that is precisely what we said: speaking in universal terms we should repay the debt, but if giving would greatly exceed repaying either in nobility or in necessity, we should incline toward that.[710] For sometimes even the return of a previous service is not equal to it, namely, when one party knows he is benefiting someone excellent, whereas the other would be returning it to someone he thinks is depraved. For sometimes you should not reciprocate by lending to someone who has lent to you. For he lent to you as someone who is decent, thinking he would be repaid, whereas you do not expect that you would be repaid by a wicked person. Therefore, if the situation is truly like that, the worth of the parties is not equal.[711] And even if it is not like that, but they think it is, what they do would not seem strange. So precisely as we have often said, accounts concerned with feelings and actions have the same determinateness as the things they are concerned with.[712]

That we should not repay everything to the same person nor everything to our father, just as we should not make all our sacrifices to Zeus, is clear enough. And since different things should be repaid to parents, brothers, companions, and benefactors, we should allocate to all what properly belongs to them and is fitting. And this is evidently what people in fact do. To weddings they invite their relatives, since these have a share in the family and so, then, in the actions that concern it. And funerals too, people think, should be attended by relatives more than anyone else, because of the same consideration.

It would seem, though, that in matters of sustenance we should assist our parents most, on the grounds of owing them this, and that it is a nobler thing to assist the causes of our existence in this way than to assist ourselves. And honor too, it would seem, we should give to our parents just as we should give it to the gods—but not every sort of honor. For we should not even give the same honor to a father as to a mother (or as to a wise person, moreover, or a general) but, rather, the paternal sort and the maternal sort respectively.

To all older people too we should give honor in accord with their age, by standing up, finding them a seat, and so on. With companions and brothers, on the other hand, we should be free speaking and share everything. And to relatives, fellow tribesmen, fellow citizens, and all the rest we should always try to allocate what properly belongs to them, and to make comparative judgments about the things accruing to each in accord with kinship, virtue, or use.

The comparative judgment is certainly easier with people of the same kind and harder work with those of different kinds. Yet we must not abandon the task because of this, at least, but, rather, to the extent possible make such determinations as far as we can.

## IX 3

There is also a puzzle about whether or not to dissolve friendships with those who do not remain the same. Or is there, as regards those who are friends because of utility or pleasure, nothing strange if the friendships are dissolved when they no longer have the relevant attributes? For it was because of these attributes that they were friends, and when these depart it is reasonable not to love. We might complain, though, if someone who liked us because of utility or pleasure pretended to do so because of our character. For, as we said at the start, most disputes arise between friends when the way in which they think they are friends is not the same as the way in which they are friends.[713]

Now when someone has deceived himself and supposed that he was being loved because of his character, although the other was doing nothing of the sort, he will hold himself responsible. But when he is deceived by the other's pretenses, he will be justified in complaining about his deceiver—more so even than about those who debase currency, inasmuch as his evildoing concerns something more estimable.

If we accept another person as a friend for being good, however, and then he becomes depraved and seems so, should we still love him? Or is that not possible, if indeed not everything is lovable but, rather, what is good?[714] What is wicked, by contrast, is neither lovable nor should be loved (for a lover of wickedness is something we must not be, nor must we become like a base person, and like, we said, is friend to like).[715] So should this sort of friendship be dissolved immediately? Or not in all cases but only when the friends are incurable in their depravity? If they do admit of rectification, we should aid them more with their character than with their property, inasmuch as that is a better thing and more properly belongs to friendship. A person who did dissolve such a friendship, however, would seem to be doing nothing strange, since it was not to a person of that sort that he was a friend. So when his friend has changed, and he is unable to restore him to what he was, he disclaims him.

But suppose one friend remained the same while the other became more decent and greatly different in virtue; should the second treat the first as a friend? Or can he not possibly do that? When the distance between them is large, the answer becomes most clear—for example, in children's friendships. For if one friend remained a child in thought while the other became a man of the best sort, how could they be friends, when they are neither satisfied with the same things nor find the same things enjoyable or painful? Not even with regard to each other, indeed, will this be so, and without it, as we saw, they cannot be friends, since they cannot share a life. But we have talked about these topics.[716]

Should the better person then behave no differently toward him than if he had never been his friend at all? Surely he should recall their former intimacy, and just as we think we should do a favor for friends rather than strangers, so we should allocate something to former friends too, because of our former friendship, when the dissolution does not occur because of extreme depravity.

## IX 4

|**1166a1**| The features fitted to friendships toward neighbors, and those definitive of the various sorts of friendship, seem to derive from the features of a person's friendship for himself. For [1] people take a friend to be someone who wishes and does what is good or is apparently good for another person's own sake or [2] who wishes his friend to exist and live for his own sake—just as mothers feel about their children and friends feel who are irritated with each other.[717] And [3] others take a friend to be someone who passes the time with his friend and [4] makes the same choices as he does or [5] suffers and enjoys together with him—this also happens most where mothers are concerned. It is by one or other of these features that people define friendship as well.

And each of these features is found in a decent person's relation to himself and in that of all other people insofar as they suppose themselves to be decent (but, as we said, virtue and the excellent person would seem to be the measure in each case).[718] For this sort of person is [4] of one mind with himself and desires the same things with all his soul, and [1] wishes, then, what is good to himself and what appears good, and does it (for it is characteristic of a good person to practice what is good) and does it for his own sake (for he does it for the sake of the thought-involving element in him, which is precisely what each of us seems to be).[719] Also, [2] he wishes himself to live and be preserved and, most of all, the element with which he thinks. For existence is a good thing for an excellent person, and each person wishes the good things to himself. But no one chooses, by becoming someone other than himself, to have everything (since even now the god has the good).[720] Rather, he chooses to have it while being whatever it is that he is. But each person would seem to be his understanding part, or it most of all.

And [3] such a person wishes to pass the time with himself, since he does so pleasantly. For his memories of what he has done are agreeable and his expectations for the future are good, and memories and expectations like that are pleasant. His thought too is well supplied with objects of contemplation. And [5] he, most of all people, suffers and is pleased together with himself, since it is always the same thing that is painful or pleasant, not different ones at different times, since he is, in a word, without regrets.[721]

A decent person, then, has each of these features [1–5] in relation to himself and is related to his friend as he is to himself, since his friend is another himself. In fact, friendship seems to be one or other of these features, and friends to be those who have them.

Whether there is or is not friendship to oneself, however, is a question we may set aside for the present.[722] There *would* seem to be friendship, though, insofar as a person is—from the features we mentioned—two or more, and in that the extreme of friendship resembles friendship to oneself.[723]

The features we mentioned, however, are apparently also found in ordinary people, base though they are. So is it only insofar as they are satisfied with themselves and suppose themselves to be decent that they share in these? Certainly no one who is altogether base and impious in his actions has them or even appears to do so.[724]

It is pretty much the case indeed that base people do not have them either, since they are at odds with themselves and, having an appetite for one set of things, wish for another, the way people who lack self-control do.[725] For instead of the things they themselves think to be good, they choose pleasant ones that are actually harmful, whereas others again, because of cowardice or idleness, shrink from doing the actions they think best for themselves. Those who have done many terrible actions because of their depravity hate and even flee from living, and ruin themselves.[726]

Besides, depraved people seek others with whom to spend their days but flee from themselves, since when they are by themselves they remember many repellant things and expect others like them in the future, whereas when they are with others they forget these. And since they have nothing lovable, they feel none of the things that are fitted to friendship toward themselves. Neither, then, do people like this enjoy or suffer together with themselves. For their soul is torn by faction, and one element in it, because of its depravity, suffers at being held back from certain things, whereas the other is pleased, and so one pulls this way and the other that, as if tearing him asunder.[727] And even if it is not possible to be pained and pleased at the same time, still after a bit he is pained that he was pleased and he wishes that these things had not become pleasant to him.[728] For base people are full of regret.

A base person, then, is apparently not so disposed as to be fitted for friendship even toward himself, because he has nothing lovable. If, then, to be very much that way is wretched, we should be intensely active in avoiding depravity and in striving to be decent, since that way a person will both be fitted for friendship to himself and become friend to another.

## IX 5

Goodwill seems to be a feature fitted to friendship, but friendship it is surely *not.* For goodwill arises even toward people we do not know and without their being aware of it, whereas friendship does not. We also said this before.[729] Nor is goodwill a way of loving.[730] For it does not include intensity of feeling or desire, whereas in the case of a way of loving these do follow along. Also, a way of loving involves intimacy, whereas goodwill can arise all of a sudden—as it does, for example, toward athletic contestants. For people come to have goodwill for them and to share in their wishes, but would never join in their actions. For people come to have goodwill all of a sudden, just as we said, and to feel an affection that is superficial.

Goodwill seems, then, to be a starting-point of friendship, just as the pleasure from sight is the starting-point of erotic love. For without first being pleased by the appearance of the other, no one falls in love, but someone who does enjoy another's appearance is none the more in love unless he also longs for the other when he is absent and has an appetite for his presence. In the same way too, then, it is not possible for people to be friends without first having goodwill, but those who have goodwill are none the more friends. For they only *wish* good things to those for whom they have goodwill but would never join in their actions or go to any trouble on their behalf.[731] Hence by transference of the term we might say that goodwill is inactive friendship, which—if it lasts through time and arrives at intimacy—becomes friendship.

This is not the friendship that exists because of utility, however, nor the one that exists because of pleasure, since even goodwill does not arise in the case of these.[732] For a person who has received a benefaction and allocates goodwill in return for what he has received does what is just. But a person who wishes another person to do well, expecting to get resources through him, seems to have goodwill not toward him but more toward himself, just as he is not a friend, either, if he takes care of another because of some use to be made of him.

Goodwill arises, on the whole, because of virtue and some sort of decency, when one person appears to another to be noble, brave, or something like that, just as in the case of the contestants we mentioned.[733]

## IX 6

Concord too is apparently a feature fitted to friendship. That is why it is not agreement in belief, since that might occur even among people who do not know each other. Nor are people said to be in concord when they are of one mind about just anything—for example, on matters related to the heavens (for concord concerning these is not fitted to friendship).[734] On the other hand, we do say that a city is in concord when people are of one mind about what is advantageous, deliberately choose the same things, and put into action the things they have resolved in common.

Things doable in action, then, is what concord is concerned with, and of these, the ones that have a certain magnitude and where it is possible for both or all parties to attain their goals. A city is in concord, for example, when all resolve to have offices be elective, to form an alliance with Sparta, or to have Pittacus rule (when he too is willing to do so).[735] But when each of the two parties wishes the rule for himself, like those in the *Phoenician Women*, they factionalize.[736] For it is not concord when each of the two parties thinks the same thing, whatever it may be, but, rather, when they think it in connection with the same party (for example, when both the common people and the decent ones think that the best people should rule), since that way all the parties get what they are seeking.[737] Concord is apparently political friendship, then, as it is in fact said to be, since it is concerned with things that are advantageous and ones that affect our life.[738]

This sort of concord is found among decent people, since they are in accord both with themselves and with others—out for the same things, in a word. For the wishes of such people are constant, not ebbing and flowing like a tidal race. They wish for just things as well as advantageous ones, and these they also seek in common.

Base people, however, cannot be in concord, except to a small extent, any more than they can be friends. For they seek a greedy share in benefits, but in labors and charitable services a deficient one. And since each one wishes these things to himself, he keeps an eye on his neighbor and stands in his way, with the excuse that if people do not keep watch, the common good gets ruined. The result is that they factionalize, compelling each other to do just things but not wishing to do them themselves.

## IX 7

Benefactors seem to love their beneficiaries more than those who have been benefited love the givers, and this is investigated on the supposition that it is contrary to reason for this to happen. Now to most people it appears that one lot are debtors whereas the other lot are creditors. Just as in the case of a loan, then, where debtors wish their creditors did not exist anymore, whereas creditors even take care to preserve the safety of their debtors, in the same way it is thought that benefactors wish their beneficiaries to exist as providers of gratitude, whereas the beneficiaries are careless about making the return. Now Epicharmus would perhaps claim that most people say this because "they are looking at the matter from a wicked point of view," yet it would seem to be a human one.[739] For ordinary people are forgetful and seek to receive benefits more than to confer them.

But the cause would seem be more deeply natural than that, and the case concerning creditors would seem to be not even a similar one.[740] For it does not involve a way of loving on their part but, rather, a wish to safeguard their debtors for the sake of recovering a debt. Benefactors, by contrast, love and like their beneficiaries even if they are of no use to them and will not become so later.

The very same happens in the case of craftsmen too, since all of them like their own work more than it would like them if it became ensouled. Perhaps this happens most where poets are concerned, since they have an excessive liking for their own poems, feeling affection for them as for |**1168a1**| children.

This, then, is the sort of case that the one of the benefactors actually resembles, since the fact that someone has been benefited is their work. It, then, they like more than the work does its producer. The cause of this is the following: existence is lovable and choiceworthy for everyone; we *are* when in activity (since we *are* by living and doing actions); and the work is in a way the producer when in activity. He feels affection for his work, then, because he feels affection for existence too. And this *is* natural, since what he is in capacity, his work is when in activity.[741]

At the same time, to the benefactor what is in accord with his action is noble, so that he enjoys the person in whom it occurs.[742] The person acted on, by contrast, finds nothing noble in the agent, but if anything, something advantageous, and this is less pleasant and less lovable.

What is pleasant, however, when it belongs to the present is activity; when it belongs to the future is expectation; and when it belongs to the past is memory. But what is most pleasant—and similarly most lovable—is what is in accord with activity. Now for the person who has produced something, his work endures (since what is noble is long lasting), whereas for the person acted on, the utility passes away.[743] As for memory, that of noble things is pleasant too, whereas that of useful ones is scarcely pleasant at all or less so; although the reverse would seem to hold of expectation. Also, loving something in some way is like producing something, whereas being loved is like having something done to you. And it is the partner who exceeds where action is concerned who—it is entailed—loves something and has the features fitted to friendship.

Further, everyone feels more affection for those things that come about by his painful labor—for example, in the case of money, those who have made it more than those who have inherited it. To be benefited, though, seems to involve no painful labor, whereas to confer benefits seems like hard work. It is also because of these factors that mothers are the more child loving ones.[744] For giving birth involves more painful labor, and they know better that the children are their own. This feature too seems to properly belong to benefactors.

## IX 8

There is also a puzzle about whether a person should love himself most or someone else. For people admonish those who like themselves most, calling them "self-lovers," on the supposition that this is actually something shameful. It seems too that a base person does all his actions for the sake of himself, and the more depraved he is the more he does so—people complain, therefore, that he "does nothing from himself."[745] A decent person, by contrast, seems to act because of what is noble, and the better he is the more he does so, and for the sake of a friend, disregarding his own interests.

With these accounts, however, our results clash, which is not surprising.[746] For the results say that we should love most the one who is most a friend, and the one who is most a friend is the one who wishes good things to the person he wishes them to for that person's own sake, even if no one will know. But these features are found most in a person's relations to himself, as of course are all the others by which a friend is defined. For, as we said, it is from oneself that all the features fitted to friendship also extend to others. All the proverbs are of one mind about this as well—for example, "one soul," and "what friends have they have in common," and "equality is friendship," and "knee is closer than shin."[747] For all these things are found most in a person's relations to himself. For he is a friend to himself most of all, and should, then, love himself most.

It is reasonable to be puzzled, then, as to which side we should follow, since both carry conviction. Now presumably in cases like these we need to draw distinctions in connection with the arguments and determine to what extent and in what ways they grasp the truth. If, then, we were to find out what those on each side mean by "self-love," perhaps that would be clear.

Now those who reduce it to a term of reproach call "self-lovers" those who allocate to themselves the greater share in money, honors, and bodily pleasures. For these are the things ordinary people desire and take seriously, on the supposition that they are the best goods—which is why they are fought about.[748] Those people, then, who are greedy where these things are concerned gratify their appetites and their feelings and the nonrational part of the soul generally. And ordinary people are like this, which is why the term has come about, deriving from the most ordinary case, which really is a base one.[749] Those who are self-lovers in this way, then, *are* justly objects of reproach.

That it is those who allocate goods of this sort to themselves that most people are used to calling "self-lovers" is clear enough. For if someone were always taking more seriously than anything else the doing of just actions or temperate ones or whatever else might be in accord with the virtues, and in general were always keeping for himself what was noble, no one would call *this* person a "self-lover" or blame him.

A person of this sort, though, would seem to be *more* of a self-lover. At any rate, he allocates to himself the good things that are noblest and the ones that are best of all and gratifies the element in himself that has most control, obeying it in everything.[750] But just as a city too or any other complex system, seems to be most of all its most controlling part, so also does a human being.[751] A person is most of all a self-lover, then, who likes this part and gratifies this part.

Also, a person is called "self-controlled" or "lacking in self-control" depending on whether or not his understanding is in control, on the supposition that this is what each person *is*, and it is actions involving reason that people seem most of all to do themselves and to do voluntarily.[752] **1169a1** So it is clear enough that this part is what each person is or is most of all and that a decent person likes this part most.[753]

That is why a decent person is most of all a self-lover, but of a different form than the one that is reproached and differing from it as much as living in accord with reason does from living in accord with feeling and as much as desiring what is noble does from desiring what seems advantageous.[754]

Those, then, who *par excellence* take seriously the doing of noble actions are welcomed and praised by everyone. And if everyone competed for what is noble and strived to do the noblest actions, everything would be as it should as regards the common good, and each person as an individual would have the greatest of goods, if indeed virtue is such. And so a good person should be a self-lover (for by doing noble actions he will both profit himself and benefit others), whereas a depraved person should not be one (for he will harm both himself and his neighbors, since he follows his base feelings).

For a depraved person, the things he should do clash with the ones he does, whereas the things a decent person should do are the very ones he does. For every understanding chooses what is best for itself, and a decent person obeys his understanding.[755]

It is true of an excellent person too that he does many actions for the sake of his friends and his fatherland, even dying for them if need be. For he will give up wealth, honors, and fought-about goods generally, in keeping for himself what is noble. For he will choose intense pleasure for a short time over weak pleasure for a long one; living life nobly for a year over many years lived in random fashion; and a single noble and great action over many small ones. This is presumably what happens with those who die for others. They are choosing, then, something of great nobility for themselves. And they will give up wealth on the condition that their friends get more. For while the friend gets wealth, the excellent person himself gets what is noble. The greater good, then, he allocates to himself.

Where honors and ruling offices are concerned he is the same way. For he will give up all these for his friend, since this is noble and praiseworthy for himself. It makes perfect sense, then, that he seems excellent, choosing as he does what is noble before anything else. It may be that he will even give up actions in favor of his friend, however, since it may be nobler to become the cause of his friend's doing the action than to do the action himself.

In the case of every praiseworthy thing, then, an excellent person evidently allocates the greater share of what is noble to himself. In this way, then, we should be self-lovers, as we said.[756] But in the way ordinary people are, we shouldn't.

## IX 9

There is also a dispute regarding a happy person as to whether he will need friends or not. For people say that those who are blessed and self-sufficient have no need of friends, since they already have the things that are good, and being self-sufficient, then, they need nothing in addition, whereas a friend, being another yourself, provides the things that you are unable to provide by yourself. Whence the saying, "When your *daimôn* does well by you, what need of friends?"[757]

It seems strange, though, to allocate all the good things to a happy person and yet not to grant him friends, who seem to be the greatest of external goods.[758] And if it is more characteristic of a friend to confer benefits than to receive them, and if it is characteristic of a good person and of virtue to do the benefiting, and if it is nobler to confer benefits on friends than on strangers, an excellent person will need people to receive his benefits. That is also why the question is asked about whether it is in good fortune that friends are needed more or in bad fortune, on the supposition that in times of bad fortune we need benefactors and in times of good fortune people to confer benefits on.[759]

It is presumably strange too to make a blessed person live a solitary life, since no one would choose to have every good thing yet be by himself, since a human being is a political being and one whose nature is to live with others.[760] To one who is happy, then, this also applies, since he has the natural goods.[761] But clearly it is better to spend his days with friends and decent people than with strangers and random ones. Hence a happy person does need friends.

What, then, are the first lot claiming and in what way are they grasping the truth?[762] Or is it that ordinary people think friends are those who are useful? Well, of friends of this sort, a blessed person *will* have no need, since he already has the things that are good. Nor, then, will he need (or only to a small extent) the ones who are friends because of pleasure (for his life, being pleasant, has no need of adventitious pleasure).[763] So since they do not need friends of these sorts, they seem not to need friends at all.

But this is presumably not true. For we said at the start that happiness is a sort of activity, and an activity is clearly something that comes to be and does not belong to us like some possession.[764] But if being happy lies in living and engaging in activity, and if the activity characteristic of a good person is intrinsically excellent and pleasant (as we said at the start), and if things that are properly our own are among the things that are pleasant, and if we are better able to contemplate our neighbors than ourselves and their actions than those that are properly our own, then the actions of excellent people who are their friends are pleasant to good people (since they have both the features that make them naturally pleasant).[765] A blessed person, then, will need friends of this sort, if indeed he deliberately chooses to contemplate decent actions that are properly his own, and the actions of a good person who is a friend are like this.[766]

People think too that a happy person must be living pleasantly. Well, for a solitary person life is difficult, since it is not easy for him, when all by himself, to be continuously in activity, whereas together with others and in relation to others it is easier.[767] His activity will be more continuous, then, since it is intrinsically pleasant, as it must be where a blessed person is concerned.[768] For an excellent person, insofar as he is excellent, enjoys actions that are in accord with virtue but is repelled by those that stem from vice, just as a musician enjoys noble melodies and is pained by those that are base. A sort of training in virtue also comes about from living together with good people, as Theognis says.[769]

If we investigate the matter from a more deeply natural point of view, an excellent friend seems to be naturally choiceworthy for an excellent person, since, as we said, what is naturally good is intrinsically good and pleasant for an excellent person.[770] Now living is defined in the case of animals by a capacity for perception and in the case of human beings by a capacity for perception or understanding, but a capacity is brought back to its activity, so that the full thing resides in the activity.[771] Living in the full sense, then, seems to be perceiving or understanding. Living, however, is among the things that are intrinsically good and pleasant, since it is something determinate, and being determinate is characteristic of the nature of the good.[772] And what is naturally good is also good for a decent person, which is why living seems pleasant to everyone. (But we should not take as an example a way of living that is depraved and ruinous or one spent in pain, since living like that is indeterminate as are the attributes that belong to it. In what follows, however, matters concerning pain will be made clearer.)[773]

But if living itself is good and pleasant (as it seems to be from the very fact that everyone desires it, and decent and blessed people most of all, since for them life is more choiceworthy and living more blessed), and if a person who sees perceives that he sees and one who hears perceives that he hears and one who walks perceives that he walks, and if in the other cases too there is similarly something that perceives that we are in activity, so that if we are perceiving, we perceive that we are perceiving; and if we are understanding, we are perceiving that we are understanding; and if perceiving that we are perceiving or understanding is perceiving that we are existing (since existing, we said, consists in perceiving or understanding) and if perceiving that we are living is one of the things that is intrinsically pleasant (since living is something naturally good, and perceiving what is good to be present in ourselves is pleasant) and if living is choiceworthy and most so for good people, because for them existing is good and pleasant (for they take pleasure in being co-perceivers of what is intrinsically good) and if in the way an excellent person is related to himself he is also related to his friend (since a friend is another himself), then just as his own existing is choiceworthy for each one, so—or to much the same extent—is that of his friend too.[774] But, as we saw, his existence is choiceworthy because he perceives himself as being good, and such perceiving is intrinsically pleasant. He must, then, also co-perceive his friend existing, something that comes about in their living together and sharing in talk and thought, since this is what living together would seem to mean in the case of human beings and not, as in the case of cattle, grazing in the same place.

If, then, his existing is intrinsically choiceworthy for the blessed person (since it is naturally good and pleasant), as to much the same extent is that of his friend, his friend too will be among the things that are choiceworthy. But what is choiceworthy for him he must have, or else he will be in this respect lacking.[775] Hence someone who is to be happy will need friends who are excellent.

## IX 10

Should we, then, make as many friends as possible? Or, as in the case of guest-friendship, where it has been appropriately said, it seems, that we should be "neither many-guest-friended nor guest-friendless," is it the case in friendship too that it is appropriate to be neither friendless nor excessively many-friended?[776]

With friends made with a view to utility, then, the saying would seem to be entirely appropriate, since to reciprocate many people's services is a laborious task and a lifetime is not enough to do so. More of them, then, than are enough for our own life are superfluous and a hindrance to living in a noble way. So we have no need of them. As for friends made with a view to pleasure, a few are sufficient, just like seasoning in food.

But what about excellent people? Should we have as many as possible as friends or is there some measure for the number of friends, as there is for the number of people in a city? (For a city cannot come about from ten people, and if there are ten times ten thousand, it is a city no longer.[777]) Presumably, though, the number is not a single number, but, rather, anything between certain determinate limits. Of friends too, then, there is a determinate number—perhaps the largest number a person could be living together with (since living together, we found, is most fitted to friendship).[778]

That a person cannot both live together with a large number of people and parcel out himself among them is clear enough. Furthermore, they too must be friends with each other, if all of them are going to be spending their days together, but this is hard work in a large group. It is also difficult for a large number of people to enjoy together and suffer together as if they were each other's own kin, since it is likely that being pleased together with one person and grieving together with another will both occur at the same time. Presumably, then, it is well not to seek to be too many-friended, but, rather, to have just as many friends as are enough for the purposes of living together. For it would not seem even possible to be extremely friendly with a large number of people, which is why we cannot be in love with more than one person. For erotic love wants to be a sort of excessive form of friendship, and that excess is toward one person.[779] Intense friendship, then, will be toward few.

This also seems to be confirmed by the things themselves. For it just does not happen that many people become friends in accord with companionate friendship, and the ones that are celebrated in song are between two people. Those who are many-friended, and treat everyone they meet as if they were their own kin, seem to be friends with no one, except in a political way—in fact, people call them "ingratiating."[780] In a political way, certainly, it is possible to be a friend to many people and yet not be ingratiating but, rather, truly decent. But to be a friend to many people because of virtue and because of the people themselves, is not possible, and it should content us to find even a few friends like that.

## IX 11

Do we need friends more in good fortune or in bad?[781] For they are sought after in both, since the unfortunate need assistance and the fortunate need people to share a life with and to benefit, since they wish to do well. Friendship is more necessary, then, in bad fortune, which is why useful friends are needed there. But it is more noble in good fortune, which is why we also seek decent friends, since it is more choiceworthy to confer benefactions on them and pass the time with them.

In fact, even the very presence of friends is pleasant in good fortune and in bad too, since our pain is alleviated when friends share our suffering. That is why someone might even be puzzled about whether they, as it were, share our burden, or whether—without this happening—the pleasantness of their presence and the thought of their sharing our suffering lessens the pain. Whether it is indeed because of these factors or because of something else that the alleviation occurs is a puzzle we may set aside. At any rate, what we have described evidently does happen.

It seems, though, that their presence is a sort of mixture of things. For the very seeing of friends is pleasant, most of all in misfortune, and comes as a sort of |**1171b1**| assistance aiming at our not feeling pain (for a friend is someone who consoles us, both by the sight of him and by his words, if he is dexterous, since he knows our character and the things that please and pain us).[782] But to see him pained at our misfortunes is painful, since everyone tries to avoid being a cause of pain to his friends. That is why people with a manly nature are wary of making their friends share their pain. And if he does not go to extremes in his painlessness, a manly person cannot endure the pain that ensues for them and in general does not allow fellow mourners, because he is not himself prone to mourning.[783] But the weaker sex and men who are like them enjoy having people to weep with and love them as friends who share their suffering. It is clear, though, that we should imitate the better person in everything.

In good fortune, by contrast, the presence of friends brings with it both a pleasant way of passing the time and the pleasant thought that they are pleased at the good things that are ours. That is why it would seem that we should eagerly invite our friends to share our good fortunes (since to be a ready benefactor is a noble thing), but be hesitant to invite them to share our misfortunes, since we should share bad things as little as possible—whence the saying, "my own misfortunes are enough."[784] We should most of all summon our friends to our aid, however, when with little trouble to themselves they are likely to benefit us greatly.

Conversely, it is presumably fitting to go uninvited to the aid of those in misfortune and to do so eagerly (since it is characteristic of a friend to confer benefits, most of all on those who are in need and have laid no claim to them, since this is nobler and pleasanter for both parties). But when they are enjoying good fortune, though we should go eagerly when it is a matter of co-working (since they need friends for this too), we should do so in a leisurely fashion when there are benefits to be received, since it is not a noble thing to be eager to receive benefits. On the other hand we should presumably be wary of getting a reputation for unpleasantness by rejecting them (which indeed sometimes happens).

The presence of friends, then, is apparently choiceworthy in all circumstances.

## IX 12

Now what those who are in love like most is the sight of the beloved, and choose this sort of perception over all the rest on the supposition that their love depends most on it for its existence and it coming to be. Hence isn't it that way with friends too, so that living together is most choiceworthy? For friendship is a community, and as a person is related to himself, so he is related to his friend as well. Where he himself is concerned, however, the perception that he exists is choiceworthy; so too, then, is the perception of his friend's existence. But this perception's activity comes about in living together, so it makes perfect sense that this is what friends seek.

And no matter what existing consists in for each sort of person, no matter what they choose to be living for the sake of, it is *this* they wish to pass their time doing in company with their friends. That is why some drink together, some play dice together, while others train together, hunt together, or do philosophy together, each sort spending their days together in whatever they most like in life. For since they wish to be living together with their friends, they do these actions and share in these things in which they think living together consists.[785]

The friendship of base people, then, turns out to be depraved, for they share in things that are base, being unstable, and become depraved too by becoming like each other.[786] The friendship of decent people, by contrast, is decent and increases along with their social interaction by its own increase. And they even seem to become better by being active and correcting each other, since they take on the imprint of those things in each other that they find pleasing—whence the saying "From noble people noble things."[787]

So much to be said for friendship, then. The next thing we should discuss is pleasure.

# Book X

## X 1

The next topic we should discuss is, presumably, pleasure.[788] For it seems to be most intimately attached to our kind, which is why those who educate the young steer them by means of pleasure and pain.[789] And it seems too that with regard to virtue of character the biggest thing is enjoying what we should and hating what we should. For these extend throughout the whole of a person's life and have a powerful influence with regard to both virtue and the happy life, since people deliberately choose pleasant things and avoid painful ones.

Topics like this, then, would seem to be ones we should least omit to discuss, since they most admit of much dispute.[790] For some say that pleasure is the good, whereas others, on the contrary, say that it is altogether bad—some presumably because they are convinced that this is how things actually are, others because they think it is better as regards our life to represent pleasure as a bad thing even if it isn't (for ordinary people, they think, incline toward it and are slaves to pleasures, which is why we should lead them in the contrary direction, since in that way they will arrive at the mean).[791]

But surely this is not the correct thing to say. For accounts of matters that lie in the sphere of actions and feelings carry less conviction than the facts, and so when they clash with what is in accord with the perceptible facts, they are despised and undermine the truth as well.[792] For if someone who puts the blame on pleasure is ever seen seeking it, he is taken to be inclining toward it as if, to him, every sort of pleasure was to be sought. For it is not characteristic of ordinary people to make distinctions.

It is true accounts, then, that seem to be most useful, not only with regard to knowledge but also with regard to our life. For since they are in tune with the facts, they carry conviction, and so they encourage those who comprehend them to live in accord with them.

Enough, then, of such issues. Let us move on to the things that have been said about pleasure.

## X 2

Now Eudoxus thought that pleasure is the good, because he saw all things, both rational and nonrational, seeking it, and because he thought that in all cases what is choiceworthy is what is decent and that what is most so is what is most excellent.[793] The fact, then, that all are drawn toward the same thing, indicated, he thought, that this is the best good for all of them (since each finds its own good as it finds its own food) and that what is good for all of them and what all of them seek is *the* good. His accounts carried conviction, though, more because of his virtuous character than because of the accounts themselves, since he seemed to be exceedingly temperate. It was not, then, as a friend of pleasure that he seemed to say what he said but because things were truly that way.

He thought that the matter was no less evident from the contrary, since for all things pain is intrinsically something to be avoided. Similarly, then, its contrary must be choiceworthy. And what is most choiceworthy is what we choose neither because of something else nor for the sake of something else, and pleasure is agreed to be like that. For nobody asks a person "For the sake of what are you getting pleasure?"—the supposition being that pleasure is intrinsically choiceworthy. Moreover, he argued that when pleasure is added to any other good (for example, acting justly or being temperate) it makes it more choiceworthy and that the good is only increased by the addition of itself.

It would seem, then, that this last argument, at least, represents pleasure as *a* good, and no more a good than any other. For every good is more choiceworthy when it is accompanied by another good than when it is on its own. It is by an argument of this sort indeed that Plato tries to confute the view that pleasure is the good.[794] For he argues that the pleasant life is more choiceworthy with the addition of wisdom than without it, and that if the mixture is more excellent, pleasure is not *the* good, since there is nothing which, when added to the good, makes *it* more choiceworthy.[795] And it is clear that nothing else will be the good, either, if it is made more choiceworthy by the addition of any intrinsic good.

What, then, is there that is like this and that we share in?[796] It is this sort of thing we are looking for.

Those on the other hand, who object to Eudoxus' argument by saying that what all seek is not good, are surely talking nonsense (for things that seem to be so to everyone, these, we say, are).[797] And a person who confutes this |1173b1| conviction about the goodwill scarcely have anything more convincing to say. For if it is creatures without understanding that desire these things, what they say would make sense, but if it is also wise ones, how could it make sense? But perhaps even in base creatures there is some naturally good element, more excellent than themselves, which seeks the good that properly belongs to them.[798]

It does not seem that the point about the contrary is correctly put either. For they say that if pain is a bad thing, it does not follow that pleasure is a good one, since bad is also opposed to bad, and both bad and good to what is neither. In saying this, they are not wrong, but in the case of the things at issue, at least, they are not speaking the truth either. For if both pleasure and pain were bad things, they would both also have to be things to be avoided, and if both were neither good nor bad, neither would have to be avoided or both would have to be similarly so. As it is, though, it is evident that people avoid pain as a bad thing and choose pleasure as a good one. This, then, must be the way they are opposed.

## X 3

Again, it does not follow, either, that if pleasure is not a quality, it is not a good either. For virtuous activities are not qualities, nor is happiness.

But they say that the good is determinate, whereas pleasure is indeterminate because it admits of degree.[799] Now if it is from people's being pleased that they discern this, the same will apply to justice and the other virtues, where we plainly say that people have more or less of these qualities and do their action in ways that are more or less in accord with the virtues (for people can be more or less just or courageous, and doing just actions and being intemperate also admit of degree). If, on the other hand, they discern it from the various pleasures, surely they are not stating the real cause, if indeed some pleasures are unmixed, others mixed.[800]

Again, what would prevent us from saying that just as health, while it is determinate, admits of degree, so it is for pleasure as well? For neither does the same proportion exist in everyone nor is there always some single proportion in the same person, but it may be loosened and yet remain present up to a point and so differ in degree.[801] It is possible, then, for the same sort of thing to hold where pleasure is concerned.

Again, by regarding the good as complete, but processes and comings to be as incomplete, they try to represent pleasure as a process and a coming to be.[802] But they do not seem to be correct even in saying that it is a process, since fastness and slowness seem to properly belong to every process—if not in relation to itself (as, for example, in the case of the universe), then in relation to something else.[803] To pleasure, by contrast, neither of these belongs. For while we can *become* pleased quickly, as we can become angry quickly, we cannot *be* pleased quickly, not even in relation to something else, whereas we can walk quickly, grow quickly, and the like. So while it is possible to change quickly (or slowly) to the state of being pleased, it is not possible to be active in relation to that state—I mean, to be pleased—quickly.

Again, how could pleasure be a coming to be? For it seems that one random thing does not come to be out of another random thing, but, rather, what a thing comes to be out of is what it is dissolved into, and so what pleasure is the coming to be of, pain would be the ruin of.[804] They also say, though, that pain is the lack of what is in accord with nature, and pleasure its replenishment.[805] And these feelings are bodily. If, then, pleasure is replenishment of what is in accord with nature, that in which the replenishment is found will also be what is being pleased— hence, the body. But it does not seem to be. Hence the replenishment is not pleasure, although someone would be pleased when the replenishing takes place, just as he would be pained when the cutting does.[806] This belief seems to be in accord with pains and pleasures connected with nourishment, since when people have developed a lack, and so an antecedent feeling of pain, they are pleased by the replenishment.[807] This does not happen in connection with all pleasures, however, since those of learning are without pain as—in the case of the pleasures of perception—are those arising through smell, and many sounds, sights, memories, and expectations are like that as well.[808] Of what, then, will they be comings to be? For no lack of something has developed of which they are the replenishment.

In reply to those who cite the disgraceful pleasures, we might say that these are not pleasant either (for if they are pleasant to people in a bad condition, we should not think that they are pleasant, except to these people, any more than we should think that things that are healthy or sweet or bitter to sick people are such, except to them, or again that things are white that appear so to people with an eye disease).[809]

Or else we might say that pleasures are choiceworthy but not from these sources, just as wealth is choiceworthy but not from treachery, and health but not from eating anything and everything.

Or perhaps pleasures differ in form, since those from noble sources are different from those from shameful ones, and we cannot feel the pleasures of a just person without being just; or those of a musician without being a musician; and similarly in the other cases.

The fact too that a friend is different from a flatterer seems to make it manifest that pleasure is not a good or that pleasures differ in form. For it is with a view to the good that a friend seems to engage in social interaction with us, whereas a flatterer does so with a view to pleasure. Also, a flatterer is reproached, whereas a friend—on the grounds that he engages in social interaction with us with a view to different things—is praised.

Also, no one would choose to live possessing a child's level of thought throughout his life, even if he were to take the fullest possible pleasure in the things children take pleasure in or to get enjoyment from doing some utterly shameful action, even if he were never going to suffer any pain. Moreover, there are many things we would consider excellent even if they brought no pleasure—for example, seeing, remembering, knowing, and possessing the virtues. But if these things necessarily entail pleasures, that makes no difference, since we would choose them even if no pleasure resulted from them.

That pleasure is not the good, then, seems to be clear, as does the fact that not every pleasure is choiceworthy and that some pleasures, being different from the others in form or in their sources, are intrinsically choiceworthy.

Enough, then, for the things said about pleasure and pain.

## X 4

What pleasure is or what sort of thing it is will become more evident if we take up the question again from the start. For seeing seems at any time to be complete, since it does not lack anything whose coming to be at a later time will complete its form.[810] Pleasure also seems to be like this. For it is some sort of whole, and we can at no given time find a pleasure that by coming to be for a longer time will have its form completed.

That is why pleasure is not a process either. For every process (for example, building) is in time and relates to some end and is complete when it has produced what it seeks to produce—in other words, in this whole time that it takes.[811] And all processes are incomplete in their parts (and during the corresponding time), which differ in form both from the whole process and from each other. For putting together the stones is different from fluting the column, and both of these are different from producing the temple. Also, the production of the temple is a complete production, since it lacks nothing as regards what was proposed. The production of the foundation and of the triglyph, though, are incomplete, since each is the production of a part.[812] They differ in form, then, and it is not possible during any part of the time taken to find a process that is complete in form, but if indeed such a process is to be found, it is in the whole time taken.

Similarly too in the case of walking and the rest. For if locomotion is a process of moving from one place to another, there are differences in form here as well—flying, walking, leaping, and so on. And not only that but there are also differences in walking itself, since the from-where and to-where are not the same in a whole stadium racecourse as they are in a part of it or the same in one part as in another; nor is traversing this line the same as traversing that one, since we do not travel only along a line but also along one that is in a certain place, and this place is different from that.[813] Well, we have discussed "process" in an exact way in other places, and it does seem that it is not complete at every time but, rather, that its many sub-processes are incomplete and different in form, if indeed the from-where and to-where constitute their form.[814]

Of pleasure, by contrast, the form is complete at every time whatsoever. So it is clear that movement and pleasure are different from each other and that pleasure is something whole and complete. This would also seem to follow from the fact that it is not possible to be in process and not take time, but it is possible to be pleased, since what occurs in the "now" is a sort of whole.[815] From these considerations it is also clear that it is not correct to say, as people do, that there is a process or a coming to be *of* pleasure, since these are not said of everything but only of things that are divisible into parts and are not wholes.[816] For there is no coming to be of seeing, either, or of a point or of a unit, nor is any of these a process or a coming to be. Of pleasure too, then, there is neither of these, since it is a sort of whole.

Since every perceptual capacity is active in relation to its perceptible object, and completely so when it is in good condition in relation to the noblest of its perceptible objects (for a complete activity seems to be most of all something of this sort, but whether it is the perceptual capacity itself that is said to be active or the subject that perceptual capacity is in makes no difference), in the case of each perceptual capacity, the best activity will be, then, the activity of the subject that is in the best condition in relation to the most excellent of its objects. And this activity will be the most complete and most pleasant. For with every perceptual capacity there is a pleasure connected, and the same holds for both thought and contemplation. But the most pleasant is the most complete, and the most complete is the activity of a subject that is in good condition in relation to the most excellent of the relevant objects. And pleasure is what completes the activity.[817]

But pleasure does not complete it in the way that the perceptible object and the perceptual capacity do when they are both excellent, just as health and a doctor are not in the same way a cause of being healthy.[818]

(That it is in connection with each of the perceptual capacities that pleasure arises is clear, since we say that sights and sounds are pleasant. It is clear too that it does so most when the perceptual capacity is at its best and is active in relation to an object that is in the same condition. And when the perceptual capacity and the object being perceived are in conditions like that, there will always be pleasure, so long, at any rate, as what will produce the effect and what will be affected are both present.)

And pleasure completes an activity not as the state does by being present in something but as a sort of supervenient end, like the bloom on men in their prime of youth.[819] So long, then, as the intelligible object or the perceptible one and what discerns or contemplates are as they should be, there will be pleasure in the activity.[820] For when what is affected |**1175a1**| and the thing producing the effect are similar and keep in the same relation to each other, the same thing naturally arises.

How is it, then, that no one is pleased continuously? Or is it that we get tired? For continuous activity is impossible for all things human. So no continuous pleasure arises either, since it is entailed by the activity. Some things delight us when they are novelties, but later delight us less, because of the same thing. For at first thought is called forth and is intensely active regarding them, as happens in the case of our sight when we look hard at something, but later the activity is no longer like that but has grown relaxed, so that the pleasure is dimmed as well.

Pleasure's being desired by everyone, we might think, is due to the fact that everyone also seeks to live. And living is a sort of activity, and each person is active in relation to those things and with those things that he likes most—for example, a musician is active with his hearing in relation to melodies and a lover of learning is so with his thought in relation to objects of contemplation, and so on for each of the others. And pleasure completes the activities and hence it completes living, which is something people find desirable. So it is quite reasonable that they seek pleasure too, since for each person it completes living, which is something choiceworthy.

But whether we choose living because of pleasure, or pleasure because of living—this is something we may set aside for the present, since the two appear to be coupled together and not to admit of separation, since without activity pleasure does not arise, and every activity too is completed by pleasure.[821]

## X 5

This is why pleasures seem to differ in form as well. For we think that things that differ in form are completed by different things (since this is apparently what happens both with natural things and with the products of craft—for example, animals, trees, a painting, a sculpture, a house, or a vessel) and, similarly, that activities that differ in form are completed by things that differ in form.

Activities of thought, however, differ in form from those of the perceptual capacities, and both differ in form among themselves. So too, then, do the pleasures that complete them. This is also evident from the fact that each of the pleasures is intimately attached to the activity it completes, since the pleasure that properly belongs to it increases the activity by its own increase.[822] For we discern each thing better and treat it with greater exactness when the activity involves pleasure; for example, those who enjoy geometry become true geometers and understand each aspect of it better and, similarly, those who are lovers of music or building or whatever it is—each makes advances in their own work by finding enjoyment in it. And so the pleasures increase the activities by their own increase. But what increases something by its own increase properly belongs to that thing, and to things that differ in form, things that also differ in form properly belong.

This will be even more evident, however, from the fact that activities are impeded by pleasures arising from other sources. For lovers of flute music are incapable of paying attention to a discussion if they happen to overhear someone playing the flute, since they enjoy flute playing more than the activity at hand. So the pleasure connected with flute playing ruins the activity related to discussion.

This also happens in a similar way in other cases, when we are involved in two activities at the same time. For the more pleasant activity knocks out the other one, and all the more so if the difference in pleasure is large, to the point where we no longer engage in the other activity. That is why when we enjoy something intensely we scarcely do anything else, but do indeed do other things when only mildly pleased—for example, people who eat sweets in theaters do so most when the actors are bad.

And since the pleasure that properly belongs to an activity makes it more exact, longer lasting, and better, whereas alien pleasures spoil it, it is clear that they differ widely. For alien pleasures do pretty much what proper pains do, since the pains that properly belong to activities ruin them—for example, if painting or rationally calculating is unpleasant and painful for someone, he does not write or rationally calculate, because the activity is painful. An activity is affected in contrary ways, then, by the pleasures and pains that properly belong to it—the ones that properly belong being the ones that supervene on the activity by itself. As for the alien pleasures, we said that they have very much the same effect as pain, since they ruin the activity, only not in the same way.

Since activities differ in decency and baseness, however, and some are choiceworthy, some to be avoided, and some neither, the same goes for pleasures as well, since for each activity there is a pleasure that properly belongs to it. So the pleasure that properly belongs to an excellent activity is decent, and the one that properly belongs to a base activity is depraved. For appetites too are praiseworthy when they are for noble activities and blameworthy when for shameful ones. And the pleasures that are in the activities more properly belong to these than do the corresponding desires. For the desires are distinguished from the activities both in time and in nature, whereas the pleasures are closely related to the activities and so little distinguished from them that disputes arise as to whether the activity and the pleasure are not the same thing. Still, pleasure does not seem to be thought or to be perception (since that would be strange), but, rather, because it is not found separated, it appears to some people to be the same as them.[823]

Just as activities differ, then, so too do the corresponding pleasures. Sight differs from touch in purity, however, as hearing and smell do from taste. The pleasures, then, also differ in the same way, as the pleasures of thought do from these, and as, within each of the two, some do from others.

Each sort of animal, though, seems to have a pleasure that properly belongs to it, just as it does a function; I mean the pleasure that is in accord with its activity. This will also become evident if we look at each.[824] For horse, dog, and human being have different pleasures, and, as Heraclitus says, "donkeys prefer sweepings to gold," since food is more pleasant to donkeys than gold.[825] So animals that differ in form also have pleasures that differ in form, and if they are the same in form, it is quite reasonable to expect their pleasures not to be different.

But in the case of human beings, at any rate, they do vary quite a lot, since the same things delight some people and give pain to others, and while to some they are painful and hateful, to others they are pleasant and lovable. This also happens in the case of sweet things. For the same things do not seem sweet to a feverish person and to a healthy one, or hot to a weak person and to one in good physical condition. And the same thing happens in other cases.

In all such cases, however, it seems that what *is* so is what appears so to an excellent person. And if this is correct, as it seems to be, and it is virtue and a good person (insofar as he is such) that are the measure of each thing, then pleasures will be those that appear to be pleasures to him, and the things that are pleasant will be the ones that he enjoys. But if the things he finds repellant seem pleasant to someone, it is no wonder, since there are many ways for human beings to get ruined or spoiled. Pleasant, however, these things are not, except to these people and to people in this condition. It is clear, then, that pleasures agreed to be shameful should be said not to be pleasures at all, except to people who have been ruined.

Of those pleasures that seem to be decent, however, which sort or which particular one should we say is characteristic of a human being? Or isn't this clear from the corresponding activities, since the pleasures are entailed by these? So whether the activities of a complete and blessed man are one or more than one, the pleasures that complete these will be said to be characteristically human pleasures in the full sense, and the rest will be so in a secondary or many-times-removed way, as are the activities.

## X 6

Now that we have discussed matters concerning the virtues, friendships, and pleasures, it remains for us to discuss happiness by giving an outline of it, since we take it to be the end in human affairs. Accordingly, our account will be more concise if we first recapitulate what we said before about this.

We said, then, that happiness is not a state, since, if it were, it might be possessed by someone who was asleep his whole life, living the life of plants or by someone suffering the greatest misfortunes.[826] If these implications are not satisfying, then, we should, rather, class happiness as a sort of activity, as we said before.[827] And if some activities are necessary and choiceworthy because of other things, whereas others are intrinsically choiceworthy, it is clear that happiness must be classed as one of those that are intrinsically choiceworthy, not as one of those choiceworthy because of something else, since happiness lacks nothing but instead is self-sufficient.[828]

The ones that are intrinsically choiceworthy, however, are those from which nothing is sought beyond the activity. And actions in accord with virtue seem to be like this, since doing noble and excellent actions is one of the things that are choiceworthy because of themselves.

Pleasant amusements, though, also seem to be like this. For we do not choose them because of other things, since people are harmed by them more than benefited, through being led to neglect their bodies and possessions. Most of those who are called "happy," however, take refuge in such pastimes, which is why those who are witty participants in them enjoy a good reputation with tyrants, since what these seek they make themselves pleasant by providing, and tyrants need people like that. So these amusements seem to bear the stamp of happiness, because people in positions of power spend their leisure in them.

Presumably, though, such people are no indication of anything. For virtue and understanding, which are the sources of excellent activities, do not depend on holding positions of power. And if, being unable to taste pure and free pleasures, people in such positions take refuge in the bodily ones, these should not for that reason either be thought more choiceworthy, since boys too think the most excellent things are the things most honored among boys. Just as different things appear estimable to boys and men, then, it is quite reasonable that it should be the same way with base people and decent ones.

So as we have often said, what *is* estimable and pleasant is what is so to the excellent person, since for each person the most choiceworthy activity is the one in accord with the state that properly belongs to him.[829] And so for the excellent one, then, it is the one in accord with virtue.

Hence happiness does not lie in amusement, since it would indeed be strange if the end were amusement and we did all the work we do and suffered evils all our lives for the sake of amusing ourselves. For, in a word, we choose everything—except happiness, since end *it* is—for the sake of something else. But to engage in serious matters and to labor for the sake of amusement would evidently be silly and utterly childish. On the contrary, "amusing ourselves so as to engage in serious matters," as Anacharsis puts it, seems to be correct.[830] For amusement is like relaxation, and it is because people cannot labor continuously that they need relaxation. End, then, relaxation is not, since it occurs for the sake of activity.

The happy life, though, seems to be in accord with virtue, and this is one that involves engagement in serious matters and does not lie in amusement. And we say that serious things are better than ridiculous ones and those that involve amusement and that in every case the activity of what is better, whether a part or a human being, is more excellent.[831] But the activity of what is better is more excellent and for this very reason bears more of the stamp of happiness.[832]

Moreover, any random person—even a slave—can enjoy bodily pleasures no less than the best person can. But no one assigns a share in happiness to a slave any more than a share of the relevant sort of life.[833] For happiness does not lie in such pastimes but in activities in accord with virtue, as we also said before.[834]

# X 7

But if happiness is activity in accord with virtue, it is quite reasonable that it should be in accord with the one that is most excellent, and this will be the virtue of the best element. Whether, then, this element is understanding or something else that seems by nature to rule, lead, and understand what is noble and divine, whether by being something divine itself or by being the most divine element in us—the activity of *it,* when in accord with the virtue that properly belongs to it, will be complete happiness.[835] That it is contemplative activity we already said.[836]

And this would seem to be in agreement both with what was said before and with the truth, since this activity is also most excellent. For not only is understanding the most excellent element in us, but also, of knowable objects, the ones that understanding is concerned with are the most excellent ones. Further, it is the most continuous activity, since we can contemplate more continuously than we can do any action whatsoever.[837]

Moreover, we think that pleasure must be mixed in with happiness, and the most pleasant of the activities in accord with virtue is agreed to be the one in accord with theoretical wisdom. At any rate, philosophy seems to involve pleasures that are wondrous for their purity and stability, and it is quite reasonable that those who have attained knowledge should pass their time more pleasantly than those who are looking for it.[838]

Moreover, the self-sufficiency that is meant will belong most of all to contemplative activity.[839] For while a theoretically-wise person as well as a just one and people with the other virtues all need the things necessary for living, when these are adequately supplied, the just one still needs people to do just actions for and with, and similarly for a temperate person, a courageous person, and each of the others. But a theoretically-wise person, even when by himself, is able to contemplate, and the more wise he is, the more he is able to do so. He will do it better, presumably, if he has co-workers, but all the same he is most self-sufficient.

Moreover, this activity, and only this, would seem to be liked because of itself [alone].[840] |**1177b1**| For nothing arises from it beyond having contemplated, whereas from the practical ones we try—to a greater or lesser extent—to get for ourselves something beyond the action.[841]

Moreover, happiness seems to reside in leisure, since we do unleisured things in order to be at leisure, and wage war in order to live in peace. Now the activity of the practical virtues occurs in politics or in warfare, and the actions concerned with these seem to be unleisured and those in warfare completely so (for no one chooses to wage war for the sake of waging war, or to foment war either, since someone would seem completely bloodthirsty, if he made enemies of his friends in order to bring about battles and killings). But the activity of a politician too is unleisured and beyond political activity itself he tries to get positions of power and honors or, at any rate, happiness for himself and his fellow citizens—this being different from the exercise of politics and something we clearly seek on the supposition of its being different.

If, then, among actions in accord with the virtues, those in politics and war stand out in nobility and magnitude but these are unleisured and seek some end rather than being choiceworthy because of themselves, whereas the activity of understanding seems to be superior in excellence because it is contemplative, to seek no end beyond itself, and to have its own proper pleasure, which increases the activity by its own increase, and if in addition the self-sufficiency, leisured quality, and unweariness (so far as this is possible for a human being), as well as all the other attributes assigned to the blessed, are evidently attributes of it, then this activity will be the complete happiness of a human being, if it receives a complete span of life (since nothing is incomplete that is characteristic of happiness).[842]

But such a life would be more excellent than one in accord with the human element, since it is not insofar as he is a human being that someone will live a life like that but insofar as he has some divine element in him, and to the degree that this element is superior to the compound, to that degree will its activity also be superior to that in accord with the other sort of virtue.[843] If, then, understanding is something divine in comparison with the human element, so also a life in accord with it is divine in comparison with human life. We should not, however, in accord with the makers of proverbs, "think human things, since you are human" or "think mortal things, since you are mortal" but, rather, we should as far as possible immortalize, and do everything to live in accord with the element in us that is most excellent.[844] For even if it is small in bulk, in its power and esteem it far exceeds everything.

It would seem too that each person actually *is* this, if indeed it is the controlling and better element.[845] So it would be strange if he were to choose not his own life but that of something else. Moreover, what we said before will fit now as well. For what properly belongs to each thing by nature is most excellent and most pleasant for each of them.[846] For each human being, then, the life in accord with understanding is so too, if indeed this most of all is a human being. Hence, this life will also be happiest.

# X 8

Happiest, but in a secondary way, is the life in accord with the other virtue, since the activities in accord with it are human. For just actions, brave actions, and other actions that we do in accord with the virtues, we do in relation to each other in contracts, catering to needs, and in every sort of action and in feelings as well, by keeping closely to what is appropriate to each person. And all of these are evidently human. Indeed, some of them even seem to arise from the body, and virtue of character seems in many ways to be intimately attached to feelings.[847]

Practical wisdom too is coupled together with virtue of character, and it with practical wisdom, if indeed the starting-points of practical wisdom are in accord with the virtues of character and the correctness of these virtues is in accord with practical wisdom.[848] And connected as these virtues also are with feelings, they will be concerned with the compound.[849] But the virtues of the compound are human. So too, then, are both the life and the happiness that is in accord with them. The virtue of understanding, though, is separated.[850] (About it, in fact, let just that much be said, since to develop an exact account of it is a greater task than the one we have set before us.[851])

It would seem too that it has little need of external supplies or less need than virtue of character does.[852] For let us grant that they both need the necessary ones and to an equal extent, even if the politician does labor more in relation to the body and suchlike, since any differences here would be small.[853] As regards the activities, though, there will be a large difference. For a generous person will need money for doing generous actions, and so will a just one, then, for repaying debts (for wishes are not manifest things, and people who are not just pretend to wish to do just actions). And a courageous person will need power, if indeed he is to bring to completion anything that is in accord with his virtue, and a temperate one will need authority. For how else will it be manifest that he or any of the others is what he is?

Moreover, it is disputed whether it is deliberate choice or action that is the more controlling element in virtue, on the supposition that it depends on both.[854] Well, its completeness clearly does depend on both.[855] For the actions, though, many things are needed and more of them the greater and more noble the actions are.

A person who is contemplating, by contrast, needs none of these things, at any rate for the activity. On the contrary, one might say that they are even impediments, at any rate to his contemplating. But insofar as he is a human being and is living with many other people, he chooses to do the actions that are in accord with virtue and so will need such things for living a human life.

But that complete happiness is some contemplative activity will also be evident from the following considerations. The gods, in fact, we suppose to be the most blessed and happy of all. But what sorts of actions should we assign to them? Just ones? Won't they appear ridiculous if they engage in transactions, return deposits, and so on? Courageous ones, then, enduring what is frightening and facing danger because it is a noble thing to do? Or generous ones? To whom will they give? It will be a strange thing, if they actually have money or anything like that. And their temperate actions, what would they be? Or isn't the praise vulgar, since they do not have base appetites?[856] If we were to go through them all, it would be evident that everything to do with actions is petty and unworthy of gods. Nonetheless, everyone supposes them to be living, at least, and hence in activity, since surely they are not sleeping like Endymion.[857] If, then, living has doing actions taken away from it and still more so producing, what is left except contemplating?[858] So the activity of a god, superior as it is in blessedness, will be contemplative. And so the activity of humans, then, that is most akin to this will most bear the stamp of happiness.

A further indication of this is that other animals do not share in happiness, being completely deprived of this sort of activity. Hence the life of the gods is blessed throughout; that of human beings is so to the extent that it has something similar to this sort of activity, whereas of the other animals, none is happy, since they in no way share in contemplation. Happiness extends indeed just as far as contemplation does, and those to whom it more belongs to contemplate, it also more belongs to be happy, not coincidentally but, rather, in accord with contemplation, since this is intrinsically estimable. And so happiness will be some sort of contemplation.

But to the extent that someone is a human being, he will also need external prosperity, since his nature is not self-sufficient for contemplation, but his body needs to be healthy and provided with food and other sorts of care.[859] Nonetheless, we should not think that a person who is going to be happy needs many things and grand ones, even if it is not possible for him to be blessed without external goods. For self-sufficiency does not lie in an extreme amount of these and neither does action. But it is possible to do many noble actions even without ruling land and sea, since even from moderate resources a person can do actions in accord with virtue. (This is plain enough to see, since private individuals seem to do decent actions no less, or even more, than people in positions of power). It is enough, then, to have that amount, since the life of a person who is active in accord with virtue will be happy.

Solon too was presumably depicting happy people correctly when he described them as moderately supplied with external goods but as having done what he regarded as the noblest actions and lived their lives temperately.[860] For it is possible with moderate possessions to do the actions we should. Anaxagoras also seems to have supposed a happy person to be neither rich nor in a position of power when he said that it would be no wonder if a happy one appeared to be a strange sort of person to ordinary people.[861] For these judge by external goods, since these are the only ones they can perceive.[862] The beliefs of wise people, then, would seem to be in harmony with our arguments.[863]

But while these sorts of considerations also carry a certain conviction, the truth in practical matters must be discerned from the facts of our life, since these are what have the controlling vote.[864] When we examine what has been previously said, then, it must be discerned by bringing it to bear on the facts of our life, and if it is in harmony with the facts, we should accept it, but if it clashes, we should suppose it mere words.[865]

The person whose activity is in accord with understanding, however, and who takes care of it, would seem to be both in the best condition and the one most loved by the gods. For if the gods exercise a sort of supervision over human affairs, as indeed they seem to, it would also be quite reasonable both that they should enjoy what is best and most akin to themselves (and this would be understanding) and that they should reward those who most like and honor it for supervising what they themselves love and for acting correctly and nobly.[866] But that all these attributes belong most of all to a wise person is quite clear. Therefore, he is most beloved by the gods. And the same person is also likely to be the happiest, so that in this way too a wise person will be most happy of all.[867]

## X 9

Well then, if we have said enough in outline form about these topics and about the virtues, and furthermore about friendship and pleasure, should we think that our deliberate choice has achieved its end?[868] Or is it, as the saying goes, that in the case of practical matters the end is not to contemplate and know each of the various things but rather |**1179b1**| to put it into action, so that knowing about virtue is not enough either, then, but, rather, we must try to have and use it or to become good in whatever other way we can?[869]

Now if arguments were self-sufficient for making people decent, "many and large the wages they would earn," as Theognis says, and justly so, and arguments would be what need to be provided.[870] As things stand, however, they appear to have the strength to encourage and stimulate those of the young who are free minded, and to make ready to be possessed by virtue a character that is well bred and that truly loves what is noble but to be unable to encourage ordinary people toward noble-goodness.

For ordinary people naturally obey not shame but fear and abstain from base things not because of their shamefulness but because of the sanctions involved.[871] For living by feeling as they do, they pursue the pleasures that are properly their own as well as the things through which these come about, and avoid the opposing pains. Of what is noble and what is truly pleasant, however, they have no understanding at all, not having tasted it.[872]

What sort of argument, then, could reform such people? For it is not possible—or not easy—to alter by argument what has long since been locked up in traits of character.[873] Presumably, though, we should be content if, when we have all the things through which it seems we become decent people, we achieve some share of virtue.

Now some people think that it is by nature that we become good, whereas some think that it is by habit and others by teaching. Well, nature's contribution, it is clear, is not up to us, but because of some divine causes is present in those who are truly fortunate.[874] Argument and teaching, on the other hand, surely do not have strength in everyone but, rather, the soul of the audience must be prepared beforehand through habits to enjoy and hate in a noble way, like earth that is to nourish seed.[875] For someone who lives in accord with his feelings will not listen to—or, what is more, comprehend—argument that encourages him to turn away. And in a state like that how is it possible to persuade him to change his ways? Moreover, feeling generally seems to yield not to argument but to force. Character, then, must in some way be there beforehand and properly suited for virtue, liking what is noble and repelled by what is shameful.

It is difficult, however, for someone to get correct guidance toward virtue from childhood if he has not been nurtured under laws of the appropriate sort, since a moderate and resilient way of living is not pleasant for ordinary people, most of all when they are young.[876] That is why laws must prescribe their nurture and practices, since these will not be painful when they have become habitual.

But it is not enough, presumably, that when people are young they get the correct nurture and supervision. |**1180a1**| On the contrary, even when they have grown into adulthood they must continue to practice the same things and be habituated to them. And so there will need to be laws concerning these matters as well and, in general, then, concerning all of life. For ordinary people obey force rather than argument; and they obey penalties rather than what is noble.

That is why some think that legislators should, on the one hand, exhort and encourage people toward virtue for the sake of what is noble (on the supposition that those who have been decently guided in the formation of habits will listen), and, on the other hand, impose punishments and sanctions on those who disobey and are not naturally well disposed, while entirely expelling those who are incurable.[877] For a decent person, they think, living as he does with a view to what is noble, will obey reason, whereas a base one, whose desire is for pleasure, needs to be punished by means of pain, like a beast of burden.[878] That too is why they say that the sorts of pains inflicted should be those that are most opposed to the pleasures liked.

Whatever about that; if, as we said, someone who is to be good should be nobly nurtured and habituated and then live that way in decent practices and neither involuntarily nor voluntarily do base actions, this would happen if people lived their life in accord with a sort of understanding and correct constitutional arrangement and this had the requisite strength.[879]

Now paternal instructions do not have such strength or the element of compulsion and neither, then, do the instructions of any individual man in general (unless he is a king or something like that).[880] The law, however, does have the power to compel, being reason that derives from a sort of practical wisdom and understanding.[881] And while people feel enmity toward human beings who oppose their impulses, even if they do so correctly, the law causes no offense in prescribing what is decent.

Yet it is in the city of the Spartans alone (or almost alone) that the legislator seems to have created the supervision of nurture and also of practices.[882] In most cities, however, such matters are utterly unsupervised, and each person lives as he wishes, Cyclops-fashion, laying down the law "for children and wife."[883]

The most excellent thing, then, is that there should be communal supervision that is correct. But if things are communally unsupervised, it would seem appropriate for each individual to further the virtue of his own children and friends—to be capable of doing it, or, at any rate, of deliberately choosing it.[884] But he would be more capable of doing this, it seems, given what has been said, if he becomes competent in legislative science.[885] For it is clear that communal types of supervision come about through laws and that decent ones do so through excellent laws. Whether the laws are written or unwritten, though, would seem to make no difference, nor would it make a difference whether one or many are thereby educated—anymore than it does in the case of music, physical training, or any of the other practices. For just as lawful things and habits have strength in cities, so in households do paternal words and habits (still more strength, in fact, because of the kinship and the benefactions involved, since children are naturally predisposed to feel affection and be ready to obey).[886]

Further, particularized education is actually superior to communal education, just as in the case of medicine. For while rest and abstinence from food are in universal terms advantageous for a feverish patient, for a particular patient, presumably, they may not be, nor does a boxing instructor prescribe the same style of fighting for everyone. It would seem, then, that a particular case is treated with more exactness when there is individual supervision, since each person is more likely to get what suits him. But the best supervision in each particular case will be provided by the doctor, athletic trainer, or whoever else has knowledge of the universal and knows what applies in all cases or in these sorts (since the sciences are said to be—and actually are—of what is common).[887]

But, despite that, there is nothing to prevent a single individual from being correctly supervised even by someone who lacks scientific knowledge but who has—due to experience—seen exactly what happens in each particular case, just as some people seem to be their own best doctors even though they would be of no assistance at all to another person. Nonetheless, it seems, presumably, that someone who *does* wish to become expert in a craft or in a theoretical science should take steps toward the universal and come to know it as well as possible, since that, we said, is what the sciences are concerned with.[888]

Maybe, then, someone who wishes to make people—whether many or few—better because of his supervision should also try to acquire legislative science, if it is through laws that we can become good. For producing a noble disposition in anyone whoever—in anyone put before him—is not a matter for some random person, but if indeed anyone can do it, it is a person who has knowledge, just as in medicine and in all other matters that involve a sort of supervision and practical wisdom.[889]

Hence shouldn't we next investigate from what sources and in what way someone might become competent in legislative science? Or isn't it, as in other cases, from politicians? For, as we saw, legislative science seems to be a part of politics.[890] Or is not evident that it is the same in the case of politics as in the other sciences and the other capacities?

For in the others, it is evident that it is the same people who impart their capacities to others as actively practice them themselves, just as with doctors or writers. In the case of politics, however, although it is the sophists who profess to teach it, it is practiced not by any of them but by politicians, and they seem to do so |**1181a1**| thanks to some sort of ability and experience rather than to thought.[891] For it is evident that they neither write nor speak about such matters (and yet that would be a nobler thing, presumably, than to compose speeches for the law courts and the assembly), and furthermore it is evident that they have not made their own sons or any other friends of theirs into politicians either.[892] But it would be quite reasonable for them to have done so, if indeed they were able to, since there is nothing better than this capacity that they could have left to their cities or could have chosen to have for themselves or, then, for their closest friends. Still, experience does seem to make no small contribution, since otherwise people could not, through intimacy with politics, have become politicians.[893] That is why those who seek to know about politics would seem to need experience in addition.

Those of the sophists who profess to teach politics, however, are evidently a long way from teaching it, since on the whole they know nothing about what sort of thing it is or what sorts of things it is concerned with. For if they did, they would not have taken it to be the same as rhetoric or even inferior to it, nor would they have thought that legislating is an easy matter for anyone who has collected together laws that enjoy a good reputation, since it amounts to selecting the best ones—as if the selection did not call for comprehension and correct discernment were not, as in matters of music, the greatest thing.[894] For those with experience in a particular area discern the works in it correctly and comprehend by what means or in what way they are brought to completion, and discern what is in tune with what, whereas those who lack experience must be content not to have it escape them whether the work is well or badly made, as in the case of painting. But laws would seem to be the works of politics, so how could someone become competent in legislative science or discern which laws are best, from *them,* |**1181b1**| since it is evident that we do not become doctors from reading textbooks either?

Yet these textbooks do try to say not only what the treatments are but also how each sort of patient might be cured and should be treated, distinguishing their various states. But while these do seem to be of benefit to experienced people, to those who lack scientific knowledge they seem useless.[895] Presumably, then, collections of laws and constitutions might also be of good use to people who are able to get a theoretical grasp on them and discern what is correctly done or the opposite and what sorts of things fit with what. In those who go through them without being in this state, however, no correct discernment would be present, unless of course by chance, although they may become better comprehenders of them.

So since our predecessors have left the subject of legislation unexamined, it is presumably better if we ourselves investigate it and indeed constitutions generally, so that as far as possible our philosophy of human affairs may be brought to completion.[896]

First, then, if there is anything that has been correctly said by our predecessors on some part of the subject, let us try to go through it and then, on the basis of the collection of constitutions, try to get a theoretical grasp on what sorts of things preserve and destroy cities, what sorts of things preserve or destroy each sort of constitution, and what causes some cities to be well governed and others the opposite.[897] For when we have gotten a theoretical grasp on these matters, maybe we shall also be better able to see which constitution is best, how each should be arranged, and what laws and habits it should use.[898]

Let us discuss this, then, starting from the beginning.

# Notes

## Book I

Note 1

**Craft:** Discussed at VI 4. **Method of inquiry** (*methodos*): A *methodos* is a *tropos tês zêtêseôs*—a way of inquiry (*APo.* I 31 46$^a$32–$^b$36). *Hodos* means "route" or "road," as at *NE* I 4 1095$^a$33. **Action** (*praxis*): The noun *praxis* (verb: *prattein*) is used in a broad sense to refer to any intentional action, including one performed by a child or wild beast (III 1 1111$^a$25–26, 2 1111$^b$8–9), and in a narrower one to refer exclusively to what results from deliberation (*bouleusis*) and deliberate choice (*prohairesis*), of which neither wild beasts nor children are capable (I 9 1099$^b$32–1100$^a$5, *EE* II 8 1224$^a$28–29). The narrower sense may be the one intended here. **Deliberate choice:** Discussed in III 2.

Note 2

**That is why they correctly declare:** Aristotle apparently commits the logical fallacy of inferring from the fact that there is a good that each seeks that there is a good that all (that is, all who practice crafts, follow lines in inquiry, do actions, and make deliberate choices) seek. This is like inferring from the fact that each boy loves a girl (but not necessarily the same one) that there is a girl all boys love. I 2 1094$^a$18–$^b$7 suggests a way to defend the inference. Any good or end is sought or desired either because of itself or because of something else. Eventually this chain of "becauses" must terminate in an end or good X that is desired solely because of itself. If all such chains terminate in the same X, as the existence of an architectonic science with an end or good that circumscribes all the others suggests, then X will be the human good—that is, the one unique good that all human beings, in seeking any good whatsoever, thereby seek. **Correctly** (*kalôs*): *Kalôs*, the adverb derived from the adjective *kalos* ("noble"), sometimes means "nobly" and sometimes, as here, means something closer to "rightly" or "correctly." **The good is "that which all** (*panta*) **seek":** One of the generally accepted accounts of the good canvassed at *Rh.* I 6 1362$^a$23–29 and treated as uncontroversial at *NE* X 2 1172$^b$35–1173$^a$6. It is attributed to Eudoxus (who may be one of "they" referred to) at X 2 1172$^b$9–10, where *panta* clearly means not "all things" but all animals, whether rational or nonrational.

Note 3

**Appears** (*phainetai*): The verb *phainesthai* ("appear") with (1) a participle is endorsing of what appears to be so and is translated "it is evident," and the cognate adjective *phaneron* is translated as "evident." *Phainesthai* with (2) an infinitive is neither endorsing nor rejecting of what appears to be so and is translated "appears." When *phainesthai* occurs without a participle or an infinitive, it may be endorsing or rejecting. Appearances (*phainomena*) are things that appear to be so but that may or may not be so. Things that appear so to everyone or to wise people who have investigated them are *endoxa,* or reputable beliefs. The role of both *phainomena* and *endoxa* in ethics are discussed at VII 1 1145$^{b}$2–7. **Ends:** "The end (*telos*) is the best and last thing for whose sake all the other things are done" (*EE* II 1 1219$^{a}$10–11; *Met.* V 16 1021$^{b}$29–30).

Note 4

**Activities:** The actualization (*entelecheia*) or use (*chrêsis*) of a capacity (*dunamis*) or state (*hexis*), as when an agent is currently engaging in deliberately chosen action, is an activity (*energeia*), by contrast with a process or movement (*kinêsis*). This contrast is employed in *NE* X 4. When the activity is something's function—as deliberately chosen action is (part of) a human being's function—then "the function is the end (*telos*), and the activity is the function" (*Met.* IX 8 1050$^{a}$21–22). A second sort of end is one that is the further end of an activity of this first sort. Thus functions are also of two sorts: "It is clear that the function is better than the state or the disposition (*diathesis*); but 'function' is said of things in two ways. In some cases, the function is a different thing beyond the use (*chrêsis*), as a house is the function of building and not the activity of building, and health is the function of medicine and not the activity of producing health or practicing medicine. In other cases, the use is the function, as seeing is the function of sight, and active contemplation (*theôria*) is the function of the scientific knowledge of mathematics. Hence it necessarily follows that when the use of a thing is its function, the use is better than the state" (*EE* II 1 1219$^{a}$11–18). So just as the house is better than the activity of building, so the actualization or use of a state or of a capacity is better than the state or capacity itself (*NE* I 1 1094$^{a}$16–18). Although one kind of further end is a product or work, such as a house or health, another can be a state. Thus the actualization of practical wisdom, which is a state of the soul, is a valuable end, choiceworthy because of itself but also choiceworthy for the sake of theoretical wisdom and its actualization (VI 13 1145$^{a}$6–11, X 7 1177$^{b}$4–26). Correlated with this difference is one in the states themselves. The actualization or use of a *productive* state or capacity, such as building, is an incomplete activity, since it is not itself an end, whereas that of other sorts of states, such as scientific knowledge, is a complete activity, since it is an end (*Met.* IX 6 1048$^{b}$18–35). Productive states are discussed in *NE* VI 4, where they are contrasted with practical or action-related ones. **Works** (*erga:* singular, *ergon*): Aristotle uses the noun *ergon* for (1) the function or activity that is the actualization or use of a state, such as the knowledge of the craft of medicine, and for (2) works (which may or may not be products in the strict sense of the term) that are the further results of that activity.

Note 5
**Sciences** (*epistêmai*: singular, *epistêmê*): Aristotle usually divides sciences into three kinds: theoretical (contemplative), practical (action-determining), and productive (crafts) (*Top.* VI 6 145ᵃ15–16, *Met.* XI 7 1064ᵃ16–19). Sometimes a more fine-grained classification is employed, in which theoretical sciences are divided into natural sciences (such as physics and biology) and strictly theoretical sciences (such as astronomy and theology) on the basis of the kinds of beings with which they deal (*Ph.* II 7 198ᵃ21–ᵇ4, *Met.* VI 1 1025ᵇ18–1026ᵃ32). In *NE*, the term *epistêmê* is sometimes reserved for the unconditional scientific knowledge provided exclusively by the strictly theoretical sciences (VI 3 1139ᵇ31–34), but here, as often elsewhere, *epistêmê* is used in the looser sense, which encompasses the natural, practical, and productive sciences as well. **Medicine . . . shipbuilding . . . generalship . . . household management:** The names of these crafts or sciences are: *iatrikê* ("medicine"), *naupêgikê* ("shipbuilding"), *stratêgikê* ("generalship"), and *oikonomikê* ("household management"). The ending *-ikê* signifies that either *epistêmê* ("science") or *technê ("craft")* should be supplied or presupposed, so that *iatrikê* is "the science of medicine," and *naupêgikê* is "the craft of shipbuilding." Since a craft is a productive science, it usually doesn't matter much which we choose.

Note 6
**Capacity (*dunamis*):** The term *dunamis* (plural: *dunameis*) is used by Aristotle to capture two different but related things. (1) As in ordinary Greek, it signifies a power or capacity something has, especially one to cause movement in something else (productive *dunamis*) or to be caused to move by something else (passive *dunamis*). (2) It signifies a way of being F, being capable of being F (or being F in potentiality) as distinguished from being actively F (or F in actuality) (see IX 7 1168ᵃ5–15). Here the use of the term indicates that Aristotle is thinking of the crafts and sciences in his usual way, as psychological capacities or states of the soul, not as abstract structures of propositions or sentences of the sort found in textbooks (see VI 3 1139ᵇ15–18, X 9 1181ᵇ2). **And, in the same way:** Reading δὲ for OCT δὴ ("in the same way, then").

Note 7
**But in all such cases:** Reading δὲ for OCT δὴ ("in all such cases, then"). **The architectonic ones:** "In each craft, the architectonic craftsmen are more estimable, know more, and are wiser than the handicraftsmen, because they know the causes of their products" (*Met.* I 1 981ᵃ30–ᵇ1).

Note 8
**The sciences we have mentioned:** Suppose that the end of someone's action is to do well in action (VI 2 1139ᵇ1–4), and that doing well in action consists in actualizing or using his virtuous state of character, then the end of his action will be the activity consisting in the actualization of that state.

Because the sciences mentioned have ends beyond their actualization or use, they are not like this.

Note 9

**If, then, there is some end that we wish for because of itself, and the others because of it, . . . this will be the good—that is, the best good:** "Since the for-the-sake-of-which is an end, and the sort of end that is not for the sake of other things but rather other things are for its sake, it follows that if there is to be a last thing of this sort, the series will not be without a limit, but if there is no such thing, there will be no for-the-sake-of-which. Those who make it unlimited are unwittingly getting rid of the nature of the good (and yet no one would try to do anything if he were not going to come to a limit). Nor would there be any understanding present in beings. For a person who has understanding, at any rate, always does the actions he does for the sake of something, and this is a limit, since the end is a limit" (*Met.* II 2 994$^{b}$9–16). **Doable in action** (*prakton*): Verbals ending in *-ton*—of which *prakton* is an example—sometimes have (1) the meaning of a perfect passive participle ("done in action") and sometimes (2) express possibility ("doable in action"). A decree (*psêphisma*) seems to be *prakton* in sense (2), since it is a prescription specific enough to be acted on without further need for deliberation (VI 8 1141$^{b}$23–28). What it specifies is thus a possibility (a type of action) that many different particular (token) actions might actualize. Particular objects of perception that are *prakton* (VI 11 1143$^{a}$32–33, $^{b}$4–5) seem to be so in sense (1). **Wish:** Discussed in III 4. **The desire will be empty and pointless:** Like their English counterparts "empty" and "pointless," *kenos* and *mataios* are somewhat vague. The primary meaning of *kenos* is "being like an empty cup or vessel." In Plato, as elsewhere, it is thus readily applied to desires: "hunger, thirst, and the like are some sort of emptiness related to the state of the body" (*Rep.* IX 585a–b). Presumably, then, a *kenos* desire is one that, as (always) empty, cannot be satisfied. This does not mean that a desire cannot be *kenos*, but when it is, a question naturally arises about the rationality of acting on it. It is this fact that lays the ground for *mataios*, the primary connotation of which is "foolish or without reason" or "pointless." Thus it is *mataios* for a young person to study a practical science like ethics or politics, since he tends to follow his feelings, not what he will learn by studying it (*NE* I 4 1095$^{a}$5).

Note 10

**Our life** (*bios*): Two Greek words correspond to the English word "life": *bios*, used here, and *zôê*, used extensively in I 7 and translated "living." *Zôê* refers to the sorts of life processes and activities studied by biologists, zoologists, and so on, such as growth, reproduction, perception, and understanding. *Bios* refers to the sort of life a natural historian or biographer might investigate—the life of the otter, the life of Pericles—and so to a span of time throughout which someone possesses *zôê* at least as a capacity

(I 13 1102b5–7). Hence, in the conclusion of the function argument, we are reminded that a certain *zôê* will not be happiness for a human being unless it occurs "in a complete *bios*" (I 7 1098a18–20). **Knowledge** (*gnôsis; verb, gignôskein*): Although there may be little difference between *gnôsis* and *epistêmê* (verb, *epistasthai*), *epistêmê* is usually applied only to demonstrative sciences, crafts, or other bodies of systematic knowledge, so that *epistêmê* is specifically *scientific* knowledge. *Gnôsis* is weaker and is used for perceptual knowledge and knowledge by acquaintance—something familiar is *gnôrimos*. If X knows that *p*, it follows that *p* is true and that X is justified in believing it. Similar entailments hold in the cases of *epistasthai* and *eidenai* but may not hold in that of *gignôskein*. **Target** (*skopos*): The notion of a *skopos*, which belongs primarily to archery, is used metaphorically to refer to an end, particularly one pursued in deliberate action (*EE* I 2 1214b6–9, II 10 1227a5–7, *Pol.* VII 13 1331b6–8, *Rh.* I 6 1362a15–20).

Note 11

**Outline:** Sometimes when Aristotle gives an outline, it means that a fuller account may be forthcoming, so that the outline is merely provisional (II 7 1107b14–16). When things in a given area hold for the most part, however, it seems that the truth about them *must* be stated in outline (II 2 1104a1–5). In this case, having to outline seems to be a function of the subject matter, so that it is because we are discussing things that hold for the most part in ethics and politics that these sciences involve outlining. Far from being a correctable flaw in such sciences, this seems to be an indication of their intellectual probity. **We should try to grasp . . . what the good is:** "Everyone who can live in accord with his own deliberate choice should adopt some target for the noble life, whether honor, reputation, wealth, or education, which he will look to in all his actions—at any rate, not to have ordered one's life in relation to some end is the sign of great foolishness. Most of all, though, and before everything else, he should define for himself in which of our possessions living well consists and what those things are without which it cannot belong to human beings" (*EE* I 2 1214b6–14). **Sciences or capacities:** Often sciences and capacities are lumped together as things that can be used to achieve opposite effects, as medicine can be used to cure but also to kill (V I 1129a13–14). Sometimes, though, a body of knowledge (such as rhetoric or dialectic) is classified as a capacity (*dunamis*) rather than a science, because its subject matter lacks the requisite sort of unity: "Rhetoric is constituted from the science of the *Analytics* [= logic and scientific explanation] and from the part of politics dealing with character [= ethics], resembling dialectic on the one hand, sophistical arguments on the other. But to the extent that someone tries to set out dialectic and rhetoric not as *dunameis* but as sciences, he unwittingly obscures their nature by the change, setting them down as sciences dealing with specific subject matters, rather than with arguments alone" (*Rh.* I 4 1359b9–16).

Note 12

**Control** (*kurios*): Control is fundamentally executive power or authority or the power to compel, so that a general is *kurios* over his army (III 8 1116ᵃ29–ᵇ2) and a political ruler is *kurios* over a city and its inhabitants. Since what is *kurios* in a sphere determines or partly determines what happens within it, it is one of the most estimable or important elements in the sphere, so that what is inferior or less important than something cannot control it (VI 12 1143ᵇ33–35, 13 1145ᵃ6–7). When Aristotle contrasts natural virtue of character with the *kurios* variety (VI 13 1144ᵇ1–32), the control exerted by the latter seems to be teleological: the natural variety is a sort of virtue because it is an early stage in the development of mature virtue (compare *Met.* IX 8 1050ᵃ21–23). Hence *kuria aretê* is "full virtue" or virtue in the full sense of the term. It is in this sense that the life of those who are active and awake is a more *kurios* life—life in a fuller sense—than that of the inactive or asleep (*NE* I 7 1098ᵃ5–8).

Note 13

**Politics** (*politikê*): *Politikê* is the practical science used in ruling a city (I 9 1099ᵇ29–32, 13 1102ᵃ18–25, II 1 1103ᵇ3–6, VI 8 1141ᵇ23–33, VII 11 1152ᵇ1–3, X 9 1180ᵇ23–1181ᵇ23). Someone who knows *politikê* is a true *politikos*—a true politician or true statesman. **City** (*polis*): A *polis* is a unique political organization, something like a city and something like a state. Unlike a typical modern city, a *polis* enjoyed the political sovereignty characteristic of a modern state: it could possess its own army and navy, enter into alliances, make war, and so on. Unlike a typical modern state, however, it was a politically, religiously, and culturally unified community, and quite small scale. The territory of a *polis* included a single (typically) walled town (*astu*) with a citadel and a marketplace, which, as the political and governmental heart of *polis,* is itself often referred to as the *polis*. But a *polis* also included the surrounding agricultural land, and the citizens lived both there and inside the town proper.

Note 14

**Rhetoric:** "Let rhetoric be [defined as] the capacity of getting a theoretical grasp on the available means of persuasion in any given case" (*Rh.* I 2 1355ᵇ25–26).

Note 15

**The other practical sciences:** Reading ταῖς λοιπαῖς πρακτικαῖς. OCT omits πρακτικαῖς ("practical"). **Circumscribe** (*periechoi*): The primary connotation of *periechein* (here "circumscribe"), which is a compound of the preposition *peri* ("around") and the verb *echein* ("have," "possess"), is that of containing by surrounding. So if that were its meaning here, the human good would have to contain all the other goods subordinate to it. Yet generalship's end—victory—does not seem to contain either trained horses or their bridles, any more than health, which is medicine's end and a certain bodily condition, contains medical instruments, medical treatment, or drugs. Just as "contain" can also mean "circumscribe" or "limit," however, so too can *periechein*. The idea would then be that the end of politics *limits* or circumscribes the ends of all the relevant sciences, including those of the other practical sciences and actions. By looking to its own end, politics sets limits as to which sciences should be in cities, which groups should practice them and to what degree, and what actions should be done and what avoided. Why a limiting end of this sort would have to be the best or human good would remain unclear. Other people's rights, for example, may set absolute limits to our pursuit of happiness and so be limiting ends. But it is not obvious that respecting the rights of others is the *best* good. In addition, whatever imposes the limit should itself be an end that all other ends further, so that this end is a better good than the other ones. This end, in other words, would have to be the common end of all of them—an idea implicit in the use of *periechein* at V I 1129$^{b}$10–11. **Human** (*anthrôpinon*): An *anthrôpos* is a human being of either sex; an *anêr* is a male human being—a man. The adjective *anthrôpinos* ("human") often seems to mean something like "*merely* human" (for example, X 7 1177$^{b}$32). *Anthrôpikos* (also "human") sometimes has similar connotations (for example, X 8 1178$^{a}$10). Indeed, *anthrôpos* itself is sometimes used to refer to the whole human animal, sometimes to the human element in human beings by contrast with the divine one (their understanding) (X 7 1177$^{b}$27–28), and sometimes to that divine element, since it is what makes human beings distinctively human (X 5 1176$^{a}$25–29). **It will be the human good:** "Since the end in every science and craft is a good, the greatest and best good is the end of the science or craft that has most control of all of them, and this is the political capacity (*politikê dunamis*). But the political good is justice, and justice is the common advantage" (*Pol.* III 12 1282$^{b}$14–18); "First, then, we must see that every science and capacity has some end, and it is something good. For no science or capacity exists for the sake of a bad end. So if of every capacity the end is something good, it is clear the end of the best one will be the best good. But the political capacity is the best one, so its end will be the best good. Hence it is about the good, it seems, that we must speak and not an unconditional one but about the good for us and not about the good for the gods" (*MM* I 1 1182$^{a}$32–$^{b}$4). In the *Metaphysics* a parallel argument is used to show that theoretical wisdom (*sophia*) "knows the end for which each thing should be done, and this is the good characteristic of each of them and, in general, the best good in all of nature" (I 2 982$^{b}$4–7).

Note 16

**If the good is the same for an individual and for a city:** "It is evident that the same life is necessarily best both for each human being individually and for cities and human beings collectively" (*Pol.* VII 3 1325$^{b}$30–32). **More complete:** The relative completeness of goods is discussed at I 7 1097$^{a}$30–34.

Note 17

**A sort of politics:** Specifically it is "the part of politics dealing with character (*ta êthê*)" (*Rh.* I 4 1359ᵇ10–11), so that *NE*, as a contribution to virtue and to politics (II 4 1105ᵃ11–12), is included in what Aristotle refers to as "those philosophical works of ours in which we draw distinctions concerning matters of character (*tôn êthikôn*)" (*Pol.* III 12 1282ᵇ20) and as "our ethical works (*tous êthikous logous*)" (VII 13 1332ᵃ22).

Note 18

**Degree of perspicuity** (*diasaphêtheiê*): *Saphêneia* is associated with explanation, which is ultimately from starting-points: "Beginning with things that are truly stated but not perspicuously, we proceed to make them perspicuous as well. . . . That is why even politicians should not regard as peripheral to their work the sort of theoretical knowledge that makes evident (*phaneron*) not only the fact that but also the explanation why" (*EE* I 6 1216ᵇ32–39). The same point is made at *NE* I 7 1098ᵇ7–8 by noting that when we have a correct definition of the starting-point of politics much else will "at the same time become evident (*sumphanê*) through it." *Saphês* and *akribês* ("exact") are often equivalent in meaning: "it is well to replace a word with a better known equivalent, for example, instead of *akribês* in describing a supposition, *saphês*" (*Top.* II 4 111ᵃ8–9).

Note 19

**Exactness** (*akribes*): "One science is more exact than another, and prior to it, if it is both of the fact and the explanation why, and not of the fact separately from giving the scientific knowledge of the explanation why; or if it is not said of an underlying subject and the other is said of an underlying subject (as, for example, arithmetic is more exact than harmonics); or if it proceeds from fewer things and the other from some additional posit (as, for example, arithmetic is more exact than geometry). By from an additional posit I mean, for example, that a unit is a substance without position and a point is a substance with position—the latter proceeds from an additional posit" (*APo.* I 27 87ᵃ31–37); "we should not demand the argumentative exactness of mathematics in all cases but only in the case of things that involve no matter" (*Met.* II 3 995ᵃ14–16). As applied to craftsmen and their products, on the other hand, *akribês* means "refinement," "finish," or "sophistication." Applied to perceptual capacities, such as seeing or smelling (*DA* II 9 421ᵃ10), it means "discriminating." Applied to virtue and nature, it may have more to do with accuracy—hitting a target (*NE* II 5 1106ᵇ14–15)—as it may when applied to definitions (VIII 7 1159ᵃ3) or distinctions (II 9 1107ᵇ15–16) or units of measurement (*Met.* X 1 1053ᵃ1).
**In all accounts** (*logois*): *Logos* (here "account") can refer among other things (1) to a word or organized string of words constituting a discussion, conversation, speech, explanation, definition, principle, reason, or piece of reasoning, or (2) to what such words or their utterances mean, express, or denote, such as, the ratio between quantities (V 3 1131ᵃ31–32), or (3) to

the capacity that enables someone to argue, give reasons, and so on (*Pol.* VII 13 1332$^b$5).

Note 20

**Noble** (*kalos*): The adjective *kalos* is often a term of vague or general commendation ("fine," "beautiful," "good"), with different connotations in different contexts: "The contrary of *to kalon* when applied to an animal is *to aischron* ["ugly in appearance"], but when applied to a house it is *to mochthêron* ["wretched"], and so *kalon* is homonymous" (*Top.* I 15 106$^a$20–22). (1) Even in this general sense, however, *kalos* has a distinctive evaluative coloration suggestive of "order (*taxis*), proportion (*summetria*), and determinateness (*hôrismenon*)" (*Met.* XIII 3 1078$^a$36–$^b$1), making a term with aesthetic connotation, such as "beauty," seem a good equivalent: to bear the stamp of happiness one must have *kallos* as opposed to being "very ugly (*panaischês*)" (*NE* I 8 1099$^b$3–4; also *Pol.* V 9 1309$^b$23–25). Moreover just as a thing need not have a purpose in order to be beautiful, a *kalon* thing can be contrasted with a purposeful one: a great-souled person is one "whose possession are more *kalon* and purposeless (*akarpa*) than purposeful and beneficial" (*NE* IV 3 1125$^a$11–12). At the same time, it seems wrong to associate *kalon* with beauty in general, since to be *kalon* a thing has to be on a certain scale: "greatness of soul requires magnitude, just as *to kallos* ('nobility of appearance') requires a large body, whereas small people are elegant and well proportioned but not *kaloi*" (IV 3 1123$^b$6–8); "any *kalon* object . . . made up of parts must not only have them properly ordered but also have a magnitude which is not random. For what is *kalon* consists in magnitude and order (*taxis*)" (*Po.* 7 1450$^b$34–37; also *Pol.* VII 4 1326$^a$33–34). It is this requirement that makes "nobility" in its more aesthetic sense a closer equivalent than "beauty." (2) In ethical or political contexts, the canonical application of *kalon* is to ends that are intrinsically choiceworthy and intrinsically commendable or praiseworthy (*epaineton*): "Of all goods, the ends are those choiceworthy for their own sake. Of these, in turn, the *kalon* ones are all those praiseworthy because of themselves" (*EE* VIII 3 1248$^b$18–20; also *NE* I 13 1103$^a$9–10). It is because ethically *kalon* actions are intrinsically choiceworthy ends that a good person can do virtuous actions because of themselves (*NE* II 4 1105$^a$32) and for the sake of what is *kalon* (III 7 1115$^b$12–13). What makes such actions choiceworthy (VI 1 1138$^a$18–20) and praiseworthy (II 6 1106$^b$24–27), however, is that they exhibit the sort of order (X 9 1180$^a$14–18), proportionality (II 2 1104$^a$18), and determinateness (II 6 1106$^b$29–30, IX 9 1170$^a$19–24) that consists in lying in a mean (*meson*) between two extremes. This brings us full circle, connecting what is ethically *kalon* to what is aesthetically noble, lending the former too an aesthetic tinge. Finally, what is ethically *kalon* includes an element of self-sacrifice that recommends "nobility," in its more ethical sense, as a good equivalent for it as well: "It is true of an excellent person too that he does many actions for the sake of his friends and his fatherland, even dying for them if need be. For he will give up wealth, honors, and fought-about goods generally, in keeping for himself what is *kalon*" (IX 8 1169a18–22). One reason people praise a *kalon* agent, indeed, is that his actions benefit them: "The greatest virtues must be those that are most useful to others, and because of this, just people and courageous ones are honored most of all; for courage is useful to others in war, justice both in war and peace" (*Rh.* I 9 1366b3–7). But since what is *kalon* is a greater good than those an excellent person gives up or confers on others, there is also a strong element of self-interest in what he does: "The greater good, then, he allocates to himself" (*NE* IX 8 1169a28–29). An excellent person does *kalon* actions for their own sake, not for an ulterior motive, because it is only as done in that way that they constitute the doing well in action (*eupraxia*) that *is* happiness. **By nature:** See V 7 1134b18–35.

Note 21
**For the most part:** The fact that things in a given area of study hold for the most part does not preclude there being a demonstrative science of them (*APr.* I 13 32b18–22, *APo.* I 30 87b19–27, *Met.* VI 2 1027a19–21). Theorems of natural sciences hold for the most part (*APr.* I 13 32b4–8), as do those of ethics or politics (*NE* V 10 1137b13–19, IX 2 1164b31–33). Only strictly theoretical sciences, such as mathematics, astronomy, and theology, have theorems that hold universally and with unconditional necessity (VI 3 1139b18–24).

Note 22
**Well-educated person:** "Regarding every branch of theoretical knowledge and every method of inquiry, the more humble and more estimable alike, there appear to be two ways for the state to be—one that may be well described as scientific knowledge of the subject matter, the other a certain sort of educatedness. For it is characteristic of a person well educated in that way to be able accurately to discern what is well said and what is not. We think of someone who is well educated about the whole of things as a person of that sort, and we think that being well educated consists in having the capacity to do that sort of discerning. But in one case we consider a single individual to have the capacity to discern in practically all subjects, in the other case we consider him to have the capacity to discern in a subject of a delimited nature—for there might be a person with the same capacity as the person we have been discussing but about a part of the whole. So it is clear in the case of inquiry into nature too that there should be certain defining marks by reference to which one can appraise the manner of its demonstrations, apart from the question of what the truth is, whether thus or otherwise" (*PA* I 1 639a1–15); "The term 'doctor' applies both to a producer of health and to an architectonic craftsman and thirdly to someone well educated in the craft. For there are people of this third sort in practically speaking all the crafts. And we assign the task of discerning to well-educated people no less than to experts" (*Pol.* III 11 1282a3–7); "Because it seems to them characteristic of a philosopher not

to speak baselessly but always in a way that involves reason, some people often unwittingly formulate reasons that are foreign to the subject and so, pointless (sometimes they do this because of ignorance, sometimes because they are boasters). By means of such reasons even people of experience and capable of doing things in action can be caught out by those with no capacity for architectonic or practical thinking. This happens to them because of their not being well educated, since not being well educated is precisely the inability to discern in each subject which arguments belong to it and which are foreign to it" (*EE* I 6 1216$^{b}$40–1217$^{a}$10); "Some people want everything expressed exactly, whereas others are annoyed by what is exact, either because they cannot string all the bits together or because they regard it as nitpicking. For exactness does have something of this quality, so that just as in business transactions so too in arguments it seems to have something unfree or ungenerous about it. That is why we should already have been well educated in what way to accept every one" (*Met.* II 3 995$^{a}$8–13). **The nature of the subject matter allows:** See *IX* 2 1164$^{b}$27–28, 1165$^{a}$2–3, 12–14.

Note 23
**Persuasive arguments** (*pithanologountos*) **from a mathematician . . . demonstrations** (*apodeixeis*) **from a rhetorician:** Rhetoric's end or goal is persuasion (*pithanon*) (*Rh.* I 2 1355$^{b}$26), and "the mode of persuasion that has the most control" is the *enthymeme*, which is "a demonstration of a sort" (I 1 1355$^{a}$4–8) whose premises are reputable beliefs (1355$^{a}$27–28). A demonstration (*apodeixis*) proper, by contrast, of the sort that we find in an exact science, is a valid deduction from scientific starting-points, which are definitions of real essences, so that the predicates belong to the subjects in every case, intrinsically, and universally (*APo.* I 4 73$^{a}$24–27). From a mathematician we should expect demonstrations, not persuasive arguments based on reputable beliefs; from a rhetorician we should expect persuasive arguments, not demonstrations from scientific starting-points.

Note 24
**Unconditionally** (*haplôs*): The adjective *haplous* means "simple" or "single-fold." The adverb *haplôs* thus points in two somewhat opposed directions. To speak *haplôs* sometimes means to put things simply or in simple terms, so that qualifications and conditions will need to be added later. Sometimes, as here, to be F *haplôs* means to be F in a way that allows for no "ifs," "ands," or "buts." In this sense, what is F *haplôs* is F unconditionally speaking, or in the strictest, most absolute, and most unqualified way (*Met.* V 5 1015$^{b}$11–12). In this sense, what is unconditionally F is what is intrinsically F (*NE* VII 9 1151$^{b}$2–3).

Note 25
**Not a suitable audience for politics:** See X 9 1179$^{b}$24–26.

Note 26

**No experience of the actions of life:** The prime time (*akmê*) for a man's service in the military is that of his body, which is somewhere between the ages of thirty and thirty-five, while the prime time for that of his soul or his capacity for thought is forty-nine or fifty (*Pol.* VII 16 $1335^b32$–35, *Rh.* II 14 $1390^b9$–11), and it is not until then that he has the experience required for practical wisdom (*Pol.* VII 9 $1328^b34$–$1329^a17$).

Note 27

**Feelings:** See II 5 $1105^b21$–23. **Not knowledge but action:** See II 2 $1103^b26$–29.

Note 28

**Those who lack self-control:** Lack of self-control (*akrasia*)—sometimes referred to as weakness of will or incontinence—is discussed briefly in I 13 and more fully in VII 1–10.

Note 29

**Ordinary people** (*hoi polloi*): Sometimes Aristotle uses *hoi polloi* (literally, "the many," "the multitude") to refer simply to a majority of people of whatever sort—to most people. But quite often, as here, he uses it somewhat pejoratively to refer to the vulgar masses (I 5 $1095^b16$) in contrast to cultivated, sophisticated, or wise people ($1095^a21$). "Ordinary people" is intended to capture both uses. **Happiness** (*eudaimonia*): See Introduction, pp. liii–lvi.

Note 30

**Intrinsically** (*kath' hauto* or *auto kath' hauto*): Something is intrinsically F or (literally) F "all by itself" or F *in its own right* or (Latin) *per se* F if it is F unconditionally, or because of what it itself essentially is. Thus Socrates is intrinsically rational, since being rational is part of being human and Socrates is essentially human, but he is not intrinsically musical, since being musical is not part of what it is to be human.

Note 31

**Presumably** (*isôs*): *Isôs* sometimes, as here, signals a presumption or probability that such-and-such is the case, and is translated "presumably." But sometimes it signals tentativeness and is translated "perhaps." **Seem to have some argument for them:** "To investigate all the beliefs about happiness held by different people is superfluous, since little children, sick people, and lunatics apparently have many views, but no one with any understanding would go through them. For these people need not arguments but, in some cases, time in which to mature, in others, medical or political correction [or punishment]—for a medical treatment is no less correctional than a flogging. Similarly there is no need to investigate the beliefs of the majority, since they speak baselessly on pretty much every topic but most of all this one. On it, only the beliefs of wise people need be investigated. . . . But since there are puzzles concerning every subject, it is clear that there are also puzzles about the most excellent life (*kratistou biou*) and the best life activity (*zôês tês aristês*). So it is good to investigate the beliefs they hold, since the refutations of the arguments of those who dispute a certain view are demonstrations of the opposing arguments" (*EE* I 3 1214$^b$28–1215$^a$7).

Note 32

**Starting-point** (*archê*): "The starting-points, though small in magnitude, are great in power. In fact this is what it is for something to be a starting-point—that it is itself the cause of many things, with nothing above it being a cause of it" (*GA* V 7 788$^a$14–16). Starting-points (or first principles) include substance, nature, the elements (earth, water, air, fire, ether), the various types of causal factors (formal, final, efficient, material), as well as practical thought and deliberate choice (*Met.* V 1 1013$^a$16–23). The starting-points referred to here are those of a science, which are of two kinds (*APo.* I 10 76$^a$37–$^b$22). Those special to it are definitions of the real (as opposed to nominal) essences of the beings with which the science deals (II 3 90$^b$24, II 10 93$^b$29–94$^a$19). Because these are definitions by genus and differentiae (II 13 96$^a$20–97$^b$39), a single science must deal with a single genus (I 7 75$^b$10–11, I 23 84$^b$17–18, 28 87$^a$38–39). Other starting-points (so-called axioms) are common to all or many sciences (I 2 72$^a$14–24, I 32 88$^a$36–$^b$3). A third sort of starting-point posits the existence of the genus with which the science deals but may often be left implicit if its existence is clear (I 10 76$^b$17–18).

Note 33

**Some are knowable to us, some unconditionally:** "All learning comes about in this way, proceeding through what is by nature less knowable toward what is more knowable. And just as in practical matters our work is to start from what is good for each and make what is entirely [= unconditionally] good also good for each, so here it is our work to start from what is more knowable to us and make what is knowable by nature also knowable to us. Now what is knowable to each person at first is often knowable to a very small extent and possesses little or nothing of what is real [or true]. All the same, we must start from what is but badly knowable to us and try, as I said, to proceed through this to a knowledge of what is entirely knowable" (*Met.* VII 3 1029$^b$3–12).

Note 34

**We must be nobly brought up:** See X 9 1179$^b$11–1180$^a$1.

Note 35

**The starting-point is the fact that something is so:** See I 7 1098$^a$34–$^b$3. **Do not also need an explanation of why it is so** (*to dioti*): If we have been brought up with sufficiently good habits, we will accept that certain things are noble and good without explanation, as a botanist recognizes that certain plants are nettles or thistles. At that point, we are ready to look for explanations (*EE* I 6 1216$^b$26–39). Since explanations supply causes, *to dioti* is specifically a causal explanation.

Note 36
**Hesiod** (c. 700 BC): One of the oldest known Greek poets, author of the *Theogony*, *Works and Days* (of which Aristotle cites lines 293, 295–297), and the *Catalogue of Women*. His works, like those of Homer, played a substantial role in Greek education.

Note 37
**Where we digressed:** At 1095$^a$22.

Note 38
**From their lives:** See X 8 1179$^a$17–22.

Note 39
**Contemplative** (*theôrêtikos*): The adjective *theôrêtikos* is usually translated as "contemplative" when applied, as here, to a type of life or activity (X 7 1177$^a$18) in contrast to a practical (*praktikos*) one or one focused on doing actions, but as "theoretical," when applied to a type of science or thought (VI 2 1139$^a$27). While in many ways apt, this opposition is also somewhat misleading. For what makes something *praktikos* for Aristotle is that it is appropriately related to *praxis* or action, considered as an end choiceworthy because of itself, and not—as with "practical"—that it is opposed to what is theoretical, speculative, or ideal. Hence *theôrêtikos* activities are more *praktikos* than those that are widely considered to be most so: "It is not necessary, as some suppose, for a *praktikos* life to involve relations with other people, nor are those thoughts alone *praktikos* that we engage in for the sake of the consequences that come from *praxeis*, on the contrary, much more so are the *theôrêtikos* activities and thoughts that are their own ends and are engaged in for their own sake. For *eupraxia* [doing well in action] is the end, so that *praxis* of a sort is too" (*Pol.* VII 3 1325$^b$16–21). If some things are *praktikos*, because, like practical ones, they are useful, effective, or feasible means to some end, others are yet more *praktikos* because they further an end by constituting it or being identical to it: "we term both health and wealth as *prakton*, as well as the actions we do for their sake, the ones that further health or the making of money, so it is clear that happiness should be set down as the best for human beings of things *prakton*" (*EE* I 7 1217$^a$37–40). So even though theoretical wisdom is not intrinsically concerned with "any of the things from which a human being will come to be happy" (*NE* VI 12 1143$^b$19–20), because it is itself what complete happiness consists in (X 7), it is much more practical even than the practical wisdom that does contemplate them.

Note 40
**Many of those in positions of power:** The thought is that if powerful people—who can, presumably, live any way they like—choose the life of indulgence, then the majority have a reason to make the same choice. The

views of the powerful about what happiness is are therefore worth considering (1095$^{a}$30), even if they are finally rejected (X 8 1178$^{b}$33–1179$^{a}$17). **Sardanapalus:** An Assyrian king (669–626 BC) whose luxurious lifestyle was legendary. Aristotle also uses him as an example of this sort at *EE* I 5 1216$^{a}$16–19.

Note 41
**Properly belongs** (*oikeios*): *Oikeios* derives from *oikos* ("household"), so that what is *oikeios* to someone belongs to him or is properly his own in the way his family belongs to him or is properly his own. Whether wealth is *oikeios* or not "depends on who has the power of its disposal, and by disposal I mean gift or sale" (*Rh.* I 5 1361$^{a}$21–22).

Note 42
**Practically-wise people:** Practical wisdom is discussed primarily in VI 5, 7–13. **Virtue** (*aretê*): Anything that has a function (*ergon*) has a correlative *aretê*. Thus it is possible to speak of the *aretê* of thieves, scandalmongers, and other bad things that are good at doing what they do (*Met.* V 16 1021$^{b}$12–23), as well as of the *aretê* of nonliving tools and instruments. For this reason *aretê* is often nowadays translated as "excellence." An advantage of the traditional translation "virtue" is that it preserves the link with so-called virtue ethics.

Note 43
**Thesis** (*thesis*): The word may be used in the technical sense in which a *thesis* is "a supposition of some eminent philosopher that is contrary to common belief (*paradoxos*)" (*Top.* I 11 104$^{b}$19–20). **At all costs:** Compare VII 13 1153$^{b}$19–21.

Note 44
**Works that are in circulation:** Works, perhaps by Aristotle, which, like "external accounts," were available outside the Lyceum.

Note 45
**Moneymaker** (*chrêmatistês*): A *chrêmatistês* is someone whose life is devoted to accumulating wealth (*chrêmata*), where wealth is anything whose value is measured by money (*nomisma*) (IV 1 1119$^{b}$26–27). **In a way forced:** The discussion of actions that occur by force in III 1 1110$^{a}$1–4, $^{b}$1–17 requires that their cause lie outside the agent. If that is the idea here, Aristotle may be thinking of the fact that the value of money is conventional and thus lies outside the agent's own control (*Pol.* I 9 1257$^{b}$10–14). Alternatively, since the life of moneymaking is only "in a way" forced, the point may simply be that we do not freely choose money, since we choose it solely as a necessary means to other things.

Note 46
**We may set them aside:** "We can distinguish between types of lives. Some of them make no claim to this sort of thriving (*euêmeria*

[= happiness]), since they are pursued only for the sake of necessities—for example, those concerned with the vulgar crafts or concerned with money-making or vulgar occupations. . . . But since there are three things thought to lead to a happy life (the ones spoken of earlier as the greatest of human goods), namely, virtue, wisdom (*phronêseôs*), and pleasure, so we also see three lives that all those who have the power to do so deliberately choose to live—the political life, the philosophical life, the life of indulgence. For of these, the philosopher wishes to concern himself with wisdom and the contemplation that is concerned with truth; the politician with the actions that are noble (these being the ones that stem from virtue); and the indulgent person with pleasures that are of the body" (*EE* I 4 $1215^a25$–$^b5$).

Note 47
**The men who introduced the forms:** Plato and some of his followers.

Note 48
**Did not furnish a form of numbers:** "Further, in things where there is priority and posteriority, there is not some common thing beyond these and separate from them. For then there would be something prior to the first, since the common separate thing would have priority because if the common one were destroyed, the first would be destroyed. For example, if multiplication by two is the first case of multiplication, the multiplication predicated of all of them in common cannot be separate from them, since it would then be prior to multiplication by two" (*EE* I 8 $1218^a1$–8).

Note 49
**Substance:** An intrinsic being is a substance (*ousia*) rather than an attribute if and only if (1) it is most of all a primary subject, or "that of which all the others are said" (*Met.* VII 3 $1028^b36$–$1029^a2$); (2) it is separate from attributes (VII 1 $1028^a23$–24); (3) it is primary in definition or account (VII 4 $1030^b4$–7), nature (V 11 $1019^a1$–3), scientific knowledge, and time (VII 1 $1028^a32$–33); and (4) it is a particular "this" (III 6 $1003^a9$, V 8 $1017^b24$–25, VII 3 $1029^a27$–28). **Coincidental:** F is a coincidental (*kata sumbebêkos*) attribute of x if and only if it is an attribute of x but not an intrinsic one. The coincidental attributes of a thing, then, are those attributes that are not part of or entailed by its essence. Being rational is an intrinsic attribute of Socrates since he is essentially human and being rational is part of being human. Being bald, by contrast, is one of Socrates' coincidental attributes.

Note 50
**Category:** "The kinds of intrinsic beings are precisely those that are signified by the types of predication (*katêgorias*), since they are said of things in as many ways as being is signified. Since among things predicated of a thing, some signify what it is, some its quality, some its quantity, some its relation to something, some its affecting something, some its being affected by something, some where it is, some when it is, therefore being signifies the same as each of these. For there is no difference between 'a

man is keeping healthy' and 'a man keeps healthy' or between 'a man is cutting or walking' and 'a man cuts or walks'; and similarly in all the other cases" (*Met.* V 7 1017ᵃ22–30). These kinds of intrinsic being are what we call categories. **The god and the understanding** (*ho theos kai ho nous*): *Ho theos* sometimes refers to (1) the divine being that is Aristotle's closest equivalent to our God. He is defined as *nous noêseôs noêsis*—"an understanding that is an active understanding of active understanding"—or, more familiarly, "thought thinking itself" (*Met.* XII 7 1074ᵇ34–35). This being is the cause of the movement of the various heavenly spheres, also conceived of us as gods, and so of the various sublunary movements they in turn explain, including the generation of animals like ourselves (XII 5 1071ᵃ13–17, 8 1073ᵃ22–ᵇ3). He does this, however, not by being himself in motion but by being the ultimate and unmoving object of wish and desire, who is identical to happiness (XII 7 1072ᵃ26–ᵇ30): "God is in a state of well-being . . . by being too good to contemplate anything besides himself. And the explanation for this is that while our well-being is in accord with something different, he is himself his own well-being" (*EE* VII 12 1245ᵇ16–19). Often, though, *ho theos* refers to (2) the human understanding, which is the divine constituent in the human soul (*NE* X 7 1177ᵇ28): "Human beings possess nothing divine or blessed that is worth taking seriously except what there is in them of understanding (*nous*) and wisdom (*phronêsis*). For this alone of our possessions seems to be immortal, this alone divine. And by dint of being able to share in the capacity, our life, however wretched and harsh by nature, is yet managed in so sophisticated a way that a human being seems a god in comparison with other things. For understanding is the god in us . . . and a mortal life has a part that is a god" (Rose, *Fr.* 61). If that is its reference here, the sense of the clause is "the god, that is, the understanding." *EE* I 8 1217ᵇ30–31 has *ho nous kai ho theos*, where the reversed order of the conjuncts more strongly suggests the identity of the two.

Note 51

**Universal:** "A universal is naturally such as to belong to many things" (*Met.* VII 13 1038ᵇ11–12). For Platonists such a universal is a "one over many": "[*Socrates*] Do you want us to begin our investigation with the following point, then, in accordance with our usual method? I mean, as you know, we usually posit some one particular form in connection with each of the manys (*hekasta ta polla*) to which we apply the same name. Or don't you understand? [*Glaucon*] I do. [*Soc.*] Then, in the present case, too, let us take any of the manys you like. For example, there are surely many couches and tables. [*G.*] Of course. [*Soc.*] But the ideas connected to these manufactured items are surely just two, one of a couch and one of a table" (Plato, *Rep.* X 596a5–b2). Such ones, they thought, were ontologically independent of or separable from the corresponding manys—a view Aristotle rejects: "No universal occurs apart from particulars and separate" (*Met.* VII 16 1040ᵇ26–27).

Note 52

**Of all goods there would also be some one science:** In *Peri Ideôn,* which exists only in fragments, Aristotle cites and criticizes three arguments the Platonists give for forms, each of which appeals to the sciences. The second of these (79.8–11) is as follows: "The things of which there are sciences, these things *are*. And the sciences are of things other and beyond the particulars: for these are indefinite and indefinable, whereas the sciences are of definable things. Therefore there are some things beyond the particulars, and these things are the forms."

Note 53

**Each-thing-itself:** Plato often refers to the form of F as the F-itself. Aristotle thinks this cloaks a fundamental misunderstanding of the difference between particulars and universals: "Those who say there are forms are right in a way to separate them, since they are substances; but in another way they are wrong, because they say the one over many [that is, a universal] is a form. The reason is that they do not know how to characterize the indestructible substances that are over and above the particular perceptible ones. So they make the former the same in kind as the destructible ones (since we know those), adding to perceptible ones the word 'itself'—for example, the man-itself and the horse-itself" (*Met.* VII 16 $1040^b27$–34); "Platonists claim that there is man-itself and horse-itself and health-itself, with no further qualification—a procedure like that of the people who said there are gods but in human form. For just as the latter were positing nothing other than eternal men, so the former are positing forms as eternal perceptible substances" (II 2 $997^b8$–12).

Note 54

**Pythagoreans:** Followers of the philosopher and mathematician Pythagoras of Samos (mid-sixth century BC), after whom the famous Pythagorean theorem is named. Aristotle discusses them at *Met.* I 5, I 6 $987^b22$–$988^a1$, I 8 $989^b29$–$990^a32$, XIV 3 $1091^a13$–22. **Column of goods:** The reference is to a column in a table of opposites. The table referred to here may be one constructed by the Pythagoreans (*Met.* I 5 $983^a22$–26, *NE* II 6 $1106^b29$–30), although Aristotle himself also makes use of a similar device: "Objects of desire and intelligible objects . . . move without being moved. Of these objects, the primary ones are the same. For that of appetite is the apparent good, and the primary object of wish is the real good. . . . And understanding is moved by intelligible objects, and intrinsically intelligible objects are in one of the two columns, and in this column, substance is primary, and in this, the simple one and an activity. . . . But the good—that is, what is choiceworthy because of itself—is also in the same column, because a best thing is always analogous to a first one" (*Met.* XII 7 $1072^a26$–$^b1$). **Speusippus:** Nephew of Plato and eventual head of his Academy (407–339 BC). That Speusippus adopted the Pythagorean view is taken as evidence of its superior plausibility.

Note 55
**Contraries:** "Things in the same genus that are furthest from them are defined as contraries" (*Cat.* 6 6$^a$17–18; also *NE* II 8 1108$^b$33–34).

Note 56
**The form will be pointless:** The form (*eidos*, *idia*) of F is what answers the question, what is (*ti esti*) F? and thus specifies the what it is of F, or what F is. The point of introducing it is to explain why particular Fs are F: they are F because they participate in the form of F. If nothing participates in the form of the good except that very form, this explanation would go on indefinitely and thus be pointless (compare what makes a desire pointless at I 2 1094$^a$20–21).

Note 57
**Homonymy resulting from luck:** It is just luck that the word "bank" applies to the sides of rivers and also to financial institutions, so "bank" is a lucky or chance homonym. "Good" as applied to such apparently intrinsic goods as practical wisdom and certain pleasures seems not to be like that. Yet "good" is not said of each of them in accord with a single form, since they are not good in exactly the same way. Two other possibilities seem open. The stronger is that the good of practical wisdom and that of certain pleasures derive from or are related to a single sort of good, as a healthy diet and healthy complexion are both related, although in different ways, to the single bodily condition that is health in a human being—one promoting it, the other being an indication of it. A weaker possibility is that the good of practical wisdom is at least analogous to that of certain pleasures, as sight is analogous to understanding: we see a red billiard ball and see how a mathematical proof goes.

Note 58
**Soul:** A soul is "the first actualization (*entelecheia*) of a natural body which has life as a capacity" (*DA* II 2 412$^a$27–28). Since actualization and activity are intimately related, the soul is also "the activity of some sort of body" (*Met.* VIII 3 1043$^a$35–36). Everything alive, whether plant, animal, or divine being, has a soul.

Note 59
**A different branch of philosophy:** The branch of philosophy to which the criticism of Plato's account of forms and the good belongs is identified at *EE* I 8 1217$^b$16–19: as "of necessity being much more like dialectic, since arguments that are both common [to many subject areas] and destructive belong to no other science."

Note 60
**Separable:** "The belief in forms came about in those who spoke about them, because, in regard to truth, they were persuaded by the Heraclitean argument that all perceptibles are always in flux, so that if there is to be scientific knowledge and wisdom (*phronêsis*) of anything, there must,

in their view, be some different natures, beyond perceptibles, which are permanent; for there is no scientific knowledge of things in flux. Socrates occupied himself with the virtues of character, and in connection with them became the first to raise the problem of universal definitions. . . . But whereas Socrates did not make the universals or the definitions separable, his successors did separate them, and these were the kinds of beings they called forms" (*Met.* XIII 4 1078$^{b}$12–32). **Doable in action or acquirable by a human being:** See X 2 1172$^{b}$34–35.

Note 61
**The same conclusion:** As at 1095$^{a}$16–17 or 1094$^{b}$6–7.

Note 62
**Complete** (*teleios*): The adjective *teleios*, which derives from *telos* ("end," "goal"), has a number of different senses. "[a] We call [*part-whole*] complete that outside of which not even one part is to be found, as, for example, the complete time of each thing is the one outside of which there is no time to be found that is part of that time, and [b] we also call [*value*] complete that which, as regards virtue or goodness, cannot be surpassed relative to its kind, as, for example, a doctor is complete and a flute-player is complete when they lack nothing as regards the form of their own proper virtue. . . . Further, virtue is a sort of completion, since each thing is complete and every substance is complete when, as regards the form of its proper virtue, it lacks no part of its natural extent. [c] Again, things that have attained a good end are called [*end*] complete, since things are complete as regards having attained their end . . . which is a last thing. . . . And the end and that for which something is done is a last thing" (*Met.* V 16 1021$^{b}$12–30).

Note 63
**By "self-sufficient," however, we mean not self-sufficient for someone who is alone, living a solitary life, but also for parents, children, wife, and friends and fellow citizens generally** (*To d'autarkes legomen [1] ouk autô[i] monô[i], tô[i] zônti bion monôtên, alla kai [2] goneusi kai teknois kai gunaiki kai holôs tois philois kai politais*): The grammar is loose. The logical subject is *autô[i]* ("someone"). He is considered as (1) living alone and as (2) living a political life in relationship with others. The relevant sort of self-sufficiency applies to happiness for him not in (1) but in (2). The sentence, however, applies "self-sufficiency" in (2) not to happiness for him but to happiness for parents, children, and so on. Since their happiness does have an impact on his own happiness (see I 8 1099$^{b}$3–6), this may be what Aristotle intends. When he returns to the topic of happiness, however, he claims that the "self-sufficiency that is meant" (presumably here) is found more in contemplation than in anything else, in part because a person can contemplate by himself without (or with minimum need for) other people (X 7 1177$^{a}$27–$^{b}$1). At the same time, he recognizes that our nature "is not self-sufficient for contemplation," so that we need other things in our lives

in order to be able to engage in contemplation, even though contemplation itself is an entirely self-sufficient end (X 8 1178$^{b}$33–35). It seems, then, that we should understand (1–2, "He is . . . with others.") as making a cognate point. Family, friends, and fellow citizens are among the external goods (IX 9 1169$^{b}$10) or added prosperity (I 8 1099$^{b}$6–7) that a person must be provided with first. When he already has these, we can then raise the question of self-sufficiency by asking about what activity, taken in isolation, would make his life choiceworthy and lacking in nothing (1097$^{b}$14–15). **Nature:** A nature (*phusis*) is an internal source of "movement and rest, whether with respect to place, growth and decay, or alteration" (*Ph.* II 1 192$^{b}$13–15). **Political** (*politikos*): Often the claim is that a human being is by nature a political animal (*NE* IX 9 1169$^{b}$18–19), where political animals are those whose function "is some one common thing" (*HA* I 1 488$^{a}$7–8). In this sense, gregarious animals such as bees, wasps, ants, and cranes also count as political animals. A human being is more fully political than any of these, however, because he has the capacity for rational speech, whose purpose is "to make clear what is beneficial or harmful, and hence also what is just or unjust. For it is special to human beings, in comparison to other animals, that they alone have perception of what is good or bad, just or unjust, and the rest. And it is community in these that makes a household and a city" (*Pol.* I 2 1253$^{a}$2–18). Human beings are political animals, then, because they are naturally *polis*- or city-dwellers (*NE* VIII 12 1162$^{a}$17–19, *Pol.* III 6 1278$^{b}$15–30).

Note 64

**Defining mark** (*horos*): The most common meaning of *horos* in the *NE* is "term" in the logical sense, in which a syllogism has three terms. But here, as often elsewhere, a *horos* is what gives definition to what would otherwise lack it (see *Pol.* I 9 1258$^{a}$18, II 8 1267$^{a}$29, VII 4 1326$^{a}$35). A boundary marker is a *horos*.

Note 65

**What is added would bring about a superabundance of goods:** "How should we look for the best good? Is it to be counted among good things? Surely, that would be absurd. For the best is the complete end, and the complete end, unconditionally speaking, seems to be nothing other than happiness, and happiness is constituted out of many goods. So if in looking for the best one, you count it among the goods, it will be better than itself, because it itself is the best one. For example, take healthy things and health, and look to see which is the best of all these. But the best one is health. So if this is the best one, it will be better than itself, which is a strange outcome" (*MM* I 3 1184$^{a}$15–21); "A larger number of goods is a greater good than one or than a smaller number of them, provided that the one or the smaller number is included in the count, since the larger number exceeds the smaller, and what is contained in the larger number is exceeded by it" (*Rh.* I 7 1363$^{b}$18–21).

Note 66

**Function:** A function (*ergon*) is the activity that is the use or actualization of a state, capacity, or disposition, or it is a work or product that is the further result of such an activity. A thing's function is intimately related to its end and final cause: "The function is the end, and the activity is the function" (*Met.* IX 8 1050$^{a}$21–22); "each thing that has a function exists for the sake of its function" (*Cael.* II 3 286$^{a}$8–9). It is true too that the "good—the doing well—seems to lie in the function" (1097$^{b}$26–27 below). But this holds only when the thing itself is not already something bad, since "in the case of bad things, the end and the activity must be worse than the capacity" (*Met.* IX 9 1051$^{a}$15–16). Finally, a thing's function is intimately related to its nature, form, and essence. For a thing's nature is "its end—that is, what it is for the sake of" (*Ph.* II 2 194$^{a}$27–28), its form is more its nature than its matter (II 1 193$^{b}$6–7), and its essence and form are the same: "by form I mean the essence of each thing" (*Met.* VII 7 1032$^{b}$1–2). Hence "all things are defined by their function" (*Mete.* IV 12 390$^{a}$10), with the result that if something cannot function, it has no more than a name in common with its functional self (*Pol.* I 2 1253$^{a}$20–25, *PA* I 1 640$^{b}$33–641$^{a}$6). Aristotle attributes functions to an enormous variety of things, whether living or non-living. These include plants (*GA* I 23 731$^{a}$24–26) and animals generally (*NE* X 5 1176$^{a}$3–5), including divine celestial ones (*Cael.* II 3 286$^{a}$8–11), parts of their bodies and souls (*PA* II 7 652$^{b}$6–14, IV 10 686$^{a}$26–29), instruments or tools of various sorts (*EE* VII 10 1242$^{a}$15–19), crafts (as here), sciences (II 1 1219$^{a}$17), philosophies (*Met.* VII 11 1037$^{a}$15) and their practitioners (*NE* VI 7 1141$^{b}$10), cities (*Pol.* VII 4 1326$^{a}$13–14), and even nature itself (I 10 1258$^{a}$35).

Note 67

**May we likewise also posit some function of a human being that is beyond all these:** "Since every instrument is for the sake of something, and each of the parts of the body is for the sake of something, and what they are for the sake of is a certain action, it is evident that the whole body too is put together for the sake of a certain complex (*polumerous*) action. For sawing is not for the sake of the saw but the saw for sawing, since sawing is a certain use. So the body too is, in a way, for the sake of the soul, and the parts of the body for the sake of those functions for which each of them has naturally developed" (*PA* I 5 645$^{b}$14–20); "Each animal, insofar as it is an animal, must possess perception, since it is by this that we distinguish being an animal from not being an animal. As for the various particular perceptual capacities, taste and touch are necessarily present in all animals, touch because of the explanation we gave in *De Anima* [III 12 434$^{b}$13–17: 'The body of an animal must be capable of touch if the animal is to survive, . . . since anything without perception that touches things will be unable to avoid some of them and take others. And if that is so, it will be impossible for the animal to survive.'], and taste because of nutrition. For it is by taste that we discern what is pleasant and what is painful where nourishment is concerned, so as to avoid the former and pursue the latter, since flavor as a whole is an affection of the nutritive part. The perceptual capacities that depend on an external medium, on the other hand, such as smell, hearing, and sight, are found only in animals that can move from place to place. All animals that possess these perceptual capacities have them for the sake of survival, in order that, guided by antecedent perception, they can pursue their food and avoid things that are bad or destructive. But in animals that have practical wisdom they are also for the sake of living well, since they inform us of many differences, from which arises practical wisdom about intelligible things (*tôn noêtôn*) and things doable in action" (*Sens.* 1 436$^{b}$10–437$^{a}$3). See also *NE* VI 13 1145$^{a}$6–11.

Note 68

**We are looking for what is special:** "People whose function, that is to say, the best thing to come from them, is to use their bodies . . . are natural slaves" (*Pol.* I 6 1254$^{b}$17–19); "If a human being is a simple animal and his substance is ordered in accord both with reason and with understanding, he has no other function than this alone, namely, the attainment of the most exact truth about the beings. But if he is naturally co-composed of several potentialities, and it is clear that he has by nature several functions to be completed, the best of them is always *his* function, as health is the function of the doctor, and safety of a ship's captain" (*Protr.* B65). Since human beings are not naturally simple (*NE* VII 14 1154$^{b}$20–22) and do have several functions (I 10 1100$^{b}$12–13), the best one will be the one that is special to them. But because human beings have not just a complex nature but also a compound one consisting of a divine element (understanding) and a human one (X 7–8 1177$^{b}$26–1178$^{a}$23), their special function may—like that of the part of the soul that has reason (VI 1 1139$^{a}$17, 2 1139$^{a}$29–31, $^{b}$12)—be compound too. Moreover, it will matter whether we are considering male or female human beings, since these have different special functions (VIII 12 1162$^{a}$22–24).

Note 69

**Next in order is some sort of perceptual living:** The *NE* is a sort of politics (I 2 1094$^{b}$10–11), and so involves some account of the soul (I 13 1102$^{a}$18–19). The reference to an "order" among life activities or functions signals that Aristotle is drawing on his own account: "In all living things that are complete there are two parts that are most necessary, the one by which they take in nourishment and the one by which they eliminate residues [= waste products]. For a living thing can neither exist nor grow without nourishment. . . . A third part [= the perceptual part] present in all animals lies between (*meson*) the most necessary ones, and within it is found the starting-point of their sort of life. Since, then, it is the nature of plants [which are also living things] to be immobile, their non-uniform parts are not of many kinds. For the use of a few instrumental parts is enough for the few actions they perform. . . . Those beings that have perception in addition to life, by contrast, are more polymorphic in appearance and of these some more than others, and there is still greater variety among those whose nature partakes not only of living but also of living well. And such is humankind, since of living beings known to us it alone, or it most all, partakes of the divine [= reason and understanding]" (*PA* II 10, 655$^b$29–656$^a$8).

Note 70

**One part has it [reason] by dint of obeying reason, the other by dint of actually having it and exercising thought:** These parts are discussed in I 13.

Note 71

**"Living" is said of things in two ways:** Things can be said to be "alive" when they have a certain capacity or state or when they are engaged in the correlative activity. See I 8 1098$^b$30–33.

Note 72

**Excellent** (*spoudaios*): Often, as here, *spoudaios* is a synonym of *agathos* ("good") but sometimes, when predicated of things, it means "serious," "weighty," or "important," as at X 6 1177$^a$1–2. **The best and most complete:** An important addendum to this conclusion is added at *Pol.* VII 13 1332$^a$7–18: "We say, and we have given this definition in our ethical works (if anything in those discussions is of service), that happiness is a complete activation or use of virtue, and not a conditional use but an unconditional one. By 'conditional uses' I mean those that are necessary; by 'unconditional' I mean those that are noble. For example, in the case of just actions, just retributions and punishments spring from virtue but are necessary uses of it and are noble only in a necessary way, since it would be more choiceworthy if no individual or city needed such things. On the other hand, just actions that aim at honors and prosperity are unconditionally noblest. The former involve choosing something that is somehow bad, whereas the latter are the opposite: they construct and generate goods." Despite the claim in the opening sentence, nothing quite like this does appear in Aristotle's ethical works as we have them.

Note 73

**Complete life:** Sometimes a complete life seems to be one that reaches normal life expectancy: "it is correctly said among ordinary people that a life's happiness should be judged in its longest time, since what is complete should exist in a complete time and a complete human being" (*MM* I 4 1185$^a$6–9). But this seems not to be its meaning in the *NE*. See, for example, IX 8 1169$^a$18–25.

Note 74

**Blessed** (*makarios*) **and happy:** "Since, as we saw, happiness is something complete, and life (*zôê*) can be either complete or incomplete, and virtue the same (for there is the whole and the part), and the activity of incomplete things is incomplete, happiness will be the activity of complete life (*zôês*) in accord with complete virtue" (*EE* II 1 1219$^{a}$35–39). The next sentence (1219$^{a}$39–40) refers to this as providing "the genus and the defining mark" of happiness. *Makarios* is often a synonym for "happy," but sometimes with the implication of being extremely happy (*NE* I 10 1101$^{a}$7) or in a condition like that of the gods (X 8 1178$^{b}$25–32).

Note 75
**Anyone can produce what is lacking:** "In the case of all discoveries, the results of previous labors, handed down from others, have been advanced bit by bit by those who took them over, whereas the discoveries of starting-points usually constitute small progress at first but were of much greater usefulness than the later ones that developed from them. For the most important thing in all cases is perhaps the starting-point, as the saying goes. That is why it is also the most difficult. . . . But when this has been discovered, it is easier to add to it and develop the rest. This is exactly what has happened where accounts of rhetoric as well as practically all the other crafts were concerned. For those who discovered the starting-points carried them forward in an altogether small way, whereas those who are highly reputed nowadays are the heirs, so to speak, of a long succession of predecessors who advanced them bit by bit and so have developed them to their present condition. . . . Hence it is no wonder that the craft is of some significance" (*SE* 34 183$^{b}$17–34).

Note 76
**What was said before:** At I 3 1094$^{b}$11–1095$^{a}$2.

Note 77
**About what it is** (*ti esti*) **or what sort of thing** (*poion ti*): Geometry tells us what a right angle is—it specifies its essence—its what it is or what it is to be (*to ti ên einai*). Its essential attributes tell us what sort of thing it is. **Contemplator of the truth** (*theatês talêthous*): Plato, *Rep.* V 475e4 describes philosophers as *tês alêtheias philotheamonas* ("those who love to contemplate truth").

Note 78
**The works themselves:** The work of the ethicist or politician is in part (X 9 1179$^{a}$33–35) to provide an outline sketch of the good or happiness, which is a starting-point of ethics or politics (I 12 1102$^{a}$1–4), that has the degree of exactness appropriate to the relevant subject matter, which consists of noble and just things. The side issues—literally, the things beyond the works (*parerga*)—are the details that can be readily filled in later once the starting-point has been properly outlined.

Note 79
**Cause** (*aitia*): The distinction between *aitia* (feminine) and *aition* (neuter) is that an *aitia* is sometimes an explanatory argument (a type of deduction) that identifies causes, whereas an *aition* is an item in the world that is

causally efficacious. Aristotle does not systematically observe the distinction, but it is *aitia* that figures in his definitions of craft knowledge and scientific knowledge (*APo.* I 2 71ᵇ9–12, II 11 94ᵃ20–27).

Note 80

**Correctly shown** (*deichthênai*) . . . **where starting-points are concerned:** *Deichthênai* is the aorist passive infinitive of the verb *deiknunai,* which means "to show" or "to prove." One way to show something is to demonstrate it from starting-points or first principles, but a starting-point cannot itself be shown in this way, precisely because it is a *first* principle (*APo.* I 3 72ᵇ18–33, 22 84ᵃ29–ᵇ1). Nonetheless it can be made evident (*phaneron*) (*APr.* I 30 46ᵃ24–27, *DA* II 2 413ᵃ11–16) or given "an adequate showing (*dedeigmenon*)" (*NE* VII 1 1145ᵇ7) through the dialectical process of solving the puzzles which, by tying our thought in knots, cloud or darken our understanding of it (*Ph.* VIII 3 253ᵃ31–33, *Met.* III 1 955ᵃ27–ᵇ4).

Note 81

**The fact that something is so is . . . a starting-point:** Compare I 4 1095ᵇ4–8.

Note 82

**Theoretical grasp** (*theôrein*): The verb *theasthai*, with which *theôria* is cognate, means to look at or gaze at. Hence *theôria* itself is sometimes what one is doing in looking closely at something, or observing, studying, or contemplating it. *Theôria* can thus be an exercise of understanding (*nous*), which is the element responsible for grasping scientific starting-points (VI 6 1141ᵃ7–8), such as (the definition of) right angle in the case of geometry, or (the definition of) happiness in the case of politics. Hence the cognate verb *theôrein* sometimes means "to be actively understanding" or "to be actively contemplating" something. In these cases, "get a theoretical grasp on" often seems to convey the right sense. **Induction:** "Induction is the route from the particulars to the universal" (*Top.* I 12 105ᵃ13). That is, it begins with perception of particulars and ends with the grasp of a universal by understanding (*APo.* II 19 99ᵇ35–100ᵇ5). **Habituation:** A process, typically involving pleasure (reward) and pain (punishment) by which we acquire a habit that is at once cognitive (as in the case of induction) and conative, because what we experience as pleasurable we tend to desire and pursue and what we experience as painful we tend to be averse to and avoid (*DA* III 7 431ᵃ8–ᵇ10, *NE* III 5 1114ᵃ31–ᵇ3, III 12 1119ᵃ25–27, *Pol.* VIII 5 1340ᵃ23–28).

Note 83

**We must investigate it:** Probably a reference not just to any starting-point but to happiness, which is a starting-point of the present method of inquiry into ethics or politics (I 12 1102ᵃ1–4). **Things we say:** The things we say about something (*legomena*), or that seem true of it (*phainomena*), or that are thought or believed about it (*doxa*) are starting-points for a philosophical investigation of it. They need not all turn out to be among the *endoxa* or reputable beliefs that must be left intact, once the puzzles to which they give rise have been gone through. See VII 2 1145$^b$2–7.

Note 84
**They soon clash with a false one:** Omitting ταληθές ("the truth"). If it is retained, the sense is: "whereas the truth soon clashes with a false one." **All the data are in tune with a true view, whereas they soon clash with a false one:** "It is well to judge separately the argument of the explanation and what is being shown in it, because . . . one should not always attend simply to things based on arguments, often one should attend more to appearances (*phainomenois* [= *legomena*])—as things stand, though, if people cannot resolve an argument, they feel compelled to believe what has been said—and because it often happens that what seems to have been shown by the argument, although true, is not true on the basis of the explanation the argument gives. For it is possible to prove a truth from a falsehood" (*EE* I 6 1217$^a$10–17).

Note 85
**Goods, then, have been divided into three sorts, with some said to be external, some relating to the soul, and some to the body:** External goods are usually those external to the soul (*EE* II 1 1218$^b$32–33). But sometimes goods relating to the body are also classed as internal goods (*Rh.* I 5 1360$^b$1–29). In either case, goods of the soul are superior to goods of the body (*MM* I 3 1184$^b$1–6, *Pol.* VII 1 1323$^a$24–$^b$29).

Note 86
**Goods of the highest degree:** Since *the* human good—happiness—consists in actions and activities of the soul in accord with virtue (I 7 1098$^a$16–17).

Note 87
**Agreed to by philosophers:** See Plato, *Euthd.* 279b–c, *Phlb.* 48e, *Lg.* 743e.

Note 88
**It is not reasonable . . . most of them:** "Human beings are naturally adequate as regards the truth and for the most part they happen upon the truth" (*Rh.* I 1 1355$^a$15–17); "Each person has something of his own to contribute to the truth" (*EE* I 6 1216$^b$30–31).

Note 89
**Those who say that happiness is virtue or some sort of virtue:** Identified at *EE* I 4 1215$^a$23–24 as "some among the older wise men." The view that virtue is (or by itself produces) happiness is often attributed to Socrates.

Note 90
**State:** A state (*hexis*) is the penultimate stage in the development or bringing to completion of a capacity, and is a relatively stable condition (*Cat.* 8

8$^{b}$25–9$^{a}$13) ensuring that a thing is "either well or badly disposed, whether intrinsically or in relation to something—for example, health is a state, since it is a disposition of this sort" (*Met.* V 20 1022$^{b}$10–12). Capacities are of two broadly different sorts, some nonrational, others involving reason. A mark of the ones that involve reason is that they are "capacities for contraries alike," whereas a single nonrational capacity is "for a single thing": what is hot can only heat things, whereas medicine can both cure a disease and cause it (IX 2 1046$^{b}$4–7; also *NE* V 1 1129$^{a}$11–17). When we possess a capacity by nature, we do not acquire it by frequently or habitually doing something, rather, we have it first and are able to do something because we have it, as we see things because we first have sight (the capacity to see), rather than acquiring sight by frequently engaging in acts of seeing. In the case of crafts and sciences, by contrast, we acquire them by engaging in the right sort of activity (II 1 1103$^{a}$32–34).

Note 91
**And he does discern them that way:** See III 4 1113$^{a}$31–34, X 5 1176$^{a}$15–19.

Note 92
**These qualities are not distinguished in the way the Delian inscriptions . . . For the best activities possess them all:** The *Eudemian Ethics* opens with this claim (I 1 1214$^{a}$1–8). The inscription in question is in the temple on the island of Delos.

Note 93
**As we said:** Aristotle has not so much said that it is impossible or not easy to do noble actions without supplies as implied that he agrees with it at I 8 1098$^{b}$26–29.

Note 94
**There are some [goods] whose deprivation disfigures blessedness:** Deprivation of external goods impedes the virtuous activities that use them as instruments, and so the happiness such activities—when unimpeded—constitute (VII 13 1153$^{b}$9–12). Disfiguring seems to be a different matter and to apply to goods (good breeding, good children, noble looks) that are not so much instruments as features of the agent that impede activities in other ways (note the reference to "goods of the body" as impeding factors at VII 13 1153$^{b}$17–19). **Good breeding:** "Good breeding is a combination of ancient wealth and virtue" (*Pol.* IV 8 1294$^{a}$21; also V 1 1301$^{b}$2); "Good breeding in a race (*ethnei*) or a city means that its members are indigenous or ancient, that its earliest leaders were distinguished men, and that from them have sprung many who were distinguished for qualities we admire. The good breeding of an individual may result from the male side or from the female one, requires legitimacy [in birth and citizenship] on both, and—as in the case of a city—that the earliest ancestors were notable for virtue, wealth, or something

else that is highly esteemed, and that many distinguished people—men, women, young and old—come from the stock" (*Rh*. I 5 1360$^b$31–38); "Good breeding (*eugenes*) is in accord with the virtue [or excellence] of the stock (*genous*), being true to one's descent (*gennaion*), though, is in accord with not being a degeneration from nature. This degeneration, for the most part, does not happen to the well born, although there are many who are worthless people. For in the generations of men, as in the fruits of the earth, there is a certain yield, and sometimes, when the stock is good, exceptional men are produced for a period of time, and then again later on [after a period of worthless ones]. Naturally good (*euphua*) stock degenerates into characters disposed to madness (for example, the offspring of Alcibiades and Dionysius), whereas steady stock degenerates into stupidity and dullness (for example, the offspring of Cimon, Pericles, and Socrates)" (II 15 1390$^b$21–31).

Note 95
**Just as we said:** Most recently at 1099$^a$32.

Note 96
**Luck:** What happens by luck (*tuchê*) in the broad sense is what happens coincidentally or contingently (*APo*. I 30 87$^b$19–22, *Met*. X 8 1065$^a$24–28). What happens by luck in the narrow sense of *practical* luck is what has a coincidental final cause. If a tree's being by the backdoor is the sort of thing that might be an outcome of deliberative thought, it is a candidate final cause of action—an end we aim at (*Ph*. II 5 197$^a$5–8, 6 197$^b$20–22). If wish, which is the desire involved in deliberation and deliberate choice, is what causes it to be there, the tree's being by the backdoor is a genuine final cause. If not, its being there is a coincidental final cause. Unlike chance (*to automaton*), which applies quite generally to whatever results from coincidental efficient causes, practical luck—applies only to what could come about because of action and deliberate choice. Hence it is the sphere relevant to action: "Luck and the results of luck are found in things that are capable of being lucky, and, in general, of action. That is why indeed luck is concerned with things doable in action" (II 6 197$^b$1–2). The sphere of practical luck is also that of the practical and productive sciences (*PA* I 1 640$^a$27–33, *Rh*. I 5 1362$^a$2). Goods external to the soul are controlled by luck (*MM* VII 3 1206$^b$33–34), goods internal to it, such as virtue, are not (*NE* I 10 1100$^b$7–21, *Pol*. VII 1 1323$^b$27–29). **Others to identify virtue with happiness:** "To live well is the same as to live justly and nobly" (Plato, *Cri*. 48b8); "The noble and good man or woman is happy, the unjust and base one wretched" (Plato, *Grg*. 470e9–11).

Note 97
**To puzzle:** Aristotle returns to this puzzle in I 10 1100$^b$7–1101$^a$13, X 9 1179$^b$20–1181$^b$15. **Training:** See IX 9 1170$^a$11–13.

Note 98

**A different investigation:** "Since it is not only practical wisdom and virtue that produce happiness (*eupragia*), but we also say that those with good luck do well, on the supposition that good luck also produces doing well in action and the same things as scientific knowledge, we must investigate whether it is by nature that one man enjoys good luck and another bad luck, or not, and how things stand regarding these matters. . . . Do people enjoy good luck because of being loved, as they say, by a god, so that success stems from something external, so that just as a badly built ship often sails better, not because of itself, but because it has a good captain, in the same way, a person who enjoys good luck has a good captain, namely, his guardian spirit (*daimona*)? But it would be strange if a god or a guardian spirit loved someone like that rather than someone who is best and most practically-wise" (*EE* VIII 2 1246$^b$37–1247$^a$29).

Note 99

**Disabled:** Someone may be disabled as the result of an injury, disease, or accident, or because of a chance natural defect, such as being born blind. No one who lacks virtue because he is disabled in these ways is reproached or blamed for this, although someone who lacks it because he had disabled himself would be (III 5 1114$^a$25–28). The same is true of those who are *by nature* disabled where *full* virtue is concerned. A female, for example, is by nature a sort of disabled male (*GA* II 3 737$^a$27–28), since in the process of embryogenesis she is formed because of a disabling or deforming of the form transmitted in her male progenitor's semen by the menstrual fluid of her female progenitor (IV 3). Human females, as result, cannot develop full virtue, since the deliberative part of their souls "lacks control (*akuron*)" (*Pol.* I 13 1260$^a$13). Females thus have a share in happiness that is less than that of males. The same is true of natural slaves, whose souls lack a deliberative part altogether (I 13 1260$^a$12), and may also be true of people in northern or southern climates: "One may pretty much grasp what these qualities citizens should have by looking at those Greek cities that have a good reputation and at the way the entire inhabited world is divided into nations. The nations in cold regions—particularly, in Europe—are full of spirit but somewhat deficient in thought and craft knowledge. That is why they remain comparatively free but are apolitical and incapable of ruling their neighbors. Those in Asia, on the other hand, have souls endowed with thought and craft knowledge but they lack spirit. That is why they remain in subjection and slavery. The Greek race, however, occupies a medial position geographically and thus shares in both sets of characteristics. For it is both spirited and capable of thought. That is why it remains free, governed in the best way, and capable, if it chances on a single constitution, of ruling all the others. Greek nations also differ from each other in these ways. For some have a nature that is one-sided, whereas in others both these capacities are well blended. It is evident, then, that people should be by nature capable in thought and spirit if they are to be easily guided to virtue by the legislator" (VII 7 1327$^{b}$20–38).

Note 100
**What we said at the start:** At I 2 1094$^{b}$7.

Note 101
**Its supervision aims above all at producing citizens of a certain sort:** Compare I 13 1102$^{a}$7–13, II 1 1103$^{b}$2–6, X 9 1179$^{b}$20–1180$^{b}$28.

Note 102
**As we said:** At I 7 1098$^{a}$16–19.

Note 103
**Priam:** Priam was the king of Troy. His family and city were destroyed by the Greeks.

Note 104
**Wretched** (*athlios*): *Athlios*, which means "wretched" or "miserable," often has no ethical connotation (as at VII 7 1150$^{b}$5). Sometimes, though, it does have such connotations, so that someone dies in a wretched way when (unlike the case of Priam) he dies in a way that shows him to be a wretch—someone without ethical virtue (I 10 1100$^{b}$9–11, 1100$^{b}$33–1101$^{a}$14).

Note 105
**Solon** (c. 640–560 BC): Athenian statesman and poet and first architect of the Athenian constitution. The story of his advice (given to the Lydian king Croesus) is recounted in Herodotus, I 30–33.

Note 106
**As a sort of chameleon and as someone with unstable foundations:** This may be a quotation from an unknown play.

Note 107
**As we said:** At I 8 1099$^{b}$6–7.

Note 108
**Estimable:** To say that something is estimable (*timios*) is to ascribe a distinct sort of goodness or value to it: "By what is estimable I mean such things as what is divine, what is superior (for example, soul, understanding), what is more time-honored, what is a starting-point, and so on" (*MM* I 2 1183$^{b}$21–23). Thus happiness, as a starting-point of ethics, is "something estimable and complete" (*NE* I 12 1102$^{a}$2–4). Ordinary people "commonly say of those they find most estimable and most love that they 'come first'" (*Cat.* 12 14$^{b}$5–7). Something is thus objectively *timios* when—like starting-points and causes—it "comes first by nature" (*Cat.* 12 14$^{b}$3–5). Since sciences inherit their level of esteem from the kinds of beings they deal with (*Met.* XI 7 1064$^{b}$3–6), the "most estimable science must deal with the most estimable genus of beings" (*Met.* VI 1 1026$^{a}$21–22). That is why things having to do with the gods are particularly *timios* (*NE* IV 2 1122$^{b}$19–21). Finally, because

the most exact science provides scientific knowledge of ultimate starting-points and causes, the most *timios* science is also the most exact one (*Met.* I 2 982a25–27). **Most of all and most continuously:** Theoretical wisdom (*sophia*) is the virtue of the scientific part of the soul (VI 12 1144a1–3) and the most exact form of scientific knowledge (VI 7 1141a9–b8). Living in accord with theoretical wisdom is the best kind of happiness (X 7–8), the kind most like that of the blessed, and something we are more capable of doing continuously than we are of continuous action (X 7 1177a21–22).

Note 109
**Forgetfulness does not occur:** See VI 5 1140b28–30.

Note 110
**Get a theoretical grasp on things in accord with virtue:** IX 9 1170a2–4 mentions getting a theoretical grasp on (or contemplating) actions that are in accord with virtue. Here the context requires it to be the theoretical grasp itself that is in accord with virtue—in particular with the virtue of theoretical wisdom. **"Good, foursquare, beyond blame":** From a poem of Simonides. Also quoted at Plato, *Prt.* 339b.

Note 111
**As we said:** At I 7 1098a12–20. **Base** (*phaulos*): *Phaulos* is often an antonym of *kalos* ("noble") and is translated as "base." Sometimes, though, it is an antonym of *agathos* ("good") and is translated as "bad."

Note 112
**Misfortunes:** See V 8 1135b16–17.

Note 113
**In the way human beings are:** God enjoys a sort of blessed happiness that, while like ours in kind, is free from the vicissitudes of fortune, continuous, and of a higher degree: "If, then, that state of well-being that we are sometimes in, the god is always in, that is a wondrous thing; but if he is in it to a higher degree (*mallon*), that is still more wondrous. But that *is* his state" (*Met.* XII 7 1072b24–26).

Note 114
**All his friends:** Here everyone that is dear to or loved by a person, including the members of his family. Friendship is discussed in VIII–IX.

Note 115
**Our deductive argument:** A reference back to I 7–8 1097b22–1098b12.

Note 116
**Praiseworthy:** We praise a moral agent or a runner not just for being of a certain quality (virtuous, in good athletic condition) but for doing something as a result of it that we value as good or excellent, such as winning a race for our city or country or doing a courageous action in its defense. "Virtue . . . is a good thing that is praiseworthy. But virtue is thought to

be a capacity for providing and safeguarding good things, or a capacity for repeatedly doing great good things of all kinds and on all occasions. . . . But if indeed virtue is a capacity for doing good (*euergetikê*), the greatest virtues must be those that are useful to others, and because of this people honor most those who are just and courageous, since courage is useful to others in war, justice both in war and in peace" (*Rh.* I 9 1366ª35–ᵇ7). **Praiseworthy . . . estimable . . . capacities:** "Goods may be divided into the estimable, the praiseworthy, and capacities. . . . The capacities include rule, wealth, and noble looks, since these are the things that the excellent man can use well and the base one badly. That is why these goods are called capacities" (*MM.* I 2 1183ᵇ20–30). As the human good, happiness cannot be used badly. Hence it cannot be a capacity and so must be either an estimable thing or a praiseworthy one.

Note 117
**Works:** Here including the activities that are the actualizations of virtuous states of character as well as whatever further works result from these (I 1 1094ª4–6). See 1101ᵇ33 below.

Note 118
**Awards of praise involve such a reference:** By praising the gods, we imply that the standard to which their actions are referred is human virtue, even though this is absurd (X 8 1178ᵇ8–22).

Note 119
**We never praise happiness:** "Why is happiness not praised? Due to the fact that other things are praised because of it, either by being referred to it, or by being parts of it" (*EE* II 1 1219ᵇ11–13).

Note 120
**Eudoxus of Cnidus** (c. 390–c. 340 BC): A celebrated mathematician, astronomer, and philosopher and an acquaintance of Plato's. Also mentioned at X 2 1172ᵇ9.

Note 121
**The god and the good:** Compare "the god and the understanding" at I 6 1096ª24–25.

Note 122
**Encomia are properly given to its works:** "Awards of praise characteristic of virtue are due to its works, and it is to its works that encomia are properly given; and it is the winners who get the victory crowns, not those who have the capacity to win but do not win. Further, it is on the basis of his works that we discern what sort of person he is" (*EE* II 1 1219ᵇ8–11).

Note 123
**The starting-point and cause of what is good:** See V 11 1152ᵇ1–3. **Estimable and divine:** Something is objectively estimable when—like starting-points and causes—it "comes first by nature" (*Cat.* 12 14ᵇ3–5).

Note 124
**Politician** (*politikos*): A *politikos* is someone who rules a city using, in the best case, his knowledge of politics (X 9 1180ᵇ23–31), and, in the less than the best case, some approximation to it, much as a doctor is someone who treats the sick using his knowledge of the craft of medicine.

Note 125
**Cretan . . . Spartan:** The constitution of Crete is discussed in *Pol.* II 7; that of Sparta in II 6, VIII 4.

Note 126
**Deliberate choice we made at the start:** The choice was to inquire about happiness, so that the appropriate method of inquiry is that of politics (I 2 1094ᵇ10–11).

Note 127
**Politics is more estimable and better than medicine:** Politics is more estimable than medicine because it is more architectonic, aims at a more estimable good (happiness rather than health), and deals with a more estimable thing (the soul rather than the body). **Sophisticated:** Sophistication here is indicated by an interest in the ultimate starting-points or first principles of one's craft or science: "Of doctors, those who are cultivated and curious say something about physics and claim to derive their starting-points from it" (*Resp.* 21 480ᵇ26–28). These are the doctors earlier described as being more philosophical: "Of doctors who pursue their craft in a more philosophical way, the vast majority begin with physics" (*Sens.* 1 436ᵃ19–ᵇ1). Similarly "the politician must have certain defining marks, derived from nature and from the truth itself, by reference to which he will discern what is just, what is noble, and what is advantageous" (*Protr.* B47).

Note 128
**External accounts:** Also mentioned at VI 4 1140ᵃ2, *Ph.* IV 10 217ᵇ30, *Met.* XIII 1 1076ᵃ28, *EE* I 8 1217ᵇ20, II 1 1218ᵇ32, *Pol.* III 6 1278ᵇ30, VII 1 1323ᵃ21. At *Cael.* I 9 279ᵃ30 we have "the philosophical works in circulation" and at *DA* I 4 407ᵇ29 "the common accounts." The references are apparently to popular works written by Aristotle himself and "in circulation" (*NE* I 5 1096ᵃ3) outside the Lyceum, or to accounts or arguments, not necessarily developed by him, that are generally known. Whatever the precise reference here, it must (as at VI 4 1140ᵃ2) be to accounts with which the audience of the *Ethics* could be safely taken to be familiar. **Another part has reason:** This comprises the scientific part and the rationally calculative or deliberative one (VI 1 1139ᵃ5–15), as well as the understanding, which is responsible for knowledge of scientific and deliberative starting-points (VI 6 1141ᵃ7–8) and so is involved in both of them. It has reason because it is able to engage in reasoning of various sorts and produce reasons.

Note 129

**In definition** (*logô[i]*): The definition of convex is different from that of concave—alternatively the being (*einai*) of concave, or what it is to be concave, is different from the being of convex, or what it is to be convex—but in a curved surface the two are inseparable in nature. **Like convex and concave:** In an account of the soul more exact than the one required by politics, it would be important to pursue this question, as at *DA* II 2 413b13–32, III 9 432a15–b7, III 10 433a31–b13.

Note 130

**Things that appear** (*phantasmata*): *Phantasmata* are "like perceptions (*aisthêmata*)" (*DA* III 8 432a9) but, as products of the imagination (*phantasia*) (*DA* III 3 428a1–2), can persist after actual perception has ceased in the form of small movements that are like those produced by a perceptual object. When someone is asleep, it is small movements of this sort that produce dream appearances (*Insomn.* 2–3). **Decent** (*epieikês*): *Epieikês* is sometimes used interchangeably with *agathos* ("good") (V 10 1137a34–b2), as it probably is here (also IX 8 1168a33–35, X 2 1172b10–11). In a narrower sense (defined at V 10 1137b34–1138a3), an *epieikês* person is characterized in particular by an attitude to legal justice that pays more attention to fairness than to the letter of the law. What makes an *epieikês* person decent is that he is fair-minded and considerate of others (VI 11 1143a19–24). When contrasted with the majority (*hoi polloi*), the *epieikeis* are the ones who are better off and more respectable (IX 6 1167a35–b1).

Note 131

**Nutritive part:** The part responsible for the life functions of nutrition and growth.

Note 132

**As we said:** At 1102b13–14.

Note 133

**Appetitive part . . . desiring part as a whole:** Besides the capacity for nutrition and growth, which they share with plants, animal souls possess two further capacities, which must occur together (*DA* II 2 413b23–24), one "to discern things and the other to cause movement with respect to place" (III 9 432a15–17). The capacity for discernment or discrimination is due, first, to the possession of a "perceptual part" (*DA* III 9 432a30), responsible for perception proper and various other functions, such as imagination. In human beings, this part consists of the primary perceptual part, located in the heart, as well as the various perceptual capacities—sight, smell, hearing, taste, touch—and the common perceptual capacity. The part responsible for movement is the desiring part, which comprises "appetite, spirit, and wish" (II 3 414b1–2). These cause movement or action by being modes of receptivity or responsiveness to aspects of reality that are discerned to be pleasant or painful or, in some other way, good or bad, end-furthering or end-frustrating (III 7 431b8–10).

Note 134
**The reason of our fathers:** See X 9 1180ᵇ4–7.

Note 135
**Theoretical wisdom . . . temperance:** Theoretical wisdom is discussed in VI 7 1141ᵃ9–ᵇ8, comprehension in VI 10, practical wisdom in VI 5 and elsewhere in VI, generosity in IV 1, and temperance in III 10–12.

## Book II

Note 136
**Character:** *EE* II 2 1220ᵇ5–7 defines character as "a quality of soul that, though nonrational itself, is capable of obedience to reason by being in accord with a prescriptive reason."

Note 137
**Teaching:** Teaching is essentially a linguistic activity: "Certain animals share at once in some learning and teaching, some from each other, some from human beings, these are the ones that have hearing—not just those that hear sounds but those that further perceive the differences between signs" (*HA* IX 1 608ᵃ17–21; also *Pol.* I 2 1253ᵃ1–18, *Po.* 19 1456ᵇ5–7). In the full sense, it involves formal instruction in a craft or science: "Teaching is what those people do who state the causes of each thing" (*Met.* I 2 982ᵃ29–30); "An indication of the one who knows, as opposed to the one who does not know, is his capacity to teach. That is why we think craft knowledge to be more like scientific knowledge than experience is, since craftsmen can teach, while experienced people cannot" (I 1 981ᵇ7–10); "Teaching is argument (*logos*) in accord with scientific knowledge" (*Rh.* I 1 1355ᵃ26). **Experience and time:** Compare VI 8 1142ᵃ11–16.

Note 138
**Stone . . . fire:** Stone or earth and fire are two of the four sublunary elements Aristotle recognizes; the other two are water and air. Each of these has a rectilinear movement that is natural to it. Thus earth naturally moves down toward the center of the universe, and fire naturally moves upward to the universe's boundary (*Cael.* IV 4). Unless compelled or restrained, then, a stone will move downward, fire upward.

Note 139
**Brought to completion:** A virtue is a sort of completion (*Ph.* VII 3 246ᵇ2), so that by acquiring the virtues we complete our functions and ourselves (*NE* I 7 1098ᵃ12–15).

Note 140
**Various** (*allôn*): An illogical but common use of *allos* (for example, Plato, *Grg.* 473d1, *Phd.* 62a2–3) not to mean "other," since this would carry the

false suggestion that virtues are themselves crafts, but to mean "various." Also II 4 1105$^{b}$1.

Note 141
**We become just people by doing just actions:** "Since all capacities are either innate (like the perceptual capacities) or come about by habit (like that of flute playing) or through learning (like that of the crafts), in the case of some capacities—namely, those that come about by habit and by reason—previous practice is necessary for their possession but this is not necessary for the ones that are not of this sort and that involve being affected" (*Met.* IX 5 1047$^{b}$31–35).

Note 142
**Constitution** (*politeia*): A *politeia* is "a sort of way of life (*bios*) of a city" (*Pol.* IV 11 1295$^{a}$40–$^{b}$1); "a certain organization of a city's inhabitants" (III 1 1274$^{b}$38) or of its various offices, "above all, the one with control of everything" (III 6 1278$^{b}$8–10). "It is by seeking happiness in different ways and by different means that individual groups of people create different ways of life and different constitutions" (VII 8 1328$^{a}$41–$^{b}$2).

Note 143
**Confidence** (*tharrein*): "Confidence is expectation of safety accompanied by the appearance that it is close at hand and that frightening things either do not exist or are far off" (*Rh.* II 5 1383$^{a}$17–19). This best characterizes the state not of those somewhat rare confident people who are entirely fearless—such as the Celts described at *NE* III 7 1115$^{b}$27–28—but that of the majority of confident people who are, in reality, "rash cowards" (III 7 1115$^{b}$32).

Note 144
**Straight from childhood:** See X 9 1179$^{b}$31–34. **All the difference:** Compare IV 1 1121$^{a}$16–30, VII 2 1146$^{a}$31–34.

Note 145
**Our others:** Since what Aristotle says about his *Ethics* might also be said about his *Politics* and *Rhetoric*, he is probably thinking of his works as divided among the four types of philosophy he recognizes. The three theoretical ones—comprising mathematical, natural, and theological philosophies (*Met.* VI 1 1026$^{a}$18–19), which aim at truth (these are collectively "our others")—and the practical ones (*NE* X 9 1181$^{b}$15), to which his ethical writings are a contribution (*Pol.* III 12 1282$^{b}$18–23). **To become good people:** "[Socrates] used to inquire about what virtue is, not how it comes about or from what sources. This is correct procedure in the case of the theoretical sciences, since there is nothing else to astronomy or natural science except knowing and getting a theoretical grasp on the nature of the things that are the underlying subject matter of these sciences—although nothing prevents them from being coincidentally useful to us where many of the necessities of life are concerned. But the end of

the productive sciences is different from scientific knowledge or knowing things—for example, health is different from medicine; good government (*eunomia*), or some such thing, is different from politics. Now it is in fact noble to know each of the noble things but, where virtue is concerned at least, the noblest thing is not knowing what it is but from what sources it comes about. For our wish is not to know what courage is but to be courageous, nor to know what justice is but to be just—just as our wish is to be healthy rather than to know what being healthy is, and to have our state in a good condition rather than to know what it is to have it good condition" (*EE* I 6 1216$^{b}$9–25).

Note 146
**As we said:** Most recently at II 1 1103$^{b}$21–23.

Note 147
**The correct reason:** The correct reason could be either the process of reasoning engaged in by the part that has reason or the proposition, principle, or prescription that is the outcome of the process. Eventually, virtue is required not just to be in accord with the correct reason but to "involve" it (VI 13 1144$^{b}$26–27). **We shall talk about it later:** See VI 1 1138$^{b}$18–20.

Note 148
**Issues relating to action:** Reading πρακτέων for OCT πρακτῶν ("the things doable in action"). **We said at the start:** At I 3 1094$^{b}$11–22.

Note 149
**Get a theoretical grasp on** (*theôrein*): *Theôrein* can just mean "look at" or "observe," but here Aristotle is inferring something about virtues and vices ("states like these") from facts we can see (*horômen*) to be true about strength and health, so "get a theoretical grasp on" seems to convey the right sense.

Note 150
**Insensible in a way:** Insensibility of the relevant sort involves being a less good discerner, since "we discern each thing better and treat it with greater exactness when the activity involves pleasure" (X 5 1175$^{a}$31–32). Because this condition is rarely found, it lacks a name in common usage (II 7 1107$^{b}$6–8).

Note 151
**Works** (*ergois*): Here *erga* are or include the agent's actions, not just the further ends of actualizing his function.

Note 152
**Someone who is pained is cowardly:** The cowardly person is pained by the very things that he should be—and that the courageous person is—pleased by. An intemperate one, by contrast, has unruly appetites that conflict with and lessen the pleasure he takes in those things but do not prevent him from doing them.

Note 153
**Virtue of character is concerned with pleasures and pains:** "All the virtues of character are concerned with bodily pleasures and pains, and these occur either in doing actions or in remembering or in expecting. Now those that occur in acting are in accord with perception, with the result that they are set in motion by something perceptible, whereas those that occur in memory or in expectation come from this (for people feel pleasure either in remembering what they have experienced or in expecting what may be going to happen in the future). So it is necessary that all pleasures of this sort come about from perceptible things" (*Ph.* VII 3 247$^{a}$7–14).

Note 154
**As Plato says:** The reference is probably to the following passage from the *Laws*: "I say that the first infantile sensations a child feels are pleasure and pain, and it is in these that virtue and vice first come about in the soul. . . . Education, then, I say, is the first coming about of virtue in a child, when pleasure and love, pain and hatred correctly come about in his soul before he is able to grasp a reason. Then, when he does grasp the reason, these feelings agree with the reason in affirming that they have been correctly habituated in appropriate habits. This harmony taken in its entirety is virtue. But the part of it consisting in being correctly trained where pleasures and pains are concerned, so as to hate what we should hate straight from the start until the end, and love what we should love—if you separate that off in an account and call it education, in my view at least you will be calling it by its correct name" (II 653a–c; also *Republic* III 401d–402a). Compare *NE* II 1 1103$^{b}$23–25, X 1 1172$^{a}$19–26, *Pol.* VIII 6 1340$^{b}$36–39.

Note 155
**Entails** (*hepetai*): The verb *hepesthai* means "follow." So pleasure and pain follow on or accompany feelings and actions. But they do not do so in a merely temporal sense or accidentally. Instead, feelings and actions essentially involve or entail pleasures and pains.

Note 156
**By means of contraries:** Medical claims like this are made by Hippocrates of Cos, a medical writer and contemporary of Socrates. See *Aphorisms* II 22, V 19, *Breaths* I. He sounds a note of caution in *On Ancient Medicine* 13. Plato also analogizes punishments to medical treatments at *Grg.* 478a–c, *Rep.* III 408c–410a, and *Lg.* V 735d–736a.

Note 157
**As we said just now:** At II 2 1104$^{a}$27–$^{b}$3.

Note 158
**The state . . . that is a doer of the best actions:** "The state from which we are doers of the best actions" (*EE* II 5 1222$^{a}$6–12).

Note 159
**Three proper objects of choice and three of avoidance:** Aristotle treats this triadic division as generally accepted and uncontroversial (*Top.* I 13 105$^{a}$27–28, III 3 118$^{b}$27–28).

Note 160
**Dyed into our lives:** Compare Plato, *Rep.* IV 429d–430b.

Note 161
**Spirit:** See VII 6. **Heraclitus of Ephesus** (flourished c. 500 BC): One of the greatest of the Presocratic philosophers and originator of the doctrine that everything flows or is in flux. Aristotle elsewhere (*Pol.* VIII 9 1315$^{a}$30–31, *EE* II 7 1223$^{b}$22–24) quotes him as saying only that it is difficult to fight "against spirit" (*DK* 22 B85). Aristotle may be referring to that passage here or he may be referring to some other, lost passage. **A better thing:** See II 9 1109$^{a}$24–30.

Note 162
**Unchangeable state:** In a discussion of what "indestructible (*aphtharton*)" means, Aristotle notes that things are said to be indestructible (1) because it is "entirely impossible" for them to be destroyed, or (2) because it is "not easy" to destroy them (*Cael.* I 11 280$^{b}$20–281$^{a}$1). Some passages suggest that a virtuous state is unchangeable in a sense parallel to (1) (*NE* I 11 1100$^{b}$33–35, III 5 1114$^{a}$16–21), others that it is so only in the weaker sense parallel to (2) (II 2 1104$^{a}$25–29, 3 1105$^{a}$15). "A base man may improve," we learn in *Categories*, "if he is being brought into a better way of life and thought" (10 13$^{a}$22–25).

Note 163
**Little or no strength:** See X 9 1179$^{b}$23–31.

Note 164
**The one who, in addition, does them:** Retaining ὁ ("the one") with the mss.

Note 165
**Ordinary people:** Probably those who think they will become good by listening to sophists. Compare X 9 1180$^{b}$23–1181$^{b}$12.

Note 166
**Since the things that come about in the soul are of three sorts—feelings, capacities, and states—virtue will be one of these:** A virtue of character is a quality (I 6 1096$^{a}$25), specifically of the desiring part of the soul (I 13 1103$^{a}$1–10). So Aristotle can rely on his discussion of qualities (*poiotêtai*) in *Cat.* 8 to define the relevant ones more narrowly: "By quality I mean that by dint of which things are said to be somehow qualified. Quality, however, is among the things that are said of things in many ways. One kind of quality we may call a state or disposition (*diathesis*). A state differs from a disposition, though, in being more steadfast and lasting longer. . . . A second kind of quality is that by dint of which we call people

boxers, runners, healthy, or sickly—simply put, anything which they do in accord with a natural capacity or absence of one. . . . A third kind of quality consists of affective qualities or feelings" ($8^b25$–$19^a29$). **Feelings** (*pathê*): The verb *paschein* means "suffer," "undergo," "be affected by," so that *pathê* are things we are passive in experiencing rather than active—"affections" and "passions" are common translations. Further, as the contrast with states implies, feelings are episodic in nature, temporary "movements of the soul" (*Pol.* VIII 3 $1337^b42$–$1138^a1$, 7 $1342^a4$–8). Occurrent appetites, desires, and emotions and whatever else is in the desiring part of the soul are *pathê*.

Note 167
**Feeling . . . pain:** Reading λυπηθῆναι with OCT. To achieve greater consistency with Aristotle's characterization of feelings as "whatever entails pleasure and pain," some editors read φοβηθῆναι ("feeling fear") instead.

Note 168
**Disposed in a certain way:** Our feelings are episodic movements in the desiring part of the soul—something reflected in the fact that we are said to be moved to anger or pity or fear on particular occasions. Virtues and vices are relatively permanent states in which we are disposed to feel these feelings in certain ways.

Note 169
**We talked about this earlier:** At II 1 $1103^a18$–26.

Note 170
**Genus** (*genos*): The starting-point of a science—whether theoretical, practical, or productive—are items whose definitions tell us what the item (or its essence) is. Since ethics is a practical science aiming to help make people virtuous, it must tell us what a virtue of character is (something it also needs to do as part of defining happiness). Scientific definitions typically assign the *definiendum* to a species (*eidos*) by specifying its genus (which tells us what it is) and its differentia (*diaphora*) (which tell us what sort of thing it is) (*Top.* VI 5–6, *NE* I 7 $1098^a29$–32). Thus having specified the genus to which virtue of character belongs (*hexis,* or state), Aristotle goes on to ask what sort of state it is (II 7 $1106^a14$).

Note 171
**We have already said:** Most recently at II 1 $1104^a11$–27.

Note 172
**In everything continuous and divisible, then, it is possible to take more, less, and equal, and these either in relation to the thing itself or in relation to us:** The claim is probably that in everything continuous and divisible there is *either* a mean in relation to the object *or* a mean in relation to us, not that there are always *both* sorts of means. There is a mean

or midpoint between the integers 2 and 10 (namely, 6) but not, it seems, a mean in relation to us.

Note 173
**Takes . . . too much** (*pleonazei*): A tendency to take too much (*pleonazei*) or more than one's fair share is *pleonexia* (greed or graspingness).

Note 174
**Minae:** A *mina* (pl. *minae*) was the weight of 100 drachmas (or, as an amount of money, the 100 drachmas themselves). A drachma weighed about 0.15 ounces. So a mina weighed 15.15 ounces, or just about 1 pound.

Note 175
**Milo of Croton** (late sixth century BC): A famous wrestler. He supposedly ate an entire cow in a single day.

Note 176
**Virtue is more exact than any craft:** The ultimate end of any craft is happiness, or doing well in action (VI 2 1139$^{b}$1–4), but no craft can achieve it unaided. For happiness is a starting-point, and about it practical wisdom is "true supposition" (VI 9 1142$^{b}$33). What makes practical wisdom's supposition true, in turn, is virtue of character, since it is "natural or habituated" virtue of character "that teaches correct belief about the starting-point" (VII 8 1151$^{a}$18–19). Just as a science S that provides scientific knowledge of the starting-point of S$^{*}$ is more exact than S$^{*}$, so virtue of character, in providing correct belief about the ultimate starting-point of the crafts, is more exact than any of them (*APo.* I 27 87$^{a}$31–37). As a result, virtue of character better achieves the ultimate end than craft alone does, since a craft can, for example, be used for vicious purposes: "Medicine can both cure a disease and cause it" (*Met.* IX 2 1046$^{b}$4–7; also *NE* V 1 1129$^{a}$11–17). **As nature also is:** Nature is more exact than craft because nature does nothing pointlessly and always acts to achieve the best (*IA* 2 704$^{b}$15–17), whereas a craft, though it "imitates nature" (*Mete.* IV 1 381$^{b}$6), can fail to achieve what is best by not being under virtue's control (*NE* VI 2 1139$^{b}$1–3). That is why "the for-the-sake-of-which and the good (*to kalon*) are present more in the works of nature than of craft" (*PA* I 1 639$^{b}$19–21). **Aim at and hit** (*stochastikê*): The verb *stochazesthai* means "to aim at." Being *stochastikê* is being skillful at aiming at, and thus able to aim at and hit, the target.

Note 177
**Similarly where actions are concerned:** "For movement is continuous and an action is a movement" (*EE* II 3 1220$^{b}$26–27).

Note 178
**Excess is in error and subject to blame:** Reading ἡ μὲν ὑπερβολὴ ἁμαρτάνεται καὶ ψέγεται, καὶ ἡ ἔλλειψις for the mss. ἡ μὲν ὑπερβολὴ

ἁμαρτάνεται καὶ ἡ ἔλλειψις ψέγεται ("excess is in error and deficiency is blamed"). OCT deletes ψέγεται ("excess and deficiency miss the mark"), losing the contrast with the mean as both praised and correct.

Note 179
**Pythagoreans portrayed it:** In their table of opposites (see I 6 1096^b^6).

Note 180
**"People are good in one way, you see, but bad in all sorts of ways":** Source unknown.

Note 181
**Deliberately choosing state:** A deliberative desire (*bouleutikê orexis*) is one that has deliberation as its "starting-point and cause" (*EE* II 10 1226^b^19–20)—likewise, desiderative understanding and thinking desire (VI 2 1139^a^22–23). Presumably, then, a deliberately choosing state is one that has deliberate choice as its starting-point and cause in that the actions resulting from it have deliberate choice (that is a deliberative desire) as their starting-point and cause. **The one by which:** Reading ᾧ with OCT. The mss. have ὡς ("in the way in which").

Note 182
**Essence** (*ousia*), **what is it to be** (*to ti ên einai*): An *ousia* is a substance, but the *ousia* or being of *x* is *x*'s essence—the thing specified by the account (*logos*) or definition (*horos*) that tells us what x is, or what it is to be x.

Note 183
**To do any of these things is to err:** "That is why, in fact, when people dispute the accusation, they do so by saying that they had sex but were not committing adultery, since they were acting in ignorance or were compelled" (*EE* II 4 1221^b^23–25).

Note 184
**The ones that apply to a part are truer:** The important question here (II 2 1103^b^26–31) is, what actions are such that doing them repeatedly will make someone virtuous? For obvious reasons, the account of courage will provide a more informative or truer answer than the universal account of virtue of character. Similarly the "truest portrayals (*alêthinôtata*) of distress or violent anger are given by the one who experiences these emotions" (*Po.* 17 1455^a^31–32). However, x can be a truer account than y even if there is no absolutely true account to which x is closer: "If what is more (*mallon*) is what is closer, there must be some truth to which the more true (*to mallon alêthes*) is closer. But even if there isn't, still there is already at least something more stable and truer (*alêthinôteron*)" (*Met.* IV 4 1009^a^1–3). **Our account should be in harmony with them:** The Greek does not specify what account should be in harmony with the particulars, but I 8 1098^b^9–12 suggests that it is the account of virtue of character.

Note 185

**Chart:** A chart of the virtues, with their associated excesses and deficiencies is given in *EE* II 3 1220$^{b}$38–1221$^{a}$12:

| EXCESS | DEFICIENCY | MEAN |
|---|---|---|
| irascibility | insensitivity to pain | mild-mannerdness |
| rashness | cowardice | courage |
| shamelessness | bashfulness | sense of shame |
| intemperance | insensibility | temperance |
| enviousness | nameless | indignation |
| profit | loss | justice |
| wastefulness | acquisitiveness | generosity |
| boastfulness | self-deprecation | truthfulness |
| flattery | surliness | friendliness |
| ingratiation | churlishness | dignity |
| luxuriousness | toughness | resilience |
| conceit | smallness of soul | greatness of soul |
| extravagance | niggardliness | magnificence |
| unscrupulousness | unworldliness | practical wisdom |

The instruction in our text suggests that this (or a similar) chart was available to Aristotle's audience, perhaps displayed on the wall of his lecture room. The list differs most conspicuously from the one employed in the *NE* in that it includes practical wisdom as a mean state.

Note 186

**Insensible:** See II 2 1104$^{a}$24–25.

Note 187

**Acquisitiveness** (*aneleutheria*): Literally un- (*an-*) generosity (*eleutheria*). Gamblers and robbers are *aneleutheros* (IV 1 1122$^{a}$7–8) in taking what they shouldn't from people they shouldn't, but we would hardly say that they were ungenerous because of it. Hence acquisitiveness.

Note 188

**Excessive in getting but deficient in giving:** Compare IV 1 1119$^{b}$28–31, 1121$^{a}$14–16, 1121$^{b}$12–1122$^{a}$16.

Note 189

**The way we have laid down:** At 1107$^{b}$14–15 above.

Note 190

**A truthful sort:** Truthful specifically about himself (IV 7).

Note 191

**There are also medial conditions in feelings** (*pathêmata*) **and concerned with feelings** (*pathê*): The mean is in *pathêmata* but concerned with *pathê*. The distinction, if one is intended, seems to be between inner feelings that do not necessarily result in deliberately chosen actions, and those that do result in such actions.

Note 192
**Similarly:** The similarity is to the opportunity for later discussion, not to saying in which way the virtues of reason (or of thought) are means, since the doctrine of the mean is not applied to these.

Note 193
**It takes work to be excellent:** A traditional saying. See, for example, Hesiod, *Works and Days* 287–292; Plato, *Prt.* 339a–341e.

Note 194
**Homer:** *Odyssey* XII. 219–220. Circe, not Calypso, gives this advice.

Note 195
**Rectifying distortions in pieces of wood:** See IX 3 1165$^{b}$19–20. Compare Plato, *Prt.* 325d.

Note 196
**Homer:** *Iliad* III. 156–160. The abduction of Helen, wife of the Greek king Menelaus, by Paris, the son of Priam, king of Troy, was the purported cause of the Trojan War. What the elders said is that Helen should be sent away, lest her irresistible beauty ruin Troy.

Note 197
**Define in an account** (*logos*): Or "define by reason," "define in words."
**Their discernment lies in perception:** Repeated almost verbatim at IV 5 1126$^{b}$3–4. Perception is in control (*kuriôs*) of our knowledge and our discernment of particulars because it alone gives us cognitive access to them and their attributes (*APo.* I 18 81$^{a}$38–$^{b}$6, *NE* VII 3 1147$^{a}$25–26). When the attributes in question are proper perceptibles, such access is largely inerrant: "By proper perceptible I mean the one that cannot be perceived by another perceptual capacity and about which we cannot be in error. . . . Each perceptual capacity is discerning about its proper perceptibles, at any rate, and does not make errors about whether there is color or whether there is sound but, rather, about what the colored thing is or where it is, or what the thing making the sound is or where it is" (*DA* II 6 418$^{a}$11–16). This presupposes, however, that the perceptual capacities (or senses) are functioning properly in conditions which do not impede their achieving their end (*NE* VII 12 1153$^{a}$15). For people "do not perceive what is presented to their eyes, if they happen to be deep in thought or afraid or hearing a lot of noise" (*Sens.* 7 447$^{a}$15–17) and cannot perceive accurately what isn't presented at the right distance (449$^{a}$21–24) or in the right way: "Each thing is more readily perceptible when presented simply by itself (*haplôs*) than when mixed with others—for example, pure rather than unmixed wine or honey, or a color or a single note rather than one in a chord—because they tend to obscure one another" (447$^{a}$17–20).

# Book III

Note 198

**Feelings:** Aristotle says nothing about what makes a feeling voluntary or involuntary, giving all his attention to actions. It may be, therefore, that he intends the voluntariness or involuntariness of feelings to be parasitic on that of actions, in the way suggested at II 9 1109ª30–ᵇ12. **It is the voluntary ones that are praised and blamed:** This could mean an action's or feeling's being voluntary is (1) a *sufficient* condition or (2) a *necessary* condition of its being praised or blamed. Since there need be nothing praiseworthy or blameworthy about an action or feeling that meets Aristotle's criteria for voluntariness (1111ª22–24), (2) is almost certainly the intended meaning. **Sympathetic consideration** (*suggnômê*): *Suggnômê*, which is like pardon or forgiveness, is discussed in VI 11. **Voluntary** (*hekousion, hekôn*), **involuntary** (*akousion, akôn*): An agent acts or undergoes something *hekôn* if and only if what he does or undergoes is *hekousion*, and does or undergoes something *akôn* if and only if what he does or undergoes is *akousion*. Broadly speaking, what is *hekousion* is an event in the history of an agent that accrues to him in such a way that he is appropriately praised or blamed, rewarded or punished. What is *akousion* is an event in his history that does not accrue to him in this way. The practical focus of the investigation is important to keep in mind.

Note 199

**The agent, or the one being affected, contributes nothing:** Aristotle is describing a case of involuntary *action*, so the agent involved here must be imagined as acting, but under the influence of an external force or starting-point. So the agent does something in being carried by the wind or by human beings with control over him, and what he does constitutes his involuntarily going to where it or they take him. If he were asleep or narcotized, he would not be *going* where he is being taken, and so would not be going there involuntarily either.

Note 200

**Something noble:** In the example this could be saving one's parents and children by giving in to the tyrant's threat or nobly refusing to do so even at the price of their lives.

Note 201

**Instrumental parts:** The instrumental parts of a living thing are parts, such as the limbs, that it can use to achieve an end (*GA* II 6 742ª28–36).

Note 202

**Unconditionally . . . intrinsically:** See VII 9 1151ᵇ2–3.

Note 203

**Euripides** (c. 480–407/6 BC): Athenian tragic playwright, author of some ninety plays, including the *Bacchae* and *Medea*. Aristotle refers to the lost

*Alcmaeon* from which he quotes at V 9 1136$^{a}$13–14. Alcmaeon's father, Amphiaraus, foresaw that he would meet his death on an expedition that his wife Eriphyle had compelled him to join. In revenge, he ordered Alcmaeon to kill Eriphyle, threatening to put a curse on him for noncompliance.

Note 204
**The actions lie in the particulars** (*hai gar praxeis en tois kath' hekasta*): Literally, "the actions [are] in the particulars." Here the preposition *en* expresses a relationship between an action and some particulars, which could be (1) the set of particulars in which the action consists or (2) the class—that of particulars—in which it is included, or (3) the particular circumstances in which it occurs. 1110$^{b}$33–1111$^{a}$1 (*hê kath' hekasta, en hois kai peri ha hê praxis*) seems to somewhat favor (1). Later, the same preposition is used to characterize one of these particulars (see *en tini* at 1111$^{a}$4), but must then have a somewhat different sense.

Note 205
**For the sake of these:** See II 3 1104$^{b}$30–1105$^{a}$1.

Note 206
**It is ridiculous, then:** Reading δὴ ("then") for OCT δὲ ("But it is ridiculous . . .")

Note 207
**Not voluntary** (*ouch hekousion*) **. . . *contra-voluntary*** (*akousion*): Aristotle usually uses *akousion* ("involuntary") as equivalent in meaning to *ouch hekousion* ("not voluntary"). Here, however, he somewhat confusingly uses the same term to apply to what is not voluntary and regretted as opposed to what is simply not voluntary. "Contra-voluntary" is intended to capture this special sense of *akousion*.

Note 208
**Drunk** (*methuôn*): Dead drunk rather than merely tipsy or merry (*oinomenos*) (VII 3 1147$^{a}$14).

Note 209
**Depraved person** (*mochthêros*): *Mochthêria* ("depravity") is much the same as vice, so that a *mochthêros* person is a vicious one. Sometimes, though, *mochthêros* is simply equivalent to *kakos* ("bad") (for example, VII 14 1154a11).

Note 210
**When someone acts, then, we can ask . . .:** Aristotle mentions seven particular elements as being those "in which the action lies and with which it is concerned (*en hois kai peri ha*)": (1) *tis* (who?), (2) *ti* (what?), (3) *peri ti* (concerning what?) or (4) *en tini* (in what?), (5) *tini* (with what?), (6) *heneka tinos* (for the sake of what?), (7) *pôs* (in what way?). In V 8, two shorter lists are given: *on* (the one affected), *hô(i)* (the instrument), *hou heneka* (the

end) (1135ᵃ25 also ᵇ15–16); *on* (the one affected), *ho* (what the agent is doing), *hô(i)* (the instrument), *hou heneka* (the end) (1135ᵇ13). In *EE* II 9 we also have two shorter lists: *on* (the one affected), *hô(i)* (the instrument), *hou heneka* (the end) (1225ᵇ2); *on* (the one affected), *hô(i)* (the instrument), *ho* (what the agent is doing) (1225ᵇ7). (2) *ti* (what?) is clearly what the shorter lists refer to as *ho* (what the agent is doing). Since a sane agent cannot be ignorant of the fact that he is the one doing the action, (1) is usually omitted (*NE* 1111ᵃ7–8). By a process of elimination, then, (3) *peri ti* (concerning what?) and (4) *en tini* (in what?) must express in greater detail what the other lists refer to simply as *on* (the one affected). Now the one affected (whether a person or a thing) by an action is the primary locus of the action—the one in which it occurs: "In all the cases where what comes to be is a different thing that is beyond the use [of the capacity], in those cases the activity is in (*en*) what is being produced—for example, the activity of building is in the house that is being built" (*Met.* IX 8 1050ᵃ30–32); "In the case of all the potentialities the activities are external, either in something other than oneself, or in oneself insofar as one is other [as when a doctor heals himself]" (*EE* VII 2 1237ᵃ36). For example, Merope's action, had she not stopped herself in time, would have occurred in her son, whom she mistakes for the enemy. Apparently, then, we should understand (4) *en tini* as making the somewhat vague (3) *peri ti* more precise, and as making more explicit that *on* (the one affected by the action) is the one in which or in whom the action occurs or is located. Thus the location of an action is one of the particular factors in which it lies. *Peri* and *en* express one thing, therefore, when they are used to characterize the relationship between an action and its many constituents (as at *NE* 1110ᵇ6, 8; 1111ᵃ1, 16), and a different thing when they are used (as at 1111ᵃ4, 18) to characterize one of those constituents.

Note 211
**Aeschylus** (?525/4–456/5 BC): Tragic playwright, author of between seventy and ninety plays, including the *Oresteia.* The religious cult of Demeter and Kore at Eleusis, included some rites—the so-called Eleusinian Mysteries—that initiates were forbidden to reveal. Aeschylus seems to have been formally charged with violating this injunction before the Court of the Areopagus in Athens but was acquitted.

Note 212
**As Merope did:** In Euripides' lost play *Cresphontes,* "Merope, on the point of killing her son, recognizes him in time" (*Po.* 14 1454ᵃ5–7). **Pumice stone:** A solidified frothy lava that is much lighter than regular stone.

Note 213
**The ones in which the action occurs** (*en hois hê praxis*) **and what it is for the sake of:** Of the seven factors in which an action lies (4) and (6) are here identified as the ones with the most control. The idea, presumably, is that if we are ignorant about either of these, it will make our knowledge or ignorance of the others irrelevant.

Note 214

**Deliberate choice:** Because what we "deliberate about and deliberately choose" is what furthers the end (III 5 1113$^b$3–4), deliberate choice (*prohairesis*) is a matter of choosing (*hairein*) one thing before (*pro*) another (1112$^a$16–17) and thus of determining what things should be done *earlier than* or *in preference to* others (*MA* 7 701$^a$17–20) in order to further the desired end in the best way: "someone with understanding chooses the better of two things in all cases" (*EE* VII 2 1237$^b$37–38). **A better discerner of people's characters than their actions are:** "When we praise or blame we look more to the deliberate choice than to the works done, even though the activity of the virtue is more choiceworthy. This is because people do base actions when they are compelled but do not deliberately choose to do them. Further, it is because it is not easy to see what sort of choice is involved that we are compelled to discern from his works what sort of person someone is. So, while the activity is more choiceworthy, the choice is more praiseworthy" (*EE* II 11 1228$^a$11–19; also *NE* II 4 1105$^a$28–33).

Note 215

**Children and other animals share in what is voluntary but not in deliberate choice:** See III 1 1111$^a$24–26.

Note 216

**Those who say:** Aristotle's reference is unclear.

Note 217

**Appetite is contrary to deliberate choice but not to appetite:** To conflict as contraries, two appetites would have to be for and against the same thing at the same time in the same respect.

Note 218

**There is wish for impossible things:** Omitting καὶ. Or (keeping it) "There is wish for impossible things as well [as possible ones]."

Note 219

**Proper object of deliberation:** A proper object of deliberation (*bouleuton*) is something that has the features (such as being up to us to bring about) that make it possible (sensible) for us to deliberate about it.

Note 220

**No one deliberates about . . .:** The classes of things Aristotle refers to as lying outside the scope of deliberation are: (1) Eternal necessities of the sort we find in mathematics and in those parts of cosmology that deal with the unmoved mover (god), who is the starting-point of all change or movement in the universe (*Met.* XII 6–7), and that involve beings (god, numbers) that do not move or change. (2a) Necessities involving beings (such as the heavenly bodies) that do involve change or movement but whose movement is always the same (the solstices, the risings of the heavenly bodies). (2b) Necessities in the natural or sublunary realm that are due to the natures of the things in that realm, that always happen in the same way. (3) Droughts and rains, which also come about naturally and so by a sort of necessity, even though they do so for the most part rather than always in the same way: "All things due to nature come about always or for the most part but nothing which is the outcome of luck or chance does that. For we do not think it is luck or coincidence when there is a lot of rain in winter but when there is a lot in summer, nor when there are heat waves in summer but when there are in winter" (*Ph.* II 7 198[b]34–199[a]3); things in (2b) and (3) are subsequently classed together as being explained by appeal to nature (*NE* 1112[a]31–33). (4) Things that come about by luck. Since it covers the entire sphere of the coincidental or contingent, the sort of luck referred to is broad luck.

Note 221
**We do deliberate about . . .:** "The things we deliberate about are clear. They are those that naturally depend on us, that is, those of which the starting-point of their coming about is up to us, since we investigate a thing until we discover whether it is possible or impossible for us to do in action" (*Rh.* I 4 1359[a]37–[b]1). The action possible for us to do or not to do is what best furthers—perhaps by constituting—our end, which, in the last analysis, is happiness or the human good. This brings understanding into the picture, since we desire what we understand to be good: "We desire something because it seems good rather than its seeming so because we desire it, since the starting-point is active understanding" (*Met.* XII 7 1072[a]28–30).

Note 222
**There is no deliberation . . .:** "The explanation of why doctors deliberate about the things with which their science deals whereas scribes do not is that there are two kinds of errors (we err either in rational calculation or in perception while actually doing the thing); in medicine it is possible to err in both ways but in writing the letters of the alphabet only in perception and action, and if they investigate [or rationally calculate] about that, they will go on without limit" (*EE* II 10 1226[a]33–[b]2).

Note 223
**More where crafts are concerned than sciences:** In place of OCT τέχνας ("crafts") some editors read δόξας ("beliefs"). **Sciences:** Since crafts are productive sciences, the sciences with which they are contrasted here, as the use of "for the most part" in the next sentence suggests, are the strictly theoretical sciences (mathematics, theology), which deal with eternal necessities, or with beings whose movement is always the same (astronomy).

Note 224
**And where there is an element of indefinability:** In place of OCT καὶ ἐν οἷς ἀδιόριστον ("and where there is an element of indefinability")

some editors read καὶ ἐν οἷς τὸ ὡς δεῖ ἀδιόριστον ("and in which what we should do is indefinable"). *MM* I 17 1189b24 has ἐν οἷς ἤδη ἀοριστόν ἐστι τὸ ὡς δεῖ ("in which there is an element of indefinability in what we should do").

Note 225
**Good government:** A city or constitution exhibits good government or is well governed if it has laws that are obeyed by the citizens and that are either the best ones available to that particular city or are unconditionally the best ones (*Pol.* IV 8 1294a4–9).

Note 226
**Last thing found in the analysis:** See VI 8 1142a28–29.

Note 227
**What comes about through our friends comes about through ourselves in a way, since the starting-point is in us:** See IX 4 1166a30–32, 8 1169a32–34, 9 1169b30–1170a4, 12 1172a10–14.

Note 228
**Through whom** (*di' hou*) **. . . through which things** (*dia tinos*): *Di' hou* could also mean "through *which* thing" (neuter instead of masculine), but that would make it difficult to distinguish this topic of deliberation from *dia tinos* ("through *which things*").

Note 229
**As we said:** At 1112b28. See also VI 2 1139b4–5. **Other things:** As Aristotle immediately makes clear in the next sentence, these are the ends we wish for and thus take for granted in deliberating about what actions of ours will best further them.

Note 230
**The leading element:** Understanding is the element in the soul that rules and leads (X 7 1177a14–15). Its role in deliberate choice is characterized at VI 2 1139a33–b5, VI 11 1143a35–b11.

Note 231
**The kings announced to the common people:** The kings are the equivalent of leading element; their announcement is the equivalent of a decree (*psêphisma*), which is the last thing reached in deliberation (VI 8 1141b26–28).

Note 232
**In accord with our deliberation:** Reading κατὰ τὴν βούλευσιν with OCT. Some mss. have κατὰ τὴν βούλησιν ("in accord with our wish"). An agent who lacks self-control, however, wishes in accord with deliberation but desires and acts in accord with appetite.

Note 233
**As we said:** At 2 1111b26.

Note 234
**Those:** See Plato, *Grg.* 466a–468e, where Socrates defends this view of wish. **The proper object of wish:** Retaining τὸ.

Note 235
**Even contrary ones:** Aristotle attributes a view like this to Protagoras at *Met.* XI 6 1062ᵇ12–19.

Note 236
**A standard and measure of them:** Repeated at IX 4 1166ᵃ12–13, X 11 1176ᵃ15–19.

Note 237
**Being good people and being bad people:** Being good or bad does not consist simply in doing good or bad actions unless these are understood as actions that are done in the way the good or bad person would do them (II 4 1105ᵇ5–10). **Will be:** Reading ἔσται with some mss. for OCT ἄρα ("being decent or base is *therefore* up to us").

Note 238
**Voluntarily evil or involuntarily blessed:** Aristotle may be adapting a saying of the fifth-century comic poet Epicharmus. The claim is a staple of Plato's works (*Prt.* 345d–e; *Grg.* 468b–c; *Men.* 77d–e; *Rep.* III 413a; *Ti.* 86d–e; *Lg.* V 731c, V 734b, IX 860d). **Wicked** (*ponêros*): *Ponêria* is ethical badness or vice (VII 8 1150ᵇ36–37), so *ponêros* means "wicked," or "knavish."

Note 239
**Said just now:** At 3 1112ᵇ31–32, explained at 1113ᵃ5–7.

Note 240
**The ones in us:** Reading ἐν ἡμῖν with OCT. Some mss. have ἐφ' ἡμῖν ("up to us"). See 1114ᵃ19.

Note 241
**Doubled in cases of drunkenness:** A law requiring "a drunken person to be punished more severely for an offense than a sober one," was peculiar to Pittacus (*Pol.* II 12 1274ᵇ18–23), who was appointed tyrant of Mytilene in 589 BC to restore order. He is referred to again at *Rh.* II 24 1402ᵇ8–12.

Note 242
**The starting-point was in him:** Reading ἐν αὐτῷ with OCT for the mss. ἐπ' αὐτῷ ("up to him").

Note 243
**Everyone would admonish:** See Plato, *Prt.* 323c–d.

Note 244
**The naturally good disposition in its complete and true form:** "A good natural disposition (*euphuia*) in its true form consists in just this—the

ability to choose the true and avoid the false. For people with natural discernment are the very ones who can do this well, since they discern correctly what is best by a correct love or hatred for what is set before them" (*Top.* VIII 14 $163^b13$–16); "a good natural disposition, good memory, readiness to learn, quick-wittedness . . . are all productive of good things" (*Rh.* I 6 $1362^b24$–25).

Note 245
**People who are cowards . . . face the loss of wealth with good confidence:** See VI 13 $1144^b30$–$1145^a1$.

Note 246
**Wanton aggression:** "The person who commits wanton aggression (*hubris*) also treats with contempt; for wanton aggression consists in doing things or saying things that involve shame for the one who suffers them, not in order that something [beneficial] may come about for the agent or because something [bad] has happened to him but for the pleasure of it; for those who are doing the same thing back are revenging themselves not committing wanton aggression. The cause of pleasure to those who commit wanton aggression is that they think they become superior themselves by ill-treating others (that is why young people and rich ones are prone to wanton aggression, since they think themselves superior when they commit wanton aggression)" (*Rh.* II 2 $1378^b23$–29). **Flogged:** That is, flogged as a punishment for the crimes he has committed.

Note 247
**In cities and by monarchs:** The contrast is between political systems with one ruler (monarchies) and those with more than one (democracies, aristocracies).

Note 248
**Unanxious** (*adeês*): Aristotle usually describes a courageous person as *aphobos* ("fearless") in the way the correct reason requires (I 13 $1102^b27$–28). Here and at $1115^b1$, he shifts to a near equivalent, *adeês*, with a slightly different coloration akin to that of *atarachos* ("calm") at III 8 $1117^a19$, 9 $1117^a31$; IV 5 $1125^b34$.

Note 249
**Seamen remain optimistic in keeping with their experience:** See III 8 $1116^b3$–15.

Note 250
**Prowess** (*alkê*): *Alkê* sometimes simply means "strength" or "vigor," as when physical exercise is said to promote "health and *alkê*" (*Pol.* VIII 3 $1338^a19$–20). But often, as probably here, it means strength (in the sense of prowess) displayed in action. **Neither holds when we come to ruin in these two ways:** What we are to imagine is a person facing death at sea or by disease who, though he has quite reasonably despaired of safety,

nonetheless remains calm or without anxiety, not because his expert knowledge and long experience of seafaring or medicine makes him optimistic about his chances of survival but because, being courageous, his fears are in a mean. To that extent, and as far as his feelings go, he exhibits his courage. Yet there is something he cannot do, namely, deliberately choose to "show his courage (*andrizontai*)" in a display of prowess, or in doing some action that would constitute dying a noble death. For death by disease or at sea are simply things to be avoided, since there is nothing noble or choiceworthy about them, and if one has rationally despaired of avoiding them, there is nothing to deliberately choose to do but accept one's grim fate.

Note 251
**This also holds, then, for a courageous person. But courage is something noble:** Reading καὶ τῷ ἀνδρειῷ δὴ ἡ δ' ἀνδρεία καλόν for OCT καὶ τῷ ἀνδρειῷ δὲ ἡ ἀνδρεία καλόν ("And so to the brave person too courage is something noble").

Note 252
**We said earlier:** At II 7 $1107^{b}1$–2. **Neither earthquake nor waves:** Apparently a quotation. "Because of spirit, the Celts, for example, take up arms and march against the waves" (*EE* III 1 $1229^{b}28$–30). Peoples from cold northern European regions are "full of spirit but somewhat deficient in thought and craft knowledge" (*Pol.* VII 7 $1327^{b}23$–25). Compare Plato, *Rep.* IV 435e.

Note 253
**Political courage:** Socrates defines such courage as the power to "preserve through everything the correct and law-inculcated belief about what is terrible and what isn't" (*Rep.* IV 430b–c).

Note 254
**Homer:** *Iliad* XXII. 100 (the speaker is Hector, son of Priam); VIII. 148–149 (the speaker is Diomedes, son of Tydeus).

Note 255
**We previously discussed:** in III 6–7.

Note 256
**Homer:** *Iliad* II. 391–393 (the speaker is Agamemnon). Hector expresses a similar thought somewhat differently at XV. 348–351.

Note 257
**Socrates thought:** "Courage is scientific knowledge of what is terrible and what confidence inspiring" (Plato, *La.* 199a–b); courage is "wisdom (*sophia*) about what is terrible and what isn't" (Plato, *Prt.* 360d).

Note 258
**Occasions that are empty of danger:** Reading κενά ("occasions that are empty of danger") with OCT. Some mss. have καινά ("surprises").

Note 259
**At the temple of Hermes:** In a battle near the city of Coronea in Boetia in 353 BC, professional mercenaries abandoned the citizen militia. Hermes is the messenger god.

Note 260
**Homer:** *Iliad* XI.11; XIV.151; XVI.529; V.470; XV.232, 594; and *Odyssey* XXIV.318–319. **His blood boiled:** Not in Homer.

Note 261
**The end:** What is added is more precisely a grasp by understanding of this end (VI 13 1144[b]1–14).

Note 262
**Taking them for Sicyonians:** This happened in a battle at Corinth in 392 BC. See Xenophon, *Hellenica* IV 4 10. Sicyonians were less formidable than Spartans.

Note 263
**Because it is small in extent:** The idea, presumably, is not that the end (victory, crown, and honors) is actually a small thing, but, rather, that it appears small because it is far off (see Plato, *Prt.* 356a–357a).

Note 264
**The nonrational parts:** The parts are probably spirit and appetite (as at III 1 1111[a]24–25), with courage being the virtue of spirit, temperance of appetite. Unlike Plato, who did think that spirit and appetite were separate parts of the soul (*Rep.* IV 435a–441c), Aristotle includes both in the soul's desiring part (I 13 1102[b]30).

Note 265
**Except coincidentally:** "By the sorts of smells we enjoy non-intrinsically [= coincidentally], I mean those we enjoy because of anticipation or memory, such as those of food and drink (for we enjoy the pleasure of these because of a different pleasure, namely, that of eating and drinking). An example of the sort we enjoy intrinsically is that of flowers. Stratonicus put it elegantly when he said that some things smell beautiful, others delicious" (*EE* III 2 1231[a]7–12). Stratonicus (c. 410–360 BC) was a famous Athenian lute player and wit. **Perfumes or gourmet dishes** (*opsôn*): In the case of perfumes, the objects in question are probably sexual; in the case of gourmet dishes, they are those of hunger and thirst. *Opsa* were literally relishes or condiments used to flavor staple foods.

Note 266
**"A deer or a wild goat":** Homer, *Iliad* III.24.

Note 267
**Slavish:** The existence of gluttons, drunks, and sex addicts attests to the power of the associated pleasures to make us their slaves (III 11 1118[b]20–21),

in part by incapacitating our reason (VII 11 1152$^{b}$16–18). Contrast "appropriate to free people" at 1118$^{b}$5. **Touch and taste:** "The primary form of perception is touch, which belongs to all animals" (*DA* II 2 413$^{b}$4–5); "Touch is the only perceptual capacity whose lack necessarily involves the animal's dying" (III 13 435$^{b}$4–5); "Taste is a sort of touch, since taste is of food and food is a tangible body. Sound, color, and smell do not nourish, nor do they produce either growth or decay. So taste too must be a sort of touch, because it is a perception of what is tangible and nourishing. These, then, are necessary to the animal, and it is evident that without touch no animal can exist" (III 12 434$^{b}$18–24).

Note 268
**Pleasures of Aphrodite:** Sexual pleasures. On the development of sexual tastes through habituation, see *HA* VII 1 581$^{b}$11–21.

Note 269
**Touching that gave the gourmand pleasure:** "Even where the pleasures of taste are concerned, not all of them are attractive to wild beasts, for example, those perceived by the tip of the tongue. But those perceived by the throat are, which is a feeling more like touch than taste. That is why gluttons pray not for a long tongue, but for the gullet of a crane—as did Philoxenus, the son of Eryxis" (*EE* III 2 1231$^{a}$12–17).

Note 270
**Insofar as we are animals:** See X 3 1173$^{b}$20–25, X 5 1176$^{a}$15–29.

Note 271
**Most appropriate to free people** (*eleutheriôtatai*): *Eleutheria* is freedom, particularly political freedom (V 3 1131$^{a}$28, V 6 1134$^{a}$27). An *eleutherios* person is free (in the appropriate way) with his wealth and is thus generous. **Certain parts:** In the cases of food and drink, these are the tongue, mouth, throat, and stomach; in the case of sexual pleasures, the genitals and related parts.

Note 272
**As Homer puts it:** *Iliad* XXIV.130–131.

Note 273
**The replenishment of a need:** See X 3 1173$^{b}$7–20; Plato, *Grg.* 493e–497d, *Rep.* IX 585d–e, *Phlb.* 31b–32b.

Note 274
**Gluttons:** Literally, "people who are belly-mad (*gastrimargoi*)."

Note 275
**Before the others:** The reference could be: (1) to pleasant things other than the most pleasant ones; or (2) to things other than the pleasant or most pleasant ones.

Note 276
**Intemperance** (*akolasia*): *Akolasia* means "lack of discipline," from the cognate verb *kolazein* ("discipline," "punish").

Note 277
**Just as:** Reading δὲ with OCT. Some mss. have ὥσπερ γὰρ ("for just as"). **Tutor** (*paidagôgos*): The *paidagôgos* was a household slave responsible for minding and bringing up a young child, taking him to and from school, and so on.

## Book IV

Note 278
**Wealth** (*chrêmata, ploutos*): Wealth consists of the store of goods required by household managers and politicians to ensure the self-sufficiency of the household or city (*Pol.* I 8 1256^b^26–39). Money (*nomisma*) is a medium of exchange, a unit of value, and a way of storing wealth for future use (*Pol.* I 9). **Giving** (*dosis*) **or getting** (*lêpsis*): *Dosis* and *lêpsis* do not mean quite what we mean by "giving" and "getting." For example, *lêpsis* does not mean getting wealth or money in exchange for something or by producing it, as a farmer or shoemaker might. That is why someone can "get" wealth or money from himself ($1120^a34–^b2$). Similarly, spending (*dapanê*) is included under *dosis* ($1121^a12$), because it is the absolute alienation of wealth, not the exchange of it for something of equal or comparable value. Someone who gives a bookseller $20 in return for a book has not "spent" anything, since his wealth remains unchanged by the transaction: he could return the book and get his $20 back. *Dosis* and *lêpsis* are not commercial activities, then, so much as they are social ones, like our gift giving and gift getting. That is why, having asked whether it is "a characteristic of the free person to get or provide himself with wealth," Aristotle answers, "No. That sort of thing is not a matter of any virtue at all" (*MM* I 24 $1192^a15$–16). Acquiring and accumulating wealth is the function of the craft of wealth acquisition, which is discussed in *Pol.* I 3–4 and 8–11; I 11 discusses the parts of it that a free person should know.

Note 279
**Take wealth more seriously than they should:** See II 7 $1107^b13$–14, IV 1 $1121^a14$–16, $1121^b12$–$1122^a16$.

Note 280
**Substance** (*ousia*): *Ousia* can mean "substance," "substantial being," or "essence," all of which are metaphysical notions. Here it means "substance" in the sense of "a person of substance" or "a substantial sum."

Note 281
**Those who have not acquired . . . poets do:** "[Socrates:] You do not seem particularly to love money. And those who have not made it

themselves are usually like that. But those who have made it themselves love it twice as much as anyone else. For just as poets love their poems, and fathers their children, so those who have made money take their money seriously both as something they have made themselves and—just as other people do—because it is useful. This makes them difficult even to be with, since they are unwilling to praise anything except money" (Plato, *Rep*. I 330b–c).

Note 282
**Simonides** (c. 556/532–466/442 BC): A poet from Iulis on Ceos. None of his surviving poems explain this allusion to him. He did, though, have a reputation for acquisitiveness, and this may be what Aristotle has in mind.

Note 283
**Contemptuously** (*oligôrôs*): Contempt (*oligôria*) is "the actively entertained belief that something is manifestly worthless. . . . There are three forms of it: despising, spite, and wanton aggression" (*Rh*. II 2 $1378^{b}10$–15).

Note 284
**In order not to be compelled to do anything shameful:** There is a hint of this thought in what Cephalus says about the advantages of wealth: "Not cheating someone, even unintentionally, not lying to him, not owing a sacrifice to some god or money to a person, and as a result departing for that other place in fear—the possession of wealth makes no small contribution to this" (Plato, *Rep*. I 331b1–4).

Note 285
**They are satisfied:** Reading ἀρέσκει with OCT. Some mss. have ἀρέσκειν ("so they are satisfied, they say"). Compare Plato, *Rep*. II 359a1–2, where those who lack the power to do injustice without suffering it "decide that it is profitable to come to an agreement with each other neither to do injustice nor to suffer it."

Note 286
**Unfree** (*aneleutheros*): *Eleutheria* is political freedom (V 3 1131a28). *Eleutheriotês* is freedom in the use of wealth, or generosity. *Aneleutheria* is acquisitiveness, or being unfree in the use of wealth. Here, though, *aneleutheria* has the broader sense—cognate with *eleutheria*—of something unfree or unsuitable for a free person: "There is a difference between the functions of the free and those of the unfree, and that they [children who are to become free citizens] should share only in such useful things as will not turn them into vulgar craftsmen. (Any function, craft, or branch of learning should be considered vulgar if it renders the body or mind of free people useless for the practices and activities of virtue. That is why the crafts that put the body into a worse condition and work done for wages are called "vulgar," since they debase the mind and deprive it of leisure.) Even in the case of some of the sciences that are suitable for a free person, while it is not unfree to participate in them up to a point, to study

them too assiduously or pedantically is liable to result in the harms just mentioned. What one acts or learns *for* also makes a big difference. For what one does for one's own sake, for the sake of friends, or on account of virtue is not unfree, but someone who does the same thing for others would often be held to be acting like a hired laborer or a slave" (*Pol.* VIII 2 1337ᵇ5–21). "Liberty," "liberality," "illiberality," and "liberal" (as in a "liberal education") preserve these relationships but are not all current in everyday English.

Note 287
**A gambler and a robber:** Omitting καὶ ὁ λῃστὴς ("and a pirate").

Note 288
**Equipping a trireme:** Athens as well as other Greek cities required wealthy private citizens to finance public projects of various sorts, from equipping a trireme (an oared warship) to putting on a theater festival.

Note 289
**What the action lies in, and what it concerns** (*en hô[i] kai peri ha*): Compare *en hois kai peri ha* at III 1 1110ᵇ33–1111ᵃ1.

Note 290
**"Gave to many a vagabond":** Homer, *Odyssey* XVII.420.

Note 291
**We will talk about these topics later:** At 1123ᵃ19–33.

Note 292
**As we said at the start, the state** (*hê hexis*): The reference could be (1) to the state of magnificence in particular and "the start" could refer to (1) the start of this chapter. Alternatively, the references could be (2) to virtuous states in general (with "the [*hê*]" serving as a universal quantifier, as in "the tiger is a quadruped") and (2) to the start of the *NE* or to the start of the discussion of virtue of character. Of these (1) is perhaps more likely, since Aristotle has not previously said that virtues are defined by their objects, which here are works (*erga*) beyond the activities of the state itself (1122ᵇ3–6), although he has said that they are defined by their activities (II 1 1103ᵇ22–23). Magnificence, on the other hand, is defined at the start of this chapter both by its great works (for example, a well-equipped trireme) and by its activities, which are expenditures suitable in scale to them—something Aristotle will now make more explicit.

Note 293
**What is worshipped** (*to daimonion*): Daimons are either gods or the children of gods (Plato, *Ap.* 27c10–d3). *To daimonion* is the sphere of such beings and thus of religious matters generally. **The common good** (*to koinon*): Literally, "the common thing," or "what is common." But here, and often, the reference is to the common good (VIII

12 1162ᵃ28–29), or common advantage (V I 1129ᵇ15, VIII 9 1160ᵃ11) of a community.

Note 294
**Something of the character of votive offerings:** When the city does something grand—such as erecting a temple, making a lavish offering to a god, or having a public feast—an individual can display his magnificence by paying the bill. Occasions like that are the canonical occasions for such display. But he can also display magnificence in entirely private occasions, such as a wedding, which are one-off affairs, and which, like other such occasions, attract a certain amount of public attention, as celebrity weddings do in our society. A magnificent private house adorns the city in much the way that a statue given to it as a gift does or as a trireme exhibits the city's wealth and power. Finally there are private events undertaken on behalf of the city, such as entertaining visiting dignitaries, and the like. These may not benefit the citizens or the city directly, but they show it off in a good light—light that is reflected back on the magnificent person who undertakes them.

Note 295
**The unconditionally most magnificent one:** Ἁπλῶς ("unconditionally") is added in OCT but omitted by many editors.

Note 296
**Dining club** (*eranos*): The members of an *eranos* took turns in paying for dinner. Feasts were supposed to be on a scale that all members—including poorer ones—could afford. **Purple . . . Megara:** Purple dye was expensive in the ancient world, and purple robes inappropriately solemn and regal for a comedy. The reference to Megara is obscure.

Note 297
**Greatness of soul:** "If we were inquiring about what greatness of soul is, we should investigate, in the case of some great-souled people we know, what one feature they have in common as such. For example, if Alcibiades, Achilles, and Ajax are great-souled, what one feature do they all have in common? Intolerance of insults, since one went to war, one became enraged, and one killed himself. Next take some other cases, such as Lysander and Socrates. If their common feature is being indifferent to good or bad luck, I take these two and investigate what feature—indifference to luck and intolerance of dishonor—they have that is the same. And if there is none, there will be two forms of greatness of soul" (*APo.* II 13 97ᵇ17–25).

Note 298
**The person who is in accord with it:** The person in accord with greatness of soul or some other state of character is the person whose actions and feelings are in accord with it.

Note 299
**Lacks understanding:** See VI 13 1144ᵇ8–14.

Note 300
**Not everyone who thinks himself worthy of great things is conceited:** A thinks he is worthy of x, when he is actually worthy of y, where y < x. B thinks he is worthy of x, and is worthy of it. If x is not great enough to make B great-souled, then it is not great enough to make A conceited either. Conceit, like greatness of soul, requires magnitude.

Note 301
**If he were not worthy of so much:** In this case, a small-souled person A is imagined to be worthy of the greatest things, x, but considers himself worthy of y, where y < x. Since the difference between x and y cannot be greater than it is in this case, anyone who is to be the most small-souled would have to be worthy of x. For suppose B is worthy of z, which is less than x, but, like A, he considers himself worthy of y. Then either (1) z > y, and B is conceited; or (2) z = y, and B is temperate or (if z is great enough) great-souled; or (3) z < y, and B is small-souled but not as small-souled as A.

Note 302
**It surely is the greatest of external goods:** Compare IX 9 1169$^{b}$8–10.

Note 303
**They think themselves worthy:** Omitting οἱ μεγάλοι ("for it is most of all of honor that *the great* think themselves worthy") with OCT.

Note 304
**Relative to himself:** That is, in relation to his own worth. Similarly, it is in relation to his own worth that the conceited person is excessive, and in relation to the worth of the great-souled person that he is not excessive.

Note 305
**Noble-goodness:** "Noble-goodness is complete virtue" (*EE* VIII 3 1249$^{a}$16–17; also *MM* II 8 1207$^{b}$20–27). Notice "virtue that is complete" at 1124$^{a}$8.

Note 306
**Good luck:** "Good luck consists in getting and keeping those good things of which luck is the explanation" (*Rh.* I 5 1361$^{b}$39–1362$^{a}$1).

Note 307
**These things make people more great-souled:** It is not clear whether Aristotle is (1) endorsing this position or (2) giving reasons why it seems (or why people think) that good luck contributes to greatness of soul.

Note 308
**Thetis does not mention . . . his behalf:** Aristotle is apparently misremembering Homer, *Iliad* I.503–527, where Thetis asks Zeus to support her son, Achilles, in his dispute with Agamemnon but does mention her good services (503–504), though without saying what they were, and does not mention his previous good services to her. **Nor did the Spartans . . . they received:** Aristotle is apparently referring to a Spartan embassy to

Athens in 369 BC to ask for aid against the Thebans. In Xenophon's account (*Hellenica* VI 5 33–36), the Spartans do mention their previous good services to Athens.

Note 309
**Except when he is being self-deprecating . . . ordinary people:** Or "except when [he speaks less than the truth] in the presence of ordinary people [because he is being moderate], not because he is self-deprecating." This avoids the implication (apparently made problematic by IV 7 1127ᵇ22–23) that the great-souled person is self-deprecating.

Note 310
**Because of wanton aggression** (*hubris*): The *hubris* (wanton aggression or insult) is probably that of the great-souled person's enemies and the one thing he will speak ill of them for. But some editors take the *hubris* to belong to the great-souled person himself, in which case the sense is that he will not speak ill even of his enemies "unless to insult them to their face."

Note 311
**They are not evildoers:** See III 2 1123ᵃ31–33.

Note 312
**More opposed:** Compare IV 1 1122ᵃ13–16.

Note 313
**Our first remarks:** At II 7 1107ᵇ24–30.

Note 314
**Our first remarks:** At II 9 1109ᵇ16–18.

Note 315
**Anger:** "Anger may be defined as a desire involving pain for manifest revenge because of a manifest act of contempt directed toward ourselves or our kin, when the contempt is inappropriate. . . . Where an act of contempt is an activity characteristic of the belief that something is manifestly of no worth" (*Rh.* II 2 1378ᵃ30–ᵇ12).

Note 316
**Spirit:** Here anger or rage (compare III 8 1116ᵇ24–1117ᵃ5).

Note 317
**Taking revenge or exacting punishment:** Reading ἢ ("or") with OCT. One ms. has ἢ καὶ ("or even"), suggesting that a harsh person seeks not simply revenge (an eye for an eye) but further punishment as well.

Note 318
**In our previous remarks:** At II 9 1109ᵇ14–23.

Note 319
**Define in an account** (*tô[i] logô[i] apodounai*): Or "define by reason," "define in words." Compare *tô(i) logô(i) aphorisai* at II 9 1109ᵇ21. **For it**

**lies in the particulars, and it is in perception that their discernment lies:** Reading ἐν γὰρ τοῖς καθ' ἕκαστα, κἀν τῇ αἰθήσει ἡ κρίσις with OCT but adding a comma to give the same sense as at II 9 $1109^b22$–23. The mss. have τοῖς καθ' ἕκαστα καὶ τῇ αἰθήσει ἡ κρίσις ("for its discernment lies in the particulars and in perception").

Note 320
**Causing pleasure:** The Greek is *sunêdunein,* which may be a neologism.

Note 321
**Guided by the consequences:** The virtuous person primarily (1) pursues what is noble, since this is the end characteristic of virtue (e.g., III 7 $1115^b12$–13), but he also (2) pursues what is advantageous (good things that are not noble), provided that doing so is consistent with (1). He (3) chooses to cause pleasure and avoid causing pain as intrinsically valuable ends provided that doing so better furthers (1) and (2).

Note 322
**Extremes appear to be opposed:** Compare IV 4 $1125^b24$–25.

Note 323
**And self-deprecation:** καὶ τῆς εἰρωνείας ("and self-deprecation") is an addition accepted by OCT and most editors.

Note 324
**Not extremely blameworthy:** Omitting ὡς ὁ ἀλαζών ("as the boaster"). If the phrase is retained, as in OCT, the reference must be to the plain boaster who boasts but not for the sake of a further end. The sense would then be: "the one who does it for reputation or honor is not extremely blameworthy, as the plain boaster isn't either." Some editors read ὡς ἀλαζών. The sense then is "the one who does it for reputation or honor is not as extremely blameworthy as a boaster."

Note 325
**Since it is in accord with his state of character:** Compare VI 2 $1139^a31$–35.

Note 326
**A prophet, a wise person, or a doctor:** Reading μάντιν σοφὸν ἰατρόν with OCT. The mss. have μάντιν σοφὸν ἢ ἰατρόν ("a wise prophet or doctor").

Note 327
**As indeed Socrates used to do:** Socrates' disavowal of expert craft or scientific knowledge of virtue is a commonplace in Plato's portrait of him (*Ap.* 20d6–e3, 21b4–5; *Hp. Ma.* 286c8–d2, 304d5–e3; *La.* 190b7–c5; *Ly.* 212a4–7, 223b4–8; *Men.* 71b1–3; *Prt.* 361c2–6; *Rep.* I 354c1–3). As a result many of his interlocutors charge him with *eirôneia* ("self-deprecation," "irony"), thinking that he must have such knowledge if he is able to refute

others (*Ap.* 38a1, *Grg.* 489e3, *Rep.* I 337a4, *Smp.* 216e4). Aristotle takes these disavowals at face value (*SE 34* 183ᵇ7–8).

Note 328
**Spartan dress:** Spartan dress was extremely austere (hence our adjective "spartan"). Wearing it could thus be a way of boasting of one's own austerity or disregard for fashion.

Note 329
**Jibing** (*ton skôptomenon*): *Skôptein* is often translated as "joking" but seems closer in meaning to "jibing" or "mocking," or "putting down," since "the person who jibes (*skôptôn*) is the one who aims to expose faults of soul or body" (*Po.* II = Janko, p. 37). Wit—jibing well—is thus "well educated insult (*pepaideumenê hubris*)" (*Rh.* II 12 1389ᵇ11–12).

Note 330
**Also to listen to:** Compare III 4 1113ᵃ31–34.

Note 331
**Old-style and new-style comedies . . . shameful language:** Old-style comedies, such as those of Aristophanes (c. 446–386 BC), used obscene and abusive language for comic affect. New comedy, whose greatest practitioner was probably Menander (344–392 BC), began in the last quarter of the fourth century and was more decorous. Aristotle's "shameful language" covers both obscenity and certain sorts of abuse: "The legislator should altogether outlaw shameful language from the city, as he would any other shameful thing, since by speaking lightly of a shameful activity one comes closer to doing it. He should particularly outlaw it among children, so that they neither say nor hear anything of the sort. If it happens, nonetheless, that any free man who is not yet old enough to have been given a seat at the messes is found saying or doing something forbidden, he should be punished by being dishonored or beaten. But if he is older than this, he should be punished with those dishonors usually reserved for the unfree, because he has acted in a slavish manner. And since we are outlawing shameful talk, we should apparently also outlaw looking at unseemly pictures or stories. So the officials should ensure that there are no statues or pictures representing unseemly actions, except those kept in the temples of those gods at whose festivals custom permits even scurrility to occur. Custom allows men of suitable age to pay this sort of honor to the gods on behalf of themselves and of their women and children. But younger people should not be permitted to witness iambus or comedy until they have reached the age when it is appropriate for them to recline at the communal table and drink wine, and their education has rendered them altogether immune to the harm such things can do" (*Pol.* VII 17 1336ᵇ3–23). In *Po.* II, comedy is explicitly distinguished from abuse: "Comedy differs from abuse (*loidoria*), since abuse rehearses the bad action and qualities of people without any concealment, whereas comedy requires so-called implication

(*emphasis*)" (= Janko, p. 37). In the same work comedy is divided, as has become traditional, into new, middle, and old: "The types of comedy are: old, which is greedy for what causes laughter; new, which abandons this, and tends more toward the dignified; and middle, which is a mixture of both" (= Janko, p. 42).

Note 332
**Do not cause pain to his listener:** "The one who can produce jibes of the sort that gives pleasure to a person of good discernment, even though the laugh is on himself, will be a mean between the vulgar person and the one who is prim. This definition is better than the one saying that the jibe must not be painful to the person who is the butt of it, no matter what sort of person he is. Rather, it should please the person in the medial condition, since he is the one who discerns well" (*EE* III 7 1234$^{a}$18–23). A similar issue about who sets the standard for correctness is raised by *NE* III 11 1118$^{b}$25–27, which refers to "ordinary people."

Note 333
**Endure listening to:** Listening to jibes primarily includes listening to and finding funny those directed at the listener himself: "There are, however, two sorts of wit: one consists in enjoying something that causes laughter and is directed at oneself, if it does happen to be that way, as a jibe is; the other consists in the ability to produce things of that sort" (*EE* III 7 1234$^{a}$14–17).

Note 334
**More like a feeling than a state:** "All these medial conditions [indignation, shame, friendliness, dignity, simplicity or candor (*haplous*), wit] are praiseworthy without being virtues, and their contraries are not vices either, since they do not involve deliberate choice. All of them are found in the classification of feelings, since each is a particular feeling. But because they are natural, they contribute to the natural virtues . . . for each virtue somehow occurs both naturally and otherwise, that is, involving practical wisdom" (*EE* III 7 1234$^{a}$23–30).

Note 335
**Live by their feelings:** See I 3 1095$^{a}$2–6, X 9 1179$^{b}$31–1180$^{a}$1.

Note 336
**It will be discussed later:** At VII 1–10.

## Book V

Note 337
**Underlying conditions** (*hupokeimena*): A *hupokeimenon* is often the underlying (*hupokeisthai*) subject, which can persist through change, as Socrates

can persist through change, from being bearded to being clean shaven. If the change in question is a substantial or existence change, so that it is the coming to be or passing away of a substance, the *hupokeimenon* is matter. Here, however, the *hupokeimena* are the underlying conditions of a state, including those that help produce it. Thus the unconditionally best constitution is contrasted with the best one achievable *ek tôn hupokeimenôn* or "given the underlying conditions" (*Pol.* IV 1 1288$^b$25–26).

Note 338
**Keys:** The clavicle, or collar bone, may be called a key (*kleis*) because it rotates on its axis when the shoulder is abducted or drawn back, or because its somewhat hooked shape was like that of an early sort of key, which was a hook pushed through a door from the outside to raise the latch.

Note 339
**So it is clear:** See 1129$^a$19–23.

Note 340
**In accord with their virtue:** Reading κατ' ἀρετὴν, omitted in OCT.

Note 341
**Happiness and its parts:** The reference is probably to happiness and external goods, which are sometimes referred to as parts of happiness: "It follows from this definition of happiness that its constituent parts are: good birth, plenty of friends, good friends, wealth, good children, plenty of children, good old age; further, the bodily virtues (for example, health, beauty, strength, height, athletic ability), reputation, honor, good luck, and virtue" (*Rh.* I 5 1360$^b$19–24). **Political community** (*politikê koinônia*): A community consists of a group of people (or other animals) who engage in a common (*koinos*) enterprise that involves sharing something with one another (*koinônein*) (*Pol.* II 1 1260$^b$39–40). It is political when it is governed by a constitution. The canonical political community is the city (*polis*).

Note 342
**"Neither the evening star nor the morning star is so wondrous":** Euripides, *Melanippe*, fr. 486. **"In justice is all virtue summed":** Theognis of Megara (late seventh or mid-sixth century BC), ln. 147.

Note 343
**Complete use:** Reading χρῆσις τελεία for OCT χρῆσις ("use"). "Since happiness is the best thing, however, and it is some sort of activity or complete use (*chrêsis tis teleios*) of virtue, and since, as it happens, some people are able to share in happiness, whereas others are able to do so only to a small degree or not at all, it is clear that this is why there are several kinds and varieties of cities and a plurality of constitutions. For it is by seeking happiness in different ways and by different means that individual groups of people create different ways of life and different constitutions" (*Pol.* VII 8 1328$^a$37–$^b$2).

Note 344
**Bias of Priene** (sixth century BC): One of the so-called Seven Sages, men famous for their wisdom.

Note 345
**The good of another:** A view defended by Thrasymachus in Plato, *Rep.* I 343c.

Note 346
**Since that is difficult work:** See II 3 1105$^{a}$9.

Note 347
**They are the same state but their being** (*einai*) **is not the same:** When something considered in one way satisfies one account or definition and satisfies another account or definition when considered in a different way, the object considered in the first way differs in being (*einai*) from the same object considered in the second way (see VI 7 1141$^{b}$23–24).

Note 348
**Pleasure of making a profit:** When an exchange of goods (such as honor, wealth, or safety) between A and B or an allocation of goods to them is just, it is in some way equal or fair. If A profits relative to B, he gets more than he should of those goods. If he arranges the exchange or allocation in order to make that profit, he is greedy and unjust in the correlative sense.

Note 349
**We distinguished:** At V 1 1129$^{a}$32–$^{b}$1.

Note 350
**The common good** (*to koinon*): "The virtue of a part must be determined by looking to the virtue of the whole. Hence both women and children [as well as men] must be educated by looking to the constitution, if indeed it makes any difference to the virtue of a city that its children be virtuous, and its women too. And it must make a difference, since half the free population are women, and from children come those who participate in the constitution" (*Pol.* I 13 1260$^{b}$14–20).

Note 351
**We must determine later:** See X 9 1180$^{a}$14–$^{b}$28.

Note 352
**A good man . . . a good citizen:** "The virtue of a citizen must be suited to his constitution. Consequently, if indeed there are several kinds of constitution, it is clear that there cannot be a single virtue that is the virtue—the complete virtue—of an excellent citizen. But a good man, we say, is so in accord with a single virtue: the complete one. Evidently, then, it is possible for someone to be an excellent citizen without having acquired the virtue with which an excellent man is in accord" (*Pol.* III 4 1276$^{b}$30–34).

Note 353
**Fair** (*to ison*), **unfair** (*to anison*): A fair share is an equal (*ison*) one, and unfair share an unequal (*anison*) one. "Fair or equal" translates *ison* when the equality aspect of it is playing a role in the argument.

Note 354
**Worth lies in freedom:** With the result that all free citizens are of equal worth. **Aristocracy, in virtue:** "Aristocracy" is understood as rule by the truly best people, that is, by the most genuinely virtuous ones (*Pol.* IV 7).

Note 355
**Numbers consisting of units:** Numbers consisting of units, or "pure" numbers, such as 1, 2, 3, 4, and so on, are proportionate: 1:2::2:4. But so too are applied numbers, such as 2 ounces, 4 feet, and 12 men.

Note 356
**Justice ensouled** (*dikaion empsuchon*): Or, "justice personified," as we might say.

Note 357
**Intermediary** (*meson*): That is, a sort of mean.

Note 358
**The second was exceeding the mean . . .:** Imagine a line AB divided into two equal segments AD (6 units), DB (6 units). ED (2 units) and DC (2 units) are equal segments of AD and DB.

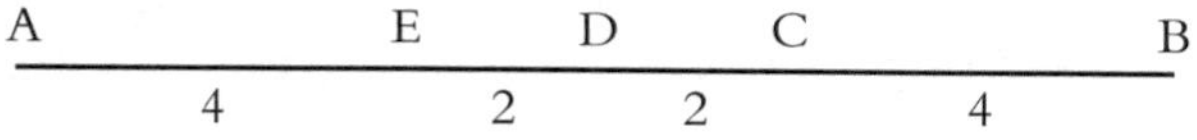

A E D C B

4 2 2 4

Aristotle is imagining that ED is subtracted from AD, resulting in AE (4 units) and added to DB, resulting in EB (8 units). EB (8 units) now exceeds AE (4 units) by (2 × 2) units. The mean is 6 units. The share EB (8 units) that is too much exceeds the mean by (1 × 2) units and the mean exceeds the share that is too little, AE (2 units), by (1 × 2) units.

Note 359
**The greatest share** (*tou megistou*): The share of the party who gets more.

Note 360
**Let the lines AA′ . . .:** This case is more general than the previous one, since it does not assume that the amount subtracted from one party in the transaction is equal to the amount added to the other.

Note 361
**This:** Probably the claim made at 1132$^{a}$26–30: "And when the whole has been divided in two, then people say that each 'has his own share' when he receives what is equal—where what is equal is a mean between too much and too little that is in accord with the arithmetic proportion." The idea is that injustice will occur if the producer produces more (or less) than the

recipient of his product receives or vice versa. **This . . . quality:** Reading ἔστι δὲ τοῦτο καὶ ἐπὶ τῶν ἄλλων τεχνῶν· ἀνῃροῦντο ἄν, εἰ μὴ ⟨ὃ⟩ ἐποίει τὸ ποιοῦν καὶ ὅσον καὶ οἷον, καὶ τὸ πάσχον ἔπασχε τοῦτο καὶ τοσοῦτον καὶ τοιοῦτον with the mss. The sentence is repeated at V 5 1133ᵃ14–16. OCT, in common with most editions, deletes it here, not there. I delete it there, not here.

Note 362
**Grants immunity:** That is, grants immunity to the one who profits, from a charge of having made an unjust transaction.

Note 363
**Counter to what is voluntary** (*para to hekousion*): Compare V 2 1131ᵃ5–9, 4 1131ᵇ25–26.

Note 364
**"If a person suffered what he did, right justice would be done":** Hesiod, Fr. 286. Rhadamanthys, the son of Zeus and Europa, was one of the judges of the dead in Hades. See Plato, *Ap.* 41a3, *Grg.* 523e8, *Lg.* 948b3.

Note 365
**Omitting 1133ᵃ14–16:** "This also holds in the case of the various crafts, since they would have been ruined if the producer (*to poioun*) did not produce something of both a certain size and a certain quality and if the recipient (*paschon*) did not receive this and in that size and that quality." Aristotle does accept a general principle of this sort: "producing (*poiein*)—for example, cutting or burning; being affected (*paschein*)—being cut, being burned" (*Cat.* 2ᵃ3–4; also *DA* III 5 430ᵃ10–19, *Met.* IX 5 1048ᵃ13–6). But it is hardly relevant here, where the point is to show that products and producers of different sorts need to be equalized.

Note 366
**If people did not need things . . .:** "[Socrates] Well then, a city comes to be, I believe, because none of us is individually self-sufficient but each has many needs he cannot satisfy. Or do you think that a city is founded on some other principle? . . . Then because we have many needs and because one of us calls on another out of one need and on a third out of a different need, we gather many into a single settlement as partners and helpers. And we call such a shared settlement a city. Isn't that so? . . . Tell me, then, how will a city be able to provide all this? Won't one person have to be a farmer, another a builder, and another a weaver? And shouldn't we add a shoemaker to them or someone else to take care of our bodily needs? . . . Well, then, should each of them contribute his own work for the common use of all? I mean, should a farmer, although he is only one person, provide food for four people and spend quadruple the time and labor to provide food to be shared by them all? Or should he not be concerned about everyone else? . . . [Adeimantus]. The first alternative, Socrates, is perhaps easier" (Plato *Rep.* II 369b–370a).

Note 367

**Money came into existence on the basis of convention:** "Since not all the natural necessities are easily transportable, the use of money had of necessity to be devised. So for the purposes of exchange people agreed with each other to give and take something that was a useful thing in its own right and that was convenient for use in acquiring the necessities of life: iron or silver or anything else of that sort. At first, its value was determined simply by size and weight, but finally people also put a stamp on it so as to save themselves the trouble of having to measure it. For the stamp was put on as an indication of the amount. . . .That is why . . . wealth is often supposed to be a pile of money. . . . On the other hand, it is also held that money itself is mere trash and wholly conventional, not natural at all. For if those who use money alter it, it has no value and is useless for acquiring the necessities, because often someone who has lots of money is unable to get the food he needs. Yet it is absurd for something to be wealth if someone who has lots of it will die of starvation, like Midas in the fable, when everything set before him turned to gold in answer to his own greedy prayer" (*Pol.* I 9 1257$^{a}$34–$^{b}$17).

Note 368

**Permit the export of corn in return for wine:** Incommensurability of goods (how much wine is equal in value to a corn export license?) can be as big an obstacle to exchange as their being unneeded.

Note 369

**Based on a hypothesis:** The hypothesis being that a convention (*nomos*) assigning a monetary value to all exchangeable goods has been adopted by the relevant parties.

Note 370

**Productive of a mean** (*mesou estin*): Literally, "of a mean." The next sentence explains.

Note 371

**A communal life with a view to self-sufficiency:** "A complete community, . . . once it reaches the limit of total self-sufficiency, practically speaking, is a city. It comes to be for the sake of living but it remains in existence for the sake of living well" (*Pol.* I 1 1252$^{b}$28–30). "Someone who is eligible to participate in deliberative and judicial office is a citizen in this city, and a city, unconditionally speaking, is a multitude of such people adequate for self-sufficiency of life" (III 1 1275$^{b}$18–21).

Note 372

**Nothing politically just in their relations with each other:** "We should take as our initial starting-point that many constitutions have come into existence because, though everyone agrees about justice (that is to say, proportional equality), they are mistaken about it, as we also mentioned earlier. For democracy arose from those who are equal in some respect thinking themselves to be unconditionally equal, since because they are equally free, they think they are unconditionally equal. Oligarchy, on the other hand, arose from those who are unequal in some respect taking themselves to be wholly unequal, since because they are unequal in property, they take themselves to be unconditionally unequal. The result is that former claim to merit an equal share of everything, on the grounds that they are all equal, whereas the latter, being unequal, seek to get more (for a bigger share is an unequal one). All these constitutions possess justice of a sort, then, although unconditionally they are mistaken. . . . Those who are outstandingly virtuous, however, . . . are alone the ones it is most reasonable to regard as unconditionally unequal" (*Pol.* V 1 1301$^a$25–$^b$1).

Note 373
**There is not always injustice:** 1134$^a$17–23 explains. Agents can do unjust actions from motives other than deliberate choice and thus without themselves being unjust. Among such agents, doing injustice exists but not injustice. Since this is true in the case of particular injustice, it will also be true in the case of political justice, when—as Aristotle is supposing (1134$^a$35–$^b$6)—the laws embodying the latter are themselves just.

Note 374
**Reason:** Most mss. have λόγον, but one has νόμον ("law"), and in fact *logos* here probably does mean the *reason* that is embodied in *law*: "Those who think it advantageous to be ruled by a king hold that laws speak only of the universal and do not prescribe with a view to actual circumstances. Consequently, it is foolish to rule in accord with written rules in any craft, and doctors in Egypt are rightly allowed to abandon the treatment prescribed by the manuals after the fourth day (although, if they do so earlier, it is at their own risk). It is evident for the same reason, therefore, that the best constitution is not one that follows written rules and laws. All the same, the rulers should possess the reason, that is, the universal one, as well. And something to which feeling [*to pathêtikon = the nonrational or desiring part of the soul*] is entirely unattached is better than something in which it is innate. This element does not belong to the law, whereas every human soul necessarily possesses it" (*Pol.* III 15 1286$^a$9–20).

Note 375
**We also said earlier:** At V 1 1130$^a$3.

Note 376
**Some sort of wage must be given to him:** "No type of craft or rule provides what is beneficial for itself but . . . it provides and enjoins what is beneficial for its subject, and aims at what is advantageous for it—the weaker, not the stronger. That is why . . . no one chooses to rule voluntarily and take other people's troubles in hand and straighten them out, but each asks for wages" (Plato, *Rep.* I 346e3–347a1).

Note 377

**Our possession:** "Something is said to be a 'possession' of someone in the same way as something is said to be a 'part' of him. For a part is not just partly another's but is *wholly* that thing's. The same is also true of a possession. That is why a master is just his slave's *master,* not simply *his,* while a slave is not simply his master's *slave* but is in fact *wholly his*" (*Pol.* I 4 1254$^a$9–13).

Note 378

**We saw . . .:** At 1134$^a$29–31 political justice is in accord with law. At 1134$^a$26–27 it "is found [1] where people share a communal life (*bios*) [2] with a view to self-sufficiency and [3] are free and equal." Since a thing's *bios* is natural to it, (1) implies that political justice is found among people naturally subject to law in their relations with each other, while (2) implies that the community such people constitute is a city. A citizen of a city, however, is "generally speaking, someone who participates [equally] in ruling" (*Pol.* III 13 1283$^b$42–1284$^a$1), and (3) implies that political justice is found among people sharing equally in ruling and being ruled.

Note 379

**Just in a household . . . politically just:** "A man rules both his wife and children as free people but not in the same way: instead, he rules his wife the way a politician does and his children the way a king does. For a male, unless he is somehow constituted contrary to nature, is naturally better fitted to command than a female, and someone older and completely developed is naturally better fitted to command than someone younger and incompletely developed. In most cases of political rule, it is true, people take turns at ruling and being ruled, because they naturally tend to be on an equal footing and to differ in nothing. Nevertheless, whenever one person is ruling and another being ruled, the one ruling tries to distinguish himself in demeanor, title, or rank from the ruled. . . . Male is always related to female in this way. The rule of a father over his children, on the other hand, is that of a king, since a parent rules on the basis both of age and affection, and this is a type of kingly rule" (*Pol.* I 12 1259$^a$39–$^b$12).

Note 380

**Brasidas** (d. 422 BC): A distinguished Spartan general (Thucydides, V 11). After his death a cult was established for his worship at Amphipolis, close to Aristotle's birthplace in Stagira. Such hero cults were common, since heroes, a bit like Christian saints, were conceived of as beings with a special status, intermediate between gods and ordinary human beings. **Decree:** A law (*nomos*) is a relatively permanent enactment, universal in scope and applicable on many different occasions even if, as here, it happens to deal with a particular person. A decree (*psêphisma*) is a singular enactment, adapted to particular circumstances (V 10 1137$^b$27–32), stating what is to be done in a single particular case, and thus the last thing reached in a piece of practical deliberation (VI 8 1141$^b$24–28). The political liabilities of government by decree rather than law are discussed in *Pol.* IV 5 1292$^a$4–37.

Note 381
**Ambidextrous:** "Of things that are just, some are so by nature, some by law. But we must not regard them as never being subject to alteration. For even the natural ones have a share in alteration. I mean, for example, that if we were all to practice always throwing with the left hand, we would become ambidextrous. Yet the left hand is such by nature, and the right hand is nonetheless naturally better than the left, even if we did everything with the left as we do with the right" (*MM* I 33 1194$^{b}$30–1195$^{a}$36; also *Pol.* II 12 1274$^{b}$12–13); "Of all animals human beings alone can become ambidextrous" (*HA* II 1 497$^{b}$31–32).

Note 382
**Constitutions are not the same everywhere:** Hence neither are laws or legal justice, since "laws should be established, and all do establish them, to suit the constitution and not the constitution to suit the laws" (*Pol.* IV 1 1289$^{a}$13–15). **One is everywhere naturally best:** This is the aristocratic constitution, in which the virtues of a citizen (including justice) coincide with those of a human being: "the only constitution that is rightly called an aristocracy is the one that consists of those who are unconditionally best as regards virtue, and not of those who are good men only given a certain supposition. For only here is it unconditionally the case that the same person is a good man and a good citizen. But those who are good in other constitutions are so relative to their constitutions" (*Pol.* IV 7 1293$^{b}$3–7). This constitution is described in *Pol.* VII–VIII.

Note 383
**Constitutional arrangement** (*taxei*): *Hê Krêtikê taxis* is the Cretan constitution (*Pol.* II 10 1271$^{b}$40–41).

Note 384
**Later** (*husteron*): The reference may be to the next chapter but *husteron* would be an odd word to choose to refer to something immediately following. Or the reference may be to a lost book of the *Politics* dealing with laws, or to *Rhetoric* I 13–14. None of these is an unimpeachable candidate.

Note 385
**Unjust *action* . . . just *action* . . .:** An action that is intrinsically just or intrinsically unjust rather than merely coincidentally so.

Note 386
**As was also said earlier:** At III 1 1111$^{a}$3–19.

Note 387
**One of the parties must be depraved:** A takes B to court for nonpayment of a legitimate bill. B claims that he has paid it, A that he has not. If A has not forgotten B's payment or B has not forgotten that he did not actually pay, then either A or B must be depraved (on the supposition that A and B engaged in the transaction knowingly, and so on).

Note 388
**Dispute about which action was just . . . the other denies it:** When A has struck B in anger at an apparent injustice done him by B, the dispute between them is not about whether A struck B but about whether doing so was a just action. B thinks he was unjustly struck; A thinks he was unjustly provoked.

Note 389
**Sympathetic consideration:** Defined at VI 11 1143ª23–24.

Note 390
**"I killed my own mother . . .":** The lines are from the lost *Alcmaeon* (to which Aristotle refers at III 1 1110ª27–29). The first line is spoken by Alcmaeon, the second possibly by Phegeus.

Note 391
**Always one or the other:** Omitting ὥσπερ καὶ τὸ ἀδικεῖν πᾶν ἑκού-σιον ("just as doing an unjust action is always voluntary"), which OCT brackets as a dittograph of the identical words in the line above.

Note 392
**Suffer a just action involuntarily:** As, for example, in the case of just punishments.

Note 393
**"Gold for bronze, a hundred oxen's worth for nine":** Homer, *Iliad* VI.236. Glaucus was an ally of the Trojans, Diomedes of the Greeks. Glaucus made the proverbially bad trade because Zeus stole away his wits.

Note 394
**Of the puzzles we deliberately chose to discuss, two remain:** The first puzzle has not been previously mentioned, the second has already been partly discussed at 1136ª31–ᵇ1.

Note 395
**Our definition of what it is to do an unjust action:** Given at 1136ᵇ3–5.

Note 396
**The starting-point of the action:** See VI 2 1139ᵇ5.

Note 397
**Because of this:** Because of thinking that doing unjust actions is up to them (1137ª4–5).

Note 398
**Of this sort:** Things that, because they are up to us or are voluntary, we are able to do or not to do.

Note 399
**Unconditionally good things:** These are: (1) intrinsically good things, such as the virtues, that are good for everyone; (2) things, such as money, honor, or external goods generally, that taken in isolation are good but that may not be good for this or that person. (2) is the kind relevant here (V 1 1129ᵃ34–ᵇ6).

Note 400
**What is decent isn't:** Omitting οὐ δίκαιον with some mss. OCT reads ἢ τὸ ἐπιεικὲς οὐ δίκαιον ("or what is decent is not just").

Note 401
**This sort of subject matter:** See I 2 1094ᵇ12–22, 7 1098ᵃ26–ᵇ8.

Note 402
**Standard used in Lesbian building:** The standard in question seems to have been a flexible lead device used to find a match for an irregularly shaped stone that was already set in position.

Note 403
**What has been said:** presumably at V 9 1136ᵃ10–1137ᵃ1.

Note 404
**Killing:** Supplying ἀποκτιννύναι as complement of μὴ κελεύει ("it forbids"). The idea is that in the case of killing, the law should be taken to forbid what it does not expressly allow and to exempt it from sanctions. Since it does not expressly allow the killing of oneself, it should be taken to forbid it. OCT reads ἃ δὲ μὴ κελεύει, ἀπαγορεύει ("and those things the law does not permit, it forbids").

Note 405
**More than one person involved:** "The same person cannot at the same time have more and less. . . . Yet the unjust agent, insofar as he does an unjust action, has more, and the one who suffers injustice, insofar as he suffers an unjust action has less. Hence, if a person does an unjust action to himself, it is possible for the same person at the same time to have more and less. But this is impossible. Hence it is impossible for a person to do an unjust action to himself" (*MM* I 33 1196ᵃ7–13).

Note 406
**Initiatory** (*proteron*): Literally, "earlier," or "before." An action is initiatory if it is not retaliatory.

Note 407
**The definition concerned with suffering an unjust action voluntarily:** Given at V 9 1136ᵇ3–5, 23–25.

Note 408
**In these accounts** (*logois*)*:* Or "in these ratios," that is, the ratio of the worth of a master to that of a slave, or that of the head of a household to

that of his wife or children. As translated, the phrase probably refers to accounts like Plato's, which speak about a person being just or unjust to himself. See *Rep.* IV 431a3–7: "It seems to me, however, that . . . within the same person's soul there is a better thing and a worse one. Whenever the naturally better one masters the worse, this is called being master of oneself. At any rate, it is praised." And 441e3–5: "Then isn't it appropriate for the rationally calculating element to rule, since it is really wise and exercises foresight on behalf of the whole soul, and for the spirited kind to obey it and be its ally?"

## Book VI

Note 409
**We have previously said that we should choose the mean:** Aristotle has not explicitly said this, but he has implied it. Virtue of character "finds the mean and chooses it" (II 6 1107$^{a}$5–6) and insofar as it is able "to hit the mean" is itself a sort of mean (II 6 1106b27–28) that we do and should choose (I 7 1097$^{b}$2–5). **As the correct reason says:** See II 2 1103$^{b}$31–34, III 5 1114$^{b}$25–30, 11 1119$^{a}$20, V 11 1138$^{a}$10.

Note 410
**The states we have discussed:** The virtues of character. **Tightens or loosens:** The metaphor derives from music, where an instrument's strings are adjusted until a certain target note is struck (*Pol.* IV 3 1290$^{a}$22–29; Plato, *Ly.* 209b). From there it is extended to vocal cords, sinews (*GA* V 7 787$^{b}$10–24), and other string-like things. Eventually it is employed wherever a certain tripartite structure is thought to exist: a continuous substrate, often referred to as "the more and the less (*to mallon kai to hêtton*)"; a pair of opposed attributes that vary in degree; and a target—typically a medial state of some sort—that can be achieved by increasing (tightening) or decreasing (relaxing) the substrate so as to change the degree of those attributes. See *NE* II 9 1109$^{b}$1–7, X 3 1173$^{a}$25–28, 9 1180$^{a}$10–14. **Defining mark** (*horos*): The root meaning of *horos* is that of a stone marking the boundary of a territory or piece of land in a visible way. Hence the doctor's *horos* is the thing "by reference to which he discerns what is healthy for a body from what isn't" (*EE* VII 15 1249$^{a}$21–22).

Note 411
**Supervision:** Supervision (*epimeleia*) of x, which involves taking care of (*epimeleisthai*) it, is often exercised by a type of craft or science that has x's welfare as its end or goal. For example, a king supervises his subjects to ensure that they do well (VIII 11 1161$^{a}$13), and medicine supervises the sick with the aim of making them healthy (X 9 1180$^{b}$17). Similarly the gods supervise the person "whose activity is in accord with understanding," since

they love and take pleasure in what is best and "most akin to themselves" (X 8 1179$^a$22–32).

Note 412
**We said:** At I 13 1103$^a$3–10.

Note 413
**Previously, then, we said:** At I 13 1102$^b$13–1103$^a$3.

Note 414
**Admit of being otherwise:** Some things do not *at all* admit of being otherwise, because, as eternal or unchanging, they are unconditionally necessary (VI 3 1139$^b$20–21, V 7 1134$^b$27–35). Of things that do admit of being otherwise, some hold for the most part and are necessary in a weaker sense, while others are the result of luck (*APr.* I 13 32$^b$4–13). Since those relevant here are known by the rationally calculative part of the soul, with which we deliberate, and since deliberation is restricted to "things that come about through ourselves" (*NE* III 3 1112$^b$3), they cannot be necessary, even in the weaker sense of holding for the most part, and so must be the result of luck. **Those that do admit of being otherwise:** Reading ᾧ τὰ ἐνδεχόμενα with OCT. Some editors read ὦ ἐνδέχονται ("those whose starting-points do admit of being otherwise"). **On the basis of a certain similarity and kinship:** "The part of the soul that has reason is divided into two subparts, these being the deliberative and the scientific. That these are different will be evident from their subject matter. For just as color, flavor, sound, and smell are different from each other, so too nature has assigned different perceptual capacities to them (for sound we know [*gnôrizomen*] by hearing, flavor by taste, and color by sight). By the same token, we must suppose it to be this way in all other cases. When, then, the subject matters are different, different too must be the parts of the soul by which we know them. Now an intelligible object (*noêton*) and a perceptible object (*aisthêton*) are different, and we know them through our soul. Hence the part of the soul concerned with perceptible objects is different from the one concerned with intelligible ones. But the deliberative and deliberately choosing part is concerned with perceptible objects and with things in the process of changing—that is, unconditionally speaking, with what comes to be and perishes. For we deliberate about things that are up to us to do or not to do in action, about which there is deliberation and deliberate choice whether to do or not do them. And these are perceptible objects that are in the process of changing, so that, according to this account, the deliberately choosing part of the soul pertains to perceptible objects" (*MM* I 34 1196$^b$15–34).

Note 415
**Deliberating** (*bouleusis*) **is the same as rationally calculating:** *Bouleusis* has a broad sense and a narrow sense. In the broad sense, a craftsman—such as a doctor, navigator, or physical trainer—can deliberate about what to

do when his craft does not provide explicit directions (III 3 1112$^{a}$34–$^{b}$9). This is the sense relevant here. In the narrow sense, the "unconditionally good deliberator is the one capable of aiming at and hitting, in accord with rational calculation, the best for a human being of things doable in action" (VI 7 1141$^{b}$12–14), so that deliberation of this sort is exclusively a practical or action-determining matter.

Note 416
**Action:** Here, action that is deliberately chosen. For of action in the broader sense, perception is a starting-point: "The things that move an animal are thought, imagination, deliberate choice, wish, and appetite. And all these can be reduced to understanding and desire. For both imagination and perception have the same place [in causing movement] as understanding" (*MA* 6 700$^{b}$17–20). **Truth:** One sort of truth Aristotle recognizes is plain, or theoretical, truth, which is a feature of propositions, statements, or thoughts: "to say that what is is and that what is not is not, is true" (*Met.* IV 7 1011$^{b}$26–28). About such truth, as about scientific knowledge, he is a realist: "It is not because of our truly thinking you to be pale that you are pale, on the contrary, it is because of you being pale that we who say this have hold of the truth" (*Met.* IX 10 1051$^{b}$6–9). A second sort of truth, discussed below, is practical truth.

Note 417
**Deliberative desire** (*bouleutikê orexis*): "I mean by something's being 'deliberative (*bouleutikên*)' that deliberation is its starting-point and cause—that is, the agent desires because of having deliberated" (*EE* II 10 1226$^{b}$19–20).

Note 418
**Understanding:** Deliberation involves understanding, because it has a starting-point (VI 11 1143$^{a}$35–$^{b}$5) and understanding is what grasps starting-points (VI 6 1141$^{a}$7–8). **A state of character:** Deliberate choice's effectiveness in achieving its end depends on whether the appetites and emotions in the soul's desiring part are in a mean, and thus on the states of character that are the desiring part's virtues (or vices) (IV 7 1127$^{b}$14–15).

Note 419
**Desiderative understanding or thought-involving desire:** Since deliberate choice is also deliberative desire, desiderative understanding, thought-involving desire, and deliberative desire must be the same thing. But deliberative desire is desire that has deliberation as its "starting-point and cause" (*EE* II 10 1226$^{b}$19–20), so desiderative understanding must be desire that has the understanding involved in deliberation as its starting-point and cause (VI 11 1143$^{a}$35–$^{b}$5). **This sort of starting-point is a human being:** This is so because wild beasts and children are incapable of deliberate choice and the "sort of control with which god presumably

rules" is the sort that results in "what does not admit of being otherwise" (*EE* II 6 1222$^{b}$22–23).

Note 420
**Agathon:** A distinguished Athenian tragedian of the late fifth century BC. Plato's *Symposium* memorializes his victory at the Lenaia (one of the annual Athenian dramatic festivals) of 416 BC. Fr. 5 is quoted here; fr. 6 at VI 4 1140$^{a}$19–22.

Note 421
**Supposition** (*hupolêpsis*): *Hupolêpsis* can be about any object of thought, whether particular or universal (*MM* I 34 1197$^{a}$30–32). That is why scientific knowledge, understanding, belief, and practical wisdom are varieties of it (*NE* VI 5 1140$^{b}$12–16, 6 1140$^{b}$31–32, 9 1142$^{b}$33). Since we can suppose falsehoods as well as truths, supposition can be mistaken. **Belief** (*doxa*): *Doxa* can be about pretty much anything, including things that are up to us (*NE* III 2 1111$^{b}$30–33), and so operates in the same territory as craft knowledge and practical wisdom—territory that includes perceptible particulars. In this regard it is like belief as we understand it. But *doxa* is unlike belief in that it presupposes rational calculation: "Perceptual appearance . . . the other animals have too, but the deliberative sort exists in those with rational calculation. . . . And that is the cause of their not seeming to have *doxa*, since they do not have the sort [of appearance] that results from deduction" (*DA* III 11 434$^{a}$5–11). The *doxastikon*, which is the part of the soul responsible for *doxa*, is thus the same as the part that rationally calculates or deliberates (VI 5 1140$^{b}$25–26, 13 1144$^{b}$14–15). But unlike rational calculation and deliberation, which are types of inquiry, a *doxa* is something "already determined," since *it* is "not inquiry but already a sort of assertion" (VI 9 1142$^{b}$11–14).

Note 422
**Outside our theoretical grasp** (*exô tou theôrein*): Or "outside observation," as suggested by *Top.* V 3 131$^{b}$21–23: "Everything perceptible has an unclear status whenever it is unperceived (*exô tês aisthêseôs*), since it is not evident whether it still holds true, because it is only through perception that this is known."

Note 423
**Some is through induction and some by deduction** (*syllogismos*): "All teaching and all learning involving thought result from already existing knowledge. This is evident if we look at all the cases, since the mathematical sciences arise in this way and so do each of the crafts as well. The same holds too where arguments are concerned, whether those that proceed by deduction or those that proceed by induction, since it is from things previously known that they both do their teaching—the former getting hold of them as if from discerning people, the latter showing the universal through the particular's [already] being clear" (*APo.* I 1 71$^{a}$1–8).

A deduction is "an argument in which, certain things having been supposed, something different from those supposed things necessarily results because of their being so" (*APr.* I 2 24[b]18–20). When the deduction is a syllogism proper (also *syllogismos*) it consists of a major premise, a minor premise, and a conclusion, where the premises have exactly one "middle" term in common, and the conclusion contains only the other two "extreme" terms. The conclusion's predicate term is the major term, contributed by the major premise; its subject is the minor term, contributed by the minor premise. At *APr.* I 32 47[a]33–35 a syllogism is distinguished from a "necessity" (or what we would call a valid deduction) on the grounds that not all necessities are syllogisms. Since Aristotle sometimes seems to use *syllogismos* and *syllogizesthai* to cover both valid deductions and syllogisms proper, I translate these as "deduction" and "deduce" rather than as "syllogism" and "syllogize."

Note 424
**In the *Analytics*:** "If we are to have scientific knowledge through demonstration, . . . we must know the starting-points better and be better convinced of them than of what is being shown, but we must also not find anything more convincing or better known among things opposed to the starting-points, from which a contrary mistaken conclusion may be deduced, since someone who has unconditional scientific knowledge must be incapable of being convinced out of it" (*APo.* I 2 72[a]37–[b]4; also *Top.* V 5 134[a]34–35).

Note 425
**External accounts:** See I 13 1102[a]26.

Note 426
**And nor:** Reading καὶ οὐδὲ ("and nor"). OCT reads διὸ οὐδὲ ("That is why").

Note 427
**Whose starting-point is in the producer:** "From craft come the things whose form is in the soul of the producer—and by form I mean the essence of each thing and the primary substance. . . . For example, health is the account in the soul, the scientific knowledge [of the form]. So the healthy thing comes to be when the doctor reasons as follows: Since health is this, necessarily if the thing is to be healthy this must be present—for example, a uniform state—and if the latter is to be present, there must be heat, and he goes on, always thinking like this, until he is led to a final "this" that he himself is able to make. Then the process from this point onward, toward health, is called production. . . . Of comings into being and processes, one part is called understanding (*noêsis*) and the other producing (*poiêsis*)—what proceeds from the starting-point and form is understanding, what proceeds from the final stage of understanding is producing" (*Met.* VII 7 1032[a]32–[b]17).

Note 428
**In accord with nature:** The starting-point of a natural thing is its nature, which is an "internal starting-point of change and staying unchanged, whether in respect of place, growth and decay, or alteration" (*Ph.* II 1 192$^b$13–15). More its form than its matter (*Ph.* II 1 193$^b$6–7), this nature is something the natural thing inherits from something else that already possesses it, just as a human being inherits his form (or nature) from his male progenitor. Consequently, a nature is at once the starting-point of a natural being's coming to be and of its persistence.

Note 429
**Craft incompetence** (*atechnia*): *Atechnia* is not mentioned elsewhere in Aristotle, although the quality of being *atechnos* is mentioned many times. *Atechnia* seems to be the cognitive condition of someone who pretends to have craft knowledge and gives false craft reasons. See IV 7 1127$^b$17–22.

Note 430
**No craft exists:** That is, the craft does not tell us how to further the end in the given case.

Note 431
**True state involving reason:** The same thing, presumably, as a state involving true reason (1140$^b$21–21).

Note 432
**Pericles** (c. 495–429 BC): The leading Athenian politician during the heyday of Athens' empire.

Note 433
**What preserves practical wisdom:** "Temperance is the savior (*sôtêria*) of wisdom (*phronêsis*)" (Plato, *Cra.* 411e4–412a1).

Note 434
**Vice is ruinous of the starting-point:** Cognate with the claim that virtue makes the target correct (VI 12 1144$^a$8). Expanded on at VII 6 1150$^a$3–5.

Note 435
**True state:** Following OCT in reading ἀληθῆ. Some mss. have ἀληθοῦς ("true [reason]"), which is perhaps to be preferred, since it makes the description of practical wisdom cognate with that of craft (VI 4 1140$^a$4) and attributes "true," in a perspicuous way, to reason rather than in an obscure one to states.

Note 436
**Of practical wisdom there isn't [forgetfulness]:** See I 10 1100$^b$12–17.

Note 437
**Since scientific knowledge involves reason:** The implication is that if a science involves reason, it involves demonstration from starting-points.

Note 438
**Phidias . . . Polyclitus:** Phidias (active c. 465–425 BC) oversaw the construction of the Parthenon, creating its most important religious images and supervising and probably designing its sculptural decoration. Polyclitus (active c. 460–410 BC), who was admired by Socrates for his wisdom (Xenophon, *Mem.* I iv 3), advocated a system of proportion in which every part of the body was related mathematically to every other. In commending these sculptors for their wisdom and *akribeia* ("exactness") Aristotle probably has in mind both the representational accuracy of their works and the aesthetic principles—definitive of classicism—that underlay them: order, proportion, and clarity of line.

Note 439
***Margites*:** A lost burlesque recounting the deeds of a ridiculous hero that Aristotle regards as having prefigured comic drama in certain respects (*Po.* 4 $1448^b28$–$1149^a2$).

Note 440
**The most exact** (*akribestatê*) **of the sciences:** When applied to a science, *akribes* has a quite technical sense: "One science is more exact than another, and prior to it, if it is both of the fact and the explanation why, and not of the fact separately from giving the scientific knowledge of the explanation why; or if it is not said of an underlying subject and the other is said of an underlying subject (as, for example, arithmetic is more exact than harmonics); or if it proceeds from fewer things and the other from some additional posit (as, for example, arithmetic is more exact than geometry). By from an additional posit I mean, for example, that a unit is a substance without position and a point is a substance with position—the latter proceeds from an additional posit" (*APo.* I 27 $87^a31$–37); "we should not demand the argumentative exactness of mathematics in all cases but only in the case of things that involve no matter" (*Met.* II 3 $995^a14$–16).

Note 441
**Head:** Understanding is of starting-points, which stand at the head of a science, containing its theorems in embryo, like the summary statement or headline that puts "a head on the body of a speech" (*Rh.* III 14 $1415^b8$–9, *NE* II 7 $1107^b14$). Understanding, which deals with the first, and so most universal, starting-points and the ones farthest from experience (*APo.* I 2 $72^a4$–5), caps off, or completes, scientific knowledge in the way a capstone (a secondary meaning of *kephalê*) does a wall or pillar.

Note 442
**Unless the best thing in the universe is a human being:** Sciences inherit their value or level of esteem (which is the relevant kind of best) from the kinds of beings they deal with (*Met.* XI 7 $1064^b3$–6) and so the "most estimable science must deal with the most estimable genus of beings" (*Met.* VI 1 $1026^a21$–22).

Note 443
**Now if health. . .:** Reading εἰ δ᾽ ("If health") at $^{a}$22 for OCT εἰ δὴ ("If, then, health") and τὸ γὰρ περὶ ἕκαστα τὸ εὖ θεωροῦν φαῖεν ἂν εἶναι φρόνιμον, καὶ τούτῳ ἐπιτρέψειαν ἂν αὐτά ("for the one that has a theoretical grasp of the good of a given sort of being is the one they would call 'practically-wise,' and it is to him that they would entrust such matters") at $^{a}$25–26 for OCT τὸ γὰρ περὶ αὑτὸ ἕκαστα τὸ εὖ θεωροῦν φησὶν εἶναι φρόνιμον, καὶ τούτῳ ἐπιτρέψει αὐτά ("For the one who sees well each of the things that concern himself is the one they call 'practically-wise,' and it is to him that they entrust such matters"). In OCT, "The one that sees well" refers to an agent, who—as the reference to different species at $^{a}$22–25 and the attribution of generic practical wisdom to wild beasts at $^{a}$26–27 both suggest—might belong to any one of a number of different species. This makes "the one they would call 'practically-wise'" difficult to understand, since we do not entrust the welfare of bees to practically-wise bees and they can hardly be credited with doing so, or with calling any bees anything. The alternative text avoids this problem. It is human beings who call a skilled apiarist (say) "practically-wise about bees" and who entrust the welfare of bees to him.

Note 444
**Some of the wild beasts are said to be practically-wise:** "The majority of other animals, indeed, possess traces of the sorts of characteristics having to do with the soul that are more clearly differentiated in the case of human beings. For tameness and wildness, gentleness and roughness, courage and cowardice, fearfulness and boldness, and spiritedness and mischievousness are present in many of them together with a semblance, where thought is concerned, of comprehension. . . . For some of these characteristics differ by degree from the human, as the human does from the majority of animals (for certain characteristics of this sort are present to a greater degree in the human case, certain others to a greater degree in other animals), whereas others differ by analogy: for corresponding to craft knowledge, theoretical wisdom, and comprehension, certain animals possess some other natural capacities similar to these" (*HA* VII 1 588$^{a}$18–31).

Note 445
**A different one for each sort:** See I 6 1096$^{a}$31–34.

Note 446
**Those from which the universe is composed:** The universe referred to is the heavens (*Cael.* I 9 278$^{b}$9–21, *Met.* XI 6 1063$^{a}$13–17). The beings that compose it are the stars and heavenly bodies, which, as divine and eternal living things, are more estimable than human beings (*Cael.* II 2 285$^{a}$29–30, *Met.* XII 7 1072$^{a}$26–30, 8 1073$^{a}$23–$^{b}$1). They are "the most evident (*phanerôtata*)" of such beings, because, as clearly visible (*phaneros* also means "visible") in the night sky for all to see, they are "the most divine of things evident [to perception]" (*Ph.* II 4 196$^{a}$33–34) and make it "quite

clear that if the divine is present anywhere," it is in the subject matter of astronomy and theology (*Met.* VI 1 1026ᵃ18–31).

Note 447
**Thales, Anaxagoras:** Thales of Miletus (sixth century BC) believed that the earth rests on water, which is the starting-point of all things, and that soul produces motion and is mixed into everything, so that the world is "full of gods" (*DA* I 2 405ᵃ19–21, 5 411ᵃ7–8, *Met.* I 3 983ᵇ6–27). Anaxagoras of Clazomenae (c. 500–428 BC), also mentioned at *NE* X 8 1179ᵃ13, believed that what initially existed was an entirely homogeneous stuff out of which the familiar elements (earth, water, fire, air) as well as perceptible objects and properties were produced by the operations of a divine mind or understanding (*Ph.* III 4 203ᵃ16–ᵇ15, *Met.* I 3 984ᵃ11–ᵇ22). What is commonly said about both philosophers is thus to some extent in keeping with Aristotle's account of them and so does reveal the existence of two kinds of wisdom. But it is only part of the story, for most people fail to see the profound bearing theory has on practice (*NE* X 8 1179ᵃ13–16). Thales' knowledge of astronomy enabled him to predict a bumper crop of olives, so that by cornering the market in olive presses during the off season when they were cheap, he was able to make a fortune by leasing them out when the crop was harvested (*Pol.* I 11 1259ᵃ5–33). Anaxagoras made the yet more important discovery that theorizing "about the heavens and the whole order of the universe" constitutes the most blessedly happy life and thus is the most practical thing of all (*EE* I 4 1215ᵇ6–14, 5 1216ᵃ10–16).

Note 448
**Those with experience:** See X 9 1180ᵇ16–23.

Note 449
**Bird meats are healthy:** Omitting κοῦφα καὶ ("light and"). **Will produce health more:** Because he can recognize birds (and so their meat) on the basis of experience and perception.

Note 450
**Or this one more:** See X 9 1180ᵇ13–28.

Note 451
**Architectonic:** See I 2 1094ᵃ14.

Note 452
**Their being** (*einai*) **is not the same:** See V 1 1130ᵃ12.

Note 453
**Legislative science:** Legislative science (*nomothetikê*) is an architectonic subbranch of politics; it drafts universal prescriptive laws with the aim of furthering the happiness of citizens by inculcating the virtues in them and directing their actions (X 9 1180ᵇ23–28) but is also concerned with constitutional questions more broadly (*Pol.* IV 1 1288ᵇ21–1289ᵃ15). Hence a politician must know, for example, when a particular city would most benefit

from having an oligarchic constitution, and must be able to establish and preserve such a constitution (even if it is not the unconditionally best one) by enacting laws that preserve it and further its ends. Since not everything can be exactly defined, even maximally exact laws cannot obviate the need for deliberation altogether (*Pol.* III 16 1287b22–23, *Rh.* I 13 1374a18–b23). Besides an architectonic legislative component, politics thus also needs a deliberative one, which, among other things, issues decrees.

Note 454
**Decree:** See V 10 1137b28–32.

Note 455
**Household management:** The part of practical wisdom (1141b32) that deals with the use of wealth or property (*Pol.* I 8 1256a10–13) and to some extent with its acquisition too (*Pol.* I 8 1256b26–30). **Judicial** (*dikastikê*): The essential parts of a city are "the warriors, those who participate in the administration of judicial justice (*dikaiosunês dikastikês*), and also those who deliberate, since deliberation is a function of political comprehension" (*Pol.* IV 4 1291a26–28).

Note 456
**Much difference:** The practical wisdom that enables an agent to know what is good for himself is of many sorts—or, more loosely, has many different aspects or facets (compare *Pol.* IV 15 1299a4–5).

Note 457
**Euripides says:** *Philoctetes,* frs. 787–788.

Note 458
**Through abstraction:** "Mathematicians produce theoretical knowledge that deals with abstractions. For in their theorizing they eliminate all perceptible attributes—such as weight and lightness, hardness and its contrary, heat and cold, and all the other perceptible contraries—and leave only the quantitative and the continuous, sometimes in one, sometimes in two, sometimes in three dimensions, and the attributes of things qua quantitative and qua continuous, and do not theorize about any of their other aspects" (*Met.* XI 3 1061a28–35). **Talk the talk:** See I 3 1095a2–11, VII 3 1147a19–22, b10–12.

Note 459
**Heavy types of water:** "Salt water is heavy and sweet water is light" (*Pr.* XIII 20 933b28–29).

Note 460
**Opposed, then, to understanding:** Understanding is concerned with the starting-points of a science (VI 6 1141a3–8), which are terms or definitions for which no reason or demonstration can be given within the science. The opposition between understanding and practical wisdom stems from this difference, since "what is most universal is furthest away [from

perception], what is particular nearest, and these are opposed (*antikeitai*) to each other" (*APo*. I 2 72ᵃ4–5).

Note 461
**Last thing among mathematical objects:** See III 3 1112ᵇ11–24. **Practical wisdom, however, is more this perception:** Reading μᾶλλον αἴσθησις ἡ φρόνησις for OCT μᾶλλον αἴσθησις ἢ φρόνησις ("[mathematical perception] is more this perception than it is practical wisdom"). A third alternative is μᾶλλον αἴσθησις ἢ ἡ φρόνησις ("[mathematical perception] is more perception than practical wisdom is").

Note 462
**Good guesswork:** The relevant sort is the sort that hits on "the middle term in an imperceptible amount of time," once "the extreme terms are recognized" (*APo*. I 34 89ᵇ10–15).

Note 463
**Without reason:** Good deliberation is not a form of belief and does not have the same sort of correctness as belief—namely, truth. And yet it does involve a reason (that is, something believed) whose correctness is truth.

Note 464
**Correctness of thought:** This seems to follow less from an argument by elimination than from the uncontroversial fact that deliberation, as some sort of inquiry and rational calculation, is some sort of thought or thinking.

Note 465
**What this correctness is:** Omitting ἡ βουλὴ ("what this deliberation is)," which OCT retains.

Note 466
**Something very bad:** See VII 1 1145ᵇ10–12.

Note 467
**Scientific knowledge as a whole:** Scientific knowledge as a whole comprises the unconditional variety, exemplified exclusively by the strictly theoretical sciences (such as geometry) as well as the less exact sort, exemplified by the natural, practical, and productive sciences (such as medicine). Comprehension cannot be identical to this entire thing, because it is not concerned with eternal and unchanging things, whereas the theoretical sciences are. Similarly, comprehension cannot be medicine or any of the other crafts or sciences dealing with things that come to be and pass away, and so admit of being otherwise, since these provide determinate answers to some questions without any need for deliberation at all (III 3 1112ᵇ2–9).

Note 468
**One might puzzle and deliberate about:** "What is comprehension and with what is it concerned? Comprehension operates in the same areas as practical wisdom also does—those concerned with matters of action.

For someone is said to have comprehension because of his capacity for deliberation—that is, in that he discerns and sees things correctly; but the discernment is about small matters and in small areas. Comprehension is a part of practical wisdom, then, and being a comprehender is part of being a practically-wise person, since to separate comprehender from practically-wise is impossible" (*MM* I 34 1197$^{b}$11–17).

Note 469
**Tend in the same direction:** To have consideration, one must be decent (1143$^{a}$19–20); to be decent one must be generally just and so be completely virtuous and have comprehension (1143$^{a}$15–16); to be fully virtuous one must have practical wisdom (1144$^{b}$16–17); to have practical wisdom one must have understanding (1143$^{b}$2–5).

Note 470
**Both directions:** The concern of understanding with both universal and particular last things is characterized as being "in both directions" for the same reason that understanding is characterized as "opposed" to practical wisdom (VI 8 1142$^{a}$25): universals are opposed to—or lie in the opposite explanatory direction from—particulars (*APo.* I 2 72$^{a}$4–5, *NE* I 4 1095$^{a}$30–$^{b}$1).

Note 471
**The unchanging and primary terms:** "That which produces movement will be one in kind, the desiring part qua desiring—but the object of desire comes first, since it produces movement without itself changing, by being grasped by understanding or imagination. In number, though, there will be more than one thing that produces movement. All movement indeed involves three things: first, the mover, second, that by means of which it moves, and third, the thing moved. And the mover is twofold, the unchanging one and the one that moves and is moved. The one that is unchanging is the good doable in action, and the one that moves and is moved is the desiring part (for the mover is moved insofar as it desires, and active desiring is a sort of movement), while the thing moved is the animal" (*DA* III 10 433$^{b}$10–18). Since the unchanging factor in movement is "the good doable in action," the unchanging major term (in a demonstration's major premise) presumably refers to it (see *NE* VI 12 1144$^{a}$31–33). **Those that are practical:** That is, in those demonstrations that are practical. **The other premise:** This is the demonstration's minor premise, which, as the last thing reached in deliberation, is a decree. In this premise, the crucial term is the middle one, since it is the one that can be predicated of something on the basis of perception and so can be acted on directly, without the need for further deliberation. Just as there is no giving a reason for or demonstrating a major term that is a starting-point of any sort, there is no giving one for a middle term in a practical demonstration. We simply see that this meat is bird meat and so do not need to justify our predicating "bird meat" of it by yet another practical demonstration that would

constitute our ground or reason for doing so: perception is one of the ways in which we grasp starting-points (I 7 1098$^{b}$3–4).

Note 472
**This is understanding:** Perception involves the concurrent grasp of universals—"we perceive particulars but perception is of universals—for example, of man and not of Callias the man"—and universals are grasped by understanding (*APo.* II 19 100$^{a}$16–$^{b}$1).

Note 473
**Understanding is both starting-point and end:** Understanding is what grasps all starting-points (VI 6 1141$^{a}$7–8); the starting-point of a practical demonstration is the end aimed at (VI 5 1140$^{b}$16–17); so understanding grasps both end and starting-point. It is said *to be* end and starting-point, as the function of the deliberative and scientific parts is said to be truth (VI 2 1139$^{b}$12), because it grasps the truth.

Note 474
**By being possessed and actualized:** "Things are produced in three ways: as health produces health, as food produces health, and as physical training does" (*Rh.* I 6 1362$^{a}$31–33).

Note 475
**Virtue makes the target correct:** Because it "teaches correct belief about the starting-point" (VII 8 1151$^{a}$18–19), thus ensuring "true supposition" about the practical good (VI 9 1142$^{b}$33), which is, as the end or target aimed at, the starting-point in practical matters (VI 5 1140$^{b}$16–17). **Practical wisdom what furthers it:** Practical wisdom is primarily a deliberative capacity (VI 5 1140$^{a}$30–31) and deliberation is concerned not with ends or targets but with what furthers hitting them (III 3 1112$^{b}$11–12).

Note 476
**To hit upon them:** Reading (1) τυγχάνειν αὐτῶν for OCT (2) τυγχάνειν αὐτοῦ ("to hit or hit upon it"). What role is being accorded to cleverness depends somewhat on which we accept. In (1) cleverness is said to hit upon "them (αὐτῶν)," that is, the things that further hitting a proposed target. In (2) it is said to hit upon or hit "it (αὐτοῦ)," that is, the target itself. The following passage favors (1): "It belongs to another capacity to hit upon all that must be done to further the end; but that the deliberate choice's end is correct—of this, virtue of character is the cause" (*EE* II 11 1227$^{b}$39–1228$^{a}$2).

Note 477
**Unscrupulous:** An unscrupulous person is one who "greedily takes anything from anywhere" (*EE* II 3 1221$^{a}$36–37; also *Pr.* XVI 4 917$^{a}$1–2). That is to say, he takes as much as he can of money, honors, bodily pleasures, and other goods of competition that are greed's particular targets (*NE* IX 8 1168$^{b}$15–21), regardless of to whom they belong.

Note 478

**That is why both practically-wise people and unscrupulous ones are said to be clever:** Reading διὸ καὶ τοὺς φρονίμους δεινοὺς καὶ τοὺς πανούργους φαμὲν εἶναι for OCT διὸ καὶ τοὺς φρονίμους δεινοὺς καὶ πανούργους φαμὲν εἶναι ("that is why even practically-wise people are said to be unscrupulous and clever").

Note 479

**Does not exist without this capacity:** "Cleverness and a clever person are not the same as practical wisdom or a practically-wise person, but a practically-wise person is certainly clever, and that is why cleverness works together in a way with practical wisdom. A base person is also said to be clever . . . but not practically-wise. For it is characteristic of a practically-wise person and of practical wisdom to seek the best things and always to deliberately choose and do them in action, whereas it is characteristic of cleverness and a clever person to discover the things from which each of the things doable in action may come about, and to provide these" (*MM* I 34 1197[b]18–26; also *NE* VII 10 1152[a]11–14).

Note 480

**This eye of the soul:** Probably understanding, which is analogized to sight—"as sight is in the case of body, so understanding is in the case of soul" (I 6 1096[b]28–29)—its lack analogized to blindness (VI 13 1144[b]8–13; compare *Protr.* B70, *Met.* IX 10 1052[a]3–4). Aristotle is probably recalling Plato's *Republic*, where an element in the soul is analogized to an eye (*Rep.*VII 533d) that accomplishes bad things when "forced to serve vice," but, through proper habituation in virtue, can accomplish good ones (VII 518c–519a).

Note 481

**Depravity produces distortion and false views about practical starting-points:** See VII 8 1151[a]18–19, X 8 1178[a]17–18.

Note 482

**Straight from birth:** "All the medial states are praiseworthy, but they are not virtues, nor are their contraries vices—for they do not involve deliberate choice. All of them belong in the class of affections, since an affection is what each of them is. But because they are natural they tend toward virtues that are natural, since . . . each virtue is in some way both natural and otherwise (that is, when it involves practical wisdom). Envy tends toward injustice (for the actions that stem from it are in relation to another), righteous indignation to justice, shame to temperance" (*EE* III 7 1234[a]23–32); "Surely people become virtuous (*agathoi*) or excellent because of three things: nature, habit, and reason. For first one must possess a certain nature from birth, namely, that of a human, and not that of some other animal. Similarly one's body and soul must be of a certain sort. But in the case of some of these qualities there is no benefit in just being born with them, since they are altered by our habits. For some qualities are naturally capable of being developed by habit either in a better direction or in a worse one. The other animals mostly live under the guidance of nature alone, although some are guided a little by habit. But human beings live under the guidance of reason as well, since they alone have reason. Consequently all three of these factors need to be harmonized with each other. For people often act contrary to their habits and their nature because of reason, if they happen to be persuaded that some other course of action is better" (*Pol.* VII 13 1332$^{a}$38–$^{b}$8).

Note 483
**Without understanding:** See III 12 1119$^{b}$8–9.

Note 484
**Socrates used to inquire:** The use of the imperfect *ezêtei* ("used to inquire") at $^{b}$19 suggests that Aristotle may be referring to the historical Socrates. The fact that he also describes him as identifying the virtues not with practical wisdom but with reason or scientific knowledge ($^{b}$29–30) suggests that he is not trying to be precise. The Socrates we find in Plato's dialogues (whether accurately modeled on the historical figure or not) does seem to think that the virtues are all cases of the scientific knowledge of good and evil (*Chrm.* 174b–c, *Men.* 87d–89a) but does not distinguish this sort of knowledge either from craft knowledge or from scientific knowledge.

Note 485
**Involve reason** (*meta logou*): "Socrates was not speaking correctly when he said that virtue was reason because it was not beneficial to do courageous and just actions unless one did them knowingly and deliberately chose them by reason. That is why he incorrectly said that virtue is reason. Present thinkers, by contrast, do better, since it is doing noble things in accord with correct reason that they say is virtue. Even they, however, are not correct. For one might do just actions with no deliberate choice whatsoever or with no knowledge of noble things but through some nonrational impulse, and yet do them correctly and in accord with correct reason (I mean where one does them as the correct reason *would* command). All the same, this sort of action is not praiseworthy. It is better, as we do, to define virtue as the impulse toward what is noble that involves reason, since that is both a virtue and praiseworthy" (*MM* I 34 1198$^{a}$10–22; also *NE* VII 4 1147$^{b}$31–32).

Note 486
**Contend dialectically:** A problem (*problêma*) is posed: Is pleasure choiceworthy or not? The answerer claims that yes, it is (or that no, it is not). The questioner must refute him by asking questions—by offering him premises to accept or reject. The questioner succeeds if he forces the answerer to accept a proposition contrary to the one he undertook to defend (*SE* 2 165$^{b}$3–4).

The questioner fails if the answerer always accepts or rejects premises in a way consistent with that proposition. Dialectic—or more precisely *plain* dialectic—is the craft or capacity that enables someone to play the role of questioner or answerer successfully (see Introduction, pp. xxxvi–xlviii). **Naturally well disposed in the highest degree** (*euphuestatos*): Something is *euphuês* if it is well (*eu*) grown (*phuê*), or favored by nature in capacities, appearance, or some other respect: the situation of a bodily organ can be *euphuês* (*PA* III 4 666ᵃ14), as can that of a city (*Pol.* V 3 1303ᵇ8); an animal can be *ephuês* as regards a function, such as reproduction (*GA* II 8 748ᵇ8, 12), or the acquisition of a capacity, such as bearing the cold (*Pol.* VII 17 1336ᵃ20) or becoming a poet (*Po.* 17 1455ᵃ32) or a musician (*EE* VIII 2 1247ᵇ22). The sort relevant here, since it consists in possession of the natural virtues of character (when these are properly developed by habituation), is the sort of natural discernment (*euphuia*) that makes the end and the deliberate choice of it correct (*NE* III 5 1114ᵇ5–12, *EE* VIII 2 1247ᵇ39).

Note 487
**The actions that the end consists in:** See I 7 1098ᵃ16–18, VI 2 1139ᵇ2–4. **The actions that further it:** See III 3 1112ᵇ11–12.

## Book VII

Note 488
**Beastliness** (*thêriotês*): The term *thêriotês* is coined by Aristotle to refer to a state of character responsible for *thêriôdês* (beast-like) behavior. Things and behavior can be *thêriôdês,* however, without stemming from *thêriotês:* "We do not see the kind of vice we called beastliness in wild beasts, but in human beings" (*MM* II 6 1203ᵃ18–19). Beasts are beast-like but not beastly.

Note 489
**Virtue that is beyond us** (*huper hêmas*): Often called "superhuman virtue." Aristotle seems to countenance the real possibility of people possessed of such virtue, just as he does beastly people who are "beyond human (*huper anthrôpon*)" (*MM* II 1200ᵇ18–19) in the other direction: "A city is among the things that exist by nature, a human being is by nature a political animal, and anyone who is without a city, not by luck but by nature, is either in base condition or else superior to a human being" (*Pol.* I 2 1253ᵃ2–4); "Anyone who cannot form a community with others or who does not need to because he is self-sufficient is no part of a city—he is either a beast or a god" (I 2 1253ᵃ28–29; also III 13 1284ᵃ3–11, VII 14 1332ᵇ16–25). **Homer:** *Iliad* XXXIV.258–259.

Note 490
**Human beings become gods:** See VIII 7 1159ᵃ5–11, IX 4 1166ᵃ19–23, X 7 1177ᵇ26–1178ᵃ8.

Note 491
**Neither is there of a god:** See VI 2 1139$^a$20, VII 6 1149$^b$31–1150$^a$1, X 8 1178$^b$8–18.

Note 492
**That of a wild beast is of a different kind than vice:** "Beastliness is a sort of excessive badness. For when we see someone who is completely base, we say that he is not a human being but a wild beast, on the supposition that beastliness is a sort of vice. The virtue opposed to it has no name, but is the sort that is beyond human—a sort that is heroic or divine. This virtue is nameless because there is no virtue that belongs to a god. For god is better than virtue, and it is not in accord with virtue that he is excellent, since in that case virtue would be better than god. That is why the virtue opposed to beastliness has no name. We take it, though, that the opposite to this kind of vice is a virtue that is divine and beyond human. For just as the vice of beastliness is also beyond human, so too is its opposing virtue" (*MM* II 5 1200$^b$9–19); "We do not see the kind of vice we called beastliness in wild beasts, but in human beings (for beastliness is a name for the excess of vice). Why is this? Because there is nothing that is an evil starting-point in a wild beast. The starting-point is reason. For which would do more evil, a lion, or Dionysius, Phalaris, Clearchus, or some other depraved person? It is clear that they would. For the existence of an evil starting-point within them is a great contributor to it, but in a wild beast there is no starting-point [of action] at all. In an intemperate person, however, there is an evil starting-point. For insofar as he does evil actions and his reason assents to them, and so he believes that these are what he should do, the starting-point that exists in him is not a healthy one. That is why a person who lacks self-control would seem to be better than an intemperate one" (II 6 1203a18–29).

Note 493
***Seios anêr*:** *Theios anêr* ("divine man") in Attic dialect.

Note 494
**Later on:** At VII 5 1148$^b$18–24.

Note 495
**Resilience** (*karteria*): Resilience is a medial state between luxuriousness (*trupherotês*) and toughness (*kakopatheia*) (*EE* II 3 1221$^a$9). It goes along with being hard (*sklêros*) and so is the opposite of being soft (*EE* III 1 1229$^b$2, *NE* VII 7 1150$^a$14). In *Cael.* II 5 287$^b$34 human conviction or certainty (*pisteuein anthrôpinôs*) is contrasted with a more resilient (*karterikôteros*) sort. **Either of the two:** The two pairs of contraries: lack of self-control and softness, self-control and resilience.

Note 496
**As in the other cases** (*hôsper epi tôn allôn*): As at *Pol.* I 1 1252$^a$18 (*hôsper epi tois allois*), the precise reference is unclear. It could be all other cases

or some more limited range. **The things that appear to be so** (*phainomena*): Basic perceptual observations and other things that appear on the face of it to be the case are *phainomena*: "This [that the earth is spherical] is also shown by the sensory *phainomena*. For how else would lunar eclipses exhibit segments shaped as we see them to be?" (*Cael.* II 14 297$^b$23–25; also 297$^a$2–6). Hence *phainomena* are typically contrasted with things that need to be supported by proof or evidence (*EE* I 6 1216$^b$26–28). Nonetheless, they need not be—and in Aristotle rarely are—devoid of a fair amount of interpretative or conceptual content (1145$^b$12–14 below). **Puzzle** (*aporia*): "There is a puzzle about whether a thing holds or not, because there are strong arguments on both sides" (*Top.* I 11 104$^b$13–14; also *NE* IX 8 1168$^b$10–12). **Reputable beliefs** (*endoxa*): "*Endoxa* are things that are held by everyone, by the majority, or by the wise—either by all of them or by most or by the most notable and most *endoxos* (reputable)" (*Top.* I 1 100$^b$21–23; repeated 101$^a$11–13). Appeals to *endoxa* mark a discussion as dialectical in nature. **Ways of being affected** (*pathê*): *Pathê* are usually feelings but here are more like conditions of the feelings.

Note 497
**An adequate showing:** "Those who wish to be free of puzzles must first go through the puzzles well, since the subsequent puzzle-free condition (*euporia*) is reached by untying the knots produced by the puzzles raised in advance, and it is not possible for someone who is unaware of a knot to untie it. A puzzle in thought, however, reveals a knot in its subject matter. For thought caught in a puzzle is like people who are tied up, since in either case it is impossible to make progress. That is why one must get a theoretical grasp on all the difficulties ahead of time, both for these reasons and because those who inquire without first going through the puzzles are like people who do not know where they have to go and in addition do not even know whether they have found what they were inquiring about, since the end is not clear to them. But to someone who has first gone through the puzzles it is clear. Besides one is necessarily in a better position to discern things when one has heard all the competing arguments, like opposing parties in a courtroom" (*Met.* III 1 995$^a$27–$^b$4; also *NE* V 2 1146$^b$6–7).

Note 498
**Excellent things and praiseworthy ones:** Reading τῶν σπουδαίων καὶ τῶν ἐπαινετῶν for OCT τῶν σπουδαίων καὶ [τῶν] ἐπαινετῶν ("excellent and praiseworthy conditions"). **Base as well as blameworthy:** Reading φαύλων τε καὶ ψεκτῶν for OCT φαύλων καὶ ψεκτῶν ("base and blameworthy").

Note 499
**Such as to depart from** (*ekstatikos*): "All change is by nature a departure (*ekstatikon*)" (*Ph.* IV 13 222$^b$16); "Every movement is a departure of the thing moved insofar as it is moved" (*DA* I 3 406$^b$12–13); "The virtues are

completions (*teleiôseis*), the vices departures (*ekstaseis*)" (*Ph.* VII 3 247ª2–3). Someone who is *ekstatikos* because of spirit or anger is, as we would say, "beside himself."

Note 500
**Things that are said:** The appearances mentioned at 1145ᵇ3.

Note 501
**What sort of correct supposition a person has when he acts in a way that is not self-controlled:** Or "in what way does a person with correct supposition act without self-control."

Note 502
**Scientific knowledge:** When Aristotle is characterizing Socrates' views (as at VI 13 1144ᵇ17–29), he treats *epistêmê* and *phronêsis* as equivalents, even though in his own account these are quite different states. **Socrates used to think:** The use of the imperfect *ô[i]eto* ("used to think") suggests a reference to the historical Socrates, but Plato's Socrates also rejects a view that he characterizes in language very similar to Aristotle's: "The belief of ordinary people about scientific knowledge is that it is not something strong that has hegemonic power and rules. They do not think of it that way at all but that often a human being who has scientific knowledge in him is ruled not by it but by something else, in one case spirit, in another pleasure, in another pain, sometimes sexual passion, often fear. They just think of scientific knowledge as a slave that gets dragged around by all the rest" (*Prt.* 352b3–c2).

Note 503
**Doer of action** (*praktikos*): The action involving the correct reason that a practically-wise person possesses and knows. **Last things:** See VI 8 1142ª23–25.

Note 504
**Good** (*chrêstai*): *Chrêstos,* which often means "useful," or "serviceable," is here, as often elsewhere, equivalent in meaning to *agathos* ("good").

Note 505
**Neoptolemus . . . it pains him to tell a falsehood:** Neoptolemus is the son of Achilles, the most prominent of the Greek heroes in the Trojan wars. Odysseus is another very prominent Greek hero. In his *Philoctetes,* Sophocles (c. 496–406 BC), the Athenian tragic playwright and author of *Oedipus Tyrannus,* makes Neoptolemus a companion of Odysseus in the expedition to Lemnos to bring the bow of Heracles, which Philoctetes possesses, back to Troy. Odysseus persuades Neoptolemus to lie, win Philoctetes' trust, and take the bow. Neoptolemus does do this but—deeply moved by the subsequent plight of Philoctetes—confesses the truth to him and returns the bow.

Note 506
**A certain sophistical argument:** An argument is sophistical when it appears to be a sound deduction establishing or refuting a conclusion but isn't (*SE* I 1).

Note 507
**They:** The sophists who use the argument. **Contrary to beliefs** (*paradoxa*): What is *paradoxos* is not what is paradoxical in our sense of the term but what is contrary to or goes against (*para*) beliefs (*doxa*) that we hold. **When they engage in ordinary discussions:** Reading ἐντύχωσιν for OCT ἐπιτύχωσιν ("they are successful"). One of dialectic's uses is in ordinary discussions (*enteuxeis*) (*Top.* I 2 101ᵃ26–27), because "once we have catalogued what most people believe, our approach to them will begin from their own views, not from those of others, and we will redirect them whenever they appear to us to be wrong" (*Top.* I 2 101ᵃ31–34).

Note 508
**Seems to be better:** This conflicts with what appears to be so, since vice (involving the deliberate choice of what is bad) is prima facie worse than lack of self-control. This *phainomenon* has not been listed earlier.

Note 509
**But he is already persuaded, yet nonetheless does something else:** Reading νῦν δὲ πεπεισμέωος οὐδὲν ἧττον ἄλλα πράττει with the ms. OCT inserts ἄλλα after δὲ and brackets ἄλλα after ἧττον ("But in fact, though already persuaded to act otherwise, he still does the act he does").

Note 510
**The resolution of a puzzle constitutes a discovery:** That is, a discovery of the solution to the puzzle, consisting of an adequate showing (VII 1 1145ᵇ7), based on the reputable beliefs that are left standing, of the conclusion about (in this case) self-control and lack of self-control that these beliefs support. Compare "process of discovery" (III 3 1112ᵇ19) and "discovering a treasure" (1112ᵃ27).

Note 511
**Know in the most exact way:** *Eidenai* ("know") not *epistasthai* ("know scientifically") here and at 1147ᵃ9 and 21.

Note 512
**Heraclitus makes clear enough:** "For if belief is intensely stable and unalterable by persuasion, it will not differ at all from scientific knowledge, since belief will carry with it the conviction that things are as they are believed to be, for example, Heraclitus of Ephesus has this sort of belief about what he believes" (*MM* II 6 1201ᵇ5–8).

Note 513
**Ways of presenting premises** (*protaseôn*): Either as the universal (or major) premise (*protasis*) of a syllogism or as the particular (or

minor) premise. **The partial one** (*tê[i] kata meros*): The premise dealing with a part, or the particular premise. **Here the particulars are what is doable in action:** See VI 7 1141$^{b}$15–16, 8 1142$^{a}$20–30, 11 1143$^{a}$2–3.

Note 514
**Whether this is of that sort:** That is, whether this food is dry. Aristotle ignores the other possibility, namely, that the agent does not have or is not activating the knowledge that *he* is of the relevant sort—that he is a human being. Presumably, Aristotle thinks that the agent could not fail to be aware of this: "As sometimes happens in asking [dialectical] questions, however, so here [in practical deliberation] thought does not stop to consider the other premise, the one that is clear. For example, if taking walks is good for a man, he does not linger over the thought that he is a man" (*MA* 7 701$^{a}$26–29; also *NE* III 1 1111$^{a}$6–7). **Does not have or is not activating:** "Does not have" could mean (1) does not have at all or (2) does not have in the way required for scientific knowledge, so that he knows (*eidenai*) it but does not scientifically know (*epistasthai*) it. Since (1) appears to conflict with the characterization of a person who lacks self-control as acting voluntarily (V 9 1136$^{a}$32–33, VII 1 1146$^{a}$7, VII 10 1152$^{a}$15–16) and so knowingly (III 1 1111$^{a}$22–24), (2) seems more likely. "Is not activating" means "is not actively contemplating it," or "is not engaging in the activity of contemplating it."

Note 515
**Tipsy** (*oinomenos*): To be distinguished, perhaps, from those who are dead drunk (*methuôn*) and thus act unknowingly and involuntarily (III 1 1110$^{b}$26). Notice the comparison of people who lack self-control to those who "quickly get drunk (*tachu methuskomenoi*)" at VII 8 1151$^{a}$4.

Note 516
**Alter the condition of the body as well:** That is, as well as altering the way in which we have scientific knowledge.

Note 517
**Empedocles of Acragas** (c. 492–432): A pre-Socratic philosopher from Sicily. Aristotle elsewhere describes Empedocles as "using the language of demonstration" (*Met.* III 4 1002$^{a}$18–25).

Note 518
**Takes time:** compare I 3 1095$^{a}$2–11, VI 8 1142$^{a}$11–20.

Note 519
**Like actors on a stage** (*hupokrinomenous*): The comparison is with those who can utter speeches suggestive of the possession of scientific knowledge, without actually having it, as actors (*hypokritai*) can (see VII 4 1148$^{b}$8). But orators also *hypokrinesthai* (*Rh.* III 12 1413$^{b}$21–23).

Note 520

**One is a universal belief:** one of the premises mentioned at 1146b35–1147a7. **Perception already controls:** See II 9 1109b21–23, III 3 1112b34–1113a2, IV 5 1126b3–4, VI 8 1142a25–30.

Note 521

**In productive cases** (*poiêtikais*): Aristotle often contrasts action (*praxis*) and action-related, or practical (*praktikos*) matters with production (*poiêsis*) and productive (*poiêtikos*) ones. But often too, as most likely here, he uses *poiêsis* and *poiêtikos* in a more inclusive sense in which no contrast is intended. Hence the example that follows is of a *praxis* not a (narrow) *poiêsis*. **In one sort of case . . . it acts straightaway:** "How does it happen that understanding is sometimes followed by action and sometimes by inaction; that is, sometimes by moving and sometimes by not moving? What happens seems parallel to the case of thinking and deducing (*sullogizomenois*) about unchanging objects. But there the end is a theoretical proposition (for when one has understood the two premises, one has understood—that is, put together—the conclusion), whereas here the conclusion that follows from the two premises being put together becomes the action. Some examples: whenever someone understands that every man should take walks, and that he is a man, straightaway he takes a walk, or if he understands that no man should take a walk now, and that he is a man, he straightaway stays put. And he does each of these things provided nothing prevents him from doing it or compels him to do something else" (*MA* 7 701a7–16).

Note 522

**Do this at once:** That is, taste this particular sweet thing.

Note 523

**And this one** (*hautê*) **is active:** The reference of the demonstrative pronoun *hautê* is unclear. I take it to refer only to "this is sweet," since that is the sort of premise whose activation is at issue at 1147a7. **From reason, in a way, and from belief, he acts without self-control:** The agent's acting without self-control—in part because of appetite—consists in his tasting x (this sweet thing). Since appetite is activated by what is pleasant (or by a perception, imagination, or belief with the appropriate content), the belief he acts from must be the belief that x is pleasant. A belief, however, must be based on rational calculation or deliberation (VI 3 1139b17). So in this case it must be derived from (1) *the bad major premise,* "everything sweet should be tasted," which, together with the active *bad minor premise,* "This is sweet," yields not *the bad conclusion,* "Pursue or taste this!" but, rather, the action of tasting (since here nothing effectively prevents the agent from tasting). Aristotle does not explicitly mention this bad deduction, but his reference to the agent's uncontrolled action as stemming from reason and belief presupposes its existence. At the same time, there is also a universal proposition in (or believed by) the agent "preventing tasting." This is (2) *the good major premise,* which the agent, since he (in some sense) has scientific knowledge, also believes. Its exact content is unspecified but is probably something like, "Nothing sweet should be tasted." Together with the active (but now) *good minor premise,* "This is sweet," it yields *the good conclusion,* namely, "the one proposition [that] says 'Avoid this.'" (The conclusion here is a proposition, not an action, because the agent's appetite prevents him from doing the requisite action of not tasting x.) It is the existence of (2) in the agent that explains why, in acting on (1), he acts from reason only *in a way,* and why, in acting from it, he acts without self-control: it is (2) not (1) that provides the correct (scientific) reason. The mere belief that x is pleasant is not intrinsically contrary to that reason, however, but as part of what explains the agent's appetite for x, it is coincidentally contrary to it, since it is part of what explains his acting contrary to it. Understood in this way, the passage presents a familiar picture of uncontrolled action as stemming from a conflict between the agent's wish (based on [2]) and his appetite (based on [1]), but explains in greater detail how uncontrolled action (and not just deliberately chosen action) can be based on reason and belief. The passage is one of the most vexed in Aristotle, and many other interpretations have been proposed of it and of $1147^{b}9$–17, which employs it.

Note 524

**Natural scientists:** "Sleep is not every disability of the perceptual part but, rather, this affection arises from the evaporation that attends eating food. For that which is vaporized must be driven on to a given point and then must turn back and change, just like the tide in a narrow strait. In every animal the hot naturally rises, but when it has reached the upper parts, it turns back and moves downward in a mass. That is why sleepiness mostly occurs after eating food, since then a large watery and earthy mass is carried upward. When this comes to a stop, therefore, it weighs a person down and makes him nod off; but when it has actually sunk downward, and, by its return, has driven back the hot, then sleepiness comes on and the animal falls asleep" (*Somn.* 3 $456^{b}17$–28); "When someone changes from drunkenness, sleep, or disease, we do not say that he has acquired scientific knowledge again—even though he was unable to use his knowledge [while drunk, asleep, or diseased]. . . . For it is due to the soul's stopping its natural restlessness that something becomes practical wisdom or scientific knowledge. . . . In some cases nature itself causes the soul to settle down and come to a state of rest, while in other cases other things do so. But in either case the result is brought about through the alteration of something in the body, as we see in the case of the use and activity of practical wisdom or scientific knowledge, when someone becomes sober or wakes from sleep" (*Ph.* VII 3 $247^{b}13$–$248^{a}6$).

Note 525

**The final premise** (*hê teleutaia protasis*): *Hê teleutaia protasis* could be the conclusion of the deduction, but it seems more likely that it is the good minor premise of the good deduction, which an agent who lacks self-control believes, namely, "this [particular perceptible thing] is sweet." For it is always a minor premise or decree (VI 8 1141$^b$24–28) that controls action, since action follows straightaway from it, provided nothing prevents this from happening. The agent does not have this premise, that is, does not have it in the way required for scientific knowledge, because, even though he actively believes (or activates) it, he does so for the reason provided by the bad deduction not for the correct reason provided by the good (scientific) deduction.

Note 526
**The last term . . . the perceptual sort:** The last term is the middle term in the final (or good minor) premise in the good deduction, namely, "sweet" (compare VI 8 1142$^a$25–27). As applicable to x on the basis of perception, the universal it refers to is the sort that Aristotle describes as "indeterminate" and "better known by perception" (*Ph.* I 1 184$^a$22–25). When analyzed into its "constituents and starting-points," it is transformed into the sort of intelligible universal, cognizable by understanding rather than perception, that is suited to play a role in scientific knowledge (*Ph.* I 1 184$^a$23). It is as so analyzed that it would figure in the good deduction and be scientifically knowable. The perceptual sort of knowledge is the sort described at VI 8 1142$^a$27–30.

Note 527
**We took:** At III 10 1118$^a$1–$^b$8.

Note 528
**The victor at the Olympic Games called "Human"** (*Anthrôpos*): Human was a boxing champion in the Olympic Games of 456 BC. He is *a* human, so that the account common to all human beings (*human$_c$*) also applies to him. At the same time, there is also an account special to him (*human$_c$* + *x*) that differs only slightly (+ *x*) from the common one. *Human$_c$* is an analogue of *lack-of-self-control$_c$*, which applies to (1) those who *lack self-control$_c$* with regard to the necessary sources of pleasure (and so are unconditionally lacking in self-control) and (2) those who *lack self-control$_c$* with regard to intrinsically choiceworthy things (and so *lack self-control$_s$*—the analogue of *human$_s$*). *Human$_c$* is the account of the proper or primary use of the term "human," because it defines what is *unconditionally human* (rather than what is *human* + *x*). Similarly, *lack-of-self-control$_c$* is the account of the proper or primary use of the term "lack-of-self-control," because it defines what *unconditionally lacks self-control* (rather than *what lacks self-control with regard to intrinsically choiceworthy things* (the analogue of *human* + *x*). In the cases of both *human* and *lack-of-self-control*, it is the special accounts that are the more exact ones: "Although sailors differ in their capacities (for one is an oarsman, another a captain, another a lookout, and others have other sorts of names), it is clear both that the most exact account of the virtue of each sort of sailor will be special to him, and similarly that

there will also be some common account that fits them all" (*Pol.* III 4 1276b21–26).

Note 529
**An indication of this:** That unconditional and partial lack of self-control are different. **An indication . . . people is:** Or "An indication of this is that lack of self-control is blamed not only as an error but also as a sort of vice, whether unconditional or partial, whereas none of these is blamed." **None of these other people:** The ones suffering from the types of partial lack of self-control (mentioned at 1147b29–31) that are concerned with non-necessary sources of pleasure, such as wealth, profit, and so on.

Note 530
**Unconditionally and solely so:** A person who lacks self-control and an intemperate person are concerned with the same pleasures and pains (1148a15). An intemperate person is concerned exclusively with the tactile pleasures of eating, drinking, and having sex, and is "more pained than he should at not getting pleasant things," because of the pain produced in him by not getting that pleasure (III 11 1118b30–32). A person who unconditionally lacks self-control, however, seems to be concerned with a wider class of things than that, since he goes to excess in avoiding the pains not just of hunger and thirst but also of heat and cold. The association of intemperance with the sorts of pleasures we share with other animals may speak in favor of the wider class, since they too avoid the extremes of heat or cold (*HA* VIII 13 598a1).

Note 531
**The others:** The ones concerned with the non-necessary sources of pleasure and pain.

Note 532
**The others:** Those who do not unconditionally lack self-control but do lack self-control where some particular thing is concerned.

Note 533
**These people . . . deliberate choice:** These people must be the ones who lack self-control and are intemperate but not the self-controlled and temperate ones. For people who lack self-control do not act from deliberate choice and intemperate ones do (VII 3 1146b22–25, VII 9 1152a4–6), whereas both self-controlled people and temperate people act from deliberate choice (III 2 1111b14–15, VII 1 1145b10–12).

Note 534
**We distinguished this group earlier:** At 1147b28–30.

Note 535
**Niobe:** Niobe boasted that she was superior to the goddess Leto because she had many children, while Leto had only two. Leto commanded her own children to take revenge for this insult by killing Niobe's children.

**Satyrus, the so-called father lover:** Satyrus supposedly committed suicide on hearing of the death of his father.

Note 536
**Savages who live around the Black Sea:** "Many nations think nothing of killing and cannibalizing people, for example, the Achaeans and the Heniochi, who live around the Black Sea. And there are similar peoples on the mainland and others that are even worse" (*Pol.* VIII 4 $1338^{b}20$–23). See also Herodotus, IV 18 (cannibalism), Thucydides, III 94 (raw meat). **Phalaris** (c. 570–c. 549 BC): Tyrant of Acragas in Sicily. He allegedly roasted his enemies alive inside a bronze bull—the action of someone with a depraved (because savagely cruel) nature. The savages around the Black Sea are presumably beast-like because of habit; the child-devouring woman because of a disability.

Note 537
**Those who have suffered wanton aggression:** Reading τοῖς ὑβριζομένοις with OCT. The reference is probably to sexual aggression, in particular, and is intended to explain why some men engage in sexual intercourse with other men. Some mss. have τοῖς ἐβιζομένοις ("those who get habituated") while others have τοῖς γυμναζομένοις ("those who get trained").

Note 538
**In a morbid condition because of habit:** "Males who are naturally effeminate are so constituted that little or no semen is excreted in the testicles and penis, where males whose condition is in accord with nature excrete it, but instead in the region around the anus. The explanation of this is that they are constituted contrary to nature, since, although they are male, the former region is necessarily disabled. A disability, however, produces either total destruction or distortion. Now here it does not produce the former, since then a woman would come about. Hence it is necessary for the secretion of semen to be perverted and moved toward some other region. That is why in fact such males are insatiable, just as women are. . . . Those in whom the semen collects in the anus desire to be passive, while those in whom it collects in both regions desire to be both active and passive, and wherever it collects more, the corresponding appetite is greater. In some, this condition even comes about as the result of habit. For people enjoy what they get used to doing, and excrete semen accordingly. So they develop an appetite for doing what produces these things, and so the habit becomes more like nature. That is why those who are habituated to submit to sexual intercourse around puberty but not before, because of the memory that arises in them during the act because of their habit, and simultaneously with the memory the pleasure, as if by nature have an appetite to play the passive role. Frequent repetition, however, and habit become just like nature" (*Pr.* IV 26 $879^{b}20$–$880^{a}4$).

Note 539
**Either not controlling them:** Reading μὴ κρατεῖν for OCT κρατεῖν ("controlling"). If we read κρατεῖν, we must understand an implicit reference to self-control later in the sentence: "On the other hand, having them and either controlling them or being controlled by them is not unconditional [self-control or] lack of self-control." **Unconditionally lacking self-control:** Reading ἀκρατῆ ἁπλῶς for OCT ἀκρατῆ ("lacking self-control").

Note 540
**Excesses of vice:** Reading ὑπερβάλλουσα κακίας for OCT ὑπερβάλλουσα ("excesses").

Note 541
**Weasel** (*galeê*): *Galeê* is the name of various animals, including weasels and polecats, some of which were kept as house pets.

Note 542
**Naturally without rational calculation** (*alogistoi*): Compare VII 3 1147$^{b}$4–5.

Note 543
**And that unconditional lack of self-control is that in accord with what is human intemperance only:** Reading with some mss. ἁπλῶς δὲ ἡ κατὰ τὴν ἀνθρωπίνην ἀκολασίαν μόνην for OCT ἁπλῶς δὲ ἡ κατὰ τὴν ἀνθρωπίνην ἀκολασίαν μόνη ("and that unconditional lack of self-control is only the kind corresponding to human intemperance").

Note 544
**Spirit** (*thumos*): Aristotle sometime uses *thumos* and *orgê* ("anger") interchangeably (*Rh.* I 4 1369$^{b}$11) and very often uses *thumos* in contexts where its aggressive side is highlighted (for example, *NE* III 8 1116$^{b}$15–1117$^{a}$9). In other places, however, he says that anger is only "in (*en*)" the spirited element (*Top.* II 7 113$^{a}$36–$^{b}$1, IV 5 126$^{a}$10) alongside other feelings, such as fear and hatred (IV 5 126$^{a}$8–9). In one passage, indeed, he identifies spirit as the source not just of "negative" feelings but also of love and friendship: "spirit (*thumos*) is what produces friendliness (*philêtikon*), since it is the capacity of the soul by which we love (*philoumen*)" (*Pol.* VII 7 1327$^{b}$40–1328$^{a}$1). This is in keeping with his claim that if hatred is in the spirited element, then love, as its contrary, must be there too (*Top.* II 7 113$^{a}$33–$^{b}$3). Presumably, then, we should think of spirit as passionate—as "hot and hasty (1149$^{a}$30)—rather than as always aggressive.

Note 545
**Instructions:** Reading προστάξεως with OCT. Some mss. have πράξεως ("actions").

Note 546
**Imagination:** "Perceptual imagination the other animals have, too . . . but the deliberative sort exists [only] in those with rationally calculative parts. For when one comes to whether to do this or that one, at the same

time comes too a task for rational calculation. And one must measure by a single [standard], since one is pursuing the greater [good]. And so one must be able to make out of many appearances a single one . . . the one resulting from a deduction" (*DA* III 11 434[a]5–11). Since uncontrolled action resulting from imagination must be contrary to reason, the imagination in question must be deliberative imagination. **As if deducing:** When, in the process of deliberation, reason or deliberative imagination reveals to a virtuous or self-controlled agent (1) that he has been wantonly injured or contemptuously treated by A, and arrives at a decree or minor premise to the effect (2) that such injury or treatment *does not* merit revenge, the agent immediately acts to avoid taking revenge on A. Once deliberation reaches (1) in an agent who lacks self-control regarding spirit, by contrast, he acts as if reason had gone on to arrive at (2′), that such treatment *does* merit taking revenge on A, and so he takes it straightaway. Here the agent's overly quick spirit prevents him from acting on *reason's* minor premise by making him act before he hears it. Thus spirit does not hear what reason orders but only what it reveals. This is the analogue of the sound the dogs hear or whatever it is the hasty servants respond to (perhaps the master says, "There's a knock at the door," and they—thinking falsely that he will instruct them to open it—rush out to do so.) Because it is spirit's quickness that prevents the action that is in accord with the reason, no actual prescriptive conclusion can have been delivered by reason *prior to* the action, since it is only *post prevention* that such a conclusion emerges.

Note 547
**Spirit follows reason, in a way, but appetite does not:** Uncontrolled spirit follows reason by being guided not by the minor premise of reason's deliberative deduction, since it acts against that, but by what it falsely takes to be reason's minor premise. Uncontrolled appetite, by contrast, does not engage with reason's minor premise at all but simply acts contrary to it once it hears about the pleasantness of what it then goes for. (Notice that "reason *or* perception" implies that the source of information on which appetite acts need not be either reason itself or deliberative imagination.)

Note 548
**More a feeling of sympathetic consideration for people who follow natural desires:** Compare III 1 1110[a]23–26.

Note 549
**Things that are not necessary:** See V 4 1147[b]23–31.

Note 550
**Aphrodite:** The goddess, especially, of sexuality and reproduction, emblematic of seductive charm and deception. **Homer:** *Iliad* XIV. 214, 217.

Note 551
**No one is pained . . . no wanton aggression in spirit:** With the implicit premises and interim conclusions supplied, Aristotle's unusually

compressed argument seems to run as follows: (1) No agent who commits an act of wanton aggression that is not self-controlled does so with pain—in fact he does so with pleasure. (From the definition of "wanton aggression.") (2) People who act out of anger in a way that is not self-controlled are pained by what they do. (From the definition of "anger.") (3) [Implicit] Therefore, no acts of wanton aggression that are not self-controlled are committed out of anger. (4) [Implicit] Anger is a spirited desire or response. (5) [Implicit] No act of wanton aggression that is not self-controlled is committed out of spirit. (6) No act of wanton aggression that is not self-controlled is performed out of wish. (From the definition of lack of "self-control.") (7) [Implicit] Wish, spirit, and appetite are the three types of desires that cause actions. (From the definition of "desiring part.") (8) Therefore, an act of wanton aggression that is not self-controlled must be committed out of appetite. (9) Acts of wanton aggression that are not self-controlled are unjust and inspire justified anger. (From the definition of "wanton aggression.") (10) [Implicit] Acts done out of anger or spirit are done in revenge for contemptuous treatment, and so should not themselves inspire anger. (From the definition of "anger.") (11) It is more just to be angry at acts of wanton aggression that are not self-controlled than at acts due to anger or spirit that are not self-controlled. (12) Acts at which it is more just to be angry are more unjust. (Anger, to be virtuous, should be in a mean and thus proportionate to the level of contempt and so to its level of injustice.) (13) Acts that are not self-controlled which come about because of appetite are more unjust than those which come about because of spirit.

Note 552
**Degeneration from nature:** "Being true to one's descent (*gennaion*) is not being a degeneration from nature" (*HA* I 1 488$^a$19–20).

Note 553
**The better thing . . . is just not present:** The better thing is the starting-point (VII 8 1151$^a$25–26), which is what vice ruins (VI 5 1140$^b$18–19). This starting-point is understanding (1150$^a$5), which wild beasts lack (*DA* II 3 414$^b$18–19), as do beastly human beings, since they are reasonless (*NE* VII 5 1149$^a$9). It is the better thing because (1) it is the most divine element in the human soul (X 7 1177$^a$16) and (2) the one whose activity is in accord with theoretical wisdom is the best sort of human happiness (X 7 1178$^a$7–8) and so the best good (I 2 1094$^a$22). The "human case" is the human scale or natural vice mentioned at 1149$^b$28, which is now being contrasted with beastliness or beast-like vice.

Note 554
**Understanding is the starting-point:** That is, a starting-point (end) of deliberately chosen (and so of vicious) action (VI 11 1143$^b$9–11).

Note 555
**Beastliness . . . as a beast:** This argument is best read as comparing natural or human-level vice to beastliness (beast-like vice). Beastly human

beings lack the understanding needed for deliberate choice and vicious action (and so are like lifeless or soulless beings), while the humanly vicious ones possess it (and so are like living beings or beings with a soul). As a result, the vicious ones are more harmful than the beastly ones, because their understanding enables them to do more of it (compare VI 13 1144[b]8–13). The comparison between the two is thus similar to that between injustice, which lacks a soul and is not alive, and an unjust human being who is, as it were, injustice ensouled (compare V 4 1132[a]21–22).

Note 556
**Beast** (*thêriou*): Best understood here as referring to a human being whose beastliness renders him relevantly similar to an actual wild beast (*thêrion*).

Note 557
**And does so:** Reading καὶ with some mss. for OCT ἢ ("or").

Note 558
**One person has a kind of softness . . . the other person is intemperate:** The avoidance of excessive pains because of deliberate choice (1150[a]23–25) is only a *kind* of softness because unlike softness proper, it is a vice. To pursue excessive pleasures because of deliberate choice, on the other hand, is to be intemperate (1150[a]19–22).

Note 559
**Theodectes** (fourth century BC): A tragic poet mentioned by Aristotle as the author of an *Ajax* (*Rh.* II 23 1400[a]27–28), an *Alcmaeon* (II 23 1397[b]2–3), a *Helen* (*Pol.* I 2 1255[a]36–38), an *Orestes* (*Rh.* II 24 1401[a]35), a *Socrates* (II 23 1399[a]8–9), and a *Tydeus* (*Po.* 16 1455[a]9). A native of Phaselis in Pamphylia, he spent most of his life in Athens. On his *Philoctetes*, see VII 2 1146[a]20. **Carcinus** (fourth century BC): An Athenian tragic poet mentioned by Aristotle as the author of an *Amphiaraos* (*Po.* 17 1455[a]26–27), an *Oedipus* (Rh. III 16 1417[b]18–19), and a *Medea* (II 23 1400[b]10). **Xenophantus:** Possibly the musician of that name in the court of Alexander the Great.

Note 560
**As female differs from male:** "All females are less spirited than males, except in the case of bear and leopard: in these the female seems to be more courageous. But in the other kinds the females are softer, more inclined to do evil, less simple, more impetuous, and more attentive to the feeding of the young, whereas males, on the contrary, are more spirited, more boorish, simpler, and less given to plotting. There are traces of these characteristics in almost all animals, but they are more evident in those that have more character and most of all in human beings, since their nature is most complete" (*HA* IX 1 608[a]33–[b]7).

Note 561
**Those who tickle first:** "Why can no one tickle himself? Or is it that we also feel less tickled by another if we are aware of it beforehand, and more if we do not see it coming?" (*Pr.* XXXV 6 965[a]11–12).

Note 562
**Passionate people** (*melagcholikoi*): A *melagcholikos* person is not melancholy in our sense of the term but someone with intense desires (VII 4 $1154^{b}11$–13), easily affected by imagination and dreams: "Passionate people most of all are moved by appearances (*phantasmata*)" (*Mem.* 2 $453^{a}19$); "People who are naturally passionate see multifarious dream visions" (*Div. Somn.* 2 $463^{b}16$).

Note 563
**As we said:** At VII 7 $1150^{a}20$–22.

Note 564
**In listing the puzzles:** At VII 2 $1146^{a}31$–$^{b}2$.

Note 565
**Those who depart** (*hoi ekstatikoi*): Not those who depart from their rational calculation (*ekstatikos tou logismou*) (VII 1 $1145^{b}11$–12), since they do not act without prior deliberation, but, rather, those who act on a strong passionate impulse (VII 7 $1150^{b}25$–28) that sets them in action contrary to the correct reason (VII 8 $1151^{a}20$–21) before deliberation has a chance to reach it (VII 6 $1149^{a}34$–$^{b}2$).

Note 566
**A person who lacks self-control:** Not one who lacks generic self-control, presumably, but one who suffers from weakness (VII 7 $1150^{b}19$–25).

Note 567
**Demodocus** (sixth century BC): A poet from the island of Leros near Miletus. Very little of his work survives.

Note 568
**Virtue preserves the starting-point, whereas depravity ruins it:** Compare VI 5 $1140^{b}13$–20, VII 6 $1150^{a}3$–5. **Hypotheses are in mathematics:** Sometimes the class of starting-points or posits (*theses*) is divided into definitions (which do not assume the existence or non-existence of the *definiendum*) and hypotheses (which do assume this) (*APo.* I 2 $72^{a}18$–24). Here, though, as often elsewhere (I 19 $81^{b}14$–15, *Ph.* II 3 $195^{a}18$–19, *Met.* V 1 $1013^{a}16$), hypotheses are probably not being distinguished from posits generally.

Note 569
**Virtue . . . teaches correct belief about the starting-point:** Compare VI 12 $1144^{a}28$–$^{b}1$, X 8 $1178^{a}17$–18. Habituated virtue is neither natural nor full virtue, apparently, but an intermediate stage: "Surely people become virtuous (*agathoi*) or excellent because of three things: nature, habit, and reason. For first one must possess a certain nature from birth, namely, that of a human and not that of some other animal. Similarly, one's body and soul must be of a certain sort. But in the case of some of these qualities, there is no benefit in just being born with them, since they are altered by

our habits. For some qualities are naturally capable of being developed by habit either in a better direction or in a worse one. The other animals mostly live under the guidance of nature alone, although some are guided a little by habit. But human beings live under the guidance of reason as well; for they alone have reason. Consequently, all three of these factors need to be harmonized with each another. For people often act contrary to their habits and their nature because of reason, if they happen to be persuaded that some other course of action is better" (*Pol.* VII 13 1332ᵃ38–ᵇ8).

Note 570
**The puzzle we raised earlier:** At VII 2 1146ᵃ16–21.

Note 571
**Lack control** (*akura*) **. . . insofar as these are like decrees:** The relevant beliefs are those expressed in the minor premises of practical deductions, which, since they have prescriptive force (VI 10 1143ᵃ8), are like decrees. When a decree is revoked or nullified it is rendered *akuron,* so that it no longer controls action. When Aristotle claims that a woman's rationally calculating or deliberative part is *akuron* (*Pol.* I 13 1260ᵃ13), he invokes the same idea.

Note 572
**Neoptolemus in Sophocles'** ***Philoctetes*****:** See VII 2 1146ᵃ19.

Note 573
**It has been shown:** At VI 12 1144ᵃ29–ᵇ1.

Note 574
**In our initial account:** At VI 12 1144ᵃ22–29.

Note 575
**He acts voluntarily:** See III 1 1111ᵃ15–18, V 8 1135ᵃ23–ᵇ2.

Note 576
**Not a plotter:** See VII 6 1149ᵇ13–15.

Note 577
**Anaxandrides' jibe:** Anaxandrides (fourth century BC) was a comic poet from Camirus in Rhodes. Aristotle mentions him at *Rh.* III 10 1411ᵃ18, 11 1412ᵇ16, and 12 1413ᵇ25.

Note 578
**Evenus** (fifth century BC): A sophist and rhetorician from Paros. Aristotle quotes from him at *Met.* V 5 1015ᵃ29–29a, *EE* II 7 1223ᵃ31–32, and *Rh.* I 11 1370ᵃ10–11.

Note 579
**Political philosopher:** Aristotle sometimes applies the term *philosophia* to any science aiming at truth rather than action: "It is also right that philosophy should be called scientific knowledge of the truth. For the end of theoretical science is truth, while that of practical science is a piece of work

(*ergon*)" (*Met.* II 1 993ᵇ19–21). In this sense of the term, all the broadly theoretical sciences count as branches of philosophy, and *philosophia* is more or less equivalent in meaning to *epistêmê*. *Philosophia* also has a narrower sense, however, in which it applies exclusively to sciences providing knowledge of starting-points. Thus "natural—that is, secondary, philosophy" has the task of providing theoretical knowledge of the starting-point of perceptible substances (VII 11 1037ᵃ14–16), whereas "the determination of the unmoving starting-point" of natural substances "is a task for a different and prior philosophy" (*GC* I 3 318ᵃ5–6). Since there are just "three theoretical philosophies, mathematical, natural, and theological" (*Met.* VI 1 1026ᵃ18–19), theological philosophy must be primary, mathematical philosophy tertiary. In addition to the theoretical philosophies, there is also the practical "philosophy of human affairs" (*NE* X 9 1181ᵇ15) to which Aristotle's ethical and political writings belong: "Everyone holds that what is just is some sort of equality, and up to a point, at least, all agree with what has been determined in those philosophical works of ours in which we draw distinctions concerning ethical matters; for justice is [a matter of giving] something to someone, and it should be something equal to those who are equal, it is said, but equality in what and inequality in what should not be overlooked, since this involves a puzzle and political philosophy" (*Pol.* III 12 1282ᵇ18–23). Since puzzles—especially those about starting-points—are the provenance of philosophy, it seems that political philosophy, like its theoretical fellows, should be primarily concerned with the starting-points of politics and with the puzzles to which these give rise. **Architectonic craftsman of the end:** See I 2 1094ᵃ26–ᵇ7, 13 1102ᵃ7–26. **In calling each thing unconditionally bad or good:** See I 12 1102ᵃ2–4.

Note 580
**Taken it:** at II 3 1104ᵇ13–28, 1105ᵃ10–16; also X 1 1171ᵃ21–23. **Happiness involves pleasure:** See I 8 1098ᵇ23–25, 1099ᵃ7–16.

Note 581
**Perceived coming to be in the natural state:** "Every process of generation . . . always takes place for the sake of some particular being, and . . . all generation taken together takes place for the sake of the existence of being as a whole . . . Now pleasure, if indeed it turns out to be a kind of generation, comes to be for the sake of some being . . . But that for whose sake something comes to be ought to be put into the class of good things, while that which comes to be for the sake of something else belongs in another class . . . So if pleasure is indeed a kind of generation, will we be placing it correctly if we put it in a class different from that of the good? . . . We ought to be grateful, then, to the person who indicated to us that there is always only generation of pleasure and that it has no being whatsoever. And it is obvious that he will laugh at those who claim that pleasure is a good thing . . . But this same person will also laugh at those who find their fulfillment in processes of generation . . . I mean those who cure their hunger

or anything else that is cured by a process of generation. They take delight in generation as a pleasure and proclaim that they would not want to live if they were not subject to hunger and thirst and if they could not experience all the other things one might want to mention in connection with such conditions. But would we not all say that destruction is the opposite of generation? . . . So whoever makes this choice would choose generation and destruction in preference to that third life, which consists of neither pleasure nor pain but is a life of thinking wise thoughts (*phronein*) in the purest degree possible" (Plato, *Phlb.* 54c2–55a8). Aristotle proposes a similar view elsewhere: "We may take it that pleasure is a process of movement in the soul, a process of intensive (*athroan*) and perceptible restoration to its original nature and that pain is the opposite. . . . So it must be for the most part pleasant to move toward the natural state, and most of all so insofar as a natural process achieves the complete recovery of that natural state" (*Rh.* I 11 1369$^{b}$33–1170$^{a}$5).

Note 582
**A temperate person avoids pleasures:** "Temperance too—even what the masses call temperance (not being carried away by one's appetites, but despising them and behaving in an orderly fashion)—belongs, doesn't it, only to . . . people who most despise the body and live in love of wisdom?" (Plato, *Phd.* 68c8–12).

Note 583
**What is painless:** See II 3 1104$^{b}$23–26.

Note 584
**Pleasures impede thinking:** "The body keeps us busy in a thousand ways because of the nourishment it must have. . . . It fills us too with multifarious passions, appetites, fears and phantoms, and with all sorts of other trash, so that we are really and truly, as the saying goes, never able to think about anything because of it" (Plato, *Phd.* 66b5–c6); "The most intense and violent pleasures . . . put countless impediments in our way and infect the souls in which they dwell, with madness" (63d3–6).

Note 585
**No craft of pleasure:** "The craft that deals with the soul I call politics. As for the one that deals with the body, I can't in the same way give you a single name for it. For though the care of the body is a single craft, I say it has two parts—physical training and medicine. In politics, I say that legislative science is the counterpart of physical training and medicine of judicial science [reading *dikastikê*]. . . . Since there are these four crafts, then, two taking care of the body and two of the soul, and always with a view to what is best, when sycophancy sees this . . . it divides itself into four, impersonates each of the parts, and pretends to be what it impersonates. It thinks nothing of what is best, but snares and deceives the ignorant with what is pleasantest at the moment. . . . Well, anyway, sycophancy is what

I call it, and I say it is a shameful sort of thing . . . because it takes aim at what is pleasant without knowing what is best. And I say it isn't a craft but a knack, because it has no account of what it is treating nor of the nature of the things it is treating it with and so can't tell you the explanation in either case. And I do not call anything a craft that lacks an [explanatory] account" (Plato, *Grg.* 464b3–465a6).

Note 586
**And not always:** Reading <ἀεὶ> δ' οὔ for OCT <ἁπλῶς> δ' οὔ ("and not unconditionally").

Note 587
**[Against 1a]:** Suppose the process of A's coming to be F is a pleasure. If A's being F is unconditionally good, so is the process of A's coming to be F. What is unconditionally good could be constituted by such processes even if processes and their ends are different in kind. Similarly, if A's coming to be F is coincidentally good, what is coincidentally good could be constituted by such processes. For some pleasant processes that seem bad, and are cited as counterexamples to the claim that what is coincidentally good is pleasure, could be coincidentally good for a particular person or at a particular time or for a short period. Finally, some processes cited as counterexamples are not really pleasures at all.

Note 588
**Residual state and nature:** As opposed to the state and nature that is being restored to its natural condition by a curative process (compare VII 14 $1154^{b}15$–20). Just what this residual state and nature is, is not entirely clear. Perhaps, Aristotle's thought is this: When someone is hungry his appetite for food is a painful unsatisfied lack needing to be restored to its natural state. But its capacity to motivate him to eat does not need any restoration. This capacity thus belongs to "the residual state and nature," which has been left unimpaired, and it is its activity (eating and filling up the lack) that is coincidentally pleasant. **The activities:** Retaining ἐνέργειαι. **No lack in the natural state:** "Not every pleasure is a coming to be. For the pleasure that comes from contemplation is not a coming to be, nor is that which comes from hearing, seeing, or smelling. For it does not arise from a lack, as in the other cases—for example, those of eating or drinking. For these come about from deficiency and excess, from the filling of a lack or the taking away of an excess. That is why they seem to be comings to be. Deficiency or excess is pain. So there is pain involved wherever pleasure is a process of coming to be. But in the cases of seeing, hearing, smelling, there certainly isn't any pain beforehand, since no one taking pleasure in seeing or smelling felt pain beforehand. Similarly, in the case of thinking, we can contemplate something with pleasure without having felt any pain beforehand" (*MM* II 7 $1204^{b}6$–17).

Note 589
**An end:** See I 1 1094ᵃ3–5. **When we use something:** Pleasures are activities, and it is the use of a (natural) state that is an activity, not our coming to be in that state (I 1 1094ᵃ4n).

Note 590
**But we should better** (*alla mallon*) **say that it is an activity of a natural state:** If this clause is identifying pleasure with an activity, as it would be if we understood *mallon* to mean "rather" or "instead," the claim it makes is apparently contradicted at X 4 1174ᵇ23–33, 5 1175ᵇ30–35. It may be, though, that it is making the somewhat weaker claim that it is better or nearer the truth—another meaning of *mallon*—to say that pleasure is an activity than to say that it is a perceived process of coming to be. The possibility of later refinement would then be left open.

Note 591
**Even contemplation:** Contemplation in accord with theoretical wisdom is complete happiness (X 7) and the best good (I 2 1094ᵃ22), so if it is sometimes harmful to health, and in that respect bad, it cannot be an argument against pleasure's being the good that some pleasures can be bad in some respects.

Note 592
**Learn all the more:** See X 5 1175ᵃ30–ᵇ1.

Note 593
**Only of the corresponding capacity:** "None of the other sciences [or crafts] transmits to the learner their use and their activity, but the state [or capacity] alone. So in this case [ethics] too the knowledge of the relevant things does not transmit their use (for happiness is an activity, we say) but the state [or capacity] alone, and happiness does not consist in knowing the things from which it arises, but arises from the use of these things" (*MM* II 10 1208ᵃ35–38).

Note 594
**In what way pleasures are good and in what way not all of them are unconditionally good:** Reading πῶς ἀγαθαὶ καὶ πῶς οὐκ ἀγαθαὶ ἁπλῶς for OCT πῶς ἀγαθαὶ ἁπλῶς καὶ πῶς οὐκ ἀγαθαὶ ("in what way pleasures are unconditionally good and in what way not all of them are good").

Note 595
**Speusippus used to propose:** The use of the imperfect *elue* ("used to propose") suggests that Aristotle is referring to historical occurrences. **Does not in fact resolve it:** To resolve the argument that pleasure—as the contrary of a bad thing—is good, Speusippus accepts that, as such a contrary, pleasure must be either good or neutral. Since pleasure can be neutral it cannot be essentially or intrinsically good, but that does not mean that it

cannot be *coincidentally* good. So the argument does entail that pleasure is coincidentally good. To resolve the argument even for that weaker conclusion, Speusippus would have to claim—quite implausibly and without the support of any of the arguments canvassed in VII 12—that pleasure cannot even be coincidentally good, which is equivalent to saying that it is intrinsically bad. **What is equal:** The analogue of what is equal in the case of pain is the neutral state of feeling neither pleasure nor pain. As we cannot infer that $x < y$ from the fact that $y \not> x$ (since the fact that $y = x$ may be what makes $y \not> x$ true), so we cannot infer that x is a pleasure from the fact that x is a state contrary to pain. A similar argument is attributed to Eudoxus at X 2 1172[b]18–20.

Note 596
**Intrinsically bad** (*hoper kakon ti*): Here, as often elsewhere in Aristotle, *hoper* is the opposite of *kata sumbebêkos* ("coincidentally") and thus equivalent in meaning to "essentially," or "intrinsically."

Note 597
**This *is* pleasure:** See VII 12 1153[a]14–15.

Note 598
**Quite reasonably:** See I 8 1098[b]24–29, 1099[a]7–31.

Note 599
**Happiness is something complete:** See I 7 1097[a]25–[b]5, X 7 1177[b]24–26.

Note 600
**Goods of the body and external goods:** See I 8 1098[b]12–16, 1099[a]31–[b]8. **The ones luck brings:** "It is not possible to be happy without external goods, which luck controls" (*MM* II 8 1206[b]33–34); "Of goods external to the soul, chance or luck is the explanation, but no one is just or temperate as a result of luck or because of luck" (*Pol.* VII 2 1323[b]27–29).

Note 601
**Broken on the rack:** "[Glaucon:] If what I say sounds crude, Socrates, remember that it is not I who speak but those who praise injustice at the expense of justice. They will say that the just person who has an unjust reputation will be whipped, stretched on a rack, chained, blinded with a red-hot iron, and, at the end, when he has suffered every sort of bad thing, he will be impaled and will realize then that one should not want to be just but to be believed to be just" (Plato, *Rep.* II 361e1–362a2).

Note 602
**All things . . . pursue pleasure:** See X 2 1172[b]9–15. **Pleasure is in some way the best good:** "Complete and unimpeded activity has enjoyment within it, so that contemplative activity must be the most pleasant of all" (*Protr.* B87; also *NE* I 8 1099[a]10–16). **"No rumor . . .":** Hesiod, *Works and Days* 763.

Note 603

**All things by nature have something divine in them:** "The most natural function in such living things as are complete and not disabled or that do not have the capacity to spontaneously generate is to produce another thing like themselves—an animal to produce an animal, a plant a plant—in order that they may partake of the everlasting and divine insofar as they can. For all of them desire this, and for its sake do all that they—in accord with their nature—do. . . . So, since they cannot share in the eternal and divine by continuous existence, because no numerically one and the same perishable thing can persist that way, they share in them insofar as each of them can, some more and some less, and what persists is not the thing itself but something like itself, not numerically one but one in form" (*DA* II 4 415$^a$26–$^b$7; also *NE* X 2 1173$^a$4). The idea goes back to Plato: "The intercourse of man and woman is in fact a begetting. And this affair is something divine: living creatures, despite their mortality, contain this immortal thing, pregnancy and procreation. . . . Mortal nature seeks, so far as it can, to exist forever and to be immortal. And it can achieve it only in this way, through coming into being, so that it always leaves behind something else that is new in place of the old" (Plato, *Smp.* 206c5–207d3; also *Lg.* 721b–c).

Note 604

**If pleasure is not a good:** Reading μὴ ἡ ἡδονὴ for OCT μὴ ἡδονὴ.

Note 605

**Of some states and processes . . . such an excess:** "For external goods have a boundary, as does any instrument and all things that are useful for something; so excessive amounts of them must harm or bring no benefit to their possessors. In the case of each of the goods of the soul, however, the more excessive it is, the more useful it is (if these goods too should be thought of as useful and not simply as noble)" (*Pol.* VII 1 1323$^b$7–12).

Note 606

**As we said:** See VII 12 1152$^b$26–33.

Note 607

**Contrive certain thirsts for themselves:** "They produce thirst for themselves, so that they may take pleasure in drinking. Some of these, which are harmless, are not objectionable. For even a decent person will try to make foods and drinks pleasant for himself through exercise and exertions. But if they devise these arrangements to their harm, then they are bad people and to be blamed—for example, those who, when they are fully satisfied, nevertheless devise for the sake of pleasure ways in which they may again eat or drink or enjoy the pleasures of sex" (Aspasius, p. 157).

Note 608

**When these are harmless:** "Harmless pleasures are suitable not only as regards the end of life but also as regards relaxation" (*Pol.* VIII 5 1339$^b$25–27).

Note 609

**As the natural scientists also testify:** "Anaxagoras said that an animal is always suffering because of its perceptual capacities" (Aspasius, p. 157).

Note 610

**In a condition that is like tipsiness:** "Heat around the region in which we think and have hopeful expectations makes us cheerful. And that is why everyone is eager to drink to the point of drunkenness, because a lot of wine makes everyone have hopeful expectations, just as youth does children. For old age is despondent, whereas youth is full of hopeful expectation. . . . In fact, this is why children are more cheerful while old people are more cheerless. For children are hot, old people cold, since old age is a sort of cooling down" (*Pr.* XXX 1 954$^{b}$9–955$^{a}$18).

Note 611

**Because of its mix:** "Straight from the beginning the passionate humor (*chumos ho melagcholikos*) is mixed, since it is a mixture of hot and cold, since its nature is constituted out of these two things. Now, black bile (*hê cholê hê melaina*) is naturally cold by nature, and not on the surface, so when it is very cold, if there is an excess of it in the body, it produces apoplexy, torpor, spiritlessness, or fear. . . . But if it gets overheated, it produces cheerfulness accompanied by song, ecstatic outbursts, breaking out in sores, and the like. . . . Those in whom such a mixture is established by nature straightaway develop all sorts of characters, different ones being in accord with different mixtures—for example, those in whom black bile is plentiful and cold become sluggish and stupid, whereas those in whom it is extremely plentiful and hot become mad, clever, erotically inclined, easily moved to anger and appetite, and—in the case of some of them—more talkative" (*Pr.* XXX 1 954$^{a}$12–34).

Note 612

**The part of us that remains healthy:** See VII 12 1152$^{b}$35.

Note 613

**Our nature is not simple but also has another element in it, in that we are mortals:** Our soul contains a divine element—understanding—which is our true nature or what we are, most of all (X 7 1177$^{b}$26–1178$^{a}$8, IX 8 1168$^{b}$31–32): "Human beings are the only animals that stand upright, and this is because their nature and substance is divine" (*PA* IV 10 686$^{a}$27–28). In contrast to the other element referred to here, which we have in us insofar as we are mortal, our understanding is immortal: "The understanding seems to be born in us as a sort of substance and not to perish" (*DA* I 4 408$^{b}$18–19); "And this [active or productive] understanding . . . is in substance [or essence] an activity . . . and it alone [of the components of the human soul] is immortal and eternal" (III 5 430$^{a}$17–23).

Note 614
**The god** (*ho theos*) **always enjoys a single simple pleasure:** Aristotle's primary god is a simple and entirely unmoving or immobile being (*Protr.* B64, *Met.* XII 7 1072$^a$21–$^b$1), whose one activity "is a pleasure" (*Met.* XII 7 1072$^b$16). It may be to him that Aristotle is referring. Our own immortal understanding is also *ho theos* (for example, *EE* VIII 3 1249$^b$6–23), however, and, when it is active in accord with theoretical wisdom, is of the same sort as the god's: "[the god's] activity (*diagôgê*) has the same character as ours has for the short time it is at its best. . . . The good state of activity that we are sometimes in, the god is always in" (*Met.* XII 7 1072$^b$14–25).

Note 615
**The poet:** Euripides, *Orestes* 234.

Note 616
**It remains for us to discuss friendship too:** The definition of happiness involves (1) virtue, (2) external goods, and (3) completeness of life (I 7 1098$^a$16–20, 10 1101$^a$14–16, I 8 1099$^a$31–$^b$6), but also (4) pleasure (I 8 1098$^b$25, 1099$^a$15–31). The division of the soul into a desiring part and a rational part requires the division of virtue into (1a) virtue of character and (1b) virtue of thought (I 13). The definition of (1a) virtue of character, in turn, involves a reference to the correct reason and so the practical wisdom that provides it (II 6 1106$^b$36–1107$^a$2)—although (4) also has a substantive role to play in it (II 3). These topics occupy Books II–V. Book VI deals with (1b) virtues of thought (practical wisdom, theoretical wisdom), and so with the correct reason. Book VII 1–10 deals primarily with self-control and the lack of it, which are defective states related to (1b), and so cast additional light on it. VII 11–14 provides an account of the pleasure and pain involved not only in the explanations of self-control and lack of self-control but also in the account of (1a) and of happiness itself (VII 11 1152$^b$1–8). It is reasonable to expect, therefore, that Aristotle will next turn to (2) to complete his account of (1a). And to some extent that is precisely what he does in Books VIII and IX, since the friendship to which they are devoted is "the greatest of external goods" (IX 9 1169$^b$10). Consequently, these books, which can seem to come somewhat out of the blue, do to some extent justify Aristotle's characterization of them as being devoted to what it "remains for us to discuss." No separate account of (3), completeness of life, exists in the *NE* as we have it.

## Book VIII

Note 617
**Most necessary:** Friendship is most necessary in that it is "choiceworthy because of something else" (X 1176$^b$3), but it is also choiceworthy for its own sake in that it is something noble (1155$^a$28–29).

Note 618
**"Two go together":** Homer, *Iliad* X.224.

Note 619
**Lovers of mankind** (*philanthrôpous*): A *philanthrôpos* is not a philanthropist in our sense of the term but a person or animal that loves human beings. Thus woodcocks are *philanthrôpos* in that they are easily domesticated (*HA* IX 26 617ᵇ23–27), whereas we are *philanthrôpos* if, for example, we are moved by seeing even a very bad person falling from good fortune into bad (*Po.* 13 1453ᵃ2) or a clever villain being deceived (*Po.* 18 1456ᵃ21).

Note 620
**Lawgivers take it more seriously than justice:** Aristotle is in part thinking of Socrates' arguments in the *Republic* (especially Books III and V): "Socrates most praises unity in a city, something that is held to be and that he himself says is the function of friendship" (*Pol.* II 4 1262ᵇ9–10). But he also defends rather similar views on his own behalf: "A city is not a sharing of a common location and does not exist to prevent mutual wrongdoing and to exchange goods. Rather, while these must be present if indeed there is to be a city, when all of them *are* present there is still not yet a city but only when households and families live well as a community for the sake of a complete and self-sufficient life. But this will not be possible unless they do inhabit one and the same location and practice intermarriage. That is why marriage connections arose in cities, as well as brotherhoods, religious sacrifices, and the leisured pursuits of living together. For things of this sort are the result of friendship, since the deliberate choice to live together constitutes friendship" (*Pol.* III 9 1280ᵇ30–1281ᵃ39).

Note 621
**Concord** (*homonoia*): Discussed in *NE* IX 6. **Faction** (*stasis*): Internal political conflict in a city, extending from tensions to actual civil war, which sometimes leads to the overthrow or modification of the constitution. Discussed extensively in *Pol.* V.

Note 622
**No need for justice:** That is to say, no need for it *in addition to friendship,* since friendship already entails it (VIII 9 1159ᵇ25–32).

Note 623
**The most just of all seem to be fitted to friendship:** The line of thought is perhaps this. The most just things of all are the decent ones (V 10 1137ᵇ34–1138ᵃ3); sympathetic consideration is the correct discernment of what is decent (VI 11 1143ᵃ20); friends are particularly likely to have sympathetic consideration for each other, especially given the close connections between friendship and equality or fairness (VIII 13–14).

Note 624
**Disputes about friendship:** Most of the disputes Aristotle mentions stem from Plato, *Ly.* 213d–216, which quotes some of the same texts. Plato, *Smp.* 187a5–6 quotes Heraclitus, DK 22 B51, which Aristotle paraphrases.

Note 625
**"Birds of a feather flock together":** Literally, "Jackdaw is drawn to jackdaw."

Note 626
**Proverbial potters:** "Potters hate potters" (Hesiod, *Works and Days* 25).

Note 627
**Euripides:** Fr. 898.

Note 628
**Heraclitus:** DK 22 B8. The final phrase may be a paraphrase of B80 and the middle one of B51.

Note 629
**Empedocles:** DK 31 frs. B22, 62, 90.

Note 630
**Some people think that there is one form** (*eidos*): The people are probably Platonists and the notion of *eidos* the Platonic one discussed in I 6, which entails, in Aristotle's view, that things that share a single form must instantiate a single universal (1096$^{a}$24, 27–28). In the case of his own notion of *eidos*, which allows things to share a single form or be of a single type or have a single account or definition without instantiating a single universal (1096$^{b}$27–28), Aristotle denies that things with different forms can admit of differences in degree: "Unconditionally speaking, unless both x and y admit the definition of the F that is under discussion, neither will be called more (*mallon*) F than the other. So not all qualifications admit of differences in degree (*to mallon kai to hêtton*)" (*Cat.* 8 11$^{a}$12–14); "Of the animals, some have all their parts mutually identical, whereas some have different ones. Some parts are identical in *eidos*—for example, one man's nose and eye are identical to another man's nose and eye. . . . In other cases—those whose genus is the same—they are indeed identical [in *eidos*], but they differ in excess or deficiency . . . for example, of colors and shapes, in that some have the same things to a greater others to a lesser degree, and additionally in greater or fewer number, and larger or smaller size, or, to put it generally, in excess or deficiency" (*HA* I 1 486$^{a}$14–$^{b}$8); "Ruling and being ruled differ in *eidos,* but things that differ in degree do not differ in that way" (*Pol.* I 13 1259$^{b}$37–38).

Note 631
**We have spoken about these earlier:** Aristotle has argued that there is not a single Platonic form of the good—a single common universal that all

good things instantiate (I 6 1096ᵃ17–ᵇ5). Things are called "good," he claims, in (at least) two different ways, either because they are intrinsically good or because they are related to intrinsic goods in some way (I 6 1096ᵇ10–13). Nonetheless, goods do admit of differences of degree, since some are more complete or more choiceworthy than others (I 7 1097ᵃ25–ᵇ21). He has also allowed that good things may all be "good" by being "related to a single thing (*pros hen*)" (I 6 1096ᵇ27–28) and pretty much asserts that the thing in question is happiness (I 12 1102ᵃ3–4, VII 11 1152ᵇ2–3). Now "friend," he argues, is also a *pros hen* term like this: "Things are good in more than one way (for we call one thing 'good' because it is [intrinsically] such (*toionde*) as it is, another because it is beneficial and useful), furthermore, what is pleasant may be either unconditionally pleasant and good, or pleasant to a particular person and only apparently good. . . . So we are friends with one person because he is [intrinsically] such as he is and because of his virtue, another in that he is beneficial and useful, and another because of pleasure. . . . Hence there are three forms (*eidê*) of friendship, and they are all so called not in virtue of a single [universal], nor are they species (*eidê*) of a single genus, nor entirely homonymously. For they are so called by relation to one case that is primary. It is like the term 'medical,' since we use it in speaking of soul, body, instrument, and function, but in the full sense in speaking of what is primary. And what is primary is the one whose account is contained in all the cases (*pasin*)—for example, a medical instrument is one that a medical man [= doctor] would use, whereas the account of the instrument is not contained in the account of a medical man. In every case, then, people look for what is primary, and because the universal is primary [in scientific knowledge] they assume that what is primary is also universal. But that is false. So, where friendship is concerned, they are unable to do justice to all the things that appear to be the case. (For since a single [universal] account does not fit all, they think the other cases are not friendships, even though they really are, but in a different way). And so, when they find that the one that is primary does not fit them, they go on to deny that the other cases are friendships at all, on the supposition that it would be universal, if indeed it were really primary. But there are in fact many forms of friendship. For this is part of what we already implied when we distinguished three ways in which people are said to be friends—because of virtue, because of utility, and because of pleasure. . . . That of the best people, though, is in accord with virtue. . . . [And] the primary friendship, the friendship of good people, is reciprocal love and reciprocal deliberate choice of each other" (*EE* VII 2 1236ᵃ7–ᵇ5). As we might expect, then, the three different forms of friendship are also comparable with respect to their degree of completeness (VIII 3–4 1156ᵇ7–1157ᵃ36). Hence Aristotle's criticism of the Platonist argument in our text is that it mistakenly infers that there is a single universal Platonic form F that all Fs instantiate from the fact that x and y can differ in their degree of F, since differences in degree of F between x and y are consistent with F having a *pros hen* definition like that of "medical."

Note 632
**The proper object of love** (*to philêton*): What friends do is love (*philein*) each other. The proper object of love is the feature in a person (such as being a source of pleasure or utility) that attracts his friend's love to him.

Note 633
**That will make no difference:** We can say either (1) what is good for each person is lovable to himself or (2) what appears good to each person is what appears lovable to himself.

Note 634
**Goodwill:** See IX 5.

Note 635
**One of the things we mentioned:** At 1155$^{b}$19 (goodness, utility, or pleasure).

Note 636
**In the case of each object of love . . . unawares:** This suggests that goodwill exists in all three forms of friendship. The next sentence is probably best read as modifying that suggestion, however, since Aristotle is later explicit that in friendships that exist because of utility or pleasure, the friends do not wish good things to each other for the other's own sake, and so do not have goodwill toward each other (IX 5 1167$^{a}$10–21).

Note 637
**Guest-friendship** (*xenikê philia*): A ritualized form of pseudo-kinship between (typically) men of equal social status but belonging to different social units (such as Athens and Sparta), involving a variety of forms of mutual support, including exchange of valuable resources (gifts, troops) and services (a home away from home). The relationship, like true kinship, was perpetual, descending from fathers to sons, so that, for example, a *xenos* was expected to show protective concern for the son of his *xenos,* including acting as his substitute father if his real father died. Such friendships are like the ones Aristotle is discussing in being in accord with mutual advantage and dependent on it, but because of the sort of mutual advantage involved, this need not entail any instability: "Guest-friendships might seem to be the most stable of all, since they have no common end about which to dispute, as, for example, fellow citizens do" (*MM* II 11 1211$^{a}$12–14).

Note 638
**As long as they are good:** See IX 3 1165$^{b}$13–36.

Note 639
**"Eaten the canonical amount of salt together":** The canonical amount is a *medimnos* or bushel (*EE* VII 2 1238$^{a}$2–3).

Note 640
**A lover and his boyfriend** (*erastê[i] kai erômenô[i]*): *Paiderasteia*, or boy love between an older man (*erastês*) and an adolescent boy (*erômenos*), was an

accepted practice in Classical Athens. Sex was common in such relationships, with the boy playing the passive role. Once the boy reached manhood, however, and his bloom of youth faded, that had to change. On pain of losing his citizen rights, he could no longer be a passive sexual partner. Instead, he was expected to marry, have children, and became an *erastês* in his turn. Though erotic in nature, the relationship was conceived as primarily educative. By associating with someone who was already a man, a boy learned virtue or excellence and how to be a man himself. Rites of passage in some primitive warrior societies also involve sexual contact between men and boys, and it is sometimes suggested that Greek *paiderasteia* also had its roots in a warrior past.

Note 641
**The ones who live together:** Not necessarily those who live under the same roof but those who engage together in the life activities they value most (IX 12 1171$^{b}$29–1172$^{a}$8).

Note 642
**"Many a friendship has broken off for want of conversation":** Source unknown.

Note 643
**Nature most avoids what is painful and seeks what is pleasant:** See X 1 1172$^{a}$19–20.

Note 644
**Deliberate choice stems from a state:** See VI 2 1139$^{a}$33–35.

Note 645
**Friendship is said to be equality:** also IX 8 2 1168$^{b}$8, *EE* VII 6 1240$^{b}$2.

Note 646
**Something of that sort:** The sort in question probably includes both complete friendship and erotic love. For erotic love is "a sort of excessive form of friendship" (IX 10 1171$^{a}$11–12), and complete friendship—as something complete—is also a kind of excess: "we call something complete when, as regards virtue or goodness, it cannot be exceeded relative to its kind, as, for example, a doctor is complete and a flute player is complete when they lack nothing as regards the form of their own proper virtue" (*Met.* V 16 1021$^{b}$12–17). Moreover, the friends in such a friendship are fully good or virtuous people, and virtue—though in essence a medial state—is an extreme or excess "in relation to the best and doing well" (*NE* II 6 1107$^{a}$6–8). **In relation to a single person:** See X 10 1170$^{b}$34–1171$^{a}$13.

Note 647
**The good itself:** That is, the Platonic form of the good discussed in I 6.

Note 648
**Achieve proportionate equality as an inferior:** See V 5 1132$^{b}$30–1133$^{b}$28, VIII 7 1158$^{b}$23–28, 13 1162$^{a}$34–$^{b}$4.

Note 649
**We have already said:** See VIII 4.

Note 650
**A different virtue and a different function:** "The soul naturally contains a part that rules and a part that is ruled, and we say that each of them has a different virtue, that is to say, one belongs to the part that has reason and one to the nonrational part. It is clear, then, that the same holds in the other cases as well, so that most instances of ruling and being ruled are natural. For free rule slaves, male rules female, and a grown man rules a child in different ways, because, while the parts of the soul are present in all these people, they are present in different ways. For a slave does not have the deliberative part of the soul at all; a woman has it but it lacks control; a child has it but it is incompletely developed. We must suppose, therefore, that the same necessarily holds of the virtues of character, too: all must share in them but not in the same way; rather, each must have a sufficient share to enable him to perform his own function. Hence a ruler must have virtue of character complete, since his function is unconditionally that of an architectonic craftsman, and reason is something architectonic but each of the others must have as much as pertains to him" (*Pol.* I 13 1260$^a$5–20).

Note 651
**Characteristic of friendship:** See VIII 5 1157$^b$36.

Note 652
**Separation:** VIII 5 1157$^b$5–13 discusses the effects of spatial separation on friendship. Here the separation between the two parties is a measure of their differences in virtue, resources, and so on.

Note 653
**The puzzle . . . good things:** If we wished the greatest goods to our friends, we would wish them to become gods. But then (1) they would be too separate from us and other human beings to have friends, which will deprive them of the greatest of external goods, since that is just what friends are (IX 9 1169$^b$9–10). Alternatively, (2) in depriving ourselves of their friendship, we would deprive *ourselves* of the greatest external goods. Although both interpretations are possible, but (2) is perhaps more plausible, since the puzzle is one about whether friends really wish to their friends the greatest goods that they wish to themselves—friendship itself being one of these.

Note 654
**Most of all for himself:** See IX 8. **If, then . . . each person wishes good things:** (1) It is to his friend *as a human being* that a friend wishes the greatest goods, which excludes the possibility of wishing him to become a god. (2) "But perhaps not all of them," might seem at first to mean that there are some greatest goods that the good man does not wish to his

friend. But that conflicts with the later claim that a good person "is related to his friend as he is to himself, since his friend is another himself" (IX 4 1166ª30–32), since it entails that a good person will wish some greatest goods to himself that he will not wish to his friend, and so his friend will not be a second himself after all. What (2) must mean, therefore, is that there are some greatest goods that the good man does not wish to his friend *as a human being,* but as the thing he most of all is, namely, his immortal and divine understanding (IX 8 1168ᵇ28–34, X 5 1176ª24–29, 7 1178ª2–8)—this being the way he wishes good things most of all for himself (IX 4 1166ª19–23). So the person who raises the puzzle is partly right and partly wrong. He is right in thinking that there are some greatest goods that a good man does not wish to his friend *as a human being,* but wrong in thinking that there are therefore some greatest goods that he does not wish to his friend *at all.*

Note 655
**Loving seems to be the virtue characteristic of friends:** We are praised for loving our friends and it is virtues that attract praise (I 13 1103ª9–10, II 5 1106ª1).

Note 656
**Steadfast in themselves:** Because their virtue is something steadfast (VII 3 1156ᵇ12).

Note 657
**They do not remain even like themselves:** "What is good is simple, but what is bad is multiform, and a good person is always the same and does not change in his character, whereas a base person or a foolish one is not the same in the evening as he was in the morning. That is why, unless they adjust to each other, base people are not friends, but fall out, since a friendship that is not steadfast is not a friendship at all" (*EE* VII 5 1239ᵇ11–16; also *NE* IX 4 1166ᵇ7–29).

Note 658
**Another discussion entirely:** See VIII 1 1155ᵇ1–9.

Note 659
**As we said at the start:** See VIII 1 1155ª22–28.

Note 660
**The extent of justice:** See V 5 1132ᵇ31–1333ᵇ28.

Note 661
**For the sake of what is advantageous:** What is advantageous is not to be identified with what is useful, but includes living nobly and well: "A complete community, constituted out of several villages, once it reaches the limit of total self-sufficiency, practically speaking, is a city. It comes to be for the sake of living, but it remains in existence for the sake of living well. That is why every city exists by nature, since the first communities

do" (*Pol.* I 2 1252$^{b}$27–31); "A human being is by nature a political animal. That is why, even when they do not need one another's aid, people no less desire to live together. Although it is also true that the common advantage brings them together, to the extent that it contributes some share of noble living to each. This above all is the end, then, whether of the community or of each individual. But human beings also join together and maintain political communities for the sake of living itself. For there is perhaps some share of the noble in living itself alone, as long as it is not too overburdened with the hardships of life. In any case, it is clear that most human beings are willing to endure much hardship in order to cling to living, as if it had a sort of joy inherent in it and a natural sweetness" (III 6 1278$^{b}$19–30).

Note 662
**What is for the common advantage is said to be just:** "It is evident, then, that those constitutions that aim at the common advantage turn out—according to what is unconditionally just—to be correct, whereas all those that aim only at the advantage of the rulers are mistaken and are deviations from the correct constitutions. For they are like rule by a master, whereas a city is a community of free people" (*Pol.* III 6 1279$^{a}$17–21).

Note 663
**Tribe** (*phylê*), **Deme:** A *phylê* ("tribe" is the canonical but somewhat misleading translation) was a principal division of the citizens of a city, which functioned—among many other things—as a constituency for the election of magistrates and other political offices. A *deme* was a local territorial district within a city, on the order of a village or township, with many different functions, including the according of citizenship to eighteen-year-olds through registering them as *deme* residents.

Note 664
**Religious guild** (*thiasos*): The members of a *thiasos* danced in processions and joined in sacrificial feasts in honor of a god, especially Bacchus or Dionysus.

Note 665
**For all of life . . .:** Something may be missing from the text here.

Note 666
**Three forms of constitution:** "A monarchy that looks to the common advantage we customarily call a kingship, and rule by a few, but more than one, an aristocracy (either because the best people rule, or because they rule with a view to what is best for the city and those who share in it). But when the multitude governs for the common advantage, the constitution is called by the name common to all constitutions: *politeia* [= polity]. Moreover, this happens quite reasonably. For while it is possible for one or a few to be outstandingly virtuous, it is already difficult for a larger number to be accomplished in every virtue, although they can be so most of all in military

virtue. That is why the class of defensive soldiers, the ones who own the weapons, has the most control in this constitution. Deviations from these are tyranny from kingship, oligarchy from aristocracy, and democracy from polity. For tyranny is rule by one person for the advantage of the monarch, oligarchy is for the advantage of the rich, and democracy is for the advantage of the poor. But none is for what profits the common good" (*Pol.* III 7 1279ᵃ32–ᵇ10).

Note 667
**Property assessment** (*timêma*): A measure of wealth or property for the purposes of taxation or determining such public services or votive offerings as the equipping of a trireme, which was used in some constitutions to determine citizenship or access to public office. Aristotle associates *timokratia* (timocracy) with *timêma*, Plato (*Rep.* VIII 545b–548d) with *timê* (honor).
**Polity** (*politeia*): Aristotle uses the term *politeia* in a number of different ways: (1) Sometimes it refers to a political system of any sort, whether constitutional or not (*Pol.* II 10 1271ᵇ20 with 1272ᵇ9–11). (2) Sometimes (in fact more often than not) it refers to a political system defined by a constitution and governed in accordance with universal laws (IV 2 1289ᵃ18–20). (3) Sometimes, as here, it refers to a system of a particular sort, namely, a polity (II 6 1265ᵇ26–28). Of it too a number of different—but roughly equivalent—accounts are given besides the one given here. A polity is: (3a) a constitution ruled by the majority for the common advantage (III 7 1279ᵃ37–39); (3b) a mixed constitution (IV 8 1293ᵇ33–34); (3c) a constitution that depends on the middle class (IV 11 1295ᵇ34–1296ᵃ9), or (3d) on the hoplite or warlike class (II 6 1265ᵇ26–28). The nature of the mixture mentioned in (3b) is variously characterized as a mixture of democracy and oligarchy (V 7 1307ᵃ10–12), of the rich and the poor (IV 8 1294ᵃ16–17), or of elements drawn from democratic and oligarchic constitutions (IV 9).

Note 668
**Titular king** (*klêrôtos*): Literally, "king appointed by lot."

Note 669
**It is the worst:** "We distinguished two kinds of tyranny while we were investigating kingship, because their power somehow also overlaps with kingship, owing to the fact that both are in accord with law. For some non-Greek peoples choose [1] autocratic monarchs, and in former times among the ancient Greeks there were [2] people called dictators who became monarchs in this way. There are, however, certain differences between these; but both were kingly, because they were in accord with law, and involved monarchical rule over willing subjects, but both were tyrannical, because the monarchs ruled like masters in accord with their own judgment. But [3] there is also a third kind of tyranny, which seems to be tyranny in the highest degree, being a counterpart to absolute kingship. Any monarchy is necessarily a tyranny of this kind if the monarch rules in a non-accountable fashion over all people who are equal to him or better, with an eye to his

own advantage not that of those he rules. That is why it is rule over involuntary subjects, subjects, since none among free people willingly endures such rule" (*Pol.* IV 10 1295ᵃ7–23).

Note 670
**Kingship is meant to be paternal rule:** "The rule of a father over his children is that of a king, since a parent rules on the basis both of age and affection, and this is a type of kingly rule. Hence Homer did well to address Zeus, who is the king of them all, as 'Father of gods and men'" (*Pol.* I 12 1259ᵇ10–14). Homer refers to Zeus as "father" at *Iliad* I.544.

Note 671
**He changes it into an oligarchy:** Presumably because he allocates what belongs to the household contrary to its members' worth (1160ᵇ13) and assign "offices"—that is authority and rule—always to the same people, namely, himself (1160ᵇ14–15). It is less clear that he gives all or most of the good things to himself (1160ᵇ14) or makes wealth the most important qualification for office (1160ᵇ15).

Note 672
**Habitation** (*oikêsis*): An *oikia* (household) is a community with a distinctive organization in which someone is master. An *oikêsis* is a place to live in, so that a bird's nest, for example, is an *oikêsis* (*HA* IX 11 614ᵇ31).

Note 673
**Homer:** *Iliad* II.243, IV.413, and often elsewhere. Agamemnon was the leader of the Greek army attacking troy.

Note 674
**A king those he rules:** "A king should be naturally superior, but belong to the same stock as those he rules; and this is the condition of older in relation to younger and father in relation to child" (*Pol.* I 12 1259ᵇ14–17).

Note 675
**In tyranny there is little or no friendship:** Friendship between a tyrant and his subjects is excluded by the fact that they are effectively his slaves. Friendship between the subjects is made difficult by the measures typically taken to preserve tyrannical power, such as: "Prohibiting messes, clubs, education, and other things of that sort. Keeping an eye on anything that typically engenders two things: thought and mutual trust. Prohibiting schools and other gatherings connected with learning, and doing everything to ensure that people are as ignorant of one another as possible, since knowledge tends to give rise to mutual trust . . . Retaining spies . . . since people speak less freely when they fear the presence of such spies. . . . Slandering people to one another, setting friend against friend, the people against the notables, and the rich against themselves" (*Pol.* VII 11 1313ᵃ41–ᵇ18).

Note 676

**Soul toward body:** "An animal is primordially constituted by soul and body: the soul is the natural ruler; the body the natural subject. But, of course, one should investigate what is natural in things whose condition is natural, not ruined. One should therefore study the human being too whose soul and body are in the best possible condition; one in whom this is clear. For in depraved people, and those in a depraved condition, the body will often seem to rule the soul, because their condition is base and contrary to nature. At any rate, it is, as I say, in an animal, that we can first observe both rule of a master and rule of a statesman. For the soul rules the body with the rule of a master, whereas understanding rules desire with rule of a statesman or with the rule of a king" (*Pol.* I 6 1254$^{a}$34–$^{b}$6).

Note 677

**Insofar as he is a human being there is:** Some people are *natural* slaves: "Those people who are as different from others as body is from soul or beast from human, and those whose function (that is to say, the best thing to come from them) is the use of their bodies are in this condition—those people are natural slaves. And it is better for them to be subject to this rule. . . . For someone who can belong to someone else (and that is why he actually does belong to someone else), and he who shares in reason to the extent of perceptually apprehending it, but does not have it himself (for the other animals do not perceptually apprehend reason but obey their feelings), is a natural slave. The difference in the use made of them is small, since both slaves and domestic animals help provide the necessities with their bodies" (*Pol.* I 6 1254$^{b}$16–26). Slaves of this sort have no deliberative element in their souls: "a slave has no deliberative part of the soul at all" (I 13 1260$^{a}$12). As a result, they are less than human, since the possession of a deliberative element is what distinguishes human beings from other animals (*NE* I 7 1097$^{b}$34–1098$^{a}$8). Other people are human beings who happen to have been enslaved. They are *legal* or *conventional* slaves: "slaves and slavery are spoken of in two ways: for there are also slaves—that is to say, people who are in a state of slavery—by *law*. The law is a sort of agreement by which what is conquered in war is said to belong to the victors" (*Pol.* I 6 1255$^{a}$4–7). Toward natural slaves neither friendship nor justice exists—or only a very minimal level of them, consequent upon the fact that even a capacity minimally to apprehend reason may qualify someone to participate to some extent in a community of law and agreement: "there is a certain mutual advantage and mutual friendship for such masters and slaves as deserve to be naturally so related" (I 6 1255$^{b}$12–14). In the case of legal slaves, friendship between them and their masters is excluded by the fact that they are being treated unjustly in being enslaved—between them the contrary of friendship and mutual advantage holds ( I 6 1255$^{b}$14–15). But there is nothing, it seems, to prevent legal slaves (to the extent that they are human beings) from being friends with each other or with other human beings who are not their masters.

Note 678
**As we said:** VIII 9.

Note 679
**Another . . . "themselves":** IX 9 1170$^b$6–7.

Note 680
**Proportionate:** That is, to their distance from their initial common ancestor (1162$^a$3–4).

Note 681
**Household is prior to and more necessary than city:** Households are necessary for the existence of cities and are thus prior to them in the way that matter is prior to form: "It is the same way in the case of anything in which an end is present: without things that have a necessary nature it could not exist, but it does not exist because of these (except in the way that a thing exists because of its matter), but for the sake of something. For example, why is a saw such as it is? So that this may be—that is, for the sake of this end. It is impossible, however, that the end it is for the sake of should come to be unless the saw is made of iron. It is necessary, then, that it should be made of iron, if there is to be a saw and the function belonging to it" (*Ph.* II 9 200$^a$7–13). Yet just as the saw does not exist for the sake of the iron that is necessary for its existence, so the city does not exist for the sake of the household, but the other way around. From that more important teleological point of view, therefore, crucial to defining what a household is, the city is prior: "The city is also prior in nature to the household and to each of us individually, since a whole is necessarily prior to its parts. For if the whole body is dead, there will no longer be a foot or a hand, except homonymously, as one might speak of a stone 'hand' (for once dead a hand will be like that); but everything is defined by its function and by its capacity; so that in such condition they should not be said to be the same things but homonymous ones" (*Pol.* I 3 1253$^a$18–25).

Note 682
**Their functions are divided:** "A man would seem a coward if he had the courage of a woman, and a woman would seem garrulous if she had the temperance of a good man, since even household management differs for the two of them, since his function is to acquire property and hers to preserve it" (*Pol.* III 5 1277$^b$21–25).

Note 683
**At the start:** VIII 3 1156$^a$6–7.

Note 684
**The one who excels . . . does not complain about his friend:** A and B are both virtuous, so each wants to do well by the other. When A tries to do well by B, B responds by trying to do well by A instead. If A excels B, he does better by B than B does by him. Normally a breach of equality

like this would be grounds for complaint by A, but here it isn't, since A is doing the good that he desires.

Note 685
**Should be content with that:** See VII 4 1157$^{a}$21–25.

Note 686
**And do so voluntarily:** Reading καὶ ἑκόντι which OCT brackets. **An involuntarily friend:** If the recipient kept as a free gift what the giver intended as loan, he would be treating him as an involuntary friend, since his motives were those of a business partner, not a friend.

Note 687
**The controlling element . . . lies in deliberate choice:** See III 1 1111$^{b}$4–6, X 8 1178$^{a}$34–$^{b}$3.

Note 688
**Charity** (*leitourgia*): Any public service paid for out of private funds (some examples are given at IV 2 1122$^{b}$22–23) is a *leitourgia*, but here and at IX 6 1167$^{b}$12 the sense is closer to our notion of a charity. **The functions** (*ta erga*): *Ta erga* could also mean "the works," or (roughly) what each party has done for the other in the relationship. But the issue is not so much about what the parties have done as about the relative worth (superiority, inferiority) of the parties themselves and how it is to be measured. The good person thinks that it should be measured in terms of relative virtue, the benefactor, in terms of relative utility. Ultimately, this seems to be a disagreement about what the functions are of the parties to a friendship (compare VIII 7 1158$^{b}$18). *Erga* are assigned to friendship itself at *EE* VII 2 1237$^{a}$34, *Pol.* III 9 1280$^{b}$38.

Note 689
**A community formed with a view to making money** (*chrêmatôn koinônia[i]*): See VIII 9 1160$^{a}$16.

Note 690
**The function of a good friend** (*to philou agathou*): Supplying an implied *ergon* ("function") from 1163$^{a}$30. Or "For the characteristic of a good friend."

Note 691
**Disputes also arise . . . the assistance of those in need:** "In friendships in accord with superiority the claims of proportionality of desert are not of the same sorts. Rather the superior party claims the proportion to be an inverse one, namely, that as he stands to the inferior party, so should what he receives from the inferior party stand to what the inferior party receives from him, his standing being like that of ruler to ruled. Or if not that, he claims that he deserves an arithmetically equal share. . . . The inferior party, on the contrary, inverts the proportion. . . . It seems that this way the superior party comes off worse, however, and that the friendship

or the community is in fact a charity. Hence equality must be restored or proportion maintained by some other means. And this is honor, which is the very thing due to a natural ruler or a god in comparison to someone he rules. But the profit must be equalized relative to the honor" (*EE* VII 10 $1242^{b}$6–21).

Note 692
**Honor is a common good:** See I 5 $1095^{b}$23.

Note 693
**As we said:** Most recently at $1162^{b}$2–4, but also at VIII 7 $1158^{b}$27–28, 8 $1159^{a}$35–$^{b}$2.

Note 694
**Disown:** Athenian parents were under no legal obligation to rear their children: exposure of unwanted infants was not uncommon. A law attributed to Solon made maltreatment of parents a prosecutable offense, but exempted a son from the obligation to support his aged father if the latter had failed to teach him a craft or prostituted him.

## Book IX

Note 695
**As we said:** Most recently at VIII 14 $1163^{b}$11–12.

Note 696
**Political friendship:** "Political friendship is in accord with utility. . . . [It] looks to equality and to the object as buyers and sellers do, whence the saying, 'Fair wages make good friends.' So when it is in accord with an agreement, this is political and legal friendship, but when people entrust things to each other, it tends to be based on character and to be companionate" (*EE* VII 10 $1242^{b}$21–37; also *NE* IX 10 $1171^{a}$15–20).

Note 697
**No longer possessed by both of them:** That is, the lover no longer possesses the quality of usefulness or the boy of pleasingness. See $1164^{a}$11.

Note 698
**As we said:** Aristotle may be referring to erotic friendships in which the lovers come to feel affection for each other's characters, since he has remarked that the parties can then remain friends beyond the period in which each gets the pleasure that he initially wanted from the relationship (VIII 4 $1157^{a}$10–12), implying, if not outright stating, that such transformed erotic friendships can be steadfast. But apparently the parties must be good men—though not necessarily equally good ones (VIII 13 $1162^{a}$36–$^{b}$1)—for this to be true (VIII 4 $1157^{a}$16–20). In any case, such friendships could not be cases of intrinsic friendship, since only good or

virtuous people can be intrinsic friends (VIII 4 1157ᵃ18–19). If, on the other hand, transformed erotic friendships can exist between men who are not good, then the sentence is a parenthetical comment about friendship in accord with virtue of character and the reference is to VIII 8 1159ᵃ35ᵇ–7.

Note 699
**Pleasure in return for pleasure:** Probably the pleasure of anticipating payment in return for the pleasure of listening.

Note 700
**Protagoras:** Protagoras of Acragas (c. 490 BC–c. 420) was a famous sophist, perhaps the first to describe himself as such and to charge fees for his teaching (Plato, *Prt.* 317b, 349a).

Note 701
**To a man his wage:** Hesiod, *Works and Days* 368.

Note 702
**Sophists:** The sophists were paid independent itinerant teachers of rhetoric and a variety of other subjects, who were central to intellectual life in Athens in the late fifth century BC and later. Aristotle defines a sophist as "one who makes money from an apparent but non-genuine wisdom" (*SE* I 1 165ᵃ22–23).

Note 703
**As we said:** At VIII 13 1162ᵇ6–13 (VIII 4 1157ᵃ25–33 shows its relevance to friendships other than those in accord with virtue).

Note 704
**Characteristic of a friend and of virtue:** See VIII 13 1162ᵇ5–13, 1163ᵃ21–23.

Note 705
**The case of gods and parents:** See VIII 14 1163ᵇ15–18.

Note 706
**Voluntary transactions:** See V 2 1131ᵃ1–5. **In the same way as we formed it:** See VIII 13 1162ᵇ29–31.

Note 707
**Whether a person should allocate everything to his father:** That is, in an attempt to repay his father for the enormous debt he owes him (VIII 14 1163ᵇ15–18, IX 1 1164ᵇ4–6). Hence the shift from *aponemein* ("allocate") here to *apodoteon* ("return") at 1165ᵃ14.

Note 708
**Nobility and necessity:** What is noble—choiceworthy because of itself or for its own sake and so chosen voluntarily—is often contrasted with what, because it is necessary, we are compelled to choose (III 8 1116ᵇ2–3, IV 1 1120ᵇ3–4, VIII 1 1155ᵃ28–29).

Note 709
**We should not return everything to the same person:** Possibly a response to the opening puzzle about what we owe our fathers. But since that puzzle is explicitly mentioned at 1165ª14–16, it may instead be a separate point, amplified in the next clause. When, as is often true, we have multiple—and sometimes conflicting—obligations, we cannot give all of the resources available to discharge them to a single person but must, rather, find a way to balance them.

Note 710
**Precisely what we said:** Most recently at 1164ᵇ27–28 (see also 1165ª12–14). **Speaking in universal terms:** See II 2 1104ª5–7.

Note 711
**The worth of the parties is not equal:** And so the evil party should not get the same thing from the decent one as the latter got from him.

Note 712
**Precisely as we have often said:** Although not always in quite the same words. See I 3 1094ᵇ11–27, II 2 1103ᵇ34–1104ª5.

Note 713
**As we said at the start:** The reference may be to VIII 13 1162ᵇ23–25 or (more plausibly) IX 1 1164ª13–14, but nothing exactly like this has been said before.

Note 714
**Not everything is lovable, but, rather, what is good:** See VIII 2 1155ᵇ17–21.

Note 715
**We said:** At VIII 3 1156ᵇ19–21, 8 1159ᵇ2–3.

Note 716
**We have talked about these topics:** At VIII 5 1157ᵇ17–24, 7 1158ᵇ33–35.

Note 717
**As mothers feel about their children:** That is, mothers who have given away their children to be raised by someone else, and whose love is therefore unidirectional and entirely disinterested (see VIII 8 1159ª27–33). **Friends feel who are irritated with each other** (*proskekroukotes*): Irritation is not uncommon in people who live together: "It is generally difficult to live together and to share in any human enterprise. . . . Travelers away from home, who share a journey together, show this clearly. For most of them start disputes because they irritate each another (*proskrouontes*) in humdrum matters and little things. Moreover, among the servants it is with those we employ most regularly for everyday services that we get most irritated (*proskrouomen*)" (*Pol.* II 5 1263ª15–21). Friends who are irritated with

each other may therefore be friends who used to live together but whose irritation with each other eventually drove them apart without otherwise affecting their high regard for one another. This would explain why they are mentioned in the same breath as mothers who have given away—and so no longer live with—their children.

Note 718
**As we said:** At III 4 1113$^a$29–33.

Note 719
**Desires the same things with all his soul:** See I 13 1102$^b$25–28. **The thought-involving element in him** (*to dianoêtikon*): Referred to in the next line as "the element with which he thinks (*phronei*)," this is more narrowly identified a few lines later with the understanding part (*to nooun*) (1166$^a$22) and later still with understanding (*nous*) itself (X 7 1177$^b$26–1178$^a$3).

Note 720
**Even now the god** (*ho theos*) **has the good** (*tagathon*): (1) *Ho theos* could refer to the god and *tagathon* to *the* good (that is, happiness). The thought would then be that no one would choose to have happiness or the good if he had to become a god to get it. (2) *Ho theos* could refer to the understanding (as at I 6 1096$^a$24–25, 12 1101$^b$30) and *tagathon* to the good under discussion, that is, the excellent person's ongoing life. The thought would then be that the excellent person, to whom life is a good, wishes good things to himself and so wishes for his ongoing life to be preserved, since this is a condition of his having these other good things. In other words he wishes to become something at each next moment, that will have those good things. If the something in question were *something else,* its having those things would not be a case of *his* having them. For as things stand, there is something in him that already has ongoing life (the good in question), namely, his own understanding, since it is immortal and eternal. Moreover, his understanding is not something other than himself, since it is what he is or is most of all. On balance (2) seems to make better sense of the entire argument than (1).

Note 721
**Always the same thing that is painful or pleasant:** See VII 14 1154$^b$20–31. A different but related point is made at I 8 1099$^a$11–13.

Note 722
**We may set aside for the present:** The question is discussed in IX 8.

Note 723
**Insofar as a person is—from the features we mentioned** (*ek tôn eirêmenôn*)**—two or more** (*duo ê pleiô*): The phrase *ek tôn eirêmenôn* must have the same reference, apparently, as *ta eirêmena* ("the features we mentioned") one line later (1166$^b$2), and so both must refer to the five features

of friendship. (1) If the preposition *ek* means "from," Aristotle is saying that "insofar as a person is or possesses two or more from the [list of] features we mentioned." But since a person possesses *all five* features, this makes the expression "two or more" difficult to justify. (2) A different way to understand the passage involves treating the preposition *ek* in its inferential sense, so that we can *infer something from* the five features, namely, that if a person has them in relation to himself, then he or his soul must be or possess two or more elements or parts. The subsequent discussion of failures of self-friendship (1166b2–29) reveals that two of these parts are wish and appetite (1166b7–8), but insofar as psychological conflict or "faction" (1166b19) is what gives rise to distinct conflicting elements, there is no reason to think that there need be only two of these—hence "two *or more*." On balance (2) is preferable and has the further advantage of making the account of the problem of self-friendship fit with those given elsewhere. "When we wish to describe a very intense friendship, we say, 'My soul and his are one.' So since the soul has more parts than one (*pleiô merê*), it will only be one soul when reason and feeling are in harmony with each other (since this way it will be at one), and it follows that when it has become one it will exhibit friendship to itself. But this friendship to self will exist only in an excellent person, since in him alone the parts of the soul are in a good state relative to each other by not being at odds" (*MM* II 11 1211a32–38); "The question about whether a person is or is not a friend to himself needs much investigation. Some people think that each person is most a friend to himself, and they use this as a standard by which to judge his friendships with his other friends. If we look to arguments and the features commonly thought to be characteristic of friends, however, the two sorts of friendship are apparently contrary in some ways and alike in others. For the present sort is somehow friendship by analogy rather than unconditionally. For loving and being loved require two distinct relata. Because of this a person is a friend to himself more in the way in which we said that a person who lacks self-control and a person who has it are voluntary or involuntary agents, depending on how the parts of their souls stand in relation to each other. In fact, all questions of this sort—whether a person can be a friend or enemy to himself or whether he can do an injustice to himself—have a similar answer, since all these relations require two distinct relata. Insofar, then, as the soul is somehow two, these relations are somehow possible, but insofar as it is not two, they are not" (*EE* VII 6 1240a7–21).

Note 724

**Impious in his actions** (*anosiourgos*): A human being is "the most impious (*anosiôtaton*) and savage of the animals when he lacks virtue" (*Pol.* I 2 1253a36).

Note 725

**It is pretty much the case indeed that base people do not have them either:** These people cannot be *altogether* base, unrestrained, and depraved, since if they were they would "certainly (*ge*)" lack the features in question ($1166^b5$) rather than its being "pretty much the case (*schedon*)" that they lack them. They are *somewhat* base and depraved, then, in that they have some depraved appetites ($1166^b20$) and sometimes act (in an uncontrolled way) on these ($1166^b10$–11) or with self-control refrain from doing so ($1166^b18$–22). Notice "very much that way (*to houtôs echein lian*)" at $1166^b27$. **The way people who lack self-control do:** Implied by I 13 $1102^b14$–21, III 2 $1111^b13$–15, V 9 $1136^b6$–7.

Note 726
**Have done many terrible actions because of their depravity hate and even flee from living their life:** Reading (1) δεινὰ πέπρακται διὰ τὴν μοχθηρίαν μισοῦσι τε καὶ. OCT reads (2) δεινὰ πέπρακται καὶ διὰ τὴν μοχθηρίαν μισοῦνται καὶ φεύγουσι τὸ ζῆν ("have done many terrible actions and because of their depravity are hated and even flee from living their life"). Reading (2) brings in a reference to other people's attitudes to the somewhat base agent's depravity. Reading (1) refers only to attitudes internal to this agent—attitudes that he seeks to assuage by surrounding himself with others ($1166^b13$–14) who must be *unaware* of his depraved actions. **For instead of the things they themselves think to be good . . . ruin themselves:** Those who are altogether base do not regret their actions or lives (VII 7 $1150^a20$–22, 8 $1150^b29$–31), since they always do what they desire and choose, whereas the somewhat base ordinary people under discussion are "full of regret" ($1166^b24$–25). This is because, unlike those who are altogether base, they will sometimes suffer from—and recognize that they suffer from—their own analogues of self-control or the lack of it and will "shrink from doing the actions *they* think to be best for themselves," because of (what *they* consider to be) idleness or cowardice. Some of them may even have some appetites that are from their own point of view depraved ($1166^b20$). If these have caused them to do many things they consider terrible, they will hate living and sometimes kill themselves.

Note 727
**Faction:** The metaphor of faction or civil war in the soul is used persistently by Plato to justify the existence of a variety of elements or parts in the soul. "And don't we often notice on other occasions that when appetite forces someone contrary to his rational calculation, he reproaches himself and feels anger at the thing in him that is doing the forcing, and just as if there were two warring factions, such a person's spirit becomes the ally of his reason?" (*Rep.* IV 440a9–b4). He also uses the existence of such complexity to justify the *intra*personal use of a variety of *inter*personal notions such as justice, friendship, and enmity: "And in a single individual too I presume, injustice will produce the very same effects that it is in its nature to produce. First, it will make him incapable of acting because of inner faction and not being of one mind with himself; second, it makes

him his own enemy as well as the enemy of just people" (*Rep*. I 352a6–9). **Besides, depraved people seek others . . . as if tearing him asunder:** As in the previous paragraph, the people under discussion are not altogether base or depraved but, rather, have appetites they themselves consider to be depraved, which have led them to do many things they consider to be terrible or objectionable and which they expect will lead them to such things in the future. Since they consider these appetites to be depraved, they wish to hold them back and so try to do so. If they succeed, the appetites are frustrated and cause suffering, whereas their wish is satisfied and gives them pleasure.

Note 728
**It is not possible to be pained and pleased at the same time:** "Surely, we say, the same thing, in the same respect of itself, in relation to the same thing, and at the same time, cannot do opposite things" (Plato, *Rep*. IV 439b5–6). **And even if it is not possible . . . pleasant to him:** The things the agent eventually "wishes . . . had not become pleasant for him" are the objects of his depraved appetites. What he is pained that he was pleased about is not, as we might at first think, the pleasure he got from satisfying his wish that those depraved appetites not be satisfied but was, rather, the pleasure he anticipated he would get from satisfying them.

Note 729
**We also said this before:** See VIII 2 1155$^b$32–1156$^a$5. See also 6 1158$^a$4–10.

Note 730
**A way of loving:** See VIII 3 1156$^a$6–7.

Note 731
**Never join in their actions** (*sumpraxaien*) **or go to any trouble on their behalf:** "[People are friendly] to those whom they would join in doing good actions (*tagatha sumprattôsin*), unless greater evils would result for themselves" (*Rh*. II 4 1381$^b$23–24).

Note 732
**Goodwill does not arise in the case of these:** See VIII 3 1156$^a$9–14.

Note 733
**We mentioned:** At 1166$^b$34–1167$^a$2.

Note 734
**Concord . . . agreement in belief . . . are of one mind:** The Greek terms *homonoia* ("concord"), *homodoxia* ("agreement in belief"), and *homognômonein* ("be of one mind") share the common prefix *homo-* ("same").

Note 735
**Pittacus:** One of the fabled Seven Sages, Pittacus was elected ruler of Mytilene in 589 BC. After ten years, against the wishes of the Mytilenians,

he stepped down. Hence Aristotle's reference to willingness. Pittacus is also mentioned at *Pol.* II 12 1274b18–23, III 14 1285a35–b1.

Note 736
**The *Phoenician Women*:** A play by Euripides dealing with the factional struggle between Eteocles and Polyneices, the sons of Oedipus, to gain the kingship of Thebes.

Note 737
**In connection with the same party** (*to en tô[i] autô[i]*): "If both parties have it in mind to rule, but one has himself in mind, and the other has *himself* in mind, are they *then* in fact in concord? Surely not. But if I wish to rule myself, and the other party wishes me to rule, that way we are in fact in concord. Concord, then, must lie in the sphere of what is doable in action and involve wish for the same thing. It is the establishment of the same ruler regarding what is doable in action, therefore, that we say is concord in the full sense" (*MM* II 12 1212a21–27).

Note 738
**Concord is apparently political friendship . . . affect our life:** See VIII 9 1160a8–23.

Note 739
**Epicharmus** (early fifth century BC): A poet from Sicily. The verse fragment Aristotle quotes is otherwise unknown, as is its precise meaning. It may refer to a bad seat in a theater.

Note 740
**More deeply natural than that:** See 1168a8–9.

Note 741
**The cause of this . . . we *are* when in activity** (*energeia[i]*) **. . . what he is in capacity** (*dunamei*) **his work is when in activity** (*energeia[i]*): Because Aristotle is drawing an analogy between a case of production and a case of benevolent action, he speaks of the benefactor as producing (*poiein*) the beneficiary—that is to say, producing him *as someone benefited*. The way the benefactor does this is to perform a benevolent action, thereby actualizing himself as a benefactor and—as a further end—benefiting someone. The beneficiary as such outlasts his being actively benefited and so outlasts "the producer in activity"—the benefactor insofar as he is actively benefiting: "In all the cases where what comes to be is a different thing that is beyond the use [of the capacity], in those cases the activity is in what is being produced—for example, the activity of building is in the house that is being built" (*Met.* IX 8 1050a30–32). That is why the beneficiary is only *in a way* the producer or benefactor in activity. The reason it is deeply natural for the benefactor to benefit people is that by doing so he is realizing the human nature that his generosity, as a virtue of character, perfects or completes. The terms *energeia* and *dunamis* are often translated as "actuality" and "potentiality" here.

Note 742

**What is in accord with his action is noble, so that he enjoys the person in whom it occurs:** When the benefactor's benevolent potentiality (capacity, state) is actualized, that actualization is his benevolent action or activity. But "in the case of all the potentialities the activities are external, either in something other than oneself or in oneself insofar as one is other [as when a doctor heals himself]" (*EE* VII 2 $1237^a36$). Thus the benevolent action or activity occurs in the beneficiary. But that action or activity, as generous, must be both noble and enjoyed by the benefactor as such (IV 1 $1120^a23$–27), and so he enjoys the beneficiary insofar as he is in accord with it or in that the enjoyable action or activity occurs in him and is occasioned by him.

Note 743

**What is noble is long lasting:** Almost an analytic truth for Aristotle, since long-lastingness is an important determinant of a work's nobility (IV 2 $1123^a8$–9). **His work endures . . . utility passes away:** The benefactor's work is in one way (1) his benevolent action or activity, which involves conferring a useful benefit on someone and in another way the further end of that activity, (2) the beneficiary. (1), however, may be "in accord with [the benefactor's] activity" for only the very short time in which the benefactor is actively conferring his benefit. The work of his that endures, then, must be (2). The previous arguments help explain how this can be so. The utility of the benefit that constituted the beneficiary as a beneficiary, by contrast, is something that need not last very long. It was useful when the benefit was bestowed; now it isn't (see VIII 3 $1156^a21$–22).

Note 744

**The more child-loving ones:** See also VIII 8 $1159^a27$–33, 12 $1161^b24$–27.

Note 745

**Does nothing from himself** (*ouden aph' heautou prattei*): The precise meaning of *aph' heautou* is obscure. If it is supposed to be cognate with "disregarding his own interests (*to d'hautou pariêsin*)" ($1168^a33$), as seems likely, *apo* has its quasi-spatial sense, so that the meaning is something like (1) a base person does nothing *away from* himself or his own interests. Another (less likely) possibility is that *apo* has its causal sense, so that the meaning is (2) a base person does nothing *of his own accord,* since he does what is just (as opposed to self-interested) only when compelled to do so by others (see IX 6 $1167^b13$–15).

Note 746

**Results** (*erga*): *Erga,* the plural of *ergon* ("function" or "work"), is usually treated here as equivalent in meaning to *ta huparchonta* ("data," "facts"), which is suggested by I 8 $1098^b11$–12. But because Aristotle later treats these *erga* as themselves accounts and the accounts with which they conflict as to some extent true (1168ᵇ12–13), and because he has previously defended them on his own behalf, it seems better not to treat *erga* as facts but, rather, as results or results of work already done.

Note 747
**"One soul":** Euripides, *Orestes* 1046. Also *MM* II 11 1211ᵃ33–34: "When we wish to describe a very intense friendship, we say 'my soul and his are one.'" **"Equality is friendship"** (*isotês philotês*): Compare "friendship is said to be equality (*philotês isotês*)" (VIII 5 1157ᵇ36). **"Knee is closer than shin":** Theocritus, *Idylls* XVI.18. The meaning is close to "Charity begins at home."

Note 748
**Fought about:** Goods of this fought-about sort are traditionally referred to as "goods of competition."

Note 749
**Ordinary people are like this:** See I 5 1095ᵇ19–20, IV 1 1121ᵇ15, VIII 8 1159ᵃ12–14, VIII 14 1163ᵇ26–27, IX 7 1167ᵇ27–28.

Note 750
**The ones that are best of all:** See 1169ᵃ10–11.

Note 751
**Just as a city:** "The governing class (*politeuma*) has control in every city, and the governing class is the constitution" (*Pol.* III 6 1278ᵇ10–11).

Note 752
**This [understanding] is what each person *is*:** X 7 1178ᵃ2–3.

Note 753
**A decent person likes this part most:** See 1168ᵃ33 with 1168ᵇ30.

Note 754
**Living in accord with reason . . . living in accord with feeling:** See I 3 1095ᵃ6–11, I 7 1098ᵃ5–8, III 12 1119ᵇ14–15, IV 9 1128ᵇ15–21. **And as much as desiring what is noble does from desiring what seems advantageous:** Reading καὶ ὀρέγεσθαι τοῦ καλοῦ ἢ τοῦ κατὰ πάθος for OCT καὶ ὀρέγεσθαι ἢ τοῦ καλοῦ ἢ τοῦ κατὰ πάθος ("and either desiring what is noble or desiring what seems advantageous").

Note 755
**Chooses what is best for itself:** "Let a good thing, then, be whatever is choiceworthy for its own sake, or that for the sake of which we choose something else, or what is sought by all things, or by all the ones having perception or understanding, or by all things if they acquire understanding, or what understanding would give to each, or what each individual's understanding would give to each (this being the good for each)" (*Rh.* I 6 1362ᵃ21–26); "We call something good that is both choiceworthy for its own sake and not for the sake of something else, or what all things seek,

or what something that has understanding and practical wisdom would choose" (I 7 1163$^{b}$12–15). **Every understanding . . . obeys his understanding:** See III 3 1113$^{a}$5–9, X 7 1177$^{a}$13–15.

Note 756
**As we said:** At 1169$^{a}$11–12.

Note 757
**When your *daimôn* does well by you** (*hotan ho daimôn eu didô[i]*): Euripides, *Orestes* 667. A *daimôn* is a god or the child of a god, who functions a bit like a guardian angel in the way that Socrates' famous *daimôn* does (Plato, *Ap.* 27c10–d3, 40a4–b2). So when a person's *daimôn* does well (*eu*) by him or benefits him, he is *eu-daimôn* ("happy").

Note 758
**The greatest of external goods:** Aristotle refers to those who argue that a blessed person does not need friends as "the first lot" at 1169$^{b}$22, suggesting the existence of a second lot who argue against the first. Since Aristotle has earlier confidently claimed that honor is the greatest external good (IV 3 1123$^{b}$19–20), the present view about friends should perhaps be attributed to these.

Note 759
**The question is asked whether it is in good fortune that friends are needed more or in bad fortune:** Aristotle answers it in IX 11.

Note 760
**A solitary life:** See I 7 1097$^{b}$6–11, 8 1099$^{a}$32–$^{b}$6.

Note 761
**Natural goods:** See VII 4 1148$^{a}$22–32.

Note 762
**The first lot:** Those who argue that a blessed person does not need friends.

Note 763
**Adventitious pleasure:** See I 8 1099$^{a}$15–16.

Note 764
**As we said at the start:** At I 7 1098$^{a}$16–20, I 8 1098$^{b}$30–1099$^{a}$7.

Note 765
**As we said at the start:** At I 8 1099$^{a}$13–15, 21–24. **Things that are properly our own are among the things that are pleasant:** See IV 1 1120$^{b}$13–14, IX 7 1167$^{b}$33–1168$^{a}$2. **Contemplate** (*theôrein*): *Theôrein* could simply mean "observe" here, with no implication that it is in particular an act of the understanding that is being referred to. But because a human being is most of all his understanding (IX 8 1168$^{b}$28–34, X 5 1176$^{a}$24–29, 7 1178$^{a}$2–8) and it is most of all to each other's understanding that virtuous friends wish good things (VII 7 1159$^{a}$5–13), it

seems more likely that *theôrein* does have this implication. What virtuous people deliberately choose to do and enjoy doing is not just to observe or to look at their friends in action—moving their bodies in certain ways that are in accord with their deliberate choices—but to understand those actions as embodiments of their friends' excellent deliberation and the correct understanding-involving reason it embodies. **Then:** Reading δὴ for OCT δὲ ("and [if]"). Following OCT postpones the conclusion of the argument to 1170ᵃ2 ("A blessed person, then [δὴ]"). Aristotle's argument, however, has the resources to reach a conclusion also at this earlier point. **Both the features that make them naturally pleasant:** The features are (1) being virtuous and (2) being properly his own. Feature (2) is puzzling because A's own actions seem to be properly his own in a way that the actions of his friend B are not. B's are of the same sort as A's, perhaps, but A (or his wish or deliberate choice) is not their starting-point. Aristotle, however, seems to think that B's actions are A's in a stronger sense than that (III 3 1112ᵇ27–28, IX 8 1169ᵃ32–34, IX 12 1172ᵃ10–14).

Note 766

**If indeed he deliberately chooses to contemplate decent actions that are properly his own:** One reason he does choose to do this is that such actions are pleasant to perceive, remember, and anticipate doing (VIII 3 1156ᵇ15–17, IX 7 1168ᵃ13–21).

Note 767

**Continuously in activity . . . together with others and in relation to others** (*meth' heterôn de kai pros allous*): The activity referred to could be (1) practical activity (action) or (2) contemplative activity. The mention of continuity suggests that (2) is at least part of the intended reference (see I 10 1100ᵇ15–16, X 7 1177ᵃ21–22). This is compatible with the claim that the relevant activity is easier "with others," even though such activity can, if one is theoretically-wise enough, be engaged in by oneself (X 7 1177ᵃ32–34). It is also compatible with the claim that the relevant activity is easier "in relation to others," since—as has just been shown—contemplation of the actions of others is easier than contemplating one's own. On the other hand, the phrase *meth' heterôn kai pros allous* is strongly suggestive of (1) a political life in a city, which is sustained by people of different genders, classes, and sorts and involves practical activities or actions (such as generous ones) that are "in relation to others" in that they positively require their existence. We might reasonably conclude that Aristotle has both (1) and (2) in view, which is what the following text also suggests. "A person's friend tends to be a sort of separated himself. Perceiving his friend, then, must in a way be perceiving himself and, in a way knowing himself. So it makes perfect sense that it is pleasant to share even vulgar pleasures with his friend and to be living together with him (since at the same time there is always a perception of him), but it is even more pleasant to share the more divine pleasures. This is so because it is always pleasant for him to contemplate himself sharing in a better good, which may be sometimes a feeling, sometimes an action, and sometimes something else. But if what he contemplates is himself living well and his friend also doing likewise, and being active in living together, their community surely lies in the things that most of all constitute their ends. That is why (*dio*) it consists in *contemplating together and feasting together*. For it is not for food and necessary pleasures that these sorts of social interaction seem to exist, in the way that indulgent ones do. But the end that each person can attain, that is the one he wishes his living together with his friend to consist in" (*EE* VII 12 1245$^a$35–$^b$8).

Note 768
**His activity will be more continuous, then, since it is continuously pleasant:** See VIII 6 1158$^a$22–26, I 8 1099$^a$13–15.

Note 769
**A sort of training in virtue:** See I 9 1099b10, 16. **Theognis:** Ln. 35.

Note 770
**More deeply natural point of view** (*phusikôteron*): See IX 7 1155$^b$2, IX 7 1167$^b$29, 1168$^a$8. **As we said:** At I 8 1099$^a$7–11, III 4 1113$^a$31–33.

Note 771
**Living is defined in the case of animals by a capacity for perception:** "It is because of this starting-point [nutritive soul], then, that living things are living, but it is because of perception first of all that they will be animal" (*DA* II 2 413$^b$1–2). **In the case of human beings by a capacity for perception or understanding:** "Some sort of animals have in addition [to perception and imagination] a part responsible for movement with respect to place and others both a thinking part and an understanding—for example, human beings and anything else that is more estimable" (*DA* II 3 414$^b$16–19). **A capacity is brought back** (*anagetai*) **to its activity:** "It is necessary for anyone who is going to investigate these capacities of soul to grasp what each of them is and in that way then proceed to investigate what follows and so on. But if we must say what each of them is—for example, what the understanding part is or the perceptual or the nutritive—we must further say what active understanding is and what active perceiving is. For activities and actions are, as regards their definitions, prior to capacities" (*DA* II 4 415$^a$14–20; also *Met.* IX 8 1049$^b$12–17). For the sense of *anagetai*, see III 3 1113$^a$6. **Living in the full sense:** See I 7 1098$^a$5–7.

Note 772
**Being determinate is characteristic of the nature of the good:** See II 6 1106$^b$29–30.

Note 773
**Living like that is indeterminate:** See II 6 1106$^b$28–30. **In what follows:** See X 1–5, especially 5 1175$^b$13–24. See also VII 13 1153$^b$14–17.

Note 774

**Something that perceives that we are in activity:** Perception proper encompasses the special perceptual capacities (sight, smell, hearing, taste, and touch), whose primary objects are *proper perceptibles,* such as colors, odors, sounds, and so on, which only a single perceptual capacity can detect. But it also includes the common perceptual capacity—or so-called common sense (*DA* III 7 431$^{b}$5, *Mem.* 1 450$^{a}$10–11)—which is the "something" responsible for the awareness of the activity or inactivity of the various special perceptual capacities (*DA* III 2 425$^{b}$12–25). The common sense is also responsible for the simultaneous perception of two or more proper perceptibles in a single act, the perception of two or more proper perceptibles as distinct, the control of waking up the special perceptual capacities or letting them sleep (*Somn.* 2 455$^{a}$12–26), and perhaps also the perception of common perceptibles (*koina aisthêta*)—which are accessible to more than one perceptual capacities—such as change, rest, shape, size, number, unity, and perhaps others (*DA* III 1 425$^{a}$14–20). **Co-perceivers** (*sunaisthanomenoi*): Aristotle sometimes uses the rare verb *sunaisthanesthai* as the interpersonal analogue of self-conscious activity: "Living together (*to suzên*) with someone is co-perceiving him (*sunaisthanesthai*) and co-knowing him (*suggnôrizein*). But for each individual, perceiving himself and knowing himself is most choiceworthy. . . . If, then, we did some cutting and made knowledge be knowledge *itself,* not knowledge *of himself* . . . in that case there would be no difference between someone's knowing himself and knowing another instead of himself and likewise no difference between another's living instead of himself. It makes perfect sense, though, that perceiving oneself and knowing oneself is more choiceworthy" (*EE* VII 12 1244$^{b}$25–34); "For suppose it were possible for many people to be living together (*suzên*) and co-perceiving (*sunaisthanesthai*) at the same time; in that case the greatest number of friends would be the most choiceworthy number of them. But, since this is in fact very difficult, the activity of co-perceiving (*sunaisthêseôs*) must be restricted to a few" (VII 12 1245$^{b}$21–24). Presumably, its sense here must be the same. Good people take pleasure in perceiving what is intrinsically good in each other as they perceive it in themselves (*NE* 1170$^{b}$2–3). At 1170$^{b}$10, the excellent person co-perceives his friend's existence as he perceives his own.

Note 775

**In this respect lacking:** And so not happy (see I 7 1097$^{b}$14–16).

Note 776

**"Neither many-guest-friended nor guest-friendless":** Hesiod, *Works and Days* 7.

Note 777

**A city cannot come about from ten people, and if there are ten times ten thousand, it is a city no longer:** "Likewise, a city that consists of too few people is not self-sufficient (whereas a city is something self-sufficient) but one that consists of too many, while it is self-sufficient in the necessities, the way a nation is, is still no city, since it is not easy for it to have a constitution. For who will be the general of an excessively large multitude, and who, unless he has the voice of Stentor, will serve as herald? Hence the first city to arise is the one composed of the first multitude large enough to be self-sufficient with regard to living well as a political community. It is also possible for a city that exceeds this one in number to be a greater city, but, as we said, this is not possible indefinitely. The defining mark of the excess can easily be seen from the facts. For a city's actions are either those of the rulers or those of the ruled. And a ruler's function is to issue orders and judge. But in order to render judgments in lawsuits and allocate offices in accord with merit, citizens must know each other and what sort of person each is. For where this cannot happen, the business of electing officials and judging lawsuits must go badly, since to decide offhand in either of these proceedings is unjust. But this is evidently what occurs in an overpopulated city. Besides, it is easy for resident aliens and foreigners to participate in the constitution, since it is not difficult to escape detection because of the excessive size of the population. It is clear, then, that the best defining mark of a city is this: it is the greatest size of multitude that furthers self-sufficiency of living and that can be easily surveyed as a whole. The size of a city, then, should be determined in this way" (*Pol.* VII 4 1326$^{b}$2–25). Stentor was a herald of the Greek forces in the Trojan War, "his voice was as powerful as fifty voices of other men" (Homer, *Iliad* V.785–786).

Note 778
**We found:** At VII 5 1157$^{b}$19, 6 1158$^{a}$7–10, IX 7 1166$^{a}$6–7.

Note 779
**Toward one person:** See VIII 6 1158$^{a}$10–15.

Note 780
**In a political way:** See IX 1 1163$^{b}$34. **Ingratiating:** See IV 6 1126$^{b}$11–14, 1127$^{b}$7–9.

Note 781
**In good fortune or in bad:** See IX 8 1169$^{b}$13–16.

Note 782
**Dexterous:** See IV 8 1128$^{a}$16–19.

Note 783
**And if does not go to extremes in his painlessness** (*kan mê huperteinê[i] tê[i] alupia[i]*): Most translators treat *alupia* as meaning "insensitive to pain," or "immune to pain," and *kan* (= *kai an*) with *mê* as meaning "unless": "unless he is extremely insensitive to pain." But it is doubtful whether *alupia* can have that meaning, which is otherwise unattested. Rather, the thought seems relevantly similar to the earlier one—that within the realm of fortune and of the external goods that luck controls, a practically-wise person pursues

an ideal of painlessness (VII 12 1153ᵃ27–35). A manly person presumably pursues a similar ideal, but unless he is excessive in its pursuit, he will not be able to endure the pain that his own sufferings cause his friends. An alternative proposal with some merit but without manuscript support reads *atuchia[i]* ("bad fortune") in place of *alupia*: "unless his bad fortune is extreme."

Note 784
**"My own misfortunes are enough":** Source unknown.

Note 785
**Share in these things** (*hois*): Reading *hois* ("these") as neuter. If *hois* is read as masculine, the sense is: "They do these things and share in these things with the ones they intend to be living with." **In which they think living together consists:** Reading οἷς οἴονται συζῆν with OCT. Some editors read ὡς οἷόν τε ("as best they can"), citing *EE* VII 12 1245ᵃ19–22: "It is evident at any rate that everyone finds it pleasant to share good things with his friends, insofar as it pertains to each to share in as good a thing as possible—in one case bodily pleasures, in another artistic contemplation, in another philosophy."

Note 786
**Being unstable** (*abebaioi*): Here (as at VIII 8 1159ᵇ7–10) it is base people who are unstable, but their friendships too are such: "Base people may be friends with each other because of both utility and pleasure. But some people say that they are not friends because the primary sort of friendship [namely, that of decent people] does not obtain between them. For a base person, they say, will do injustice to another base person, and those who do injustice to each other do not love each other. But in fact they do love, only not with the love of primary friendship. Nothing, though, prevents them from doing so with the other sorts. For because of pleasure they put up with each other although it is harmful to them, doing as people who lack self-control do. But those who love each other because of pleasure do not seem to be friends either, when people investigate the matter in an exact way, because their friendship is not of the primary sort. For the primary sort is stable, whereas this one is unstable (*abebaios*)" (*EE* VII 2 1236ᵇ10–19).

Note 787
**"From noble people noble things":** Theognis, Ln. 35 (as at IX 9 1170ᵃ11–13). The entire phrase is *esthlôn men gar ap' esthla didaxeai* ("from noble people you will learn noble things"). Also quoted at Plato, *Men*. 95d.

## Book X

Note 788
**Next . . . we should discuss . . . pleasure:** As was already said at IX 12 1172ᵃ15.

Note 789
**It seems to be most intimately attached to our kind** (*malista . . . sunô[i]keiôsthai tô[i] genei hêmôn*): The verb *sunô[i]keiôsthai* ("closely belong to") is used to describe the intimate relationship between a mother and her child at VIII 12 1161ᵇ21 and the intimate connection between a pleasure and the activity it completes at X 5 1175ᵃ29. The involvement of pleasure in human life is certainly intimate (see II 3 especially 1105ᵃ1–3), but *malista* together with *genei hêmôn* suggests a double contrast: (1) that of pleasures with other things that belong less intimately in human life and (2) that of our human kind with other kinds in whose life pleasure figures less intimately. It may be, therefore, that Aristotle is thinking of Plato's *Philebus,* where the role of pleasure in human life is contrasted (1) with that of other goods and (2) with its role in the life of the gods. For whereas no human being "would choose to live in possession of every kind of wisdom, understanding, knowledge, and memory of all things, while having no part, whether large or small, of pleasure or pain" (21d9–e1), this is not true—or not so clearly true—of gods, who may choose a life consisting of "thinking wise thoughts in the purest degree possible," without regard to the pleasure or pain involved (55a6–8).

Note 790
**Topics like this, then:** Reading δὴ for OCT δὲ ("and [topics like this would seem]").

Note 791
**Arrive at the mean:** See II 9 1139ᵃ30–ᵇ12.

Note 792
**Facts** (*ergois*): *Ergon* is usually translated as "function" or "work." **Clash with what is in accord with the perceptible facts:** See I 8 1098ᵇ9–12.

Note 793
**Eudoxus:** See I 12 1101ᵇ27.

Note 794
**It is by an argument of *this* sort that Plato:** See *Phlb.* 60d–e.

Note 795
**Wisdom** (*phronêsis*): Plato does use the word *phronêsis* in the argument under discussion, as he does the word *epistêmê* (*Phlb.* 60d4–5), but he isn't necessarily distinguishing distinctively practical wisdom from theoretical wisdom (Aristotle's *sophia*) or from wisdom generally. **Nothing which, when added to the good, makes *it* more choiceworthy:** See I 7 1097ᵇ16–20, IX 9 1170ᵇ17–19.

Note 796
**And that we share in:** See I 6 1096ᵇ32–35.

Note 797

**For things that seem to be so to everyone, these, we say, are:** This could be (1) a general claim to the effect that things that seem to be *the case* to everyone are (a) *presumptively* the case, or (b) *genuinely* the case. Or it could be (2) a specific claim to the effect that things that seem to be *good* to everyone are (a) *presumptively* good or (b) *genuinely* good. The fact that something seems so to all or most people leads us "to trust it as something in accord with experience" (*Div. Somn.* 1 462$^b$14–16). For "human beings are naturally adequate as regards the truth and for the most part happen upon it" (*Rh.* I 1 1355$^a$15–17; also *EE* I 6 1216$^b$30–31). That is why something that seems so to everyone is a reputable belief which can be accepted as presumptively true. If there are other reputable beliefs that conflict with it (*Top.* I 10 104$^a$11–12), however, that presumption is cancelled, pending further investigation into the puzzle created by the conflict. This may result in the reputable belief being modified or rejected outright (*NE* VII 1 1145$^b$2–7). (1a) is something Aristotle does claim, then, whereas (1b) is something he rejects. (2a), as a special case of (1a), is something to which he is at least committed, but he also accepts (2b), provided that practically-wise people are included among those to whom the thing in question seems good (see III 4 1113$^a$29–33, X 5 1176$^a$15–19).

Note 798

**Some naturally good element, more excellent than themselves:** Reading τι φυσικὸν ἀγαθὸν κρεῖττον ἢ καθ' αὑτά with OCT. Many editors omit either (1) φυσικὸν ἀγαθὸν or (2) ἀγαθὸν and read (1) "some element better than themselves" or (2) "some natural element better than themselves." This element is discussed at VII 13 1153$^b$29–32.

Note 799

**They say:** See Plato, *Phlb.* 24e–25a, 31a.

Note 800

**Some pleasures are mixed, others unmixed:** Plato, *Phlb.* 52b–d, distinguishes between pleasures that are mixed with pain (such as hunger or sexual desire, which are preceded by pain) and pure pleasures (such as that of learning) that are not mixed with pain, characterizing the mixed ones as indeterminate, or lacking in measure, the pure ones as measured, or determinate.

Note 801

**The same proportion:** "Health is the proportion of hot elements to cold ones" (*Top.* VI 2 139$^b$21). The relativity of this proportion to individuals and, within a single individual, to various factors and circumstances, is explained at *NE* II 2 1104$^a$1–18, 6 1106$^a$36–$^b$7. **It may be loosened and yet remain present up to a point:** See VI 1 1138$^b$23.

Note 802

**They try to represent pleasure as a process and a coming to be:** See Plato, *Phlb.* 53c–54d.

Note 803
**The universe:** As at VI 7 1141ᵇ1, the universe here is not the universe as a whole but the heavens, in particular the outermost sphere of the fixed stars (the so-called primary heaven). Its circular motion is absolutely uniform and unchanging, and so it cannot at one time be moving faster or slower "in relation to itself (*kath' hautên*)" at another time: "To claim that the [primary] heaven is by turns faster and slower in its movement is completely absurd and like a fairy story" (*Cael.* II 6 289ᵃ5–6).

Note 804
**A thing comes to be out of what it is dissolved into:** "Everything can be dissolved into that from which it is constituted" (*Ph.* III 5 204ᵇ33–34).

Note 805
**They also say:** Plato, *Phlb.* 31e–32b, 42c–d.

Note 806
**Cutting:** Reading τεμνόμενος with OCT. Some editors read κενούμενος ("becoming empty"). See Plato, *Ti.* 65b. The point is that being cut is not identical to being in pain but is usually accompanied by being in pain.

Note 807
**This belief:** The belief that pleasure is a replenishment with what is in accord with nature.

Note 808
**Those of learning** (*hai mathêmatikai*): Not just the pleasures of mathematics (*hê mathêmatikê*) but also those of activating a state of theoretical knowledge acquired by the process of learning (*mathêsis*). See VII 12 1153ᵃ1, X 4 1174ᵇ21.

Note 809
**Who cite the disgraceful pleasures:** If some pleasures are disgraceful, some are bad. If some are bad, not all are good. If not all are good, pleasure cannot be the good.

Note 810
**Seeing seems at any time to be complete:** Aristotle usually tries to capture this sort of completeness by noting that the present tense of the relevant verb has perfective meaning, whereas in the case of a verb designating a process the present tense has imperfective meaning: "At the same time, one is seeing [a thing] and has seen [it], is being practically-wise and has been practically-wise, is understanding [something] and has understood [it], whereas it is not the case that [at the same time,] one is learning [something] and has learned [it] nor that one is being cured and has been cured. Someone who is living well, however, at the same time has lived well and is happy and has been happy [at the same time]. If this were not so, these would have to come to an end at some time, as when one is slimming [something]. But as things stand, there is no such time,

but one is living and has lived. Of these, then, one group should be called processes and the other activities. For every *process* is incomplete, for example, slimming, learning, walking, building. These are processes and are certainly incomplete. For it is not the case that at the same time one is walking and has taken a walk nor that one is building [something] and has built [it] or is coming to be [something] and has come to be [it] or is being changed [in some way] and has been changed [in that way], but they are different, as are someone's changing and having changed [something]. By contrast, one has seen and is seeing the same thing at the same time or is understanding and has understood. The latter sort, then, I call an activity; the former a process" (*Met.* IX 6 1048$^{b}$23–35).

Note 811
**Building:** Reading οἰκοδόμησις for OCT οἰκοδομική ("craft of building"). **This whole time that it takes:** Reading χρόνῳ τούτῳ for OCT χρόνῳ ἢ τούτῳ. The sense of the entire OCT clause is: "in other words, in the whole time, then, that it takes or at this [final] one."

Note 812
**Triglyph:** Vertical three-grooved tablet in the frieze of a temple.

Note 813
**This line . . . that one:** The audience is apparently being directed to look at lines on a diagram representing different segments of a stadium racecourse. Compare II 7 1107$^{a}$32–33.

Note 814
**In other places:** *Ph.* VI–VIII. **Its many sub-processes** (*hai pollai*): Literally, "the many [processes]."

Note 815
**In the "now":** "Necessarily too, the now—the one that is so-called not on the basis of something else but rather intrinsically and primarily—is indivisible, and this sort of now is found in every time" (*Ph.* VI 3 233$^{b}$33–35).

Note 816
***Of* pleasure:** Reading τῆς ἡδονῆς, as at 1174$^{b}$13, for OCT τὴν ἡδονήν ("pleasure"). If we follow OCT, we should translate: "It is not right to say, as people do, that pleasure is a process or a coming to be."

Note 817
**Pleasure is what completes the activity:** Compare VII 12 1153$^{a}$9–15.

Note 818
**Health and a doctor are not in the same way a cause of being healthy:** See VI 12 1144$^{a}$3–6.

Note 819
**The state:** That is, the excellent state of the relevant perceptual or intellectual capacity. **The bloom** (*hôra*) **on men in their prime of youth**

(*tois akmaiois*): Only young men, whose beards have not yet begun to grow, have a *hôra* (see VIII 4 1157ª6). This occurs well before their physical prime, which is thirty to thirty-five, in Aristotle's view (I 3 1095ª3). Hence the prime referred to here must be the prime of youth, not of life.

Note 820
**Intelligible object** (*noêton*): An object of understanding (*nous*).

Note 821
**Coupled together** (*sunezeuchthai*): See X 8 1178ª16.

Note 822
**Increases . . . by its own increase** (*sunauxei*): *Sunauxein* means "to increase or enlarge along with or together," the implication being that as the pleasure increases so does the activity. "Increases . . . by its own increase" attempts to capture this implication.

Note 823
**It appears to some people to be the same as them:** See VII 12 1153ª9–15.

Note 824
**Look at** (*theôrountai*): See I 7 1098ᵇ3.

Note 825
**Heraclitus:** DK 22 fr. B9.

Note 826
**We said:** At I 5 1095ᵇ32–1096ª2, 8 1098ᵇ31–1099ª7.

Note 827
**As we said before:** At I 7 1098ª5–6.

Note 828
**Self-sufficient:** See I 7 1097ᵇ6–21.

Note 829
**As we have often said:** Most recently at X 6 1176ª15–22, also III 4 1113ª22–33, IX 4 1166ª12–13, IX 9 1170ª14–16.

Note 830
**Anacharsis:** A largely legendary Scythian prince, sometimes included among the Seven Sages on account of his supposed extraordinary wisdom.

Note 831
**Excellent** (*spoudaios*): *Spoudaios*, translated as "serious" in the previous paragraphs, needs now, as subsequently, to be translated as "excellent" (see I 7 1098ª9).

Note 832
**The activity of what is better** (*tou beltionos*) **is more excellent** (*kreittôn*): *Beltiôn* is the comparative of *agathos* ("good"), whereas *kreittôn*, which

is also used as the comparative of *agathos*, comes from *kratus* ("strong"). Often the two comparatives have the same meaning, but here the slight difference in connotation between them prepares for the conclusion reached at X 7 $1177^{b}34$–$1178^{a}2$, where the activity of the *kratiston* (superlative of *kratus*) element in us is most excellent, since it is the activity of the element that exceeds everything in power and esteem.

Note 833
**Any more than of the relevant sort of life:** Literally, "if not also of life (*biou*)." Like non-human animals, (natural) slaves have souls that lack a deliberative element and so cannot participate in the deliberately chosen life of virtue in which happiness consists. People do not constitute a city "only for the sake of living, but rather for the sake of living well, since otherwise there could be a city of slaves or of other animals, whereas in fact there isn't, because these share neither in happiness nor in a life in accord with deliberate choice" (*Pol.* III 9 $1280^{a}31$–34).

Note 834
**As we also said before:** Most recently at $1176^{a}35$–$^{b}9$.

Note 835
**This element is understanding or something else that seems by nature to rule, lead, and understand what is noble and divine:** See III 3 $1113^{a}5$–7, IX 8 $1169^{a}17$–18. **Complete happiness:** Aristotle has said that happiness is activity in accord with complete virtue (I 10 $1101^{a}14$–15) or with the best and most complete one (I 7 $1098^{a}16$–18) and that it itself is something complete, but he has not previously distinguished complete happiness from happiness of another sort, as he seems to do here and explicitly does at X 7–8 $1178^{a}7$–10.

Note 836
**We already said:** This has not in fact been said in so many words, but see I 5 $1095^{b}14$–$1096^{a}5$, VI 7 $1141^{a}18$–$^{b}3$, 12 $1143^{b}33$–$1144^{a}6$, 13 $1145^{a}6$–11.

Note 837
**The most continuous activity:** See I 10 $1100^{b}11$–17.

Note 838
**Philosophy:** That is, the love (*philia*) of theoretical wisdom (*sophia*).

Note 839
**The self-sufficiency that is meant** (*legomenê autarkeia*): A reference back to *to d'autarkes legomen* ("by 'self-sufficient,' however, we mean") at I 7 $1097^{b}7$.

Note 840
**This activity, and only this, should seem to be liked because of itself [alone]:** The next sentence favors the addition of [alone]. Other things are liked because of themselves, but only happiness is liked solely because of itself.

Note 841

**For nothing arises from it beyond having contemplated:** "It was when pretty much all the necessities of life, as well as those related to ease and passing the time, had been supplied that such wisdom began to be sought. So clearly we do not seek it because of any utility for something else, but rather just as a human being is free, we say, when he exists for his own sake and not for someone else's, in the same way it alone among the sciences is free, since it alone exists for its own sake. It is because of this indeed that the possession of this science might be justly regarded as not for human beings, since in many ways the nature of human beings is enslaved, so that, according to Simonides, 'god alone can have this privilege,' and it is not fitting that man should not be content to seek the science that is in accord with himself. If, then, there is something in what the poets say, and jealousy is natural to the divine, it would probably occur in this case most of all, and all those who went too far [in this science] would be unlucky. The divine, however, cannot be jealous—but, as the proverb says, 'Bards often do speak falsely.' Moreover, no science should be regarded as more estimable than this. For the most divine science is also the most estimable. And a science would be such in only two ways: if god most of all would have it, then it will be the divine one among the sciences, or if it were a science of divine things. And this science alone is divine in both these ways. For the god seems to be among the causes of all things and to be a sort of starting-point, and this is the sort of science that god alone, or that he most of all, would have. Hence all the sciences are more necessary than this one, but none is better" (*Met.* I 2 982$^{b}$22–983$^{a}$11).

Note 842

**These are unleisured and seek some end:** That is, some end beyond the activity itself. **A complete span of life:** See I 7 1098$^{a}$18.

Note 843

**The compound:** This could be either (1) the compound of soul and body or (2) the compound of the understanding and the other less divine elements in the soul. The reference to virtues of character and feelings (X 8 1178$^{a}$9–14) suggests (2); the association of some of these specifically with the body (X 8 1178$^{a}$14–15) suggests (1).

Note 844

**We should as far as possible immortalize** (*athanatizein*): The verb *athanatizein* is rare and its precise meaning difficult to determine. However, its one other occurrence in a text of Aristotle's (although it may be spurious) helps somewhat with its interpretation: "Aristotle himself, in his defense against the charge of impiety—if the speech is not a forgery—says: 'You see, if I had deliberately chosen to sacrifice to Hermias as an immortal, I would not have prepared a memorial to him as a mortal, and if I had wished to immortalize (*athanatizein*) his nature, I would not have adorned his body with burial honors'" (Rose, *Fr.* 645). Since there is no inconsistency and slim basis for a charge of impiety in preparing a memorial for someone and adorning his body with burial honors on the one hand and regarding him as like an immortal on the other, *athanatizein* must mean something like "make or treat as really being immortal." Aristotle's advice, then, would be to immortalize ourselves by contemplating, that is, by living in accord with the immortal element in us, which is what we most of all are. Compare Plato, *Ti.* 90b1–c4: "If a man has become wholly engaged in his appetites or spirited love of victory and takes great pains to further them, all his beliefs must become merely mortal. And so far as it is at all possible he will become thoroughly mortal, and not fall short of it even to the least degree, seeing that he has strengthened these all along. On the other hand, if someone has seriously devoted himself to the love of learning and to truly wise thoughts, if he has exercised these aspects of himself above all, then there is absolutely no way his thinking can fail to be immortal and divine. And to the degree that human nature can partake of immortality, he can in no way fail to achieve this." **Most excellent** (*kratiston*): Also at 1178ᵃ5.

Note 845
**Each person actually *is* this:** See IX 8 1168ᵇ28–1169ᵃ6.

Note 846
**Most excellent and most pleasant for each of them:** See X 5 1175ᵃ26–ᵇ33.

Note 847
**Arise from the body:** See VI 13 1144ᵇ1–14. **Intimately attached:** See X 1 1172ᵃ20.

Note 848
**Coupled together** (*sunezeuktai*): See X 4 1175ᵃ19. **If indeed the starting-points of practical wisdom are in accord with the virtues of character:** See VI 12 1144ᵃ28–ᵇ1, VII 8 1151ᵃ18–19. **The correctness of these is in accord with practical wisdom:** See VI 13 1144ᵇ20–32.

Note 849
**The compound:** See X 7 1177ᵇ28-29.

Note 850
**The virtue of understanding, though, is separated:** Active understanding is separate from the body and from the other elements in the soul that are the body's form: "And this [active] understanding is separate, impassive, and unmixed, being in essence an activity. . . . And when separated it is precisely what it is and nothing else, and it alone is immortal and eternal" (*DA* III 5 430ᵃ17–23); "Understanding seems to be born in us as a sort of substance, and not to pass away. . . . Understanding and contemplation are extinguished because something else within passes away, but it itself is unaffected" (I 4 408ᵇ18–25); "It remains then that

understanding alone enters [the body of the male seed in the process of embryogenesis] additionally from outside and alone is divine, since bodily activity is in no way associated with its activity" (*GA* II 3 736b15–29); "Consider now the body of the seed, in and with which is emitted the starting-point of soul, part of which is separate from the body and belongs to those beings in which something divine is included (and this is what is called understanding), while the other is not separate from the body" (II 3 737a7–11). Theoretical wisdom is separate from the body and the other psychic elements, in turn, because it is the virtue of something separate from them.

Note 851
**The one we have set before us:** The task that has been set before us is a contribution to politics (I 2 1094b10–11, 13 1102a12–13) which, as the same state of the soul as practical wisdom (VI 8 1141b23–24), does not control or use theoretical wisdom but "sees to its coming into being" (VI 13 1145a6–11).

Note 852
**External supplies:** Elsewhere referred to as external goods.

Note 853
**The necessary ones:** Those necessary for life (X 7 1177a28–29). **The politician does labor more in relation to the body:** The politician aims to develop the virtues of character in the citizens (I 13 1102a7–10). These involve bodily appetites and feelings and so also the bodily pleasures and pains (II 3) that allow the citizens to be properly habituated through rewards (pleasures) and punishments (pains) (X 1179b4–1180b28).

Note 854
**The more controlling element:** See VIII 13 1163a22–23, also III 2 1111b4–6, IX 1 1164b1–2.

Note 855
**Its completeness:** "Of the actions that have a [temporal] limit, none is an end but all are in relation to an end—as for example, slimming is. For the things themselves, when one is slimming them, are in process (*en kinêsei*), since what the process (*kinêsis*) is for the sake of [namely, its end] does not yet belong to them. Hence these are not cases of action, at least not of complete action, since none is an end. But it is the sort in which the end belongs that is a [complete] action" (*Met.* IX 6 1048b18–23).

Note 856
**The praise:** The praise involved in calling them "temperate" (see I 12 1101b16).

Note 857
**Endymion:** Loved for his great beauty by Selene, goddess of the Moon, Endymion was made immortal by her but was cast into a deep sleep in a

cave on Mount Latmus in Caria so that she might descend and visit him during the dark phase of the lunar month.

Note 858
**What is left except contemplating:** Happiness is activity in accord with some sort of virtue. This activity could be (1) practical, and so in accord with practical wisdom and the virtues of character, (2) productive, and so in accord with the virtues associated with craft (VI 7 1141$^{a}$9–12) and—ultimately—with practical wisdom (VI 2 1139$^{b}$1), or (3) contemplative, and so in accord with theoretical wisdom. (1) is excluded by the previous considerations, and (2) is implicitly excluded by them too, leaving (3) as the only possibility (VI 1–2 1138$^{b}$35–1139$^{b}$4).

Note 859
**External prosperity:** See I 8 1099$^{a}$31–$^{b}$8.

Note 860
**Solon too was presumably depicting happy people correctly:** Croesus, the fabulously wealthy and powerful king of Lydia, confident that he was the "most blessed (*olbiôtaton*)" of human beings (Herodotus, I 30 2), invited Solon to confirm his self-estimation. Solon famously demurred, citing Tellus the Athenian as most happy, and justifying himself by describing Tellus' life as follows: "In the first place, Tellus' city was in a prosperous condition (*eu hêkousês*) when he had sons who were noble and good, and he saw children in turn born to all of them, and all surviving. Secondly, when he himself had come prosperously to a moment of his life—that is prosperously, by our standards—he had an ending for it that was most glorious: in a battle between the Athenians and their neighbors in Eleusis he made a sally, routed the enemy, and died most nobly, and the Athenians gave him a public funeral where he fell and so honored him greatly" (I 30 3–5).

Note 861
**Anaxagoras:** See VI 7 1141$^{b}$3n. DK 59 A30 quotes this comment on Anaxagoras along with VI 7 1141$^{b}$3–8 and the following two passages: "Anaxagoras of Clazomenae, when asked who was happiest, said, 'none of those whom you acknowledge, but one who would appear strange to you.' He responded in this way because he saw that the questioner supposed it was impossible for someone who was not grand, handsome (*kalon*), or rich to deserve the name, whereas he himself presumably thought that someone who was living free of pain and was pure as regards what is just, or who participated in some divine sort of contemplation, that person was as blessed as any human being could be said to be" (*EE* I 4 1215$^{b}$6–14); "They say that Anaxagoras, when confronted with puzzles about this sort of thing and cross-questioned about why someone should choose to be born rather than not to be born, replied, 'to contemplate the heavens and the order of the whole universe'" (I 5 1216$^{a}$10–14).

Note 862
**Since these are the only ones they can perceive:** See X 9 1179ᵇ7–31, especially 15–16, 26–28.

Note 863
**The beliefs of wise people, then, would seem to be in harmony with our arguments:** With the result that these arguments are in harmony with reputable beliefs.

Note 864
**From the facts of our life** (*ek tôn ergôn kai tou biou*): See I 5 1095ᵇ14–16, I 8 1098ᵇ9–12.

Note 865
**We should suppose it mere words** (*logous*): See II 4 1105ᵇ10–18, X 1 1172ᵃ34–ᵇ1.

Note 866
**If the gods exercise a sort of supervision, as indeed they seem to:** The gods in question live exclusively contemplative lives (X 8 1178ᵇ8–23) and so whatever supervision they exercise over human affairs must be of a somewhat special sort. Aristotle does not tell us what it is, but his identification of these gods with the heavenly spheres (*Met.* XII 8 1074ᵃ38–ᵇ14) suggests an answer. For the orderly revolutions of these spheres govern the seasons as well as the cycles of fertility and infertility of land and animals (*GA* IV 10 778ᵃ4–9). Hence they confer benefits on all beings, but especially on those wise people who, through astronomical contemplation of the heavens, learn about these cycles, and adjust their lives accordingly.

Note 867
**In this way too:** Compare Plato, *Rep.* X 612a–c.

Note 868
**Our deliberate choice has achieved its end:** See I 13 1102ᵃ12–13.

Note 869
**As the saying goes:** See II 2 1103ᵇ26–31.

Note 870
**Theognis:** Lines 432–434: "If the god had given the power to doctors/To cure men's badness and muddled wits/Many and large the wages they would earn." Lines 437–438 read: "But by teaching/You will never make a bad man good." Plato quotes line 434 at *Men.* 95e.

Note 871
**Not shame but fear:** See III 8 1116ᵃ31–32.

Note 872
**Not having tasted it:** See X 6 1176ᵇ19–21.

Note 873
**Locked up in traits of character:** Reading τοῖς ἤθεσι κατειλημμένα with OCT. Some editors read τοῖς ἔθεσι κατειλημμένα ("locked up as a result of habits").

Note 874
**Nature's contribution:** See III 5 1114ᵃ31–ᵇ13. **Because of some divine causes:** See I 9 1099ᵇ9–20.

Note 875
**The soul of the audience:** Compare I 3 1094ᵇ27–1095ᵃ11. **Through habits:** Compare I 4 1095ᵇ4–8, *Met.* II 3 994ᵇ32–995ᵃ6.

Note 876
**From childhood:** See II 1 1103ᵇ23, 3 1104ᵇ11–13. **Resilient:** See VII 7 1150ᵃ32–1150ᵇ1.

Note 877
**Some think:** Plato, *Lg.* 718c–723d. **Not naturally well disposed** (*aphuesteroi*): *Aphuês* is the contrary of *euphuês* (see VI 13 1144ᵇ34). Those who are not naturally well disposed lack the natural contribution (1179ᵇ20–23) requisite to develop virtue but (unlike the incurably bad) can be made to act in accord with law and virtue through fear of sanctions (1179ᵇ11–13). **Impose . . . sanctions . . . incurable:** Plato, *Prt.* 325a–b.

Note 878
**Will obey reason** (*logos*): *Logos*, which is best understood as "argument" in what has preceded, now shifts its meaning more toward the "reason" that argument embodies and expresses.

Note 879
**Constitutional arrangement** (*taxis*): See V 7 1135ᵃ10. Notice "the laws must prescribe (*tetachthai*)" at 1179ᵇ34 and "paternal instructions (*prostaxis*)" at 1180ᵃ19–20.

Note 880
**Paternal instructions:** See VII 10 1160ᵇ24–27.

Note 881
**Reason that derives from a sort of wisdom and understanding:** "Anyone who instructs law to rule would seem to be asking god and the understanding alone to rule, whereas someone who asks a human being asks a wild beast as well. For appetite is like a wild beast, and anger distorts [the understanding of] rulers even when they are the best men. That is why law is understanding without desire" (*Pol.* III 16 1287ᵃ28–32). The sort of practical wisdom and understanding from which law derives and which it embodies is identified at *NE* VI 8 1141ᵇ23–33, 13 1144ᵇ1–14.

Note 882
**The legislator:** Lycurgus. Aristotle discusses the Spartan constitution in *Pol.* II 9.

Note 883
**"For children and wife":** Homer, *Odyssey* IX.114–115. Aristotle correctly quotes the lines at *Pol.* I 2 1253$^b$22–23, but here he has "wife" instead of "wives."

Note 884
**To be capable of doing it:** Transposing καὶ δρᾶν αὐτὸ δύνασθαι from 1180$^a$30 (where it is deleted in the OCT) to 1180$^a$32. **Deliberately choosing it:** See 1179$^a$34 and 1178$^a$34–$^b$3.

Note 885
**Legislative science:** See VI 8 1141$^b$25.

Note 886
**Habits:** Reading ἔθη ("habits") on both occasions for OCT ἤθη ("types of character"). **Paternal words** (*patrikoi logoi*): Or "paternal reasons." See I 13 1103$^a$3.

Note 887
**Of what is common:** That is, of universals, which are common to many things.

Note 888
**We said:** At VI 6 1140$^b$31. **But, despite that, there is nothing to prevent . . . is what the sciences are concerned with:** "With a view to action, experience seems no different from craft knowledge—on the contrary, we even see experienced people to be more successful than those who have an account (*logos*) but lack experience. The cause of this is that experience is knowledge (*gnôsis*) of particulars, whereas craft knowledge is of universals, and actions and productions are all concerned with particulars. For the doctor does not cure *human being,* except coincidentally but rather Callias or Socrates or someone else spoken of in that way, who happens coincidentally to be a human being. If, then, someone without experience has the account and knows the universal but does not know the particular included under it, he will often make an error in treatment, since it is the particular that admits of treatment. Nevertheless, we regard knowledge and comprehension as characteristic of craft rather than of experience and assume that craftsmen are wiser than experienced people, on the supposition that wisdom in every case follows along with knowledge rather than with experience. This is because craftsmen know (*eidenai*) the cause, whereas experienced people do not. For experienced people know the fact but do not know the explanation why, whereas craftsmen know the explanation why, that is, the cause" (*Met.* I 1 981$^a$12–30).

Note 889
**Practical wisdom:** See VI 5 1140ᵃ28–30.

Note 890
**As we saw:** At VI 8 1141ᵇ24–25.

Note 891
**Politics:** Aristotle switches from *politikê* to *ta politika*, but the reference seems to be the same. **Thought:** See IX 4 1166ᵃ17.

Note 892
**They have not made their own sons or any other friends of theirs into politicians:** Politics, as a virtue of thought identical to practical wisdom (VI 8 1141ᵇ23–24), is acquired by teaching (II 1 1103ᵃ15). Being able to teach is a mark of possessing scientific knowledge rather than just an experienced-based ability: "On the whole too an indication of the one who knows, as opposed to the one who does not know, is his capacity to teach. That is why we think craft knowledge to be more like scientific knowledge than experience is, since craftsmen can teach, while experienced people cannot" (*Met.* I 1 981ᵇ7–10). Compare Plato, *Men.* 93a–94e.

Note 893
**Through intimacy with politics** (*politikê*): See VI 7–8 1141ᵇ14–33.

Note 894
**Comprehension:** Discussed in VI 10. **As in matters of music, the greatest thing:** "Everyone who listens to representations comes to have the corresponding emotions, even when the rhythms and melodies these representations contain are taken in isolation. And since music happens to be one of the pleasures, and virtue is a matter of enjoying, loving, and hating in the correct way, it is clear that nothing is more important than that we should most of all learn and be habituated to discern correctly and enjoy decent characters and noble actions" (*Pol.* VIII 5 1340ᵃ12–18).

Note 895
**Those who lack scientific knowledge:** Compare 1180ᵇ17.

Note 896
**Unexamined:** "The majority of those who have expressed views about constitutions, even if what they say is correct in other respects, certainly fail to give useful advice. For one should not get a theoretical grasp on only the best constitution but also the one that is possible and similarly the one that is easier and more attainable by all cities. As it is, however, some seek only the constitution that is highest and requires a lot of resources, while others, though they discuss a more attainable constitution, do away with the constitutions actually in place and praise the Spartan or some other. But what should be done is to describe the sort of organization that people will be easily persuaded to accept and participate in, given what they already have, as it is no less a task to reform a constitution than to establish one from the

start, just as it is no less a task to change what we have learned than to learn it at the start. That is why . . . a politician should also be able to help existing constitutions. . . . But this is impossible if he does not know how many kinds of constitutions there are. As things stand, however, some people think that there is just one kind of democracy and one of oligarchy. But this is not true. So one must not overlook the varieties of each of the constitutions, how many they are and how many ways they can be combined. And it is with this same practical wisdom that one should try to see both which laws are best and which are fitting for each of the constitutions. For laws should be established, and all do establish them, to suit the constitution and not the constitution to suit the laws" (*Pol.* IV 1 1288ᵇ35–1289ᵃ15). **Philosophy of human affairs:** See II 2 1103ᵇ27, VII 11 1152ᵇ2.

Note 897
**Anything that has been correctly . . . go through it:** In *Pol.* II, Aristotle discusses the constitutions described in Plato's *Republic* and *Laws,* as well as various other constitutions, including the Spartan, Cretan, and Carthaginian. **The collection of constitutions:** A reference to the 158 constitutions compiled under Aristotle's supervision, of which only the *Constitution of the Athenians* survives complete. **What sorts of things preserve . . . the opposite:** Primarily discussed in *Pol.* IV–VI.

Note 898
**Which constitution is best:** See V 7 1135ᵃ5 and *Pol.* VII–VIII. **Habits:** Reading ἔθεσι with OCT, some mss. read ἤθεσι ("sorts of characters").

# Further Reading

A detailed annotated bibliography of works on Aristotle's *Ethics* by Thornton Lockwood is available in the Classics section at Oxford Bibliography Online: http://www.oxfordbibliographies.com/obo/page/classics.

The on-line *Stanford Encyclopedia of Philosophy* (http://plato.stanford.edu) has many useful articles on Aristotle, as well as on Plato and other relevant topics.

Perseus under PhiloLogic (http://perseus.uchicago.edu) has excellent searchable Greek texts and English translations of many of Aristotle's writings, including the *Eudemian Ethics, Nicomachean Ethics,* and *Politics,* as well as many linked Greek grammars and dictionaries.

*The following are some of the works that I think most useful:*

## *Aristotle Life and Works*

Ackrill, J. L. *Aristotle the Philosopher* (Oxford, 1981).

Lear, J. *Aristotle: The Desire to Understand* (Cambridge, 1988).

Natali, C. *Aristotle: His Life and School* (Princeton, 2013).

Shields, C. *Aristotle* (New York, 2007).

## *Ethical Writings in English Translation*

Ackrill, J. L. *Aristotle's Ethics* (London, 1973).

Broadie, S. and C. Rowe. *Aristotle: Nicomachean Ethics* (New York, 2002).

Crisp, R. *Aristotle: Nicomachean Ethics* (Cambridge, 2000).

Inwood, B. and R. Woolf, *Aristotle Eudemian Ethics* (Cambridge, 2013).

Irwin, T. H. *Aristotle: Nicomachean Ethics*. 2d ed. (Indianapolis, 1999).

Ostwald, M. *Aristotle: The Nicomachean Ethics* (Indianapolis, 1962).

Pakaluk, M. *Aristotle Nicomachean Ethics Books VIII–IX* (Oxford, 1999).

Rackham, H. *Aristotle: The Nicomachean Ethics* (Cambridge, Mass., 1934).

Ross, W. D. *Aristotle: The Nicomachean Ethics* (Oxford, 1925).

Taylor, C. C. W. *Aristotle Nicomachean Ethics Books II–IV* (Oxford, 2006).

Woods, M. *Aristotle Eudemian Ethics, Books I, II, and VIII.* 2d. ed. (Oxford, 1992).

## Books, Commentaries, and Collections of Papers

Bostock, D. *Aristotle's Ethics* (Oxford, 2000).

Burnet, J. *The Ethics of Aristotle* (London, 1900).

Charles, D. *Aristotle's Philosophy of Action* (London, 1984).

Cooper, J. M. *Reason and Emotion: Essays on Ancient Moral Psychology and Ethical Theory* (Princeton, 1999).

Curzer, H. *Aristotle and the Virtues* (Oxford, 2012).

Destrée, P. and M. Zingano (eds.) *Theoria: Studies on the Status and Meaning of Contemplation in Aristotle's Ethics* (Louvain-La-Neuve, 2013).

Gauthier, R.A., and J. Y. Jolif. *L'Éthique à Nicomaque: Introduction, Traduction et Commentaire.* 2d ed. (Louvain-La-Neuve, 2002).

Gottlieb, P. *The Virtue of Aristotle's Ethics* (Cambridge, 2009).

Greenwood, L. H. G. *Aristotle Nicomachean Ethics Book Six with Essays, Notes, and Translation* (Cambridge, 1909).

Kontos, P. *Aristotle's Moral Realism Reconsidered: Phenomenological Ethics* (London, 2011).

Kraut, R. *Aristotle on the Human Good* (Princeton, 1989).

———. (ed.) *The Blackwell Guide to Aristotle's Nicomachean Ethics* (Oxford, 2006).

Lear, G. R. *Happy Lives and the Highest Good* (Princeton, 2004).

Meyer, S. S. *Aristotle on Moral Responsibility: Character and Cause* (Oxford, 2012).

Miller, J. (ed.) *Aristotle's Nicomachean Ethics: A Critical Guide* (Cambridge, 2011).

Moss, J. *Aristotle on the Apparent Good: Perception, Phantasia, Thought, & Desire* (Oxford, 2012).

Natali, C. (ed.) *Aristotle's Nicomachean Ethics Book VII* (Oxford, 2009).

Pakaluk, M. *Aristotle's Nicomachean Ethics: An Introduction* (Cambridge, 2005).

———. and G. Pearson (eds.) *Moral Psychology and Human Action in Aristotle* (Oxford, 2011).

Pearson, G. *Aristotle on Desire* (Cambridge, 2012).

Price, A. W. *Love and Friendship in Plato and Aristotle* (Oxford, 1997).

Rorty, A. (ed.) *Essays on Aristotle's Ethics* (Berkeley, 1980).

Stewart, J. A. *Notes on the Nicomachean Ethics* (Oxford, 1882).

*The following are relevant works of my own:*

*Practices of Reason: Aristotle's Nicomachean Ethics* (Oxford, 1992).

"Philosophy, Politics, and Rhetoric in Aristotle." Amélie Rorty (ed.), *Essays on Aristotle's Rhetoric* (Berkeley, 1996), pp. 191–205.

*Aristotle: Politics* (Indianapolis, 1998).

"Aristotelian Education." Amélie Rorty (ed.), *Philosophers on Education* (London, 1998), pp. 51–65.

*Substantial Knowledge: Aristotle's Metaphysics* (Indianapolis, 2000).

*Action, Contemplation, and Happiness: An Essay on Aristotle* (Cambridge, Mass., 2012).

"Aristotle's Method of Philosophy." Christopher Shields (ed.), *The Oxford Handbook of Aristotle* (Oxford, 2012), pp. 150–70.

*Aristotle on Practical Wisdom: Nicomachean Ethics VI* (Cambridge, Mass., 2013).

# Index

Line references are to the Greek text but closely approximate those in the translation. 1094$^{a}$1–1099$^{b}$34 omit the initial 10, 1100$^{a}$1–1181$^{b}$24 omit the initial 1. Boldface entries signal attached notes.

Aid (*boêthêma*), 97a6, 138a2, 155a14, 165b19

**Aim (at and hit)**, (*stochastikos*), **106b15**, 28, 109a23, 109a30, 126b29, 127a8, 128a6, 129b15, 141b13, 160a13

**Alcmaeon**, **110a28**

Alleviate (*kouphizontai*), 171a29, 33

Alliances (*summachiai*), 157a27

Allocate, allocation (*dianomê*), 130b31, 131b10, 27+ [justice in an a.], 134a3, 136b18+, 171a2

Allow (*ean*), 138a10

*Alope*, 150b10

**Ambidextrous** (*amphidexios*), **134b34**

Amusement (*paidia*), 108a13, 23, 127b34, 128a14, 20, b4, 6, 150b17, 176b9, 28, 30, 33

Amusement-lover (*paidiôdês*), 150b16, 18

**Anacharsis**, **176b33**

Analogy, analogous (*analogia*), 96b28, 103b9, 108b26, 148b10. *See also* proportion

Analysis, analyze (*analusis, analuein*), 112b20, 23 [a deliberator seems to inquire and a.]

*Analytics, The*, 139b27, 32

**Anaxagoras of Clazomenae**, **141b3**, **179a13**

**Anaxandrides**, **152a22**

Ancestor, starting (*archêgos*), 162a4

Ancient (*archaios*), 113a8, 160a25

**Anger** (*orgê*), 103b18, 105b22, 108a4, 109b16, 117a6, **125b26**, 30, 126a16, 22, 24, 34, 130a31, 135b27, 29, 138a9, 148a11, 149b20

Announce (*anaggellein*), 113a9

Annoyed (*achthomenos*), 104b6, 121a6

**Aphrodite**, **149b15**. *See also* sex

**Appear**, what appears to be so, apparent, evident, open (*phainesthai, phainomenon, phaneros*), **94a3**, b8, 26, 95a22, b6, 23, 31, 96a9, 97a16, 25, 28, 97b6, 20, 23, 34, 98a2, b8, 22, 99a31, b14, 17, 25, b6, 12, 101a18 [not e.], 23, 27, 101b19, 23, 102b3, 16, 26, 104a13 [we must use e. cases to testify on behalf of obscure ones], 30, b29, 105a5, 106a25, 108b19, 31, 109a14, 110a28, 111b7, 112a14, b21, 26, 113a16, 20, 22, 30, 113b1, 19, 114a32, b1, 15, 17, 115a7, b31, 116a2, b8, 117a17, 21, 22, b6, 27, 118a22, 25, 121a9, 122a2, 123b22, 33, 124b29, 125a31, b22, 126a17, 23, 127a11, b8, 11, b23, 28, 31, 32, 128b14, 129a19, 20, 130a32, b21, 135b28, 136b25, 137a34, b3, 34, 138a4, 28, 139b18, 140b18, 141a28, b1, 142a24, 144a34, 36, b9, **145b3**, 28, 31, 147b23, 151a6, 27, b29, 31, 152b32, 154a1, 24, 26, 31, 155b17, 26, 156a2, b29, 157b16, 158a28, b7, 10, 35, 159b16, 160a28, 34, b8, 31, 33, 161a10, 162a31, b15, 163b5, 164b12, 18, 21, 165a18, 166a4, 15, b2, 6, 25, 167a19, 22, b2, 19, 169a35, 171a34, b28, 172b18, 173a11, b25, 174a13, 175a20, 23, 29, 35, b2, 176a5, 16, 19, b23, 32, 177b24, 178a14, b8, 17, 21, 179a15, b7, 180b31, 33, 181a4, 13, b2

**Appearance** (*phantasma*), **102b10**

Appearance (*phantasia*), 114a32, b3, 150b28. *Also* imagination

Appearance (*idea*) 99b4 [extremely ugly in a.], 129a29, 167a5. *See also* form

**Appetite, appetitive part** (*epithumia*), **102b30**, 103b18, 105b21 [a. is a feeling], 106b18, 111a25+ [actions done because of spirit or a. are presumably not correctly said to be involuntary], 32 [things in accord with a. are pleasant], 111b2, 11+, 17 [a. is concerned with what is pleasant and what is painful], 117a1, 118a13+, b8+ [some a. seem to be shared, others to be peculiar to individuals and

they b. than others do about what they know scientifically], 147a25+ [one is a universal b., whereas the other is concerned with particulars], b9, 151a19 [it is virtue, whether natural or habituated, that teaches correct b. about the starting-point], b3+, 159a23, 167a23+ [agreement in b.], 173b13, 179a17 [the b. of wise people]. *See also* reputable

Belief, contrary to (*paradoxos*), 146a22 [sophists wish to refute in a way that is c.], b24+, 26 [some people with b. are not hesitant but think they know in the most rigorous way]

**Belongs, properly**, properly its own, properly suited for, akin, kin, kinship (*oikeios*), **95b26**, 96a15, 96b31, 98a15 [virtue], 29, 99b14, 101b34, 111b5, 119b33, 120a17, 124a7, 126a8, 128a17, 129b33, 139a11, 155a21 [every human being is k. to every other], b9 [puzzles proper to natural science do not p. to an ethical investigation of friendship], 159a23, 161b22, 162a3, 11, 165a17, 31, 33, b20, 167b34, 168a2, 27, 169b33, 170b26 [life], 171a7, 16, 173a5 [good], 32, 175a31, 35, 36, 175b14, 17 [pain], 21 [pain], 176b26 [state], 177a17 [virtue], 178a5

Benefaction, benefactor, beneficence, benefit, beneficiary (*euergesia, euergetês*), 120a34, 124b9, 16, 155a8, 161a12, 16, 163a1+, b4, 7, 164b31, 167a14, b17, 23, 169b12, 15, 171a27, b16, 180b6

Beneficial, benefit (*ôphelimon*), 95a5 [pointless and not b.], 11 [of great b.], 96b15 [b. vs. intrinsic goods], 97a8, 103b29, 108a29, 120a22, 121a29 [an acquisitive person b. no one, not even himself], 125a12 [more noble and purposeless than purposeful and b.], 126b29 [referring to what is noble and what is b.], 127a8 [b. in terms of wealth], 134a8 [b. vs. harmful], 10 [unconditionally b.], 137a29, 30 [b. up to a point for some, harmful to others], 141a30 [b. for themselves], 142b28 [correctness with regard to the b. thing to do], 155a7, 156a26 [b. vs. pleasure], b14, 157a20, 157b20, 158b3, 26 [more b.], 159b12, 160b5 [b. not to himself but to those he rules], 161a35 [b. vs. friendship], 162b2, 17, 36 [b. vs. noble], 163a10+, 28+, b20+, 164b32 [we should repay a loan to the one who conferred the b. rather than give it to a companion], 167b11, 168a13, 171b19, 25 [it is not a noble thing to be eager to receive b.], 176b11, 181b6

Benefit v. (*onêsetai*), 169a12

Benefits to be received (*eupatheia*), 159a21, 171b24

Best people (*aristoi*), 129b16, 167b1. *See also* aristocracy

Betrayal (*pseudomarturia*), 131a7

Better, best (*beltion*), 145b27, 33 [nothing b. than scientific knowledge], 150a2 [the b. has not been corrupted], 151a25 [the b. is preserved in him—the starting-point], 154a14 [of some states and processes there cannot be an excess that is b.], 177a4 [the activity of what is b. is b.]

Beware (*eulabeisthai*), 121b24, 127a3, b6, 171b7, 26

**Bias of Priene**, **130a1**

Bind together (*sunechein*), 132b32, 133a27, b7, 155a23, 162a29

Birth, from, congenital (*ek genetês*), 144b6, 154a33, 162a12

Citizen (*politês*), 97b10, 99b31, 102a8, 103b3, 116a18, b18, 130b29 [good man vs. good citizen], 160a2, 5, 161a28, 165a31, 177b14

**City** (*polis*), **94a28**, b8 [the good of a c. is more complete than that of an individual], 10, 103b3, 115a32, 122a5, b23, 123a2, 132b34 [it is proportionate reciprocity that keeps a c. together], 138a11, 13 [the c. imposes a penalty on a person who has done away with himself, on the supposition that he is doing something unjust to the c.], 141b25 [the practical wisdom concerned with the c.], 145a11 [politics prescribes with regard to everything in the c.], 152a20, 155a22 [friendship holds c. together], 157a27, 160a17, b13, 162a19 [household is prior to and more necessary than c.], 167a26, 30, 168b31 [a c. or any other complex system, seems to be most of all its most controlling part], 170b30, 31 [ten people will not yet constitute a c., nor will ten times ten thousand still constitute one], 180a25 [the c. of the Spartans], 27, b4 [laws and habits have strength in c.], 181a7, b18

Clash (*diaphônein*), 98b12, 132b27, 155b22, 169a15

Classmate (*sumphoitêtês*), 162a33

Clever, cleverness (*deinos*), 144a24+, 145b19, 146a23 [sophists], 152a10 [c. people can lack self-control], 158a32 [c. at doing what is prescribed]. *See also* terrible

Close, closeness, closely related (*suneggus*), 111b20, 129a27, 162a3, 175b32

**Coincidental(ly)** (*sumbebêkos*), **96a22**, 118a9, 17, 135a18, 26, b3, 6, 7, 136a25, 137a12, 23, 138b1, 3, 139b35, 147b2, 151a33, b2, 152b9, 34, 154b1, 17, 156a16, b11, 157a35 [things that are c. to a subject are scarcely ever coupled], b4, 159a18, b20, 178b30

Collection (*sunagôgê*), 181a16 [c. of constitutions], b7 [c. of laws and constitutions], 17

Colors (*chrômata*), 118a4

**Column of goods** (*sustoichia tôn agathôn*), **96b6**

Comedy (*kômô[i]dia*), 123a23, 128a22

Coming to be, process of (*genesis*), 139b24 [eternal things cannot c.], 140a11+ [very craft is concerned with c.], 143a5, b20 [theoretical wisdom is not concerned with c.], 145a9 [practical wisdom is concerned with the c. of theoretical wisdom], 152b13 [pleasure a perceived c.], 14 [no c. is the same kind of thing as its end], 23, 153a9 [end better than c.], 10 [pleasure isn't a c. and doesn't involve a c.], 13, 15, 16, 154b1 [being in a good state is better than c. in it], 169b30 [an activity is clearly something that c., and does not belong to us like some possession], 173a30+ [pleasure not a c.], b16+ [c. vs. completeness], 174b10+ [no c. *of* pleasure]

Commands (*prostagma*), 119b13

Commensurable (*sumblêta*), 133a19

Common (*koinos*), 96a23 [c. Platonic form], 28 [c. universal], b25 [the good is not something c.], 32 [predicated in c.], 104a32 [c. view and to be taken as basic], 107a30 [universal accounts are c. to more cases], 122a2, b7 [a feature c. to the virtues], 123a5, 129b11 [this term circumscribes the two cases and is what they have in c.], 15 [c. advantage], 131b28+ [c. funds], 135a13 [c. type of just action],

do and should abstain from, and it is because of this sort of e. that bad people come about], 111a34 [e. made on the basis of rational calculation vs. those made on the basis of spirit], 115b15 [the way e. comes about is that we fear what we shouldn't], 118b16+ [e. in the natural appetites vs. e. in the pleasures peculiar to individuals], 119a34 [children's e. have a certain similarity to intemperance], 121a8 [e. of a wasteful person], 122a15 [people e. more in the direction of acquisitiveness than wastefulness], 125a19 [small-souled and conceited people are not bad but are in e.], 126a1 [mild-mannerdness e. more toward deficiency], 34 [it is not easy to define e. in the case of anger], 128b18 [young people live by their feelings and so make many e.], 135b12+ [of the three sorts of harm found in communities, those involving ignorance are *errors*], 136a7 [e. that merit sympathetic consideration vs. e. that don't], 137b16+ [the law picks what holds for the most part, not unaware of the e. involved], 140b23 [voluntary e. is preferable in a craft but not in a virtue], 142a21 [e. in deliberation may be about the universal or about the particular], b8, 10 [no e. of scientific knowledge], 144b19 [Socrates' e.], 148a3 [lack of self-control is blamed not only as an e.but also as a sort of vice], 149a28 [the e. in spirit's lack of self-control], 155a13 [friends are necessary to young people with a view to the avoidance of e.], 159b7 [it is characteristic of good people not to commit e. themselves nor to allow their friends to do so], 160b31 [the Persian form of rule is apparently e.], 163a3 [e. in receiving benefits]

Escape notice, keep from being noticed (*lanthanein*) 109b20, 124b27, 129a28, 139b22, 150b36

Essence (*ousia*). *See* substance

**Estimable** (*timios*), **100b15** [the most estimable sciences], 101b11, 102a1 [happiness is included among things both e. and complete], 4 [the starting-point and cause of what is good is something e. and divine], 20 [politics is more e. and better than medicine], 122b16 [the most e. work is the one that is great and noble], 19 [the sorts of expenditure that are called e.], 141a20 [theoretical wisdom must be scientific knowledge of the most e. things], b3, 145a26 [a god's state is more e. than virtue], 165b12, 176b25 [what *is* e. is what is so to the excellent person], 178a1 [in its power and e. understanding exceeds everything], b31 [contemplation is intrinsically e.], 179a27

**Eudoxus of Cnidus**, **101b27**, 172b9+

**Evenus of Paros**, **152a31**

**Euripides**, **110a28**, 136a11, 142a2, 155b2

Evident beforehand, things that are (*ta prophanê*), 117a22

Evildoing, evildoer (*kakourgia*), 114a6, b4, 125a19, 165b12

**Exact**, exactness (*akribeia*), **94b13** [we must not look for the same degree of e. in all accounts], 24 [characteristic of a well educated person to look for the degree of e. that the nature of the subject allows], 96b30 [an e. treatment more properly belongs to a different branch of philosophy], 98a27,

intrinsically excellent and pleasant], 170a12 [a sort of training in virtue also comes about from living together with g. people], 15+ [what is naturally g.], 20+ [intrinsically g.], 21 [being determinate is characteristic of the nature of the g.], 171b14 [the g. things that are ours], 172a28+ [is pleasure the g?], b27+ [every g. is more choiceworthy when it is accompanied by another g. than when it is on its own], 34 [intrinsic g.], 173a4 [some naturally g. element], 16 [the g. is determinate], 174a9 [that pleasure is not the g. seems to be clear], 176a18 [it is virtue and a g. person (insofar as he is such) that are the measure of each thing], 179a2+ [external g.], 179a16 [ordinary people judge by external g.], 180a15 [someone who is to be g. should be nobly nurtured and habituated]

**Good breeding**, well bred (*eugeneia*), **99b3**, 100b32, 122b31, 124a21, 131a28, 179b8

**Good government** (*eunomia*), **112b14**

**Good guesswork** (*eustochia*), 142a33, b1, **2**

Good physical condition, what conduces to a good state (*euektikos*), 129a20, 23, 138a31, 143b25, 176a15

Goods fought about (*perimachêta agatha*), 168b19, 169a21

Goodwill (*eunoia, eunoein*), IX 5 and 155b32+, 156a4, 157b18, 158a7

Gossiper, inveterate (*diêgêtikos*), 117b34

Gourmand (*opsophagos*), 118a32

Gourmet chef (*opsopoiêtikê*), 153a26

**Gourmet dishes** (*opsa*), **118a12**, 29, 154a18

Graces (*Charites*), 133a3

Graciousness, gracious (*euschêmosunê*), 101a1, 128a7, 25

Grammarian, grammatical (*grammatikos*), 105a20+

Gratitude, favor (*charis*), 120a15 [gratitude goes to the person who gives not to the one who does not get], 133a4, 137a1 [greedy for a f.], 167b24

Grazing (*nomê*), 117a1

Greatness of soul (*megalopsuchia*), IV 3, 100b32, 107b22, 26, 123a34+, 125b3

Greed, greedy, greedy for (*pleonexia*), 106a31 [takes too much], 129a32, b1, 9, 10, 130a17, 20, 26, 136b22 [getting a larger share], 137a1, 167b10, 168b19

Grievance (*mempsis*), 162b5, 18

Grieve together with (*sunachthesthai*), 171a8

Growth, growing (*auxêsis*), 103a16, 104a27, 119b4, 154b10

Grudge, burden (*baros*), 126a23, 171a31

Guard v. (*phulattein*), 109b7, 121b25

Guardian (*phulax*), 134b1 [a ruler is a g. of what is just]

Guest-friendship (*xenikê philia*), 156a31, 161b16, 170b21+

Guidance (*agôgê*), 179b31 [g. toward virtue]

Habit (*ethos*), 103a17 [virtue of character results from h.], 26 [virtues are brought to completion through h.], 148b17 [disability, h., depraved natures], 27+ [morbid conditions arising from h.], 152a30 [h. is easier to change than nature, but is also difficult to change because it is like nature], 179b21 [do we become good by nature, by h., or by teaching?], 25 [the audience must be prepared beforehand by means of h. to enjoy and hate in a noble way, like earth that is to nourish seed], 180a8 [those who

**Margites**, 141a14

Mathematics, mathematician (*mathêmatika*), 94b26, 102b33 [the reason of m.], 112b22 [m. inquiry], 131b13, 142a12+ [young people can become geometers and m. and wise in such things], 18 [the objects in m. are given through abstraction], 28 [the last thing among m. objects is a triangle], 151a17 [hypotheses are starting-points in m.], 18 [reason does not teach the starting-points in m.], 173b17 [the pleasure of m.]

Matter, subject m. (*hulê*), 94b12, 98a28, 104a3, 116b33 [*en hulê(i)* = in a forest], 137b19

Mean, medial, middle (*mesos, mesotês*), II 3–9, 106a34+ [m. in relation to us vs. mean in the thing], 108b14 [m. disposition], 109b25 [m. point of a circle], 121b12 [reach the m. and be as he should], 124b20 [those in the m.], 126b5+ [m. state], 127a6 [m. person], 23+ [m. person], 128a16 [m. state], 33 [m. person], 132a19 [a m. between loss and profit], 24 [a judge is a sort of m.], 142b24 [m. term]

Measure (*metron*), 113a33, 133b16, 135a1, 2, 163a17, 22, 166a12, 170b30, 176a18. *See also* standard

Mediators (*mesidioi*), 132a23

Medicine, medical science, medical treatment (*iatrikê, iatreia, iatreuein*), 94a8, 96a33, 97a10, 13, 17, 19, 102a21, 104a9, b17, 112b4, 137a24, 138a31, b31, 141a32, 143a3, b27, 33, 144a4, 145a8, 152b32, 154a28, 30, 34, b12, 18, 180b8, 27, 181a2. *See also* doctor

Megara, 123a24

Melody (*melê*), 118a8, 170a10, 175a14

Memory, remember (*mnêmê*), 124b12, 125a3, 147b5 [imagination and m. of particulars], 165b33, 166a25 [an excellent person's m. are pleasant], 168a14, 17, 173b18, 174a6 [m. would be excellent even if it brought no pleasure]

Menial (*thêtikos*), 125a2

**Merope, 111a12**

**Method of inquiry** (*methodos*), **94a1**, b11, 98a29, 129a6

Mild-mannered, mild-mannerdness (*praos, praotês*), IV 5 and 103a8, b19, 108a6, 109b17, 129b22

Milesians, 151a8, 9

**Milo of Croton, 106b3**

**Mina** (*mna*), **106b1**, 2, 133b23, 24, 134b22

Mind, of one (*homognômonein*), 166a13 [a virtuous person is o. with himself], 167a24, 27, 168b7

Minimizing (*katamikrizontes*), 163a14

Misers (*pheidôloi*), 121b22

Misfortune (*atuchêma*), 101a10, 28, 135b17 [m. defined]

Misfortunes (*dustuchiai*), 100a21, 153b19, 155a11

Mistrust (*apistein*), 112b10

Mix (*krasis*), 154b13

Mixed (*miktos*), 110a11 [m. actions], 128b34 [m. state], 171a35, 172b30, 173a23 [pleasures]

Moderate, moderately (*metrios, metriôs*), 96a25, 33, 110a23, 119a14, 17, b10, 121a2, b6, 122a26, 123b10, 124a6, 15, b20, 125b5, 13, 127b30, 136b20, 179a10, 12

**Moderation** (*kosmiotês*), **109a16**

Monarch, monarchy (*monarchia*), 115a32, 160b1, 11

Money, currency (*nomisma, argurion*), 109a27, 119b26, 127b13, 133a20+, b11+, 137a4, 164a1, 28, 32, 165b12, 178b15

Money, receive (*chrêmatizesthai*), 163b8

**Moneymaker**, (craft of) moneymaking (*chrêmatistikê*), **96a5** [life of m.], 112b4, 153a18

that are wondrous for their purity and dependability], 27 [those who have attained knowledge pass their time more p. than those who are looking for it], 21, 178a6 [what properly belongs to each thing by nature is most p. for each of them], 179a34, b13, 15 [of what is truly p., they have no understanding at all, because they have had no taste of it], 33, 180a11, 14 [the sorts of pains inflicted should be those that are most opposed to the p. liked]

Pleasure, cause (*sunêdunein*), 126b32, 127a2, 7

Pledge, pledging (*egguê*), 131a4, 133b12

Plotting (*epiboulos*), 149b13, 14, 152a18

Poems (*poiêmata*), 168a2

Poets (*poiêtês*), 120b14, 154b29, 168a1

Point (*stigmê*), 174b12

Pointless, vain (*mataios*), **94a21**, 95a5, 29, 96b20, 127b11 [v. and foolish vs. bad]

Poisoning (*pharmakeia*), 131a6

**Political** (*politikos*), 95b18+ [p. life], **97b11** [a human being is by nature p.], 99b1 [p. power], 116a17 [p. courage], 129b19 [p. community], 134a26+ [p. just], 160a9 [all communities seem to be parts of the p. community], 11 [the p. community seems both to have come together at the start and to remain in existence for the sake of what is advantageous], 21 [the p. community seeks not the advantage that is present at hand but the one that is for all of life], 161b13 [p. friendships], 162a17 [a human being seems to be by nature more couple-forming than p.], 163b34 [p. friendship], 167b2 [p. friendship], 169b18 [a human being is a p. being], 171a17 [friends in a p. way],

Political community (*politeia*). *See* constitution

**Politician** (*politikos*), **94a27**, **102a8** [someone who is truly a p. will have worked most of all on virtue, since he wishes to make the citizens good and obedient to the laws], 18 [a p. must in a way know about what pertains to the soul], 23 [a p. must get a theoretical grasp on what concerns the soul], 112b14 [a p. does not deliberate about whether to produce good government], 152b1 [it belongs to the p. philosopher to have a theoretical grasp on pleasure and pain, since he is the architectonic craftsman of the end to which we look in calling each thing unconditionally bad or good], 177b12+ [the activity of a p. is unleisured], 178a27 [the p. does labor more in relation to the body], 180b30 [we must acquire legislative science from ps.], 181a5, 11 [experience does seem to make no small contribution, since otherwise people could not, through intimacy with politics have become p.]

**Politics** (*politikê*), **94a27** [p. has the most control and is most architectonic], b11 [our method of inquiry is a sort of p.], 15 [p. investigates noble and just things], 95a2 [a young person is not a suitable audience for p.], 16 [p. seeks the topmost of all the good things doable in action], 95b5 [noble things, just things, and the topics of p. as a whole], 99b29 [p. supervision aims at producing citizens of a certain sort—that is, good people and doers of noble actions], 102a12, 21 [p. is more estimable and better than

Readiness of wit (*agchinoia*), 142$^{b}$5

**Reason**, rational (*logos*), 98$^{a}$3+ [some sort of practical life of what has r.], **102$^{a}$28** [one part of the soul is non-r. whereas another has r.], $^{b}$14+ [it is nonrational but shares in r. in a way], 103$^{a}$1+ [the part that has r. is double—one part having it fully and within itself, the other as something able to listen to it as to a father], 107$^{a}$1 [defined by a r. and the one by which a practically-wise person would define it], 108$^{b}$10 [virtues of r.], 111$^{b}$1 [non-r. feelings], 13 [deliberate choice is not something shared by non-r. creatures, whereas appetite and spirit are], 112$^{a}$16 [deliberate choice involves r.], 115$^{b}$12 [as r. prescribes], 20, 117$^{a}$8, 21 [r. calculation and r.], $^{b}$24 [non-r. parts of the soul], 119$^{b}$11+ [appetite should not oppose r. in any way], 126$^{a}$35, 134$^{a}$35 [it is not a human being we allow to rule but r.], 138$^{b}$9, 22, 139$^{a}$4+ [division of the part that has r.], 24 [r. must be true], 32 [r. that is for the sake of something], 140$^{a}$4+ [state involving r.], 22 [state involving false r.], 140$^{b}$5 [true state involving r.], 20+, 33 [scientific knowledge involves r.], 142$^{a}$26 [the terms for which there is no r.], $^{b}$3 [good guesswork is without r.], 12 [without r. there is no deliberation], 143$^{b}$1 [concerning the primary terms and the things that come last, there is understanding but no r.], 144$^{a}$2 [the correct r. is the one in accord with practical wisdom], 29 [Socrates thought the virtues were cases of r. (all being cases of scientific knowledge); we think they involve r.], 145$^{b}$14 [a self-controlled person, knowing that his appetites are base, does not follow them, because of his r.], 147$^{b}$1 [from r. in a way, and from belief, he acts in a way that lacks self-control], 148$^{a}$29 [contrary to r.], 149$^{a}$26+ [spirit seems to listen to what r. says but to mishear it], 150$^{b}$28 [they do not wait for r., because they are the sort people who follow appearances], 151$^{a}$1 [have the r. but do not stand by it], 17 [r. does not teach the starting-points], 29+ [any r. whatsoever], 34 [the true r. and the correct deliberate choice], $^{b}$10, 24+, 152$^{a}$3 [not to feel pleasure contrary to r.], 152$^{a}$13 [close as regards r.], 167$^{b}$18 [contrary to r.], 168$^{b}$20 [non-r], 169$^{a}$1 [actions involving r.], 5 [living in accord with r.], 172$^{b}$10 [r. and nonrational], 180$^{a}$11 [a decent person will obey r.], 21 [r. that derives from a sort of practical wisdom and understanding]. *See also* account, argument, ratio, word

**Reason, correct** (*orthos logos*), 103$^{b}$32, 114$^{b}$29, 119$^{a}$20, 138$^{a}$10 [contrary to c.], $^{b}$20, 25, 29, 35 [we must determine what the c. is and what its defining-mark], 144$^{b}$23, 26 [it is not the state that is only *in accord with* c that is virtue but the one that also *involves* c.], 147$^{b}$2 [coincidentally contrary to c.], 31 [contrary to the c. that is in them], 151$^{a}$12 [contrary to c.], 21 [contrary to c.]

Reasonable expectation, against (*paralogôs*), 135$^{b}$16, 17

Reasonless people (*alogistoi*), 149$^{a}$9 [= beast like people]

Reciprocate, reciprocal, reciprocity, recipient (*antipaschein*), 132$^{b}$21+, 133$^{b}$6, 155$^{b}$33, 163$^{a}$1

of what makes deliberate choice correct and what should be done to carry it out], $^{b}$29 [Socrates, then, thought that the virtues were all cases of s.], 145$^{b}$22, 23 [can a person who lacks self-control have s.?], 32 [nothing is stronger than s.], 34, 146$^{b}$24, 28, 29, 30 [some people have no less conviction about what they believe than others do about what they s.], 31 [we speak of s. in two ways, since both the person who has but is not using his s. and the one who is using it are said to s.], 147$^{a}$2 [acting against s.], 10 [among those who have s. but are not using it we see a difference in the having of it, so that someone both has it in a way and does not have it—for example, if he is asleep, mad, or tipsy], 19 [words that stem from s.], 147$^{b}$6 [recovers his s.], 11, 13 [the last term is not universal and does not seem to be s. in the way the universal is], $^{b}$15 [full s.], 17 [perceptible type of s.], 153$^{b}$8 [some s. might be the best good], 164$^{a}$26, 32, 180$^{b}$15 [the s. are of what is common]

Science, those who lack (*anepistêmôn*), 180$^{b}$17, 181$^{b}$6

Sculptor (*agalmatopoios*), 97$^{b}$25; s. in bronze (*andriantopoios*), 141$^{a}$11; s. in stone (*lithourgos*), 141$^{a}$10

Scythians, 112$^{a}$28, 150$^{b}$14

Sea (*thalassa*), 115$^{a}$29, 179$^{a}$4

Seamen (*thalattioi*), 115$^{b}$1

Seasoning (*hêdusma*), 170$^{b}$29

Second, second best, secondarily, secondary way (*deuteros*), 109$^{a}$34, 158$^{b}$30 [s. vs. primarily], 176$^{a}$29 [s. vs. full], 178$^{a}$9 [happiest in a s.]

Secret (*aporrêtos*), 111$^{a}$9

See (*oran*), 96$^{b}$17, 106$^{a}$19, 154$^{b}$8, 157$^{a}$7, 170$^{a}$29, 171$^{a}$35, $^{b}$29, 174$^{a}$5, 14, $^{b}$12

Seed (*sperma*), 179$^{b}$26

Segment of a line (*tmêma*), 132$^{a}$26, 27

*Seios anêr*, 145$^{a}$29

Selection (*eklogê*), 181$^{a}$17, 18

Self-control (*enkrateia*), lack of (*akrasia*), VII 1–10 and 95$^{a}$12 [knowledge is profitless to those who lack s.], 102$^{b}$14 [we praise the reason of those who have s. and those who lack s.], 102$^{b}$21 [the impulses of people who lack s. are in contrary directions], 27 [the nonrational part is obedient to the reason of a s. person—and listens still better, presumably, to that of a temperate and courageous one, since there it chimes with reason in everything], 14+ [a person who lacks s. acts from appetite but not from deliberate choice, whereas a person who has s. does the reverse], 114$^{a}$15 [living a life that lacks s.], 119$^{a}$31 [we call people who lack s.wasteful], 128$^{b}$34 [s. is not a virtue but a sort of mixed state], 136$^{a}$32+, 142$^{b}$18 [a person who lacks s. will reach what he proposes should be done as a result of rational calculation and so will have deliberated correctly but will have got hold of something very bad], 154$^{b}$32, 166$^{b}$8 [people who lack s. have an appetite for one set of things but wish for another], 168$^{b}$34 [a person is called s. or lacking in s. depending on whether or not his understanding is in control, on the supposition that this is what each person *is*],

Self-deprecating, self-deprecation (*eirôneia*), 108$^{a}$22, 124$^{b}$30, 127$^{a}$14, 22, $^{b}$22, 30, $^{b}$31

Self-esteem, lacking in (*oknêros*), 125$^{a}$24

Self-lover (*philautos*), 168$^{a}$30, 168$^{b}$15+

Self-ruination (*apôleia hautou*), 120$^{a}$2

**Self-sufficiency**, self-sufficient (*autarkeia*), **97$^b$7** [definition of s.], 8, 112$^b$1 [no deliberation in sciences that are rigorous and s.], 125$^a$12 [characteristic of s. people to have possessions that are noble and purposeless], 134$^a$27 [what is politically just is found where people share a common life with a view to s.], 160$^b$4 [a king is s. and superior in all good things], 169$^b$5 [do s. people need friends?], 177$^a$27 [s. found in contemplation], $^b$1, 21, 178$^b$34, 179$^a$5, $^b$4
Selling (*prasis*), 131$^a$3
Selling. *See* buying
**Separable** (*chôriston*), **96$^b$33**
Separate v. (*chôrizein*), 96$^b$14 [s. off the intrinsic goods], 102$^a$30 [in-s. by nature], 121$^b$19 [acquisitiveness sometimes comes about in s. bits], 134$^b$11, 144$^b$33 [someone might contend dialectically that the virtues are s. from each other], 157$^b$8 [friends in s. places], 161$^b$29 [children s. from parents], 175$^a$20 [activity and the pleasure in it do not admit of s.], 175$^b$35 [pleasure and perception not found s.], 178$^a$22 [the virtue of understanding is s.]
Separation, degree of (*apostêmasi*), 100$^a$26
Serious. *See* excellent
Servant (*oiketês*), 136$^b$31
Servants (*diakonoi*), 149$^a$27
Service, do a s. for (*hupêretein*), 124$^b$18, 158$^a$17, 159$^b$5, 164$^b$25
Services to be rendered (*hupourgia*), 163$^a$34
Set aside, topics and questions Aristotle thinks we may (*apheisthô*), 96$^a$10, 130$^b$20, 155$^b$8, 159$^b$23, 166$^a$34, 171$^a$34, 175$^a$19
Sex, sexual (*aphrodisia*), 118$^a$31 [pleasures of Aphrodite], 147$^a$15 [appetites], $^b$27, 148$^b$29, 149$^a$14 [strange s. pleasure], 152$^b$17, 154$^a$18; have s. with a woman (*sugginesthai gunaiki*), 134$^a$20, 137$^a$6, 20. *See also* erotic desire
Shame, shameful, ashamed (*aidôs*), 96$^b$3, 108$^a$32, 111$^b$32, 112$^a$21, 116$^a$28, 31, 128$^b$10, 18, 139$^b$24, 179$^b$11
Shame, sense of (*aidêmôn*), IV 9 and 108$^a$32, 35, 115$^a$14, 129$^b$19,
Shameful (*aischros*), 128$^b$21, 25
Shameful language (*aischrologia*), 128$^a$23
Shamefully, acting (*aischropragein*), 120$^a$15
Shameless, shamelessness (*anaischuntia*), 107$^a$11, 108$^a$35, 115$^a$14, 128$^b$31
Shape, figure (*schêma*), 118$^a$4, 125$^a$30, 133$^b$1, 137$^b$31, 160$^b$25
Share, no (*amoiros*), 102$^b$12
Shield (*aspis*), 130$^a$18, 137$^a$21
Ship n. (*ploion*), 94$^a$9
Shipbuilding (*naupêgikê*), 94$^a$8
Shoe (*hupodêma*), 101$^a$5, 133$^a$8, 22, 23, 163$^b$34
Shoemaker (*skuteus*, *skutotomos*), 97$^b$29, 101$^a$4 [a good s. makes the noblest shoe out of the hides he has been given], 133$^a$7+, $^b$5
Show v. (*deiknunai*), 94$^b$20, 98$^b$2, 130$^a$2, 145$^b$4, 7, 146$^a$8, 152$^a$8
Sick, dead (*kamnontes, kekmêkotes*), 101$^a$35, $^b$6, 105$^b$15, 150$^b$5, 152$^b$33, 164$^b$23, 173$^b$24, 175$^a$4
Sicyonians, 117$^a$27
Sides of a square (*pleura*), 112$^a$23
Sight, seeing (*opsis*), 96$^b$29, 114$^b$7, 118$^a$3, 144$^b$11, 12, 171$^b$3, 167$^a$4 [the pleasure of s.], 175$^a$8
Sights (*horamata*), 173$^b$18, 174$^b$27
Silly (*êlithios*), 111$^b$22, 112$^a$20, 121$^a$27, 122$^b$28, 123$^b$4, 125$^a$23, 28, 126$^a$5, 176$^b$32
Similarity (*homiotês*), 108$^b$31, 119$^b$1, 139$^a$10, $^b$19, 148$^b$6, 155$^a$33, 156$^b$20, 157a1, 159$^b$3, 4, 160$^b$22, 178$^b$27

constituent of s. is nonrational], 15, 20 [in people who lack self-control the impulses of in their s. are in contrary directions], 22, 23 [in the s. there is something countering reason and going against it], 104$^{b}$19 [the things that naturally cause every state of s. to become worse or better are the ones it is naturally related to and concerned with], 105$^{b}$17 [people who do philosophy without doing the actions it prescribes will not have s. that are in a good state], 20 [the things that come about in s. are of three kinds—feelings, capacities, and states], 114$^{a}$22 [it is not only vices of s. that are voluntary], 138$^{b}$9 [in these accounts the part of the s. that has reason is distinguished from the nonrational part], 33 [states of the s.], 35 [some virtues of s. are virtues of character and some of thought], 139$^{a}$4 [two parts of s. that have reason], 9 [where beings differ in kind, parts of s. that differ in kind are naturally suited to each of them], 18 [three things in s. control action and truth—perception, understanding, and desire], 139$^{b}$15 [the states in which the s. grasps the truth by way of assertion and denial], 140$^{b}$25 [practical wisdom a virtue of the part of s. that forms beliefs], 143$^{b}$16 [practical wisdom and theoretical wisdom are virtues of different parts of s.], 144$^{a}$9 [of the nutritive part of s. there is no ethical virtue], 30 [this eye of s.], 147$^{a}$28 [when a single belief comes about from a universal belief and a particular belief, s. necessarily asserts what has been concluded or acts straightaway], 161$^{a}$35 [no friendship of body toward s.], 166$^{a}$14 [an excellent person desires the same things with all his s.], 166$^{b}$19 [s. of depraved people torn by faction], 168$^{b}$21 [those greedy for money, honors, and bodily pleasures gratify the nonrational part of s.], 179$^{b}$25 [argument and teaching do not have strength in everyone, but rather the s. of the audience must be prepared beforehand by means of habits to enjoy and hate in a noble way]

Soul, belonging to (*psuchikos*), 98$^{b}$16, 99$^{a}$8, 101$^{b}$34 [encomia given to works b.], 117$^{b}$28 [pleasures b.]

Soulless (*apsuchos*), 136$^{b}$30, 150$^{a}$3, 155$^{b}$27 [love for s. objects is not friendship], 157$^{b}$30, 161$^{b}$2, 4. *See also* ensouled

Sounds (*akousmata, akroamata*), 173$^{b}$18

Sour-tempered people (*struphnoi*), 157$^{b}$14, 158$^{a}$2, 6

Sparring partners (*akrocheirizomenoi*), 111$^{a}$15

Spartans (*Lakedaimonioi, Lakônes*), 102$^{a}$11, 112$^{a}$29, 117$^{a}$27, 124$^{b}$16, 127$^{b}$28, 145$^{a}$28, 167$^{a}$31, 180$^{a}$25

**Special** (*idion*), **97$^{b}$34** [s. function], 113$^{a}$31 [each state has it own s. set of things that are pleasant or noble], 131$^{a}$30 [being proportionate is s. to number in general], 133$^{a}$4 [the s. character of gratitude], 142$^{a}$27 [s. objects of perception], 147$^{b}$8 [not s. to this way of being affected], 148$^{a}$1 [common account vs. s. one], 162$^{a}$24 [s. functions of man and woman]

Speech, those uttering a (*hupokrinomenoi*), 147$^{a}$23

Speeches for the law courts (*dikanikoi logoi*), 141$^{b}$33

Spend their days together (*sunêmereuein*), 156$^{b}$4, 157$^{b}$15, 20, 158$^{a}$9, 162$^{b}$16, 166$^{b}$14, 169$^{b}$21, 171$^{a}$5, 172$^{a}$5

**Spending**, expenditure (*dapanê*), **119b25** [s. vs. giving, getting], 31, 120a8, b27, 121a12, b9, 122a21+, b2+, 19 [e. that are called estimable], 34, 123a4, 11+

**Speusippus**, **96b7**, 153b5

Spirit, spirited (*thumos*), **102b30**, 105a8, 111a34, b2, 116b24+ [s. and courage], 126a21 [= anger], 135b21, 26, 145b20, 147a15, b34, 148b13, 149a3, 26

Spite (*epichairekakia*), 107a10, 108b1, 5

Spoil (*lumainesthai*), 100b28, 175b15, 176a21

Stable, stability (*bebaios*), 100b13, 105a33, 159b8, 162a15, 172a9 [base people are un-s.], 177a26

Stadium racecourse, in a (*en tô[i] stadiô[i]*), 95b1, 174a33

Stand by (a belief or deliberate choice) (*emmenein*), 110a31, 145b11, 146a17, 20, 150b30, 151a26, 30, 35, b3+, 152a18

Standard (*kanôn*), 105a4 [we measure our actions, some more and others less, by the s. of pleasure and pain], 113a33, 137b30+ [the s. of what is indeterminate is itself indeterminate]. *See also* measure

**Starting-point** (*archê*), **95a31+** [reasons leading *from* s. and reasons leading *to* s. are different], b6 [the s. is the fact that something is so], 8 [nobly brought up person, then, either has the s. or can easily get hold of them], 98b2 [in the case of s. it will be adequate explanation if the fact that they are so has been correctly brought to light], 4 [*that something is so* is a first thing and a s.], 4 [we get a theoretical grasp of some s. by means of induction, some by means of perception, some by means of some sort of habituation, and others by other means], 7 [the s. is more than half the whole and many of things we were inquiring about become quite evident because of it], 102a2 [happiness is a s., since it is for the sake of it that we all do all the other actions that we do, and we suppose that the s. and cause of what is good is something estimable and divine], 110a1+ [what is forced is what has an external s.], 112b28 [what comes about because of our friends comes about because of our own agency in a way, since the s. is in us], b32 [a human being is a s. of actions], 113a6 [each of us stops inquiring about what way to act when he brings back the s. to himself and, within himself, to the leading element], 113b18+, 114b31 [s. of actions vs. s. of states], 131a5, 134a21 [deliberate choice was not the s. of his action but rather feeling], 135b18, 26, 136b28, 139a7 [beings whose s. do not admit of being otherwise], 18 [perception is not a s. of action], 31 [the s. of action is deliberate choice, and of it desire and reason for the sake of something], 139b5 [this sort of s. is a human being], 28 [in science induction leads to the s., that is, the universal], 34 [if the s. are not better known than the conclusion, it is in a coincidental sense that he will have scientific knowledge], 140a13 [s. in the producer and not in the product], 16 [things that are in accord with nature have their s. within themselves], 34 [things whose s. admit of being otherwise cannot be demonstrated], b16 [the s. of things doable in action is the end for which they are done], 20 [vice is corruptive of the s.], 33+

[understanding is what grasps s.], 141a17 [a theoretically-wise person must not only know what follows from the s. but also must grasp the truth about the s.], 142a19 [the s. in theoretical wisdom or natural science come from experience], 143b4 [these are s. of the end, since it is from particulars that universals come], 10 [understanding is both s. and end], 144a13, 32 [practical syllogisms have a s.], 35 [depravity produces distortion and false views about practical s.], 146b14 [the s. of the investigation], 150a5 [the baseness of what does not possess the s. is always less destructive, and understanding is the s.], 151a15 [virtue preserves the s. and depravity corrupts it], 16 [in actions the end for which we act is the s.], 18 [reason does not teach the s., instead, it is virtue, whether natural or habituated, that teaches correct belief about the s.], 26 [the best thing is preserved in him—the s.], 167a3 [goodwill is a s. of friendship], 178a18 [the s. of practical wisdom are in accord with the virtues of character]

**State** (*hexis*), **98b33** [does the best good consist in virtue's possession or in its use—that is, in the s. or in the activity], 103a9 [it is the praiseworthy s. that we call virtues], b22+ [s. come about from activities that are similar to them], 31 [actions control s.], 104a12 [s. like these are naturally ruined by deficiency and excess], b4 [the pleasures and pains that supervene on a person's works are an indication of his s.], 19, 25 [definition of s. of character], 105a27+ [s. in crafts vs. s. in virtues], b17, 20 [feelings, capacities, and s.], 25+ [by s. I mean the things by dint of which we are well or badly off in relation to feelings], 106a12 [s. are the genus of virtue], 14 [what sort of s.], 22, b36 [a deliberately choosing s.], 108b17 [mean s.], 109b24 [mean s.], 113a31 [each s. has it own special set of things that are pleasant or noble], 114a10 [it is from engaging in the activity that the corresponding s. comes about], b2+ [each individual is somehow responsible for his own s.], 115b21 [the end of every activity is the one in accord with the corresponding s.], 116a5, 117a20+ [more the result of his s., because it was less the result of preparation], 120b9, 122a30, b1 [s. defined by its activities and objects], 123a31 [these s. are vices], b1, 124a15 [moderate s.], 125b20, 126b5+ [mean s. praiseworthy], 9 [we should cling to the mean s.], 17 [blameworthy s.], 21 [nameless s.], 127b2, 15, 128a17, b11, 15, 34 [not a virtue but a sort of mixed s.], 129a7, 13+ [s. doesn't operate in the same way as a capacity, craft, or science], 18+ [s. can often be known from their underlying conditions], 130a13 [the same s. but their being is not the same], 137a8+ [doing them because of being in a certain s. is not easy and not up to ourselves], 138a1+, b21, 32, 139a16, 22 [deliberately choosing state], 34, 139b13 [the s. in accord with which each most grasps the truth], 31 [s. affording demonstrations], 140a4+ [practical s. vs. productive s.], 22 [s. involving false reason], 140b5 [true s.], 20 [true s.], 28+ [forgetfulness of a s.], 141b24 [the same s. but their being is not the same],

179$^{a}$18 [the t. in practical matters must be discerned from the facts of our life]

Truth, grasp the, be truthful (*alêtheuein*), 139$^{b}$13 [virtues as states that g.], 15 [the five states of the soul that g. by way of assertion and denial], 141$^{a}$3, 151$^{b}$20, 168$^{b}$13 [which of two accounts of friendship g.], 169$^{b}$23, 173$^{a}$9

**Truthful sort of person** (*euparakolouthêtos*), IV 7 and **108$^{a}$19+**

Turn completely around (*anakukleisthai*), 100$^{b}$3

Turn over something to someone (*epitrepein*), 164$^{a}$24, $^{b}$15, 16

Turn pale (*ôchriôsin*), 128$^{b}$14 [those who fear death t.]

**Tutor** (*paidagôgos*), **119$^{b}$14**, 121$^{b}$11 [left un-t.]

**Tyranny**, tyrant (*turannis*), 110$^{a}$5, 120$^{b}$25, 122$^{a}$5, 134$^{b}$1, 8, 160$^{b}$1, 2, **160$^{b}$7** [t. is the worst constitution], 11, 160$^{b}$28, 30, 161$^{a}$32, $^{b}$9, 176$^{b}$13

Ugly, very (*panaischês*), 99$^{b}$4

**Unanxious** (*adeês*), **115$^{a}$33**, $^{b}$1

**Unbearable** (*aphorêtos*), 126$^{a}$13

Unbiased (*adekastoi*), 109$^{b}$8 [we are not u. discerners of pleasure]

Unclear (*adêlon*), 112$^{b}$9 [u. and so requiring deliberation], 178$^{a}$30 [wishes u.]

**Unconditional, unconditionally,** simply (*haplôs*), **95$^{a}$1** [u. good discerner], $^{b}$3 [knowable u.], 97$^{a}$33 [u. complete], 98$^{a}$10, 101$^{b}$3 [u. so vs. so for them], 104$^{b}$25 [say this u.], 105$^{b}$33 [s. gets angry], 106$^{a}$8 [capacity s. to feel things], 107$^{a}$17 [s. to do any of these things is to err], 108$^{b}$7 [justice is not said of things only u.], 110$^{a}$9 [u. speaking, no one throws cargo overboard voluntarily], 18 [u. speaking mixed actions are involuntary], 110$^{b}$1 [u. forced], 113$^{a}$23 [u. and in truth the proper object of wish is the good], 115$^{a}$8 [u. speaking frightening things are bad things], 123$^{a}$12 [u. most magnificent], 129$^{b}$3 [u. speaking always good, but for this or that person not always so], 5 [we should pray that u. good things will also be good for us], 8 [u. bad things], 26 [u. vs. in relation to another person], 130$^{a}$13 [insofar as it is u. a state of a certain sort it is virtue], $^{b}$27 [u. a good man], 132$^{b}$21+ [u. just], 134$^{a}$10 [u. beneficial], 25 [u. just vs. politically just], 34+ [u. good, u. bad], 136$^{a}$31 [to do what is u. an unjust action], $^{b}$21 [u. noble], 137$^{a}$26 [u. good things], 33 [neither u. the same nor different in genus], $^{b}$22+ [made an error in pronouncing u.], 138$^{a}$33 [complete and u. vice], 139$^{b}$2 [what is u. an end vs. in relation to something and for something else], 24 [u. necessary], 141$^{b}$13 [u. good deliberator], 142$^{b}$29+ [deliberate well u. vs. to further a specific end], 145$^{a}$1 [u. good person], 146$^{b}$5+ [u. lacking in self-control], 19+, 147$^{b}$20+, 148$^{a}$4 [u. or partial], $^{b}$16 [u. pleasant], 149$^{a}$2 [u. vs. by resemblance], 16+ [u. depravity], 24 [u. vs. by transference], $^{b}$18, 151$^{a}$25 [not u. base], $^{b}$2+ [what is u. = what is intrinsically], 152$^{b}$3 [the end to which we look in calling each thing u. bad or good], 27+ [u. good or bad vs. for some particular person], 153$^{a}$4+ [u. pleasant], 30 [in what way u. good], $^{b}$2 [u. bad vs. being in some way an impediment to activity], 14, 155$^{b}$24 [u. lovable vs. lovable to each person], 156$^{b}$14+

Work = *NE* (*pragmateia*), 103$^{b}$26, 105$^{a}$6, 11

Work, hard, n. (*ergôdês*), 102$^{a}$25, 165$^{a}$34, 168$^{a}$24, 171$^{a}$5

**Works in circulation** (*egkuklia*), **96$^{a}$3**. *See also* external accounts

Worshipped, worthy of worship (*daimonion*), 122$^{b}$21, 141$^{b}$7

Worth, worthy, deserve (*axia*), 117$^{a}$24, 119$^{a}$20, $^{b}$26, 122$^{b}$33, 123$^{a}$2, 18, $^{b}$17, 19, 25, 124$^{b}$19, 126$^{b}$36, 131$^{a}$26, 163$^{a}$2, 30, 164$^{a}$22, $^{b}$4+, 165$^{a}$11

Worth, contrary to (*para tên axian*), 122$^{b}$29, 136$^{b}$16, 160$^{b}$13, 36

Worth, in, in accord with, (*kat' axian*), 122$^{a}$26, 123$^{a}$18, $^{b}$3, 131$^{a}$24, 158$^{b}$27, 31 [equality in w. vs. equality in quantity], 159$^{a}$35, 160$^{b}$33, 161$^{a}$22 [in accord with w. vs. the same], 163$^{b}$11, 35

Wounds (*traumata*), 117$^{b}$8

Wrestling (*palê*), 106$^{b}$5

**Wretched** (*athlios*), **100$^{a}$9**, $^{b}$5, 34 [no blessed person will ever become w., since he will never do hateful or base actions], 101$^{a}$6, 102$^{b}$7, 150$^{b}$5, 166$^{b}$27 [to be very ill fitted for friendship is w.]

Writing, written (*graphê*), 112$^{b}$2 [w. = a rigorous and self-sufficient science], 180$^{a}$35 [w. vs. unwritten laws], $^{b}$34, 181$^{a}$3. *See also* painting

**Xenophantus**, **150$^{b}$12**

Yes (*to nai*), 113$^{b}$8

Young, youth, stages of life, age (*hêlikia*), 95$^{a}$6, 100$^{a}$3, 121$^{a}$20, 128$^{b}$16, 143$^{b}$8, 156$^{a}$33, 161$^{a}$5, 26, $^{b}$34, 165$^{a}$28

Young person (*neos*), 95$^{a}$3, 6, 118$^{b}$11, 128$^{b}$16, 19, 142$^{a}$12, 20, 154$^{b}$10, 11, 155$^{a}$12, 156$^{a}$26, 158$^{a}$5, 20, $^{b}$13, 172$^{a}$21 [those who educate the y. steer them by means of pleasure and pain], 179$^{b}$8, 31, 34, 180$^{a}$1. *See also* childhood, from

Zeus, 124$^{b}$16, 160$^{b}$26, 165$^{a}$15